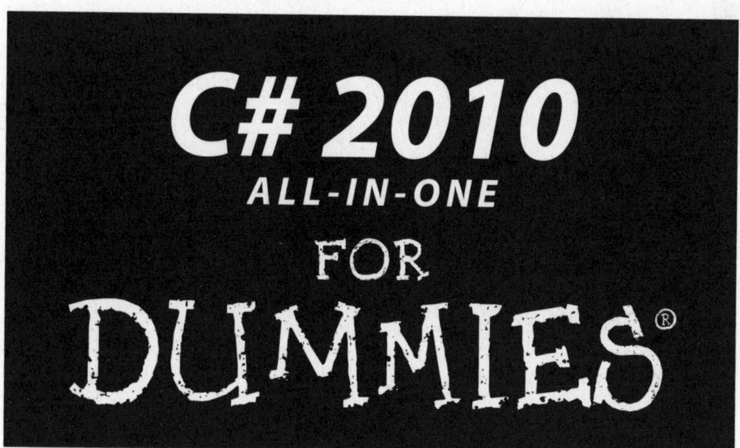

by Bill Sempf, Chuck Sphar, and Stephen Randy Davis

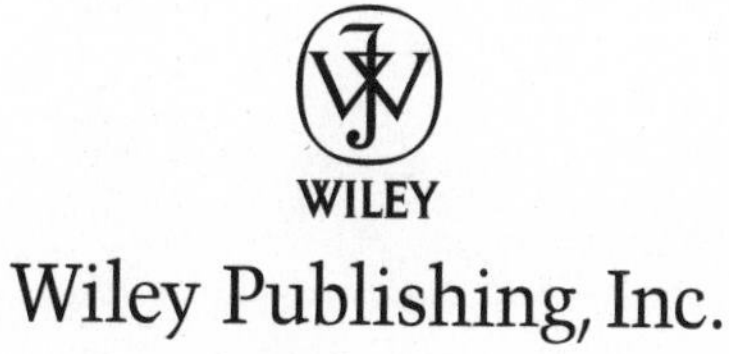

Wiley Publishing, Inc.

C# 2010 All-in-One For Dummies®

Published by
Wiley Publishing, Inc.
111 River Street
Hoboken, NJ 07030-5774

www.wiley.com

Published by Wiley Publishing, Inc., Indianapolis, Indiana

Published simultaneously in Canada

For general information on our other products and services, please contact our Customer Care Department within the U.S. at 877-762-2974, outside the U.S. at 317-572-3993, or fax 317-572-4002.

For technical support, please visit www.wiley.com/techsupport.

Wiley also publishes its books in a variety of electronic formats. Some content that appears in print may not be available in electronic books.

Library of Congress Control Number: TK

ISBN: 978-0-470-56348-9

Manufactured in the United States of America

10 9 8 7 6 5 4 3 2

About the Authors

Hi, my name is **Bill Sempf**, and I am a software architect. Although I used to hate the term *architect,* it's clearly the only thing out there that defines what I do. My breadth of experience includes business and technical analysis, software design, development, testing, server management and maintenance, and security. In my 17 years of professional experience, I have participated in the creation of well over 200 applications for large and small companies, managed the software infrastructure of two Internet service providers, coded complex software happily in every environment imaginable, and made mainframes talk to cellphones. In short, I make the technology products that people are using every day play nicely together.

I started playing with computers in 1979 and haven't looked back since. In 1985 I was helping my father (also named Bill) manage Apple IIe systems at the local library. Since then I have built applications for the likes of Bank One, Lucent Technologies, Nationwide Insurance, and Sears, Roebuck and Co. I am the author of *Visual Basic 2008 For Dummies* and *Visual Basic 2005 For Dummies*; a coauthor of *Effective Visual Studio.NET, Professional ASP. NET Web Services,* and *Professional VB.NET*; a frequent contributor to MSDN, Builder.com, Hardcore Web Services, Cloud Computing Journal, Inside Web Development Journal, and Intranet Journal; and have recently been an invited speaker for the ACM and IEEE, DevEssentials, the International XML Web Services Expo, and the Association of Information Technology Professionals. I am a graduate of The Ohio State University with a bachelor's of science degree in business administration, a Microsoft Certified Professional, a Certified Internet Business Strategist, and a Certified Internet Webmaster. My company is Products Of Innovative New Technology (usually called POINT), and you can reach me at `bill@pointWeb.net`.

Chuck Sphar escaped the Microsoft C++ documentation camps after six years of hard labor as a senior technical writer. You can reach Chuck for praise and minor nits at `csharp@chucksphar.com`. His C# material Web page (references throughout the book) is `csharp102.info`.

Stephen R. Davis, who goes by the name Randy, lives with his wife and son near Dallas, Texas.

Dedication

This book goes to the active community of Microsoft developers that I get to work with every day. Thanks for your commitment to getting things done right, sharing what you know, and having a good time doing it.

Also, for Gabrielle and Adam, who had to put up with another six months of Daddy hiding in the basement.

—Sempf

Acknowledgments

A lot of people work to make a book of this size. Don't think, just because the authors are listed on the front page, that they conceived every idea in the book. It takes a community.

First, thanks to Chuck Sphar and Randy Davis for the fantastic source material that is the backbone of this book. I learned much just editing the first two minibooks for use in this *All-in-One.* Also, thanks to Katie Feltman and Chris Morris for their editorial expertise.

A number of community members had a huge part in the creation of this book. Carey Payette and Phil Japikse built Book V (about WPF) basically from the goodness of their hearts, and I couldn't have completed it without them — my WPF skills aren't worth writing about. These two get the award for Biggest Contribution, and I thank them both.

The developers at Information Control Corporation were also essential in formulating the initial scope of this book and then fact-checking the details. Steve Webb, Stephen Giffin, John Hannah, Larry Beall, Michael Birchmeyer, and Azher Muhammad all had a big part, especially in the information related specifically to C# 4.0. Thanks to them and all the other ICC experts who gave me ideas and tips.

Kevin Pilch-Bisson at Microsoft provided some C# clarity via Twitter throughout the scope of this book. Steve Andrews provided the structure for the T4 chapter in Book IV. Mads Torgerson reviewed the table of contents, and I thank him for the "It looks delicious" phrase, which I think was my most quoted phrase of the year.

Lars Corneliussen provided a few choice pointers for the book, and Julie Lerman's Entity Framework writing was the basis of my own additions to the ADO.NET chapter.

As always, thanks to my wife, Gabrielle, for her support. Sometimes I just can't believe how lucky I am.

Publisher's Acknowledgments

We're proud of this book; please send us your comments at http://dummies.custhelp.com. For other comments, please contact our Customer Care Department within the U.S. at 877-762-2974, outside the U.S. at 317-572-3993, or fax 317-572-4002.

Some of the people who helped bring this book to market include the following:

Acquisitions, Editorial, and Media Development

Senior Project Editor: Christopher Morris

Acquisitions Editor: Katie Feltman

Copy Editors: Debbye Butler, Heidi Unger, Becky Whitney

Technical Editor: Mike Spivey

Editorial Manager: Kevin Kirschner

Media Development Project Manager: Laura Moss-Hollister

Media Development Assistant Project Manager: Jenny Swisher

Media Development Associate Producers: Josh Frank, Marilyn Hummel, Douglas Kuhn, Shawn Patrick

Editorial Assistant: Amanda Graham

Sr. Editorial Assistant: Cherie Case

Cartoons: Rich Tennant (www.the5thwave.com)

Composition Services

Project Coordinator: Sheree Montgomery

Layout and Graphics: Samantha K. Cherolis, Nikki Gately, Joyce Haughey

Proofreader: Christine Sabooni

Indexer: Broccoli Information Mgt.

Publishing and Editorial for Technology Dummies

Richard Swadley, Vice President and Executive Group Publisher

Andy Cummings, Vice President and Publisher

Mary Bednarek, Executive Acquisitions Director

Mary C. Corder, Editorial Director

Publishing for Consumer Dummies

Diane Graves Steele, Vice President and Publisher

Composition Services

Debbie Stailey, Director of Composition Services

Contents at a Glance

Table of Contents

Chapter 4: Practical WPF 601

Book VI: Web Development with ASP.NET 627

Chapter 1: Looking at How ASP.NET Works with C# 629

Chapter 2: Building Web Applications 641

Chapter 3: Controlling Your Development Experience 659

Introduction

C# *2010 All-in-One For Dummies* represents a different way of looking at programming languages. Rather than present the standard *For Dummies* format, which includes only 350 pages on quite a large subject, the book was expanded to include a broader scope and just a *few* pages were added.

So, although you find all the original *C# For Dummies* goodness in this book, you also find discussions about Visual Studio, Windows Presentation Foundation (WPF), service-oriented development, Web development, and a host of other topics. This book is a one-stop shop for a C# developer.

The C# programming language is a powerful and, at some nine years old, relatively mature descendant of the earlier C, C++, and Java languages. Programming with C# is lots of fun, as you're about to find out in this book.

Microsoft created C# as a major part of its .NET initiative. The company turned over the specifications for the C# language to the ECMA (pronounced "ek-ma") international standards committee in the summer of 2000 so that any company can, in theory, come up with its own version of C# written to run on any operating system, on any machine larger than a calculator.

When the first edition of this book was published, the Microsoft C# compiler was the only game in town, and its Visual Studio .NET suite of tools was the only way to program C# (other than at the Windows command line). Since then, however, Visual Studio has undergone three major revisions — the latest is Visual Studio 2010. And, at least two other players have entered the C# game.

You can now write and compile C# programs on Windows and a variety of Unix-based machines using implementations of .NET and C#, such as Mono (`www. mono-project.com`), an open source software project sponsored by Novell Corporation. Version 1.2 was released in November 2006. Though Mono lags Microsoft .NET by half a version or so, it appears to be moving fast, having implemented basically all of .NET 1.1 and much of .NET 2.0, along with those versions of C#.

Both Mono and a less well developed competitor, Portable .NET (`www. dotgnu.org/pnet.htm`), claim to run C# programs on Windows and a variety of Unix flavors, including Linux and the Apple Macintosh operating system. At the time of this writing, Portable .NET reaches the greater number of flavors, whereas Mono boasts a more complete .NET implementation. So choosing between them can be complicated, depending on your project, your platform, and your goals. (Books about programming for these platforms are becoming available already. Check online booksellers.)

Open source software is written by collaborating groups of volunteer programmers and is usually free to the world.

A description of how to make C# and other .NET languages portable to other operating systems is far beyond the scope of this book. But you can expect that within a few years, the C# Windows programs you discover how to write in this book will run on all sorts of hardware under all sorts of operating systems — matching the claim of Sun Microsystems' Java language to run on any machine. That's undoubtedly a good thing, even for Microsoft. The road to that point is still under construction, so it's no doubt riddled with potholes and obstacles to true universal portability for C#. But it's no longer just Microsoft's road.

For the moment, however, Microsoft Visual Studio has the most mature versions of C# and .NET and the most feature-filled toolset for programming with them.

Note: Though three authors contributed to this book, saying *I* rather than *we* throughout the main text seemed more economical, so that's what we (or I) do throughout.

What's New in C# 4.0

Although much of C# 4.0 is still virtually the same as the previous version, this new version adds some exciting new features, most of which revolve around COM Interop, to assist with Office development. The big new additions that this book covers include these topics:

- **Dynamic types:** Functional programming is all the rage these days, with the cool kids programming in Ruby and Haskell. Functional programming certainly has some benefits that have a place in the more tightly woven world of C#, and dynamic typing is one of them. As supported in C++ and Visual Basic, dynamic types allow runtime declaration when you don't know the type of a variable and then have the compiler figure it out. Properly used, dynamic typing is quite powerful; poorly used, it's quite dangerous.
- **Named and optional parameters:** In C# 3.0, you had to provide a value for every parameter in a method call. In C# 4.0 — again, to optimize interactions with COM — you can mark parameters as optional and accept outside objects that have optional parameters.
- **Variance in generics:** Although objects in previous versions of C# are variant, generic collections of objects are invariant. This statement means that although the compiler accepts an apple when you're asked for a fruit, it doesn't accept a basket of apples when you're asked for a basket of fruit. This issue is fixed in C# 4.0.

Leaving aside a few of the more esoteric and advanced additions, we mention a few smaller items here and there as appropriate. (Don't worry if parts of this introduction are Geek to you. You'll get there.)

Because the features of C# 4.0 all tie together for use in a single major operation — COM Interop — we bundled discussions of these features in the back of this book, in Book VIII. Throughout this book, we have updated chapters from the original C# 3.0 material wherever it seemed appropriate.

About This Book

The goal of this book is to explain C# to you. To write usable programs, you need a specific coding environment. We're betting that most readers will use Microsoft Visual Studio, although we suggest alternatives. Because this book is an *All-in-One,* we give you comprehensive coverage of Visual Studio in Book IV.

The original version of *C# For Dummies* (like all programming language books) focused on C# as a language, not all of the things you *do* with C#. This version of the book — in the mondo-size *All-in-One* format — covers Windows development, Web development, service development, and .NET Framework development, such as graphics and databases.

Our goal is to make a one-stop shop for development with Microsoft products, though there is indeed more to the topics than fits in this book. Office development isn't covered, for instance. SharePoint has way too much going on to cover it along with everything else (although Bill co-authored *VSTO For Dummies*). This book is designed to handle the vast majority of C# users, though 20 percent of our readers will be working on something that we don't cover. Sorry about that — we'll try to stretch the book to 1,000 pages next time.

Another point is that every programming problem is different. Although many different situations are covered between the covers of this book, your specific situation is different. Some interpolation has to be taking place. If you have a question about how your personal situation fits in, send the author an e-mail at `csharpfordummies.net` and we'll try to help.

What You Need in Order to Use This Book

You need, at minimum, the .NET Common Language Runtime (CLR) before you can even execute the programs generated by C#. Visual Studio 2010 copies the CLR onto your machine as part of its installation procedure. Alternatively, you can download the entire .NET package, including the C# compiler and many other useful tools, from the Microsoft Web site at `msdn.microsoft.com`. Look for the .NET Software Development Kit (SDK). The book's Web site at `csharpfordummies.net` explains how to get these items.

If all you need is C#, you can download the free version of Visual Studio, Visual C# 2010 Express, from msdn.microsoft.com/vstudio/express. The Express versions include the new C# 4.0 features. Alternatively, see SharpDevelop (www.icsharpcode.net), a good, free Visual Studio "workalike," which are provided on the Web site for this book.

You can still create most of the programs in this book using earlier versions of Visual Studio, such as Visual Studio 2008, if you need to. The exceptions are the programs that cover the new features available only in C# 4.0, which we describe in Book VIII.

How to Use This Book

We've made this book as easy to use as possible. Figuring out a new language is hard enough — why make it any more complicated than it needs to be? Though this book is divided into eight minibooks, we use an even *easier* subdivision.

Books I and II comprise the bulk of the original *C# For Dummies* book, and they cover the C# language, updated for version 4.0. Books III and IV cover technologies that are peripheral to C#. Books V, VI, and VII cover the three main types of development you do in C# — Windows Presentation Foundation, Web development, and service-oriented programming. We finish with the (thankfully short) Book VIII, about new C# 4.0 features.

If you're brand new, start at the beginning and read the first two minibooks. You'll discover a lot. Really. It will seem as though you're reading a lot of text, but it is engaging and has interesting examples.

If you're using the .NET Framework (which you probably are), read Book III as well. If you're using Visual Studio, read Book IV. (Note that we use Visual Studio 2010 Professional edition, so if you're using Express or Ultimate, your screens might look slightly different.)

Finally, you can focus on your project type — Books V, VI, and VII are specific to project type, and you can pick and choose what to read. These three minibooks are organized more as a collection of related articles than as discrete book units. You'll find them easier to use that way.

How This Book Is Organized

Here's a brief rundown of what you'll find in each part of this book.

Book I: The Basics of C# Programming

This minibook is the first of two that are based on the original *C# For Dummies.*

Book II: Object-Oriented C# Programming

In Book II, we dig into the meat of the matter and discuss which tasks C# is good for. This minibook covers how to create good class libraries and use the built-in libraries correctly. We also give you a good dose of theory and practical knowledge.

Book III: Designing for C#

.NET is essentially the set of libraries that you get to use with C#. This broad topic covers almost everything that Microsoft products can do, from coding for Windows Mobile to accessing XML files. Book III covers four of the most-needed topics:

- Databases
- Files
- Graphics
- Security

Book IV: A Tour of Visual Studio

Because Visual Studio is the tool that 95 percent of C# programmers use, it's the tool that is the focus of Book IV. It covers the use, optimization, and customization of this graphical user interface.

Book V: Windows Development with WPF

This minibook is an unconventional choice for Windows development. For years in .NET — since its inception — the choice for Windows developers was Windows Forms, the successor to the Ruby engine in Visual Basic 6. That's just how you build Windows applications.

Even with the introduction of C# 4.0 and Visual Studio 2010, Windows Forms is likely the most common choice for development of Windows applications. However, it's not the future. Windows Presentation Foundation — built on the XML derivative XAML — is the future.

For that reason, we include chapters on Windows development with WPF. If you're looking for Windows Forms 101, we include it at `csharpfordummies.net`.

Book VI: Web Development with ASP.NET

Some people would argue that ASP.NET Web Forms is falling by the wayside because of ASP.NET MVC, but we believe that it's a version or two away. In this book, we look at ASP.NET application creation and form controls and the other usual suspects. (Look for MVC in the next edition of this book, though.)

Book VII: Service-Oriented Development

On the topic of Web services, we decided to give you an overview. Our experience shows that ASP.NET Web Services, Windows Communication Foundation (WCF), and REpresentational State Transfer, or ReST, are all used in the wild, so we describe a piece of all of them.

Book VIII: New Features in C# 4.0

In the last minibook in this book, we describe some of the new features in C# 4.0, with a focus on the COM Interop changes.

Icons Used in This Book

Throughout the pages of this book, we use the following icons to highlight important information:

This scary-sounding icon flags technical information that you can skip on your first pass through the book.

The Tip icon highlights a point that can save you a lot of time and effort.

Remember this information. It's important.

Try to retain any Warning information you come across, too. This one can sneak up on you when you least expect it and generate one of those extremely hard-to-find bugs. Or, it may lead you down the garden path to La-La Land.

This icon identifies code samples you can find on the book's Web sites. `Csharp102.info` has the samples for Book I and II, and many of the articles. `Csharpfordummies.net` has a current blog, errata, and examples for the rest of the book. This feature is designed to save you some typing time when your fingers start to cramp, but don't abuse it: You gain a better understanding of C# when you enter the programs yourself and then use them as test beds for your explorations and experiments in C#.

Conventions Used in This Book

Throughout this book, we use several conventions to help you get your bearings. Terms that aren't "real words," such as the names of program variables, appear in `this font` to minimize confusion. Program listings are offset from the text this way:

```
use System;
namespace MyNameSpace
{
  public class MyClass
  {
  }
}
```

Each listing is followed by a clever, insightful explanation. Complete programs are included on the Web site for your viewing pleasure; small code segments are not.

When you see a command arrow, as in the instruction "Choose File➪Open With➪Notepad," you simply choose the File menu option. Then, from the menu that appears, choose Open With. Finally, from the resulting submenu, choose Notepad.

About this book's Web site

Two main Web sites expand on the content in this book.

✦ At `csharp102.info`, you can find support for the original *C# For Dummies* book as well as a host of bonus material. A set of utilities is also included. We've used the SharpDevelop utility enough to know that it can handle the task of writing almost any program example in this book (with the possible exception, for now, of the new LINQ features). The Reflector tool lets you peek under the covers to see what the compiler has created from your lovely C# source code. The NUnit testing tool, wildly popular among C# programmers, makes testing your code easy, whether it's in Visual Studio or SharpDevelop.

- At csharpfordummies.net, you can find the source code for all projects in this book, updated for Visual Studio 2010. We give you a set of links to other resources and a (short, we hope) list of any errata found in this book. You can also contact the authors at this site.

Additionally, you can find access to both sites at this book's companion Web site — check out www.dummies.com/go/csharp2010aiofd.

If you encounter a situation that you can't figure out, check the Frequently Asked Questions (FAQ) list at the original Web site for the *C# For Dummies* book, at csharp102.info.

In addition, both sites include bonus chapters, a list of any mistakes that may have crept into the book, and other material on C# and programming that you may find useful. Finally, you can find links to the authors' e-mail addresses, in case you can't find the answer to your question on the site.

Where to Go from Here

Obviously, your first step is to figure out the C# language — ideally, by using *C# 2010 All-in-One For Dummies,* of course. You may want to give yourself a few months of practice in writing simple C# programs before taking the next step of discovering how to create graphical Windows applications. Give yourself many months of Windows application experience before you branch out into writing programs intended to be distributed over the Internet.

In the meantime, you can keep up with C# goings and comings in several locations. First, check out the official source: msdn.microsoft.com/msdn. In addition, various programmer Web sites have extensive material on C#, including lively discussions all the way from how to save a source file to the relative merits of deterministic versus nondeterministic garbage collection. (Around Bill's house, garbage collection is quite deterministic: It's every Wednesday morning.) Here's a description of a few large C# sites:

- msdn.microsoft.com/vcsharp, the C# home page, directs you to all sorts of C# and .NET resources.
- blogs.msdn.com/csharpfaq is a C# blog with Frequently Asked Questions.
- msdn.microsoft.com/vcsharp/team/blogs is composed of the personal blogs of C# team members.
- www.c-sharpcorner.com and www.codeproject.com are two major C# sites that have articles, blogs, code, job information, and other C#-related resources.

Book I

Basics of C# Programming

"Before I go on to explain more advanced procedures like the 'Zap-Rowdy-Students-Who-Don't-Pay-Attention' function, we'll begin with some basics."

Contents at a Glance

Chapter 1: Creating Your First C# Console Application

In This Chapter

- A quick introduction to programming
- Creating a simple console application
- Reviewing the console application
- Saving code for later

In this chapter, I explain a little bit about computers, computer languages — including the computer language C# (pronounced *see sharp*) — and Visual Studio 2010. Then I take you through the steps for creating a simple program written in C#.

Getting a Handle on Computer Languages, C#, and .NET

A computer is an amazingly fast but incredibly stupid servant. Computers will do anything you ask them to (within reason); they do it extremely fast — and they're getting faster all the time.

Unfortunately, computers don't understand anything that resembles a human language. Oh, you may come back at me and say something like, "Hey, my telephone lets me dial my friend by just speaking his name. I know that a tiny computer runs my telephone. So that computer speaks English." But that's a computer *program* that understands English, not the computer itself.

The language that computers truly understand is *machine language*. It's possible, but extremely difficult and error-prone, for humans to write machine language.

Humans and computers have decided to meet somewhere in the middle. Programmers create programs in a language that isn't nearly as free as human speech, but it's a lot more flexible and easy to use than machine language. The languages occupying this middle ground — C#, for example — are *high-level* computer languages. (*High* is a relative term here.)

What's a program?

What is a program? In a practical sense, a Windows program is an executable file that you can run by double-clicking its icon. For example, the version of Microsoft Word that I'm using to write this book is a program. You call that an *executable program,* or *executable* for short. The names of executable program files generally end with the extension `.exe`. Word, for example, is `Winword.exe`.

But a program is something else, as well. An executable program consists of one or more *source files*. A C# *source file,* for instance, is a text file that contains a sequence of C# commands, which fit together according to the laws of C# grammar. This file is known as a *source file,* probably because it's a source of frustration and anxiety.

Uh, grammar? There's going to be grammar? Just the C# kind, which is much easier than the kind most of us struggled with in junior high school.

What's C#?

The C# programming language is one of those intermediate languages that programmers use to create executable programs. C# combines the range of the powerful but complicated C++ (pronounced "see plus plus") with the ease of use of the friendly but more verbose Visual Basic. (Visual Basic's newer .NET incarnation is almost on par with C# in most respects. As the flagship language of .NET, C# tends to introduce most new features first.) A C# program file carries the extension `.cs`.

Some wags have pointed out that C-sharp and D-flat are the same note, but you shouldn't refer to this new language as "D-flat" within earshot of Redmond, Washington.

C# is

- **Flexible:** C# programs can execute on the current machine, or they can be transmitted over the Web and executed on some distant computer.
- **Powerful:** C# has essentially the same command set as C++ but with the rough edges filed smooth.
- **Easier to use:** C# error-proofs the commands responsible for most C++ errors, so you spend far less time chasing down those errors.
- **Visually oriented:** The .NET code library that C# uses for many of its capabilities provides the help needed to readily create complicated display frames with drop-down lists, tabbed windows, grouped buttons, scroll bars, and background images, to name just a few.

- **Internet-friendly:** C# plays a pivotal role in the .NET Framework, Microsoft's current approach to programming for Windows, the Internet, and beyond.

  .NET is pronounced *dot net.*
- **Secure:** Any language intended for use on the Internet must include serious security to protect against malevolent hackers.

Finally, C# is an integral part of .NET.

This book is primarily about the C# language. If your primary goal is to use Visual Studio, program Windows applications, or use ASP.NET, the *For Dummies* books on those topics go well with this book. You can find a good amount of information later in this book on how to use C# to write Windows, Web, and service applications. You can also find good stuff about robots, compilers, and artificial intelligence — in case you're thinking of building a robot to take over the world.

What's .NET?

.NET began several years ago as Microsoft's strategy to open up the Web to mere mortals like you and me. Today, it's bigger than that, encompassing everything Microsoft does. In particular, it's the new way to program for Windows. It also gives a C-based language, C#, the simple, visual tools that made Visual Basic so popular.

A little background helps you see the roots of C# and .NET. Internet programming was traditionally very difficult in older languages such as C and C++. Sun Microsystems responded to that problem by creating the Java programming language. To create Java, Sun took the grammar of C++, made it a lot more user-friendly, and centered it around distributed development.

When programmers say "distributed," they're describing geographically dispersed computers running programs that talk to each other — in many cases, via the Internet.

When Microsoft licensed Java some years ago, it ran into legal difficulties with Sun over changes it wanted to make to the language. As a result, Microsoft more or less gave up on Java and started looking for ways to compete with it.

Being forced out of Java was just as well because Java has a serious problem: Although Java is a capable language, you pretty much have to write your entire program *in* Java to get the full benefit. Microsoft had too many developers and too many millions of lines of existing source code, so Microsoft had to come up with some way to support multiple languages. Enter .NET.

.NET is a framework, in many ways similar to Java's libraries — and the C# language is highly similar to the Java language. Just as *Java* is both the language itself and its extensive code library, *C#* is really much more than just the keywords and syntax of the C# language. It's those things empowered by a well-organized library containing thousands of code elements that simplify doing about any kind of programming you can imagine, from Web-based databases to cryptography to the humble Windows dialog box.

Microsoft would claim that .NET is much superior to Sun's suite of Web tools based on Java, but that's not the point. Unlike Java, .NET doesn't require you to rewrite existing programs. A Visual Basic programmer can add just a few lines to make an existing program *Web-knowledgeable* (meaning that it knows how to get data off the Internet). .NET supports all the common Microsoft languages — and hundreds of other languages written by third-party vendors. However, C# is the flagship language of the .NET fleet. C# is always the first language to access every new feature of .NET.

What is Visual Studio 2010? What about Visual C#?

(You sure ask lots of questions.) The first "Visual" language from Microsoft was Visual Basic. The first popular C-based language from Microsoft was Visual C++. Like Visual Basic, it had Visual in its name because it had a built-in graphical user interface (GUI — pronounced "GOO-ee"). This GUI included everything you needed to develop nifty-gifty C++ programs.

Eventually, Microsoft rolled all its languages into a single environment — Visual Studio. As Visual Studio 6.0 started getting a little long in the tooth, developers anxiously awaited version 7. Shortly before its release, however, Microsoft decided to rename it Visual Studio .NET to highlight this new environment's relationship to .NET.

That sounded like a marketing ploy to me — until I started delving into it. Visual Studio .NET differed quite a bit from its predecessors — enough to warrant a new name. Visual Studio 2010 is the third-generation successor to the original Visual Studio .NET. (Book IV is full of Visual Studio goodness, including instructions for customizing it.)

Microsoft calls its implementation of the language Visual C#. In reality, Visual C# is nothing more than the C# component of Visual Studio. C# is C#, with or without Visual Studio.

Okay, that's it. No more questions. (For now, anyway.)

Creating Your First Console Application

Visual Studio 2010 includes an Application Wizard that builds template programs and saves you a lot of the dirty work you'd have to do if you did everything from scratch. (I don't recommend the from-scratch approach.)

Typically, starter programs don't really do anything — at least, not anything useful. (Sounds like most of my programs.) However, they do get you beyond that initial hurdle of getting started. Some starter programs are reasonably sophisticated. In fact, you'll be amazed at how much capability the App Wizard can build on its own, especially for graphical programs.

This starter program isn't even a graphical program, though. A *console* application is one that runs in the "console" within Windows, usually referred to as the DOS prompt or command window. If you press Ctrl+R and then type `cmd`, you see a command window. It's the console where the application will run.

The following instructions are for Visual Studio. If you use anything other than Visual Studio, you have to refer to the documentation that came with your environment. Alternatively, you can just type the source code directly into your C# environment. See the Introduction to this book for some alternatives to Visual Studio.

Creating the source program

To start Visual Studio, choose Start➪All Programs➪Microsoft Visual Studio 2010➪Microsoft Visual Studio 2010.

Complete these steps to create your C# console app:

1. **Open Visual Studio 2010 and click the New Project icon, shown in Figure 1-1.**

   Visual Studio presents you with lots of icons representing the different types of applications you can create, as shown in Figure 1-2.

2. **In this New Project window, click the Console Application icon.**

   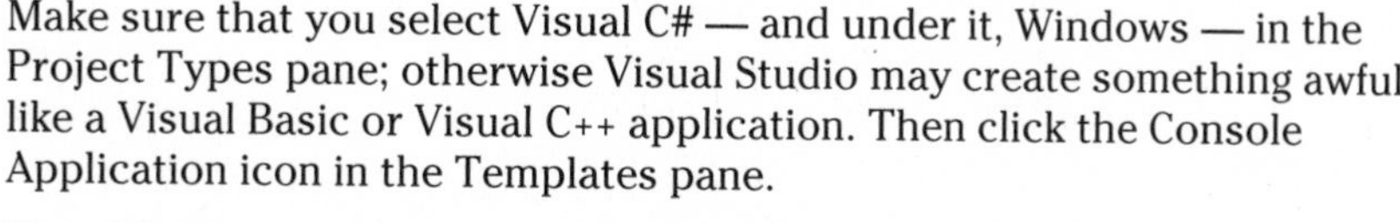
   Make sure that you select Visual C# — and under it, Windows — in the Project Types pane; otherwise Visual Studio may create something awful like a Visual Basic or Visual C++ application. Then click the Console Application icon in the Templates pane.

   Visual Studio requires you to create a project before you can start entering your C# program. A *project* is a folder in which you throw all the files that go into making your program. It has a set of configuration files that help the compiler do its work. When you tell your compiler to build (*compile*) the program, it sorts through the project to find the files it needs in order to re-create the executable program.

3. **The default name for your first application is `ConsoleApplication1`, but change it this time to** Program1 **by typing in the Name field.**

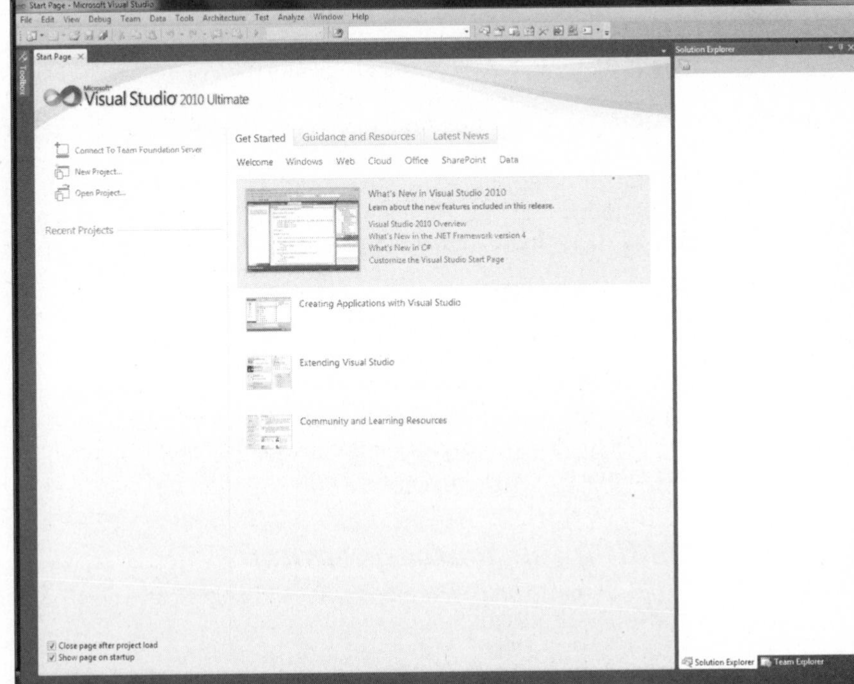

Figure 1-1: Creating a new project starts you down the road to a better Windows application.

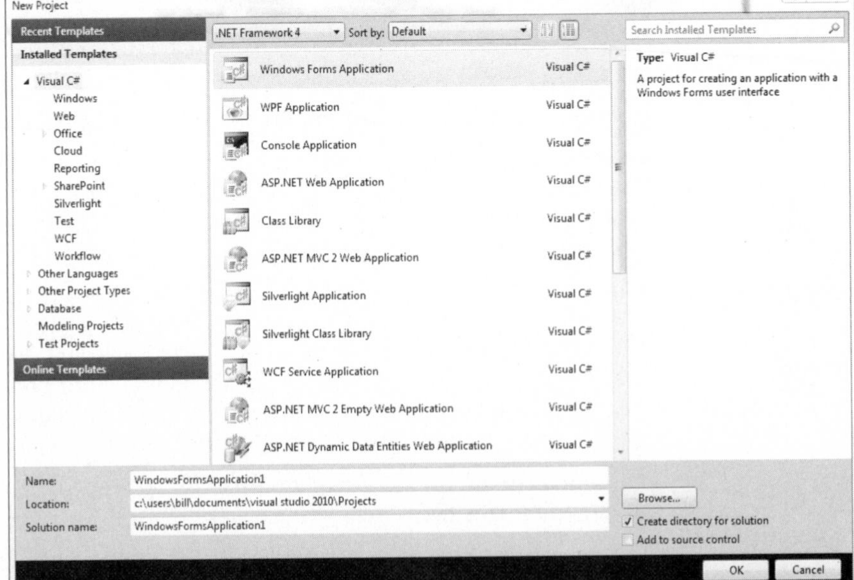

Figure 1-2: The Visual Studio App Wizard is eager to create a new program for you.

The default place to store this file is somewhere deep in your `Documents` directory. Maybe because I'm difficult (or maybe because I'm writing a book), I like to put my programs where I want them to go, not necessarily where Visual Studio wants them. To simplify working with this book, you can change the default program location. Follow these steps to make that happen:

a. *Choose Tools⇨Options.*

   The Options dialog box opens.

b. *Choose Projects and Solutions⇨General.*

c. *Select the new location in the Projects Location field, and click OK.*

   (I recommend `C:\C#Programs` for this book.)

   You can create the new directory in the Projects Location dialog box at the same time. Click the folder icon with a small sunburst at the top of the dialog box. (The directory may already exist if you've installed the example programs from the Web site.)

You can see the Options dialog box in Figure 1-3. Leave the other fields in the project settings alone for now. Read more about customization of Visual Studio in Book IV.

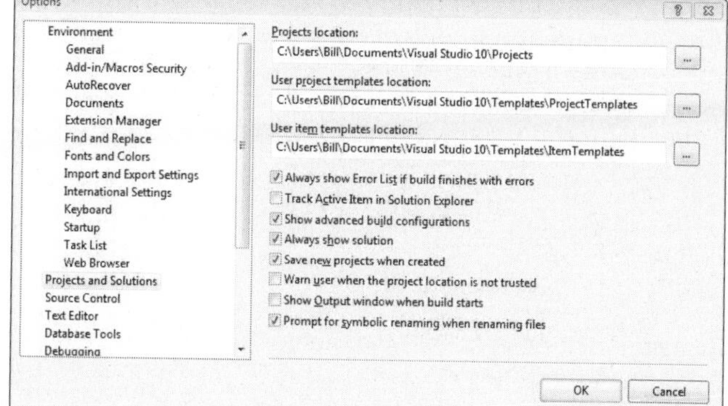

Figure 1-3: Changing the default project location.

4. **Click the OK button.**

   After a bit of disk whirring and chattering, Visual Studio generates a file named `Program.cs`. (If you look in the window labeled Solution Explorer, you see some other files; ignore them for now. If Solution Explorer isn't visible, choose View⇨Solution Explorer.)

   C# source files carry the extension `.cs`. The name `Program` is the default name assigned for the program file.

The contents of your first console app appear this way:

```
using ...

namespace Program1
{
  class Program
  {
    static void Main(string[] args)
    {

    }
  }
}
```

Along the left edge of the code window, you see several small plus (+) and minus (–) signs in boxes. Click the + sign next to `using ....` This expands a *code region,* a handy Visual Studio feature that minimizes clutter. Here are the directives that appear when you expand the region in the default console app:

```
using System;
using System.Collections.Generic;
using System.Linq;
using System.Text;
```

Regions help you focus on the code you're working on by hiding code that you aren't. Certain blocks of code — such as the `namespace` block, `class` block, methods, and other code items — get a +/– automatically without a `#region` directive. You can add your own collapsible regions, if you like, by typing `#region` above a code section and `#endregion` after it. It helps to supply a name for the region, such as `Public methods`. This code section looks like this:

```
#region Public methods
... your code
#endregion Public methods
```

This name can include spaces. Also, you can nest one region inside another, but regions can't overlap.

For now, `using System;` is the only `using` directive you really need. You can delete the others; the compiler lets you know whether you're missing one.

Taking it out for a test drive

To convert your C# program into an executable program, choose Build➪Build Program1. Visual Studio responds with the following message:

```
- Build started: Project: Program1, Configuration: Debug Any CPU -

Csc.exe /noconfig /nowarn ... (and much more)
```

```
Compile complete -- 0 errors, 0 warnings
Program1 -> C:\C#Programs\ ... (and more)==Build: 1 succeeded or up-to-date, 0
    failed, 0 skipped==
```

The key point here is the `1 succeeded` part on the last line.

As a general rule of programming, `succeeded` is good; `failed` is bad. The bad — the exceptions — is covered in Chapter 9 of this minibook.

To execute the program, choose Debug➪Start. The program brings up a black console window and terminates immediately. (If you have a fast computer, the appearance of this window is just a flash on the screen.) The program has seemingly done nothing. In fact, this is the case. The template is nothing but an empty shell.

An alternative command, Debug➪Start Without Debugging, behaves a bit better at this point. Try it out.

Making Your Console App Do Something

Edit the `Program.cs` template file until it appears this way:

```
using System;

namespace Program1
{
  public class Program
  {
    // This is where your program starts.
    static void Main(string[] args)
    {
      // Prompt user to enter a name.
      Console.WriteLine("Enter your name, please:");

      // Now read the name entered.
      string name = Console.ReadLine();

      // Greet the user with the name that was entered.
      Console.WriteLine("Hello, " + name);

      // Wait for user to acknowledge the results.
      Console.WriteLine("Press Enter to terminate...");
      Console.Read();
    }
  }
}
```

Don't sweat the stuff following the double or triple slashes (`//` or `///`), and don't worry about whether to enter one or two spaces or one or two new lines. However, do pay attention to capitalization.

Choose Build⇨Build Program1 to convert this new version of `Program.cs` into the `Program1.exe` program.

From within Visual Studio 2008, choose Debug⇨Start Without Debugging. The black console window appears and prompts you for your name. (You may need to activate the console window by clicking it.) Then the window shows `Hello`, followed by the name entered, and displays `Press Enter to terminate . . .` . Pressing Enter closes the window.

You can also execute the program from the DOS command line. To do so, open a Command Prompt window and enter the following:

```
CD \C#Programs\Program1\bin\Debug
```

Now enter **Program1** to execute the program. The output should be identical to what you saw earlier. You can also navigate to the `\C#Programs\Program1\bin\Debug` folder in Windows Explorer and then double-click the `Program1.exe` file.

To open a Command Prompt window, try choosing Tools⇨Command Prompt. If that command isn't available on your Visual Studio Tools menu, choose Start⇨All Programs⇨Microsoft Visual Studio 2008⇨Visual Studio Tools⇨Visual Studio 2008 Command Prompt.

Reviewing Your Console Application

In the following sections, you take this first C# console app apart one section at a time to understand how it works.

The program framework

The basic framework for all console applications starts as the following:

```
using System;
using System.Collections.Generic;
using System.Linq;
using System.Text;

namespace Program1
{
  public class Program
  {
    // This is where your program starts.
    public static void Main(string[] args)
    {
       // Your code goes here.
    }
  }
}
```

The program starts executing right after the statement containing `Main()` and ends at the closed curly brace (}) following `Main()`. (I explain the meaning of these statements in due course. More than that, I cannot say for now.)

The list of `using` directives can come immediately before or immediately after the phrase `namespace Program1 {`. The order doesn't matter. You can apply `using` to lots of things in .NET. I explain the whole business of namespaces and `using` in the object-oriented programming chapters in Book II.

Comments

The template already has lots of lines, and I've added several other lines, such as the following (in boldface):

```
// This is where your program starts.
public static void Main(string[] args)
```

C# ignores the first line in this example. This line is known as a *comment.*

Any line that begins with `//` or `///` is free text, and C# ignores it. Consider `//` and `///` to be equivalent for now.

Why include lines if the computer ignores them? Because comments explain your C# statements. A program, even in C#, isn't easy to understand. Remember that a programming language is a compromise between what computers understand and what humans understand. These comments are useful while you write the code, and they're especially helpful to the poor sap — possibly you — who tries to re-create your logic a year later. Comments make the job much easier.

Comment early and often.

The meat of the program

The real core of this program is embedded within the block of code marked with `Main()`, like this:

```
// Prompt user to enter a name.
Console.WriteLine("Enter your name, please:");

// Now read the name entered.
string name = Console.ReadLine();

// Greet the user with the name that was entered.
Console.WriteLine("Hello, " + name);
```

Save a ton of routine typing with the new C# Code Snippets feature. Snippets are great for common statements like `Console.WriteLine`. Press Ctrl+K and then Ctrl+X to see a pop-up menu of snippets. (You may need to press Tab once or twice to open the Visual C# folder or other folders on that menu.) Scroll down the menu to `cw` and press Enter. Visual Studio inserts the body of a `Console.WriteLine()` statement with the insertion point between the parentheses, ready to go. When you have a few of the shortcuts, such as `cw`, `for`, and `if`, memorized, use the even quicker technique: Type **cw** and press Tab twice. (Also try selecting some lines of code, pressing Ctrl+K, and then pressing Ctrl+S. Choose something like `if`. An `if` statement *surrounds* the selected code lines.)

The program begins executing with the first C# statement: `Console.WriteLine`. This command writes the character string `Enter your name, please:` to the console.

The next statement reads in the user's answer and stores it in a *variable* (a kind of workbox) named `name`. (See Chapter 2 of this minibook for more on these storage locations.) The last line combines the string `Hello,` with the user's name and outputs the result to the console.

The final three lines cause the computer to wait for the user to press Enter before proceeding. These lines ensure that the user has time to read the output before the program continues:

```
// Wait for user to acknowledge the results.
Console.WriteLine("Press Enter to terminate...");
Console.Read();
```

This step can be important, depending on how you execute the program and depending on the environment. In particular, running your console app inside Visual Studio, or from Windows Explorer, makes the preceding lines necessary — otherwise, the console window closes so fast you can't read the output. If you open a console window and run the program from there, the window stays open regardless.

Introducing the Toolbox Trick

The key part of the program you create in the preceding section consists of the final two lines of code:

```
// Wait for user to acknowledge the results.
Console.WriteLine("Press Enter to terminate...");
Console.Read();
```

The easiest way to re-create those key lines in each future console application you write is described in the following sections.

Saving code in the Toolbox

The first step is to save those lines in a handy location for future use in a handy place: the Toolbox window. With your `Program1` console application open in Visual Studio, follow these steps:

1. **In the `Main()` method of class `Program`, select the lines you want to save — in this case, the three lines mentioned previously.**
2. **Make sure the Toolbox window is open on the left. (If it isn't, open it by choosing View⇨Toolbox.)**
3. **Drag the selected lines into the General tab of the Toolbox window and drop them. (Or copy the lines and paste them into the Toolbox.)**

   The Toolbox stores the lines there for you in perpetuity. Figure 1-4 shows the lines placed in the Toolbox.

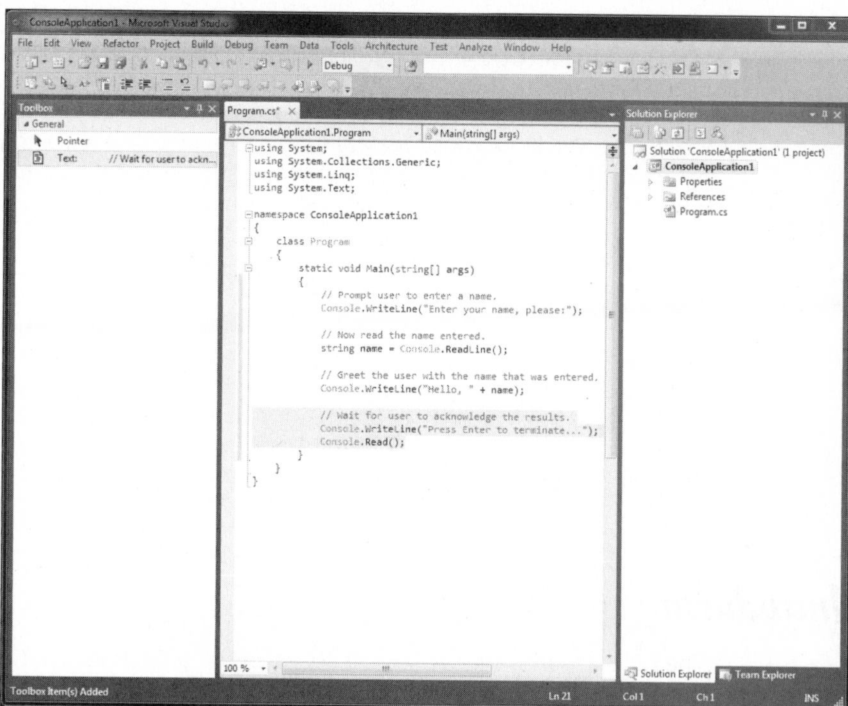

Figure 1-4: Setting up the Toolbox with some handy saved text for future use.

Reusing code from the Toolbox

Now that you have your template text stored in the Toolbox, you can reuse it in all console applications you write henceforth. Here's how to use it:

1. **In Visual Studio, create a new console application as described earlier in this chapter.**
2. **Click in the editor at the spot where you'd like to insert some Toolbox text.**
3. **With the `Program.cs` file open for editing, make sure the Toolbox window is open. (If it isn't, see the procedure above.)**
4. **In the General tab of the Toolbox window (other tabs could be showing), find the saved text you want to use and double-click it.**

   The selected item is inserted at the insertion point in the editor window.

With that boilerplate text in place, you can write the rest of your application above those lines. That's it. You now have a finished console app. Try it out for about 30 seconds. Then you can check out Chapter 2 of this minibook.

Chapter 2: Living with Variability — Declaring Value-Type Variables

In This Chapter

- **Visiting the train station — the C# variable as storage locker**
- **Using integers — you can count on it**
- **Handling fractional values — what's half a duck?**
- **Declaring other types of variables — dates, characters, strings**
- **Handling numeric constants — Π in the sky**
- **Changing types — cast doesn't mean toss**
- **Letting the compiler figure out the type — var magic**

The most fundamental of all concepts in programming is that of the variable. A C# variable is like a small box in which you can store things, particularly numbers, for later use. (The term *variable* is borrowed from the world of mathematics.)

Unfortunately for programmers, C# places several limitations on variables — limitations that mathematicians don't have to consider. This chapter takes you through the steps for declaring, initializing, and using variables. It also introduces several of the most basic *data types* in C#.

Declaring a Variable

When the mathematician says, "*n* is equal to 1," that means the term *n* is equivalent to 1 in some ethereal way. The mathematician is free to introduce variables in a willy-nilly fashion. For example, the mathematician may say this:

```
x = y² + 2y + y
if k = y + 1 then
x = k²
```

Programmers must define variables in a particular way that's more demanding than the mathematician's looser style. For example, a C# programmer may write the following bit of code:

```
int n;
n = 1;
```

The first line means, "Carve off a small amount of storage in the computer's memory and assign it the name *n*." This step is analogous to reserving one of those storage lockers at the train station and slapping the label *n* on the side. The second line says, "Store the value 1 in the variable *n*, thereby replacing whatever that storage location already contains." The train-locker equivalent is, "Open the train locker, rip out whatever happens to be in there, and shove a 1 in its place."

The equals symbol (=) is called the *assignment operator.*

The mathematician says, "*n* equals 1." The C# programmer says in a more precise way, "Store the value 1 in the variable `n`." (Think about the train locker, and you see why that's preferable.) C# operators tell the computer what you want to do. In other words, operators are verbs and not descriptors. The assignment operator takes the value on its right and stores it in the variable on the left. We say a lot more about operators in Chapter 3 of this minibook.

What's an int?

In C#, each variable has a fixed type. When you allocate one of those train lockers, you have to pick the size you need. If you pick an integer locker, for instance, you can't turn around and hope to stuff the entire state of Texas in it — maybe Rhode Island, but not Texas.

For the example in the preceding section of this chapter, you select a locker that's designed to handle an integer — C# calls it an `int`. Integers are the counting numbers 1, 2, 3, and so on, plus 0 and the negative numbers –1, –2, –3, and so on.

Before you can use a variable, you must *declare* it. After you declare a variable as `int`, it can hold and regurgitate integer values, as this example demonstrates:

```
// Declare a variable named n - an empty train locker.
int n;
// Declare an int variable m and initialize it with the value 2.
int m = 2;
// Assign the value stored in m to the variable n.
n = m;
```

The first line after the comment is a *declaration* that creates a little storage area, `n`, designed to hold an integer value. The initial value of `n` is not specified until it is *assigned* a value. The second declaration not only declares an `int` variable `m` but also *initializes* it with a value of 2, all in one shot.

The term *initialize* means to assign an initial value. To initialize a variable is to assign it a value for the first time. You don't know for sure what the value of a variable is until it has been initialized. Nobody knows.

The final statement in the program assigns the value stored in m, which is 2, to the variable n. The variable n continues to contain the value 2 until it is assigned a new value. (The variable n doesn't lose its value when you assign its value to m. It's like cloning n.)

Rules for declaring variables

You can initialize a variable as part of the declaration, like this:

```
// Declare another int variable and give it the initial value of 1.
int p = 1;
```

This is equivalent to sticking a 1 into that int storage locker when you first rent it, rather than opening the locker and stuffing in the value later.

Initialize a variable when you declare it. In most (but not all) cases, C# initializes the variable for you — but don't rely on it to do that.

You may declare variables anywhere (well, almost anywhere) within a program.

However, you may not use a variable until you declare it and set it to some value. Thus the last two assignments shown here are *not* legal:

```
// The following is illegal because m is not assigned
// a value before it is used.
int m;
n = m;
// The following is illegal because p has not been
// declared before it is used.
p = 2;
int p;
```

Finally, you cannot declare the same variable twice in the same scope (a function, for example).

Variations on a theme: Different types of int

Most simple numeric variables are of type int. However, C# provides a number of twists to the int variable type for special occasions.

All integer variable types are limited to whole numbers. The int type suffers from other limitations as well. For example, an int variable can store values only in the range from roughly –2 billion to 2 billion.

A distance of 2 billion inches is greater than the circumference of the Earth. In case 2 billion isn't quite large enough for you, C# provides an integer type called long (short for long int) that can represent numbers almost as large as you can imagine. The only problem with a long is that it takes a larger train locker: A long consumes 8 bytes (64 bits) — twice as much as a garden-variety 4-byte (32-bit) int. C# provides several other integer variable types, as shown in Table 2-1.

Table 2-1 Size and Range of C# Integer Types

Type	*Bytes*	*Range of Values*	*In Use*
`sbyte`	1	–128 to 127	`sbyte sb = 12;`
`byte`	1	0 to 255	`byte b = 12;`
`short`	2	–32,768 to 32,767	`short sh = 12345;`
`ushort`	2	0 to 65,535	`ushort ush = 62345;`
`int`	4	–2 billion to 2 billion	`int n = 1234567890;`
`uint`	4	0 to 4 billion (exact values listed in the Cheat Sheet on this book's Web site)	`uint un = 3234567890U`
`long`	8	-10^{20} to 10^{20} — "a whole lot"	`long l = 123456789012L`
`Ulong`	8	0 to 2×10^{20}	`long ul = 123456789012UL`

As I explain in the section "Declaring Numeric Constants," later in this chapter, fixed values such as 1 also have a type. By default, a simple constant such as 1 is assumed to be an `int`. Constants other than an `int` must be marked with their variable type. For example, 123U is an unsigned integer, `uint`.

Most integer variables are called *signed,* which means they can represent negative values. Unsigned integers can represent only positive values, but you get twice the range in return. As you can see from Table 2-1, the names of most unsigned integer types start with a `u`, while the signed types generally don't have a prefix.

You don't need any unsigned integer versions in this book.

Representing Fractions

Integers are useful for most calculations. One of this book's authors made it into the sixth grade before he ever found out that anything else existed, and he still hasn't forgiven his sixth-grade teacher for starting him down the slippery slope of fractions.

Many calculations involve fractions, which simple integers can't accurately represent. The common equation for converting from Fahrenheit to Celsius temperatures demonstrates the problem, like this:

```
// Convert the temperature 41 degrees Fahrenheit.
int fahr = 41;
int celsius = (fahr - 32) * (5 / 9)
```

This equation works just fine for some values. For example, 41 degrees Fahrenheit is 5 degrees Celsius. "Correct, Mr. Davis," says Stephen's sixth-grade teacher.

Okay, try a different value: 100 degrees Fahrenheit. Working through the equation, 100–32 is 68; 68 times 5⁄9 is 37. "No," she says, "The answer is 37.78." Even that's wrong because it's really 37.777 . . . with the 7s repeating forever, but I don't push the point.

An int can represent only integer numbers. The integer equivalent of 37.78 is 37. This lopping off of the fractional part of a number to get it to fit into an integer variable is called *integer truncation.*

Truncation is not the same thing as *rounding.* Truncation lops off the fractional part. Goodbye, Charlie. Rounding picks the closest integer value. Thus, truncating 1.9 results in 1. Rounding 1.9 results in 2.

For temperatures, 37 may be good enough. It's not like you wear short-sleeve shirts at 37.7 degrees but pull on a sweater at 37 degrees. But integer truncation is unacceptable for many, if not most, applications.

Actually, the problem is much worse than that. An int can't handle the ratio 5⁄9 either; it always yields the value 0. Consequently, the equation as written in this example calculates celsius as 0 for all values of fahr. Even I admit that's unacceptable.

This book's Web site includes an int-based temperature-conversion program contained in the ConvertTemperatureWithRoundOff directory. At this point, you may not understand all the details, but you can see the conversion equations and execute the program ConvertTemperatureWithRoundOff.exe to see the results. (Review Chapter 1 of this minibook if you need a hand running it.)

Handling Floating-Point Variables

The limitations of an int variable are unacceptable for some applications. The range generally isn't a problem — the double-zillion range of a 64-bit-long integer should be enough for almost anyone. However, the fact that an int is limited to whole numbers is a bit harder to swallow.

In some cases, you need numbers that can have a nonzero fractional part. Mathematicians call these *real numbers.* (Somehow that always seemed like a ridiculous name for a number. Are integer numbers somehow unreal?)

Notice that I said a real number *can* have a nonzero fractional part — that is, 1.5 is a real number, but so is 1.0. For example, 1.0 + 0.1 is 1.1. Just keep that point in mind as you read the rest of this chapter.

Fortunately, C# understands real numbers. Real numbers come in two flavors: floating-point and decimal. Floating-point is the most common type. I describe the decimal type a little later in this chapter.

Declaring a floating-point variable

A floating-point variable carries the designation `float`, and you declare one as shown in this example:

```
float f = 1.0;
```

After you declare it as `float`, the variable `f` is a `float` for the rest of its natural instructions.

Table 2-2 describes the two kinds of floating-point types. All floating-point variables are signed. (There's no such thing as a floating-point variable that can't represent a negative value.)

Table 2-2 Size and Range of Floating-Point Variable Types

Type	*Bytes*	*Range of Values*	*Accuracy to Number of Digits*	*In Use*
`float`	8	$1.5 * 10^{-45}$ to $3.4 * 10^{38}$	6 to 7	`float f = 1.2F;`
`double`	16	$5.0 * 10^{-324}$ to $1.7 * 10^{308}$	15 to 16	`double d = 1.2;`

You might think `float` is the default floating-point variable type, but actually the `double` is the default in C#. If you don't specify the type for, say, 12.3, C# calls it a `double`.

The Accuracy column in Table 2-2 refers to the number of significant digits that such a variable type can represent. For example, 5⁄9 is actually 0.555 . . . with an unending sequence of 5s. However, a `float` variable is said to have six significant digits of accuracy — which means numbers after the sixth digit are ignored. Thus 5⁄9 may appear this way when expressed as a `float`:

```
0.5555551457382
```

Here you know that all the digits after the sixth 5 are untrustworthy.

The same number — 5⁄9 — may appear this way when expressed as a `double`:

```
0.55555555555555557823
```

The `double` packs a whopping 15 to 16 significant digits.

Use `double` variable types unless you have a specific reason to do otherwise.

Converting some more temperatures

Here's the formula for converting from Fahrenheit to Celsius temperatures using floating-point variables:

```
double celsius = (fahr - 32.0) * (5.0 / 9.0)
```

The Web site contains a floating-point version of the temperature-conversion program called `ConvertTemperatureWithFloat`.

The following example shows the result of executing the `double`-based `ConvertTemperatureWithFloat` program:

```
Enter temp in degrees Fahrenheit:100
Temperature in degrees Celsius = 37.7777777777778
Press Enter to terminate...
```

Examining some limitations of floating-point variables

You may be tempted to use floating-point variables all the time because they solve the truncation problem so nicely. Sure, they use up a bit more memory. But memory is cheap these days, so why not? But floating-point variables also have limitations, which I discuss in the following sections.

Counting

You can't use floating-point variables as counting numbers. Some C# structures need to count (as in 1, 2, 3, and so on). You know that 1.0, 2.0, and 3.0 are counting numbers just as well as 1, 2, and 3, but C# doesn't know that. For example, given the accuracy limitations of floating-points, how does C# know that you aren't *actually* saying 1.000001?

Whether you find that argument convincing, you can't use a floating-point variable when counting things.

Comparing numbers

You have to be careful when comparing floating-point numbers. For example, 12.5 may be represented as 12.500001. Most people don't care about that little extra bit on the end. However, the computer takes things extremely literally. To C#, 12.500000 and 12.500001 are not the same numbers.

So, if you add 1.1 to 1.1, you can't tell whether the result is 2.2 or 2.200001. And if you ask, "Is `doubleVariable` equal to 2.2?" you may not get the results you expect. Generally, you have to resort to some bogus comparison like this: "Is the absolute value of the difference between `doubleVariable` and 2.2 less than .000001?" In other words, "within an acceptable margin of error."

The Pentium processor plays a trick to make this problem less troublesome than it otherwise may be: It performs floating-point arithmetic in an especially long `double` format — that is, rather than using 64 bits, it uses a whopping 80 bits. When rounding off an 80-bit `float` into a 64-bit `float`, you (almost) always get the expected result, even if the 80-bit number was off a bit or two.

Calculation speed

Processors such as the *x*86 varieties used in older Windows-based PCs could perform integer arithmetic much faster than arithmetic of the floating-point persuasion. In those days, programmers would go out of their way to limit a program to integer arithmetic.

The ratio in additional speed on a Pentium III processor for a simple (perhaps too simple) test of about 300,000,000 additions and subtractions was about 3 to 1. That is, for every `double` add, you could have done three `int` adds. (Computations involving multiplication and division may show different results.)

Not-so-limited range

In the past, a floating-point variable could represent a considerably larger range of numbers than an integer type. It still can, but the range of the `long` is large enough to render the point moot.

Even though a simple `float` can represent a very large number, the number of significant digits is limited to about six. For example, `123,456,789F` is the same as `123,456,000F`. (For an explanation of the `F` notation at the end of these numbers, see "Declaring Numeric Constants," later in this chapter.)

Using the Decimal Type: Is It an Integer or a Float?

As I explain in previous sections of this chapter, both the integer and floating-point types have their problems. Floating-point variables have rounding problems associated with limits to their accuracy, while `int` variables just lop off the fractional part of a variable. In some cases, you need a variable type that offers the best of two worlds:

- ✦ Like a floating-point variable, it can store fractions.
- ✦ Like an integer, numbers of this type offer exact values for use in computations — for example, 12.5 is really 12.5 and not 12.500001.

Fortunately, C# provides such a variable type, called `decimal`. A `decimal` variable can represent a number between 10^{-28} and 10^{28} — that's a lot of zeros! And it does so without rounding problems.

Declaring a decimal

Decimal variables are declared and used like any variable type, like this:

```
decimal m1 = 100;    // Good
decimal m2 = 100M;   // Better
```

The first declaration shown here creates a variable `m1` and initializes it to a value of `100`. What isn't obvious is that 100 is actually of type `int`. Thus, C# must convert the `int` into a `decimal` type before performing the initialization. Fortunately, C# understands what you mean — and performs the conversion for you.

The declaration of `m2` is the best. This clever declaration initializes `m2` with the `decimal` constant 100M. The letter *M* at the end of the number specifies that the constant is of type `decimal`. No conversion is required. (See the section "Declaring Numeric Constants," later in this chapter.)

Comparing decimals, integers, and floating-point types

The `decimal` variable type seems to have all the advantages and none of the disadvantages of `int` or `double` types. Variables of this type have a very large range, they don't suffer from rounding problems, and 25.0 is 25.0 and not 25.00001.

The `decimal` variable type has two significant limitations, however. First, a `decimal` is not considered a counting number because it may contain a fractional value. Consequently, you can't use them in flow-control loops, which I explain in Chapter 5 of this minibook.

The second problem with `decimal` variables is equally as serious or even more so. Computations involving `decimal` values are significantly slower than those involving either simple integer or floating-point values — and I do mean *significant.* On a crude benchmark test of 300,000,000 adds and subtracts, the operations involving `decimal` variables were approximately 50 times slower than those involving simple `int` variables. The relative computational speed gets even worse for more complex operations. Besides that, most computational functions, such as calculating sines or exponents, are not available for the `decimal` number type.

Clearly, the `decimal` variable type is most appropriate for applications such as banking, in which accuracy is extremely important but the number of calculations is relatively small.

Examining the bool Type: Is It Logical?

Finally, a logical variable type. Except in this case, I really mean a type "logical." The Boolean type `bool` can have two values: `true` or `false`. I kid thee not — a whole variable type for just two values. Not even a "maybe."

Former C and C++ programmers are accustomed to using the `int` value 0 (zero) to mean `false` and nonzero to mean `true`. That doesn't work in C#.

You declare a `bool` variable this way:

```
bool thisIsABool = true;
```

No conversion path exists between `bool` variables and any other types. In other words, you can't convert a `bool` directly into something else. (Even if you could, you shouldn't because it doesn't make any sense.) In particular, you can't convert a `bool` into an `int` (such as `false` becoming 0) or a `string` (such as `false` becoming the word "false").

Checking Out Character Types

A program that can do nothing more than spit out numbers may be fine for mathematicians, accountants, insurance agents with their mortality figures, and folks calculating cannon-shell trajectories. (Don't laugh. The original computers were built to generate tables of cannon-shell trajectories to help artillery gunners.) However, for most applications, programs must deal with letters as well as numbers.

C# treats letters in two distinctly different ways: individual characters of type `char` (usually pronounced *char*, as in singe or burn) and strings of characters — a type called, cleverly enough, `string`.

The char variable type

The `char` variable is a box capable of holding a single character. A character constant appears as a character surrounded by a pair of single quotation marks, as in this example:

```
char c = 'a';
```

You can store any single character from the Roman, Hebrew, Arabic, Cyrillic, and most other alphabets. You can also store Japanese katakana and hiragana characters, as well as many Japanese and Chinese kanjis.

In addition, `char` is considered a counting type. That means you can use a `char` type to control the looping structures that I describe in Chapter 5 of this minibook. Character variables do not suffer from rounding problems.

The character variable includes no font information. So you may store in a `char` variable what you think is a perfectly good kanji (and it may well be) — but when you view the character, it can look like garbage if you're not looking at it through the eyes of the proper font.

Special chars

Some characters within a given font are not printable, in the sense that you don't see anything when you look at them on the computer screen or printer. The most obvious example of this is the space, which is represented by the character `' '` (single quote, space, single quote). Other characters have no letter equivalent — for example, the tab character. C# uses the backslash to flag these characters, as shown in Table 2-3.

Table 2-3 Special Characters

Character Constant	*Value*
`'\n'`	New line
`'\t'`	Tab
`'\0'`	Null character
`'\r'`	Carriage return
`'\\'`	Backslash

The string type

Another extremely common variable type is the `string`. The following examples show how you declare and initialize `string` variables:

```
// Declare now, initialize later.
string someString1;
someString1 = "this is a string";
// Or initialize when declared - preferable.
string someString2 = "this is a string";
```

A `string` constant, often called a `string` *literal*, is a set of characters surrounded by double quotes. The characters in a `string` can include the special characters shown in Table 2-3. A `string` cannot be written across a line in the C# source file, but it can contain the new-line character, as the following examples show (see boldface):

```
// The following is not legal.
string someString = "This is a line
and so is this";
// However, the following is legal.
string someString = "This is a line\and so is this";
```

When written out with `Console.WriteLine`, the last line in this example places the two phrases on separate lines, like this:

```
This is a line
and so is this
```

A `string` is not a counting type. A `string` is also not a value-type — no "string" exists that's intrinsic (built in) to the processor. Only one of the common operators works on `string` objects: The + operator concatenates two strings into one. For example:

```
string s = "this is a phrase"
         + " and so is this";
```

These lines of code set the `string` variable `s` equal to this character string:

```
"this is a phrase and so is this"
```

The `string` with no characters, written `""` (two double quotes in a row), is a valid `string`, called an empty `string` (or sometimes a null `string`). A null `string` (`""`) is different from a null `char` (`'\0'`) and from a `string` containing any amount of space, even one (`" "`).

I like to initialize strings using the `String.Empty` value, which means the same thing as `""` and is less prone to misinterpretation:

```
string mySecretName = String.Empty;  // A property of the String type
```

By the way, all the other data types in this chapter are *value types*. The `string` type, however, is not a value type, as I explain in the following section. Chapter 3 of this minibook goes into much more detail about the `string` type.

What's a Value Type?

The variable types that I describe in this chapter are of fixed length — again with the exception of `string`. A fixed-length variable type always occupies the same amount of memory. So if you assign `a = b`, C# can transfer the value of `b` into `a` without taking extra measures designed to handle variable-length types. This characteristic is why these types of variables are called *value types*.

The types `int`, `double`, and `bool`, and their close derivatives (like unsigned `int`) are intrinsic variable types built right into the processor. The intrinsic variable types plus `decimal` are also known as value types because variables store the actual data. The `string` type is neither — because the variable actually stores a sort of "pointer" to the string's data, called a *reference*. The data in the string is actually off in another location.

The programmer-defined types that I explain in Chapter 8 of this minibook, known as reference types, are neither value types nor intrinsic. The `string` type is a reference type, although the C# compiler does accord it some special treatment because `string`s are so widely used.

Comparing string and char

Although strings deal with characters, the `string` type is amazingly different from the `char`. Of course, certain trivial differences exist. You enclose a character with single quotes, as in this example:

```
'a'
```

On the other hand, you put double quotes around a string:

```
"this is a string"
"a"   // So is this -- see the double quotes?
```

The rules concerning strings are not the same as those concerning characters. For one thing, you know right up front that a `char` is a single character, and that's it. For example, the following code makes no sense, either as addition or as concatenation:

```
char c1 = 'a';
char c2 = 'b';
char c3 = c1 + c2
```

Actually, this bit of code almost compiles — but with a completely different meaning from what was intended. These statements convert `c1` into an `int` consisting of the numeric value of `c1`. C# also converts `c2` into an `int` and then adds the two integers. The error occurs when trying to store the results back into `c3` — numeric data may be lost storing an `int` into the smaller `char`. In any case, the operation makes no sense.

A string, on the other hand, can be any length. So concatenating two strings, as shown here, *does* make sense:

```
string s1 = "a";
string s2 = "b";
string s3 = s1 + s2;  // Result is "ab"
```

As part of its library, C# defines an entire suite of string operations. I describe them in Chapter 3 of this minibook.

Naming conventions

Programming is hard enough without programmers making it harder. To make your C# source code easier to wade through, adopt a naming convention and stick to it. As much as possible, your naming convention should follow that adopted by other C# programmers:

- **The names of things other than variables start with a capital letter, and variables start with a lowercase letter.** Make these names as descriptive as possible — which often means that a name consists of multiple words. These words should be capitalized but butted up against each other with no underscore between them — for example, `ThisIsALongName`. Names that start with a capital are *Pascal-cased,* from the way a 1970s-era language called Pascal named things. (My first book was about Pascal.)
- **The names of variables start with a lowercase letter.** A typical variable name looks like this: `thisIsALongVariableName`. This variable naming style is called *camel-casing* because it has humps in the middle.

Prior to the .NET era, it was common among Windows programmers to use a convention in which the first letter of the variable name indicated the type of the variable. Most of these letters were straightforward: `f` for `float`, `d` for `double`, `s` for `string`, and so on. The only one that was even the slightest bit different was `n` for `int`. One exception to this rule existed: For reasons that stretch way back into the Fortran programming language of the 1960s, the single letters `i`, `j`, and `k` were also used as common names for an `int`, and they still are in C#. This style of naming variables was called Hungarian notation, after Charles Simonyi, a famous Microsoftie who recently went to the International Space Station as a space tourist. (Martha Stewart packed his sack lunch.)

Hungarian notation has fallen out of favor, at least in .NET programming circles. With recent Visual Studio versions, you can simply rest the cursor on a variable in the debugger to have its data type revealed in a tooltip box. That makes the Hungarian prefix a bit less useful, although a few folks still hold out for Hungarian.

Calculating Leap Years: DateTime

What if you had to write a program that calculates whether this year is a leap year?

The algorithm looks like this:

```
It's a leap year if
  year is evenly divisible by 4
  and, if it happens to be evenly divisible by 100,
    it's also evenly divisible by 400
```

You don't have enough tools yet to tackle that in C#. But you could just ask the `DateTime` type (which is a value type, like `int`):

```
DateTime thisYear = new DateTime(2011, 1, 1);
bool isLeapYear = DateTime.IsLeapYear(thisYear.Year);
```

The result for 2011 is `false`, but for 2012, it's `true`. (For now, don't worry about that first line of code, which uses some things you haven't gotten to yet.)

With the `DateTime` data type, you can do something like 80 different operations, such as pull out just the month; get the day of the week; add days, hours, minutes, seconds, milliseconds, months, or years to a given date; get the number of days in a given month; subtract two dates.

The following sample lines use a convenient property of `DateTime` called `Now` to capture the present date and time, and one of the numerous `DateTime` methods that let you convert one time into another:

```
DateTime thisMoment = DateTime.Now;
DateTime anHourFromNow = thisMoment.AddHours(1);
```

You can also extract specific parts of a `DateTime`:

```
int year = DateTime.Now.Year;                    // For example, 2007
DayOfWeek dayOfWeek = DateTime.Now.DayOfWeek;  // For example, Sunday
```

If you print out that `DayOfWeek` object, it prints something like "Sunday." And you can do other handy manipulations of `DateTimes`:

```
DateTime date = DateTime.Today;                 // Get just the date part.
TimeSpan time = thisMoment.TimeOfDay;           // Get just the time part.
TimeSpan duration = new TimeSpan(3, 0, 0, 0);  // Specify duration in days.
DateTime threeDaysFromNow = thisMoment.Add(duration);
```

The first two lines just extract portions of the information in a `DateTime`. The next two lines add a *duration* to a `DateTime`. A duration, or amount of time, differs from a moment in time; you specify durations with the `TimeSpan` class, and moments with `DateTime`. So the third line sets up a `TimeSpan` of three days, zero hours, zero minutes, and zero seconds. The fourth line adds the three-day duration to the `DateTime` representing right now, resulting in a new `DateTime` whose day component is three greater than the day component for `thisMoment`.

Subtracting a `DateTime` from another `DateTime` (or a `TimeSpan` from a `DateTime`) returns a `DateTime`:

```
TimeSpan duration1 = new TimeSpan(1, 0, 0);  // One hour later.
// Since Today gives 12:00:00 AM (midnight), the following gives 1:00:00 AM:
DateTime anHourAfterMidnight = DateTime.Today.Add(duration1);
Console.WriteLine("An hour from midnight will be {0}", anHourAfterMidnight);
DateTime midnight = anHourAfterMidnight.Subtract(duration1);
Console.WriteLine("An hour before 1 AM is {0}", midnight);
```

The first line of the preceding code creates a `TimeSpan` of one hour. The next line gets the date (actually, midnight this morning) and adds the one-hour span to it, resulting in a `DateTime` representing 1:00 a.m. today. The next-to-last line subtracts a one-hour duration from 1:00 a.m. to get 12:00 a.m. (midnight).

For more information, search for *DateTime structure* in the Visual Studio Help system and take a look at the `DateTimeExample` program on this book's Web site.

Declaring Numeric Constants

There are very few absolutes in life; however, I'm about to give you a C# absolute: Every expression has a value and a type. In a declaration such as `int n`, you can easily see that the variable `n` is an `int`. Further, you can reasonably assume that the type of a calculation `n + 1` is an `int`. However, what type is the constant `1`?

The type of a constant depends on two things: its value and the presence of an optional descriptor letter at the end of the constant. Any integer type less than 2 billion is assumed to be an `int`. Numbers larger than 2 billion are assumed to be `long`. Any floating-point number is assumed to be a `double`.

Table 2-4 demonstrates constants that have been declared to be of a particular type. The case of these descriptors is not important; `1U` and `1u` are equivalent.

Table 2-4 Common Constants Declared along with Their Types

Constant	*Type*
`1`	`int`
`1U`	`unsigned int`
`1L`	`long int` (avoid lowercase *l*; it's too much like the digit 1)
`1.0`	`double`
`1.0F`	`float`
`1M`	`decimal`
`true`	`bool`
`false`	`bool`
`'a'`	`char`
`'\n'`	`char` (the character newline)
`'\x123'`	`char` (the character whose numeric value is hex 123)[1]
`"a string"`	`string`
`""`	`string` (an empty string); same as `String.Empty`

[1] *"hex" is short for hexadecimal (numbers in base 16 rather than in base 10).*

Changing Types: The Cast

Humans don't treat different types of counting numbers differently. For example, a normal person (as distinguished from a C# programmer) doesn't think about the number 1 as being signed, unsigned, short, or long. Although C# considers these types to be different, even C# realizes that a relationship exists between them. For example, this bit of code converts an `int` into a `long`:

```
int intValue = 10;
long longValue;
longValue = intValue;  // This is OK.
```

An `int` variable can be converted into a `long` because any possible value of an `int` can be stored in a `long` — and because they are both counting numbers. C# makes the conversion for you automatically without comment. This is called an *implicit* type conversion.

A conversion in the opposite direction can cause problems, however. For example, this line is illegal:

```
long longValue = 10;
int intValue;
intValue = longValue;  // This is illegal.
```

Some values that you can store in a `long` don't fit in an `int` (4 billion, for example). If you try to shoehorn such a value into an `int`, C# generates an error because data may be lost during the conversion process. This type of bug is difficult to catch.

But what if you know that the conversion is okay? For example, even though `longValue` is a `long`, maybe you know that its value can't exceed 100 in this particular program. In that case, converting the `long` variable `longValue` into the `int` variable `intValue` would be okay.

You can tell C# that you know what you're doing by means of a cast:

```
long longValue = 10;
int intValue;
intValue = (int)longValue;  // This is now OK.
```

In a *cast,* you place the name of the type you want in parentheses and put it immediately in front of the value you want to convert. This cast says, "Go ahead and convert the `long` named `longValue` into an `int` — I know what I'm doing." In retrospect, the assertion that you know what you're doing may seem overly confident, but it's often valid.

A counting number can be converted into a floating-point number automatically, but converting a floating-point into a counting number requires a cast:

```
double doubleValue = 10.0;
long longValue = (long)doubleValue;
```

All conversions to and from a `decimal` require a cast. In fact, all numeric types can be converted into all other numeric types through the application of a cast. Neither `bool` nor `string` can be converted directly into any other type.

Built-in C# methods can convert a number, character, or Boolean into its string equivalent, so to speak. For example, you can convert the `bool` value `true` into the `string` "true"; however, you cannot consider this change a direct conversion. The `bool true` and the `string` "true" are completely different things.

Letting the C# Compiler Infer Data Types

So far in this book — well, so far in this chapter — when you declared a variable, you *always* specified its exact data type, like this:

```
int i = 5;
string s = "Hello C#";
double d = 1.0;
```

You're allowed to offload some of that work onto the C# compiler, using the `var` keyword:

```
var i = 5;
var s = "Hello C# 4.0";
var d = 1.0;
```

Now the compiler *infers* the data type for you — it looks at the stuff on the right side of the assignment to see what type the left side is.

For what it's worth, Chapter 3 of this minibook shows how to calculate the type of an expression like the ones on the right side of the assignments in the preceding example. Not that you need to do that — the compiler mostly does it for you. Suppose, for example, you have an initializing expression like this:

```
var x = 3.0 + 2 - 1.5;
```

The compiler can figure out that `x` is a `double` value. It looks at `3.0` and `1.5` and sees that they're of type `double`. Then it notices that `2` is an `int`, which the compiler can convert *implicitly* to a `double` for the calculation. All of the addition terms in `x`'s initialization expression end up as `doubles`. So the *inferred type* of `x` is `double`.

But now, you can simply utter the magic word `var` and supply an initialization expression, and the compiler does the rest:

```
var aVariable = <initialization expression here>;
```

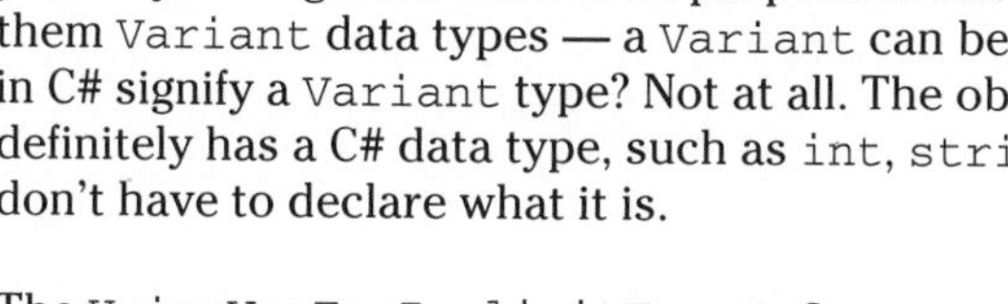

If you've worked with a scripting language such as JavaScript or VBScript, you may have gotten used to all-purpose-in-one data types. VBScript calls them `Variant` data types — a `Variant` can be anything at all. But does `var` in C# signify a `Variant` type? Not at all. The object you declare with `var` definitely has a C# data type, such as `int`, `string`, or `double`. You just don't have to declare what it is.

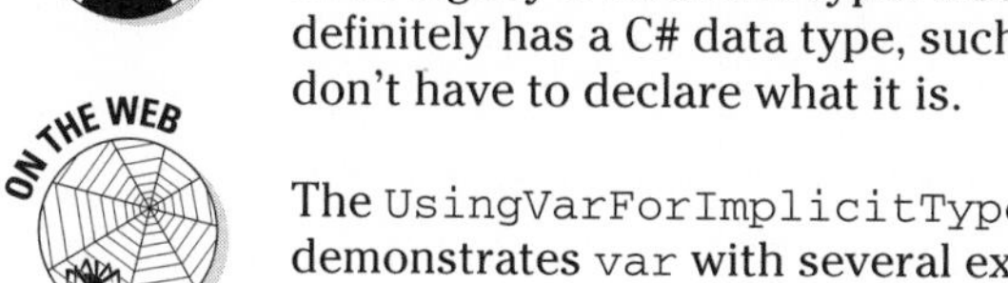

The `UsingVarForImplicitTypeInference` example on the Web site demonstrates `var` with several examples. Here's a taste.

What's really lurking in the variables declared in this example with `var`? Take a look at this:

```
var aString = "Hello C# 3.0";
Console.WriteLine(aString.GetType().ToString());
```

The mumbo jumbo in that `WriteLine` statement calls the `String.GetType()` method on `aString` to get its C# type. Then it calls the resulting object's `ToString()` method to display the object's type. (Yadda yadda.) Here's what you see in the console window:

```
System.String
```

It proves that the compiler correctly inferred the type of `aString`.

Most of the time, I recommend that you don't use `var`. Save it for when it's necessary. Being explicit about the type of a variable is clearer to anyone reading your code than using `var`. However, common usage in the C# world may change so much that everybody uses `var` all the time, in spite of my good advice. In that case, you can go along with the crowd.

You see examples later in which `var` is definitely called for, and I use it part of the time throughout this book, even sometimes where it's not strictly necessary. You need to see it used, and use it yourself, to internalize it. I'm still getting used to it myself. (I can't help it if I'm a slow learner.)

You can see `var` used in other ways: with arrays and collections of data, in Chapter 6 of this minibook, and with anonymous types, in Book II. Anonymous? Bet you can't wait.

What's more, a new type in C# 4.0 is even more flexible than `var`: The `dynamic` type takes `var` a step further.

The `var` type causes the compiler to infer the type of the variable based on expected input. The `dynamic` keyword does this at runtime, using a totally new set of tools called the Dynamic Language Runtime. You can find more about the `dynamic` type in Book VIII.

Chapter 3: Pulling Strings

In This Chapter

- Pulling and twisting a string with C# — just don't string me along
- Comparing strings
- Other string operations, such as searching, trimming, splitting, and concatenating
- Parsing strings read into the program
- Formatting output strings manually or using the `String.Format()` method

For many applications, you can treat a `string` like one of the built-in value-type variable types such as `int` or `char`. Certain operations that are otherwise reserved for these intrinsic types are available to strings:

```
int i = 1;           // Declare and initialize an int.
string s = "abc";    // Declare and initialize a string.
```

In other respects, as shown in the following example, a `string` is treated like a user-defined class (I cover classes in Book II):

```
string s1 = new String();
string s2 = "abcd";
int lengthOfString = s2.Length;
```

Which is it — a value type or a class? In fact, `String` is a class for which C# offers special treatment because strings are so widely used in programs. For example, the keyword `string` is synonymous with the class name `String`, as shown in this bit of code:

```
String s1 = "abcd"; // Assign a string literal to a String obj.
string s2 = s1;     // Assign a String obj to a string variable.
```

In this example, `s1` is declared to be an object of class `String` (spelled with an uppercase *S*) whereas `s2` is declared as a simple `string` (spelled with a lowercase *s*). However, the two assignments demonstrate that `string` and `String` are of the same (or compatible) types.

In fact, this same property is true of the other intrinsic variable types, to a more limited extent. Even the lowly `int` type has a corresponding class `Int32`, `double` has the class `Double`, and so on. The distinction here is that `string` and `String` truly are the same thing.

In the rest of the chapter, I cover `Strings` and `strings` and all the tasks you can accomplish by using them.

The Union Is Indivisible, and So Are Strings

You need to know at least one thing that you didn't learn before the sixth grade: You can't change a `string` object itself after it has been created. Even though I may speak of modifying a string, C# doesn't have an operation that modifies the actual `string` object. Plenty of operations appear to modify the `string` that you're working with, but they always return the modified `string` as a new object, instead. One string becomes two.

For example, the operation `"His name is " + "Randy"` changes neither of the two strings, but it generates a third string, `"His name is Randy"`. One side effect of this behavior is that you don't have to worry about someone modifying a `string` out from under you.

Consider this simplistic example program:

```
// ModifyString -- The methods provided by class String do
//    not modify the object itself. (s.ToUpper() doesn't
//    modify 's'; rather it returns a new string that has
//    been converted.)
using System;
namespace ModifyString
{
  class Program
  {
    public static void Main(string[] args)
    {
      // Create a student object.
      Student s1 = new Student();
      s1.Name = "Jenny";
      // Now make a new object with the same name.
      Student s2 = new Student();
      s2.Name = s1.Name;
      // "Changing" the name in the s1 object does not
      // change the object itself because ToUpper() returns
      // a new string without modifying the original.
      s2.Name = s1.Name.ToUpper();
      Console.WriteLine("s1 - " + s1.Name + ", s2 - " + s2.Name);
      // Wait for user to acknowledge the results.
      Console.WriteLine("Press Enter to terminate...");
      Console.Read();
    }
  }

  // Student -- You just need a class with a string in it.
  class Student
  {
    public String Name;
  }
}
```

I fully discuss classes in Book II, but for now, you can see that the `Student` class contains a data variable called `Name`, of type `String`. The `Student` objects `s1` and `s2` are set up so the student `Name` data in each points to the same string data. `ToUpper()` converts the string `s1.Name` to all uppercase characters. Normally, this would be a problem because both `s1` and `s2` point to the same object. However, `ToUpper()` does not change `Name` — it creates a new, independent uppercase string and stores it in the object `s2`. Now the two `Students` don't point to the same string data.

The following output of the program is simple:

```
s1 - Jenny, s2 - JENNY
Press Enter to terminate...
```

This property of strings is called *immutability* (meaning, unchangeability).

The immutability of strings is also important for `string` constants. A string such as `"this is a string"` is a form of a `string` constant, just as 1 is an `int` constant. In the same way that I reuse my shirts to reduce the size of my wardrobe (and go easy on my bank account), a compiler may choose to combine all accesses to the single constant `"this is a string"`. Reusing `string` constants can reduce the *footprint* of the resulting program (its size on disk or in memory) but would be impossible if a `string` could be modified.

Performing Common Operations on a String

C# programmers perform more operations on strings than Beverly Hills plastic surgeons do on Hollywood hopefuls. Virtually every program uses the addition operator that's used on `strings`, as shown in this example:

```
string name = "Randy";
Console.WriteLine("His name is " + name); // + means concatenate.
```

The `String` class provides this special operator. However, the `String` class also provides other, more direct methods for manipulating strings. You can see the complete list by looking up "String class" in the Visual Studio Help index, and you'll meet many of the usual suspects in this chapter. Among the string-related tasks I cover here are the ones described in this list:

- Comparing strings — for equality or for tasks like alphabetizing
- Changing and converting strings in various ways: replacing part of a string, changing case, and converting between strings and other things
- Accessing the individual characters in a string
- Finding characters or substrings inside a string

- Handling input from the command line
- Managing formatted output
- Working efficiently with strings using the `StringBuilder`

In addition to the examples shown in the rest of this chapter, take a look at the `StringCaseChanging` and `VariousStringTechniques` examples on the Web site.

Comparing Strings

It's very common to need to compare two strings. For example, did the user input the expected value? Or maybe you have a list of strings and need to alphabetize them.

If all you need to know is whether two strings are equal (same length and same characters in the same order), you can use the == operator (or its inverse, `!=`, or *not equal*):

```
string a = "programming";
string b = "Programming";
if(a == b) ... // True if you don't consider case, false otherwise.
if(a != b) ... // False if you don't consider case, true otherwise.
```

But comparing two strings for anything but equality or inequality is another matter. It doesn't work to say

```
if(a < b) ...
```

So if you need to ask, Is string A greater than string B? or Is string A less than string B?, you need another approach.

Equality for all strings: The Compare ( ) method

Numerous operations treat a string as a single object — for example, the `Compare()` method. `Compare()`, with the following properties, compares two strings as though they were numbers:

- If the left-hand string is *greater than* the right string, `Compare(`*`left`*`, `*`right`*`)` returns 1.
- If the left-hand string is *less than* the right string, it returns –1.
- If the two strings are equal, it returns 0.

The algorithm works as follows when written in *notational* C# (that is, C# without all the details, also known as *pseudocode):*

```
compare(string s1, string s2)
{
  // Loop through each character of the strings until
  // a character in one string is greater than the
  // corresponding character in the other string.
  foreach character in the shorter string
    if (s1's character > s2's character when treated as a number)
      return 1
    if (s2's character < s1's character)
      return -1
  // Okay, every letter matches, but if the string s1 is longer,
  // then it's greater.
  if s1 has more characters left
    return 1
  // If s2 is longer, it's greater.
  if s2 has more characters left
    return -1
  // If every character matches and the two strings are the same
  // length, then they are "equal."
  return 0
}
```

Thus, `"abcd"` is greater than `"abbd"`, and `"abcde"` is greater than `"abcd"`. More often than not, you don't care whether one string is greater than the other, but only whether the two strings are equal.

You *do* want to know which string is bigger when performing a sort.

The `Compare()` operation returns 0 when two strings are identical. The following test program uses the equality feature of `Compare()` to perform a certain operation when the program encounters a particular string or strings.

`BuildASentence` prompts the user to enter lines of text. Each line is concatenated to the previous line to build a single sentence. This program exits if the user enters the word *EXIT*, *exit*, *QUIT*, or *quit*:

```
// BuildASentence -- The following program constructs sentences
//   by concatenating user input until the user enters one of the
//   termination characters. This program shows when you need to look for
//   string equality.
using System;
namespace BuildASentence
{
  public class Program
  {
    public static void Main(string[] args)
    {
      Console.WriteLine("Each line you enter will be "
                      + "added to a sentence until you "
                      + "enter EXIT or QUIT");
      // Ask the user for input; continue concatenating
      // the phrases input until the user enters exit or
      // quit (start with an empty sentence).
      string sentence = "";
      for (; ; )
      {
```

```
        // Get the next line.
        Console.WriteLine("Enter a string ");
        string line = Console.ReadLine();
        // Exit the loop if line is a terminator.
        string[] terms = { "EXIT", "exit", "QUIT", "quit" };
        // Compare the string entered to each of the
        // legal exit commands.
        bool quitting = false;
        foreach (string term in terms)
        {
          // Break out of the for loop if you have a match.
          if (String.Compare(line, term) == 0)
          {
            quitting = true;
          }
        }
        if (quitting == true)
        {
          break;
        }
        // Otherwise, add it to the sentence.
        sentence = String.Concat(sentence, line);
        // Let the user know how she's doing.
        Console.WriteLine("\nyou've entered: " + sentence);
      }
      Console.WriteLine("\ntotal sentence:\n" + sentence);
      // Wait for user to acknowledge the results.
      Console.WriteLine("Press Enter to terminate...");
      Console.Read();
    }
  }
}
```

After prompting the user for what the program expects, the program creates an empty initial sentence string called `sentence`. From there, the program enters an infinite loop.

The controls `while(true)` and `for(;;)` loop forever, or at least long enough for some internal `break` or `return` to break you out. The two loops are equivalent, and in practice, you'll see them both. (Looping is covered in Chapter 5 of this minibook.)

`BuildASentence` prompts the user to enter a line of text, which the program reads using the `ReadLine()` method. Having read the line, the program checks to see whether it is a terminator using the boldfaced lines in the preceding example.

The termination section of the program defines an array of strings called `terms` and a `bool` variable `quitting`, initialized to `false`. Each member of the `terms` array is one of the strings you're looking for. Any of these strings causes the program to quit faster than a programmer forced to write COBOL.

The program must include both `"EXIT"` and `"exit"` because `Compare()` considers the two strings different by default. (The way the program is written, these are the only two ways to spell *exit.* Strings such as `"Exit"` and "eXit" aren't recognized as terminators.) You can also use other string operations to check for various spellings of exit. I show you this in the next section.

The termination section loops through each of the strings in the array of target strings. If `Compare()` reports a match to any of the terminator phrases, `quitting` is set to `true`. If `quitting` remains `false` after the termination section and `line` is not one of the terminator strings, it is concatenated to the end of the sentence using the `String.Concat()` method. The program outputs the immediate result just so the user can see what's going on.

Iterating through an array is a classic way to look for one of various possible values. (I'll show you another way in the next section, and an even cooler way in Book II.)

Here's a sample run of the `BuildASentence` program:

```
Each line you enter will be added to a
sentence until you enter EXIT or QUIT
Enter a string
Programming with

You've entered: Programming with
Enter a string
 C# is fun

You've entered: Programming with C# is fun
Enter a string
 (more or less)

You've entered: Programming with C# is fun (more or less)
Enter a string
EXIT

Total sentence:
Programming with C# is fun (more or less)
Press Enter to terminate...
```

I've flagged my input in bold to make the output easier to read.

Would you like your compares with or without case?

The `Compare()` method used in the previous example considers `"EXIT"` and `"exit"` to be different strings. However, the `Compare()` method has a second version that includes a third argument. This argument indicates whether the comparison should ignore the letter case. A `true` indicates "ignore."

The following version of the lengthy termination section in the `BuildASentence` example sets `quitting` to `true` whether the string passed is uppercase, lowercase, or a combination of the two:

```
  // Indicate true if passed either exit or quit,
  // irrespective of case.
  if (String.Compare("exit", source, true) == 0) ||
       (String.Compare("quit", source, true) == 0)
  {
    quitting = true;
  }
}
```

This version is simpler than the previous looping version. This code doesn't need to worry about case, and it can use a single conditional expression because it now has only two options to consider instead of a longer list: any spelling variation of QUIT or EXIT.

What If I Want to Switch Case?

You may be interested in whether all of the characters (or just one) in a string are uppercase or lowercase characters. And you may need to convert from one to the other.

Distinguishing between all-uppercase and all-lowercase strings

I almost hate to bring it up, but you can use the `switch` command (see Chapter 5 of this minibook) to look for a particular string. Normally, you use the `switch` command to compare a counting number to some set of possible values; however, `switch` does work on `string` objects, as well. This version of the termination section in `BuildASentence` uses the `switch` construct:

```
switch(line)
{
  case "EXIT":
  case "exit":
  case "QUIT":
  case "quit":
    return true;
}
return false;
```

This approach works because you're comparing only a limited number of strings. The `for` loop offers a much more flexible approach for searching for string values. Using the case-less `Compare()` in the previous section gives the program greater flexibility in understanding the user.

Converting a string to upper- or lowercase

Suppose you have a string in lowercase and need to convert it to uppercase. You can use the `ToUpper()` method:

```
string lowcase = "armadillo";
string upcase = lowcase.ToUpper();  // ARMADILLO.
```

Similarly, you can convert uppercase to lowercase with `ToLower()`.

What if you want to convert just the first character in a string to uppercase? The following rather convoluted code will do it (but you can see a better way in the last section of this chapter):

```
string name = "chuck";
string properName =
   char.ToUpper(name[0]).ToString() + name.Substring(1, name.Length - 1);
```

The idea in this example is to extract the first `char` in `name` (that's `name[0]`), convert it to a one-character string with `ToString()`, and then tack on the remainder of `name` after removing the old lowercase first character with `Substring()`.

You can tell whether a string is uppercased or lowercased by using this scary-looking `if` statement:

```
if (string.Compare(line.ToUpper(CultureInfo.InvariantCulture),
                   line, false) == 0) ...  // True if line is all upper.
```

Here the `Compare()` method is comparing an uppercase version of `line` to `line` itself. There should be no difference if `line` is already uppercase. You can puzzle over the `CultureInfo.InvariantCulture` gizmo in Help, 'cause I'm not going to explain it here. For "is it all lowercase," stick a not (`!`) operator in front of the `Compare()` call. Alternatively, you can use a loop, as described in the next section.

The `StringCaseChanging` example on the Web site illustrates these and other techniques, including a brief explanation of cultures.

Looping through a String

You can access individual characters of a string in a `foreach` loop. The following code steps through the characters and writes each to the console — just another (roundabout) way to write out the string:

```
string favoriteFood = "cheeseburgers";
foreach(char c in favoriteFood)
{
  Console.Write(c);  // Could do things to the char here.
}
Console.WriteLine();
```

You can use that loop to solve the problem of deciding whether `favoriteFood` is all uppercase. (See the previous section for more about case.)

```
bool isUppercase = true;  // Start with the assumption that it's uppercase.
foreach(char c in favoriteFood)
{
  if(!char.IsUpper(c))
  {
    isUppercase = false;  // Disproves all uppercase, so get out.
    break;
  }
}
```

At the end of the loop, `isUppercase` will either be `true` or `false`.

As shown in the final example in the previous section on switching case, you can also access individual characters in a string by using an array index notation.

Arrays start with zero, so if you want the first character, you ask for `[0]`. If you want the third, you ask for `[2]`.

```
char thirdChar = favoriteFood[2];   // First 'e' in "cheeseburgers"
```

Searching Strings

What if you need to find a particular word, or a particular character, inside a string? Maybe you need its index so you can use `Substring()`, `Replace()`, `Remove()`, or some other method on it. In this section, you'll see how to find individual characters or substrings. (I'm still using the `favoriteFood` variable from the previous section.)

Can I find it?

The simplest thing is finding an individual character with `IndexOf()`:

```
int indexOfLetterS = favoriteFood.IndexOf('s');  // 4.
```

Class `String` also has other methods for finding things, either individual characters or substrings:

- `IndexOfAny()` takes an array of `char`s and searches the string for any of them, returning the index of the first one found.

  ```
  char[] charsToLookFor = { 'a', 'b', 'c' };
  int indexOfFirstFound = favoriteFood.IndexOfAny(charsToLookFor); // 0.
  ```

  That call is often written more briefly this way:

  ```
  int index = name.IndexOfAny(new char[] { 'a', 'b', 'c' });
  ```

- `LastIndexOf()` finds not the first occurrence of a character but the last.
- `LastIndexOfAny()` works like `IndexOfAny()`, but starting at the end of the string.

✦ `Contains()` returns `true` if a given substring can be found within the target string:

```
if(favoriteFood.Contains("ee")) ...            // True
```

✦ And `Substring()` returns the string (if it's there), or empty (if not):

```
string sub = favoriteFood.Substring(6, favoriteFood.Length - 6);
```

(I go into `Substring()` in greater detail later in this chapter.)

Is my string empty?

How can you tell if a target string is empty (`""`) or has the value `null`? (`null` means that no value has been assigned yet, not even to the empty string.) Use the `IsNullOrEmpty()` method, like this:

```
bool notThere = string.IsNullOrEmpty(favoriteFood);  // False
```

Notice how you call `IsNullOrEmpty()`: **`string.`**`IsNullOrEmpty(s)`.

You can set a string to the empty string in these two ways:

```
string name = "";
string name = string.Empty;
```

Getting Input from the Command Line

A common task in console applications is getting the information that the user types in when you prompt her for, say, an interest rate or a name. You need to read the information that comes in as a string. (Everything coming from the command line comes as a string.) Then you sometimes need to parse the input to extract a number from it. And sometimes you need to process lots of input numbers.

Trimming excess white space

First, consider that in some cases, you don't want to mess with any white space on either end of the string. The term *white space* refers to the characters that don't normally display on the screen, for example, space, newline (or `\n`), and tab (`\t`). You may sometimes also encounter the carriage return character, `\r`.

You can use the `Trim()` method to trim off the edges of the string, like this:

```
// Get rid of any extra spaces on either end of the string.
random = random.Trim();
```

Class `String` also provides `TrimFront()` and `TrimEnd()` methods for getting more specific, and you can pass an array of `chars` to be included in the trimming along with white space. For example, you might trim a leading currency sign, such as `'$'`.Cleaning up a string can make it easier to parse. The trim methods return a new string.

Parsing numeric input

A program can read from the keyboard one character at a time, but you have to worry about newlines and so on. An easier approach reads a string and then *parses* the characters out of the string.

Parsing characters out of a string is another topic I don't like to mention, for fear that programmers will abuse this technique. In some cases, programmers are too quick to jump into the middle of a string and start pulling out what they find there. This is particularly true of C++ programmers because that's the only way they could deal with strings — until the addition of a string class.

The `ReadLine()` method used for reading from the console returns a `string` object. A program that expects numeric input must convert this `string`. C# provides just the conversion tool you need in the `Convert` class. This class provides a conversion method from `string` to each built-in variable type. Thus, this code segment reads a number from the keyboard and stores it in an `int` variable:

```
string s = Console.ReadLine();  // Keyboard input is string data
int n = Convert.ToInt32(s);     // but you know it's meant to be a number.
```

The other conversion methods are a bit more obvious: `ToDouble()`, `ToFloat()`, and `ToBoolean()`.

`ToInt32()` refers to a 32-bit, signed integer (32 bits is the size of a normal `int`), so this is the conversion method for `ints`. `ToInt64()` handles the size of a `long`.

When `Convert()` encounters an unexpected character type, it can generate unexpected results. Thus, you must know for sure what type of data you're processing and ensure that no extraneous characters are present.

Although I haven't fully discussed methods yet (see Book II), here's one anyway. The following method returns `true` if the string passed to it consists of only digits. You can call this method prior to converting into a type of integer, assuming that a sequence of nothing but digits is probably a legal number.

To be truly complete, you need to include the decimal point for floating-point variables and include a leading minus sign for negative numbers — but hey, you get the idea.

Here's the method:

```
// IsAllDigits -- Return true if all characters
//   in the string are digits.
public static bool IsAllDigits(string raw)
{
  // First get rid of any benign characters at either end;
  // if there's nothing left, you don't have a number.
  string s = raw.Trim();  // Ignore white space on either side.
  if (s.Length == 0) return false;
  // Loop through the string.
  for(int index = 0; index < s.Length; index++)
  {
    // A nondigit indicates that the string probably isn't a number.
    if (Char.IsDigit(s[index]) == false) return false;
  }
  // No nondigits found; it's probably okay.
  return true;
}
```

The method `IsAllDigits()` first removes any harmless white space at either end of the string. If nothing is left, the string was blank and could not be an integer. The method then loops through each character in the string. If any of these characters turns out to be a nondigit, the method returns `false`, indicating that the string is probably not a number. If this method returns `true`, the probability is high that the string can be converted into an integer successfully.

The following code sample inputs a number from the keyboard and prints it back out to the console. (I omitted the `IsAllDigits()` method from the listing to save space, but I've boldfaced where this program calls it.)

```
// IsAllDigits -- Demonstrate the IsAllDigits method.
using System;
namespace IsAllDigits
{
  class Program
  {
    public static void Main(string[] args)
    {
      // Input a string from the keyboard.
      Console.WriteLine("Enter an integer number");
      string s = Console.ReadLine();
      // First check to see if this could be a number.
      if (!IsAllDigits(s)) // Call the special method.
      {
        Console.WriteLine("Hey! That isn't a number");
      }
      else
      {
        // Convert the string into an integer.
        int n = Int32.Parse(s);
```

```
            // Now write out the number times 2.
            Console.WriteLine("2 * " + n + ", = " + (2 * n));
          }
          // Wait for user to acknowledge the results.
          Console.WriteLine("Press Enter to terminate...");
          Console.Read();
        }
        // IsAllDigits here.
      }
    }
```

The program reads a line of input from the console keyboard. If `IsAllDigits()` returns `false`, the program alerts the user. If not, the program converts the string into a number using an alternative to `Convert.ToInt32(aString)` — the `Int32.Parse(aString)` call. Finally, the program outputs both the number and two times the number (the latter to prove that the program did, in fact, convert the string as advertised).

The output from a sample run of the program appears this way:

```
Enter an integer number
1A3
Hey! That isn't a number
Press Enter to terminate...
```

You could let `Convert` try to convert garbage and handle any exception it may decide to throw. However, a better-than-even chance exists that it won't throw an exception but will just return incorrect results — for example, returning 1 when presented with 1A3. You should validate input data yourself.

You could instead use `Int32.TryParse(s, n)`, which returns `false` if the parse fails or `true` if it succeeds. If it does work, the converted number is found in the second parameter, an `int` that I named `n`. This won't throw exceptions. See the next section for an example.

Handling a series of numbers

Often, a program receives a series of numbers in a single line from the keyboard. Using the `String.Split()` method, you can easily break the string into a number of substrings, one for each number, and parse them separately.

The `Split()` method chops a single string into an array of smaller strings using some delimiter. For example, if you tell `Split()` to divide a string using a comma (`,`) as the delimiter, `"1,2,3"` becomes three strings, `"1"`, `"2"`, and `"3"`. (The *delimiter* is whichever character you use to split collections.)

The following program uses the `Split()` method to input a sequence of numbers to be summed. (Again, I've omitted the `IsAllDigits()` method to save trees.)

```
// ParseSequenceWithSplit -- Input a series of numbers separated by commas,
//    parse them into integers and output the sum.
namespace ParseSequenceWithSplit
{
  using System;
  class Program
  {
    public static void Main(string[] args)
    {
      // Prompt the user to input a sequence of numbers.
      Console.WriteLine(
           "Input a series of numbers separated by commas:");
      // Read a line of text.
      string input = Console.ReadLine();
      Console.WriteLine();
      // Now convert the line into individual segments
      // based upon either commas or spaces.
      char[] dividers = {',', ' '};
      string[] segments = input.Split(dividers);
      // Convert each segment into a number.
      int sum = 0;
      foreach(string s in segments)
      {
        // Skip any empty segments.
        if (s.Length > 0)
        {
          // Skip strings that aren't numbers.
          if (IsAllDigits(s))
          {
            // Convert the string into a 32-bit int.
            int num = 0;
            if (Int32.TryParse(s, out num))
            {
              Console.WriteLine("Next number = {0}", num);
              // Add this number into the sum.
              sum += num;
            }
            // If parse fails, move on to next number.
          }
        }
      }
      // Output the sum.
      Console.WriteLine("Sum = {0}", sum);
      // Wait for user to acknowledge the results.
      Console.WriteLine("Press Enter to terminate...");
      Console.Read();
    }
    // IsAllDigits here.
  }
}
```

The `ParseSequenceWithSplit` program begins by reading a string from the keyboard. The program passes the `dividers` array of `char` to the `Split()` method to indicate that the comma and the space are the characters used to separate individual numbers. Either character will cause a split there.

The program iterates through each of the smaller subarrays created by `Split()` using the `foreach` loop control. The program skips any zero-length subarrays. (This would result from two dividers in a row.) The program next uses the `IsAllDigits()` method to make sure that the string contains a number. (It won't if, for instance, you type `,.3` with an extra nondigit, nonseparator character.) Valid numbers are converted into integers and then added to an accumulator, `sum`. Invalid numbers are ignored. (I chose not to generate an error message to keep this short.)

Here's the output of a typical run:

```
Input a series of numbers separated by commas:
1,2, a, 3 4

Next number = 1
Next number = 2
Next number = 3
Next number = 4
Sum = 10
Press Enter to terminate...
```

The program splits the list, accepting commas, spaces, or both as separators. It successfully skips over the `a` to generate the result of `10`. In a real-world program, however, you probably don't want to skip over incorrect input without comment. You almost always want to draw the user's attention to garbage in the input stream.

Joining an array of strings into one string

Class `String` also has a `Join()` method. If you have an array of strings, you can use `Join()` to concatenate all of the strings. You can even tell it to put a certain character string between each item and the next in the array:

```
string[] brothers = { "Chuck", "Bob", "Steve", "Mike" };
string theBrothers = string.Join(":", brothers);
```

The result in `theBrothers` is `"Chuck:Bob:Steve:Mike"`, with the names separated by colons. You can put any separator string between the names: `", "`, `"\t"`, `"     "`. The first item is a comma and a space. The second is a tab character. The third is a string of several spaces.

Controlling Output Manually

Controlling the output from programs is an important aspect of string manipulation. Face it: The output from the program is what the user sees. No matter how elegant the internal logic of the program may be, the user probably won't be impressed if the output looks shabby.

The `String` class provides help in directly formatting string data for output. The following sections examine the `Pad()`, `PadRight()`, `PadLeft()`, `Substring()`, and `Concat()` methods.

Using the Trim() and Pad() methods

I show earlier how to use `Trim()` and its more specialized variants, `TrimFront()` and `TrimEnd()`. Here, I discuss another common method for formatting output. You can use the `Pad` methods, which add characters to either end of a string to expand the string to some predetermined length. For example, you may add spaces to the left or right of a string to left- or right-justify it, or you can add `"*"` characters to the left of a currency number, and so on.

The following small `AlignOutput` program uses both `Trim()` and `Pad()` to trim up and justify a series of names:

```
// AlignOutput -- Left justify and align a set of strings
//    to improve the appearance of program output.
namespace AlignOutput
{
  using System;
  using System.Collections.Generic;
  class Program
  {
    public static void Main(string[] args)
    {
      List<string> names = new List<string> {"Christa  ",
                                             "  Sarah",
                                             "Jonathan",
                                             "Sam",
                                             " Schmekowitz "};
      // First output the names as they start out.
      Console.WriteLine("The following names are of "
                        + "different lengths");
      foreach(string s in names)
      {
        Console.WriteLine("This is the name '" + s + "' before");
      }
      Console.WriteLine();

      // This time, fix the strings so they are
      // left justified and all the same length.
      // First, copy the source array into an array that you can manipulate.
      List<string> stringsToAlign = new List<string>();
      // At the same time, remove any unnecessary spaces from either end
      // of the names.
      for (int i = 0; i < names.Count; i++)
      {
        string trimmedName = names[i].Trim();
        stringsToAlign.Add(trimmedName);
      }
      // Now find the length of the longest string so that
      // all other strings line up with that string.
      int maxLength = 0;
      foreach (string s in stringsToAlign)
      {
```

```
        if (s.Length > maxLength)
        {
          maxLength = s.Length;
        }
      }
      // Now justify all the strings to the length of the maximum string.
      for (int i = 0; i < stringsToAlign.Count; i++)
      {
        stringsToAlign[i] = stringsToAlign[i].PadRight(maxLength + 1);
      }
      // Finally output the resulting padded, justified strings.
      Console.WriteLine("The following are the same names "
                      + "normalized to the same length");
      foreach(string s in stringsToAlign)
      {
        Console.WriteLine("This is the name '" + s + "' afterwards");
      }
      // Wait for user to acknowledge.
      Console.WriteLine("\nPress Enter to terminate...");
      Console.Read();
    }
  }
}
```

AlignOutput defines a List<string> of names of uneven alignment and length. (You could just as easily write the program to read these names from the console or from a file.) The Main() method first displays the names as they are. Main() then aligns the names using the Trim() and PadRight() methods before redisplaying the resulting trimmed up strings:

```
The following names are of different lengths:
This is the name 'Christa  ' before
This is the name '  Sarah' before
This is the name 'Jonathan' before
This is the name 'Sam' before
This is the name ' Schmekowitz ' before

The following are the same names rationalized to the same length:
This is the name 'Christa     ' afterwards
This is the name 'Sarah       ' afterwards
This is the name 'Jonathan    ' afterwards
This is the name 'Sam         ' afterwards
This is the name 'Schmekowitz ' afterwards
```

The alignment process begins by making a copy of the input names list.

The code first loops through the list, calling Trim() on each element to remove unneeded white space on either end. The method loops again through the list to find the longest member. The code loops one final time, calling PadRight() to expand each string to match the length of the longest member in the list. Note how the padded names form a neat column in the output.

PadRight(10) expands a string to be at least ten characters long. For example, PadRight(10) adds four spaces to the right of a six-character string.

Finally, the code displays the list of trimmed and padded strings for output. Voilà.

Using the Concatenate( ) method

You often face the problem of breaking up a string or inserting some substring into the middle of another. Replacing one character with another is most easily handled with the `Replace()` method, like this:

```
string s = "Danger NoSmoking";
s = s.Replace(' ', '!')
```

This example converts the string into `"Danger!NoSmoking"`.

Replacing all appearances of one character (in this case, a space) with another (an exclamation mark) is especially useful when generating comma-separated strings for easier parsing. However, the more common and more difficult case involves breaking a single string into substrings, manipulating them separately, and then recombining them into a single, modified string.

The following `RemoveWhiteSpace` sample program uses the `Replace()` method to remove white space (spaces, tabs, and newlines — all instances of a set of special characters) from a string:

```
// RemoveWhiteSpace -- Remove any of a set of chars from a given string.
//    Use this method to remove whitespace from a sample string.
namespace RemoveWhiteSpace
{
 using System;
  public class Program
  {
    public static void Main(string[] args)
    {
      // Define the white space characters.
      char[] whiteSpace = {' ', '\n', '\t'};
      // Start with a string embedded with whitespace.
      string s = " this is a\nstring"; // Contains spaces & newline.
      Console.WriteLine("before:" + s);
      // Output the string with the whitespace missing.
      Console.Write("after:");
      // Start looking for the white space characters.
      for(;;)
      {
        // Find the offset of the character; exit the loop
        // if there are no more.
        int offset = s.IndexOfAny(whiteSpace);
        if (offset == -1)
        {
          break;
        }
        // Break the string into the part prior to the
        // character and the part after the character.
        string before = s.Substring(0, offset);
        string after  = s.Substring(offset + 1);
        // Now put the two substrings back together with the
        // character in the middle missing.
        s = String.Concat(before, after);
        // Loop back up to find next whitespace char in
        // this modified s.
      }
```

```
      Console.WriteLine(s);
      // Wait for user to acknowledge the results.
      Console.WriteLine("Press Enter to terminate...");
      Console.Read();
    }
  }
}
```

The key to this program is the boldfaced loop. This loop continually refines a string consisting of the input string, `s`, removing every one of a set of characters contained in the array `whiteSpace`.

The loop uses `IndexOfAny()` to find the first occurrence of any of the `chars` in the `whiteSpace` array. It doesn't return until every instance of any of those `chars` has been removed. The `IndexOfAny()` method returns the index within the array of the first white space `char` that it can find. A return value of `-1` indicates that no items in the array were found in the string.

The first pass through the loop removes the leading blank on the target string. `IndexOfAny()` finds the blank at index 0. The first `Substring()` call returns an empty string, and the second call returns the whole string after the blank. These are then concatenated with `Concat()`, producing a string with the leading blank squeezed out.

The second pass through the loop finds the space after `"this"` and squeezes that out the same way, concatenating the strings `"this"` and `"is a\nstring"`. After this pass, `s` has become `"thisis a\nstring"`.

The third pass finds the `\n` character and squeezes that out. On the fourth pass, `IndexOfAny()` runs out of white space characters to find and returns `-1` (not found). That ends the loop.

The `RemoveWhiteSpace` program prints out a string containing several forms of white space. The program then strips out white space characters. The output from this program appears as follows:

```
before: this is a
string
after:thisisastring
Press Enter to terminate...
```

Let's Split() that concatenate program

The `RemoveWhiteSpace` program demonstrates the use of the `Concat()` and `IndexOf()` methods; however, it doesn't use the most efficient approach. As usual, a little examination reveals a more efficient approach using our old friend `Split()`. You can find the program containing this code — now in another example of a method — on the Web site under `RemoveWhiteSpaceWithSplit`. The method that does the work is shown here:

```
// RemoveWhiteSpace -- The RemoveSpecialChars method removes every
//    occurrence of the specified characters from the string.
// Note: The rest of the program is not shown here.
public static string RemoveSpecialChars(string input, char[] targets)
{
  // Split the input string up using the target
  // characters as the delimiters.
  string[] subStrings = input.Split(targets);

  // output will contain the eventual output information.
  string output = "";

  // Loop through the substrings originating from the split.
  foreach(string subString in subStrings)
  {
    output = String.Concat(output, subString);
  }
  return output;
}
```

This version uses the `Split()` method to break the input string into a set of substrings, using the characters to be removed as delimiters. The delimiter is not included in the substrings created, which has the effect of removing the character(s). The logic here is much simpler and less error-prone.

The `foreach` loop in the second half of the program puts the pieces back together again using `Concat()`. The output from the program is unchanged.

Pulling the code out into a method further simplifies it and makes it clearer.

Formatting Your Strings Precisely

The `String` class also provides the `Format()` method for formatting output, especially the output of numbers. In its simplest form, `Format()` allows the insertion of string, numeric, or Boolean input in the middle of a format string. For example, consider this call:

```
string myString = String.Format("{0} times {1} equals {2}", 2, 5, 2*5);
```

The first argument to `Format()` is known as the *format string* — the quoted string you see. The `{n}` items in the middle of the format string indicate that the *n*th argument following the format string is to be inserted at that point. `{0}` refers to the first argument (in this case, the value 2), `{1}` refers to the next (that is, 5), and so on.

This returns a string, `myString`. The resulting string is

```
"2 times 5 equals 10"
```

Unless otherwise directed, `Format()` uses a default output format for each argument type. `Format()` enables you to affect the output format by including *specifiers* (modifiers or controls) in the placeholders. See Table 3-1 for a listing of some of these specifiers. For example, `{0:E6}` says, "Output the number in exponential form, using six spaces for the fractional part."

Table 3-1 Format Specifiers Using String.Format()

Control	*Example*	*Result*	*Notes*
`C` — currency	`{0:C}` of 123.456	$123.45	The currency sign depends on the Region setting.
	`{0:C}` of –123.456	($123.45)	(Specify Region in Windows control panel.)
`D` — decimal	`{0:D5}` of 123	00123	Integers only.
`E` — exponential	`{0:E}` of 123.45	1.2345E+002	Also known as scientific notation.
`F` — fixed	`{0:F2}` of 123.4567	123.45	The number after the `F` indicates the number of digits after the decimal point.
`N` — number	`{0:N}` of 123456.789	123,456.79	Adds commas and rounds off to nearest 100th.
	`{0:N1}` of 123456.789	123,456.8	Controls the number of digits after the decimal point.
	`{0:N0}` of 123456.789	123,457	
`X` — hexadecimal	`{0:X}` of 123	0x7B	7B hex = 123 decimal (integers only).
`{0:0...}`	`{0:000.00}` of 12.3	012.30	Forces a 0 if a digit is not already present.
`{0:#...}`	`{0:###.##}` of 12.3	12.3	Forces the space to be left blank; no other field can encroach on the three digits to the left and two digits after the decimal point (useful for maintaining decimal-point alignment).
	`{0:##0.0#}` of 0	0.0	Combining the # and zeros forces space to be allocated by the #s and forces at least one digit to appear, even if the number is 0.
`{0:# or 0%}`	`{0:#00.#%}` of .1234	12.3%	The % displays the number as a percentage (multiplies by 100 and adds the % sign).
	`{0:#00.#%}` of .0234	02.3%	

The Console.WriteLine() method uses the same placeholder system. The first placeholder, {0}, takes the first variable or value listed after the format string part of the statement, and so on. Given the exact same arguments as in the earlier Format() call, Console.WriteLine() would write the same string to the console. You also have access to the format specifiers. From now on, I use the formatted form of WriteLine() much of the time, rather than concatenate items to form the final output string with the + operator.

These format specifiers can seem a bit bewildering. (I didn't even mention the detailed currency and date controls.) Explore the topic "format specifiers" in the Help Index for more information. To help you wade through these options, the following OutputFormatControls program enables you to enter a floating-point number followed by a specifier sequence. The program then displays the number, using the specified Format() control:

```
// OutputFormatControls -- Allow the user to reformat input numbers
//     using a variety of format specifiers input at run time.
namespace OutputFormatControls
{
  using System;
  public class Program
  {
    public static void Main(string[] args)
    {
      // Keep looping -- inputting numbers until the user
      // enters a blank line rather than a number.
      for(;;)
      {
        // First input a number -- terminate when the user
        // inputs nothing but a blank line.
        Console.WriteLine("Enter a double number");
        string numberInput = Console.ReadLine();
        if (numberInput.Length == 0)
        {
          break;
        }
        double number = Double.Parse(numberInput);
        // Now input the specifier codes; split them
        // using spaces as dividers.
        Console.WriteLine("Enter the format specifiers"
                    + " separated by a blank "
                    + "(Example: C E F1 N0 0000000.00000)");
        char[] separator = {' '};
        string formatString = Console.ReadLine();
        string[] formats = formatString.Split(separator);
        // Loop through the list of format specifiers.
        foreach(string s in formats)
        {
          if (s.Length != 0)
          {
            // Create a complete format specifier
            // from the letters entered earlier.
            string formatCommand = "{0:" + s + "}";
            // Output the number entered using the
            // reconstructed format specifier.
            Console.Write(
```

```
                "The format specifier {0} results in ", formatCommand);
            try
            {
              Console.WriteLine(formatCommand, number);
            }
            catch(Exception)
            {
              Console.WriteLine("<illegal control>");
            }
            Console.WriteLine();
          }
        }
      }
      // Wait for user to acknowledge.
      Console.WriteLine("Press Enter to terminate...");
      Console.Read();
    }
  }
}
```

The `OutputFormatControls` program continues to read floating-point numbers into a variable `numberInput` until the user enters a blank line. (Because the input is a bit tricky, I include an example for the user to imitate as part of the message asking for input.) Notice that the program does not include tests to determine whether the input is a legal floating-point number. I just assume that the user is smart enough to know what a number looks like (a dangerous assumption!).

The program then reads a series of specifier strings separated by spaces. Each specifier is then combined with a `"{0}"` string (the number before the colon, which corresponds to the placeholder in the format string) into the variable `formatCommand`. For example, if you entered **N4**, the program would store the specifier `"{0:N4}"`. The following statement writes the number `number` using the newly constructed `formatCommand`:

```
Console.WriteLine(formatCommand, number);
```

In the case of the lowly N4, the command would be rendered this way:

```
Console.WriteLine("{0:N4}", number);
```

Typical output from the program appears this way (I boldfaced my input):

```
Enter a double number
12345.6789
Enter the specifiers separated by a blank (Example: C E F1 N0 0000000.00000)
C E F1 N0 0000000.00000
The format specifier {0:C} results in $12,345.68

The format specifier {0:E} results in 1.234568E+004

The format specifier {0:F1} results in 12345.7

The format specifier {0:N0} results in 12,346
```

```
The format specifier {0:0000000.00000} results in 0012345.67890

Enter a double number
.12345
Enter the specifiers separated by a blank (Example: C E F1 N0 0000000.00000)
00.0%
The format specifier {0:00.0%} results in 12.3%
Enter a double number

Press Enter to terminate...
```

When applied to the number `12345.6789`, the specifier `N0` adds commas in the proper place (the `N` part) and lops off everything after the decimal point (the `0` portion) to render `12,346`. (The last digit was rounded off, not truncated.)

Similarly, when applied to `0.12345`, the control `00.0%` outputs `12.3%`. The percent sign multiplies the number by 100 and adds `%`. The `00.0` indicates that the output should include at least two digits to the left of the decimal point and only one digit after the decimal point. The number 0.01 is displayed as `01.0%`, using the same `00.0%` specifier.

The mysterious `try . . . catch` catches any errors that spew forth in the event you enter an illegal format command such as a `D`, which stands for decimal. (I cover exceptions in Chapter 9 of this minibook.)

StringBuilder: Manipulating Strings More Efficiently

Building longer strings out of a bunch of shorter strings can cost you an arm and its elbow. Because a string, after it's created, can't be changed — it's immutable, as I say at the beginning of this chapter. This example doesn't tack "ly" onto `s1`:

```
string s1 = "rapid";
string s2 = s1 + "ly";           // s2 = rapidly.
```

It creates a new string composed of the combination. (`s1` is unchanged.) Similarly, other operations that appear to modify a string, such as `Substring()` and `Replace()`, do the same.

The result is that each operation on a string produces yet another string. Suppose you need to concatenate 1000 strings into one huge one. You're going to create a new string for each concatenation:

```
string[] listOfNames = ...  // 1000 pet names
string s = string.Empty;
for(int i = 0; i < 1000; i++)
{
  s += listOfNames[i];
}
```

To avoid such costs when you're doing lots of modifications to strings, use the companion class `StringBuilder`. Be sure to add this line at the top of your file:

```
using System.Text;  // Tells the compiler where to find StringBuilder.
```

Unlike `String` manipulations, the manipulations you do on a `StringBuilder` directly change the underlying string. Here's an example:

```
StringBuilder builder = new StringBuilder("012");
builder.Append("34");
builder.Append("56");
string result = builder.ToString();  // result = 0123456
```

Create a `StringBuilder` instance initialized with an existing string, as just shown. Or create an empty `StringBuilder` with no initial value:

```
StringBuilder builder = new StringBuilder();  // Defaults to 16 characters
```

You can also create the `StringBuilder` with the capacity you expect it to need, which reduces the overhead of increasing the builder's capacity frequently:

```
StringBuilder builder = new StringBuilder(256); // 256 characters.
```

Use the `Append()` method to add text to the end of the current contents. Use `ToString()` to retrieve the string inside the `StringBuilder` when you finish your modifications. Here's the `StringBuilder` version of the loop just shown, with retrieval of the final concatenated string in boldface:

```
StringBuilder sb = new StringBuilder(20000);  // Allocate a bunch.
for(int i = 0; i < 1000; i++)
{
  sb.Append(listOfNames[i]);     // Same list of names as earlier
}
string result = sb.ToString();  // Retrieve the results.
```

`StringBuilder` has a number of other useful string manipulation methods, including `Insert()`, `Remove()`, and `Replace()`. It lacks many of `string`'s methods, though, such as `Substring()`, `CopyTo()`, and `IndexOf()`.

Suppose that you want to make uppercase just the first character of a string, as in the earlier section "Converting a string to upper- or lowercase." With `StringBuilder`, it's much cleaner looking than the code I gave earlier.

```
StringBuilder sb = new StringBuilder("jones");
sb[0] = char.ToUpper(sb[0]);
string fixedString = sb.ToString();
```

This puts the lowercase string `"jones"` into a `StringBuilder`, accesses the first `char` in the `StringBuilder`'s underlying string directly with `sb[0]`, uses the `char.ToUpper()` method to uppercase the character, and reassigns the uppercased character to `sb[0]`. Finally, it extracts the improved string `"Jones"` from the `StringBuilder`.

The `BuildASentence` example presented earlier in this chapter could benefit from using a `StringBuilder`. I use `StringBuilder` quite a bit.

The `StringCaseChanging` and `VariousStringTechniques` examples on this book's Web site show `StringBuilder` in action.

TIP

Book II introduces a C# feature called *extension methods*. The example there adds several handy methods to the `String` class. Later in that minibook, we describe how to convert between `strings`, arrays of `char`, and arrays of `byte`. Those are operations you may need to do frequently (and are shown in the `StringCaseChanging` example on this book's Web site).

Chapter 4: Smooth Operators

In This Chapter

- Performing a little arithmetic
- Doing some logical arithmetic
- Complicating matters with compound logical operators

Mathematicians create variables and manipulate them in various ways, adding them, multiplying them, and — here's a toughie — even integrating them. Chapter 2 of this minibook describes how to declare and define variables. However, it says little about how to use variables to get anything done after you declare them. This chapter looks at the operations you can perform on variables to do some work. Operations require *operators,* such as +, −, =, <, and &. I cover arithmetic, logical, and other types of operators in this chapter.

Writing programs that get things done is good. You'll never make it as a C# programmer if your programs don't *do* something — unless, of course, you're a consultant.

Performing Arithmetic

The set of arithmetic operators breaks down into several groups: the simple arithmetic operators, the assignment operators, and a set of special operators unique to programming. After you digest these, you also need to digest a separate set of logical operators. *Bon appétit!*

Simple operators

You most likely learned in elementary school how to use most of the simple operators. Table 4-1 lists them. ***Note:*** Computers use an asterisk (*), not the multiplication sign (×), for multiplication.

Table 4-1 Simple Operators

Operator	*What It Means*
– (unary)	Take the negative of
*	Multiply
/	Divide
+	Add
- (binary)	Subtract
%	Modulo

Most of these operators in the table are *binary* operators because they operate on two values: one on the left side of the operator and one on the right side. The lone exception is the unary negative. However, it's just as straightforward as the others, as shown in this example:

```
int n1 = 5;
int n2 = -n1;  // n2 now has the value -5.
```

The value of `-n` is the negative of the value of `n`.

The modulo operator may not be quite as familiar to you as the others. Modulo is similar to the remainder after division. Thus, `5 % 3` is 2 (5 / 3 = 1, remainder 2), and `25 % 3` is 1 (25 / 3 = 8, remainder 1). Read it "five modulo three" or simply "five mod three." Even numbers mod 2 are 0: `6 % 2 = 0` (6/2 = 3, remainder 0).

The arithmetic operators other than modulo are defined for all numeric types. The modulo operator isn't defined for floating-point numbers because you have no remainder after the division of floating-point values.

Operating orders

The value of some expressions may not be clear. Consider, for example, the following expression:

```
int n = 5 * 3 + 2;
```

Does the programmer mean "multiply 5 times 3 and then add 2," which is 17, or "multiply 5 times the sum of 3 and 2," which gives you 25?

C# generally executes common operators from left to right. So, the preceding example assigns the value 17 to the variable `n`.

C# determines the value of n in the following example by first dividing 24 by 6 and then dividing the result of that operation by 2 (as opposed to dividing 24 by the ratio 6 over 2). The result is 2:

```
int n = 24 / 6 / 2
```

However, the various operators have a *hierarchy,* or order of precedence. C# scans an expression and performs the operations of higher precedence before those of lower precedence. For example, multiplication has higher precedence than addition. Many books take great pains to explain the order of precedence, but, frankly, that's a complete waste of time (and brain cells).

Don't rely on yourself or someone else to know the precedence order. Use parentheses to make your meaning explicit to human readers of the code as well as to the compiler. (You can find the precedences on the Cheat Sheet for this book, if you need to do some language-lawyering.)

The value of the following expression is clear, regardless of the operators' order of precedence:

```
int n = (7 % 3) * (4 + (6 / 3));
```

Parentheses can override the order of precedence by stating exactly how the compiler is to interpret the expression. To find the first expression to evaluate, C# looks for the innermost parentheses, dividing 6 by 3 to yield 2:

```
int n = (7 % 3) * (4 + 2);    // 6 / 3 = 2
```

Then C# works its way outward, evaluating each set of parentheses in turn, from innermost to outermost:

```
int n = 1 * 6;    // (4 + 2) = 6
```

So the final result, and the value of n, is 6.

The assignment operator

C# has inherited an interesting concept from C and C++: Assignment is itself a binary operator. The assignment operator has the value of the argument to the right. The assignment has the same type as both arguments, which must match.

This view of the assignment operator has no effect on the other expressions I've described in this chapter:

```
n = 5 * 3;
```

In this example, 5 * 3 is 15 and an `int`. The assignment operator stores the `int` on the right into the `int` on the left and returns the value 15. However, this view of the assignment operator allows the following line:

```
m = n = 5 * 3;
```

Assignments are evaluated in series from right to left. The right-hand assignment stores the value 15 into `n` and returns 15. The left-hand assignment stores 15 into `m` and returns 15, which is then dropped, leaving the value of each variable as 15.

This strange definition for assignment makes the following rather bizarre expressions legal:

```
int n;
int m;
n = m = 2;
```

Avoid chaining assignments because it's less clear to human readers. Anything that can confuse people reading your code (including you) is worth avoiding because confusion breeds errors.

The increment operator

Of all the additions that you may perform in programming, adding 1 to a variable is the most common:

```
n = n + 1;  // Increment n by 1.
```

C# extends the simple operators with a set of operators constructed from other binary operators. For example, `n += 1;` is equivalent to `n = n + 1;`.

An assignment operator exists for just about every binary operator: `+=`, `-=`, `*=`, `/=`, `%=`, `&=`, `|=`, `^=`. Look up *C# language, operators* in Help for full details on them.

Yet even n += 1 is not good enough. C# provides this even shorter version:

```
++n;        // Increment n by 1.
```

All these forms of incrementing a number are equivalent — they all increment `n` by 1.

The increment operator is strange enough, but believe it or not, C# has two increment operators: `++n` and `n++`. The first one, `++n`, is the *preincrement* operator, and `n++` is the *postincrement* operator. The difference is subtle but important.

Remember that every expression has a type and a value. In the following code, both ++n and n++ are of type int:

```
int n;
n = 1;
int p = ++n;
n = 1;
int m = n++;
```

But what are the resulting values of m and p? (***Hint:*** The choices are 1 and 2.) The value of p is 2, and the value of m is 1. That is, the value of the expression ++n is the value of n *after* being incremented, and the value of the expression n++ is the value of n *before* it's incremented. Either way, the resulting value of n itself is 2.

C# has equivalent decrement operators — n-- and --n. They work in exactly the same way as the increment operators.

Performing Logical Comparisons — Is That Logical?

C# provides a set of logical comparison operators, as shown in Table 4-2. These operators are *logical* comparisons because they return either a true or a false value of type bool.

Table 4-2 Logical Comparison Operators

Operator	*Operator Is True If*
a == b	a has the same value as b
a > b	a is greater than b
a >= b	a is greater than or equal to b
a < b	a is less than b
a <= b	a is less than or equal to b
a != b	a is not equal to b

Here's an example that involves a logical comparison:

```
int m = 5;
int n = 6;
bool b = m > n;
```

This example assigns the value false to the variable b because 5 is *not* greater than 6.

The logical comparisons are defined for all numeric types, including `float`, `double`, `decimal`, and `char`. All the following statements are legal:

```
bool b;
b = 3 > 2;        // true
b = 3.0 > 2.0;    // true
b = 'a' > 'b';    // false -- Alphabetically, later = greater.
b = 'A' < 'a';    // true  -- Upper A is less than lower a.
b = 'A' < 'b';    // true  -- All upper are less than all lower.
b = 10M > 12M;    // false
```

The comparison operators always produce results of type `bool`. The comparison operators other than == are not valid for variables of type `string`. (Not to worry: C# offers other ways to compare `strings`.)

Comparing floating-point numbers: Is your float bigger than mine?

Comparing two floating-point values can get dicey, and you need to be careful with these comparisons. Consider the following comparison:

```
float f1;
float f2;
f1 = 10;
f2 = f1 / 3;
bool b1 = (3 * f2) == f1;  // b1 is true if (3 * f2) equals f1.
f1 = 9;
f2 = f1 / 3;
bool b2 = (3 * f2) == f1;
```

Notice that both the fifth and eighth lines in the preceding example contain first an assignment operator (=) and then a logical comparison (==). These are different animals, so don't type = when you mean ==. C# does the logical comparison and then assigns the result to the variable on the left.

The only difference between the calculations of `b1` and `b2` is the original value of `f1`. So, what are the values of `b1` and `b2`? The value of `b2` is clearly `true`: 9 / 3 is 3; 3 * 3 is 9; and 9 equals 9. Voilà!

The value of `b1` isn't obvious: 10 / 3 is 3.333 . . . and 3.333 . . . * 3 is 9.999 . . . . Is 9.999 . . . equal to 10? That depends on how clever your processor and compiler are. On a Pentium or later processor, C# isn't smart enough to realize that `b1` should be `true` if the calculations are moved away from the comparison.

You can use the system absolute value method to compare `f1` and `f2`:

```
Math.Abs(f1 - 3.0 * f2) < .00001; // Use whatever level of accuracy.
```

This calculation returns `true` for both cases. You can use the constant `Double.Epsilon` instead of .00001 to produce the maximum level of accuracy. `Epsilon` is the smallest possible difference between two nonequal `double` variables.

For a self-guided tour of the `System.Math` class, where `Abs` and many other useful mathematical functions live, look for *math* in Help.

Compounding the confusion with compound logical operations

The `bool` variables have another set of operators defined just for them, as shown in Table 4-3.

Table 4-3 The Compound Logical Operators

Operator	Operator Is True If
`!a`	a is false (also known as the "not" operator).
`a & b`	a and b are true (also known as the "and" operator).
`a | b`	Either a or b or else both are true (also known as a *and/or* b).
`a ^ b`	a is true or b is true but not both (also known as *a xor b*).
`a && b`	a is true and b is true with short-circuit evaluation.
`a || b`	a is true or b is true with short-circuit evaluation. (I discuss short-circuit evaluation in this section.)

The `!` operator (NOT) is the logical equivalent of the minus sign. For example, `!a` (read "not a") is true if `a` is false and false if `a` is true. Can that be true?

The next two operators in the table are straightforward. First, `a & b` is true only if both `a` and `b` are true. And `a | b` is true if either `a` or `b` is true (or both are). The exclusive or (xor) operator, or `^`, is sort of an odd beast. An exclusive or is true if either `a` or `b` is true but not if both `a` and `b` are true.

All three operators produce a logical `bool` value as their result.

The `&`, `|`, and `^` operators also have a *bitwise operator* version. When applied to `int` variables, these operators perform their magic on a bit-by-bit basis. Thus 6 & 3 is 2 (0110_2 & 0011_2 is 0010_2), 6 | 3 is 7 (0110_2 | 0011_2 is 0111_2), and 6 ^ 3 is 5 (0110_2 ^ 0011_2 is 0101_2). Binary arithmetic is cool but beyond the scope of this book. You can search for it at your favorite search engine.

The remaining two logical operators are similar to, but subtly different from, the first three. Consider the following example:

```
bool b = (boolExpression1) & (boolExpression2);
```

In this case, C# evaluates boolExpression1 and boolExpression2. It then looks to see whether they both are true before deciding the value of b. However, this may be a wasted effort. If one expression is false, there's no reason to perform the other. Regardless of the value of the second expression, the result will be false. Nevertheless, & goes on to evaluate both expressions.

The && operator avoids evaluating both expressions unnecessarily, as shown in the following example:

```
bool b = (boolExpression1) && (boolExpression2);
```

In this case, C# evaluates boolExpression1. If it's false, then b is set to false and the program continues on its merry way. On the other hand, if boolExpression1 is true, then C# evaluates boolExpression2 and stores the result in b. The && operator uses this *short-circuit evaluation* because it short-circuits around the second Boolean expression, if necessary.

Most programmers use the doubled forms most of the time.

The || operator works the same way, as shown in the following expression:

```
bool b = (boolExpression1) || (boolExpression2);
```

If boolExpression1 is true, there's no point in evaluating boolExpression2 because the result is always true.

You can read these operators as "short-circuit and" and "short-circuit or."

Matching Expression Types at TrackDownAMate.com

In calculations, an expression's type is just as important as its value. Consider the following expression:

```
int n;
n = (5 * 5) + 7;
```

My calculator says the resulting value of n is 32. However, that expression also has an overall type based on the types of its parts.

Written in "type language," the preceding expression becomes

```
int [=] (int * int) + int;
```

To evaluate the type of an expression, follow the same pattern you use to evaluate the expression's value. Multiplication takes precedence over addition. An int times an int is an int. Addition comes next. An int plus an int is an int. In this way, you can reduce the preceding expression this way:

```
 (int * int) + int
int + int
int
```

Calculating the type of an operation

Most operators come in various flavors. For example, the multiplication operator comes in the following forms (the arrow means "produces"):

```
int     * int     ⇨ int
uint    * uint    ⇨ uint
long    * long    ⇨ long
float   * float   ⇨ float
decimal * decimal ⇨ decimal
double  * double  ⇨ double
```

Thus, 2 * 3 uses the int * int version of the * operator to produce the int 6.

Implicit type conversion

The * symbol works well for multiplying two ints or two floats. But imagine what happens when the left- and right-hand arguments aren't of the same type. For example, consider what happens in this case:

```
int anInt = 10;
double aDouble = 5.0;
double result = anInt * aDouble;
```

First, C# doesn't have an int * double operation. C# could just generate an error message and leave it at that; however, it tries to make sense of the programmer's intention. C# has int * int and double * double versions of multiplication and could convert aDouble into its int equivalent, but that would involve losing any fractional part of the number (the digits to the right of the decimal point). Instead, in *implicit promotion,* C# converts the int anInt into a double and uses the double * double operator.

An implicit promotion is implicit because C# does it automatically, and it's a promotion because it involves the natural concept of uphill and downhill. The list of multiplication operators is in promotion order from int to double or from int to decimal — *from narrower type to wider type*. No implicit conversion exists between the floating-point types and decimal. Converting from the more capable type, such as double, to a less capable type, such as int, is known as a *demotion.*

Implicit demotions aren't allowed; C# generates an error message.

Explicit type conversion — the cast

Imagine what happens if C# was wrong about implicit conversion and the programmer *wanted* to perform integer multiplication?

You can change the type of any value-type variable by using the cast operator. A *cast* consists of a type enclosed in parentheses and placed immediately in front of the variable or expression in question.

Thus the following expression uses the `int * int` operator:

```
int anInt = 10;
double aDouble = 5.0;
int result = anInt * (int)aDouble;
```

The cast of `aDouble` to an `int` is known as an *explicit demotion* or *downcast.* The conversion is explicit because the programmer explicitly declared her intent. (Duh.)

You can make an explicit conversion between any two value types, whether it's up or down the promotion ladder.

Avoid implicit type conversion. Make any changes in value types explicit by using a cast. Doing so reduces the possibility of error and makes code much easier for humans to read.

Leave logical alone

C# offers no type conversion path to or from the `bool` type.

Assigning types

The same matching of types that you find in conversions applies to the assignment operator.

Inadvertent type mismatches that generate compiler error messages usually occur in the assignment operator, not at the point of the mismatch.

Consider the following multiplication example:

```
int n1 = 10;
int n2 = 5.0 * n1;
```

The second line in this example generates an error message because of a type mismatch, but the error occurs *at the assignment* — not at the multiplication. Here's the horrible tale: To perform the multiplication, C# implicitly converts n1 to a double. C# can then perform double multiplication, the result of which is the all-powerful double.

The type of the right-hand and left-hand operators of the assignment operator must match, but the type of the left-hand operator cannot change. Because C# refuses to demote an expression implicitly, the compiler generates the error message Cannot implicitly convert type double to int.

C# allows this expression with an explicit cast:

```
int n1 = 10;
int n2 = (int)(5.0 * n1);
```

(The parentheses are necessary because the cast operator has very high precedence.) This example works — *explicit* demotion is okay. The n1 is promoted to a double, the multiplication is performed, and the double result is demoted to an int. In this case, however, you would worry about the sanity of the programmer because 5 * n1 is so much easier for both the programmer and the C# compiler to read.

Chapter 5: Getting Into the Program Flow

In This Chapter

- **Making decisions `if` you can**
- **Deciding what `else` to do**
- **Looping without going in a circle**
- **Using the `while` and `do . . . while` loops**
- **Using the `for` loop and understanding scope**

Consider this simple program:

```
using System;
namespace HelloWorld
{
  public class Program
  {
    // This is where the program starts.
    static void Main(string[] args)
    {
      // Prompt user to enter a name.
      Console.WriteLine("Enter your name, please:");
      // Now read the name entered.
      string name = Console.ReadLine();
      // Greet the user with the entered name.
      Console.WriteLine("Hello, " + name);
      // Wait for user to acknowledge the results.
      Console.WriteLine("Press Enter to terminate . . . ");
      Console.Read();
    }
  }
}
```

Beyond introducing you to a few fundamentals of C# programming, this program is almost worthless. It simply spits back out whatever you entered. You can imagine more complicated program examples that accept input, perform some type of calculations, generate some type of output (otherwise, why do the calculations?), and then exit at the bottom. However, even a program such as this one can be of only limited use.

One key element of any computer processor is its ability to make decisions. When I say "make decisions," I mean that the processor sends the flow of execution down one path of instructions if a condition is true or down another path if the condition is not true. Any programming language must offer this fundamental capability to control the flow of execution.

The three basic types of *flow control* are the `if` statement, the loop, and the jump. (I describe one of the looping controls, the `foreach`, in Chapter 6 of this minibook.)

Branching Out with if and switch

The basis of all C# decision-making capability is the `if` statement (and the basis of all my decisions is the `maybe`):

```
if (bool-expression)
{
    // Control goes here if the expression is true.
}
// Control passes to this statement whether the expression is true or not.
```

A pair of parentheses immediately following the keyword `if` contains a *conditional expression* of type `bool`. (See Chapter 2 of this minibook for a discussion of `bool` expressions.) Immediately following the expression is a block of code set off by a pair of braces. If the expression is true, the program executes the code within the braces; if the expression is not true, the program skips the code in the braces. (If the program executes the code in braces, it ends just after the closing brace and continues from there.)

The `if` statement is easier to understand by looking at a concrete example:

```
// Make sure that a is not negative:
// If a is less than 0 . . .
if (a < 0)
{
    // . . . then assign 0 to it so that it's no longer negative.
    a = 0;
}
```

This segment of code ensures that the variable `a` is nonnegative — greater than or equal to 0. The `if` statement says, "If `a` is less than 0, assign 0 to `a`." (In other words, turn `a` into a positive value.)

The braces aren't required. C# treats `if(bool-expression) statement;` as though it had been written `if(bool-expression) {statement;}`. The general consensus (and my preference) is to always use braces for better clarity. In other words, don't ask — just do it.

Introducing the if statement

Consider a small program that calculates interest. The user enters the principal amount and the interest rate, and the program spits out the resulting value for each year. (This program isn't sophisticated.) The simplistic calculation appears as follows in C#:

```
// Calculate the value of the principal plus interest.
decimal interestPaid;
interestPaid = principal * (interest / 100);
// Now calculate the total.
decimal total = principal + interestPaid;
```

The first equation multiplies the principal `principal` times the interest `interest` to produce the interest to be paid — `interestPaid`. (You divide by 100 because interest is usually calculated by entering a percentage amount.) The interest to be paid is then added back into the principal, resulting in a new principal, which is stored in the variable `total`.

The program must anticipate almost anything when dealing with human input. For example, you don't want your program to accept a negative principal or interest amount (well, maybe a negative interest). The following `CalculateInterest` program includes checks to ensure that neither of these entries happens:

```
// CalculateInterest -- Calculate the interest amount paid
//    on a given principal. If either the principal or the
//    interest rate is negative, generate an error message.
using System;
namespace CalculateInterest
{
  public class Program
  {
    public static void Main(string[] args)
    {
      // Prompt user to enter source principal.
      Console.Write("Enter principal: ");
      string principalInput = Console.ReadLine();
      decimal principal = Convert.ToDecimal(principalInput);
      // Make sure that the principal is not negative.
      if (principal < 0)
      {
        Console.WriteLine("Principal cannot be negative");
        principal = 0;
      }
      // Enter the interest rate.
      Console.Write("Enter interest: ");
      string interestInput = Console.ReadLine();
      decimal interest = Convert.ToDecimal(interestInput);
      // Make sure that the interest is not negative either.
      if (interest < 0)
      {
        Console.WriteLine("Interest cannot be negative");
        interest = 0;
      }
      // Calculate the value of the principal plus interest.
      decimal interestPaid = principal * (interest / 100);
      // Now calculate the total.
      decimal total = principal + interestPaid;
      // Output the result.
      Console.WriteLine(); // Skip a line.
      Console.WriteLine("Principal     = " + principal);
      Console.WriteLine("Interest      = " + interest + "%");
      Console.WriteLine();
      Console.WriteLine("Interest paid = " + interestPaid);
```

```
        Console.WriteLine("Total         = " + total);
        // Wait for user to acknowledge the results.
        Console.WriteLine("Press Enter to terminate . . . ");
        Console.Read();
      }
    }
  }
```

The CalculateInterest program begins by prompting the user for his name using WriteLine() to write a string to the console. Tell the user exactly what you want and, if possible, specify the format. Users don't respond well to uninformative prompts, such as >.

The sample program uses the ReadLine() command to read in whatever the user types; the program returns the value entered, in the form of a string, when the user presses Enter. Because the program is looking for the principal in the form of a decimal, the input string must be converted using the Convert.ToDecimal() command. The result is stored in principalInput.

The ReadLine(), WriteLine(), and ToDecimal() commands are all examples of method calls. A *method call* delegates some work to another part of the program, called a method. I describe method calls in detail in Book II; these particular method calls are straightforward. You should be able to get the gist of the meaning using my extraordinarily insightful explanatory narrative. If that doesn't work, ignore the narrative. If *that* doesn't work, see Book II.

The next line in the example checks principal. If it's negative, the program outputs a polite "nastygram" indicating that the user has fouled up. The program does the same thing for the interest rate, and then it performs the simplistic interest calculation outlined earlier, in the "Introducing the If Statement," and spits out the result, using a series of WriteLine() commands.

The program generates the following output with a legitimate principal amount and a usurious interest rate that is perfectly legal in most states:

```
Enter principal: 1234
Enter interest: 21

Principal     = 1234
Interest      = 21%

Interest paid = 259.14
Total         = 1493.14
Press Enter to terminate . . .
```

Executing the program with illegal input generates the following output:

```
Enter principal: 1234
Enter interest: -12.5
Interest cannot be negative

Principal     = 1234
Interest      = 0%
```

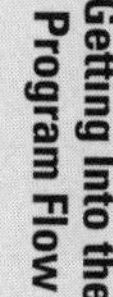


```
Interest paid = 0
Total         = 1234
Press Enter to terminate . . .
```

Indent the lines within an `if` clause to enhance readability. This type of indentation is ignored by C# but is helpful to us humans. Most programming editors support autoindenting, whereby the editor automatically indents as soon as you enter the `if` command. To set autoindenting in Visual Studio, choose Tools➪Options. Then expand the Text Editor node. From there, expand C#. Finally, click Tabs. On this page, enable Smart Indenting and set the number of spaces per indent to your preference. (I use two spaces per indent in this book.) Set the tab size to the same value.

Examining the else statement

Sometimes, your code must check for mutually exclusive conditions. For example, the following code segment stores the maximum of two numbers, `a` and `b`, in the variable `max`:

```
// Store the maximum of a and b into the variable max.
int max;
// If a is greater than b . . .
if (a > b)
{
    //  . . . save a as the maximum.
    max = a;
}
// If a is less than or equal to b . . .
if (a <= b)
{
    //  . . . save b as the maximum.
    max = b;
}
```

The second `if` statement causes needless processing because the two conditions are mutually exclusive. If `a` is greater than `b`, `a` can't possibly be less than or equal to `b`. C# defines an `else` clause for just this case. The `else` keyword defines a block of code that's executed if the `if` block is not.

The code segment to calculate the maximum now appears this way:

```
// Store the maximum of a and b into the variable max.
int max;
// If a is greater than b . . .
if (a > b)
{
    //  . . . save a as the maximum; otherwise . . .
    max = a;
}
else
{
    //  . . . save b as the maximum.
    max = b;
}
```

If a is greater than b, the first block is executed; otherwise, the second block is executed. In the end, max contains the greater of a or b.

Avoiding even the else

Sequences of else clauses can become confusing. Some programmers like to avoid them when doing so doesn't cause even more confusion. You could write the maximum calculation like this:

```
// Store the maximum of a and b into the variable max.
int max;
// Start by assuming that a is greater than b.
max = a;
// If it is not . . .
if (b > a)
{
  //  . . . then you can change your mind.
  max = b;
}
```

Some programmers avoid this style like the plague, and I can sympathize. (That doesn't mean that I'm going to change; it just means that I sympathize.) You see both this style and the "else style" in common use.

Programmers who like to be cool and cryptic often use the *ternary operator*, :?, equivalent to an if/else on one line:

```
bool informal = true;
string name = informal : "Chuck" ? "Charles";  // Returns "Chuck"
```

This chunk evaluates the expression before the colon. If the expression is true, return it after the colon but before the question mark. If the expression is false, return it after the question mark. This process turns an if/else into an expression.

I generally advise using ternary only rarely because it truly *is* cryptic.

Nesting if statements

The CalculateInterest program warns the user of illegal input; however, continuing with the interest calculation, even if one of the values is illogical, doesn't seem quite right. It causes no real harm here because the interest calculation takes little or no time and the user can ignore the results, but some calculations aren't nearly as quick. In addition, why ask the user for an interest rate after she has already entered an invalid value for the principal? The user knows that the results of the calculation will be invalid no matter what she enters next. (You'd be amazed at how much it infuriates users.)

The program should ask the user for an interest rate only if the principal is reasonable and perform the interest calculation only if both values are valid. To accomplish this, you need two if statements, one within the other.

An `if` statement found within the body of another `if` statement is an *embedded,* or *nested,* statement.

The following program, `CalculateInterestWithEmbeddedTest`, uses embedded `if` statements to avoid stupid questions if a problem is detected in the input:

```
// CalculateInterestWithEmbeddedTest -- Calculate the interest amount
//    paid on a given principal. If either the principal or the
//    interest rate is negative, then generate an error message
//    and don't proceed with the calculation.
using System;
namespace CalculateInterestWithEmbeddedTest
{
  public class Program
  {
    public static void Main(string[] args)
    {
      // Define a maximum interest rate.
      int maximumInterest = 50;
      // Prompt user to enter source principal.
      Console.Write("Enter principal: ");
      string principalInput = Console.ReadLine();
      decimal principal = Convert.ToDecimal(principalInput);
      // If the principal is negative . . .
      if (principal < 0)
      {
        // . . . generate an error message . . .
        Console.WriteLine("Principal cannot be negative");
      }
      else  // Go here only if principal was > 0: thus valid.
      {
        //  . . . otherwise, enter the interest rate.
        Console.Write("Enter interest: ");
        string interestInput = Console.ReadLine();
        decimal interest = Convert.ToDecimal(interestInput);
        // If the interest is negative or too large . . .
        if (interest < 0 || interest > maximumInterest)
        {
          //  . . . generate an error message as well.
          Console.WriteLine("Interest cannot be negative " +
                            "or greater than " + maximumInterest);
          interest = 0;
        }
        else  // Reach this point only if all is well.
        {
          // Both the principal and the interest appear to be legal;
          // calculate the value of the principal plus interest.
          decimal interestPaid;
          interestPaid = principal * (interest / 100);
          // Now calculate the total.
          decimal total = principal + interestPaid;
          // Output the result.
          Console.WriteLine();  // Skip a line.
          Console.WriteLine("Principal     = " + principal);
          Console.WriteLine("Interest      = " + interest + "%");
          Console.WriteLine();
          Console.WriteLine("Interest paid = " + interestPaid);
          Console.WriteLine("Total         = " + total);
        }
```

```
      }
      // Wait for user to acknowledge the results.
      Console.WriteLine("Press Enter to terminate . . . ");
      Console.Read();
    }
  }
}
```

The program first reads the principal from the user. If the principal is negative, the program outputs an error message and quits. If the principal is not negative, control passes to the `else` clause, where the program continues executing.

The interest rate test has been improved in this example. Here, the program requires an interest rate that's nonnegative (a mathematical law) and less than a maximum rate (a judiciary law — I can only wish that credit cards had an interest rate limit). This `if` statement uses the following compound test:

```
if (interest < 0 || interest > maximumInterest)
```

This statement is true if `interest` is less than 0 or greater than `maximumInterest`. Notice that I declare `maximumInterest` at the top of the program rather than *hard-code* it as a constant number here. *Hard-coding* refers to using values directly in your code, rather than creating a constant to hold them.

Define important constants at the top of your program. Giving a constant a descriptive name (rather than just a number) makes it easy to find and easier to change. If the constant appears ten times in your code, you still have to make only one change to change all references.

Entering a correct principal but a negative interest rate generates this output:

```
Enter principal: 1234
Enter interest: -12.5
Interest cannot be negative or greater than 50.
Press Enter to terminate . . .
```

Only when the user enters both a legal principal and a legal interest rate does the program generate the correct calculation:

```
Enter principal: 1234
Enter interest: 12.5

Principal     = 1234
Interest      = 12.5%

Interest paid = 154.250
Total         = 1388.250
Press Enter to terminate . . .
```

Running the switchboard

You often want to test a variable for numerous different values. For example, `maritalStatus` may be 0 for unmarried, 1 for married, 2 for divorced, 3 for widowed (surely I covered all the options — oh, wait), or 4 for none of your business. To differentiate among these values, you could use the following series of if statements:

```
if (maritalStatus == 0)
{
  // Must be unmarried . . .
  //  . . . do something . . .
}
else
{
  if (maritalStatus == 1)
  {
    // Must be married . . .
    //  . . . do something else . . .
```

And so on.

You can see that these repetitive if statements grow tiresome quickly. Testing for multiple cases is such a common occurrence that C# provides a special construct to decide between a set of mutually exclusive conditions. This control, the switch, works as follows:

```
switch(maritalStatus)
{
  case 0:
           //  . . . do the unmarried stuff . . .
           break;
  case 1:
           //  . . . do the married stuff . . .
           break;
  case 2:
           //  . . . do the divorced stuff . . .
           break;
  case 3:
           //  . . . do the widowed stuff . . .
           break;
  case 4:
           //  . . . get out of my face . . .
           break;
  default:
           // Goes here if it fails to pass a case;
           // this is probably an error condition.
           break;
}
```

The expression at the top of the switch statement is evaluated. In this case, the expression is simply the variable maritalStatus. The value of that expression is then compared against the value of each of the cases. Control passes to the default clause if no match is found.

The argument to the switch statement can also be a string:

```
string s = "Davis";
switch(s)
{
  case "Davis":
```

```
        // . . . control will actually pass here . . .
        break;
case "Smith":
        // . . . do Smith stuff . . .
        break;
case "Jones":
        // . . . do Jones stuff . . .
        break;
case "Hvidsten":
        // . . . do Hvidsten stuff . . .
        break;
default:
        // Goes here if it doesn't pass any cases.
        break;
}
```

Using the `switch` statement involves these severe restrictions:

- The argument to the `switch()` must be one of the counting types (including `char`) or a `string`. Floating-point values are excluded.
- The various `case` values must refer to values of the same type as the `switch` expression.
- The `case` values must be constant in the sense that their value must be known at compile time. (A statement such as `case x` isn't legal unless `x` is a type of constant.)
- Each clause must end in a `break` statement (or another exit command, such as `return`). The `break` statement passes control out of the `switch`.

  You can omit a break statement if two cases lead to the same actions: A single `case` clause may have more than one `case` label, as in this example:

  ```
  string s = "Davis";
  switch(s)
  {
    case "Davis":
    case "Hvidsten":
          // Do the same thing whether s is Davis or Hvidsten
          // since they're related.
            break;
    case "Smith":
            // . . . do Smith stuff . . .
            break;
    default:
            // Goes here if it doesn't pass any cases.
            break;
  }
  ```

This approach enables the program to perform the same operation, whether the input is Davis or Hvidsten. The `SwitchSyntaxTest` example on the Web site illustrates a variety of advice about using `switch`. The final section of this chapter supplies a small addendum to the `switch` story. You can find the code at `csharp102.info`.

Here We Go Loop-the-Loop

The `if` statement enables a program to take different paths through the code being executed depending on the results of a `bool` expression. This statement provides for drastically more interesting programs than programs without decision-making capability. Adding the ability to execute a set of instructions *repeatedly* adds another quantum jump in capability.

Consider the `CalculateInterest` program from the section "Introducing the if statement," earlier in this chapter. Performing this simple interest calculation by using a calculator (or by hand, using a piece of paper) would be much easier than writing and executing a program.

If you could calculate the amount of principal for each of several succeeding years, that would even more useful. A simple macro in a Microsoft Excel spreadsheet is still easier to handle, but at least you're getting closer.

What you need is a way for the computer to execute the same short sequence of instructions multiple times — known as a *loop.*

Looping for a while

The C# keyword `while` introduces the most basic form of execution loop:

```
while(bool-expression)
{
    //  . . . repeatedly executed as long as the expression is true.
}
```

When the `while` loop is first encountered, the `bool` expression is evaluated. If the expression is true, the code within the block is executed. When the block of code reaches the closed brace, control returns to the top and the whole process starts over again. (It's kind of the way I feel when I'm walking the dog. The dog and I loop around and around the yard until the dog . . . well, until he's finished.) Control passes beyond the closed brace the first time the `bool` expression is evaluated and turns out to be false.

If the condition is not true the first time the `while` loop is encountered, the set of commands within the braces is never executed.

Programmers often become sloppy in their speech. (Programmers are sloppy most of the time.) If a programmer says that a loop is executed until a condition is false, it implies that control passes outside the loop — no matter where the program happens to be executing — as soon as the condition becomes false. This definitely isn't the case. The program doesn't check whether the condition is still true until control specifically passes back to the top of the loop.

You can use the `while` loop to create the `CalculateInterestTable` program, a looping version of the `CalculateInterest` program. `CalculateInterestTable` calculates a table of principals showing accumulated annual payments:

```
// CalculateInterestTable -- Calculate the interest paid on a given
//    principal over a period of years.
using System;
namespace CalculateInterestTable
{
  using System;
  public class Program
    {
    public static void Main(string[] args)
    {
      // Define a maximum interest rate.
      int maximumInterest = 50;
      // Prompt user to enter source principal.
      Console.Write("Enter principal: ");
      string principalInput = Console.ReadLine();
      decimal principal = Convert.ToDecimal(principalInput);
      // If the principal is negative . . .
      if (principal < 0)
      {
        // . . . generate an error message . . .
        Console.WriteLine("Principal cannot be negative");
      }
      else  // Go here only if principal was > 0: thus valid.
      {
        //  . . . otherwise, enter the interest rate.
        Console.Write("Enter interest: ");
        string interestInput = Console.ReadLine();
        decimal interest = Convert.ToDecimal(interestInput);
        // If the interest is negative or too large . . .
        if (interest < 0 || interest > maximumInterest)
        {
          //  . . . generate an error message as well.
          Console.WriteLine("Interest cannot be negative " +
                          "or greater than " + maximumInterest);
          interest = 0;
        }
        else  // Reach this point only if all is well.
        {
          // Both the principal and the interest appear to be
          // legal; finally, input the number of years.
          Console.Write("Enter number of years: ");
          string durationInput = Console.ReadLine();
          int duration = Convert.ToInt32(durationInput);
          // Verify the input.
          Console.WriteLine();  // Skip a line.
          Console.WriteLine("Principal     = " + principal);
          Console.WriteLine("Interest      = " + interest + "%");
          Console.WriteLine("Duration      = " + duration + " years");
          Console.WriteLine();

          // Now loop through the specified number of years.
          int year = 1;
          while(year <= duration)
          {
            // Calculate the value of the principal plus interest.
            decimal interestPaid;
            interestPaid = principal * (interest / 100);
```

```
            // Now calculate the new principal by adding
            // the interest to the previous principal amount.
            principal = principal + interestPaid;
            // Round off the principal to the nearest cent.
            principal = decimal.Round(principal, 2);
            // Output the result.
            Console.WriteLine(year + "-" + principal);
            // Skip over to next year.
            year = year + 1;
          }
        }
      }
      // Wait for user to acknowledge the results.
      Console.WriteLine("\nPress Enter to terminate . . . ");
      Console.Read();
    }
  }
}
```

The output from a trial run of `CalculateInterestTable` appears this way:

```
Enter principal: 1234
Enter interest: 12.5
Enter number of years: 10

Principal      = 1234
Interest       = 12.5%
Duration       = 10 years

1-1388.25
2-1561.78
3-1757.00
4-1976.62
5-2223.70
6-2501.66
7-2814.37
8-3166.17
9-3561.94
10-4007.18

Press Enter to terminate . . .
```

Each value represents the total principal after the number of years elapsed, assuming simple interest compounded annually. For example, the value of $1,234 at 12.5 percent is $3,561.94 after nine years.

Most of the values show two decimal places for the cents in the amount. Because trailing zeros aren't displayed in all versions of C#, some values may show only a single digit — or even no digit — after the decimal point. Thus, $12.70 may be displayed as `12.7`. If so, you can fix the problem by using the special formatting characters described in Chapter 3 of this minibook. (C# 2.0 and later appear to show trailing zeros by default.)

The `CalculateInterestTable` program begins by reading the principal and interest values from the user and checking to make sure that they're valid. `CalculateInterestTable` then reads the number of years over which to iterate and stores this value in the variable `duration`.

Before entering the while loop, the program declares a variable year, which it initializes to 1. This will be the "current year" — that is, this number changes "each year" as the program loops. If the year number contained in year is less than the total duration contained in duration, the principal for "this year" is recalculated by calculating the interest based on the "previous year." The calculated principal is output along with the current-year offset.

The statement decimal.Round() rounds the calculated value to the nearest fraction of a cent.

The key to the program lies in the last line within the block. The statement year = year + 1; increments year by 1. If year begins with the value 3, its value will be 4 after this expression. This incrementing moves the calculations along from one year to the next.

After the year has been incremented, control returns to the top of the loop, where the value year is compared to the requested duration. In the sample run, if the current year is less than 10, the calculation continues. After being incremented ten times, the value of year becomes 11, which is greater than 10, and program control passes to the first statement after the while loop — the program stops looping.

Most looping commands follow this basic principle of incrementing a counter until it exceeds a previously defined value.

The counting variable year in CalculateInterestTable must be declared and initialized before the while loop in which it is used. In addition, the year variable must be incremented, usually as the last statement within the loop. As this example demonstrates, you have to look ahead to see which variables you need. This pattern is easier to use after you've written a few thousand while loops, like I have.

When writing while loops, don't forget to increment the counting variable, as I did in this example:

```
int nYear = 1;
while (nYear < 10)
{
    //  . . . whatever . . .
}
```

(We left off the year = year + 1;.) Without the increment, year is always 1 and the program loops forever. The only way to exit this *infinite loop* is to terminate the program or reboot. (So nothing is truly infinite, with the possible exception of a particle passing through the event horizon of a black hole.)

Make sure that the terminating condition can be satisfied. Usually, this means your counting variable is being incremented properly. Otherwise, you're looking at an infinite loop, an angry user, bad press, and 50 years of drought.

Infinite loops are a common mistake, so don't be embarrassed when you get caught in one.

Doing the do . . . while loop

A variation of the `while` loop is the `do . . . while` loop. In this example, the condition isn't checked until the *end* of the loop:

```
int year = 1;
do
{
    //  . . . some calculation . . .
    year = year + 1;
} while (year < duration);
```

In contrast to the `while` loop, the `do . . . while` loop is executed at least once, regardless of the value of `duration`.

Breaking up is easy to do

You can use two special commands to bail out of a loop: `break` and `continue`. Executing the `break` command causes control to pass to the first expression immediately following the loop. The similar `continue` command passes control straight back up to the conditional expression at the top of the loop to start over and get it right this time.

I have rarely used `continue` in my programming career, and I doubt that many programmers even remember that it exists. Don't forget about it completely because it may be a trick question in an interview or a crossword puzzle.

Suppose that you want to take your money out of the bank as soon as the principal exceeds a certain number of times the original amount, irrespective of the duration in years. (After all, how much money do you really need?) You could easily accommodate this amount by adding the following code within the loop:

```
if (principal > (maxPower * originalPrincipal))
{
  break;
}
```

Anyone who watches *The Simpsons* as much as I do knows who `maxPower` is. (***Hint:*** D'oh!)

The `break` clause isn't executed until the condition within the `if` comparison is true — in this case, until the calculated principal is `maxPower` times the original principal or more. Executing the `break` statement passes control outside the `while(year <= duration)` statement, and the program resumes execution immediately after the loop.

For a version of the interest table program with this addition, see the `CalculateInterestTableWithBreak` program at `csharp102.info`. (I don't include the listing here, for brevity's sake.)

An example of output from this program looks like this:

```
Enter principal: 100
Enter interest: 25
Enter number of years: 100

Principal     = 100
Interest      = 25%
Duration      = 100 years
Quit if a multiplier of 10 is reached

1-125.00
2-156.25
3-195.31
4-244.14
5-305.18
6-381.48
7-476.85
8-596.06
9-745.08
10-931.35
11-1164.19
Press Enter to terminate . . .
```

The program terminates as soon as the calculated principal exceeds $1,000 — thank goodness, you didn't have to wait 100 years!

Looping until you get it right

The `CalculateInterestTable` program is smart enough to terminate in the event that the user enters an invalid balance or interest amount. However, jumping immediately out of the program just because the user mistypes something seems harsh. Even my user-unfriendly accounting program gives me three chances to enter the correct password before it gives up.

A combination of `while` and `break` enables the program to be a little more flexible. The `CalculateInterestTableMoreForgiving` program demonstrates the principle this way:

```
// CalculateInterestTableMoreForgiving -- Calculate the interest paid on a
//    given principal over a period of years. This version gives the user
//    multiple chances to input the legal principal and interest.
using System;
namespace CalculateInterestTableMoreForgiving
{
  using System;
  public class Program
  {
    public static void Main(string[] args)
    {
      // Define a maximum interest rate.
      int maximumInterest = 50;
```

```
// Prompt user to enter source principal; keep prompting
// until the correct value is entered.
decimal principal;
while(true)
{
  Console.Write("Enter principal: ");
  string principalInput = Console.ReadLine();
  principal = Convert.ToDecimal(principalInput);
  // Exit if the value entered is correct.
  if (principal >= 0)
  {
    break;
  }
  // Generate an error on incorrect input.
  Console.WriteLine("Principal cannot be negative");
  Console.WriteLine("Try again");
  Console.WriteLine();
}
// Now enter the interest rate.
decimal interest;
while(true)
{
  Console.Write("Enter interest: ");
  string interestInput = Console.ReadLine();
  interest = Convert.ToDecimal(interestInput);
  // Don't accept interest that is negative or too large . . .
  if (interest >= 0 && interest <= maximumInterest)
  {
    break;
  }
  //  . . . generate an error message as well.
  Console.WriteLine("Interest cannot be negative " +
                    "or greater than " + maximumInterest);
  Console.WriteLine("Try again");
  Console.WriteLine();
}
// Both the principal and the interest appear to be
// legal; finally, input the number of years.
Console.Write("Enter number of years: ");
string durationInput = Console.ReadLine();
int duration = Convert.ToInt32(durationInput);
// Verify the input.
Console.WriteLine();  // Skip a line.
Console.WriteLine("Principal     = " + principal);
Console.WriteLine("Interest      = " + interest + "%");
Console.WriteLine("Duration      = " + duration + " years");
Console.WriteLine();
// Now loop through the specified number of years.
int year = 1;
while(year <= duration)
{
  // Calculate the value of the principal plus interest.
  decimal interestPaid;
  interestPaid = principal * (interest / 100);
  // Now calculate the new principal by adding
  // the interest to the previous principal.
  principal = principal + interestPaid;
  // Round off the principal to the nearest cent.
  principal = decimal.Round(principal, 2);
  // Output the result.
  Console.WriteLine(year + "-" + principal);
  // Skip over to next year.
```

```
        year = year + 1;
      }
      // Wait for user to acknowledge the results.
      Console.WriteLine("Press Enter to terminate . . . ");
      Console.Read();
    }
  }
}
```

This program works largely the same way as do the examples in previous sections of this chapter, except in the area of user input. This time, a `while` loop replaces the `if` statement used in earlier examples to detect invalid input:

```
decimal principal;
while(true)
{
  Console.Write("Enter principal: ");
  string principalInput = Console.ReadLine();
  principal = Convert.ToDecimal(principalInput);
  // Exit when the value entered is correct.
  if (principal >= 0)
  {
    break;
  }
  // Generate an error on incorrect input.
  Console.WriteLine("Principal cannot be negative");
  Console.WriteLine("Try again");
  Console.WriteLine();
}
```

This section of code inputs a value from the user within a loop. If the value of the text is okay, the program exits the input loop and continues. However, if the input has an error, the user sees an error message and control passes back to the program flow to start over.

The program continues to loop until the user enters the correct input. (In the worst case, the program could loop until an obtuse user dies of old age.)

Notice that the conditionals have been reversed because the question is no longer whether illegal input should generate an error message but, rather, whether the correct input should exit the loop. In the interest section, for example, consider this test:

```
principal < 0 || principal > maximumInterest
```

This test changes to this:

```
interest >= 0 && interest <= maximumInterest
```

Clearly, `interest >= 0` is the opposite of `interest < 0`. What may not be as obvious is that the OR (`||`) operator is replaced with an AND (`&&`) operator. It says, "Exit the loop if the interest is greater than zero AND less than the maximum amount (in other words, if it is correct)."

By the way, how could you revise `CalculateInterestTableMoreForgiving` to let the user run calculation after calculation and enter new principal and interest figures every time until she wants to quit? ***Hint:*** Use another `while(true)` loop with its own exit condition.

Note that the `principal` variable must be declared outside the loop because of scope rules, which I explain in the next section.

It may sound obvious, but the expression `true` evaluates to `true`. Therefore, `while(true)` is your archetypical infinite loop. It's the embedded `break` command that exits the loop. Therefore, if you use the `while(true)` loop, make sure that your break condition can occur.

The output from a sample execution of this program (showing one of the author's ignorance) appears this way:

```
Enter principal: -1000
Principal cannot be negative
Try again

Enter principal: 1000
Enter interest: -10
Interest cannot be negative or greater than 50
Try again

Enter interest: 10
Enter number of years: 5

Principal     = 1000
Interest      = 10%
Duration      = 5 years

1-1100.0
2-1210.00
3-1331.00
4-1464.10
5-1610.51
Press Enter to terminate . . .
```

The program refuses to accept a negative principal or interest amount and patiently explains the mistake on each loop.

Explain exactly what the user did wrong before looping back for further input or else that person will become extremely confused. Showing an example may also help, especially for formatting problems. A little diplomacy can't hurt, either, as Grandma may have pointed out.

Focusing on scope rules

A variable declared within the body of a loop is *only defined within* that loop. Consider this code snippet:

```
int days = 1;
while(days < duration)
{
    int average = value / days;
    // . . . some series of commands . . .
    days = days + 1;
}
```

The variable `average` isn't defined outside the `while` loop. Various reasons for this exist, but consider this one: The first time the loop executes, the program encounters the declaration `int average` and the variable is defined. On the second loop, the program again encounters the declaration for `average`, and were it not for scope rules, it would be an error because the variable is already defined.

I could provide other, more convincing reasons than this one, but this one should do for now.

Suffice it to say that the variable `average` goes away, as far as C# is concerned, as soon as the program reaches the closed brace — and is redefined each time through the loop.

Experienced programmers say that the *scope* of the variable `average` is limited to the `while` loop.

Looping a Specified Number of Times with for

The `while` loop is the simplest and second most commonly used looping structure in C#. Compared to the `for` loop, however, the `while` loop is used about as often as metric tools in an American machine shop.

The `for` loop has this structure:

```
for(initExpression; condition; incrementExpression)
{
    // . . . body of code . . .
}
```

When the `for` loop is encountered, the program first executes the `initExpression` expression and then executes the `condition`. If the `condition` expression is true, the program executes the body of the loop, which is surrounded by the braces immediately following the `for` command. When the program reaches the closed brace, control passes to `incrementExpression` and then back to `condition`, where the next pass through the loop begins.

In fact, the definition of a `for` loop can be converted into this `while` loop:

```
initExpression;
while(condition)
{
```

```
    // . . . body of code . . .
    incrementExpression;
}
```


An example

You can better see how the for loop works in this example:

```
// Here is one C# expression or another.
a = 1;
// Now loop for awhile.
for(int year = 1; year < duration; year = year + 1)
{
    // . . . body of code . . .
}
// The program continues here.
a = 2;
```

Assume that the program has just executed the `a = 1;` expression. Next, the program declares the variable `year` and initializes it to `1`. Then the program compares `year` to `duration`. If `year` is less than `duration`, the body of code within the braces is executed. After encountering the closed brace, the program jumps back to the top and executes the `year = year + 1` clause before sliding back over to the `year < duration` comparison.

The `year` variable is undefined outside the scope of the `for` loop. The loop's scope includes the loop's heading as well as its body.

Why do you need another loop?

Why do you need the `for` loop if C# has an equivalent `while` loop? The short answer is that you don't — the `for` loop doesn't bring anything to the table that the `while` loop can't already do.

However, the sections of the `for` loop exist for convenience — and to clearly establish the three parts that every loop should have: the setup, exit criteria, and increment. Not only is this arrangement easier to read, but it's also easier to get right. (Remember that the most common mistakes in a `while` loop are forgetting to increment the counting variable and failing to provide the proper exit criteria.)

Beyond any sort of song-and-dance justification that I may make, the most important reason to understand the `for` loop is that it's the loop everyone uses — and it (along with its cousin, `foreach`) is the one you see 90 percent of the time when you're reading other people's code.

The `for` loop is designed so that the first expression initializes a counting variable and the last section increments it; however, the C# language doesn't enforce any such rule. You can do anything you want in these two sections — however, you would be ill advised to do anything *but* initialize and increment the counting variable.

The increment operator is particularly popular when writing for loops. (I describe the increment operator along with other operators in Chapter 4 of this minibook.) The previous for loop is usually written this way:

```
for(int year = 1; year < nDuration; year++)
{
    //  . . . body of code . . .
}
```

You almost always see the postincrement operator used in a for loop instead of the preincrement operator, although the effect in this case is the same. There's no reason other than habit and the fact that it looks cooler. (The next time you want to break the ice, just haul out your C# listing full of postincrement operators to show how cool you are. It almost never works, but it's worth a try.)

The for loop has one variation that I can't claim to understand. If the logical condition expression is missing, it's assumed to be true. Thus for(;;) is an infinite loop.

You see for(;;) used as an infinite loop more often than while(true). I have no idea why that's the case.

Nesting Loops

An inner loop can appear within an outer loop, this way:

```
for( . . .some condition . . .)
{
  for( . . .some other condition . . .)
  {
    //  . . . do whatever . . .
  }
}
```

The inner loop is executed to completion after each pass through the outer loop. The loop variable (such as year) used in the inner for loop isn't defined outside the inner loop's scope.

A loop contained within another loop is a *nested* loop. Nested loops cannot "cross." For example, the following code won't work:

```
do                   // Start a do..while loop.
{
  for( . . .)        // Start some for loop.
  {
  } while( . . .)    // End do..while loop.
}                    // End for loop.
```

I'm not even sure what this chunk would mean, but it doesn't matter because the compiler tells you that it's not legal anyway.

A break statement within a nested loop breaks out of the inner loop only. In the following example, the break statement exits loop B and goes back into loop A:

```
// for loop A
for( . . .some condition . . .)
{
  // for loop B
  for( . . .some other condition . . .)
  {
    //  . . . do whatever . . .
    if (something is true)
    {
      break;        // Breaks out of loop B and not loop A
    }
  }
}
```

C# doesn't have a break command that exits both loops simultaneously.

That's not as big a limitation as it sounds. In practice, the often-complex logic contained within such nested loops is better encapsulated in a method. Executing a return from within any of the loops exits the method — thereby bailing out of all loops, no matter how nested they are. We describe methods and the return statement in Chapter 7 of this minibook.

The DisplayXWithNestedLoops example (not shown here) illustrates nesting one loop inside another to do some primitive drawing on the screen.

Don't goto Pieces

You can transfer control in an unstructured fashion by using the goto statement. It's followed by one of these items:

- A label
- A case in a switch statement
- The keyword default (the default clause of a switch statement)

The idea behind the latter two items is to "jump" from one case to another.

This snippet demonstrates how the goto statement is used:

```
// If the condition is true . . .
if (a > b)
{
  //  . . . control passes unconditionally from the goto to the label.
  goto exitLabel;
}
//  . . . whatever other code goes here . . .
exitLabel:
  // Control continues here.
```

The goto statement is unpopular for the very reason that makes it such a powerful control: It is almost completely unstructured. Tracking the flow of control through anything larger than a trivial piece of code can be difficult if you use goto. (Can you say "spaghetti code"?)

Religious wars have sprung up over the use of the goto statement. In fact, the C# language itself has been criticized for its inclusion of the control. Actually, goto is neither all that horrible nor necessary. Because you can almost always avoid using goto, I recommend staying away from it, other than *occasionally* using it to link two cases within a switch statement, like this:

```
switch(n)  // This example becomes gnarly in the logic department . . .
{
  case 0:
    // Do something for the 0 case, then  . . .
    goto 3;  // jump to another case; no break statement needed.
  case 1:
    // Do something for the 1 case.
    break;
  case 3:     // Case 0 jumps to here after doing its thing.
    // Add some case 3 stuff to what case 0 did, thus "chaining" the cases.
    break;
  default:
    // Default case.
    break;
}
```

Don't get addicted to goto, though. Really.

Chapter 6: Lining Up Your Ducks with Collections

In This Chapter

- **Creating variables that contain multiple items of data: Arrays**
- **Going arrays one better with flexible "collections"**
- **New features: Array and collection initializers and set-type collections**

Simple one-value variables of the sort you may encounter in this book fall a bit short in dealing with lots of items of the same kind: ten ducks instead of just one, for example. C# fills the gap with two kinds of variables that store multiple items, generally called *collections.* The two species of collection are the *array* and the more general purpose *collection class*. Usually, if I mean *array,* I say so, and if I mean *collection class,* I just call it that. If I refer to a *collection* or a *list,* I usually mean that it can be either one.

An *array* is a data type that holds a list of items, all of which must be of the same type: all `int` or all `double`, for example.

C# gives you quite a collection of collection classes, and they come in various shapes, such as flexible lists (like strings of beads), queues (like the line to buy your *Spider-Man XII* tickets), stacks (like the semistack of junk on someone's desk), and more. Most collection classes are like arrays in that they can hold just apples or just oranges. But C# also gives you a few collection classes that can hold both apples and oranges at a time — which is useful only rarely. (And you have much better ways to manage the feat than using these elderly collections.)

For now, if you can master the array and the `List` collection (although this chapter introduces two other kinds of collections), you'll do fine throughout most of this book. But circle back here later if you want to pump up your collection repertoire.

The C# Array

Variables that contain single values are plenty useful. Even class structures that can describe compound objects made up of parts (such as a vehicle with its engine and transmission) are critical. But you also need a construct for holding a bunch of objects, such as Bill Gates' extensive collection of vintage cars or a certain author's vintage sock collection. The built-in class `Array` is a structure that can contain a series of elements of the same type (all `int` values and all `double` values, for example, or all `Vehicle` objects and `Motor` objects — you meet these latter sorts of objects in Chapter 7 of this minibook).

The argument for the array

Consider the problem of averaging a set of six floating-point numbers. Each of the six numbers requires its own `double` storage:

```
double d0 = 5;
double d1 = 2;
double d2 = 7;
double d3 = 3.5;
double d4 = 6.5;
double d5 = 8;
```

(Averaging `int` variables can result in rounding errors, as described in Chapter 2 of this minibook.)

Computing the average of those variables might look like this:

```
double sum = d0 + d1 + d2 + d3 + d4 + d5;
double average = sum / 6;
```

Listing each element by name is tedious. Okay, maybe it's not so tedious when you have only 6 numbers to average, but imagine averaging 600 (or even 6 million) floating-point values.

The fixed-value array

Fortunately, you don't need to name each element separately. C# provides the array structure that can store a sequence of values. Using an array, you can put all your `double`s into one variable, like this:

```
double[] doublesArray = {5, 2, 7, 3.5, 6.5, 8, 1, 9, 1, 3};
```

You can also declare an empty array without initializing it:

```
double[] doublesArray = new double[6];
```

This line allocates space for six `double`s but doesn't initialize them.

The `Array` class, on which all C# arrays are based, provides a special syntax that makes it more convenient to use. The paired brackets `[]` refer to the way you access individual elements in the array:

```
doublesArray[0] // Corresponds to d0 (that is, 5)
doublesArray[1] // Corresponds to d1 (that is, 2)
. . .
```

The 0th element of the array corresponds to d0, the 1th element to d1, the 2th element to d2, and so on. Programmers commonly refer to the 0th element as "doublesArray sub-0," to the first element as "doublesArray sub-1," and so on.

The array's element numbers — 0, 1, 2, . . . — are known as the *index*.

In C#, the array index starts at 0 and not at 1. Therefore, you typically don't refer to the element at index 1 as the first element but, rather, as the "oneth element" or the "element at index 1." *The first element is the zeroth element.* If you insist on using normal speech, just be aware that the first element is always at index 0 and the second element is at index 1.

The doublesArray variable wouldn't be much of an improvement, were it not for the possibility that the index of the array is a variable. Using a for loop is easier than writing out each element by hand, as this program demonstrates:

```
// FixedArrayAverage -- Average a fixed array of numbers using a loop.
namespace FixedArrayAverage
{
  using System;
  public class Program
  {
    public static void Main(string[] args)
    {
      double[] doublesArray = {5, 2, 7, 3.5, 6.5, 8, 1, 9, 1, 3};
      // Accumulate the values in the array into the variable sum.
      double sum = 0;
      for (int i = 0; i < 10; i++)
      {
        sum = sum + doublesArray[i];
      }
      // Now calculate the average.
      double average = sum / 10;
      Console.WriteLine(average);
      Console.WriteLine("Press Enter to terminate...");
      Console.Read();
    }
  }
}
```

The program begins by initializing a variable sum to 0. Then it loops through the values stored in doublesArray, adding each one to sum. By the end of the loop, sum has accumulated the sum of all values in the array. The resulting sum is divided by the number of elements to create the average. The output from executing this program is the expected 4.6. (You can check it with your calculator.)

Checking array bounds

Fortunately, the `FixedArrayAverage` program (in the preceding section "The fixed-value array") loops through all ten elements. But what if you goof and don't iterate through the loop properly? You have these two cases to consider:

You iterate through only nine elements: C# doesn't consider it an error. If you want to read nine elements of a ten-element array, who is C# to say any differently? Of course, the average is incorrect, but the program doesn't know that.

You iterate through 11 (or more) elements: *Now* C# cares a lot. It doesn't let you index beyond the end of an array, for fear that you may overwrite an important value in memory. To test it, change the comparison in `FixedArrayAverage`'s `for` loop to the following, replacing the value 10 with 11:

```
for(int i = 0; i < 11; i++)
```

When you execute the program, you see a dialog box with this error message:

```
IndexOutOfRangeException was unhandled
Index was outside the bounds of the
      array.
```

At first glance, this error message seems imposing. However, you can get the gist rather quickly: Clearly, the `IndexOutOfRangeException` tells you that the program tried to access an array beyond the end of its *range* — accessing element 11 in a 10-element array. (In Chapter 9 of this minibook, I show you how to find out more about that error.)

The variable-length array

The array used in the `FixedArrayAverage` program example suffers from these two serious problems:

- The size of the array is fixed at ten elements.
- Worse, the elements' values are specified directly in the program.

A program that could read in a variable number of values, perhaps determined by the user during execution, would be much more flexible. It would work not only for the ten values specified in `FixedArrayAverage` but also for any other set of values, regardless of their number.

The format for declaring a variable-size array differs slightly from that of a fixed-size, fixed-value array:

```
double[] doublesArrayVariable = new double[N];  // Variable, versus ...
double[] doublesArrayFixed = new double[10];    // Fixed
```

Here, `N` represents the number of elements to allocate.

The updated program `VariableArrayAverage` enables the user to specify the number of values to enter. (`N` has to come from somewhere.) Because the program retains the values entered, not only does it calculate the average, but it also displays the results in a pleasant format, as shown here:

```
// VariableArrayAverage -- Average an array whose size is
//    determined by the user at runtime, accumulating the values
//    in an array. Allows them to be referenced as often as
//    desired. In this case, the array creates an attractive output.
namespace VariableArrayAverage
{
  using System;
  public class Program
  {
    public static void Main(string[] args)
    {
      // First read in the number of doubles the user intends to enter.
      Console.Write("Enter the number of values to average: ");
      string numElementsInput = Console.ReadLine();
      int numElements = Convert.ToInt32(numElementsInput);
      Console.WriteLine();
      // Now declare an array of that size.
      double[] doublesArray = new double[numElements]; // Here's the 'N'.
      // Accumulate the values into an array.
      for (int i = 0; i < numElements; i++)
      {
        // Prompt the user for another double.
        Console.Write("enter double #" + (i + 1) + ": ");
        string val = Console.ReadLine();
        double value = Convert.ToDouble(val);
        // Add this to the array using bracket notation.
        doublesArray[i] = value;
      }
      // Accumulate 'numElements' values from
      // the array in the variable sum.
      double sum = 0;
      for (int i = 0; i < numElements; i++)
      {
        sum = sum + doublesArray[i];
      }

      // Now calculate the average.
      double average = sum / numElements;
      // Output the results in an attractive format.
      Console.WriteLine();
      Console.Write(average + " is the average of (" + doublesArray[0]);
      for (int i = 1; i < numElements; i++)
      {
        Console.Write(" + " + doublesArray[i]);
      }
      Console.WriteLine(") / " + numElements);
      // Wait for user to acknowledge the results.
      Console.WriteLine("Press Enter to terminate...");
      Console.Read();
    }
  }
}
```

Look at the following output of a sample run in which you enter five sequential values, 1 through 5, and the program calculates the average to be 3:

```
Enter the number of values to average:5

enter double #1: 1
enter double #2: 2
enter double #3: 3
```

```
enter double #4: 4
enter double #5: 5

3 is the average of (1 + 2 + 3 + 4 + 5) / 5
Press Enter to terminate...
```

The `VariableArrayAverage` program begins by prompting the user for the number of values she intends to average. (That's the `N` we mention a little earlier.) The result is stored in the `int` variable `numElements`. In the example, the number entered is `5`.

The program continues by allocating an array `doublesArray` with the specified number of elements. In this case, the program allocates an array with five elements. The program loops the number of times specified by `numElements`, reading a new value from the user each time. After the last value, the program calculates the average.

Getting console output just right, as in this example, is a little tricky. Follow each statement in `VariableArrayAverage` carefully as the program outputs open parentheses, equal signs, plus signs, and each of the numbers in the sequence, and compare it with the output.

The `VariableArrayAverage` program probably doesn't completely satisfy your thirst for flexibility. You don't want to have to tell the program how many numbers you want to average. What you really want is to enter numbers to average as long as you want — and then tell the program to average what you entered. That's where the C# collections come in. They give you a powerful, flexible alternative to arrays. Getting input directly from the user isn't the only way to fill up your array or another collection, either.

The Length property

The `for` loop that's used to populate the array in the `VariableArrayAverage` program begins this way:

```
// Now declare an array of that size.
double[] doublesArray = new double[numElements];
// Accumulate the values into an array.
for (int i = 0; i < numElements; i++)
{
  . . .
}
```

The `doublesArray` is declared to be `numElements` items long. Thus the clever programmer used a `for` loop to iterate through `numElements` items of the array. (*Iterate* means to loop through the array one element at a time, as with a `for` loop.)

It would be a shame and a crime to have to schlep around the variable `numElements` with `doublesArray` everywhere it goes just so that you know how long it is. Fortunately, that isn't necessary. An array has a property named Length that contains its length. doublesArray.Length has the same value as numElements.

The following for loop is preferable:

```
// Accumulate the values into an array.
for (int i = 0; i < doublesArray.Length; i++) ...
```

Initializing an array

The following lines show an array with its initializer and then one that allocates space but doesn't initialize the elements' values:

```
double[] fixedLengthArray = {5, 2, 7, 3.5, 6.5, 8, 1, 9, 1, 3};
double[] variableLengthArray = new double[10];
```

You can do it all yourself using the following code:

```
double[] fixedLengthArray = new double[10] {5, 2, 7, 3.5, 6.5, 8, 1, 9, 1, 3};
```

Here, you have specifically allocated the memory using new and then followed that declaration with the initial values for the members of the array. I think I can predict which form you prefer. (***Hint:*** Line 1?)

A Loop Made foreach Array

Given an array of strings, the following loop averages their lengths:

```
public class Student  // Read about classes in Book II.
{
  public string name;
  public double gpa;          // Grade point average
}
public class Program
{
  public static void Main(string[] args)
  {
    //  . . .create the array somehow . . .
    // Now average the students you have.
    double sum = 0.0;
    for (int i = 0; i < students.Length; i++)
    {
      sum += students[i].gpa;
    }
    double avg = sum / students.Length;
    //  . . .do something with the average . . .
  }
}
```

The for loop iterates through the members of the array. (Yes, you can have arrays of any sort of object, not just of simple types such as double and string. You most likely haven't been formally introduced to classes yet, so bear with me a bit longer. I get into them in the next book.)

students.Length contains the number of elements in the array.

C# provides another loop, named foreach, designed specifically for iterating through collections such as the array. It works this way:

```
// Now average the students that you have.
double sum = 0.0;
foreach (Student student in students)
{
  sum += student.gpa;  // This extracts the current student's GPA.
}
double avg = sum / students.Length;
```

The first time through the loop, foreach fetches the first Student object in the array and stores it in the variable student. On each subsequent pass, foreach retrieves the next element. Control passes out of the foreach loop when all elements in the array have been processed.

Notice that no index appears in the foreach statement. The lack of an index greatly reduces the chance of error and is simpler to write than the for statement, although sometimes that index is handy and you prefer a for loop.

The foreach loop is even more powerful than it would seem from the example. This statement works on other collection types in addition to arrays. In addition, foreach handles *multidimensional* arrays (arrays of arrays, in effect), a topic I don't describe in this book. To find out all about multidimensional arrays, look up *multidimensional arrays* in the C# Help system.

Sorting Arrays of Data

A common programming challenge is the need to sort the elements within an array. Just because an array cannot grow or shrink doesn't mean that the elements within it cannot be moved, removed, or added. For example, the following code snippet swaps the location of two string elements within the array strings:

```
string temp = strings[i]; // Save the i'th string.
strings[i] = strings[k];  // Replace it with the kth.
strings[k] = temp;        // Replace kth with temp.
```

In this example, the object reference in the *i*th location in the strings array is saved so that it isn't lost when the second statement replaces it with another element. Finally, the temp variable is saved back into the *k*th location. Pictorially, this process looks like Figure 6-1.

The data collections discussed in the rest of this chapter are more versatile than the array for adding and removing elements.

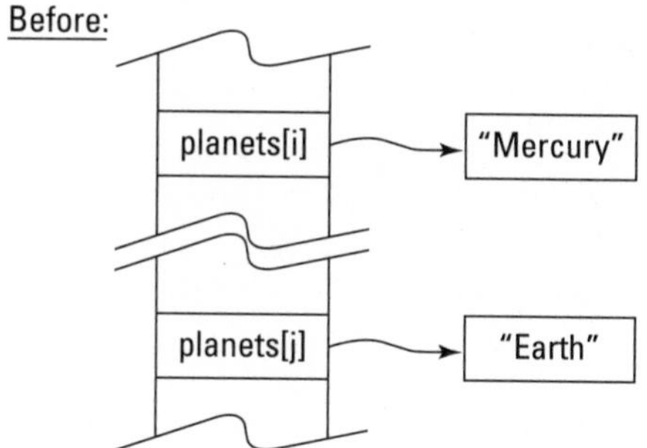

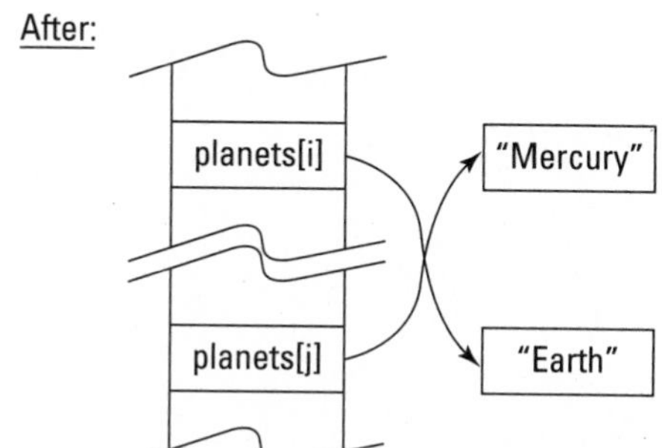

Figure 6-1: The term *swapping two objects* means swapping *references* to two objects.

The following program demonstrates how to use the ability to manipulate elements within an array as part of a sort. This particular sorting algorithm is the *bubble sort.* Though it's not so great on large arrays with thousands of elements, it's simple and effective on small arrays:

```
// BubbleSortArray -- Given a list of planets, sort their
//    names: first, in alphabetical order.
//    Second, by the length of their names, shortest to longest.
//    Third, from longest to shortest.
//    This demonstrates using and sorting arrays, working with
//    them by array index. Two sort algorithms are used:
//    1. The Sort algorithm used by class Array's Sort() method.
//    2. The classic Bubble Sort algorithm.
using System;

namespace BubbleSortArray
{
  class Program
  {
    static void Main(string[] args)
    {
      Console.WriteLine("The 5 planets closest to the sun, in order: ");
      string[] planets =
        new string[] { "Mercury", "Venus", "Earth", "Mars", "Jupiter" };
      foreach (string planet in planets)
      {
        // Use the special char \t to insert a tab in the printed line.
        Console.WriteLine("\t" +  planet);
      }
```

```
      Console.WriteLine("\nNow listed alphabetically: ");
      // Array.Sort() is a method on the Array class.
      // Array.Sort() does its work in-place in the planets array,
      // which leaves you without a copy of the original array. The
      // solution is to copy the old array to a new one and sort it.
      string[] sortedNames = planets;
      Array.Sort(sortedNames);
      // This demonstrates that (a) sortedNames contains the same
      // strings as planets and (b) that they're now sorted.
      foreach (string planet in sortedNames)
      {
        Console.WriteLine("\t" + planet);
      }

      Console.WriteLine("\nList by name length - shortest first: ");
      // This algorithm is called "Bubble Sort": It's the simplest
      // but worst-performing sort. The Array.Sort() method is much
      // more efficient, but I couldn't use it directly to sort the
      // planets in order of name length because it sorts strings,
      // not their lengths.
      int outer;  // Index of the outer loop
      int inner;  // Index of the inner loop
      // Loop DOWN from last index to first: planets[4] to planets[0].
      for (outer = planets.Length - 1; outer >= 0; outer--)
      {
        // On each outer loop, loop through all elements BEYOND the
        // current outer element. This loop goes up, from planets[1]
        // to planets[4]. Using the for loop, you can traverse the
        // array in either direction.
        for (inner = 1; inner <= outer; inner++)
        {
          // Compare adjacent elements. If the earlier one is longer
          // than the later one, swap them. This shows how you can
          // swap one array element with another when they're out of order.
          if (planets[inner - 1].Length > planets[inner].Length)
          {
            // Temporarily store one planet.
            string temp = planets[inner - 1];
            // Now overwrite that planet with the other one.
            planets[inner - 1] = planets[inner];
            // Finally, reclaim the planet stored in temp and put
            // it in place of the other.
            planets[inner] = temp;
          }
        }
      }
      foreach (string planet in planets)
      {
        Console.WriteLine("\t" + planet);
      }

      Console.WriteLine("\nNow listed longest first: ");
      // That is, just loop down through the sorted planets.
      for(int i = planets.Length - 1; i >= 0; i--)
      {
        Console.WriteLine("\t" + planets[i]);
      }

      Console.WriteLine("\nPress Enter to terminate...");
      Console.Read();
    }
  }
}
```

The program begins with an array containing the names of the first five planets closest to the sun. (To keep the figures small, I didn't include the outer planets, so I didn't have to decide about poor Pluto, which is, what now? — a planetoid or something?)

The program then invokes the array's own `Sort()` method. After sorting with the built-in `Sort()` method on the `Array` class, the program sorts the lengths of the planets' names using a custom sort just to amaze you.

The built-in `Sort()` method for arrays (and other collections) is, without a doubt, more efficient than the custom bubble sort. Don't roll your own unless you have good reason to.

The algorithm for the second sort works by continuously looping through the list of strings until the list is sorted. On each pass through the `sortedNames` array, the program compares each string to its neighbor. If the two are found to be out of order, the method swaps them and then flags the list as not sorted. Figures 6-2 through 6-5 show the `planets` list after each pass. In Figure 6-5, note that the next-to-last pass results in a sorted list and that the final pass terminates the sort because nothing changes.

Mercury ←	And they're off and running!
Venus	
Earth	
Mars	
Jupiter	

Figure 6-2: Before starting the bubble sort.

Earth ←	Earth edges its way into the lead...
Mercury	
Venus	
Mars	
Jupiter	

Figure 6-3: After Pass 1 of the bubble sort.

Earth	
Mars ←	Mars jumps past Mercury and Venus for second place
Mercury	
Venus	
Jupiter	

Figure 6-4: After Pass 2 of the bubble sort.

Figure 6-5: The final pass terminates the sort because nothing changes.

Earth	←	At the finish, it's Earth crossing the line in first place for the win...
Jupiter	←	...and Jupiter noses out Mars to place.
Mars	←	Meanwhile, Mars struggles to show.
Mercury		
Venus		

Eventually, longer planet names "bubble" their way to the top of the list; hence the name *bubble sort.*

Give single-item variables singular names, as in `planet` or `student`. The name of the variable should somehow include the name of the class, as in `badStudent` or `goodStudent` or `sexyCoedStudent`. Give arrays (or other collections) plural names, as in `students` or `phoneNumbers` or `phoneNumbersInMyPalmPilot`. As always, this tip reflects the opinion of the authors and not of this book's publisher nor any of its shareholders — C# doesn't care how you name your variables.

New Feature: Using var for Arrays

Traditionally, you used one of the following forms (which are as old as C# — almost six years old at the time this book was written) to initialize an array:

```
int[] numbers = new int[3];             // Size but no initializer, or ...
int[] numbers = new int[] { 1, 2, 3 }; // Initializer but no size, or ...
int[] numbers = new int[3] { 1, 2, 3 };// Size and initializer, or ...
int[] numbers = { 1, 2, 3 };            // No 'new' keyword -- extreme short form.
```

Chapter 2 of this minibook introduces the new `var` keyword, which tells the C# compiler, "*You* figure out the variable type from the initializer expression I'm providing."

Happily, `var` works with arrays, too:

```
// myArray is an int[] with 6 elements.
var myArray = new [] { 2, 3, 5, 7, 11, 13 };  // Initializer required!
```

The new syntax has only two changes:

- `var` is used instead of the explicit type information for the `numbers` array on the left side of the assignment.
- The `int` keyword is omitted before the brackets on the right side of the assignment. It's the part that the compiler can infer.

In the var version, the initializer is required. The compiler uses it to infer the type of the array elements without the int keyword.

Here are a few more examples:

```
var names = new [] { "John", "Paul", "George", "Ringo" };        // Strings
var averages = new [] { 3.0, 3.34, 4.0, 2.0, 1.8 };              // Doubles
var prez = new []{new President("FDR"), new President("JFK")};   // Presidents
```

You can't use the extreme short form for initializing an array when you use var. The following line doesn't compile:

```
var names = { "John", "Paul", "George", "Ringo" };  // Needs 'new []'
```

The var way is less concise, but when used in some other situations not involving arrays, it truly shines and in some cases is mandatory. (You can see examples in Chapter 7.)

The UsingVarWithArraysAndCollections sample program on this book's Web site demonstrates var with array initializers. Note that you can't use var as a variable name now, as you could in the past. It's a crummy variable name anyway.

Loosening Up with C# Collections

Often an array is the simplest, most straightforward way to deal with a list of Students or a list of doubles. You also encounter many places in the .NET Framework class library that require the use of arrays.

But arrays have a couple of fairly serious limitations that sometimes get in your way. At such times, you'll appreciate the extensive C# repertoire of more flexible collection classes.

Although arrays have the advantage of simplicity and can have multiple dimensions, they suffer from two important limitations:

- **A program must declare the size of an array when it's created.** Unlike Visual Basic, C# doesn't let you change the size of an array after it's defined. For example, you might not know up front how big the array needs to be.
- **Inserting or removing an element in the middle of an array is wildly inefficient.** You have to move around all the elements to make room. In a big array, that can be a huge, time-consuming job.

Most collections, on the other hand, make it much easier to add, insert, or remove elements, and you can resize them as needed, right in midstream. In fact, most collections usually take care of resizing automatically.

If you need a multidimensional data structure, use an array. No collection allows multiple dimensions (although you can create some elaborate data structures, such as collections of arrays or collections of collections).

Arrays and collections have some characteristics in common:

- Each can contain elements of only one type. You must specify that type in your code, at compile time, and after you declare the type, it can't change.
- As with arrays, you can access most collections with array-like syntax using square brackets to specify an index: `myList[3] = "Joe"`.
- Both collections and arrays have methods and properties. Thus, to find the number of elements in the following `smallPrimeNumbers` array, you call its `Length` property:

  ```
  var smallPrimeNumbers = new [] { 2, 3, 5, 7, 11, 13 };
  int numElements = smallPrimeNumbers.Length;  // Result is 6.
  ```

  With a collection, you call its `Count` property:

  ```
  List<int> smallPrimes = new List<int> { 2, 3, 5, 7, 11, 13 };
  int numElements = smallPrimes.Count; // Collections have a Count
      property.
  ```

  Check out class `Array` in Help to see what other methods and properties it has (7 public properties and 36 public methods).

Understanding Collection Syntax

In this section, I'll get you up and running with collection syntax and introduce the most important and most frequently used collection classes.

Table 6-1 lists the main collection classes in C#. I find it useful to think of collections as having various "shapes" — the list shape or dictionary shape, for example.

Table 6-1 The Most Common Collection "Shapes"

Class	*Description*
`List<T>`	This dynamic array contains objects of type `T`.
`LinkedList<T>`	This is a linked list of objects of type `T`.
`Queue<T>`	Start at the back end of the line and end up at the front.
`Stack<T>`	Always add or delete items at the "top" of the list, like a stack of cafeteria trays.
`Dictionary<TKey, TValue>`	This structure works like a dictionary. Look up a key (a word, for example) and retrieve its corresponding value (for example, definition).
`HashSet<T>`	This structure resembles a mathematical set, with no duplicate items. It works much like a list but provides mathematical set operations, such as union and intersection.

Figuring out <T>

In the mysterious-looking `<T>` notation you see in Table 6-1, `<T>` is a placeholder for a particular data type. To bring this symbolic object to life, *instantiate* it by inserting a real type, like this:

```
List<int> intList = new List<int>(); // Instantiating for int
```

Instantiate is geekspeak for "Create an object (instance) of this type."

For example, you might create different `List<T>` instantiations for types `int`, `string`, and `Student`, for example. By the way, `T` isn't a sacred name. You can use anything you like — for instance, `<dummy>` or `<aType>`. It's common to use `T`, `U`, `V`, and so on.

Notice how I express the `Dictionary<TKey, TValue>` collection in Table 6-1. Here, two types are needed: one for the dictionary's keys and one for the values associated with the keys. I cover dictionaries later, in the section "Using Dictionaries."

If this notation seems a bit forbidding, don't worry. You get used to it.

Going generic

These modern collections are known as *generic* collections, in the sense that you can fill in a blank template, of sorts, with a type (or types) in order to create a custom collection. If the generic List<T> seems puzzling, check out Chapter 8 in this minibook. That chapter discusses the generic C# facilities in more detail. In particular, the chapter shows you how to roll your own generic collections, classes, methods, and other types.

Using Lists

Suppose you need to store a list of MP3 objects, each of which represents one item in your MP3 music collection. As an array, it might look like this:

```
MP3[] myMP3s = new MP3[50];          // Start with an empty array.
myPP3s[0] = new MP3("Norah Jones"); // Create an MP3 and add it to the array.
// ... and so on.
```

With a list collection, it looks like this:

```
List<MP3> myMP3s = new List<MP3>();    // An empty list
myMP3s.Add(new MP3("Avril Lavigne")); // Call the list's Add() method to add.
// ... and so on.
```

So what, you say? These examples look similar, and the list doesn't appear to provide any advantage over the array. But what happens when you add the 50th MP3 to the array and then want to add a 51st? You're out of room. Your only course is to declare a new, larger array and then copy all MP3s from the old array into the new one. Also, if you remove an MP3 from the array, your array is left with a gaping hole. What do you put into that empty slot to take the place of the MP3 you ditched? The value null, maybe?

The list collection sails happily on, in the face of those same obstacles. Want to add MP3 number 51? No problem. Want to junk your old Pat Boone MP3s? (Are there any?) No problem. The list takes care of healing itself after you delete old Pat.

If your list (or array, for that matter) can contain null items, be sure to check for null when you're looping through with for or foreach. You don't want to call the Play() method on a null MP3 item. It results in an error.

The ListCollection example on this book's Web site shows some of the things you can do with List<T>. In the following code listing, I'll intersperse explanations with bits of code.

The following code (excerpted from the example) shows how to instantiate a new, empty list for the `string` type. In other words, this list can hold only strings:

```
// List<T>: note angle brackets plus parentheses in
// List<T> declaration; T is a "type parameter",
// List<T> is a "parameterized type."
// Instantiate for string type.
List<string> nameList = new List<string>();
sList.Add("one");
sList.Add(3);                              // Compiler error here!
sList.Add(new Student("du Bois"));         // Compiler error here!
```

You add items to a `List<T>` by using its `Add()` method. The preceding code snippet successfully adds one string to the list, but then it runs into trouble trying to add first an integer and then a `Student`. The list was instantiated for strings, so the compiler rejects both attempts.

The next code fragment instantiates a completely new list for type `int` and then adds two `int` values to the list. Afterward, the `foreach` loop iterates the `int` list, printing out the `ints`:

```
// Instantiate for int.
List<int> intList = new List<int>();
intList.Add(3);                            // Fine.
intList.Add(4);
Console.WriteLine("Printing intList:");
foreach(int i in intList)  // foreach just works for all collections.
{
  Console.WriteLine("int i = " + i);
}
```

The following bit of code instantiates a new list to hold `Students` and adds two students with its `Add()` method. But then notice the *array* of `Students`, which I add to the student list using its `AddRange()` method. `AddRange()` lets you add a whole array or (almost) any other collection to the list, all at once:

```
// Instantiate for Student.
List<Student> studentList = new List<Student>();
Student student1 = new Student("Vigil");
Student student2 = new Student("Finch");
studentList.Add(student1);
studentList.Add(student2);
Student[] students = { new Student("Mox"), new Student("Fox") };
studentList.AddRange(students); // Add whole array to List.
Console.WriteLine("Num students in studentList = " + studentList.Count);
```

(Don't worry about the "new Student" stuff. I get to that topic in Book II.)

You can easily convert lists to arrays and vice versa. To put an array into a list, use the list's `AddRange()` method as just described. To convert a list to an array, call the list's `ToArray()` method:

```
Student[] students = studentList.ToArray();  // studentList is a List<Student>.
```

`List<T>` also has a number of other methods for adding items, including methods to insert one or more items anywhere in the list and methods to remove items or clear the list. Note that `List<T>` also has a `Count` property. (This single nit can trip you up if you're used to the `Length` property on arrays and strings. For collections, it's `Count`.)

The next snippet demonstrates several ways to search a list: `IndexOf()` returns the array-style index of an item within the list, if found, or `-1` if not found. The code also demonstrates accessing an item with array-style indexing and via the `Contains()` method. Other searching methods include `BinarySearch()`, not shown:

```
// Search with IndexOf().
Console.WriteLine("Student2 at " + studentList.IndexOf(student2));
string name = studentList[3].Name;  // Access list by index.
if(studentList.Contains(student1))  // student1 is a Student object.
{
  Console.WriteLine(student1.Name + " contained in list");
}
```

The final code segment demonstrates several more `List<T>` operations, including sorting, inserting, and removing items:

```
studentList.Sort(); // Assumes Student implements IComparable interface  (Ch 14).
studentList.Insert(3, new Student("Ross"));
studentList.RemoveAt(3);  // Deletes the third element.
Console.WriteLine("removed " + name);          // Name defined above
```

That's only a sampling of the `List<T>` methods. You can look up the full list in Help.

To look up generic collections you have to look in the Help index for the term *List<T>*. If you try searching for just *List,* you'll be lost in a list of lists of lists. If you want to see information about the whole set of collection classes (well, the generic ones), search the index for *generic collections.*

Using Dictionaries

You've no doubt used *Webster's* or another dictionary. It's organized as a bunch of words in alphabetical order. Associated with each word is a body of information including pronunciations, definitions, and other information. To use a dictionary, you look up a word and retrieve its information.

In C#, the dictionary "shape" differs from the list shape. Dictionaries are represented by the `Dictionary<TKey, TValue>` class. `TKey` represents the data type used for the dictionary's *keys* (similar to the words in a standard dictionary or the terms you look up). `TValue` represents the data type used

to store the information or data associated with a key (similar to the word's definitions in *Webster's*).

.NET dictionaries are based on the idea of a hash table. Imagine a group of buckets spread around the floor. When you compute a hash, using a hash function, you get a value that specifies only one of the buckets. That same hash always points to the same bucket. If the hash is computed properly, you should see a good, fairly even distribution of items spread among the buckets. Thus the hash is a key to one of the buckets. Provide the key to retrieve the bucket's contents — its *value*.

Using dictionaries is no harder in C# than in high school. The following `DictionaryExample` program (excerpts) shows a few things you can do with dictionaries. To save a little space, we show just parts of the `Main()` method.

If you find the going a bit rough here, you may want to circle back later.

The first piece of the code just creates a new `Dictionary` object that has `string` keys and `string` values. You aren't limited to strings, though. Either the key or the value, or both, can be any type. Note that the `Add()` method requires both a key and a value.

```
Dictionary<string, string> dict = new Dictionary<string, string>();
//  Add(key, value).
dict.Add("C#", "cool");
dict.Add("C++", "like writing Sanskrit poetry in Morse code");
dict.Add("VB", "a simple but wordy language");
dict.Add("Java", "good, but not C#");
dict.Add("Fortran", "ANCNT");  // 6-letters-max variable name for "ancient."
dict.Add("Cobol", "even more wordy, or is it wordier, and verbose than VB");
```

The `ContainsKey()` method tells you whether the dictionary contains a particular key. There's a corresponding `ContainsValue()` method too:

```
// See if the dictionary contains a particular key.
Console.WriteLine("Contains key C# " + dict.ContainsKey("C#"));     // True
Console.WriteLine("Contains key Ruby " + dict.ContainsKey("Ruby")); // False
```

You can, of course, iterate the dictionary in a loop just as you can in any collection. But keep in mind that the dictionary is like a list of *pairs* of items — think of each pair as an object that contains both the key and the value. So to iterate the whole dictionary with `foreach`, you need to retrieve one of the *pairs* each time through the loop. The pairs are objects of type `KeyValuePair<TKey, TValue>`. In the `WriteLine()` call, I use the pair's `Key` and `Value` properties to extract the items. Here's what it looks like:

```
// Iterate the dictionary's contents with foreach.
// Note that you're iterating pairs of keys and values.
Console.WriteLine("\nContents of the dictionary:");
foreach (KeyValuePair<string, string> pair in dict)
```

```
{
  // Because the key happens to be a string, we can call string methods on it.
  Console.WriteLine("Key: " + pair.Key.PadRight(8) + "Value: " + pair.Value);
}
```

In the final segment of the example program, you can see how to iterate just the keys or just the values. The dictionary's `Keys` property returns another collection: a list-shaped collection of type `Dictionary<TKey, TValue>.KeyCollection`. Because the keys happen to be strings, you can iterate the keys as strings and call string methods on them. The `Values` property is similar. The final bit of code uses the dictionary's `Count` property to see how many key/value pairs it contains.

```
// List the keys, which are in no particular order.
Console.WriteLine("\nJust the keys:");
// Dictionary<TKey, TValue>.KeyCollection is a collection of just the keys,
// in this case strings. So here's how to retrieve the keys:
Dictionary<string, string>.KeyCollection keys = dict.Keys;
foreach(string key in keys)
{
  Console.WriteLine("Key: " + key);
}

// List the values, which are in same order as key collection above.
Console.WriteLine("\nJust the values:");
Dictionary<string, string>.ValueCollection values = dict.Values;
foreach (string value in values)
{
  Console.WriteLine("Value: " + value);
}
Console.Write("\nNumber of items in the dictionary: " + dict.Count);
```

Of course, that doesn't exhaust the possibilities for working with dictionaries. Look up *generic dictionary* in the Help index for all the details.

Dictionary pairs are in no particular order, and you can't sort a dictionary. It really is just like a bunch of buckets spread around the floor.

Array and Collection Initializers

In this section, I summarize initialization techniques for both arrays and collections — both old-style and new. You may want to bend the page corner.

Initializing arrays

As a reminder, given the new `var` syntax covered earlier in this chapter, an array declaration can look like either of these examples:

```
int[] numbers = { 1, 2, 3 };            // Shorter form -- can't use var.
var numbers = new [] { 1, 2, 3 };       // Full initializer mandatory with var.
```

Initializing collections

Meanwhile, the traditional way to initialize a collection, such as a `List<T>` — or a `Queue<T>` or `Stack<T>` — back in the C# 2.0 days (a number of years ago), was this:

```
List<int> numList = new List<int>();        // New empty list.
numbers.Add(1);                             // Add elements one at a time.
numbers.Add(2);
numbers.Add(3);                             // ...tedious!
```

Or, if you had the numbers in an array or another collection already, it went like this:

```
List<int> numList = new List<int>(numbers); // Initializing from an array or...
List<int> numList2 = new List<int>(numList);// from another collection or...
numList.AddRange(numbers);                  // using AddRange
```

When initializing lists, queues, or stacks as shown here, you can pass in any array or *list-like* collection, including lists, queues, stacks, and the new sets, which I cover in the next section (but not dictionaries — their shape is wrong). The `MoreCollections` example on the Web site illustrates several cases of initializing one collection from another.

Since C# 3.0, collection initializers resemble the new array initializers and are much easier to use than most of the earlier forms. The new initializers look like this:

```
List<int> numList = new List<int> { 1, 2, 3 };  // List
int[] intArray = { 1, 2, 3 };                   // Array
```

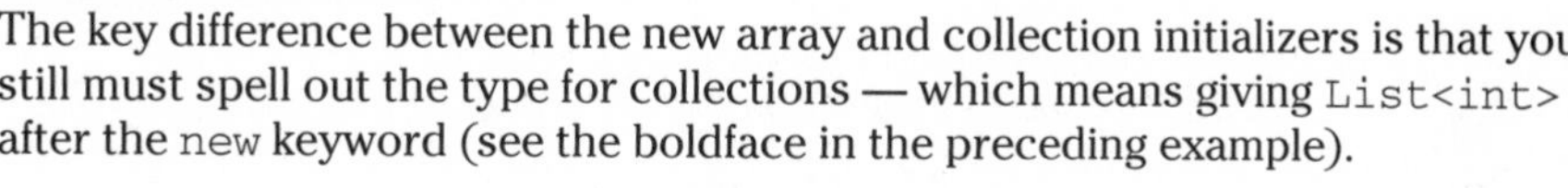

The key difference between the new array and collection initializers is that you still must spell out the type for collections — which means giving `List<int>` after the `new` keyword (see the boldface in the preceding example).

Of course, you can also use the `var` keyword with collections:

```
var list = new List<string> { "Head", "Heart", "Hands", "Health" };
```

You can also use the new `dynamic` keyword:

```
Dynamic list = new List<string> { "Head", "Heart", "Hands", "Health" };
```

Initializing dictionaries with the new syntax looks like this:

```
Dictionary<int, string> dict =
  new Dictionary<int, string> { { 1, "Sam" }, { 2, "Joe" } };
```

Outwardly, this example looks the same as for `List<T>`, but inside the outer curly braces, you see a second level of curly-brace-enclosed items, one per entry in the dictionary. Because this dictionary `dict` has integer keys and string values, each inner pair of curly braces contains one of each, separated by a comma. The key/value pairs are separated by commas as well.

Initializing sets (see the next section) is much like initializing lists:

```
HashSet<int> biggerPrimes = new HashSet<int> { 19, 23, 29, 31, 37, 41 };
```

The `UsingVarWithArraysAndCollections` example on this book's Web site demonstrates the `var` keyword used with arrays and collections.

Using Sets

C# 3.0 added the new collection type `HashSet<T>`. A *set* is an unordered collection with no duplicate items.

The set concept comes from mathematics. Think of the set of genders (female and male), the set of days in a week, or the set of variations on the triangle (isosceles, equilateral, scalene, right, obtuse). Unlike math sets, C# sets can't be infinite, though they can be as large as available memory.

You can do things to a set in common with other collections, such as add, delete, and find items. But you can also perform several specifically set-like operations, such as union and intersection. *Union* joins the members of two sets into one. *Intersection* finds the overlap between two sets and results in a set containing only the overlapping members. So sets are good for combining and eliminating items.

Like dictionaries, sets are implemented using hash tables. Sets resemble dictionaries with keys but no values, making them list-like in shape. See the earlier section "Using Dictionaries" for details.

To create a `HashSet<T>`, you can do this:

```
HashSet<int> smallPrimeNumbers = new HashSet<int>();
smallPrimeNumbers.Add(2);
smallPrimeNumbers.Add(3);
```

Or, more conveniently, you can use a collection initializer:

```
HashSet<int> smallPrimeNumbers = new HashSet<int> { 2, 3, 5, 7, 11, 13 };
```

Or create the set from an existing collection of any list-like kind, including arrays:

```
List<int> intList = new List<int> { 0, 1, 2, 3, 4, 5, 6, 7 };
HashSet<int> numbers = new HashSet<int>(intList);
```

If you attempt to add to a hash set an item that the set already contains, as in this example:

```
smallPrimeNumbers.Add(2);
```

the compiler doesn't treat the duplication as an error (and doesn't change the hash set, which can't have duplicates). Actually, `Add()` returns `true` if the addition occurred and `false` if it didn't. You don't have to use that fact, but it can be useful if you want to do something when an attempt is made to add a duplicate:

```
bool successful = smallPrimeNumbers.Add(2);
if(successful)
{
  // 2 was added, now do something useful.
}
// If successful is false, not added because it was already there
```

The following example — the `HashSetExample` on the Web site — shows off several `HashSet<T>` methods but, more important, demonstrates using a `HashSet<T>` *as a tool for working with other collections*. You can do strictly mathematical operations with `HashSet<T>`, but we find its ability to combine collections in various ways quite handy.

The first segment of this code starts with a `List<string>` and an array. Each contains color names. Though you could combine the two by simply calling the list's `AddRange()` method:

```
colors.AddRange(moreColors);
```

the resulting list contains some duplicates (`yellow`, `orange`). Using a `HashSet<T>` and the `UnionWith()` method, on the other hand, you can combine two collections and eliminate any duplicates in one shot, as the following example shows.

Here's the beginning of the `HashSetExample` on this book's Web site:

```
Console.WriteLine("Combining two collections with no duplicates:");
List<string> colors = new List<string> { "red", "orange", "yellow" };
string[] moreColors = { "orange", "yellow", "green", "blue", "violet" };
// Want to combine but without any duplicates.
// Following is just the first stage ...
HashSet<string> combined = new HashSet<string>(colors);
// ... now for the second stage.
// UnionWith() collects items in both lists that aren't duplicated,
// resulting in a combined collection whose members are all unique.
combined.UnionWith(moreColors);
foreach (string color in combined)
{
  Console.WriteLine(color);
}
```

The result given here contains `"red"`, `"orange"`, `"yellow"`, `"green"`, `"blue"`, and `"violet"`. The first stage uses the `colors` list to initialize a new `HashSet<T>`. The second stage then calls the set's `UnionWith()` method to add in the `moreColors` array — but adding only the ones not already in the set. The set ends up containing just the colors in both original lists. Green, blue, and violet come from the second list; red, orange, and yellow come from the first. The moreColors array's orange and yellow would duplicate the ones already in the set, so they're screened out.

But suppose that you want to end up with a List<T> containing those colors, not a HashSet<T>. The next segment shows how to create a new List<T> initialized with the combined set:

```
Console.WriteLine("\nConverting the combined set to a list:");
// Initialize a new List from the combined set above.
List<string> spectrum = new List<string>(combined);
foreach(string color in spectrum)
{
  Console.WriteLine(color);
}
```

Back when these examples were written, the 2008 U.S. presidential campaign was in full swing, with about ten early candidates in each major party. A good many of those candidates were also members of the U.S. Senate. How can you produce a list of just the candidates who are also in the Senate? The HashSet<T> IntersectWith() method gives you the overlapping items between the candidate list and the Senate list — items in both lists, but only those items:

```
Console.WriteLine("\nFinding the overlap in two lists:");
List<string> presidentialCandidates =
  new List<string> { "Clinton", "Edwards", "Giuliani", "McCain", "Obama",
    "Romney" };
List<string> senators = new List<string> { "Alexander", "Boxer", "Clinton",
    "McCain", "Obama", "Snowe" };
HashSet<string> senatorsRunning = new HashSet<string>(presidentialCandidates);
// IntersectWith() collects items that appear in both lists, eliminates others.
senatorsRunning.IntersectWith(senators);
foreach (string senator in senatorsRunning)
{
  Console.WriteLine(senator);
}
```

The result is "Clinton", "McCain", "Obama" because those are the only ones in both lists. The opposite trick is to remove any items that appear in both of two lists so that you end up with just the items in your target list that aren't duplicated in the other list. This calls for the HashSet<T> method ExceptWith():

```
Console.WriteLine("\nExcluding items from a list:");
Queue<int> queue =
  new Queue<int>(new int[] { 0, 1, 2, 3, 4, 5, 6, 7, 8, 9, 17 });
HashSet<int> unique = new HashSet<int> { 1, 3, 5, 7, 9, 11, 13, 15 };
// ExceptWith() removes items in unique that are also in queue: 1, 3, 5, 7.
unique.ExceptWith(queue);
foreach (int n in unique)
{
  Console.WriteLine(n.ToString());
}
```

After this code, `unique` excludes its own items that duplicate items in `queue` (1, 3, 5, 7, and 9) and also excludes items in `queue` that aren't in `unique` (0, 2, 4, 6, 8, and 17). You end up with 11, 13, and 15 in `unique`.

Meanwhile, the next code segment uses the `SymmetricExceptWith()` method to create the opposite result from `IntersectWith()`. Whereas intersection gives you the overlapping items, `SymmetricExceptWith()` gives you the items in both lists *that don't overlap*. The `uniqueToOne` set ends up containing just 5, 3, 1, 12, and 10:

```
  Console.WriteLine("\nFinding just the non-overlapping items in two lists:");
  Stack<int> stackOne = new Stack<int>(new int[] { 1, 2, 3, 4, 5, 6, 7, 8 });
  Stack<int> stackTwo = new Stack<int>(new int[] { 2, 4, 6, 7, 8, 10, 12 });
  HashSet<int> nonoverlapping = new HashSet<int>(stackOne);
  // SymmetricExceptWith() collects items that are in one collection but not
  // the other: the items that don't overlap.
  nonoverlapping.SymmetricExceptWith(stackTwo);
  foreach(int n in nonoverlapping)
  {
    Console.WriteLine(n.ToString());
  }
  Console.WriteLine("Press Enter to terminate...");
  Console.Read();
}
```

My use of stacks here is a bit unorthodox because I add all members at one time rather than *push* each one, and I remove a bunch at a time rather than *pop* each one. Those operations — pushing and popping — are the correct ways to interact with a stack.

Notice that all the `HashSet<T>` methods I demonstrate are `void` methods — they don't return a value. Thus the results are reflected directly in the hash set on which you call these methods: `nonoverlapping` in the preceding code example.

We found the behavior of `UnionWith()` and `IntersectWith()` a bit awkward at first because I wanted a new resulting set, with the original (input) sets remaining the same when I applied these methods. But in Book II you meet (I'm happy to report) the new LINQ query operators, which add versions of these methods that return a whole new set object. Combining what you see here with what you see there, you get the best of both worlds. More than that I'd better not say now.

When would you use `HashSet<T>`? Any time you're working with two or more collections and you want to find such items as the overlap — or create a collection that contains two other collections or exclude a group of items from a collection — sets can be useful. Many of the `HashSet<T>` methods can relate sets and other collection classes. You can do more with sets, of course, so look up the term *HashSet<T>* in Help and play with `HashSetExample`.

On Not Using Old-Fashioned Collections

At the dawn of time, before C# 2.0, when Zarathustra spake, all collection classes were implemented as collections of type `Object`. You couldn't create a collection just for `string`s or just for `int`s. Such a collection lets you store any type of data, because all objects in C# are derived from class `Object`. Thus you can add both `int`s and `string`s to *the same collection* without seeing error messages (because of the inheritance and polymorphism of C#, which I discuss in Book II).

But a serious drawback occurs in the `Object`-based arrangement: To extract the `int` that you know you put *into* a collection, you must cast out to an `int` the `Object` you get:

```
ArrayList ints = new ArrayList();  // An old-fashioned list of Objects
int myInt = (int)ints[0];          // Extract the first int in the list.
```

It's as though your `int`s were hidden inside Easter eggs. If you don't cast, you create errors because, for instance, `Object` doesn't support the + operation or other methods, properties, and operators that you expect on `int`s. You can work with these limitations, but this kind of code is error-prone, and it's just plain tedious to do all that casting. (Besides, as I discuss in Book II, working with Easter eggs adds some processing overhead because of the "boxing" phenomenon. Too much boxing slows your program.)

And, if the collection happens to contain objects of more than one type — pomegranates and basketballs, say — the problem becomes tougher. Somehow, you have to detect that the object you fish out is a pomegranate or a basketball so that you can cast it correctly.

With those limitations on the older, nongeneric collections, the newer generic ones are a gale of fresh air. You never have to cast, and you always know what you're getting because you can put only one type into any given collection. But you still see the older collections occasionally, in code that other people write — and sometimes you may even have a legitimate reason to stick apples and oranges in the same collection.

The nongeneric collections are found in the `System.Collections` and `System.Collections.Specialized` namespaces. The Specialized collections are interesting, sometimes useful, oddball collections, and mainly nongeneric. The modern, generic ones are found in `System.Collections.Generic`. (I explain namespaces and generics in Book II, in my discussion of object-oriented programming).

Chapter 7: Stepping through Collections

In This Chapter

- **Handling a directory as a collection of files and a file as a collection of bytes**
- **Implementing a `LinkedList` collection**
- **"Enumerating," or iterating, `LinkedList`**
- **Implementing an indexer for easy access to collection objects**
- **Easily looping through a collection with the C# iterator blocks**

Chapter 6 in this minibook explores the *collection classes* provided by the .NET Framework class library for use with C# and other .NET languages. As you probably remember, collection classes are constructs in .NET that can be instantiated to hold groups of items. If you don't remember, you can read Chapter 6 for a reminder.

The first part of this chapter extends the notion of *collections* a bit. For instance, consider the following collections: a file as a collection of lines or records of data, and a directory as a collection of files. Thus this chapter builds on both the collection material in Chapter 6 of this minibook and the file material in Book III.

However, the focus in this chapter is on several ways to step through, or *iterate*, all sorts of collections, from file directories to arrays and lists of all sorts. You also see how to write your own collection class, or *linked list*.

Iterating through a Directory of Files

Reading and writing are the basic skills you need to get ahead in this world. That's what makes the `FileRead` and `FileWrite` programs in Book IV important. In some cases, however, you simply want to skim a directory of files, looking for something.

The following `LoopThroughFiles` program looks at all files in a given directory, reading each file and dumping out its contents in hexadecimal format to the console. (That may sound like a silly thing to do, but this program also demonstrates how to write out a file in a format other than just `string`s. I describe hexadecimal format in the following sidebar, "Getting hexed.")

If you run this program in a directory with lots of files, the hex dump can take a while. Also, long files take a while to loop through. Either pick a directory with few files or stop a lengthy program run by pressing Ctrl+C. This command interrupts a program running in any console window.

```
// LoopThroughFiles -- Loop through all files contained in a directory;
//   this time perform a hex dump, though it could have been anything.
using System;
using System.IO;

namespace LoopThroughFiles
{
  public class Program
  {
    public static void Main(string[] args)
    {
      // If no directory name provided...
      string directoryName;
      if (args.Length == 0)
      {
        // ...get the name of the current directory...
        directoryName = Directory.GetCurrentDirectory();
      }
      else
      {
        // ...otherwise, assume that the first argument
        // is the name of the directory to use.
        directoryName = args[0];
      }
      Console.WriteLine(directoryName);

      // Get a list of all files in that directory.
      FileInfo[] files = GetFileList(directoryName);

      // Now iterate through the files in that list,
      // performing a hex dump of each file.
      foreach(FileInfo file in files)
      {
        // Write out the name of the file.
        Console.WriteLine("\n\nhex dump of file {0}:", file.FullName);

        // Now "dump" the file to the console.
        DumpHex(file);

        // Wait before outputting next file.
        Console.WriteLine("\nenter return to continue to next file");
        Console.ReadLine();
      }

      // That's it!
      Console.WriteLine("\no files left");

      // Wait for user to acknowledge the results.
      Console.WriteLine("Press Enter to terminate...");
      Console.Read();
    }
```

```
// GetFileList -- Get a list of all files in a specified directory.
public static FileInfo[] GetFileList(string directoryName)
{
  // Start with an empty list.
  FileInfo[] files = new FileInfo[0];
  try
  {
    // Get directory information.
    DirectoryInfo di = new DirectoryInfo(directoryName);

    // That information object has a list of the contents.
    files = di.GetFiles();
  }
  catch(Exception e)
  {
    Console.WriteLine("Directory \"{0}\" invalid", directoryName);
    Console.WriteLine(e.Message);
  }
  return files;
}

// DumpHex -- Given a file, dump out the contents of the file to the console.
public static void DumpHex(FileInfo file)
{
  // Open the file.
  FileStream fs;
  BinaryReader reader;
  try
  {
    fs = file.OpenRead();
    // Wrap the file stream in a BinaryReader.
    reader = new BinaryReader(fs);
  }
  catch(Exception e)
  {
    Console.WriteLine("\ncan't read from \"{0}\"", file.FullName);
    Console.WriteLine(e.Message);
    return;
  }

  // Iterate through the contents of the file one line at a time.
  for(int line = 1; true; line++)
  {
    // Read another 10 bytes across (all that will fit on a single
    // line) -- return when no data remains.
    byte[] buffer = new byte[10];
    // Use the BinaryReader to read bytes.
    // Note: Using the bare FileStream would have been just as easy in this
case.
    int numBytes = reader.Read(buffer, 0, buffer.Length);
    if (numBytes == 0)
    {
      return;
    }

    // Write out the data just read, in a single line preceded by line
number.
    Console.Write("{0:D3} - ", line);
    DumpBuffer(buffer, numBytes);
```

```
        // Stop every 20 lines so that the data doesn't scroll
        // off the top of the Console screen.
        if ((line % 20) == 0)
        {
          Console.WriteLine("Enter return to continue another 20 lines");
          Console.ReadLine();
        }
      }
    }

    // DumpBuffer -- Write a buffer of characters as a single line in hex format.
    public static void DumpBuffer(byte[] buffer, int numBytes)
    {
      for(int index = 0; index < numBytes; index++)
      {
        byte b = buffer[index];
        Console.Write("{0:X2}, ", b);
      }
      Console.WriteLine();
    }
  }
}
```

From the command line, the user specifies the directory to use as an argument to the program. The following command "hex-dumps" each file in the `temp` directory (including binary files as well as text files):

```
loopthroughfiles c:\randy\temp
```

If you don't enter a directory name, the program uses the current directory by default. (A *hex dump* displays the output as numbers in the hexadecimal — base 16 — system. See the nearby sidebar, "Getting hexed.")

Both `FileRead` and `FileWrite` read the input filename from the console, whereas this program takes its input from the command line. I truly am not trying to confuse you — I'm trying to show different ways of approaching the same problem.

Getting hexed

Like binary numbers (0 and 1), hexadecimal, or "hex," numbers are fundamental to computer programming. In base 16, the digits are 0 through 9 and then A, B, C, D, E, F — where A=10, B=11 . . . F=15. To illustrate (using the zero-x prefix to indicate hex):

```
0xD = 13 decimal
0x10 = 16 decimal: 1*16 + 0*1
0x2A = 42 decimal: 2*16 + A*1 (where A*1
         = 10*1)
```

The alphabetic digits can be uppercase or lowercase: *C* is the same as *c*. It's weird, but quite useful, especially when you're debugging or working close to the metal with memory contents.

The first line in `LoopThroughFiles` looks for a program argument. If the argument list is empty (`args.Length` is zero), the program calls `Directory.GetCurrentDirectory()`. If you run inside Visual Studio rather than from the command line, that value defaults to the `bin\Debug` subdirectory of your `LoopThroughFiles` project directory.

TIP

The `Directory` class gives the user a set of methods for manipulating directories. The `FileInfo` class provides methods for moving, copying, and deleting files, among other tasks.

The program then creates a list of all files in the specified directory by calling the local `GetFileList()`. This method returns an array of `FileInfo` objects. Each `FileInfo` object contains information about a file — for example, the filename (with the full path to the file, `FullName`, or without the path, `Name`), the creation date, and the last modified date. `Main()` iterates through the list of files using your old friend, the `foreach` statement. It displays the name of each file and then passes off the file to the `DumpHex()` method for display to the console.

At the end of the loop, it pauses to allow the programmer a chance to gaze on the output from `DumpHex()`.

The `GetFileList()` method begins by creating an empty `FileInfo` list. This list is the one it returns in the event of an error.

Here's a neat trick to remember when coding any `Get...List()` method: If an error occurs, display an error message and return a zero-length list.

Be careful about returning a reference to an object. For instance, don't return a reference to one of the underlying queues wrapped up in the `PriorityQueue` class, described in Chapter 8 of this minibook — unless you want to invite folks to mess with those queues through the reference instead of through your class methods, that is. That's a sure ticket to a corrupt, unpredictable queue. But `GetFileList()` doesn't expose the innards of one of your classes here, so it's okay.

`GetFileList()` then creates a `DirectoryInfo` object. Just as its name implies, a `DirectoryInfo` object contains the same type of information about a directory that a `FileInfo` object does about a file: name, rank, and serial-number-type stuff. However, the `DirectoryInfo` object has access to one thing that a `FileInfo` doesn't: a list of the files in the directory, in the form of a `FileInfo` array.

As usual, `GetFileList()` wraps the directory- and file-related code in a big `try` block. The `catch` at the end traps any errors that are generated. Just to embarrass you further, the `catch` block flaunts the name of the directory (which probably doesn't exist, because you entered it incorrectly).

The `DumpHex()` method is a little tricky only because of the difficulties in formatting the output just right.

`DumpHex()` starts out by opening `file`. A `FileInfo` object contains information about the file — it doesn't open the file. `DumpHex()` gets the full name of the file, including the path, and then opens a `FileStream` in read-only mode using that name. The `catch` block throws an exception if `FileStream` can't read the file for some reason.

`DumpHex()` then reads through the file, 10 bytes at a time. It displays every 10 bytes in hexadecimal format as a single line. Every 20 lines, it pauses until the user presses Enter. I use the modulo operator, `%`, to accomplish that task.

Vertically, a console window has room for 25 lines by default. (The user can change the window's size, of course, allowing more or fewer lines.) That means you have to pause every 20 lines or so. Otherwise, the data just streams off the top of the screen before the user can read it.

The modulo operator (`%`) returns the remainder after division. Thus `(line % 20) == 0` is true when `line` equals 20, 40, 60, 80 — you get the idea. This trick is valuable, useful in all sorts of looping situations where you want to perform an operation only so often.

`DumpBuffer()` writes out each member of a byte array using the X2 format control. Although X2 sounds like the name of a secret military experiment, it *simply* means "display a number as two hexadecimal digits."

The range of a `byte` is 0 to 255, or 0xFF — two hex digits per byte.

Here are the first 20 lines of the `output.txt` file (even its own mother wouldn't recognize this picture):

```
Hex dump of file C:\C#ProgramsVi\holdtank\Test2\bin\output.txt:
001 - 53, 74, 72, 65, 61, 6D, 20, 28, 70, 72,
002 - 6F, 74, 65, 63, 74, 65, 64, 29, 0D, 0A,
003 - 20, 20, 46, 69, 6C, 65, 53, 74, 72, 65,
004 - 61, 6D, 28, 73, 74, 72, 69, 6E, 67, 2C,
005 - 20, 46, 69, 6C, 65, 4D, 6F, 64, 65, 2C,
006 - 20, 46, 69, 6C, 65, 41, 63, 63, 65, 73,
007 - 73, 29, 0D, 0A, 20, 20, 4D, 65, 6D, 6F,
008 - 72, 79, 53, 74, 72, 65, 61, 6D, 28, 29,
009 - 3B, 0D, 0A, 20, 20, 4E, 65, 74, 77, 6F,
010 - 72, 6B, 53, 74, 72, 65, 61, 6D, 0D, 0A,
011 - 20, 20, 42, 75, 66, 66, 65, 72, 53, 74,
012 - 72, 65, 61, 6D, 20, 2D, 20, 62, 75, 66,
013 - 66, 65, 72, 73, 20, 61, 6E, 20, 65, 78,
014 - 69, 73, 74, 69, 6E, 67, 20, 73, 74, 72,
015 - 65, 61, 6D, 20, 6F, 62, 6A, 65, 63, 74,
016 - 0D, 0A, 0D, 0A, 42, 69, 6E, 61, 72, 79,
017 - 52, 65, 61, 64, 65, 72, 20, 2D, 20, 72,
018 - 65, 61, 64, 20, 69, 6E, 20, 76, 61, 72,
019 - 69, 6F, 75, 73, 20, 74, 79, 70, 65, 73,
020 - 20, 28, 43, 68, 61, 72, 2C, 20, 49, 6E,
Enter return to continue another 20 lines
```

You could reconstruct the file as a `string` from the hex display. The 0x61 value is the numeric equivalent of the character *a*. The letters of the alphabet are arranged in order, so 0x65 should be the character *e;* 0x20 is a space. The first line in this example (after the line number) is `s)\n\r Nemo`, where `\n` is a new line and `\r` is a carriage return. Intriguing, eh? That's about as far as I want to go. You can search Google or another search engine for *ASCII table.*

Those codes are also valid for the lower part of the much vaster Unicode character set, which C# uses by default. (You can look on a search engine on the Web for the term *Unicode characters,* and I explain the basics in the article "Converting Between Byte and Char Arrays" on the `http://csharp102.info` Web site.)

The following example shows what happens when the user specifies the invalid directory `x`:

```
Directory "x" invalid
Could not find a part of the path "C:\C#Programs\LoopThroughFiles\bin\Debug\x".

No files left
Press Enter to terminate...
```

Impressive, no?

Iterating `foreach` Collections: Iterators

In the rest of this chapter, you see three different approaches to the general problem of iterating a collection. In this section, I continue discussing the most traditional approach (at least for C# programmers), the iterator class, or enumerator, which implements the `IEnumerator` interface. As an example, I take you deeper into the iterator for the linked list, presented in the previous section.

The terms *iterator* and *enumerator* are synonymous. The term *iterator* is more common despite the name of the interface, but *enumerator* has been popular at Microsoft. Verb forms of these two nouns are also available: You iterate or enumerate through a container or collection. Note that the indexers and the new iterator blocks discussed later in this chapter are other approaches to the same problem.

Accessing a collection: The general problem

Different collection types may have different accessing schemes. Not all types of collections can be accessed efficiently with an index like an array's — the linked list, for example. Differences between collection types make it impossible to write a method such as the following without special provisions:

```
// Pass in any kind of collection:
void MyClearMethod(Collection aColl, int index)
{
  aColl[index] = 0; // Indexing doesn't work for all types of collections.
  // ...continues...
}
```

Each collection type can (and does) define its own access methods. For example, a linked list may offer a `GetNext()` method to fetch the next element in the chain of objects or a stack collection may offer a `Push()` and `Pop()` to add and remove objects.

A more general approach is to provide for each collection class a separate *iterator class,* which is wise in the ways of navigating that particular collection. Each collection `X` defines its own class `IteratorX`. Unlike `X`, `IteratorX` offers a common `IEnumerator` interface, the gold standard of iterating. This technique uses a second object, the *iterator,* as a kind of pointer, or cursor, into the collection.

The iterator (enumerator) approach offers these advantages:

- Each collection class can define its own iteration class. Because the iteration class implements the standard `IEnumerator` interface, it's usually straightforward to code.
- The application code doesn't need to know how the collection code works. As long as the programmer understands how to use the iterator, the iteration class can handle the details. That's good encapsulation.
- The application code can create multiple independent iterator objects for the same collection. Because the iterator contains its own state information ("knows where it is," in the iteration), each iterator can navigate through the collection independently. You can have several iterations going at one time, each one at a different location in the collection.

To make the `foreach` loop possible, the `IEnumerator` interface must support all different types of collections, from arrays to linked lists. Consequently, its methods must be as general as possible. For example, you can't use the iterator to access locations within the collection class randomly because most collections don't provide random access. (You'd need to invent a different enumeration interface with that ability, but it wouldn't work with `foreach`.)

`IEnumerator` provides these three methods:

- `Reset()`: Sets the enumerator to point to the beginning of the collection. ***Note:*** The generic version of `IEnumerator`, `IEnumerator<T>`, doesn't provide a `Reset()` method. With the generic `LinkedList`, just begin with a call to `MoveNext()`.

- `MoveNext()`: Moves the enumerator from the current object in the collection to the next one.
- `Current`: A property, rather than a method, that retrieves the data object stored at the current position of the enumerator.

The following method demonstrates this principle. The programmer of the `MyCollection` class (not shown) creates a corresponding iterator class — say, `IteratorMyCollection` (using the `IteratorX` naming convention that I describe earlier in this chapter). The application programmer has stored numerous `ContainedDataObjects` in `MyCollection`. The following code segment uses the three standard `IEnumerator` methods to read these objects back out:

```
// The MyCollection class holds ContainedDataObject type objects as data.
void MyMethod(MyCollection myColl)
{
  // The programmer who created the MyCollection class also
  // creates an iterator class IteratorMyCollection;
  // the application program creates an iterator object
  // in order to navigate through the myColl object.
  IEnumerator iterator = new IteratorMyCollection(myColl);
  // Move the enumerator to the "next location" within the collection.
  while(iterator.MoveNext())
  {
    // Fetch a reference to the data object at the current location
    // in the collection.
    ContainedDataObject contained;  // Data
    contained = (ContainedDataObject)iterator.Current;
    // ...use the contained data object...
  }
}
```

The method `MyMethod()` accepts as its argument the collection of `ContainedDataObjects`. It begins by creating an `iterator` of class `IteratorMyCollection`. The method starts a loop by calling `MoveNext()`. On this first call, `MoveNext()` moves the iterator to the first element in the collection. On each subsequent call, `MoveNext()` moves the pointer "over one position." `MoveNext()` returns `false` when the collection is exhausted and the iterator cannot be moved any farther.

The `Current` property returns a reference to the data object at the current location of the iterator. The program converts the object returned into a `ContainedDataObject` before assigning it to `contained`. Calls to `Current` are invalid if the `MoveNext()` method didn't return `true` on the previous call or if `MoveNext()` hasn't yet been called.

Letting C# access data foreach container

The `IEnumerator` methods are standard enough that C# uses them automatically to implement the `foreach` statement.

The foreach statement can access any class that implements IEnumerable or IEnumerable<T>. I discuss foreach in terms of IEnumerable<T> in this section, as shown in this general method that is capable of processing any such class, from arrays to linked lists to stacks and queues:

```
void MyMethod(IEnumerable<T> containerOfThings)
{
  foreach(string s in containerOfThings)
  {
    Console.WriteLine("The next thing is {0}", s);
  }
}
```

A class implements IEnumerable<T> by defining the method GetEnumerator(), which returns an instance of IEnumerator<T>. Under the hood, foreach invokes the GetEnumerator() method to retrieve an iterator. It uses this iterator to make its way through the collection. Each element it retrieves has been cast appropriately before continuing into the block of code contained within the braces. Note that IEnumer**able**<T> and IEnumer**ator**<T> are different, but related, interfaces. C# provides nongeneric versions of both as well, but you should prefer the generic versions for their increased type safety.

IEnumerable<T> looks like this:

```
interface IEnumerable<T>
{
  IEnumerator<T> GetEnumerator();
}
```

while IEnumerator<T> looks like this:

```
interface IEnumerator<T>
{
  bool MoveNext();
  T Current { get; }
}
```

The nongeneric IEnumerator interface adds a Reset() method that moves the iterator back to the beginning of the collection, and its Current property returns type Object. Note that IEnumerator<T> inherits from IEnumerator — and recall that interface inheritance (covered in Book II, Chapter 8) is different from normal object inheritance.

C# arrays (embodied in the Array class they're based on) and all the .NET collection classes already implement both interfaces. So it's only when you're writing your own custom collection class that you need to take care of implementing these interfaces. For built-in collections, you can just use them. See the System.Collections.Generic namespace topic in Help.

Thus you can write the foreach loop this way:

```
foreach(int nValue in myCollection)
{
  // ...
}
```

I *strongly* advise you to use foreach to iterate collections rather than do it directly with IEnumerator or IEnumerator<T>. Chapter 8 of this minibook shows how easily you can go wrong with the raw iterator. The foreach loop is a helpful tool.

Accessing Collections the Array Way: Indexers

Accessing the elements of an array is simple: The command container[n] (read "container sub-n") accesses the *n*th element of the container array. The value in brackets is a *subscript.* If only indexing into other types of collections were so simple.

Stop the presses! C# enables you to write your own implementation of the index operation. You can provide an index feature for collections that wouldn't otherwise enjoy such a feature. In addition, you can index on subscript types other than the simple integers to which C# arrays are limited; for example, strings: for another example, try container["Joe"].

Indexer format

The indexer looks much like an ordinary get/set property, except for the appearance of the keyword this and the index operator [] instead of the property name, as shown in this bit of code:

```
class MyArray
{
  public string this[int index]    // Notice the "this" keyword.
  {
    get
    {
      return array[index];
    }
    set
    {
      array[index] = value;
    }
  }
}
```

Under the hood, the expression s = myArray[i]; invokes the get accessor method, passing it the value of i as the index. In addition, the expression myArray[i] = "some string"; invokes the set accessor method, passing it the same index i and "some string" as value.

An indexer program example

The index type isn't limited to `int`. You may choose to index a collection of houses by their owners' names, by house address, or by any number of other indices. In addition, the indexer property can be overloaded with multiple index types, so you can index on a variety of elements in the same collection.

The following `Indexer` program generates the virtual array class `KeyedArray`. This virtual array looks and acts like an array except that it uses a `string` value as the index:

```
// Indexer -- This program demonstrates the use of the index operator
//    to provide access to an array using a string as an index.
//    This version is nongeneric, but see the IndexerGeneric example.
using System;

namespace Indexer
{
  public class KeyedArray
  {
    // The following string provides the "key" into the array --
    // the key is the string used to identify an element.
    private string[] _keys;

    // The object is the actual data associated with that key.
    private object[] _arrayElements;

    // KeyedArray -- Create a fixed-size KeyedArray.
    public KeyedArray(int size)
    {
      _keys = new string[size];
      _arrayElements = new object[size];
    }

    // Find -- Find the index of the element corresponding to the
    //    string targetKey (return a negative if it can't be found).
    private int Find(string targetKey)
    {
      for(int i = 0; i < _keys.Length; i++)
      {
        if (String.Compare(_keys[i], targetKey) == 0)
        {
          return i;
        }
      }
      return -1;
    }

    // FindEmpty -- Find room in the array for a new entry.
    private int FindEmpty()
    {
      for (int i = 0; i < _keys.Length; i++)
      {
        if (_keys[i] == null)
        {
          return i;
        }
      }
```

```
      throw new Exception("Array is full");
    }

    // Look up contents by string key -- this is the indexer.
    public object this[string key]
    {
      set
      {
        // See if the string is already there.
        int index = Find(key);
        if (index < 0)
        {
          // It isn't -- find a new spot.
          index = FindEmpty();
          _keys[index] = key;
        }

        // Save the object in the corresponding spot.
        _arrayElements[index] = value;
      }

      get
      {
        int index = Find(key);
        if (index < 0)
        {
          return null;
        }
        return _arrayElements[index];
      }
    }
  }

  public class Program
  {
    public static void Main(string[] args)
    {
      // Create an array with enough room.
      KeyedArray ma = new KeyedArray(100);

      // Save the ages of the Simpson kids.
      ma["Bart"] = 8;
      ma["Lisa"] = 10;
      ma["Maggie"] = 2;

      // Look up the age of Lisa.
      Console.WriteLine("Let's find Lisa's age");
      int age = (int)ma["Lisa"];
      Console.WriteLine("Lisa is {0}", age);

      // Wait for user to acknowledge the results.
      Console.WriteLine("Press Enter to terminate...");
      Console.Read();
    }
  }
}
```

The class `KeyedArray` holds two ordinary arrays. The `_arrayElements` array of objects contains the actual `KeyedArray` data. The `string`s that inhabit the `_keys` array act as identifiers for the object array. The *i*th element of _keys corresponds to the *i*th entry of _arrayElements. The application program can then index KeyedArray via string identifiers that have meaning to the application.

A noninteger index is referred to as a *key*. By the way, you can implement KeyedArray with an underlying List<T> instead of the fixed-size array. List<T> is indexable like an array because both implement the IList (or IList<T>) interface. This allows KeyedArray to be generic and to be much more flexible than using the inner array.

The set[string] indexer starts by checking to see whether the specified index already exists by calling the method Find(). If Find() returns an index, set[] stores the new data object into the corresponding index in _arrayElements. If Find() can't find the key, set[] calls FindEmpty() to return an empty slot in which to store the object provided.

The get[] side of the index follows similar logic. It first searches for the specified key using the Find() method. If Find() returns a nonnegative index, get[] returns the corresponding member of _arrayElements where the data is stored. If Find() returns -1, get[] returns null, indicating that it can't find the provided key anywhere in the list.

The Find() method loops through the members of _keys to look for the element with the same value as the string targetKey passed in. Find() returns the index of the found element (or -1 if none was found). FindEmpty() returns the index of the first element that has no key element.

Neither Find() nor FindEmpty() is written in an efficient manner. Any number of ways exist to make these methods faster, none of which has anything to do with indexers.

Hey, wouldn't it be cool to provide an indexer for the LinkedList class? Sure, you can do that. But notice that even in KeyedArray, you must loop through the underlying _keys array to locate a specified key — which is why I provide Find() and FindEmpty(), which do just that. You would also have to implement an indexer for LinkedList by looping through the list, and the only way to do that is the same way you iterate it with LinkedListIterator — by following the forward links from node to node. An indexer would be convenient but wouldn't speed things up.

Notice that you can't remove an element by providing a null key. As they used to say in college textbooks, "This problem is left as an exercise for the reader."

The `Main()` method demonstrates the `Indexer` class in a trivial way:

```
public class Program
{
  public static void Main(string[] args)
  {
    // Create an array with enough room.
    KeyedArray ma = new KeyedArray(100);

    // Save the ages of the Simpson kids.
    ma["Bart"] = 8;
    ma["Lisa"] = 10;
    ma["Maggie"] = 2;

    // Look up the age of Lisa.
    Console.WriteLine("Let's find Lisa's age");
    int age = (int)ma["Lisa"];
    Console.WriteLine("Lisa is {0}", age);

    // Wait for user to acknowledge the results.
    Console.WriteLine("Press Enter to terminate...");
    Console.Read();
  }
}
```

The program creates a `KeyedArray` object `ma` of length 100 (that is, with 100 free elements). It continues by storing the ages of the children in *The Simpsons* TV show, indexed by each child's name. Finally, the program retrieves Lisa's age using the expression `ma["Lisa"]` and displays the result. The expression `ma["Lisa"]` is read as "`ma` sub-Lisa."

Notice that the program has to cast the value returned from `ma[]` because `KeyedArray` is written to hold any type of object. The cast wouldn't be necessary if the indexer were written to handle only `int` values — or if the `KeyedArray` were generic. (For more information about generics, see Chapter 8 in this minibook.)

The output of the program is simple yet elegant:

```
Let's find Lisa's age
Lisa is 10
Press Enter to terminate...
```

As an aside, the `IList` interface describes a class that provides an array-like integer indexer of the form `object this[int]`. C# also has an `IList<T>` interface, which you can use to replace `object` with your choice of type `T`. This would eliminate the need for a cast in the previous example.

For a generic version of the `Indexer` program, see the `IndexerGeneric` example on this book's Web site.

Looping Around the Iterator Block

Here's a piece of the code from the Main() method to demonstrate the custom LinkedList (that chunk of code is in the LinkedListContainer program on this book's Web site):

```
public class Program
{
  public static void Main(string[] args)
  {
    // Create a container and add three elements to it.
    LinkedList llc = new LinkedList();
    LLNode first = llc.AddObject("This is first string");
    LLNode second = llc.AddObject("This is second string");
    LLNode third = llc.AddObject("This is last string");

    // Add one at the beginning and one in the middle.
    LLNode newfirst = llc.AddObject(null, "Insert before the first string");
    LLNode newmiddle = llc.AddObject(second, "Insert between the second and
       third strings");

    // You can manipulate the iterator "manually."
    Console.WriteLine("Iterate through the container manually:");
    LinkedListIterator lli = (LinkedListIterator)llc.GetEnumerator();
    lli.Reset();
    while(lli.MoveNext())
    {
      string s = (string)lli.Current;
      Console.WriteLine(s);
    }
    ...
```

This code gets a LinkedListIterator and uses its MoveNext() method and Current property to iterate a linked list. Just when you thought you had mastered iterating, it turns out that C# 2.0 has simplified this process so that

- You don't have to call GetEnumerator() (and cast the results).
- You don't have to call MoveNext().
- You don't have to call Current and cast its return value.
- You can simply use foreach to iterate the collection. (C# does the rest for you under the hood — it even writes the enumerator class.)

  Well, to be fair, foreach works for the LinkedList class in this chapter, too. That comes from providing a GetEnumerator() method. But I still had to write the LinkedListIterator class ourselves. The new wrinkle is that you can skip that part in your roll-your-own collection classes, if you choose.

Rather than implement all those interface methods in collection classes you write, you can provide an iterator block — and you don't have to write your own iterator class to support the collection. Iterator blocks were introduced in C# 2.0, which shipped with Visual Studio 2005.

You can use iterator blocks for a host of other chores, too, as I show you in the next example.

The best approach to iteration now uses iterator blocks. When you write a collection class — and the need still exists for custom collection classes such as KeyedList and PriorityQueue — you implement an iterator block in its code rather than implement the IEnumerator interface. Then users of that class can simply iterate the collection with foreach. I walk you through it a piece at a time, to show you several variations on iterator blocks.

Every example in this section is part of the IteratorBlocks example on this book's Web site:

```
// IteratorBlocks -- Demonstrates using the C# 2.0 iterator
//    block approach to writing collection iterators
using System;
namespace IteratorBlocks
{
  class IteratorBlocks
  {
    //Main -- Demonstrate five different applications of
    //   iterator blocks.
    static void Main(string[] args)
    {
      // Instantiate a MonthDays "collection" class.
      MonthDays md = new MonthDays();
      // Iterate it.
      Console.WriteLine("Stream of months:\n");
      foreach (string month in md)
      {
        Console.WriteLine(month);
      }

      // Instantiate a StringChunks "collection" class.
      StringChunks sc = new StringChunks();
      // Iterate it: prints pieces of text.
      // This iteration puts each chunk on its own line.
      Console.WriteLine("\nstream of string chunks:\n");
      foreach (string chunk in sc)
      {
        Console.WriteLine(chunk);
      }
      // And this iteration puts it all on one line.
      Console.WriteLine("\nstream of string chunks on one line:\n");
      foreach (string chunk in sc)
      {
        Console.Write(chunk);
      }
      Console.WriteLine();

      // Instantiate a YieldBreakEx "collection" class.
      YieldBreakEx yb = new YieldBreakEx();
      // Iterate it, but stop after 13.
      Console.WriteLine("\nstream of primes:\n");
      foreach (int prime in yb)
      {
        Console.WriteLine(prime);
      }
```

```
      // Instantiate an EvenNumbers "collection" class.
      EvenNumbers en = new EvenNumbers();
      // Iterate it: prints even numbers from 10 down to 4.
      Console.WriteLine("\nstream of descending evens :\n");
      foreach (int even in en.DescendingEvens(11, 3))
      {
        Console.WriteLine(even);
      }

      // Instantiate a PropertyIterator "collection" class.
      PropertyIterator prop = new PropertyIterator();
      // Iterate it: produces one double at a time.
      Console.WriteLine("\nstream of double values:\n");
      foreach (double db in prop.DoubleProp)
      {
        Console.WriteLine(db);
      }

      // Wait for the user to acknowledge.
      Console.WriteLine("Press enter to terminate...");
      Console.Read();

    }
  }

  // MonthDays -- Define an iterator that returns the months
  //   and their lengths in days -- sort of a "collection" class.
  class MonthDays
  {
    // Here's the "collection."
    string[] months =
            { "January 31", "February 28", "March 31",
              "April 30", "May 31", "June 30", "July 31",
              "August 31", "September 30", "October 31",
              "November 30", "December 31" };

    // GetEnumerator -- Here's the iterator. See how it's invoked
    //   in Main() with foreach.
    public System.Collections.IEnumerator GetEnumerator()
    {
      foreach (string month in months)
      {
        // Return one month per iteration.
        yield return month;
      }
    }
  }

  // StringChunks -- Define an iterator that returns chunks of text,
  //   one per iteration -- another oddball "collection" class.
  class StringChunks
  {
    // GetEnumerator -- This is an iterator; see how it's invoked
    //   (twice) in Main.
    public System.Collections.IEnumerator GetEnumerator()
    {
      // Return a different chunk of text on each iteration.
      yield return "Using iterator ";
      yield return "blocks ";
      yield return "isn't all ";
      yield return "that hard";
      yield return ".";
    }
  }
```

```
  //YieldBreakEx -- Another example of the yield break keyword
  class YieldBreakEx
  {
    int[] primes = { 2, 3, 5, 7, 11, 13, 17, 19, 23 };
    //GetEnumerator -- Returns a sequence of prime numbers
    //   Demonstrates yield return and yield break
    public System.Collections.IEnumerator GetEnumerator()
    {
      foreach (int prime in primes)
      {
        if (prime > 13) yield break;
        yield return prime;
      }
    }
  }

  //EvenNumbers -- Define a named iterator that returns even numbers
  //   from the "top" value you pass in DOWN to the "stop" value.
  //   Another oddball "collection" class
  class EvenNumbers
  {
    //DescendingEvens -- This is a "named iterator."
    //   Also demonstrates the yield break keyword.
    //   See how it's invoked in Main() with foreach.
    public System.Collections.IEnumerable DescendingEvens(int top,
                                                           int stop)
    {
      // Start top at nearest lower even number.
      if (top % 2 != 0) // If remainder after top / 2 isn't 0.
        top -= 1;
      // Iterate from top down to nearest even above stop.
      for (int i = top; i >= stop; i -= 2)
      {
        if (i < stop)
          yield break;
        // Return the next even number on each iteration.
        yield return i;
      }
    }
  }

  //PropertyIterator -- Demonstrate implementing a class
  //   property's get accessor as an iterator block.
  class PropertyIterator
  {
    double[] doubles = { 1.0, 2.0, 3.5, 4.67 };
    // DoubleProp -- A "get" property with an iterator block
    public System.Collections.IEnumerable DoubleProp
    {
      get
      {
        foreach (double db in doubles)
        {
          yield return db;
        }
      }
    }
  }
}
```

For a more real-world illustration of iterator blocks, see the example `PackageFactoryWithIterator`, available with this chapter. The example extends the `PriorityQueue` example in Chapter 8 of this minibook.

Iterating days of the month: A first example

The following fragment from the `IteratorBlocks` example provides an iterator that steps through the months of the year:

```
//MonthDays -- Define an iterator that returns the months
//   and their lengths in days -- sort of a "collection" class.
class MonthDays
{
  // Here's the "collection."
  string[] months =
          { "January 31", "February 28", "March 31",
            "April 30", "May 31", "June 30", "July 31",
            "August 31", "September 30", "October 31",
            "November 30", "December 31" };

  //GetEnumerator -- Here's the iterator. See how it's invoked
  //   in Main() with foreach.
  public System.Collections.IEnumerator GetEnumerator()
  {
    foreach (string month in months)
    {
      // Return one month per iteration.
      yield return month;
    }
  }
}
```

Here's part of a `Main()` method that iterates this collection using a `foreach` loop:

```
// Instantiate a MonthDays "collection" class.
MonthDays md = new MonthDays();
// Iterate it.
foreach (string month in md)
{
  Console.WriteLine(month);
}
```

This extremely simple collection class is based on an array, as `KeyedArray` is. The class contains an array whose items are `string`s. When a client iterates this collection, the collection's iterator block delivers `string`s one by one. Each `string` contains the name of a month (in sequence), with the number of days in the month tacked on to the `string`. It isn't useful, but, boy, is it simple — and different!

The class defines its own iterator block, in this case as a method named `GetEnumerator()`, which returns an object of type `System.Collections.IEnumerator`. Now, it's true that you had to write such a method before, but you also had to write your own enumerator class to support your custom collection class. Here, *you just write a fairly simple method to return an enumerator* based on the new `yield return` keywords. C# does the rest for you: It creates the underlying enumerator class and takes care of calling `MoveNext()` to iterate the array. You get away with much less work and much simpler code.

Less code and less work fit my work ethic to a *T.*

REMEMBER

Your class containing the `GetEnumerator()` method no longer needs to implement the `IEnumerator` interface. In fact, you don't want it to.

In the following sections, I show you several varieties of iterator blocks:

- Ordinary iterators
- Named iterators
- Class properties implemented as iterators

Note that class `MonthDays`' `GetEnumerator()` method contains a `foreach` loop to yield the strings in its inner array. Iterator blocks often use a loop of some kind to do this, as you can see in several later examples. In effect, you have in your own calling code an inner `foreach` loop serving up item after item that can be iterated in another `foreach` loop outside `GetEnumerator()`.

What a collection is, really

Take a moment to compare the little collection in this example with an elaborate `LinkedList` collection. Whereas `LinkedList` has a complex structure of nodes connected by pointers, this little `months` collection is based on a simple array — with canned content, at that. I'm expanding the *collection* notion a bit, and I expand it even more before this chapter concludes.

(Your collection class may not contain canned content — most collections are designed to hold things you put into them via `Add()` methods and the like. The `KeyedArray` class in the earlier section "Accessing Collections the Array Way: Indexers," for example, uses the `[]` indexer to add items. Your collection could also provide an `Add()` method as well as add an iterator block so that it can work with `foreach`.)

The point of a collection, in the most general sense, is to store multiple objects and to allow you to iterate those objects, retrieving them one at a time sequentially — and sometimes randomly, or apparently randomly, as well, as in the `Indexer` example. (Of course, an array can do that, even without the extra apparatus of a class such as `MonthDays`, but iterators go well beyond the `MonthDays` example, as I'll show you.)

More generally, regardless of what an iterable collection does under the hood, it produces a "stream" of values, which you get at with `foreach`. (I cover file streams in Book III — I'm liberating the stream concept to make a point about iterators.)

To drive home the point, here's another simple collection class from `IteratorBlocks`, one that stretches the idea of a collection about as far as possible (you may think):

```
//StringChunks -- Define an iterator that returns chunks of text,
//   one per iteration -- another oddball "collection" class.
class StringChunks
{
  //GetEnumerator -- This is an iterator; see how it's invoked
  //   (twice) in Main.
  public System.Collections.IEnumerator GetEnumerator()
  {
    // Return a different chunk of text on each iteration.
    yield return "Using iterator ";
    yield return "blocks ";
    yield return "isn't all ";
    yield return "that hard";
    yield return ".";
  }
}
```

Oddly, the `StringChunks` collection *stores* nothing in the usual sense. It doesn't even contain an array. So where's the collection? It's in that sequence of `yield return` calls, which use a special syntax to return one item at a time until all have been returned. The collection "contains" five objects, each a simple `string` much like the ones stored in an array in the previous `MonthDays` example. And, from outside the class, in `Main()`, you can iterate those objects with a simple `foreach` loop because the `yield return` statements deliver *one* `string` *at a time,* in sequence. Here's part of a simple `Main()` method that iterates a `StringChunks` collection:

```
// Instantiate a StringChunks "collection" class.
StringChunks sc = new StringChunks();
// Iterate it: prints pieces of text.
foreach (string chunk in sc)
{
  Console.WriteLine(chunk);
}
```

Iterator syntax gives up so easily

As of C# 2.0, the language introduced two new bits of iterator syntax. The `yield return` statement resembles the old combination of `MoveNext()` and `Current` for retrieving the next item in a collection. The `yield break` statement resembles the C# `break` statement, which lets you break out of a loop or `switch` statement.

Yield return: Okay, I give up

The `yield return` syntax works this way:

1. The first time it's called, it returns the first value in the collection.
2. The next time it's called, it returns the second value.
3. And so on. . . .

Using `yield` is much like calling an old-fashioned iterator's `MoveNext()` method explicitly, as in the `LinkedList` code. Each `MoveNext()` call produces a new item from the collection. But here you don't need to call `MoveNext()`. (You can bet, though, that it's being done for you somewhere behind that `yield return` syntax, and that's fine with us.)

You might wonder what I mean by "the next time it's called"? Here again, the `foreach` loop is used to iterate the `StringChunks` collection:

```
foreach (string chunk in sc)
{
  Console.WriteLine(chunk);
}
```

Each time the loop obtains a new chunk from the iterator (on each pass through the loop), the iterator stores the position it has reached in the collection (as all iterators do). On the next pass through the `foreach` loop, the iterator returns the next value in the collection, and so on.

Yield break: I want out of here!

I need to mention one bit of syntax related to `yield`. You can stop the progress of the iterator at some point by specifying the `yield break` statement in the iterator. Say a threshold is reached after testing a condition in the collection class's iterator block, and you want to stop the iteration at that point. Here's a brief example of an iterator block that uses `yield break` in just that way:

```
//YieldBreakEx -- Another example of the yield break keyword
class YieldBreakEx
{
  int[] primes = { 2, 3, 5, 7, 11, 13, 17, 19, 23 };
  //GetEnumerator -- Returns a sequence of prime numbers
  //   Demonstrates yield return and yield break
  public System.Collections.IEnumerator GetEnumerator()
  {
    foreach (int prime in primes)
    {
      if (prime > 13) yield break;
      yield return prime;
    }
  }
}
```

In this case, the iterator block contains an `if` statement that checks each prime number as the iterator reaches it in the collection (using another `foreach` inside the iterator, by the way). If the prime number is greater than 13, the block invokes `yield break` to stop producing primes. Otherwise, it continues — with each `yield return` giving up another prime number until the collection is exhausted.

Besides using iterator blocks in formal collection classes, using them to implement enumerators, you could simply write any of the iterator blocks in this chapter as, say, static methods parallel to `Main()` in the `Program` class. In cases such as many of the examples in this chapter, the collection is inside the method. Such special-purpose collections can have many uses, and they're typically quick and easy to write.

You can also write an *extension method* on a class (or another type) that behaves as an iterator block. That can be quite useful when you have a class that can be thought of in some sense as a collection. My favorite example comes from the Language Integrated Query (LINQ) realm in C# 3.0. Using a bit of C# *reflection*, you can get at the contents of a C# type, such as `String`, to enumerate its members. I give several examples of this concept in the `MoreExtensionMethods` example on this book's Web site. I cover extension methods in Book 2.

Iterator blocks of all shapes and sizes

In earlier examples in this chapter, iterator blocks have looked like this:

```
public System.Collections.IEnumerator GetEnumerator()
{
  yield return something;
}
```

But iterator blocks can also take a couple of other forms: as named iterators and as class properties.

An iterator named Fred

Rather than always write an iterator block presented as a method named `GetEnumerator()`, you can write a *named iterator* — a method that returns the `System.Collections.IEnumerable` interface instead of `IEnumerator` and that you don't have to name `GetEnumerator()` — you can name it something like `MyMethod()` instead.

For example, you can use this simple method to iterate the even numbers from a "top" value that you specify *down* to a "stop" value — yes, in *descending* order — iterators can do just about anything:

```
//EvenNumbers -- Define a named iterator that returns even numbers
//   from the "top" value you pass in DOWN to the "stop" value.
//   Another oddball "collection" class
class EvenNumbers
```

```
{
  //DescendingEvens -- This is a "named iterator."
  //   Also demonstrates the yield break keyword
  //   See how it's invoked in Main() with foreach.
  public System.Collections.IEnumerable DescendingEvens(int top,
                                                         int stop)
  {
    // Start top at nearest lower even number.
    if (top % 2 != 0) // If remainder after top / 2 isn't 0.
      top -= 1;
    // Iterate from top down to nearest even above stop.
    for (int i = top; i >= stop; i -= 2)
    {
      if (i < stop)
        yield break;
      // Return the next even number on each iteration.
      yield return i;
    }
  }
}
```

The `DescendingEvens()` method takes two parameters (a handy addition), which set the upper limit of even numbers that you want to start from and the lower limit where you want to stop. The first even number that's generated will equal the top parameter or, if `top` is odd, the nearest even number below it. The last even number generated will equal the value of the `stop` parameter (or if `stop` is odd, the nearest even number above it). The method doesn't return an `int` itself, however; it returns the `IEnumerable` interface. But it still contains a `yield return` statement to return one even number and then waits until the next time it's invoked from a `foreach` loop. That's where the `int` is yielded up.

This example shows another collection with no underlying collection — such as `StringChunks`, mentioned earlier in this chapter. Note that this one is *computed* — the method "yield returns" a computed value rather than a stored or hard-coded value. That's another way to implement a collectionless collection. (You can also retrieve items from a data source or Web service.) And, finally, the example shows that you can iterate a collection pretty much any way you like: down instead of up or by steps of two instead of one, for example.

An iterator needn't be finite, either. Consider the following iterator, which delivers a new number as long as you care to request them:

```
public System.Collections.IEnumerable PositiveIntegers()
{
  for (int i = 0; ; i++)
  {
    yield return i;
  }
}
```

This example is, in effect, an infinite loop. You might want to pass a value used to stop the iteration. Here's how you would call `DescendingEvens()` from a `foreach` loop in `Main()`. (Calling `PositiveIntegers()` in the preceding example would work similarly.) This example demonstrates what happens if you pass odd numbers as the limit values, too — another use of the % operator:

```
// Instantiate an EvenNumbers "collection" class.
EvenNumbers en = new EvenNumbers();
// Iterate it: prints even numbers from 10 down to 4.
Console.WriteLine("\nstream of descending evens :\n");
foreach (int even in en.DescendingEvens(11, 3))
{
  Console.WriteLine(even);
}
```

This call produces a list of even-numbered integers from 10 down through 4. Notice also how the `foreach` is specified. You have to instantiate an `EvenNumbers` object (the collection class). Then, in the `foreach` statement, you invoke the named iterator method through that object:

```
EvenNumbers en = new EvenNumbers();
foreach(int even in en.DescendingEvens(nTop, nStop)) ...
```

If `DescendingEvens()` were static, you wouldn't even need the class instance. You would call it through the class itself, as usual:

```
foreach(int even in EvenNumbers.DescendingEvens(nTop, nStop)) ...
```

It's a regular wetland out there!

If you can produce a "stream" of even numbers with a `foreach` statement, think of all the other useful things you may produce with special-purpose collections like these: streams of powers of two or of terms in a mathematical series such as prime numbers or squares — or even something exotic such as Fibonacci numbers. Or, how about a stream of random numbers (that's what the `Random` class already does) or of randomly generated objects?

If you look at the `PriorityQueue` example in Chapter 8 of this minibook, you may want to check out the `PackageFactoryWithIterator` example — which appears only on this book's Web site. The example illustrates the use of an iterator block to generate a stream of randomly generated objects representing packages coming into a shipping company. It performs the same function as the `PackageFactory` class in the original `PriorityQueue` example, but with an iterator block.

Iterated property doesn't mean "a house that keeps getting sold"

You can also implement an iterator block as a *property* of a class — specifically in the `get()` accessor for the property. In this simple class with a `DoubleProp` property, the property's `get()` accessor acts as an iterator block to return a stream of `double` values:

```
//PropertyIterator -- Demonstrate implementing a class
//   property's get accessor as an iterator block.
class PropertyIterator
{
  double[] doubles = { 1.0, 2.0, 3.5, 4.67 };
  // DoubleProp -- A "get" property with an iterator block
  public System.Collections.IEnumerable DoubleProp
  {
    get
    {
      foreach (double db in doubles)
      {
        yield return db;
      }
    }
  }
}
```

You write the `DoubleProp` header in much the same way as you write the `DescendingEvens()` method's header in the named iterators example. The header returns an `IEnumerable` interface, but as a property it has no parentheses after the property name and it has a `get()` accessor — though no `set()`. The `get()` accessor is implemented as a `foreach` loop that iterates the collection and uses the standard `yield return` to yield up, in turn, each item in the collection of `doubles`.

Here's the way the property is accessed in `Main()`:

```
// Instantiate a PropertyIterator "collection" class.
PropertyIterator prop = new PropertyIterator();
// Iterate it: produces one double at a time.
Console.WriteLine("\nstream of double values:\n");
foreach (double db in prop.DoubleProp)
{
  Console.WriteLine(db);
}
```

You can also have a generic iterator. Look up *iterators, using* in Help. The "Using Iterators" topic for C# includes an example of a named iterator that also happens to be generic.

Where you can put your iterator

Hmm, I *have* to be careful about my phrasing.

In the small special-purpose iterator classes in the `IteratorBlocks` example, earlier in this chapter, I put the collection itself *inside the iterator class,* as in `MonthDays`. In some cases, that's just right — for instance, when the collection is something like `SentenceChunks`, which returns canned bits of text, or something like `DescendingEvens`, in which the return is calculated on the spot. But suppose that you want to supply an iterator based on an iterator block for a real collection class, such as `LinkedList`.

That's what I did in the LinkedListWithIteratorBlock example on this book's Web site. That example rewrites the roll-your-own LinkedList with a GetEnumerator() method implemented as an iterator block. It completely replaces the old LinkedListIterator class. The following listing gives just the new version of GetEnumerator() (you can see the whole example on this book's Web site):

```
// LinkedListWithIteratorBlock -- Implements iterator for the linked list as
//    an iterator block.
class LinkedList   // No longer need ": IEnumerator" here.
{
  ... rest of the class.
  ...
  // Here's the iterator, implemented as an iterator block.
  public IEnumerator GetEnumerator()
  {
    // Make sure the current node is legal.
    // If it's null, it hasn't yet been set to point into the list,
    // so point it at the head.
    if (currentNode == null)
    {
      currentNode = head;
    }
    // Here's the iteration for the enumerator that
    // GetEnumerator() returns.
    while (currentNode != null)
    {
      yield return currentNode.Object;
      currentNode = currentNode.forward;
    }
  }
}
```

I show the following basic form of an iterator block in several sections earlier in this chapter, including the section "Iterating days of the month: A first example":

```
public System.Collections.IEnumerator GetEnumerator() {}
```

This line looks exactly like the IEnumerator object returned by GetEnumerator() in the original LinkedList class. But implementing the GetEnumerator() method now works quite differently, as explained in this list:

- ✦ When you write an iterator block, C# creates the underlying LinkedListIterator class for you. You don't even write the class, and you never see its code. It's no longer part of the LinkedList WithIteratorBlock example.
- ✦ In your GetEnumerator() method, you just use a loop to step through the linked list's nodes and yield return the data item stored at each node. You can see this code in the previous listing.

✦ You no longer need to specify that your collection class implements `IEnumerator`, as in this class header:

```
public class LinkedList      // No longer need ": IEnumerator" here
```

Well, of course, it isn't quite that simple

A few possible "gotchas" are inevitable here:

✦ You have to make sure you start stepping at the beginning of the list.

To make this happen, the new `LinkedList` class adds a data member, `currentNode`, with which it tracks the iterator's progress through the list. (That member used to reside in the `LinkedListIterator` class.) The `currentNode` member is initially `null`, so the iterator needs to check for it. If so, it sets `currentNode` to point to the list's `head` node.

Unless `head` is `null` itself (the list is empty), `currentNode` is now non-null for the rest of the iteration. When the iterator finally reaches the end of the list, it indeed returns `null`, which signals the `foreach` loop to stop.

✦ Each step through the list needs to do what `MoveNext()` used to do — advance to the next node; hence the `while` loop:

```
// This does what MoveNext() did.
while(currentNode != null)
{
  // This does what Current did.
  yield return currentNode...;      // Portions omitted for a moment
  currentNode = currentNode.forward;
}
```

Most iterator block implementations employ a loop to step through the collection — sometimes even an inner `foreach` loop. (But `StringChunks` shows that it isn't the only way.)

✦ When you step through the list and start to `yield return` data, you have to dig inside the `LLNode` object to extract its stored data. A list node is just a storage bin for a `string`, an `int`, a `Student`, and so on. It requires that you `yield return` not `currentNode`, but, rather, this:

```
yield return currentNode.Data;          // Now complete
currentNode = currentNode.forward;
```

Under the hood, the original enumerator did that too. The `Data` property of `LLNode` returns the node's data as an `object`. I intentionally designed the original nongeneric linked list to be as general as possible — back in the bad old days before generics. Hence it stores `objects`.

Now the `while` loop, with its `yield break` statement, is doing the work that you used to have to do with more effort, and the resulting `GetEnumerator()` method works with `foreach`, as it did before, in `Main()`.

If you think about it, this implementation simply moves the functionality of the old custom iterator class, LinkedListIterator, into the LinkedList class itself. It's all swept under the iterator block, you might say.

Under the hood, foreach makes the necessary cast for you (assuming that it's a legal cast). So if you stored strings in the list, your foreach loop looks like this:

```
foreach(string s in llc)  // foreach does the cast for you here.
{
  Console.WriteLine(s);
}
```

For a generic version of this chapter's linked list, complete with an iterator block enumerator, see the GenericLinkedListContainer example on this book's Web site. (It isn't shown here.) That example demonstrates instantiating the generic LinkedList for string and then int. You'll get a kick out of stepping through the example in the debugger to see how foreach works. For comparison, see the new, built-in LinkedList<T> class in the System.Collections.Generic namespace.

Leave behind the whole nongeneric collection world — except for the good old array, which of course is still quite useful and still type-safe. Use generic collections. (Of course, I'm about to violate this tip in the next section.)

One more wrinkle

The original iterator implementation in LinkedList implemented its iterator as a separate iterator class designed as a companion to the LinkedList. That setup had one nice feature that's missing now from the iterator block versions I describe in the preceding section: You could easily create multiple instances of the iterator object and use each one for an independent iteration of the linked list. So iterator1 may be halfway through the list when iterator2 is just starting.

But the next example in this chapter remedies that problem (although for a simpler collection, not LinkedList). IteratorBlockIterator sticks with the separate companion iterator object, with intimate access to the collection's internal values. But that iterator object is itself implemented using an iterator block:

```
// In file Program.cs:

// IteratorBlockIterator -- Implements a separate iterator object as a
//    companion to a collection class, a la LinkedList, but
//    implements the actual iterator with an iterator block
using System;
using System.Collections;
namespace IteratorBlockIterator
{
  class Program
  {
```

```
// Create a collection and use two iterator objects to iterate
// it independently (each using an iterator block).
static void Main(string[] args)
{
  string[] strs = new string[] { "Joe", "Bob", "Tony", "Fred" };
  MyCollection mc = new MyCollection(strs);
  // Create the first iterator and start the iteration.
  MyCollectionIterator mci1 = mc.GetEnumerator();
  foreach (string s1 in mci1)  // Uses the first iterator object
  {
    // Do some useful work with each string.
    Console.WriteLine(s1);
    // Find Tony's boss.
    if (s1 == "Tony")
    {
      // In the middle of that iteration, start a new one, using
      // a second iterator, repeated for each outer loop pass.
      MyCollectionIterator mci2 = mc.GetEnumerator();
      foreach (string s2 in mci2)  // Uses the second iterator object
      {
        // Do some useful work with each string.
        if (s2 == "Bob")
        {
          Console.WriteLine("\t{0} is {1}'s boss", s2, s1);
        }
      }
    }
  }
  // Wait for user to acknowledge the results.
  Console.WriteLine("Press Enter to terminate...");
  Console.Read();
}
// A simple collection of strings
public class MyCollection
{
  // Implement collection with an old-fashioned ArrayList.
  // Internal, so separate iterator object can access the strings.
  internal ArrayList _list = new ArrayList();
  public MyCollection(string[] strs)
  {
    foreach (string s in strs)
    {
      _list.Add(s);
    }
  }
  // GetEnumerator -- As in LinkedList, returns one of your
  //    iterator objects.
  public MyCollectionIterator GetEnumerator()
  {
    return new MyCollectionIterator(this);
  }
}
// MyCollectionIterator -- The iterator class for MyCollection
//    (MyCollection is in a separate file.)
public class MyCollectionIterator
{
  // Store a reference to the collection.
  private MyCollection _mc;
  public MyCollectionIterator(MyCollection mc)
  {
    this._mc = mc;
  }
```

```
      // GetEnumerator -- This is the iterator block, which carries
      //    out the actual iteration for the iterator object.
      public System.Collections.IEnumerator GetEnumerator()
      {
        // Iterate the associated collection's underlying list,
        // which is accessible because it's declared internal.
        foreach (string s in _mc._list)
        {
          yield return s;    // The iterator block's heart
        }
      }
    }
  }
}
```

The collection in `IteratorBlockIterator` isn't much to write home about: a simple class wrapped around a `List` of `strings`. Its `GetEnumerator()` method simply returns a new instantiation of the companion iterator class, as in `LinkedList`:

```
// GetEnumerator -- As in LinkedList, returns one of your
//    iterator objects.
public MyCollectionIterator GetEnumerator()
{
  return new MyCollectionIterator(this);
}
```

It's what's inside that iterator class that's interesting. It too contains a `GetEnumerator()` method. Implemented with an iterator block, this one does the iteration work. Here's that method:

```
// GetEnumerator -- This is the iterator block, which carries
//    out the actual iteration for the iterator object.
public System.Collections.IEnumerator GetEnumerator()
{
  // Iterate the associated collection's underlying list,
  // which is accessible because it's declared internal.
  foreach (string s in mc.list)
  {
    yield return s;    // The iterator block's heart
  }
}
```

This method has access to the companion collection's contained `List<string>`, so its `yield return` statement can return each `string` in turn.

But the payoff is in `Main()`, where two copies of the iterator object are created. The `foreach` loop for the second one is nested in the `foreach` loop for the first, so the output looks like this:

```
Joe
Bob
Tony
        Bob is Tony's boss
Fred
```

The indented line is produced by the nested iteration.

Here are those nested loops in `Main()` again:

```
MyCollectionIterator mci1 = mc.GetEnumerator();
foreach (string s1 in mci1)  // Uses the first iterator block
{
  // Do some useful work with each string.
  Console.WriteLine(s1);
  // Find Tony's boss.
  if(s1 == "Tony")
  {
    // In the middle of that iteration, start a new one, using
    // a second iterator; this is repeated for each outer loop pass.
    MyCollectionIterator mci2 = mc.GetEnumerator();
    foreach (string s2 in mci2)  // Uses the second iterator block
    {
      // Do some useful work with each string.
      if(s2 == "Bob")
      {
        Console.WriteLine("\t{0} is {1}'s boss", s2, s1);
      }
    }
  }
}
```

The original iterator, with `MoveNext()` and `Current`, is still more flexible, but this example comes close — and is easier to do.

Chapter 8: Buying Generic

In This Chapter

- Making your code generic — and truly powerful
- Writing your own generic class
- Writing generic methods
- Using generic interfaces and delegates

The problem with collections is that you need to know exactly what is going in them. Can you imagine a recipe that accepts only the exact listed ingredients and no others? No substitutions — nothing even named differently? That's how most collections treat you, but not generics.

As with prescriptions at your local pharmacy, you can save big by opting for the generic version. *Generics*, introduced in C# 2.0, are fill-in-the-blanks classes, methods, interfaces, and delegates. For example, the `List<T>` class defines a generic array-like list that's quite comparable to the older, non-generic `ArrayList` — but better! When you pull `List<T>` off the shelf to instantiate your own list of, say, `int`s, you replace `T` with `int`:

```
List<int> myList = new List<int>();  // A list limited to ints
```

The versatile part is that you can instantiate `List<T>` for *any single* data type (`string`, `Student`, `BankAccount`, `CorduroyPants` — whatever) and it's still type-safe like an array, without nongeneric costs. It's the superarray. (I explain type-safety and the costs of nongeneric collections next.)

Generics come in two flavors in C#: the built-in generics, such as `List<T>`, and a variety of roll-your-own items. After a quick tour of generic concepts, this chapter covers roll-your-own generic classes, generic methods, and generic interfaces and delegates.

Writing a New Prescription: Generics

What's so hot about generics? They excel for two reasons: safety and performance.

Generics are type-safe

When you declare an array, you must specify the exact type of data it can hold. If you specify `int`, the array can't hold anything other than `int`s or other numeric types that C# can convert implicitly to `int`. You see compiler errors at build-time if you try to put the wrong kind of data into an array. Thus the compiler enforces *type-safety,* enabling you to fix a problem before it ever gets out the door.

A compiler error beats the heck out of a runtime error. In fact, a compiler error beats everything except a royal flush or a raspberry sundae. Compiler errors are useful because they help you spot problems now.

The old-fashioned nongeneric collections aren't type-safe. In C#, everything IS_A `Object` because `Object` is the base type for all other types, both value-types and reference-types. But when you store *value-types* (numbers, `char`s, `bool`s, and `struct`s) in a collection, they must be *boxed* going in and *unboxed* coming back out. It's as though you're putting items in an egg carton and having to stuff them inside the eggs so that they fit, and then breaking the eggshells to get the items back out. (Reference-types such as `string`, `Student`, and `BankAccount` don't undergo boxing.)

The first consequence of nongenerics lacking type-safety is that you need a cast, as shown in the following code, to get the original object out of the `ArrayList` because it's hidden inside an egg, er, `Object`:

```
ArrayList aList = new ArrayList();
// Add five or six items, then ...
string myString = (string)aList[4];  // Cast to string.
```

Fine, but the second consequence is this: You can put eggs in the carton, sure. But you can also add marbles, rocks, diamonds, fudge — you name it. An `ArrayList` can hold many *different types* of objects *at the same time.* So it's legal to write this:

```
ArrayList aList = new ArrayList();
aList.Add("a string");       // string -- OK
aList.Add(3);                // int -- OK
aList.Add(aStudent);         // Student -- OK
```

However, if you put a mixture of incompatible types into an `ArrayList` (or another nongeneric collection), how do you know what type is in, say, `aList[3]`? If it's a `Student` and you try to cast it to `string`, you get a runtime error. It's just like Harry Potter reaching into a box of Bertie Botts's Every Flavor Beans: He doesn't know whether he'll grab raspberry beans or earwax.

To be safe, you have to resort to using the `is` operator (discussed in Book II) or the alternative, the `as` operator:

```
// See if the object is the right type, then cast it ...
if(aList[i] is Student)                 // Is the object there a Student?
{
  Student aStudent = (Student)aList[i]; // Yes, so it's safe to cast.
}
// Or do the conversion and see if it went well...
Student aStudent = aList[i] as Student; // Extract a Student, if present;
if(aStudent != null)                    // if not, "as" returns null.
{
  // OK to use aStudent; "as" operator worked.
}
```

You can avoid all this extra work by using generics. Generic collections work like arrays: You specify the one and only type they can hold when you declare them.

Generics are efficient

Polymorphism allows the type `Object` to hold any other type — as with the egg carton analogy in the previous section. But you can incur a penalty by putting in value-type objects — numeric, `char`, and `bool` types and `structs` — and taking them out. That's because value-type objects that you add have to be boxed. (See Book II for more on polymorphism.)

Boxing isn't worrisome unless your collection is big (although the amount of boxing going on can startle you and be more costly than you imagined). If you're stuffing a thousand, or a million, `ints` into a nongeneric collection, it takes about 20 times as long, plus extra space on the memory heap, where reference-type objects are stored. Boxing can also lead to subtle errors that will have you tearing your hair out. Generic collections eliminate boxing and unboxing.

Don't get me wrong: Boxing allows C# to have a unified type system, which has great benefits that usually outweigh the inconvenience and cost of boxing.

Classy Generics: Writing Your Own

Besides the built-in generic collection classes, C# lets you write your own generic classes, whether they're collections or not. The point is that you can create generic versions of classes that *you* design.

Picture a class definition full of `<T>` notations. When you instantiate such a class, you specify a type to replace its generic placeholders, just as you do with the generic collections. Note how similar these declarations are:

```
LinkedList<int> aList = new LinkedList<int>(); // Built-in LinkedList class
MyClass<int> aClass = new MyClass<int>();      // Custom class
```

Both are instantiations of classes — one built-in and one programmer-defined. Not every class makes sense as a generic; later in this chapter, I show you an example of one that does.

Classes that logically could do the same things for different types of data make the best generic classes. Collections of one sort or another are the prime example. If you find yourself mumbling, "I'll probably have to write a version of this for `Student` objects, too," it's probably a good candidate for generics.

To show you how to write your own generic class, the following example develops a special kind of queue collection class, a priority queue.

Shipping packages at OOPs

Here's the scene for an example: a busy shipping warehouse similar to UPS or FedEx. Packages stream in the front door at OOPs, Inc., and are shipped out the back as soon as they can be processed. Some packages need to be delivered by way of superfast next-day teleportation; others can travel a tiny bit slower, by second-day cargo pigeon; and most can take the snail route: ground delivery in your cousin Fred's '82 Volvo.

But the packages don't arrive at the warehouse in any particular order, so as they come in, you need to expedite some of them as next-day or second-day. Because some packages are more equal than others, they are prioritized and the folks in the warehouse give the high-priority packages special treatment.

Except for the priority aspect, this situation is tailor-made for a queue data structure. A queue is perfect for anything that involves turn-taking. You've stood (or driven) in thousands of queues in your life, waiting for your turn to buy Twinkies or pay too much for prescription medicines. You know the drill.

The shipping warehouse scenario is similar: New packages arrive and go to the back of the line — normally. But because some have higher priorities, they're privileged characters, like those Premium Class folks at the airport ticket counter. They get to jump ahead, either to the front of the line or not far from the front.

Queuing at OOPs: PriorityQueue

The shipping queue at OOPs deals with high-, medium-, and low-priority packages coming in. Here are the queuing rules:

- **High-priority packages** (next-day) go to the front of the queue — but behind any other high-priority packages that are already there.
- **Medium-priority packages** (second-day) go as far forward as possible — but behind all the high-priority packages, even the ones that a laggard will drop off later, and also behind other medium-priority packages that are already in the queue.

✦ **Low-priority ground-pounders** must join at the back of the queue. They get to watch all the high priorities sail by to cut in front of them — sometimes, *way* in front of them.

C# comes with built-in queues, even generic ones. But it doesn't come with a priority queue, so you have to build your own. How? A common approach is to embed several actual queues within a wrapper class, sort of like this:

```
class Wrapper        // Or PriorityQueue
{
  Queue queueHigh   = new Queue ();
  Queue queueMedium = new Queue ();
  Queue queueLow    = new Queue ();
  // Methods to manipulate the underlying queues...
```

Wrappers are classes (or methods) that encapsulate complexity. A wrapper may have an interface quite different from the interfaces of what's inside it — that's an *adapter.*

The wrapper encapsulates three actual queues here (they could be generic), and the wrapper must manage what goes into which underlying queue and how. The standard interface to the `Queue` class, as implemented in C#, includes these two key methods:

✦ `Enqueue()` (pronounced "N-Q") inserts items into a queue *at the back.*

✦ `Dequeue()` (pronounced "D-Q") removes items from the queue *at the front.*

For the shipping-priority queue, the wrapper provides the same interface as a normal queue, thus pretending to be a normal queue itself. It implements an `Enqueue()` method that determines an incoming package's priority and decides which underlying queue it gets to join. The wrapper's `Dequeue()` method finds the highest-priority `Package` in any of the underlying queues. The formal name of this wrapper class is `PriorityQueue`.

Here's the code for the `PriorityQueue` example on this book's Web site:

```
// PriorityQueue -- Demonstrates using lower-level queue collection objects
//    (generic ones at that) to implement a higher-level generic
//    Queue that stores objects in priority order
using System;
using System.Collections.Generic;
namespace PriorityQueue
{
  class Program
  {
    // Main -- Fill the priority queue with packages, then
    // remove a random number of them.
    static void Main(string[] args)
    {
      Console.WriteLine("Create a priority queue:");
      PriorityQueue<Package> pq = new PriorityQueue<Package>();
```

```
      Console.WriteLine(
        "Add a random number (0 - 20) of random packages to queue:");
      Package pack;
      PackageFactory fact = new PackageFactory();
      // You want a random number less than 20.
      Random rand = new Random();
      int numToCreate = rand.Next(20); // Random int from 0 - 20
      Console.WriteLine("\tCreating {0} packages: ", numToCreate);
      for (int i = 0; i < numToCreate; i++)
      {
        Console.Write("\t\tGenerating and adding random package {0}", i);
        pack = fact.CreatePackage();
        Console.WriteLine(" with priority {0}", pack.Priority);
        pq.Enqueue(pack);
      }
      Console.WriteLine("See what we got:");
      int total = pq.Count;
      Console.WriteLine("Packages received: {0}", total);

      Console.WriteLine("Remove a random number of packages (0-20): ");
      int numToRemove = rand.Next(20);
      Console.WriteLine("\tRemoving up to {0} packages", numToRemove);
      for (int i = 0; i < numToRemove; i++)
      {
        pack = pq.Dequeue();
        if (pack != null)
        {
          Console.WriteLine("\t\tShipped package with priority {0}",
              pack.Priority);
        }
      }
      // See how many were "shipped."
      Console.WriteLine("Shipped {0} packages", total - pq.Count);

      // Wait for user to acknowledge the results.
      Console.WriteLine("Press Enter to terminate...");
      Console.Read();
    }
  }

  // Priority enumeration -- Defines a set of priorities
  //    instead of priorities like 1, 2, 3, ... these have names.
  //    For information on enumerations,
  //    see the article "Enumerating the Charms of the Enum"
  //    on csharp102.info.
  enum Priority
  {
    Low, Medium, High
  }

  // IPrioritizable interface -- Defines ability to prioritize.
  //    Define a custom interface: Classes that can be added to
  //    PriorityQueue must implement this interface.
  interface IPrioritizable
  {
    Priority Priority { get; } // Example of a property in an interface
  }

  //PriorityQueue -- A generic priority queue class
  //   Types to be added to the queue *must* implement IPrioritizable interface.
  class PriorityQueue<T> where T : IPrioritizable
  {
```

```
//Queues -- the three underlying queues: all generic!
private Queue<T> _queueHigh = new Queue<T>();
private Queue<T> _queueMedium = new Queue<T>();
private Queue<T> _queueLow = new Queue<T>();

//Enqueue -- Prioritize T and add it to correct queue; an item of type T.
//   The item must know its own priority.
public void Enqueue(T item)
{
  switch (item.Priority) // Require IPrioritizable to ensure this property.
  {
    case Priority.High:
      _queueHigh.Enqueue(item);
      break;
    case Priority.Medium:
      _queueMedium.Enqueue(item);
      break;
    case Priority.Low:
      _queueLow.Enqueue(item);
      break;
    default:
      throw new ArgumentOutOfRangeException(
        item.Priority.ToString(),
        "bad priority in PriorityQueue.Enqueue");
  }
}

//Dequeue -- Get T from highest-priority queue available.
public T Dequeue()
{
  // Find highest-priority queue with items.
  Queue<T> queueTop = TopQueue();
  // If a non-empty queue is found.
  if (queueTop != null & queueTop.Count > 0)
  {
    return queueTop.Dequeue(); // Return its front item.
  }
  // If all queues empty, return null (you could throw exception).
  return default(T); // What's this? See discussion.
}

//TopQueue -- What's the highest-priority underlying queue with items?
private Queue<T> TopQueue()
{
  if (_queueHigh.Count > 0)   // Anything in high-priority queue?
    return _queueHigh;
  if (_queueMedium.Count > 0) // Anything in medium-priority queue?
    return _queueMedium;
  if (_queueLow.Count > 0)    // Anything in low-priority queue?
    return _queueLow;
  return _queueLow;           // All empty, so return an empty queue.
}

//IsEmpty -- Check whether there's anything to deqeue.
public bool IsEmpty()
{
  // True if all queues are empty
  return (_queueHigh.Count == 0) & (_queueMedium.Count == 0) &
      (_queueLow.Count == 0);
}
```

```
    //Count -- How many items are in all queues combined?
    public int Count  // Implement this one as a read-only property.
    {
      get { return _queueHigh.Count + _queueMedium.Count + _queueLow.Count; }
    }
  }

  //Package -- An example of a prioritizable class that can be stored in
  //   the priority queue; any class that implements
  //   IPrioritizable would look something like Package.
  class Package : IPrioritizable
  {
    private Priority _priority;
    //Constructor
    public Package(Priority priority)
    {
      this._priority = priority;
    }

    //Priority -- Return package priority -- read-only.
    public Priority Priority
    {
      get { return _priority; }
    }
    // Plus ToAddress, FromAddress, Insurance, etc.
  }

  //PackageFactory -- You need a class that knows how to create a new
  //   package of any desired type on demand; such a class
  //   is a factory class.
  class PackageFactory
  {
    //A random-number generator
    Random _randGen = new Random();

    //CreatePackage -- The factory method selects a random priority,
    //   then creates a package with that priority.
    //   Could implement this as iterator block.
public Package CreatePackage()
    {
      // Return a randomly selected package priority.
      // Need a 0, 1, or 2 (values less than 3).
      int rand = _randGen.Next(3);
      // Use that to generate a new package.
      // Casting int to enum is clunky, but it saves
      // having to use ifs or a switch statement.
      return new Package((Priority)rand);
    }
  }
}
```

PriorityQueue is a bit long, so you need to look at each part carefully. After a look at the target class, Package, you can follow a package's journey through the Main() method near the top.

When you run PriorityQueue, run it several times. Because it's built around random numbers, you get varying results on each run. Sometimes it may "receive" zero packages, for instance. (Slow days happen, I guess.)

Unwrapping the package

Class Package, which is intentionally simple for this example (see the listing in the previous section), focuses on the priority part, although a real Package object would include other members. All that Package needs for the example are

- ✦ A private data member to store its priority
- ✦ A constructor to create a package with a specific priority
- ✦ A method (implemented as a read-only property here) to return the priority

Two aspects of class Package require some explanation: the Priority type and the IPrioritizable interface that Package implements. Read on.

Specifying the possible priorities

Priorities are measured with an enumerated type, or enum, named Priority. The Priority enum looks like this:

```
//Priority -- Instead of priorities like 1, 2, 3, they have names.
enum Priority      // See the article "Enumerating the Charms
                   // of the Enum" on this book's Web site.
{
  Low, Medium, High
}
```

Implementing the IPrioritizable interface

Any object going into the PriorityQueue must "know" its own priority. (A general object-oriented principle states that objects should be responsible for themselves.)

You can informally "promise" that class Package has a member to retrieve its priority, but you should make it a requirement that the compiler can enforce. You require any object placed in the PriorityQueue to have such a member.

One way to enforce this requirement is to insist that all shippable objects implement the IPrioritizable interface, which follows:

```
//IPrioritizable -- Define a custom interface: Classes that can be added to
//                  PriorityQueue must implement this interface.
interface IPrioritizable  // Any class can implement this interface.
{
  Priority Priority { get; }
}
```

The notation { get; } is how to write a property in an interface declaration.

Class Package implements the interface by providing a fleshed-out implementation for the Priority property:

```
public Priority Priority
{
  get { return _priority; }
}
```

You encounter the other side of this enforceable requirement in the declaration of class PriorityQueue, in the later section "Saving PriorityQueue for last."

Touring Main()

Before you spelunk the PriorityQueue class itself, it's useful to get an overview of how it works in practice at OOPs, Inc. Here's the Main() method for the PriorityQueue example:

```
static void Main(string[] args)
{
  Console.WriteLine("Create a priority queue:");
  PriorityQueue<Package> pq = new PriorityQueue<Package>();
  Console.WriteLine(
    "Add a random number (0 - 20) of random packages to queue:");
  Package pack;
  PackageFactory fact = new PackageFactory();
  // You want a random number less than 20.
  Random rand = new Random();
  int numToCreate = rand.Next(20); // Random int from 0-20.
  Console.WriteLine("\tCreating {0} packages: ", numToCreate);
  for (int i = 0; i < numToCreate; i++)
  {
    Console.Write("\t\tGenerating and adding random package {0}", i);
    pack = fact.CreatePackage();
    Console.WriteLine(" with priority {0}", pack.Priority);
    pq.Enqueue(pack);
  }
  Console.WriteLine("See what we got:");
  int total = pq.Count;
  Console.WriteLine("Packages received: {0}", total);

  Console.WriteLine("Remove a random number of packages (0-20): ");
  int numToRemove = rand.Next(20);
  Console.WriteLine("\tRemoving up to {0} packages", numToRemove);
  for (int i = 0; i < numToRemove; i++)
  {
    pack = pq.Dequeue();
    if (pack != null)
    {
      Console.WriteLine("\t\tShipped package with priority {0}",
          pack.Priority);
    }
  }
  // See how many were "shipped."
  Console.WriteLine("Shipped {0} packages", total - pq.Count);
```

```
    // Wait for user to acknowledge the results.
    Console.WriteLine("Press Enter to terminate...");
    Console.Read();
  }
```

Here's what happens in `Main()`:

1. Instantiate a `PriorityQueue` object for type `Package`.
2. Create a `PackageFactory` object whose job is to create new packages with randomly selected priorities, on demand.

   A *factory* is a class or method that creates objects for you. You tour `PackageFactory` in the section "Using a (nongeneric) Simple Factory class," later in this chapter.
3. Use the .NET library class `Random` to generate a random number and then call `PackageFactory` to create that number of new `Package` objects with random priorities.
4. Add each package to the `PriorityQueue` by using `pq.Enqueue(pack)`.
5. Write the number of packages created and then randomly remove some of them from the `PriorityQueue` by using `pq.Dequeue()`.
6. End after displaying the number of packages removed.

Writing generic code the easy way

Now you have to figure out how to go about writing a generic class, with all those `<T>`s. Looks confusing, doesn't it? Well, it's not so hard, as this section demonstrates.

The simple way to write a generic class is to write a nongeneric version first and then substitute the `<T>`s. For example, you would write the `PriorityQueue` class for `Package` objects, test it, and then "genericize" it.

Here's a small piece of a nongeneric `PriorityQueue`, to illustrate:

```
public class PriorityQueue
{
  //Queues -- The three underlying queues: all generic!
  private Queue<Package> _queueHigh   = new Queue<Package>();
  private Queue<Package> _queueMedium = new Queue<Package>();
  private Queue<Package> _queueLow    = new Queue<Package>();
  //Enqueue -- Prioritize a Package and add it to correct queue.
  public void Enqueue(Package item)
  {
    switch(item.Priority)  // Package has this property.
    {
      case Priority.High:
        queueHigh.Enqueue(item);
        break;
```

```
        case Priority.Low:
          queueLow.Enqueue(item);
          break;
        case Priority.Medium:
          queueMedium.Enqueue(item);
          break;
      }
    }
    // And so on ...
```

Testing the logic of the class is easier when you write the class nongenerically first. When all the logic is straight, you can use find-and-replace to replace the name `Package` with `T`. (I explain a little later that there's a bit more to it than that, but not much.)

Saving PriorityQueue for last

Why would a priority queue be last? Seems a little backward to us. But you've seen the rest. Now it's time to examine the `PriorityQueue` class itself. This section shows the code and then walks you through it and shows you how to deal with a couple of small issues. Take it a piece at a time.

The underlying queues

`PriorityQueue` is a wrapper class that hides three ordinary `Queue<T>` objects, one for each priority level. Here's the first part of `PriorityQueue`, showing the three underlying queues (now generic):

```
//PriorityQueue -- A generic priority queue class
//   Types to be added to the queue *must* implement IPrioritizable interface.
class PriorityQueue<T> where T : IPrioritizable
{
  // Queues -- the three underlying queues: all generic!
  private Queue<T> _queueHigh = new Queue<T>();
  private Queue<T> _queueMedium = new Queue<T>();
  private Queue<T> _queueLow = new Queue<T>();
  // The rest will follow shortly ...
```

These lines declare three private data members of type `Queue<T>` and initialize them by creating the `Queue<T>` objects. I say more later in this chapter about that odd-looking class declaration line above the "subqueue" declarations.

The Enqueue() method

`Enqueue()` adds an item of type `T` to the `PriorityQueue`. This method's job is to look at the item's priority and put it into the correct underlying queue. In the first line, it gets the item's `Priority` property and switches based on that value. To add the item to the high-priority queue, for example, `Enqueue()` turns around and enqueues the item in the underlying `queueHigh`. Here's `PriorityQueue`'s `Enqueue()` method:

```
//Enqueue -- Prioritize T and add it to correct queue; an item of type T.
//   The item must know its own priority.
public void Enqueue(T item)
{
  switch (item.Priority) // Require IPrioritizable to ensure this property.
  {
    case Priority.High:
      _queueHigh.Enqueue(item);
      break;
    case Priority.Medium:
      _queueMedium.Enqueue(item);
      break;
    case Priority.Low:
      _queueLow.Enqueue(item);
      break;
    default:
      throw new ArgumentOutOfRangeException(
        item.Priority.ToString(),
        "bad priority in PriorityQueue.Enqueue");
  }
}
```

The Dequeue() method

Dequeue()'s job is a bit trickier than Enqueue()'s: It must locate the highest-priority underlying queue that has contents and then retrieve the front item from that subqueue. Dequeue() delegates the first part of the task, finding the highest-priority queue that isn't empty, to a private TopQueue() method (described in the next section). Then Dequeue() calls the underlying queue's Dequeue() method to retrieve the frontmost object, which it returns. Here's how Dequeue() works:

```
//Dequeue -- Get T from highest-priority queue available.
public T Dequeue()
{
  // Find highest-priority queue with items.
  Queue<T> queueTop = TopQueue();
  // If a non-empty queue is found
  if (queueTop != null & queueTop.Count > 0)
  {
    return queueTop.Dequeue(); // Return its front item.
  }
  // If all queues empty, return null (you could throw exception).
  return default(T); // What's this? See discussion.
}
```

A difficulty arises only if none of the underlying queues have any packages — in other words, the whole PriorityQueue is empty. What do you return in that case? Dequeue() returns null. The client — the code that calls PriorityQueue.Dequeue() — should check the Dequeue() return value in case it's null. Where's the null it returns? It's that odd duck, default(T), at the end. I deal with default(T) a little later in this chapter.

The TopQueue() utility method

Dequeue() relies on the private method TopQueue() to find the highest-priority, nonempty underlying queue. TopQueue() just starts with queueHigh and asks for its Count property. If it's greater than zero, the queue contains items, so TopQueue() returns a reference to the whole underlying queue that it found. (The TopQueue() return type is Queue<T>.) On the other hand, if queueHigh is empty, TopQueue() tries queueMedium and then queueLow.

What happens if all subqueues are empty? TopQueue() could return null, but it's more useful to simply return one of the empty queues. When Dequeue() then calls the returned queue's Dequeue() method, it returns null. TopQueue() works like this:

```
//TopQueue -- What's the highest-priority underlying queue with items?
private Queue<T> TopQueue()
{
  if (_queueHigh.Count > 0)    // Anything in high-priority queue?
    return _queueHigh;
  if (_queueMedium.Count > 0) // Anything in medium-priority queue?
    return _queueMedium;
  if (_queueLow.Count > 0)     // Anything in low-priority queue?
    return _queueLow;
  return _queueLow;            // All empty, so return an empty queue.
}
```

The remaining PriorityQueue members

PriorityQueue is useful when it knows whether it's empty and, if not, how many items it contains. (An object should be responsible for itself.) Look at PriorityQueue's IsEmpty() method and Count property in the earlier listing. You might also find it useful to include methods that return the number of items in each of the underlying queues. *Be careful:* Doing so may reveal too much about how the priority queue is implemented. Keep your implementation private.

Using a (nongeneric) Simple Factory class

Earlier in this chapter, I use a Simple Factory object (although I just call it a "Factory" there) to generate an endless stream of Package objects with randomized priority levels. At long last, that simple class can be revealed:

```
    // PackageFactory is part of the PriorityQueue example on the Web site.
// PackageFactory -- You need a class that knows how to create a new
//     package of any desired type on demand; such a
//     class is a factory class.
class PackageFactory
{
  Random _randGen = new Random();  // C#'s random-number generator
  //CreatePackage -- This factory method selects a random priority,
  //   then creates a package with that priority.
  public Package CreatePackage()
```

```
    {
      // Return a randomly selected package priority:
      // need a 0, 1, or 2 (values less than 3).
      int rand = _randGen.Next(3);
      // Use that to generate a new package.
      // Casting int to enum is clunky, but it saves
      // having to use ifs or a switch statement.
      return new Package((Priority)rand);
    }
  }
```

Class `PackageFactory` has one data member and one method. (You can just as easily implement a simple factory as a method rather than as a class — for example, a method in class `Program`.) When you instantiate a `PackageFactory` object, it creates an object of class `Random` and stores it in the data member `rand`. `Random` is a .NET library class that generates random numbers.

Take a look at the `PackageFactoryWithIterator` example on `csharp102.info`.

Using PackageFactory

To generate a randomly prioritized `Package` object, you call your factory object's `CreatePackage()` method this way:

```
PackageFactory fact = new PackageFactory();
IPrioritizable pack = fact.CreatePackage(); // Note the interface here.
```

`CreatePackage()` tells its random-number generator to generate a number from 0 to 2 (inclusive) and uses the number to set the priority of a new `Package`, which the method returns (to a `Package` or, better, to an `IPrioritizable` variable).

Note that I have `CreatePackage` return a reference to `IPrioritizable`, which is more general than returning a reference to `Package`. This example shows *indirection* — `Main()` refers to a `Package` indirectly, through an interface that `Package` implements. Indirection insulates `Main()` from the details of what `CreatePackage` returns. You then have greater freedom to alter the underlying implementation of the factory without affecting `Main()`.

More about factories

Factories are helpful for generating lots of test data. (A factory needn't use random numbers — that's just what was needed for the `PriorityQueue` example.)

Factories improve programs by isolating object creation. Every time you mention a specific class by name in your code, you create a *dependency* on that class. The more such dependencies you have, the more *tightly coupled* (bound together) your classes become.

Programmers have long known that they should avoid tight coupling. (One of the more *decoupled* approaches is to use the factory indirectly via an interface, such as `IPrioritizable`, rather than a concrete class, such as `Package`.) Programmers still create objects directly all the time, using the `new` operator, and that's fine. But factories can make code less coupled — and therefore more flexible.

Tending to unfinished business

`PriorityQueue` needs a couple of small bits of "spackling." Here are the issues:

- By itself, `PriorityQueue` wouldn't prevent you from trying to instantiate it for, say, `int` or `string` or `Student` — elements that don't have priorities. You need to *constrain* the class so that it can be instantiated only for types that implement `IPrioritizable`. Attempting to instantiate for a non-`IPrioritizable` class should result in a compiler error.
- The `Dequeue()` method for `PriorityQueue` returns the value `null` instead of an actual object. But generic types such as `<T>` don't have a natural default `null` value the way elements such as `int`s, `string`s, and down-and-out object references do. That part of it needs to be genericized, too.

Adding constraints

`PriorityQueue` must be able to ask an object what its priority is. To make it work, all classes that are storable in `PriorityQueue` must implement the `IPrioritizable` interface, as `Package` does. `Package` lists `IPrioritizable` in its class declaration heading, like this:

```
class Package : IPrioritizable
```

Then it implements `IPrioritizable`'s `Priority` property.

A matching limitation is needed for `PriorityQueue`. You want the compiler to squawk if you try to instantiate for a type that doesn't implement `IPrioritizable`. In the nongeneric form of `PriorityQueue` (written specifically for type `Package`, say), the compiler squeals automatically (I recommend earplugs) when one of your priority queue methods tries to call a method that `Package` doesn't have. But, for generic classes, you can go to the next level with an explicit *constraint.* Because you could instantiate the generic class with literally any type, you need a way to tell the compiler which types are acceptable — because they're guaranteed to have the right methods.

You add the constraint by specifying `IPrioritizable` in the heading for `PriorityQueue`, like this:

```
class PriorityQueue<T> where T: IPrioritizable
```

Did you notice the `where` clause earlier? This boldfaced `where` clause specifies that `T` must implement `IPrioritizable`. *That's the enforcer.* It means, "Make sure that `T` implements the `IPrioritizable` interface — or else!"

REMEMBER

You specify constraints by listing *one or more* of the following elements (separated by commas) in a `where` clause:

- The name of a required base class that `T` must derive from (or be).
- The name of an interface that `T` must implement, as shown in the previous example.
- You can see more — Table 8-1 has the complete list.

For information about these constraints, look up *Generics [C#], constraints* in the Help index.

Table 8-1 Generic Constraint Options

Constraint	*Meaning*	*Example*
`MyBaseClass`	T must be, or extend, `MyBaseClass`.	`where T: MyBaseClass`
`IMyInterface`	T must implement `IMyInterface`.	`where T: IMyInterface`
`struct`	T must be any value type.	`where T: struct`
`class`	T must be any reference type.	`where T: class`
`new()`	T must have a parameterless constructor.	`where T: new()`

Note the `struct` and `class` options in particular. Specifying `struct` means that `T` can be any value type: a numeric type, a `char`, a `bool`, or any object declared with the `struct` keyword. Specifying `class` means that `T` can be any reference type: any *class* type.

These constraint options give you quite a bit of flexibility for making your new generic class behave just as you want. And a well-behaved class is a pearl beyond price.

You aren't limited to just one constraint, either. Here's an example of a hypothetical generic class declared with multiple constraints on `T`:

```
class MyClass<T> : where T: class, IPrioritizable, new()
{ ... }
```

In this line, T must be a class, not a value type; it must implement IPrioritizable; and it must contain a constructor without parameters. Strict!

You might have two generic parameters and both need to be constrained. (Yes, you can have more than one generic parameter — think of Dictionary<TKey, TValue>.) Here's how to use two where clauses:

```
class MyClass<T, U> : where T: IPrioritizable, where U: new()
```

You see two where clauses, separated by a comma. The first constrains T to any object that implements the IPrioritizable interface. The second constrains U to any object that has a default (parameterless) constructor.

Determining the null value for type T: Default(T)

In case you read the last paragraph in the previous section and are confused, well, each type has (as mentioned earlier) a default value that signifies "nothing" for that type. For ints, doubles, and other types of numbers, it's 0 (or 0.0). For bool, it's false. And, for all reference types, such as Package, it's null. As with all reference types, the default for string is null.

But because a generic class such as PriorityQueue can be instantiated for almost any data type, C# can't predict the proper null value to use in the generic class's code. For example, if you use the Dequeue() method of PriorityQueue, you may face this situation: You call Dequeue() to get a package, but none is available. What do you return to signify "nothing"? Because Package is a class type, it should return null. That signals the caller of Dequeue() that there was nothing to return (and the caller must check for a null return value).

The compiler can't make sense of the null keyword in a generic class because the class may be instantiated for all sorts of data types. That's why Dequeue() uses this line instead:

```
return default(T);  // Return the right null for whatever T is.
```

This line tells the compiler to look at T and return the right kind of null value for that type. In the case of Package, which as a class is a reference type, the right null to return is, well, null. But, for some other T, it may be different and the compiler can figure out what to use.

If you think PriorityQueue is flexible, take a look at an even more flexible version of it — and encounter some object-oriented design principles — in the ProgrammingToAnInterface program, available with this chapter.

Chapter 9: Some Exceptional Exceptions

In This Chapter

- Handling errors via return codes
- Using the exception mechanism instead of return codes
- Plotting your exception-handling strategy

I know it's difficult to accept, but occasionally a method doesn't do what it's supposed to do. Even the ones I write — especially the ones I write — don't always do what they're supposed to. Users are notoriously unreliable as well. No sooner do you ask for an `int` than a user inputs a `double`. Sometimes, the method goes merrily along, blissfully ignorant that it is spewing out garbage. However, good programmers write their methods to anticipate problems and report them as they occur.

I'm talking about runtime errors, not compile-time errors, which C# spits out when you try to build your program. *Runtime errors* occur when the program is running, not at compile time.

The C# *exception mechanism* is a means for reporting these errors in a way that the calling method can best understand and use to handle the problem. This mechanism has a lot of advantages over the ways that programmers handled errors in the, uh, good old days. Let's revisit yesteryear so that you can see.

This chapter walks you through the fundamentals of exception handling. You have a lot to digest here, so lean back in your old, beat-up recliner.

Using an Exceptional Error-Reporting Mechanism

C# introduces a completely different mechanism for capturing and handling errors: the *exception*. This mechanism is based on the keywords `try`, `catch`, `throw`, and `finally`. In outline form, it works like this: A method will `try` to execute a piece of code. If the code detects a problem, it will `throw` an error indication, which your code can `catch`, and no matter what happens, it `finally` executes a special block of code at the end, as shown in this snippet:

```
public class MyClass
{
  public void SomeMethod()
  {
    // Set up to catch an error.
    try
    {
      // Call a method or do something that could throw an exception.
      SomeOtherMethod();
      // . . . make whatever other calls you want . . .
    }
    catch(Exception e)
    {
      // Control passes here in the event of an error anywhere
      // within the try block.
      // The Exception object e describes the error in detail.
    }
    finally
    {
      // Clean up here: close files, release resources, etc.
      // This block runs even if an exception was caught.
    }
  }
  public void SomeOtherMethod()
  {
     // . . . error occurs somewhere within this method . . .
     // . . . and the exception bubbles up the call chain.
     throw new Exception("Description of error");
     // . . . method continues if throw didn't happen . . .
  }
}
```

The combination of `try`, `catch`, and (possibly) `finally` is an *exception handler.*

The `SomeMethod()` method surrounds a section of code in a block labeled with the keyword `try`. Any method called within that block (or any method that it calls or on up the tree . . .) is considered to be within the `try` block. If you have a `try` block, you must have either a `catch` block or a `finally` block, or both.

A variable declared inside a `try`, `catch`, or `finally` block isn't accessible from outside the block. If you need access, declare the variable outside, before the block:

```
int aVariable;  // Declare aVariable outside the block.
try
{
  aVariable = 1;
  // Declare aString inside the block.
  string aString = aVariable.ToString(); // Use aVariable in block.
}
// aVariable is visible here; aString is not.
```

About try blocks

Think of using the try block as putting the C# runtime on alert. If an exception pops up while executing any code within this block, hang a lantern in the old church tower (one if by land, two if by sea — or, call 911).

Then, if any line of code in the try block throws an exception — or if any method called within that method throws an exception, or any method called by those methods does, and so on — try to catch it.

Potentially, a try block may "cover" a lot of code, including all methods called by its contents. Exceptions can percolate up (sometimes a *long* way) from the depths of the execution tree. I show you examples.

About catch blocks

A try block is usually followed immediately by the keyword catch, which is followed by the catch keyword's block. Control passes to the catch block in the event of an error anywhere within the try block. The argument to the catch block is an object of class Exception or, more likely, a subclass of Exception.

If your catch doesn't need to access any information from the exception object it catches, you can specify only the exception type:

```
catch(SomeException)  // No object specified here (no "Exception e")
{
  // Do something that doesn't require access to exception object.
}
```

However, a catch block doesn't have to have arguments: A bare catch catches any exception, equivalent to catch(Exception):

```
catch
{
}
```

I have a lot more to say about what goes inside catch blocks in two articles on csharp102.info: "Creating your own exception class" and "Responding to exceptions."

Unlike a C++ exception, in which the object in the catch argument can be any arbitrary object, a C# exception requires that the catch argument be a class that derives from Exception. (The Exception class and its numerous predefined subclasses are defined in the System namespace. Book II, Chapter 10 covers namespaces.)

About finally blocks

A `finally` block, if you supply one, runs regardless of whether the `try` block throws an exception. The `finally` block is called after a successful `try` or after a `catch`. You can use `finally` even if you don't have a `catch`. Use the `finally` block to clean up before moving on so that files aren't left open. Examples appear in the two exception-related articles on `csharp102.info`.

A common use of `finally` is to clean up after the code in the `try` block, whether an exception occurs or not. So you often see code that looks like this:

```
try
{
  ...
}
finally
{
  // Clean up code, such as close a file opened in the try block.
}
```

In fact, you should use `finally` blocks liberally — only one per `try`.

A method can have multiple `try/catch` handlers. You can even nest a `try/catch` inside a `try`, a `try/catch` inside a `catch`, or a `try/catch` inside a `finally` — or all of the above. (And you can substitute `try/finally` for all of the above.) See the discussion of the `using` clause in Book II.

What happens when an exception is thrown

When an exception occurs, a variation of this sequence of events takes place:

1. **An exception is thrown.** Somewhere deep in the bowels of `SomeOtherMethod()`, an error occurs. Always at the ready, the method reports a runtime error with the `throw` of an `Exception` object back to the first block that knows enough to `catch` and "handle" it.

   Note that because an exception is a *runtime error,* not a compile error, it occurs as the program executes. So an error can occur after you release your masterpiece to the public. Oops!

2. **C# "unwinds the call stack," looking for a `catch` block.** The exception works its way back to the calling method, and then to the method that called that method, and so on, even all the way to the top of the program in `Main()` if no `catch` block is found to handle the exception. (We say more about unwinding the call stack, or *call chain,* in an article on `csharp102.info`. The article, which describes responding to an exception, explores your options.)

   Figure 9-1 shows the path that's followed as C# searches for an exception handler.

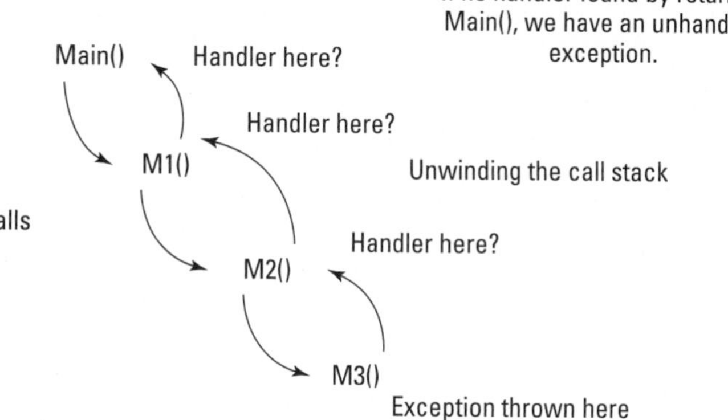

Figure 9-1: Where, oh where, can a handler be found?

3. **If an appropriate `catch` block is found, it executes.** An *appropriate* `catch` block is one that's looking for the right exception class (or any of its base classes). This `catch` block might do any of a number of things, which we cover in an article on `csharp102.info`. As the stack unwinds, if a given method doesn't have enough context — that is, doesn't know enough — to correct the exceptional condition, it simply doesn't provide a `catch` block for that exception. The right `catch` may be high up the stack.

The exception mechanism beats the old-fashioned error-return mechanism described at the beginning of this chapter all hollow, for these reasons:

- When the calling method gets an old-style return value and can't do anything useful, it must explicitly return the error itself to *its* caller, and so on. If the method that can handle the problem is far up the call chain, then returning a return that returned a return that . . . grows awkward, leading to some ugly design kludge. (*Kludge* is an engineer's term for something that works but is lame and ugly. Think "spit and baling wire.")
- With exceptions, in contrast, the exception automatically climbs the call chain until it runs into an exception handler. You don't have to keep forwarding the message, which eliminates a lot of kludgy code.

4. **If a `finally` block accompanies the `try` block, it executes,** whether an exception was caught or not. The `finally` is called before the stack unwinds to the next-higher method in the call chain. *All* `finally` blocks anywhere up the call chain also execute.
5. **If no `catch` block is found anywhere, the program crashes.** If C# gets to `Main()` and doesn't find a `catch` block there, the user sees an "unhandled exception" message and the program exits. This is a *crash.* However, you can deal with exceptions not caught elsewhere by using an exception handler in `Main()`. See the section "Grabbing Your Last Chance to Catch an Exception," later in this chapter.

This exception mechanism is undoubtedly more complex and difficult to handle than using error codes. You have to balance the increased difficulty against these considerations, as shown in Figure 9-1:

- Exceptions provide a more "expressive" model — one that lets you express a wide variety of error-handling strategies.
- An exception object carries far more information with it, thus aiding in debugging — far more than error codes ever could.
- Exceptions lead to more readable code — and less code.
- Exceptions are an integral part of C# rather than an ad hoc, tacked-on afterthought such as error-code schemes, no two of which are much alike. A consistent model promotes understanding.

Throwing Exceptions Yourself

If classes in the .NET class library can throw exceptions, so can you.

To throw an exception when you detect an error worthy of an exception, use the `throw` keyword:

```
throw new ArgumentException("Don't argue with me!");
```

You have as much right to throw things as anybody. Because the .NET class library has no awareness of your custom `BadHairDayException`, who will throw it but you?

If one of the .NET predefined exceptions fits your situation, throw it. But if none fits, you can invent your own custom exception class.

.NET has some exception types that you should never throw or catch: `StackOverflowException`, `OutOfMemoryException`, `Execution EngineException`, and a few more advanced items related to working with non-.NET code. The system owns them.

Knowing What Exceptions Are For

Software that can't complete what it set out to do should throw exceptions. If a method is supposed to process all of an array, for example, or read all of a file — and for some reason can't complete the job — it should throw an appropriate exception.

A method can fail at its task for various reasons: bad input values or unexpected conditions (such as a missing or smaller than expected file), for example. The task is incomplete or can't even be undertaken. If any of these conditions occurs in your methods, you should throw an exception.

The overall point here is that whoever called the method needs to know that its task wasn't completed. Throwing an exception is almost always better than using any error-return code.

What the caller does with the exception depends on the nature and severity of the problem. Some problems are worse than others. We use the rest of this chapter — plus the article "Responding to an exception" on `csharp102.info` — to explore the caller's options when your method "throws."

Can I Get an Exceptional Example?

The following `FactorialException` program demonstrates the key elements of the exception mechanism:

```
    // FactorialException -- Create a factorial program that reports illegal
//    Factorial() arguments using an Exception.
using System;

namespace FactorialException
{
  // MyMathFunctions -- A collection of mathematical functions
  //    we created (it's not much to look at yet)
  public class MyMathFunctions
  {
    // Factorial -- Return the factorial of the provided value.
    public static int Factorial(int value)
    {
      // Don't allow negative numbers.
      if (value < 0)
      {
        // Report negative argument.
        string s = String.Format(
             "Illegal negative argument to Factorial {0}", value);

        throw new ArgumentException(s);
      }

      // Begin with an "accumulator" of 1.
      int factorial = 1;

      // Loop from value down to 1, each time multiplying
      // the previous accumulator value by the result.
      do
      {
        factorial *= value;
      } while(--value > 1);

      // Return the accumulated value.
      return factorial;
    }
  }

  public class Program
  {
    public static void Main(string[] args)
    {
```

```
      // Here's the exception handler.
      try
      {
        // Call factorial in a loop from 6 down to -6.
        for (int i = 6; i > -6; i--)
        {
          // Calculate the factorial of the number.
          int factorial = MyMathFunctions.Factorial(i);

          // Display the result of each pass.
          Console.WriteLine("i = {0}, factorial = {1}",
                            i, factorial);
        }
      }
      catch(ArgumentException e)
      {
        // This is a "last-chance" exception handler -- the buck stops at Main().
        // Probably all you can do here is alert the user before quitting.
        Console.WriteLine("Fatal error:");
        // When you're ready to release the program, change this
        // output to something in plain English, preferably with guide-
        // lines for what to do about the problem.
        Console.WriteLine(e.ToString());
      }

      // Wait for user to acknowledge.
      Console.WriteLine("Press Enter to terminate...");
      Console.Read();
    }
  }
}
```

This "exceptional" version of `Main()` wraps almost its entire contents in a `try` block. The `catch` block at the end of `Main()` catches the `ArgumentException` object and uses its `ToString()` method to display most of the error information contained within the `exception` object in a single `string`.

I chose to use `ArgumentException` here because it most accurately describes the problem: an unacceptable argument to `Factorial()`.

Knowing what makes the example exceptional

The version of the `Factorial()` method in the preceding section includes the same check for a negative argument as the previous version. (The test for an integer is no longer relevant because we changed the `Factorial()` parameter and return types to `int`.) If its argument is negative, `Factorial()` can't continue, so it formats an error message that describes the problem, including the value it found to be offensive. `Factorial()` then bundles this information into a newly created `ArgumentException` object, which it throws back to the calling method.

I recommend running the program in the debugger to watch the exception occur in real time. (I tell you more about the debugger in Book IV.)

The output from this program appears as follows (we trimmed the error messages to make them more readable):

```
i = 6, factorial = 720
i = 5, factorial = 120
i = 4, factorial = 24
i = 3, factorial = 6
i = 2, factorial = 2
i = 1, factorial = 1
i = 0, factorial = 0
Fatal error:
System.ArgumentException: Illegal negative argument to Factorial -1
   at Factorial(Int32 value) in c:\c#programs\Factorial\Program.cs:line 21
   at FactorialException.Program.Main(String[] args) in c:\c#programs\Factorial\
     Program.cs:line 49
Press Enter to terminate...
```

The first few lines display the actual factorial of the numbers 6 through 0. Attempting to calculate the factorial of –1 generates the message starting with `Fatal error` — that doesn't sound good.

The first line in the error message was formatted back in `Factorial()` itself. This line describes the nature of the problem, including the offending value of –1.

Tracing the stack

The remainder of the output is a *stack trace.* The first line of the stack trace describes where the exception was thrown. In this case, the exception was thrown in `Factorial(int)` — more specifically, Line 21 within the source file `Program.cs`. `Factorial()` was invoked in the method `Main(string[])` on Line 50 within the same file. The stack trace stops with `Main()` because that's the module in which the exception was caught — end of stack trace.

You have to admit that this process is impressive — the message describes the problem and identifies the offending argument. The stack trace tells you where the exception was thrown and how the program got there. Using that information, you should be drawn to the problem like a tornado to a trailer park.

If you run the previous example and examine the stack trace it prints to the console, you see `Main()` at the *bottom* of the listing and deeper methods above it. The trace builds upward from `Main()`, so, technically, unwinding the call stack goes *down* the trace toward `Main()`. You should think of it the other way around, though: Callers are higher in the call chain (refer to Figure 9-1).

Returning geeky information such as the stack trace works just fine during development, but you would probably want real users to see more intelligible information. Still, you may want to write the stack trace to a log file somewhere.

The versions of `Factorial()` that I describe earlier in this chapter use a *nonrecursive* algorithm, which uses a loop to calculate the factorial. For a recursive version, see the `RecursiveFactorial` example on the Web. A *recursive* method *calls itself*, possibly repeatedly until a *stopping condition* occurs. The recursive `Factorial()` calls itself repeatedly (recurses), stopping when the value that's passed in becomes negative. Recursion is the most common way to implement `Factorial()`. **Caution:** Make sure that the recursion will stop. You can compare the results of `RecursiveFactorial` with those of the less exotic `NonrecursiveFactorial` example, and the `DeadlyRecursion` example shows what happens if the recursion doesn't stop — it results in quite an unpleasant `StackOverflowException`.

While the program is running in the debugger, the stack trace is available in one of the Visual Studio debugger windows.

Assigning Multiple catch Blocks

I mention earlier in this chapter that you can define your own custom exception types. Suppose that you defined a `CustomException` class. (I describe this process in the article "Creating Your Own Exception Class," which you can find on `csharp102.info`.) Now consider the `catch` clause used here:

```
public void SomeMethod()
{
  try
  {
    SomeOtherMethod();
  }
  catch(CustomException ce)
  {
  }
}
```

What if `SomeOtherMethod()` had thrown a simple `Exception` or another non-`CustomException` type of exception? It would be like trying to catch a football with a baseball glove — the catch doesn't match the throw.

Fortunately, C# enables the program to define numerous `catch` clauses, each designed for a different type of exception. Assuming that this is the right place to handle the other exceptions, you can tack on one after another.

Don't be alarmed by my use of the word *numerous*. In practice, you don't use many `catch` blocks in one place.

Multiple `catch` clauses for different exception types must be lined up nose to tail after the `try` block. C# checks each `catch` block sequentially, comparing the object thrown with the `catch` clause's argument type, as shown in this chunk of code:

```
public void SomeMethod()
{
  try
  {
    SomeOtherMethod();
  }
  catch(CustomException ce)  // Most specific exception type
  {
    // All CustomException objects are caught here.
  } // You could insert other exception types between these two.
  catch(Exception e)         // Most general exception type
  {
    // All otherwise uncaught exceptions are caught here.
    // Not that you should always do so -- but when it makes sense ...
  }
}
```

Were `SomeOtherMethod()` to throw an `Exception` object, it would pass over the `catch(CustomException)` because an `Exception` isn't a type of `CustomException`. It would be caught by the next `catch` clause: the `catch(Exception)`.

Always line up the `catch` clauses from most specific to most general. Never place the more general `catch` clause first, as in this fairly awful bit of code:

```
public void SomeMethod()
{
  try
  {
    SomeOtherMethod();
  }
  catch(Exception e)    // Most general first -- not good!
  {
    // All exceptions are caught here.
    // The dingo ate everything.
  }
  catch(CustomException ce)
  {
    // No exception ever gets this far, because it's
    // caught and consumed by the more general catch clause.
  }
}
```

The more general `catch` clause starves the `catch` clause that follows by intercepting any `throw`. The compiler alerts you to this error.

Any class that inherits `CustomException` IS_A `CustomException`:

```
class MySpecialException : CustomException
{
  // . . . whatever .. .
}
```

Given the chance, a `CustomException catch` grabs a `MySpecial Exception` object like a frog nabs flies.

Planning Your Exception-Handling Strategy

It makes sense to have a plan for how your program will deal with errors. Choosing to use exceptions instead of error codes is just one choice to make.

Due to space limitations, we can't fully explore all the options you have in responding to exceptions. This overview — a set of guidelines and some crucial techniques — should get you well oriented. Refer to the article on `csharp102.info` to dig much deeper into the basic question "What can I do when code throws an exception?"

Some questions to guide your planning

Several questions should be on your mind as you develop your program:

- **What could go wrong?** Ask this question about each bit of code you write.
- **If it does go wrong, can I fix it?** If so, you may be able to recover from the problem, and the program may be able to continue. If not, you probably need to pack your bags and get out of town.
- **Does the problem put user data at risk?** If so, you must do everything in your power to keep from losing or damaging that data. Knowingly releasing code that can mangle user data is akin to software malpractice.
- **Where should I put my exception handler for this problem?** Trying to handle an exception in the method where it occurs may not be the best approach. Often, another method higher up in the chain of method calls has better information and may be able to do something more intelligent and useful with the exception. Put your `try/catch` there so that the `try` block surrounds the call that leads to the place where the exception can occur.
- **Which exceptions should I handle?** Catch any exception that you can recover from somehow. Try hard to find a way to recover, as discussed in the article "Responding to an Exception" on `csharp102.info`. Then, during development and testing, the unhandled exceptions will reach the top of your program. Before you release the program to real users, fix the underlying causes of any exceptions that go unhandled — if you can. But sometimes an exception *should* require terminating the program prematurely because things are hopelessly fouled up.
- **What about exceptions that slip through the cracks and elude my handlers?** The section "Grabbing Your Last Chance to Catch an Exception," later in this chapter, describes providing a "last-chance" exception handler to catch strays.
- **How robust (unbreakable) does my code need to be?** If your code operates an air-traffic control system, it should be robust indeed. If it's just a little one-off utility, you can relax a bit.

Guidelines for code that handles errors well

You should keep the questions in the previous section in mind as you work. These guidelines may help too:

- **Protect the user's data at all costs.** This is the Top Dog guideline. See the "For More Information" sidebar at the end of this chapter Also see the next bullet item.
- **Don't crash.** Recover if you can, but be prepared to go down as gracefully as possible. Don't let your program just squeak out a cryptic, geeky message and go belly up. *Gracefully* means that you provide clear messages containing as much helpful information as possible before shutting down. Users truly hate crashes. But you probably knew that.
- **Don't let your program continue running if you can't recover from a problem.** The program could be unstable or the user's data left in an inconsistent state. When all is most certainly lost, you can display a message and call `System.Environment.FailFast()` to terminate the program immediately rather than throw an exception. It isn't a crash — it's deliberate.
- **Treat class libraries differently from applications.** In *class libraries*, let exceptions reach the caller, who is best equipped to decide how to deal with the problem. Don't keep the caller in the dark about problems. But in *applications*, handle any exceptions you can. Your goal is to keep the code running if possible and protect the user's data without putting a lot of inconsequential messages in her face.
- **Throw exceptions when, for any reason, a method can't complete its task.** The caller needs to know about the problem. (The caller may be a method higher up the call stack in your code or a method in code by another developer using your code). If you check input values for validity before using them and they aren't valid — such as an unexpected `null` value — fix them and continue if you can. Otherwise, throw an exception.

  This advice is contrary to statements you may see elsewhere, but it comes from Jeffrey Richter, one of the foremost experts on .NET and C# programming. Often you hear statements such as "Exceptions are for unexpected situations only — don't use them for problems that are likely to occur in the normal course of operations." That's not accurate. An exception is the .NET way to deal with most types of errors. You can sometimes use an error code or another approach — such as having a collection method return –1 for "item not found" — but not often. Heed the previous paragraph.

  Try to write code that doesn't need to throw exceptions — and correct bugs when you find them — rather than rely on exceptions to patch it up. But use exceptions as your main method of reporting and handling errors.

- **In most cases, don't catch exceptions in a particular method unless you can handle them in a useful way, preferably by recovering from the error.** Catching an exception that you can't handle is like catching a wasp in your bare hand. Now what? Most methods don't contain exception handlers.
- **Test your code thoroughly**, especially for any category of bad input you can think of. Can your method handle negative input? Zero? A very large value? An empty string? A `null` value? What could the user do to cause an exception? What fallible resources, such as files, databases, or URLs, does your code use? See the two previous bullet paragraphs.

  Find out how to write unit tests for your code. It's reasonably easy and lots of fun.
- **Catch the most specific exception you can.** Don't write many `catch` blocks for high-level exception classes such as `Exception` or `ApplicationException`. You risk starving handlers higher up the chain.
- **Always put a last-chance exception handler block in** `Main()` — or wherever the "top" of your program is (except in reusable class libraries). You can catch type `Exception` in this block. Catch and handle the ones you can and let the last-chance exception handler pick up any stragglers. (We explain last-chance handlers in the later section "Grabbing Your Last Chance to Catch an Exception.")
- **Don't use exceptions as part of the normal flow of execution.** For example, don't throw an exception as a way to get out of a loop or exit a method.
- **Consider writing your own custom exception classes** if they bring something to the table — such as more information to help in debugging or more meaningful error messages for users. We introduce custom exceptions in an article on `csharp102.info`.

The rest of this chapter (along with the articles on `csharp102.info`) gives you the tools needed to follow those guidelines. For more information, look up *exception handling, design guidelines* in the Help system, but be prepared for some technical reading.

If a public method throws any exceptions that the caller may need to catch, those exceptions are part of your class's public interface. You need to document them, preferably with the XML documentation comments discussed in Book IV.

How to analyze a method for possible exceptions

In the following method, which is Step 1 in setting up exception handlers, consider which exceptions it can throw:

```
public string FixNamespaceLine(string line)
{
  const string COMPANY_PREFIX = "CMSCo";
  int spaceIndex = line.IndexOf(' ');
  int nameStart = GetNameStartAfterNamespaceKeyword(line, spaceIndex);
  string newline = string.Empty;
  newline = PlugInNamespaceCompanyQualifier(line, COMPANY_PREFIX, nameStart);
  return newline.Trim();
}
```

Given a C# file, this method is part of some code intended to find the `namespace` keyword in the file and insert a string representing a company name (one of ours) as a prefix on the namespace name. (See Book II, Chapter 10 for information about namespaces.) The following example illustrates where the `namespace` keyword is likely to be found in a C# file:

```
using System;
namespace SomeName
{
  // Code within the namespace . . .
}
```

The result of running the `FixNamespaceLine()` method on this type of file should convert the first line into the second:

```
namespace SomeName
namespace CmsCo.SomeName
```

The overall program reads .CS files. Then it steps through the lines one by one, feeding each one to the `FixNamespaceLine()` method. Given a line of code, the method calls `String.IndexOf()` to find the index of the namespace name (normally, 10). Then it calls `GetNameStartAfterNamespaceKeyword()` to locate the beginning of the namespace name. Finally, it calls another method, `PlugInNamespaceCompanyQualifier()` to plug the company name into the correct spot in the line, which it then returns. Much of the work is done by the subordinate methods.

First, even without knowing what this code is for or what the two called methods do, consider the input. The `line` argument could have at least one problem for the call to `String.IndexOf()`. If `line` is `null`, the `IndexOf()` call results in an `ArgumentNullException`. You can't call a method on a `null` object. Also, at first blush, will calling `IndexOf()` on an empty string work? It turns out that it will, so no exception occurs there, but what happens if you pass an empty `line` to one of those methods with the long names? We recommend adding, if warranted, a guard clause before the first line of code in `FixNamespaceLine()` — and at least checking for `null`:

```
if(String.IsNullOrEmpty(name))  // A handy string method
{
  return name; // You can get away with a reasonable return value here
               // instead of throwing an exception.
}
```

Second, after you're safely past the `IndexOf()` call, one of the two method calls can throw an exception, even with `line` carefully checked out first. If `spaceIndex` turns out to be –1 (not found) — as can happen because the line that's passed in doesn't usually contain a `namespace` keyword — passing it to the first method can be a problem. You can guard for that outcome, of course, like this:

```
if(spaceIndex > -1) ...
```

If `spaceIndex` is negative, the line doesn't contain the `namespace` keyword. *That's not an error.* You just skip that line by returning the original line and then move on to the next line. In any event, don't call the subordinate methods.

Method calls in your method require exploring each one to see which exceptions it can throw and then digging into any methods that those methods call, and so on, until you reach the bottom of this particular call chain.

With this possibility in mind, and given that `FixNamespaceLine()` needs additional bulletproofing guard clauses first, where might you put an exception handler?

You may be tempted to put most of `FixNamespaceLine()` in a `try` block. But you have to consider whether this the best place for it. This method is low-level, so it should just throw exceptions as needed — or just pass on any exceptions that occur in the methods it calls. We recommend looking up the call chain to see which method might be a good location for a handler.

As you move up the call chain, ask yourself the questions in the earlier section "Some questions to guide your planning." What would be the consequences if `FixNamespaceLine()` threw an exception? That depends on how its result is used higher up the chain. Also, how dire would the results need to be? If you can't "fix" the namespace line for the current file, does the user lose anything major? Maybe you can get away with an occasional unfixed file, in which case you might choose to "swallow" the exception at some level in the call chain and just notify the user of the unprocessed file. Or maybe not. You get the idea. We discuss these and other exception-handling options in the article "Responding to an Exception" on `csharp102.info`.

The moral is that correctly setting up exception handlers requires some analysis and thought.

However, keep in mind that *any* method call can throw exceptions — for example, the application *could* run out of memory, or the assembly it's in might not be found and loaded. You can't do much about that.

How to find out which methods throw which exceptions

To find out whether calling a particular method in the .NET class libraries, such as `String.IndexOf()` — or even one of your own methods — can throw an exception, consider these guidelines:

✦ **Visual Studio provides immediate help with tooltips.** When you hover the mouse pointer over a method name in the Visual Studio editor, a yellow tooltip window lists not only the method's parameters and return type but also the exceptions it can throw.

✦ **If you have used XML comments to comment your own methods**, Visual Studio shows the information in those comments in its IntelliSense tool tips just as it does for .NET methods. If you documented the exceptions your method can throw (see the previous section), you see them in a tooltip. The article "Getting Help in Visual Studio" on `csharp102.info` shows how to use XML comments, and the `FactorialException` example illustrates documenting `Factorial()` with XML comments. Plug in the `<exception>` line inside your `<summary>` comment to make it show in the tooltip.

✦ **The Help files provide even more.** When you look up a .NET method in Help, you find a list of exceptions that the method can throw, along with additional descriptions not provided via the yellow Visual Studio tooltip. To open the Help page for a given method, click the method name in your code and press F1. You can also supply similar help for your own classes and methods.

You should look at each of the exceptions you see listed, decide how likely it is to occur, and (if warranted for your program) guard against it using the techniques covered in the rest of this chapter.

Grabbing Your Last Chance to Catch an Exception

The `FactorialException` example in the earlier section "Can I Get an Exceptional Example?" wraps all of `Main()`, except for the final console calls, in an outer, "last-chance" exception handler.

If you're writing an application, always sandwich the contents of `Main()` in a `try` block because `Main()` is the starting point for the program and thus the ending point as well. (If you're writing a class library intended for reuse, don't worry about unhandled exceptions — whoever is using your library needs to know about all exceptions, so let them bubble up through your methods.)

Any exception not caught somewhere else percolates up to `Main()`. This is your last opportunity to grab the error before it ends up back in Windows, where the error message is much harder to interpret and may frustrate — or scare the bejabbers out of — the program's user.

All the serious code in `FactorialException`'s `Main()` is inside a `try` block. The associated `catch` block catches any exception whatsoever and outputs a message to the console, and the application exits.

This `catch` block serves to prevent hard crashes by intercepting all exceptions not handled elsewhere. And it's your chance to explain why the application is quitting.

Experiment. To see why you need this last-chance handler, deliberately throw an exception in a little program without handling it. You see what the user would see without your efforts to make the landing a bit softer.

During development, you *want* to see exceptions that occur as you test the code, in their natural habitat — so you want all of the geekspeak. In the version you release, convert the programmerish details to normal English, display the message to the user, including, if possible, what he might do to run successfully next time, and exit stage right. Make this plain-English version of the exception handler one of the last chores you complete before you release your program into the wild.

Your last-chance handler should certainly log the exception information somehow, for later forensic analysis.

For more information

We want to be able to say that we tell you the whole story on exceptions. We want that very much. But we don't, and it's a fairly long story.

To track down the rest of the story, we recommend that you adjourn to the Web site `csharp102.info`, where you can find articles on these topics:

- **Creating your own exception class:** The .NET Framework class library developers aren't the only ones who can extend class `Exception` with new exception subclasses. You can extend `Exception` yourself. For the whats and whys and hows, see the article "Creating Your Own Exception Class" on this book's site.
- **Responding to an exception — what you can do when code throws exceptions:** Your options are to fix the problem and try again, partially fix the problem and hand it off to a higher-level exception handler that may be able to fix the rest, convert the exception into a different exception type, or just do nothing. The article "Responding to an Exception" on this book's site explores the options by using several examples.

Book II

Object-Oriented C# Programming

"Well, here's your problem. You're running applications written in C# on a B♭ server."

Contents at a Glance

Chapter 1: Object-Oriented Programming: What's It All About?

In This Chapter

- **Reviewing the basics of object-oriented programming**
- **Getting a handle on abstraction and classification**
- **Understanding why object-oriented programming is important**

This chapter answers the two-pronged musical question: "What are the concepts behind object-oriented programming, and how do they differ from the procedural concepts covered in Book I?"

Object-Oriented Concept #1: Abstraction

Sometimes, when my son and I are watching football, I whip up a terribly unhealthy batch of nachos. I dump chips on a plate, throw on some beans and cheese and lots of jalapeños, and nuke the whole mess in the microwave oven for a few minutes.

To use my microwave, I open the door, throw in the plate of food, and punch a few buttons on the front. After a few minutes, the nachos are done. (I try not to stand in front of the microwave while it's working, lest my eyes start glowing in the dark.)

Now think for a minute about all the things I *don't* do in order to use my microwave. I don't

- Rewire or change anything inside the microwave to get it to work. The microwave has an interface — the front panel with all the buttons and the little time display — that lets me do everything I need.
- Reprogram the software used to drive the little processor inside the microwave, even if I cooked a different dish the last time I used the microwave.
- Look inside the microwave's case.

Even if I were a microwave designer and knew all about the inner workings of a microwave, including its software, I still wouldn't think about all those concepts while using it to heat nachos.

These observations aren't profound: You can deal with only so much stress in your life. To reduce the number of issues you deal with, you work at a certain level of detail. In object-oriented (OO) computerese, the level of detail at which you're working is the *level of abstraction.* To introduce another OO term while I have the chance, I *abstract away* the details of the microwave's innards.

Happily, computer scientists — and thousands of geeks — have invented object orientation and numerous other concepts that reduce the level of complexity at which programmers have to work. Using powerful abstractions makes the job simpler and far less error-prone than it used to be. In a sense, that's what the past half-century or so of computing progress has been about: managing ever more complex concepts and structures with ever fewer errors.

When I'm working on nachos, I view my microwave oven as a box. (While I'm trying to knock out a snack, I can't worry about the innards of the microwave oven and still follow the Dallas Cowboys on the tube.) As long as I use the microwave only by way of its interface (the keypad), nothing I can do should cause the microwave to enter an inconsistent state and crash or, worse, turn my nachos — or my house — into a blackened, flaming mass.

Preparing procedural nachos

Suppose that I ask my son to write an algorithm for how to make nachos. After he understands what I want, he can write, "Open a can of beans, grate some cheese, cut the jalapeños," and so on. When he reaches the part about microwaving the concoction, he might write (on a good day) something like this: "Cook in the microwave for five minutes."

That description is straightforward and complete. But it isn't the way a procedural programmer would code a program to make nachos. Procedural programmers live in a world devoid of objects such as microwave ovens and other appliances. They tend to worry about flowcharts with their myriad procedural paths. In a procedural solution to the nachos problem, the flow of control would pass through my finger to the front panel and then to the internals of the microwave. Soon, flow would wiggle through complex logic paths about how long to turn on the microwave tube and whether to sound the "come and get it" tone.

In that world of procedural programming, you can't easily think in terms of levels of abstraction. You have no objects and no abstractions behind which to hide inherent complexity.

Preparing object-oriented nachos

In an object-oriented approach to making nachos, you first identify the types of objects in the problem: chips, beans, cheese, jalapeños, and an oven. Then you begin the task of modeling those objects in software, without regard for the details of how they might be used in the final program. For example, you can model cheese as an object in isolation from the other objects and then combine it with the beans, the chips, the jalapeños, and the oven and make them interact. (And you might decide that some of these objects don't need to be objects in the software: cheese, for instance.)

While you do that, you're said to be working (and thinking) at the level of the basic objects. You need to think about making a useful oven, but you don't have to think about the logical process of making nachos — yet. After all, the microwave designers didn't think about the specific problem of you making a snack. Rather, they set about solving the problem of designing and building a useful microwave.

After you successfully code and test the objects you need, you can ratchet up to the next level of abstraction and start thinking at the nacho-making level rather than at the microwave-making level.

(And, at this point, I can translate my son's instructions directly into C# code.)

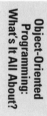

Object-Oriented Concept #2: Classification

Critical to the concept of abstraction is that of classification. If I were to ask my son, "What's a microwave?" he might say, "It's an oven that. . . ." If I then ask, "What's an oven?" he might reply "It's a kitchen appliance that. . . ." If I then ask "What's a kitchen appliance?" he would probably say "Why are you asking so many stupid questions?"

The answers my son might give stems from his understanding of this particular microwave as an example of the type of item known as a microwave oven. In addition, he might see a microwave oven as just a special type of oven, which itself is just a special type of kitchen appliance.

In object-oriented computerese, the microwave is an *instance* of the class `microwave`. The class `microwave` is a *subclass* of the class `oven`, and the class `oven` is a subclass of the class `kitchen appliance`.

Humans classify. Everything about our world is ordered into taxonomies. We do this to reduce the number of items we have to remember. For example, the first time you saw an SUV, the advertisement probably referred to the SUV as "revolutionary, the likes of which have never been seen." But you and I know that it just isn't so. I like the looks of certain SUVs (others need to go back to take another crack at it), but hey, an SUV is a car. As such, it shares all (or at least most of) the properties of other cars. It has a steering wheel, seats, a motor, and brakes, for example. I would bet that I could even drive one without reading the user's manual first.

I don't have to clutter the limited amount of storage space in my head with all the features that an SUV has in common with other cars. All I have to remember is "An SUV is a car that . . ." and tack on those few characteristics that are unique to an SUV (such as the price tag). I can go further. Cars are a subclass of wheeled vehicles along with other members, such as trucks and pickups. Maybe wheeled vehicles are a subclass of vehicles, which include boats and planes — and so on.

Why Classify?

Why should you classify? It sounds like a lot of trouble. Besides, people have been using the procedural approach for a long time — why change now?

Designing and building a microwave oven specifically for this problem may seem easier than building a separate, more generic oven object. Suppose that you want to build a microwave oven to cook only nachos. You wouldn't need to put a front panel on it, other than a Start button. You probably always cook nachos for the same length of time. You could dispense with all that Defrost and Temp Cook nonsense in the options. The oven needs to hold only one flat, little plate. Three cubic feet of space would be wasted on nachos.

For that matter, you can dispense with the concept of "microwave oven." All you need is the guts of the oven. Then, in the recipe, you put the instructions to make it work: "Put nachos in the box. Connect the red wire to the black wire. Bring the radar tube to about 3,000 volts. Notice a slight hum. Try not to stand too close if you intend to have children." Stuff like that.

But the procedural approach has these problems:

- **It's too complex.** You don't want the details of oven-building mixed into the details of nacho-building. If you can't define the objects and pull them from the morass of details to deal with separately, you must deal with all the complexities of the problem at the same time.
- **It isn't flexible.** Someday, you may need to replace the microwave oven with another type of oven. You should be able to do so as long as the two ovens have the same interface. Without being clearly delineated and developed separately, one object type can't be cleanly removed and replaced with another.

✦ **It isn't reusable.** Ovens are used to make lots of different dishes. You don't want to create a new oven every time you encounter a new recipe. Having solved a problem once, you want to be able to reuse the solution in other places within my program. If you're lucky, you may be able to reuse it in future programs as well.

Object-Oriented Concept #3: Usable Interfaces

An object must be able to project an external interface that is sufficient but as simple as possible. This concept is sort of the reverse of Concept #4 (described in the next section). If the device interface is insufficient, users may start ripping the top off the device, in direct violation of the laws of God and society — or at least the liability laws of the Great State of Texas. And believe me, you do not want to violate the laws of the Great State of Texas. On the flip side, if the device interface is too complex, no one will buy the device — or at least no one will use all its features.

People complain continually that their DVD players are too complex, though it's less of a problem with today's onscreen controls. These devices have too many buttons with too many different functions. Often, the same button has different functions, depending on the state of the machine. In addition, no two DVD players seem to have the same interface. For whatever reason, the DVD player projects an interface that's too difficult and too nonstandard for most people to use beyond the bare basics.

Compare the VCR with an automobile. It would be difficult to argue that a car is less complicated than a VCR. However, people don't seem to have much trouble driving cars.

All automobiles offer more or less the same controls in more or less the same place. For example, my sister once had a car (need I say a French car?) that had the headlight control on the left side of the steering wheel, where the turn signal handle normally lives. You pushed down on the light lever to turn off the lights, and you raised the lever to turn them on. This difference may seem trivial, but I never did learn to turn left in that car at night without turning off the lights.

A well-designed auto doesn't use the same control to perform more than one operation, depending on the state of the car. I can think of only one exception to this rule: Some buttons on most cruise controls are overloaded with multiple functions.

Object-Oriented Concept #4: Access Control

A microwave oven must be built so that no combination of keystrokes that you can enter on the front keypad can cause the oven to hurt you. Certainly, some combinations don't do anything. However, no sequence of keystrokes should

- ✦ **Break the device:** You may be able to put the device into a strange state in which it doesn't do anything until you reset it (say, by throwing an internal breaker). However, you shouldn't be able to break the device by using the front panel — unless, of course, you throw it to the ground in frustration. The manufacturer of this type of device would probably have to send out some type of fix for it.
- ✦ **Cause the device to catch fire and burn down the house:** As bad as it may be for the device to break itself, catching fire is much worse. We live in a litigious society. The manufacturer's corporate officers would likely end up in jail, especially if I have anything to say about it.

However, to enforce these two rules, you have to take some responsibility. You can't make modifications to the inside of the device.

Almost all kitchen devices of any complexity, including microwave ovens, have a small seal to keep consumers from reaching inside them. If the seal is broken, indicating that the cover of the device has been removed, the manufacturer no longer bears responsibility. If you modify the internal workings of an oven, you're responsible if it subsequently catches fire and burns down the house.

Similarly, a class must be able to control access to its data members. No sequence of calls to class members should cause your program to crash. The class cannot possibly ensure control of this access if external elements have access to the internal state of the class. The class must be able to keep critical data members inaccessible to the outside world.

How C# Supports Object-Oriented Concepts

Okay, how does C# implement object-oriented programming? In a sense, this is the wrong question. C# is an object-oriented language; however, it doesn't implement object-oriented programming — the programmer does. You can certainly write a non-object-oriented program in C# or any other language (by, for instance, writing all of Microsoft Word in `Main()`). Something like "you can lead a horse to water" comes to mind. But you can easily write an object-oriented program in C#.

These C# features are necessary for writing object-oriented programs:

- **Controlled access:** C# controls the way in which class members can be accessed. C# keywords enable you to declare some members wide open to the `public` whereas `internal` members are `protected` from view and some secrets are kept `private`. Notice the little hints. Access control secrets are revealed in Chapter 5 of this minibook.
- **Specialization:** C# supports specialization through a mechanism known as *class inheritance*. One class inherits the members of another class. For example, you can create a `Car` class as a particular type of `Vehicle`. Chapter 6 in this minibook specializes in specialization.
- **Polymorphism:** This feature enables an object to perform an operation the way it wants to. The `Rocket` type of `Vehicle` may implement the `Start` operation much differently from the way the `Car` type of `Vehicle` does. At least, I hope it does every time I turn the key in my car. (With my car, you never know.) But all `Vehicles` have a Start operation, and you can rely on that. Chapter 7 in this minibook finds its own way of describing polymorphism.
- **Indirection.** Objects frequently use the services of other objects — by calling their public methods. But classes can "know too much" about the classes they use. The two classes are then said to be "too tightly coupled," which makes the using class too dependent on the used class. The design is too brittle — liable to break if you make changes. But change is inevitable in software, so you should find more *indirect* ways to connect the two classes. That's where the C# `interface` construct comes in. (You can get the scoop on interfaces in Chapter 8 of this minibook.)

Chapter 2: Showing Some Class

In This Chapter

- Introducing the C# class
- Storing data in an object
- Assigning and using object references
- Examining classes that contain classes
- Identifying static and instance class members
- Using constants in C#

You can freely declare and use all the intrinsic data types — such as `int`, `double`, and `bool` — to store the information necessary to make your program the best it can be. For some programs, these simple variables are enough. However, most programs need a way to bundle related data into a neat package.

As shown in Book I, C# provides arrays and other collections for gathering into one structure groups of *like-typed* variables, such as `string`s or `int`s. A hypothetical college, for example, might track its students by using an array. But a student is much more than just a name — how should this type of program represent a student?

Some programs need to bundle pieces of data that logically belong together but aren't of the same type. A college enrollment application handles students, each with her own name, rank (grade-point average), and serial number. Logically, the student's name may be a `string`; the grade-point average, a `double`; and the serial number, a `long`. That type of program needs a way to bundle these three different types of variables into a single structure named `Student`. Fortunately, C# provides a structure known as the *class* for accommodating groupings of unlike-typed variables.

Defining a Class and an Object

A *class* is a bundling of unlike data and functions that logically belong together into one tidy package. C# gives you the freedom to foul up your classes any way you want, but good classes are designed to represent *concepts.*

Computer science models the world via structures that represent concepts or things in the world, such as bank accounts, tic-tac-toe games, customers, game boards, documents, and products. Analysts say that "a class maps concepts from the problem into the program." For example, your problem might be to build a traffic simulator that models traffic patterns for the purpose of building streets, intersections, and highways. (I really want you to build traffic simulators that can fix the intersections in front of my house.)

Any description of a problem concerning traffic would include the term *vehicle* in its solution. Vehicles have a top speed that must be figured into the equation. They also have a weight, and some of them are clunkers. In addition, vehicles stop and vehicles go. Thus, as a concept, *vehicle* is part of the problem domain.

A good C# traffic-simulator program would necessarily include the class `Vehicle`, which describes the relevant properties of a vehicle. The C# `Vehicle` class would have properties such as `topSpeed`, `weight`, and `isClunker`.

Because the class is central to C# programming, the rest of Book II spelunks the ins and outs of classes in much more detail. This chapter gets you started.

Defining a class

An example of the class `Vehicle` may appear this way:

```
public class Vehicle
{
  public string model;          // Name of the model
  public string manufacturer;   // Ditto
  public int numOfDoors;        // The number of doors on the vehicle
  public int numOfWheels;       // You get the idea.
}
```

A class definition begins with the words `public class`, followed by the name of the class — in this case, `Vehicle`.

Like all names in C#, the name of the class is case sensitive. C# doesn't enforce any rules concerning class names, but an unofficial rule holds that the name of a class starts with a capital letter.

The class name is followed by a pair of open and closed braces. Within the braces, you have zero or more *members*. The members of a class are variables that make up the parts of the class. In this example, class `Vehicle` starts with the member `string model`, which contains the name of the model of the vehicle. If the vehicle were a car, its model name could be Trooper II. (Have you ever seen or heard of a Trooper I?) The second member of this Vehicle class example is string manufacturer. The other two properties are the number of doors and the number of wheels on the vehicle.

As with any variable, make the names of the members as descriptive as possible. Although I added comments to the data members, it isn't necessary. A good variable name says it all.

The public modifier in front of the class name makes the class universally accessible throughout the program. Similarly, the public modifier in front of the member names makes them accessible to everything else in the program. Other modifiers are possible. (Chapter 10 in this minibook covers the topic of accessibility in more detail and shows how you can hide some members.)

The class definition should describe the properties of the object that are salient to the problem at hand. That's a little hard to do right now because you don't know what the problem is, but you can see where I'm headed.

What's the object?

Defining a Vehicle design isn't the same task as building a car. Someone has to cut some sheet metal and turn some bolts before anyone can drive an actual vehicle. A class object is declared in a similar (but not identical) fashion to declaring an intrinsic object such as an int.

The term *object* is used universally to mean a "thing." Okay, that isn't helpful. An int variable is an int object. A vehicle is a Vehicle object. You are a reader object. I am an author obj — okay, forget that one.

The following code segment creates a car of class Vehicle:

```
Vehicle myCar;
myCar = new Vehicle();
```

The first line declares a variable myCar of type Vehicle, just like you can declare a somethingOrOther of class int. (Yes, a class is a type, and all C# objects are defined as classes.) The new Vehicle() command creates a specific object of type Vehicle and stores the location into the variable myCar. The new has nothing to do with the age of myCar. (My car could qualify for an antique license plate if it weren't so ugly.) The new operator creates a new block of memory in which your program can store the properties of myCar.

In C# terms, you say that myCar is an object of class Vehicle. You also say that myCar is an instance of Vehicle. In this context, *instance* means "an example of" or "one of." You can also use the word *instance* as a verb, as in *instantiating* Vehicle. That's what *new* does.

Compare the declaration of `myCar` with that of an `int` variable named `num`:

```
int num;
num = 1;
```

The first line declares the variable `num`, and the second line assigns an already created constant of type `int` into the location of the variable `num`.

The intrinsic `num` and the object `myCar` are stored differently in memory. The constant `1` doesn't occupy memory because both the CPU and the C# compiler already know what `1` is. Your CPU doesn't have the concept of `Vehicle`. The `new Vehicle` expression allocates the memory necessary to describe a vehicle to the CPU, to C#, to the world, and yes, to the universe!

Accessing the Members of an Object

Each object of class `Vehicle` has its own set of members. The following expression stores the number 1 into the `numberOfDoors` member of the object referenced by `myCar`:

```
myCar.numberOfDoors = 1;
```

Every C# operation must be evaluated by type as well as by value. The object `myCar` is an object of type `Vehicle`. The variable `Vehicle.numberOfDoors` is of type `int`. (Look again at the definition of the `Vehicle` class.) The constant 5 is also of type `int`, so the type of the variable on the right side of the assignment operator matches the type of the variable on the left.

Similarly, the following code stores a reference to the `strings` describing the model and manufacturer name of `myCar`:

```
myCar.manufacturer = "BMW";       // Don't get your hopes up.
myCar.model = "Isetta";            // The Urkel-mobile
```

The Isetta was a small car built during the 1950s with a single door that opened the entire front of the car. I leave *Urkel* to you and your favorite search engine.

An Object-Based Program Example

The simple `VehicleDataOnly` program performs these tasks:

- Define the class `Vehicle`.
- Create an object `myCar`.

- ✦ Assign properties to `myCar`.
- ✦ Retrieve those values from the object for display.

Here's the code for the `VehicleDataOnly` program:

```
// VehicleDataOnly -- Create a Vehicle object, populate its
//    members from the keyboard, and then write it back out.
using System;
namespace VehicleDataOnly
{
  public class Vehicle
  {
    public string model;         // Name of the model
    public string manufacturer;  // Ditto
    public int numOfDoors;       // The number of doors on the vehicle
    public int numOfWheels;      // You get the idea.
  }
  public class Program
  {
    // This is where the program starts.
    static void Main(string[] args)
    {
      // Prompt user to enter her name.
      Console.WriteLine("Enter the properties of your vehicle");
      // Create an instance of Vehicle.
      Vehicle myCar = new Vehicle();
      // Populate a data member via a temporary variable.
      Console.Write("Model name = ");
      string s = Console.ReadLine();
      myCar.model = s;
      // Or you can populate the data member directly.
      Console.Write("Manufacturer name = ");
      myCar.manufacturer = Console.ReadLine();
      // Enter the remainder of the data.
      // A temp is useful for reading ints.
      Console.Write("Number of doors = ");
      s = Console.ReadLine();
      myCar.numOfDoors = Convert.ToInt32(s);
      Console.Write("Number of wheels = ");
      s = Console.ReadLine();
      myCar.numOfWheels = Convert.ToInt32(s);
      // Now display the results.
      Console.WriteLine("\nYour vehicle is a ");
      Console.WriteLine(myCar.manufacturer + " " + myCar.model);
      Console.WriteLine("with " + myCar.numOfDoors + " doors, "
                      + "riding on " + myCar.numOfWheels
                      + " wheels.");
      // Wait for user to acknowledge the results.
      Console.WriteLine("Press Enter to terminate...");
      Console.Read();
    }
  }
}
```

The program listing begins with a definition of the `Vehicle` class.

The definition of a class can appear either before or after class `Program` — it doesn't matter. However, you should, unlike me, adopt a style and stick with it. Book IV, which talks about Visual Studio, shows the more conventional technique of creating a separate `.cs` file to contain each class, but just put the extra class in your `Program.cs` file for now.

The program creates an object `myCar` of class `Vehicle` and then populates each field by reading the appropriate data from the keyboard. (The input data isn't — but should be — checked for legality.) The program then writes `myCar`'s properties in a slightly different format.

The output from executing this program appears this way:

```
Enter the properties of your vehicle
Model name = Metropolitan
Manufacturer name = Nash
Number of doors = 2
Number of wheels = 4

Your vehicle is a
Nash Metropolitan
with 2 doors, riding on 4 wheels
Press Enter to terminate...
```

The calls to `Read()` as opposed to `ReadLine()` leave the cursor directly after the output string, which makes the user's input appear on the same line as the prompt. In addition, inserting the newline character `'\n'` in a write generates a blank line without the need to execute `WriteLine()` separately.

Discriminating between Objects

Detroit car manufacturers can track every car they make without getting the cars confused. Similarly, a program can create numerous objects of the same class, as shown in this example:

```
Vehicle car1 = new Vehicle();
car1.manufacturer = "Studebaker";
car1.model = "Avanti";
// The following has no effect on car1.
Vehicle car2 = new Vehicle();
car2.manufacturer = "Hudson";
car2.model = "Hornet";
```

Creating an object `car2` and assigning it the manufacturer name `Hudson` has no effect on the `car1` object (with the manufacturer name `Studebaker`).

In part, the ability to discriminate between objects is the real power of the class construct. The object associated with the Hudson Hornet can be created, manipulated, and dispensed with as a single entity, separate from other objects, including the Avanti. (Both are classic automobiles, especially the latter.)

Can You Give Me References?

The dot operator and the assignment operator are the only two operators defined on reference types:

```
// Create a null reference.
Vehicle yourCar;
// Assign the reference a value.
yourCar = new Vehicle();
// Use dot to access a member.
yourCar.manufacturer = "Rambler";
// Create a new reference and point it to the same object.
Vehicle yourSpousalCar = yourCar;
```

The first line creates an object `yourCar` without assigning it a value. A reference that hasn't been initialized is said to point to the *null object.* Any attempt to use an uninitialized (null) reference generates an immediate error that terminates the program.

The C# compiler can catch most attempts to use an uninitialized reference and generate a warning at build-time. If you somehow slip one past the compiler, accessing an uninitialized reference terminates the program immediately.

The second statement creates a new `Vehicle` object and assigns it to `yourCar`. The last statement in this code snippet assigns the reference `yourSpousalCar` to the reference `yourCar`. This action causes `yourSpousalCar` to refer to the same object as `yourCar`. This relationship is shown in Figure 2-1.

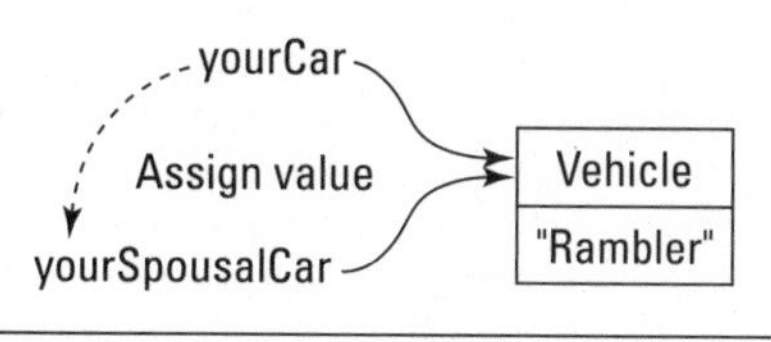

Figure 2-1: Two references to the same object.

The following two calls have the same effect:

```
// Build your car.
Vehicle yourCar = new Vehicle();
yourCar.model = "Kaiser";
// It also belongs to your spouse.
Vehicle yourSpousalCar = yourCar;
// Changing one changes the other.
yourSpousalCar.model = "Henry J";
Console.WriteLine("Your car is a " + yourCar.model);
```

Executing this program would output `Henry J` and not `Kaiser`. Notice that `yourSpousalCar` doesn't point to `yourCar`; rather, both `yourCar` and `yourSpousalCar` refer to the same vehicle.

In addition, the reference `yourSpousalCar` would still be valid, even if the variable `yourCar` were somehow "lost" (if it went out of scope, for example), as shown in this chunk of code:

```
// Build your car.
Vehicle yourCar = new Vehicle();
yourCar.model = "Kaiser";
// It also belongs to your spouse.
Vehicle yourSpousalCar = yourCar;
// When your spouse takes your car away . . .
yourCar = null;           // yourCar now references the "null object."
//  . . .yourSpousalCar still references the same vehicle
Console.WriteLine("your car was a " + yourSpousalCar.model);
```

Executing this program generates the output `Your car was a Kaiser`, even though the reference `yourCar` is no longer valid.

The object is no longer *reachable* from the reference `yourCar`. The object doesn't become completely unreachable until both `yourCar` and `yourSpousalCar` are "lost" or nulled out.

At that point — well, at some unpredictable later point, anyway — the C# *garbage collector* steps in and returns the space formerly used by that particular `Vehicle` object to the pool of space available for allocating more `Vehicles` (or `Students`, for that matter). (I say a little more about garbage collection in a sidebar at the end of Chapter 6 in this minibook.)

Making one *object variable* (a variable of a reference type, such as `Vehicle` or `Student`, rather than one of a simple type such as `int` or `double`) point to a different object — as I did here — makes storing and manipulating reference objects in arrays and collections quite efficient. Each element of the array stores a reference to an object, and when you swap elements within the array, you're just moving references, not the objects themselves. References have a fixed size in memory, unlike the objects they refer to.

Classes That Contain Classes Are the Happiest Classes in the World

The members of a class can themselves be references to other classes. For example, vehicles have motors, which have power and efficiency factors, including displacement. You could throw these factors directly into the class this way:

```
public class Vehicle
{
  public string model;          // Name of the model
  public string manufacturer;   // Ditto
  public int numOfDoors;        // The number of doors on the vehicle
  public int numOfWheels;       // You get the idea.
  // New stuff:
  public int power;             // Power of the motor [horsepower]
  public double displacement;   // Engine displacement [liter]
}
```

However, power and engine displacement aren't properties of the car. For example, your friend's Jeep might be supplied with two different motor options that have drastically different levels of horsepower. The 2.4-liter Jeep is a snail, and the same car outfitted with the 4.0-liter engine is quite peppy.

The motor is a concept of its own and deserves its own class:

```
public class Motor
{
  public int power;             // Power [horsepower]
  public double displacement;   // Engine displacement [liter]
}
```

You can combine this class into the `Vehicle` (see boldfaced text):

```
public class Vehicle
{
  public string model;          // Name of the model
  public string manufacturer;   // Ditto
  public int numOfDoors;        // The number of doors on the vehicle
  public int numOfWheels;       // You get the idea.
  public Motor motor;
}
```

Creating `myCar` now appears this way:

```
// First create a Motor.
Motor largerMotor = new Motor();
largerMotor.power = 230;
largerMotor.displacement = 4.0;
```

```
// Now create the car.
Vehicle friendsCar = new Vehicle();
friendsCar.model = "Cherokee Sport";
friendsCar.manfacturer = "Jeep";
friendsCar.numOfDoors = 2;
friendsCar.numOfWheels = 4;
// Attach the motor to the car.
friendsCar.motor = largerMotor;
```

From `Vehicle`, you can access the motor displacement in two stages. You can take one step at a time, as this bit of code shows:

```
Motor m = friendsCar.motor;
Console.WriteLine("The motor displacement is " + m.displacement);
```

Or, you can access it directly, as shown here:

```
Console.Writeline("The motor displacement is " + friendsCar.motor.displacement);
```

Either way, you can access the `displacement` only through the `Motor`.

ON THE WEB

This example is bundled into the simple program `VehicleAndMotor` on this book's Web site, not shown in full here.

Generating Static in Class Members

Most data members of a class are specific to their containing object, not to any other objects. Consider the `Car` class:

```
public class Car
{
  public string licensePlate;      // The license plate ID
}
```

Because the license plate ID is an *object property,* it describes each object of class `Car` uniquely. For example, thank goodness that my car has a license plate that's different from yours; otherwise, you may not make it out of your driveway, as shown in this bit of code:

```
Car myCar = new Car();
myCar.licensePlate = "XYZ123";

Car yourCar = new Car();
yourCar.licensePlate = "ABC789";
```

However, some properties exist that all cars share. For example, the number of cars built is a property of the class `Car` but not of any single object. These *class properties* are flagged in C# with the keyword `static`:

```
public class Car
{
  public static int numberOfCars; // The number of cars built
  public string licensePlate;     // The license plate ID
}
```

Static members aren't accessed through the object. Instead, you access them by way of the class itself, as this code snippet demonstrates:

```
// Create a new object of class Car.
Car newCar = new Car();
newCar.licensePlate = "ABC123";
// Now increment the count of cars to reflect the new one.
Car.numberOfCars++;
```


The object member `newCar.licensePlate` is accessed through the object `newCar`, and the class (static) member `Car.numberOfCars` is accessed through the class `Car`. All `Cars` share the same `numberOfCars` member, so each car contains exactly the same value as all other cars.

Class members are static members. Nonstatic members are specific to each "instance" (each individual object) and are *instance members*. The italicized phrases you see here are the generic way to refer to these types of members.

Defining const and readonly Data Members

One special type of static member is the `const` data member, which represents a constant. You must establish the value of a `const` variable in the declaration, and you cannot change it anywhere within the program, as shown here:

```
class Program
{
  // Number of days in the year (including leap day)
  public const int daysInYear = 366;  // Must have initializer.
  public static void Main(string[] args)
  {
    // This is an array, covered later in this chapter.
    int[] maxTemperatures = new int[daysInYear];
    for(int index = 0; index < daysInYear; index++)
    {
      //  . . .accumulate the maximum temperature for each
      // day of the year . . .
    }
  }
}
```

You can use the constant `daysInYear` in place of the value `366` anywhere within your program. The `const` variable is useful because it can replace a mysterious number such as `366` with the descriptive name `daysInYear` to enhance the readability of your program.

C# provides another way to declare constants — you can preface a variable declaration with the `readonly` modifier, like so:

```
public readonly int daysInYear = 366;  // This could also be static.
```

As with `const`, after you assign the initial value, it can't be changed. Although the reasons are too technical for this book, the `readonly` approach to declaring constants is usually preferable to `const`.

You can use `const` with class data members like those you might have seen in this chapter and inside class methods. But `readonly` isn't allowed in a method. Chapter 3 of this minibook dives into methods.

An alternative convention also exists for naming constants. Rather than name them like variables (as in `daysInYear`), many programmers prefer to use uppercase letters separated by underscores, as in `DAYS_IN_YEAR`. This convention separates constants clearly from ordinary read-write variables.

Chapter 3: We Have Our Methods

In This Chapter

- Defining a method
- Passing arguments to a method
- Getting results back
- Reviewing the `WriteLine()` method

Programmers need to be able to break large programs into smaller chunks that are easy to handle. For example, the programs contained in previous chapters of this minibook reach the limit of the amount of programming information a person can digest at one time.

C# lets you divide your class code into chunks known as *methods.* Properly designed and implemented methods can greatly simplify the job of writing complex programs.

A method is equivalent to a function, procedure, or subroutine in other languages. The difference is that a method is always part of a class.

Defining and Using a Method

Consider the following example:

```
class Example
{
  public int anInt;                  // Nonstatic
  public static int staticInt        // Static
  public void InstanceMethod()       // Nonstatic
  {
    Console.WriteLine("this is an instance method");
  }
  public static void ClassMethod()   // Static
  {
    Console.WriteLine("this is a class method");
  }
}
```

The element `anInt` is a *data member*, just like those shown in Book I. However, the element `InstanceMethod()` is new. `InstanceMethod()` is known as an *instance method* (duh!), which is a set of C# statements that you can execute by referencing the method's name. This concept is best explained by example — even I'm confused right now. (`Main()` and `WriteLine()` are used in nearly every example in this book, and they're methods.)

Note: The distinction between static and nonstatic members is important. I cover part of that story in this chapter and continue in more detail in Chapter 4 of this minibook with a focus on nonstatic, or instance, methods.

To invoke a nonstatic — instance — method, you need an instance of the class. To invoke a static — class — method, you call via the class name, not an instance. The following code snippet assigns a value to the object data member `anInt` and the class, or static, member `staticInt`:

```
Example example = new Example(); // Create an instance of class Example.
example.anInt = 1;               // Initialize instance member through instance.
Example.staticInt = 2;           // Initialize class member through class.
```

The following snippet defines and accesses `InstanceMethod()` and `ClassMethod()` in almost the same way:

```
Example example = new Example(); // Create an instance.
example.InstanceMethod();        // Invoke the instance method
                                 // with that instance.
Example.ClassMethod();           // Invoke the class method with the class.
// The following lines won't compile.
example.ClassMethod();           // Can't access class methods via an instance.
Example.InstanceMethod();        // Can't access instance methods via a class.
```

Every instance of a class has its own, private copy of any instance members. But all instances of the same class share the same class members — both data members and methods — and their values.

The expression `example.InstanceMethod()` passes control to the code contained within the method. C# follows an almost identical process for `Example.ClassMethod()`. Executing the lines just shown (after commenting out the last two lines, which don't compile) generates this output:

```
this is an instance method
this is a class method
```

After a method completes execution, it returns control to the point where it was called. That is, control moves to the next statement after the call.

The bit of C# code given in the two sample methods does nothing more than write a silly `string` to the console, but methods generally perform useful (and sometimes complex) operations such as calculate sines, concatenate two `strings`, sort an array of students, or surreptitiously e-mail your URL to Microsoft (not really). A method can be as large and complex as you want, but try to strive for shorter methods, using the approach described next.

I include the parentheses when describing methods in text — as in `InstanceMethod()` — to make them a little easier to recognize. Otherwise, you might become confused trying to understand what I'm saying.

A Method Example for Your Files

In this section, I divide the monolithic `CalculateInterestTable` programs from Book I, Chapter 5 into several reasonable methods; the demonstration shows how the proper definition of methods can help make a program easier to write and understand. The process of dividing working code this way is known as *refactoring*, and Visual Studio 2010 provides a handy Refactor menu that automates the most common refactorings.

I explain the exact details of the method definitions and method calls in later sections of this chapter. This example simply gives an overview.

By reading the comments *with the C# code removed*, you should be able to get a good idea of a program's intention. If you cannot, you aren't commenting properly. Conversely, if you can't strip out most comments and still understand the intention from the method and variable names, you aren't naming your methods clearly enough or aren't making them small enough (or both). Smaller methods are preferable, and using good method names beat using comments. (That's why real-world code has far fewer comments than the code examples in this book. I comment more heavily here to explain more.)

In outline form, the `CalculateInterestTable` program appears this way:

```
public static void Main(string[] args)
{
  // Prompt user to enter source principal.
  // If the principal is negative, generate an error message.
  // Prompt user to enter the interest rate.
  // If the interest is negative, generate an error message.
  // Finally, prompt user to input the number of years.
  // Display the input back to the user.
  // Now loop through the specified number of years.
  while(year <= duration)
  {
    // Calculate the value of the principal plus interest.
    // Output the result.
  }
}
```

This bit of code illustrates a good technique for planning a method. If you stand back and study the program from a distance, you can see that it's divided into these three sections:

✦ An initial input section in which the user inputs the principal, interest, and duration information

✦ A section mirroring the input data so that the user can verify the entry of the correct data

✦ A section that creates and outputs the table

Use this list to start looking for ways to refactor the program. In fact, if you further examine the input section of that program, you can see that *the same basic code* is used to input these amounts:

✦ Principal

✦ Interest

✦ Duration

Your observation gives you another good place to look. Alternatively, you can write empty methods for some of those comments and then fill them in one by one. That's *programming by intention.*

I used the techniques for planning a method to create the following version of the `CalculateInterestTableWithMethods` program:

```
// CalculateInterestTableWithMethods -- Generate an interest table
//    much like the other interest table programs, but this time using a
//    reasonable division of labor among several methods.
using System;
namespace CalculateInterestTableWithMethods
{
  public class Program
  {
    public static void Main(string[] args)
    {
      // Section 1 -- Input the data you need to create the table.
      decimal principal = 0M;
      decimal interest = 0M;
      decimal duration = 0M;
      InputInterestData(ref principal, ref interest, ref duration);
      // Section 2 -- Verify the data by mirroring it back to the user.
      Console.WriteLine();  // Skip a line.
      Console.WriteLine("Principal     = " + principal);
      Console.WriteLine("Interest      = " + interest + "%");
      Console.WriteLine("Duration      = " + duration + " years");
      Console.WriteLine();
      // Section 3 -- Finally, output the interest table.
      OutputInterestTable(principal, interest, duration);
      // Wait for user to acknowledge the results.
      Console.WriteLine("Press Enter to terminate...");
      Console.Read();
    }
    // InputInterestData -- Retrieve from the keyboard the
    //    principal, interest, and duration information needed
    //    to create the future value table. (Implements Section 1.)
    public static void InputInterestData(ref decimal principal,
                                         ref decimal interest,
                                         ref decimal duration)
    {
```

```
      // 1a -- Retrieve the principal.
      principal = InputPositiveDecimal("principal");
      // 1b -- Now enter the interest rate.
      interest = InputPositiveDecimal("interest");
      // 1c -- Finally, the duration
      duration = InputPositiveDecimal("duration");
    }
    // InputPositiveDecimal -- Return a positive decimal number
    //    from the keyboard.
    public static decimal InputPositiveDecimal(string prompt)
    {
      // Keep trying until the user gets it right.
      while(true)
      {
        // Prompt the user for input.
        Console.Write("Enter " + prompt + ":");
        // Retrieve a decimal value from the keyboard.
        string input = Console.ReadLine();
        decimal value = Convert.ToDecimal(input);
        // Exit the loop if the value that's entered is correct.
        if (value >= 0)
        {
          // Return the valid decimal value entered by the user.
          return value;
        }
        // Otherwise, generate an error on incorrect input.
        Console.WriteLine(prompt + " cannot be negative");
        Console.WriteLine("Try again");
        Console.WriteLine();
      }
    }
    // OutputInterestTable -- Given the principal and interest,
    //    generate a future value table for the number of periods
    //    indicated in duration. (Implements Section 3.)
    public static void OutputInterestTable(decimal principal,
                                           decimal interest,
                                           decimal duration)
    {
      for (int year = 1; year <= duration; year++)
      {
        // Calculate the value of the principal plus interest.
        decimal interestPaid;
        interestPaid = principal * (interest / 100);
        // Now calculate the new principal by adding
        // the interest to the previous principal.
        principal = principal + interestPaid;
        // Round off the principal to the nearest cent.
        principal = decimal.Round(principal, 2);
        // Output the result.
        Console.WriteLine(year + "-" + principal);
      }
    }
  }
}
```

I divided the `Main()` method into three clearly distinguishable parts, each marked with boldfaced comments. I further divided the first section into subsections labeled 1a, 1b, and 1c.

Normally, you don't include the boldfaced comments. If you did, the listings would grow rather complicated because of all the numbers and letters. In practice, those types of comments aren't necessary if the methods are well thought out and their names clearly express the intent of each one.

Part 1 calls the method `InputInterestData()` to input the three variables the program needs in order to create the table: `principal`, `interest`, and `duration`. Part 2 displays these three values for verification just as earlier versions of the program do. Part 3 outputs the table via the method `OutputInterestTable()`.

From the bottom and working upward, the `OutputInterestTable()` method contains an output loop with the interest rate calculations. This loop is the same one used in the inline, nonmethod `CalculateInterestTable` program. The advantage of this version, however, is that when writing this section of code, you don't need to concern yourself with any details of inputting or verifying data. When writing this method, think of it this way: "Given the three numbers — `principal`, `interest`, and `duration` — output an interest table," and that's it. After you're done, you can return to the line that called the `OutputInterestTable()` method and continue from there.

`OutputInterestTable()` offers a target for trying the Visual Studio 2010 Refactor menu. Take these steps to give it a whirl:

1. **Using the `CalculateInterestTableMoreForgiving` example from Book I, Chapter 5 as a starting point, select the code from the declaration of the `year` variable through the end of the `while` loop:**

   ```
   int year = 0;                // You grab the loop variable
   while(year <= duration)      // and the entire while loop.
   {
     //...
   }
   ```

2. **Choose Refactor⇨Extract Method.**
3. **In the Extract Method dialog box, type** OutputInterestTable. **Examine the Preview Method Signature box.**

   Notice that the proposed signature for the new method begins with the `private static` keywords and includes `principal`, `interest`, and `duration` in parentheses. (I introduce `private`, an alternative to `public`, in Book I. For now, you can make the method `public` after the refactoring, if you like.)

   ```
   private static decimal OutputInterestTable(decimal principal,
     decimal interest, int duration)
   ```

4. **Click OK and then Apply to complete the Extract Method refactoring.**

   The code you selected in Step 1 is moved to a new method, located below `Main()` and named `OutputInterestTable()`. In the spot that it formerly occupied, you see this method call:

   ```
   principal = OuputInterestTable(principal, interest, duration);
   ```

   The Preview Changes window shows two panes so that you can preview exactly which information will change. The top pane shows the code you're fixing as it looks now. The lower pane shows the code as it will look when it changes. For more sweeping refactorings, each pane may have numerous lines. You can select or deselect them individually to determine which specific elements to refactor.

If, after refactoring, you suffer "buyer's remorse," click Undo or press Ctrl+Z.

Suppose that the previous refactoring did something you don't like, such as fail to include `principal` as a parameter. (Because this situation is possible, you must always check a refactoring to be certain that it's what you want.)

This situation happened the first time this section was written, in fact. (I'm writing this chapter based on beta software.) Rather than make `principal` a parameter, the Extract Method refactoring made it a local variable. To move `principal` into the parameter list, you can use the Promote Local Variable to Parameter refactoring. But before you do that, you need to initialize the local variable `principal` (the promotion refactoring doesn't work if the variable is uninitialized):

```
decimal principal = 0M;  // M means decimal.
```

To carry out the Promote Local Variable to Parameter refactoring, you right-click the local `principal` variable's name and click Promote Local Variable to Parameter to move the local variable definition to the parameter list:

```
private static decimal OutputInterestTable(decimal interest,
                                           int duration,
                                           decimal principal) ...
```

However, `principal` is at the end of the list and you want it at the beginning. You can use the Reorder Parameters refactoring to fix this problem.

To carry out Reorder Parameters, right-click the new `principal` parameter and click the Reorder Parameters link. In the dialog box, click the `principal` line to select it. Then click the ↑ button twice to move `principal` to the top of the list. Click OK.

Why you should bother with methods

When FORTRAN introduced the function concept — methods, in C# — during the 1950s, its sole purpose was to avoid duplication of code by combining similar sections into a common element. Suppose that you were to write a program to calculate ratios in multiple places. Your program could call the `CalculateRatio()` method when needed, for more or less the sole purpose of avoiding duplicate code. The savings may not seem important for a method as small as `CalculateRatio()`, but methods can grow much larger. Besides, a common method such as `WriteLine()` may be invoked in hundreds of different places.

Quickly, a second advantage became obvious: Coding a single method correctly is easier than coding many — and is doubly easier if the method is small. The `CalculateRatio()` method includes a check to ensure that the denominator isn't zero. If you repeat the calculation code throughout your program, you can easily remember this test in some cases — and in other places, forget.

Not as obvious is a third advantage: A carefully crafted method reduces the complexity of the program. A well-defined method should stand for a concept. You should be able to describe the purpose of the method without using the words *and* or *or*. The method should do only one thing.

A method such as `CalculateSin()` is an ideal example. The programmer who's tasked with this assignment can implement this complex operation with no concern about how it may be used. The applications programmer can use `CalculateSin()` with no concern about how this operation is performed internally, which greatly reduces the number of issues she must monitor. After the number of "variables" is reduced, a large job is accomplished by implementing two smaller, easier jobs.

Large programs, such as word processors, are built up from many layers of methods at ever-increasing levels of abstraction. For example, a `RedisplayDocument()` method would undoubtedly call a `Reparagraph()` method to redisplay the paragraphs within the document. `Reparagraph()` would need to invoke a `CalculateWordWrap()` method to decide where to wrap the lines that make up the paragraph. `CalculateWordWrap()` would have to call a `LookUpWordBreak()` method to decide where to break a word at the end of the line, to make the sentences wrap more naturally. Each of these methods was described in a single, simple sentence. (Notice that these methods are well named.)

Without the ability to *abstract* complex concepts, someone writing programs of even moderate complexity would find that the task becomes almost impossible — let alone creating an operating system such as Windows Vista, a utility such as WinZip, a word processor such as WordPerfect, or a game such as *Halo*.

The result of all this refactoring consists of these two pieces:

- A new `private static` method below `Main()`, named `OutputInterestTable()`
- The following line of code within `Main()` where the extracted code was:

```
principal = OutputInterestTable(principal, interest, duration);
```

Cool! The same divide-and-conquer logic holds for `InputInterestData()`. However, that type of refactoring is more complex, so I do it by hand and don't show the steps. A description of the full art of refactoring is beyond the scope of this book, though you can find an introduction at `csharp102.info`. Experiment with the Refactor menu and use it often for building better-factored code. But always check the results.

Because C# 4.0 now supports named parameters, you can call the parameters in whichever order you want, by specifying the name of the expected parameter before the value when calling a method. I cover more of this topic later in Book 8, but in C# 4.0, reordering parameters is less of an issue.

For `InputInterestData()`, you can focus solely on inputting the three decimal values. However, in this case, you realize that inputting each one involves identical operations on three different input variables. The `InputPositiveDecimal()` method bundles these operations into a set of general code that you can apply to principal, interest, and duration alike. Notice that the three `while` loops that take input in the original program are collapsed into one `while` loop inside `InputPositiveDecimal()`. This process reduces code duplication.

Avoid duplicating code. Refactoring folks call it the worst "code smell."

This `InputPositiveDecimal()` method displays the prompt it was given and awaits input from the user. The method returns the value to the caller if it isn't negative. If the value is negative, the method outputs an error message and loops back to try again.

From the user's standpoint, the modified program acts exactly the same as the inline version, which is just the point:

```
Enter principal:100
Enter interest:-10
interest cannot be negative
Try again

Enter interest:10
Enter duration:10

Principal      = 100
Interest       = 10%
Duration       = 10 years

1-110.0
2-121.00
3-133.10
4-146.41
5-161.05
6-177.16
7-194.88
8-214.37
9-235.81
10-259.39
Press Enter to terminate...
```

I've refactored a lengthy, somewhat difficult program into smaller, more understandable pieces — while reducing some duplication. As they say in my neck of the woods, "You can't beat that with a stick."

Having Arguments with Methods

A method such as the following example is about as useful as Bill Sempf's hairbrush because no data passes into or out of the method:

```
public static void Output()
{
  Console.WriteLine("this is a method");
}
```

Compare this example to real-world methods that *do* something. For example, the mathematical sine operation requires some type of input — after all, you have to calculate the sine of something. Similarly, to concatenate two `strings`, you need two `strings`. So the `Concatenate()` method requires at least two `strings` as input. (As The Beav might say, "Gee, Wally, that sounds logical.") You need to find a way to move data into and out of a method.

Passing an argument to a method

The values you input to a method are *method* arguments, or *parameters*. Most methods require some type of arguments if they're going to do something. (In this way, methods remind me of my son: We need to have an argument before he'll do anything.) You pass arguments to a method by listing them in the parentheses that follow the method name. Consider this small addition to the earlier `Example` class:

```
public class Example
{
  public static void Output(string someString)
  {
    Console.WriteLine("Output() was passed the argument: " + someString);
  }
}
```

I could invoke this method from within the same class, like this:

```
Output("Hello");
```

I would then see this not-too-exciting output:

```
Output() was passed the argument: Hello
```

The program passes to the method `Output()` a reference to the `string` `"Hello"`. The method receives the reference and assigns it the name `some String`. The `Output()` method can use `someString` within the method just as it would use any other `string` variable.

I can change the example in one minor way:

```
string myString = "Hello";
Output(myString);
```

This code snippet assigns the variable `myString` to reference the `string` `"Hello"`. The call `Output(myString)` passes the object referenced by `myString`, which is your old friend `"Hello"`. Figure 3-1 depicts this process. From there, the effect is the same as before.

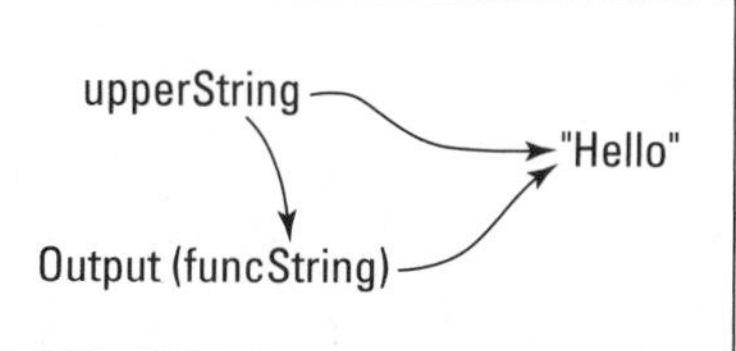

Figure 3-1: Copying the value of `myString` to `someString`.

The placeholders you specify for arguments when you write a method — for example, `someString` in `Output()` — are *parameters*. The values you pass to a method via a parameter are *arguments*. I use the terms more or less interchangeably in this book.

A similar idea is passing arguments to a program. For example, you may have noticed that `Main()` usually takes an array argument.

Passing multiple arguments to methods

When I ask my daughter to wash the car, she usually gives me more than just a single argument. Because she has lots of time on the couch to think about it, she can keep several at the ready.

You can define a method with multiple arguments of varying types. Consider the following sample method `AverageAndDisplay()`:

```
// AverageAndDisplay -- Demonstrate argument passing.
using System;
namespace Example
{
  public class Program
  {
    public static void Main(string[] args)
    {
      // Access the member method.
      AverageAndDisplay("grade 1", 3.5, "grade 2", 4.0);
      // Wait for user to acknowledge.
      Console.WriteLine("Press Enter to terminate...");
      Console.Read();
    }
```

```
    // AverageAndDisplay -- Average two numbers with their
    //    labels and display the results.
    public static void AverageAndDisplay(string s1, double d1,
                                         string s2, double d2)
    {
      double average = (d1 + d2) / 2;
      Console.WriteLine("The average of "  + s1
                      + " whose value is " + d1
                      + " and "            + s2
                      + " whose value is " + d2
                      + " is " + average);
    }
  }
}
```

Executing this simple program generates this output:

```
The average of grade 1 whose value is 3.5 and grade 2 whose value is 4 is 3.75
Press Enter to terminate...
```

The method `AverageAndDisplay()` is declared with several parameters in the order in which arguments are to be passed to them.

As usual, execution of the sample program begins with the first statement after `Main()`. The first noncomment line in `Main()` invokes the method `AverageAndDisplay()`, passing the two `strings` `"grade 1"` and `"grade 2"` and the two `double` values 3.5 and 4.0.

The method `AverageAndDisplay()` calculates the average of the two `double` values, `d1` and `d2`, passed to it along with their names contained in `s1` and `s2`, and the calculated average is stored in `average`.

Changing the value of an argument inside the method can lead to confusion and errors, so be wise and assign the value to a temporary variable and modify it instead.

Matching argument definitions with usage

Each argument in a method call must match the method definition in both type *and order* if you call them without naming them. The following (illegal) example generates a build-time error:

```
// AverageWithCompilerError -- This version does not compile!
using System;
namespace Example
{
  public class Program
  {
    public static void Main(string[] args)
    {
      // Access the member method.
      AverageAndDisplay("grade 1", "grade 2", 3.5, 4.0);
```

```
      // Wait for user to acknowledge.
      Console.WriteLine("Press Enter to terminate...");
      Console.Read();
    }
    // AverageAndDisplay -- Average two numbers with their
    //    labels and display the results.
    public static void AverageAndDisplay(string s1, double d1,
                                         string s2, double d2)
    {
      // var okay here, but it's really double.
      var average = (d1 + d2) / 2;
      Console.WriteLine("The average of "  + s1
                      + " whose value is " + d1
                      + " and "            + s2
                      + " whose value is " + d2
                      + " is " + average);
    }
  }
}
```


C# can't match the type of each argument in the call to `AverageAndDisplay()` with the corresponding argument in the method definition. The `string` `"grade 1"` matches the first `string` in the method definition; however, the method definition calls for a `double` as its second argument rather than the `string` that's passed.

You can easily see that I simply transposed the second and third arguments. (That's what I hate about computers — they take me too literally. I know what I *said*, but it's obvious what I *meant!*)

To fix the problem, swap the second and third arguments.

Overloading a method doesn't mean giving it too much to do

You can give two methods within a given class the same name — known as *overloading* the method name — as long as their arguments differ.

This example demonstrates overloading:

```
// AverageAndDisplayOverloaded -- This version demonstrates that
//    the AverageAndDisplay method can be overloaded.
using System;
namespace AverageAndDisplayOverloaded
{
  public class Program
  {
    public static void Main(string[] args)
    {
      // Access the first version of the method.
      AverageAndDisplay("my GPA", 3.5, "your GPA", 4.0);
      Console.WriteLine();
      // Access the second version of the method.
```

```
      AverageAndDisplay(3.5, 4.0);
      // Wait for user to acknowledge.
      Console.WriteLine("Press Enter to terminate...");
      Console.Read();
    }
    // AverageAndDisplay -- Average two numbers with their
    //    labels and display the results.
    public static void AverageAndDisplay(string s1, double d1,
                                         string s2, double d2)
    {
      double average = (d1 + d2) / 2;
      Console.WriteLine("The average of "  + s1
                      + " whose value is " + d1);
      Console.WriteLine("and "            + s2
                      + " whose value is " + d2
                      + " is " + average);
    }
    public static void AverageAndDisplay(double d1, double d2)
    {
      double average = (d1 + d2) / 2;
      Console.WriteLine("The average of " + d1
                      + " and "           + d2
                      + " is " + average);
    }
  }
}
```

This program defines two versions of `AverageAndDisplay()`. The program invokes one and then the other by passing the proper arguments. C# can tell which method the program wants by comparing the call with the definition. The program compiles properly and generates this output when executed:

```
The average of my GPA whose value is 3.5
and your GPA whose value is 4 is 3.75

The average of 3.5 and 4 is 3.75
Press Enter to terminate...
```

C# generally doesn't allow two methods in the same class to have the same name unless the number or type of the methods' arguments differs (or if both differ). Thus C# differentiates between these two methods:

- `AverageAndDisplay(string, double, string, double)`
- `AverageAndDisplay(double, double)`

When you say it that way, it's clear that the two methods are different.

Implementing default arguments

Often, you want to supply two (or more) versions of a method:

- **Complicated:** Provides complete flexibility but requires numerous arguments from the calling routine, several of which the user may not even understand.

The word *user* doesn't always refer to the user of a program. References to the user of a method often mean, in practice, the programmer who is making use of the method. Another term is *client* (which is often you).

✦ **Acceptable (if somewhat bland):** Assumes default values for certain arguments.

You can easily implement default arguments using method overloading. Consider this pair of `DisplayRoundedDecimal()` methods:

```
// MethodsWithDefaultArguments -- Provide variations of the same methods,
//    some with default arguments, by overloading the method name.
using System;
namespace MethodsWithDefaultArguments
{
  public class Program
  {
    public static void Main(string[] args)
    {
      // Access the member method.
      Console.WriteLine(DisplayRoundedDecimal(12.345678M, 3));
      // Wait for user to acknowledge.
      Console.WriteLine("Press Enter to terminate...");
      Console.Read();
    }
    // DisplayRoundedDecimal -- Convert a decimal value into a string
    //    with the specified number of signficant digits.
    public static string DisplayRoundedDecimal(decimal value,
                                   int numberOfSignificantDigits)
    {
      // First round off the number to the specified number
      // of significant digits.
      decimal roundedValue =
                  decimal.Round(value,
                                numberOfSignificantDigits);
      // Convert that to a string.
      string s = Convert.ToString(roundedValue);
      return s;
    }
    public static string DisplayRoundedDecimal(decimal value)
    {
      // Invoke DisplayRoundedDecimal(decimal, int) specifying
      // the default number of digits.
      string s = DisplayRoundedDecimal(value, 2);
      return s;
    }
  }
}
```

The `DisplayRoundedDecimal(decimal, int)` method converts the `decimal` value that's provided into a `string` with the specified number of digits after the decimal point. Because decimals are often used to display monetary values, the most common choice is to place two digits after the decimal point. Therefore, the `DisplayRoundedDecimal(decimal)` method provides the same conversion service — but defaults the number of significant digits to two, thereby removing any worry about the meaning of the second argument.

The generic (decimal) version of the method calls the more specific (decimal, int) version to perform its magic. This stacked method calling is more common than not because it reduces duplication. The generic methods simply provide arguments that the programmer doesn't have the inclination to find in the documentation, and shouldn't have to unless she needs them.

Having to unnecessarily consult the reference documentation for the meanings of normally defaulted arguments distracts the programmer from the main job at hand — thereby making it more difficult, wasting time, and increasing the likelihood of mistakes.

Providing default arguments does more than just save lazy programmers from exerting a tiny bit of effort (programming requires lots of concentration). The author of the method understands the relationship between the arguments — and therefore bears the onus of providing friendlier, overloaded versions of methods.

Visual Basic, C, and C++ programmers should be accustomed to supplying a default value for a parameter directly in the method signature. Until C# 4.0 was released, you couldn't do that in C#. Now you can.

For instance, although overloading the method in the preceding example is a perfectly acceptable way to implement a default parameter, you can also give default parameters by using the equal sign (=), just as in Visual Basic:

```
// MethodsWithDefaultArguments2-- Provide optional parameters to a method
// to avoid overloading. It's another way to do the same thing.
using System;
namespace MethodsWithDefaultArguments2
{
  public class Program
  {
    public static void Main(string[] args)
    {
      // Access the member method.
      Console.WriteLine(DisplayRoundedDecimal(12.345678M, 3));
      // Wait for user to acknowledge.
      Console.WriteLine("Press Enter to terminate...");
      Console.Read();
    }
    // DisplayRoundedDecimal -- Convert a decimal value into a string
    //    that has the specified number of signficant digits. That argument
    //    is optional and has a default value. If you call the method
    //    without the second argument, it uses the default value.
    public static string DisplayRoundedDecimal(decimal value,
                                            int numberOfSignificantDigits = 2)
    {
      // First round off the number to the specified number
      // of significant digits.
```

```
      decimal roundedValue =
                 decimal.Round(value,
                               numberOfSignificantDigits);
      // Convert that to a string.
      string s = Convert.ToString(roundedValue);
      return s;
    }
  }
}
```

Why would Microsoft make these changes? The answer is COM. The Component Object Model (COM) was the architectural paradigm of choice for Microsoft products before .NET was released, and it's still quite prevalent. (Notice that I didn't say *popular.*) Office, for one, is entirely developed using COM. COM applications are developed in C++ or Visual Basic 6 and earlier, and methods from those classes allow for optional parameters. Thus, communicating with COM without using optional parameters can become difficult. To address this imbalance, optional parameters (along with a number of other features) were added to C# 4.0.

I cover named and optional parameters ad nauseam in Book III.

Returning Values after Christmas

Many real-world operations create values to return to the caller. For example, `Sin()` accepts an argument and returns the trigonometric sine. A method can return a value to the caller in two ways — most commonly via the `return` statement; however, a second method uses the *call-by-reference* feature.

Returning a value via return postage

The following code snippet demonstrates a small method that returns the average of its input arguments:

```
public class Example
{
  public static double Average(double d1, double d2)
  {
    double average = (d1 + d2) / 2;
    return average;
  }
  public static void Main(string[] args)
  {
    double v1 = 1.0;
    double v2 = 3.0;
    double averageValue = Average(v1, v2);
    Console.WriteLine("The average of " + v1
                    + " and " + v2 + " is "
                    + averageValue);
```

```
        // This also works.
        Console.WriteLine("The average of " + v1
                        + " and " + v2 + " is "
                        + Average(v1, v2));
    }
}
```

Notice first that I declare the method as public static double Average() — the double in front of its name indicates that the Average() method returns a double-precision value to the caller.

The Average() method applies the names d1 and d2 to the double values passed to it. This method creates a variable average to which it assigns the average of d1 and d2 and returns to the caller the value contained in average.

People sometimes use this careless but common shorthand: "The method returns average." Saying that average or any other variable is passed or returned anywhere is imprecise. In this case, the *value* contained within average is returned to the caller.

The call to Average() from the Test() method appears the same as any other method call; however, the double value returned by Average() via the return keyword is stored in the variable averageValue.

A method that returns a value, such as Average(), cannot return to the caller by merely encountering the closed brace of the method. If it did, C# wouldn't know which value to return. You need a return statement.

Defining a method with no value

The declaration public static double Average(double, double) declares a method Average() that returns the average of its arguments as a double. (The number returned had better be the average of the input values or else someone has some serious explaining to do.)

Some methods don't need to return a value to the caller. An earlier method AverageAndDisplay() example displays the average of its input arguments but doesn't return that average to the caller. (That idea may not be a good one, but mine is not to question.) Rather than leave the return type blank, you declare a method such as AverageAndDisplay() this way:

```
public void AverageAndDisplay(double, double)
```

The keyword void, where the return type is normally used, means *nontype*. That is, the declaration void indicates that the AverageAndDisplay() method returns no value to the caller. (Regardless, every method declaration specifies a return type, even if it's void.)

A *void method* returns no value. This definition doesn't mean that the method is empty or that it's used for medical or astronautical purposes; it simply refers to the initial keyword. By comparison, a method that returns a value is a *nonvoid method.*

A nonvoid method must pass control back to the caller by executing a `return` followed by the value to return to the caller. A `void` method has no value to return. A `void` method returns when it encounters a `return` with no value attached. Or, by default (if no `return` exists), a `void` method exits automatically when control reaches the closing brace of the method.

Consider this `DisplayRatio()` method:

```
public class Example
{
  public static void DisplayRatio(double numerator,
                                  double denominator)
  {
    // If the denominator is zero . . .
    if (denominator == 0.0)
    {
      //  . . .output an error message and . . .
      Console.WriteLine("The denominator of a ratio cannot be 0");
      //  . . .return to the caller.
      return;  // An early return due to the error
    }
    // This code is executed only if denominator is nonzero.
    double ratio = numerator / denominator;
    Console.WriteLine("The ratio of " + numerator
                    + " over " + denominator
                    + " is " + ratio);
  }  // If the denominator isn't zero, the method exits here.
}
```

The `DisplayRatio()` method checks whether the `denominator` value is zero:

- **If the value is zero:** The program displays an error message and returns to the caller without attempting to calculate a ratio. Doing so would divide the numerator value by zero and cause a CPU processor fault, also known by the more descriptive name *processor upchuck.*
- **If the value is nonzero:** The program displays the ratio. The closed brace immediately following `WriteLine()` is the closed brace of the method `DisplayRatio()` and therefore acts as the return point for the program.

If that were the only difference, it wouldn't be much to write home about. However, the second form of `WriteLine()` also provides a number of controls on the output format. I describe these format controls in Book I, Chapter 3.

The WriteLine() method

You may have noticed that the `WriteLine()` construct I've used in program examples earlier in this book is nothing more than a method call that's invoked by a `Console` class:

```
Console.WriteLine("this is a method call");
```

`WriteLine()` is one of many predefined methods provided by the .NET Framework library. The `Console` predefined class refers to the application console (also known as the command prompt or command window).

The argument to the `WriteLine()` method I've used until now is a single `string`. The `+` operator enables the programmer to combine `string`s, or to combine a `string` and an intrinsic variable, before the sum is passed to `WriteLine()`:

```
string s = "Sarah"
Console.WriteLine("My name is " + s + " and my age is " + 3);
```

All that `WriteLine()` sees in this case is "My name is Sarah and my age is 3."

A second form of `WriteLine()` provides a more flexible set of arguments:

```
Console.WriteLine("My name is {0} and my age is {1}.", "Sarah", 3);
```

The first argument is a format string. The `string "Sarah"` is inserted where the symbol {0} appears — 0 refers to the first argument after the format string. The integer 3 is inserted at the position marked by {1}. This form is more efficient than in the previous example because concatenating `string`s isn't as easy as it might sound. It's a time-consuming business.

Chapter 4: Let Me Say This about `this`

In This Chapter

- How to pass an object to a method
- Class methods versus instance methods
- Understanding what `this` is
- When you don't have `this`
- When a class doesn't have a method that you need it to have

This chapter moves from the static methods that Chapter 3 in this minibook emphasizes to the nonstatic methods of a class. Static methods belong to the whole class, and nonstatic methods belong to each instance created from the class. Important differences exist between static and nonstatic class members.

Passing an Object to a Method

You pass object references as arguments to methods in the same way as you pass value-type variables, with one difference: You always pass objects by reference.

The following small program demonstrates how you pass objects — to methods, that is:

```
// PassObject -- Demonstrate how to pass an object to a method.
using System;
namespace PassObject
{
  public class Student
  {
    public string name;
  }
  public class Program
  {
    public static void Main(string[] args)
    {
      Student student = new Student();
      // Set the name by accessing it directly.
      Console.WriteLine("The first time:");
      student.name = "Madeleine";
```

```
      OutputName(student);
      // Change the name using a method.
      Console.WriteLine("After being modified:");
      SetName(student, "Willa");
      OutputName(student);
      // Wait for user to acknowledge.
      Console.WriteLine("Press Enter to terminate...");
      Console.Read();
    }
    // OutputName -- Output the student's name.
    public static void OutputName(Student student)
    {
      // Output current student's name.
      Console.WriteLine("Student's name is {0}", student.name);
    }
    // SetName -- Modify the student object's name.
    public static void SetName(Student student, string name)
    {
      student.name = name;
    }
  }
}
```

The program creates a `student` object consisting of nothing but a name. The program first sets the name of the `student` directly and passes the *student object* to the output method `OutputName()`. `OutputName()` displays the name of any `Student` object it receives.

The program then updates the name of the `student` by calling `SetName()`. Because all reference-type objects are passed by reference in C#, the changes made to `student` are retained in the calling method. When `Main()` outputs the `student` object again, the name has changed, as shown in this bit of code:

```
The first time:
Student's name is Madeleine
After being modified:
Student's name is Willa
Press Enter to terminate...
```

The `SetName()` method can change the name within the `Student` object and make it stick.

You don't use the `ref` keyword when passing a *reference-type* object. Yet the effect is that the object's contents can be modified *through the reference*. However, if `SetName()` tries to assign a whole new `Student` object to its `Student` parameter, it doesn't affect the original `Student` object outside the method, as this chunk of code shows:

```
Student student = new Student();
SetName(student, "Pam");
Console.WriteLine(student.name);  // Still "Pam"
...
```

```
// A revised SetName():
public static void SetName(Student student, string name)
{
  student = new Student(); // Doesn't replace student outside SetName().
  student.Name = name;
}
```

Defining Methods

A class is supposed to collect the elements that describe a real-world object or concept. For example, a `Vehicle` class may contain data elements for maximum velocity, weight, and carrying capacity, for example. However, a `Vehicle` has active properties — *behaviors* — as well: the ability to start and stop and the like. These active properties are described by the methods related to that vehicular data. These methods are just as much a part of the `Vehicle` class as the data elements.

Defining a static method

For example, you could rewrite the program from the previous section in a slightly better way:

```
// StudentClassWithMethods -- Demonstrate putting methods that
//    operate on a class's data inside the class. A class is
//    responsible for its own data and any operations on it.
using System;
namespace StudentClassWithMethods
{
  // Now the OutputName and SetName methods are members of
  // class Student, not class Program.
  public class Student
  {
    public string name;
    // OutputName -- Output the student's name.
    public static void OutputName(Student student)
    {
      // Output current student's name.
      Console.WriteLine("Student's name is {0}", student.name);
    }
    // SetName -- Modify the student object's name.
    public static void SetName(Student student, string name)
    {
      student.name = name;
    }
  }
  public class Program
  {
    public static void Main(string[] args)
    {
      Student student = new Student();
      // Set the name by accessing it directly.
      Console.WriteLine("The first time:");
      student.name = "Madeleine";
```

```
            Student.OutputName(student); // Method now belongs to Student.
            // Change the name using a method.
            Console.WriteLine("After being modified:");
            Student.SetName(student, "Willa");
            Student.OutputName(student);
            // Wait for user to acknowledge.
            Console.WriteLine("Press Enter to terminate...");
            Console.Read();
        }
    }
}
```

Other than its name, this program has only one significant change from the PassObject program in the previous section: I put the OutputName() and SetName() methods in the Student class.

Rather than say "in" the class, many programmers speak of members "on" the class.

Because of that change, Main() must reference the Student class in the calls to SetName() and OutputName(). The methods are now members of the class Student and not Program, the class in which Main() resides.

This step is small but significant. Placing OutputName() within the class leads to a higher level of reuse: Outside methods that need to display the object can find OutputName() right there as part of the class. It doesn't have to be written separately by each program using the Student class.

This solution is also better on a philosophical level. Class Program shouldn't need to worry about how to initialize the name of a Student object nor about how to output important material. The Student class should contain that information. *Objects are responsible for themselves.*

In fact, Main() shouldn't initialize the name to Madeleine in the first place. It should call SetName() instead.

From within Student, one member method can invoke another without explicitly applying the class name. SetName() could invoke OutputName() without needing to reference the class name. If you leave off the class name, C# assumes that the method being accessed is in or on the same class.

Defining an instance method

Although OutputName() and SetName() are static methods, they could as easily be nonstatic, or *instance*, methods.

All static members of a class are *class members*, and all nonstatic members are *instance members*. This includes methods.

The nonstatic *data members* of an object — an *instance* of a class — are accessed with the object and not with the class. Thus, you may say

```
Student student = new Student(); // Create an instance of Student.
student.name = "Madeleine";      // Access the member via the instance.
```

C# enables you to invoke nonstatic member *methods* in the same way:

```
student.SetName("Madeleine");
```

The following example demonstrates this technique:

```
// InvokeMethod -- Invoke a member method through the object.
using System;
namespace InvokeMethod
{
  class Student
  {
    // The name information to describe a student
    public string firstName;
    public string lastName;
    // SetName -- Save name information. (Nonstatic.)
    public void SetName(string fName, string lName)
    {
      firstName = fName;
      lastName  = lName;
    }
    // ToNameString -- Convert the student object into a
    //    string for display. (Nonstatic.)
    public string ToNameString()
    {
      string s = firstName + " " + lastName;
      return s;
    }
  }
  public class Program
  {
    public static void Main()
    {
      Student student = new Student();
      student.SetName("Stephen", "Davis"); // Call instance method.
      Console.WriteLine("Student's name is "
                        + student.ToNameString());
      // Wait for user to acknowledge.
      Console.WriteLine("Press Enter to terminate...");
      Console.Read();
    }
  }
}
```

The output from this program is this simple line:

```
Student's name is Stephen Davis
```

Other than having a much shorter name, this program is quite similar to the earlier `StudentClassWithMethods` program. This version uses *nonstatic* methods to manipulate both a first and last name.

The program begins by creating a new Student object, student. The program then invokes the SetName() method, which stores the two strings "Stephen" and "Davis" into the data members firstName and last Name. Finally, the program calls the member method ToNameString(), which returns the name of the student by concatenating the two strings.

Look again at the SetName() method, which updates the first and last name fields in the Student object. To see which object SetName() modifies, consider this example:

```
Student christa = new Student();   // Here's one student.
Student sarah = new Student();     // And here's a completely different one.
christa.SetName("Christa", "Smith");
sarah.SetName("Sarah", "Jones");
```

The first call to SetName() updates the first and last name of the christa object. The second call updates the sarah object.

Thus, C# programmers say that a method operates on the *current* object. In the first call, the current object is christa; in the second, it's sarah.

Expanding a method's full name

A subtle but important problem exists with my description of method names. To see the problem, consider this sample code snippet:

```
public class Person
{
  public void Address()
  {
    Console.WriteLine("Hi");
  }
}
public class Letter
{
  string address;
  // Store the address.
  public void Address(string newAddress)
  {
    address = newAddress;
  }
}
```

Any subsequent discussion of the Address() method is now ambiguous. The Address() method within Person has nothing to do with the Address() method in Letter. If my programmer friend tells me to access the Address() method, which Address() does he mean?

The problem lies not with the methods themselves, but, rather, with my description. In fact, no Address() method exists as an independent entity — only a Person.Address() and a Letter.Address() method. Attaching the class name to the beginning of the method name clearly indicates which method is intended.

This description is quite similar to people's names. Within my family, I am known as Stephen. (Actually, within my family, I am known by my middle name, but you get the point.) No other Stephens are within my family (at least not within my close family). However, two other Stephens work where I do.

If I'm at lunch with coworkers and the other two Stephens aren't present, the name *Stephen* clearly refers to me. Back in the trenches (or cubicles), shouting "Stephen" is ambiguous because it can refer to any one of us. In that context, you need to yell out "Stephen Davis" as opposed to "Stephen Williams" or "Stephen Leija."

Thus, you can consider `Address()` to be the first name or nickname of a method, with its class as the family name.

Accessing the Current Object

Consider the following `Student.SetName()` method:

```
class Student
{
  // The name information to describe a student
  public string firstName;
  public string lastName;
  // SetName -- Save name information.
  public void SetName(string firstName, string lastName)
  {
    firstName = firstName;
    lastName  = lastName;
  }
}
public class Program
{
  public static void Main()
  {
    Student student1 = new Student();
    student1.SetName("Joseph", "Smith");
    Student student2 = new Student();
    student2.SetName("John", "Davis");
  }
}
```

The method `Main()` uses the `SetName()` method to update first `student1` and then `student2`. But you don't see a reference to either `Student` object *within* `SetName()` *itself.* In fact, no reference to a `Student` object exists. A method is said to operate on "the current object." How does a method know which one is the current object? Will the real current object please stand up?

The answer is simple. The current object is passed as an implicit argument in the call to a method — for example:

```
student1.SetName("Joseph", "Smith");
```

This call is equivalent to the following:

```
Student.SetName(student1, "Joseph", "Smith"); // Equivalent call,
                                       // (but this won't build properly).
```

I'm not saying that you can invoke `SetName()` in two different ways; just that the two calls are semantically equivalent. The object identifying the current object — the hidden first argument — is passed to the method, just like other arguments. Leave that task to the compiler.

Passing an object implicitly is easy to swallow, but what about a reference from one method to another? The following code snippet illustrates calling one method from another:

```
public class Student
{
  public string firstName;
  public string lastName;
  public void SetName(string firstName, string lastName)
  {
    SetFirstName(firstName);
    SetLastName(lastName);
  }
  public void SetFirstName(string name)
  {
    firstName = name;
  }
  public void SetLastName(string name)
  {
    lastName = name;
  }
}
```

No object appears in the call to `SetFirstName()`. The current object continues to be passed along silently from one method call to the next. An access to any member from within an object method is assumed to be with respect to the current object. The upshot is that a method "knows" which object it belongs to. "Current object" (or "current instance") means something like "me."

What is the `this` *keyword?*

Unlike most arguments, the current object doesn't appear in the method argument list, so it isn't assigned a name by the programmer. Instead, C# assigns this object the less-than-imaginative name `this`, useful in the few situations where you need to refer directly to the current object.

The C# keyword `this` cannot be used for any other purpose, at least not without the express written permission of the National Football League.

Thus you could write the previous example this way:

```
public class Student
{
  public string firstName;
  public string lastName;
  public void SetName(string firstName, string lastName)
  {
    // Explicitly reference the "current object" referenced by this.
    this.SetFirstName(firstName);
    this.SetLastName(lastName);
  }
  public void SetFirstName(string name)
  {
    this.firstName = name;
  }
  public void SetLastName(string name)
  {
    this.lastName = name;
  }
}
```


Notice the explicit addition of the keyword `this`. Adding it to the member references doesn't add anything because `this` is assumed. However, when `Main()` makes the following call, `this` references `student1` throughout `SetName()` and any other method it may call:

```
student1.SetName("John", "Smith");
```

When is `this` *explicit?*

You don't normally need to refer to `this` explicitly because it is understood where necessary by the compiler. However, two common cases require `this`. You may need it when initializing data members, as in this example:

```
class Person
{
  public string name;  // This is this.name below.
  public int id;       // And this is this.id below.
  public void Init(string name, int id)  // These are method arguments.
  {
    this.name = name;  // Argument names same as data member names
    this.id = id;
  }
}
```

The arguments to the `Init()` method are named `name` and `id`, which match the names of the corresponding data members. The method is then easy to read because you know immediately which argument is stored where. The only problem is that the name `name` in the argument list obscures the name of the data member. The compiler complains about it.

The addition of `this` clarifies which `name` is intended. Within `Init()`, the name `name` refers to the method argument, but `this.name` refers to the data member.

You also need `this` when storing the current object for use later or by some other method. Consider this program example `ReferencingThisExplicitly`:

```
// ReferencingThisExplicitly -- Demonstrates how to explicitly use
//    the reference to 'this'.
using System;
namespace ReferencingThisExplicitly
{
  public class Program
  {
    public static void Main(string[] strings)
    {
      // Create a student.
      Student student = new Student();
      student.Init("Stephen Davis", 1234);
      // Now enroll the student in a course.
      Console.WriteLine
              ("Enrolling Stephen Davis in Biology 101");
      student.Enroll("Biology 101");
      // Display student course.
      Console.WriteLine("Resulting student record:");
      student.DisplayCourse();
      // Wait for user to acknowledge the results.
      Console.WriteLine("Press Enter to terminate...");
      Console.Read();
    }
  }
  // Student -- The class for university students.
  public class Student
  {
    // All students have a name and an id.
    public string _name;
    public int _id;
    // The course in which the student is enrolled
    CourseInstance _courseInstance;
    // Init -- Initialize the student object.
    public void Init(string name, int id)
    {
      this._name = name;
      this._id = id;
      _courseInstance = null;
    }
    // Enroll -- Enroll the current student in a course.
    public void Enroll(string courseID)
    {
      _courseInstance = new CourseInstance();
      _courseInstance.Init(this, courseID);    // Here's the explicit reference.
    }
    // Display the name of the student and the course.
    public void DisplayCourse()
    {
```

```
      Console.WriteLine(_name);
      _courseInstance.Display();
    }
  }
  // CourseInstance -- A combination of a student with
  //    a university course.
  public class CourseInstance
  {
    public Student _student;
    public string _courseID;
    // Init -- Tie the student to the course.
    public void Init(Student student, string courseID)
    {
      this._student = student;
      this._courseID = courseID;
    }
    // Display -- Output the name of the course.
    public void Display()
    {
      Console.WriteLine(_courseID);
    }
  }
}
```


This program is fairly mundane. The `Student` object has room for a name, an ID, and a single instance of a university course (not an industrious student). `Main()` creates the `student` instance and then invokes `Init()` to initialize the instance. At this point, the `_courseInstance` reference is set to `null` because the student isn't yet enrolled in a class.

The `Enroll()` method enrolls the student by initializing `_courseInstance` with a new object. However, the `CourseInstance.Init()` method takes an instance of `Student` as its first argument along with the course ID as the second argument. Which `Student` should you pass? Clearly, you need to pass the current `Student` — the `Student` referred to by `this`. (Thus you can say that `Enroll()` enrolls `this` student in the `CourseInstance`.)

Some programmers (and that includes me) like to differentiate data members from other variables more clearly by prefixing an underscore to the name of each data member, like this: `_name`. You see me adopt this convention most of the time, but of course, it's only a convention, and you may do as you like. If you use the convention, you don't need to preface the item with `this`, as in `this._id`. It's completely unambiguous with just the underscore prefix.

What happens when you don't have `this`?

Mixing class (static) methods and instance (nonstatic) methods is like mixing sheepmen and ranchers. Fortunately, C# gives you some ways around the problems between the two. To see the problem, consider this program snippet `MixingStaticAndInstanceMethods`:

```
// MixingStaticAndInstanceMethods -- Mixing class (static) methods
//    and instance (nonstatic) methods can cause problems.
using System;
namespace MixingStaticAndInstanceMethods
{
  public class Student
  {
    public string _firstName;
    public string _lastName;
    // InitStudent -- Initialize the student object.
    public void InitStudent(string firstName, string lastName)
    {
      _firstName = firstName;
      _lastName = lastName;
    }
    // OutputBanner (static) -- Output the introduction.
    public static void OutputBanner()
    {
      Console.WriteLine("Aren't we clever:");
      // Console.WriteLine(? what student do we use ?); ▪ The problem!
    }
    // OutputBannerAndName (nonstatic) -- Output intro.
    public void OutputBannerAndName()
    {
      // The class Student is implied but no this
      // object is passed to the static method.
      OutputBanner();
      // The current Student object is passed explicitly.
      OutputName(this);
    }
    // OutputName -- Output the student's name.
    public static void OutputName(Student student)
    {
      // Here, the Student object is referenced explicitly.
      Console.WriteLine("Student's name is {0}",
                        student.ToNameString());
    }
    // ToNameString -- Fetch the student's name.
    public string ToNameString()
    {
      // Here, the current object is implicit --
      // this could have been written:
      // return this._firstName + " " + this._lastName;
      return _firstName + " " + _lastName;
    }
  }
  public class Program
  {
    public static void Main(string[] args)
    {
      Student student = new Student();
      student.InitStudent("Madeleine", "Cather");
      // Output the banner and name statically.
      Student.OutputBanner();
      Student.OutputName(student);
      Console.WriteLine();
```

```
            // Output the banner and name again using instance.
            student.OutputBannerAndName();
            // Wait for user to acknowledge.
            Console.WriteLine("Press Enter to terminate...");
            Console.Read();
        }
    }
}
```

Start at the bottom of the program with `Main()` so that you can better see the problems. The program begins by creating a `Student` object and initializing its name. The simpleton program now wants to do nothing more than output the name preceded by a short message and banner.

`Main()` first outputs the banner and message using the class or static method approach. The program invokes the `OutputBanner()` method for the banner line and the `OutputName()` method to output the message and the student name. The method `OutputBanner()` outputs a simple message to the console. `Main()` passes the `student` object as an argument to `OutputName()` so that it can display the student's name.

Next, `Main()` uses the instance method approach to outputting the banner and message by calling `student.OutputBannerAndName()`.

`OutputBannerAndName()` first invokes the static method `OutputBanner()`. The class `Student` is assumed. No object is passed because the static `OutputBanner` doesn't need one. Next, `OutputBannerAndName()` calls the `OutputName()` method. `OutputName()` is also a static method, but it takes a `Student` object as its argument. `OutputBannerAndName()` passes `this` for that argument.

A more interesting case is the call to `ToNameString()` from within `OutputName()`. `OutputName()` is declared `static` and therefore has no `this`. It has an explicit `Student` object, which it uses to make the call.

The `OutputBanner()` method would probably like to call `ToNameString()` as well; however, it has no `Student` object to use. It has no `this` reference because it's a static method and wasn't passed an object explicitly. Note the first boldfaced line in the sample code: The static method cannot call the instance method.

A static method cannot call a nonstatic method without explicitly providing an object. No object, no call. In general, static methods cannot access any nonstatic items in the class. But nonstatic (instance) methods can access static as well as instance items: static data members and static methods.

Chapter 5: Holding a Class Responsible

In This Chapter

- Letting the class protect itself through access control
- Introducing the property, a specialized kind of method
- Allowing an object to initialize itself via the constructor
- Defining multiple constructors for the same class
- Constructing static or class members

A class must be held responsible for its actions. Just as a microwave oven shouldn't burst into flames if you press the wrong key, a class shouldn't allow itself to roll over and die when presented with incorrect data.

To be held responsible for its actions, a class must ensure that its initial state is correct and then control its subsequent state so that it remains valid. C# provides both these capabilities.

Restricting Access to Class Members

Simple classes define all their members as `public`. Consider a `BankAccount` program that maintains a `balance` data member to retain the balance in each account. Making that data member `public` puts everyone on the honor system.

I don't know about your bank, but my bank isn't nearly so forthcoming as to leave a pile of money and a register for me to mark down every time I add money to or take money away from the pile. After all, I may forget to mark my withdrawals in the register.

Controlling access avoids little mistakes, such as forgetting to mark a withdrawal here or there, and manages to avoid some truly big mistakes with withdrawals.

I know exactly what you procedural types out there are thinking: "Just make a rule that other classes can't access the `balance` data member directly, and that's that." That approach may work in theory, but in practice it never does. People start out with good intentions (like my intentions to work out every day), but those good intentions get crushed under the weight of schedule pressures to get the product out the door. Speaking of weight. . . .

A public example of public BankAccount

The following `BankAccount` class example declares all its methods `public` but declares its data members, including `_accountNumber` and `_balance`, to be `private`. Note that I've left it in an incorrect state to make a point. The following code chunk doesn't compile correctly yet:

```
// BankAccount -- Create a bank account using a double variable
//    to store the account balance (keep the balance in a private
//    variable to hide its implementation from the outside world).
// Note: Until you correct it, this program fails to compile
// because Main() refers to a private member of class BankAccount.
using System;
namespace BankAccount
{
  public class Program
  {
    public static void Main(string[] args)
    {
      Console.WriteLine("This program doesn't compile in its present state.");
      // Open a bank account.
      Console.WriteLine("Create a bank account object");
      BankAccount ba = new BankAccount();
      ba.InitBankAccount();
      // Accessing the balance via the Deposit() method is okay --
      // Deposit() has access to all the data members.
      ba.Deposit(10);
      // Accessing the data member directly is a compile-time error.
      Console.WriteLine("Just in case you get this far the following is "
                      + "supposed to generate a compile error");
      ba._balance += 10;
      // Wait for user to acknowledge the results.
      Console.WriteLine("Press Enter to terminate...");
      Console.Read();
    }
  }

  // BankAccount -- Define a class that represents a simple account.
  public class BankAccount
  {
    private static int _nextAccountNumber = 1000;
    private int _accountNumber;
    // Maintain the balance as a double variable.
    private double _balance;
    // Init -- Initialize a bank account with the next
    //    account id and a balance of 0.
    public void InitBankAccount()
    {
      _accountNumber = ++_nextAccountNumber;
      _balance = 0.0;
    }
    // GetBalance -- Return the current balance.
    public double GetBalance()
    {
      return _balance;
    }
```

```
    // AccountNumber
    public int GetAccountNumber()
    {
      return _accountNumber;
    }
    public void SetAccountNumber(int accountNumber)
    {
      this._accountNumber = accountNumber;
    }
    // Deposit -- Any positive deposit is allowed.
    public void Deposit(double amount)
    {
      if (amount > 0.0)
      {
        _balance += amount;
      }
    }
    // Withdraw -- You can withdraw any amount up to the
    //    balance; return the amount withdrawn.
    public double Withdraw(double withdrawal)
    {
      if (_balance <= withdrawal)
      {
        withdrawal = _balance;
      }
      _balance -= withdrawal;
      return withdrawal;
    }
    // GetString -- Return the account data as a string.
    public string GetString()
    {
      string s = String.Format("#{0} = {1:C}",
                               GetAccountNumber(), GetBalance());
      return s;
    }
  }
}
```

In this code example, `_balance -= withdrawal` is the same as `_balance = _balance - withdrawal`. (C# programmers tend to use the shortest notation available.)

Marking a member `public` makes that member available to any other code within your program.

The `BankAccount` class provides an `InitBankAccount()` method to initialize the members of the class, a `Deposit()` method to handle deposits, and a `Withdraw()` method to perform withdrawals. The `Deposit()` and `Withdraw()` methods even provide some rudimentary rules, such as "You can't deposit a negative number" and "You can't withdraw more than you have in your account" (both good rules for a bank, as I'm sure you'll agree). However, everyone's on the honor system as long as `_balance` is accessible to external methods. (In this context, *external* means "external to the class but within the same program.") The honor system can be a problem on big programs written by teams of programmers. It can even be a problem for you (and me), given general human fallibility.

Well-written code with rules that the compiler can enforce saves everyone from the occasional bullet to the big toe.

Before you get too excited, however, notice that the program doesn't build. Attempts to do so generate this error message:

```
'BankAccount.BankAccount._balance' is inaccessible due to its protection level.
```

I don't know why it doesn't just come out and say, "Hey, this is private, so keep your mitts off." The statement `ba._balance += 10;` is illegal because `_balance` isn't accessible to `Main()`, a method outside the `BankAccount` class. Replacing this line with `ba.Deposit(10)` solves the problem. The `BankAccount.Deposit()` method is public and therefore accessible to `Main()` and other parts of your program.

Not declaring a class member's access type explicitly is the same as declaring it `private`.

The default access type is `private`. However, you should include the `private` keyword to remove any doubt. Good programmers make their intentions explicit, which is another way to reduce errors.

Jumping ahead — other levels of security

Understanding this section depends on your having some knowledge of inheritance (see Chapter 6 in this minibook) and namespaces (Chapter 10 in this minibook). You can skip this section for now if you want, but just know that it's here when you need it.

C# provides these levels of security:

- A `public` member is accessible to any class in the program.
- A `private` member is accessible only from the current class.
- A `protected` member is accessible from the current class and any of its subclasses.
- An `internal` member is accessible from any class within the same program module or assembly.

  A C# "module," or *assembly,* is a separately compiled piece of code, either an executable program in an `.EXE` file or a supporting library module in a `.DLL` file. A single namespace can extend across multiple assemblies. (Chapter 10 in this minibook explains C# assemblies and namespaces and discusses access levels other than `public` and `private`.)

- An `internal protected` member is accessible from the current class and any subclass, and from classes within the same module.

Keeping a member hidden by declaring it `private` offers the maximum amount of security. However, in many cases, you don't need that level of security. After all, the members of a subclass already depend on the members of the base class, so `protected` offers a comfortable level of security.

Why You Should Worry about Access Control

Declaring the internal members of a class `public` is a bad idea for at least these reasons:

- **With all data members `public`, you can't easily determine when and how data members are being modified.** Why bother building safety checks into the `Deposit()` and `Withdraw()` methods? In fact, why even bother with these methods? Any method of any class can modify these elements at any time. If other methods can access these data members, they almost certainly will.

  Your `BankAccount` program may execute for an hour or so before you notice that one of the accounts has a negative balance. The `Withdraw()` method would have ensured that this situation didn't happen, so obviously another method accessed the balance without going through `Withdraw()`. Figuring out which method is responsible and under which conditions is a difficult problem.

- **Exposing all data members of the class makes the interface too complicated.** As a programmer using the `BankAccount` class, you *don't want* to know about the internal workings of the class. You just need to know that you can deposit and withdraw funds. It's like a candy machine that has 50 buttons versus 1 with just a few buttons — the ones you need.

- **Exposing internal elements leads to a distribution of the class rules.** For example, my `BankAccount` class doesn't allow the balance to be negative under any circumstances. That required *business rule* should be isolated within the `Withdraw()` method. Otherwise, you have to add this check everywhere the balance is updated.

  Sometimes, a bank decides to change the rules so that "valued customers" are allowed to carry slightly negative balances for a short period, to avoid unintended overdrafts. Then you have to search through the program to update every section of code that accesses the balance, to ensure that the safety checks are changed.

Make your classes and methods no more accessible than necessary. I give you this advice not so much to cause paranoia about snoopy hackers as to suggest a prudent step that helps reduce errors as you code. Use `private`, if possible, and then escalate to `protected`, `internal`, `internal protected`, or `public` as necessary.

Accessor methods

If you look more carefully at the BankAccount class, you see a few other methods. One, GetString(), returns a string version of the account fit for presentation to any Console.WriteLine() for display. However, displaying the contents of a BankAccount object may be difficult if its contents are inaccessible. The class should have the right to decide how it is displayed.

In addition, you see two "getter" methods, GetBalance() and GetAccountNumber(), and one "setter" method, SetAccountNumber(). You may wonder why I would bother to declare a data member such as _balance private but provide a public GetBalance() method to return its value. I have *two* reasons:

- **GetBalance() doesn't provide a way to modify _balance — it merely returns its value.** The balance is read-only. To use the analogy of an actual bank, you can look at your balance any time you want; you just can't withdraw money from your account without using the bank's withdrawal mechanism.
- **GetBalance() hides the internal format of the class from external methods.** GetBalance() may perform an extensive calculation by reading receipts, adding account charges, and accounting for any other amounts your bank may want to subtract from your balance. External methods don't know and don't care. Of course, you care which fees are being charged — you just can't do anything about them, short of changing banks.

Finally, GetBalance() provides a mechanism for making internal changes to the class without the need to change the users of BankAccount. If the Federal Deposit Insurance Corporation (FDIC) mandates that your bank store deposits differently, the mandate shouldn't change the way you access your account.

Access control to the rescue — an example

The following DoubleBankAccount program demonstrates a potential flaw in the BankAccount program. The entire program is on your Web site; however, the following listing shows just Main() — the only portion of the program that differs from the earlier BankAccount program:

```
// DoubleBankAccount -- Create a bank account using a double variable
//    to store the account balance (keep the balance in a private
//    variable to hide its implementation from the outside world).
using System;
namespace DoubleBankAccount
{
```

```
public class Program
{
  public static void Main(string[] args)
  {
    // Open a bank account.
    Console.WriteLine("Create a bank account object");
    BankAccount ba = new BankAccount();
    ba.InitBankAccount();
    // Make a deposit.
    double deposit = 123.454;
    Console.WriteLine("Depositing {0:C}", deposit);
    ba.Deposit(deposit);
    // Account balance
    Console.WriteLine("Account = {0}", ba.GetString());
    // Here's the problem.
    double fractionalAddition = 0.002;
    Console.WriteLine("Adding {0:C}", fractionalAddition);
    ba.Deposit(fractionalAddition);
    // Resulting balance
    Console.WriteLine("Resulting account = {0}", ba.GetString());
    // Wait for user to acknowledge the results.
    Console.WriteLine("Press Enter to terminate...");
    Console.Read();
  }
}
```


The `Main()` method creates a bank account and then deposits $123.454, an amount that contains a fractional number of cents. `Main()` then deposits a small fraction of a cent to the balance and displays the resulting balance.

The output from this program appears this way:

```
Create a bank account object
Depositing $123.45
Account = #1001 = $123.45
Adding $0.00
Resulting account = #1001 = $123.46
Press Enter to terminate...
```

Users start to complain: "I just can't reconcile my checkbook with my bank statement." Personally, I'm happy if I can get to the nearest $100, but some people insist that their accounts match to the penny. Apparently, the program has a bug.

The problem, of course, is that $123.454 shows up as $123.45. To avoid the problem, the bank decides to round deposits and withdrawals to the nearest cent. Deposit $123.454 and the bank takes that extra 0.4 cent. On the other side, the bank gives up enough 0.4 amounts that everything balances out in the long run. Well, in theory, it does.

The easiest way to solve the rounding problem is by converting the bank accounts to `decimal` and using the `Decimal.Round()` method, as shown in this `DecimalBankAccount` program:

```
// DecimalBankAccount -- Create a bank account using a decimal
//     variable to store the account balance.
using System;
namespace DecimalBankAccount
{
  public class Program
  {
    public static void Main(string[] args)
    {
      // Open a bank account.
      Console.WriteLine("Create a bank account object");
      BankAccount ba = new BankAccount();
      ba.InitBankAccount();
      // Make a deposit.
      double deposit = 123.454;
      Console.WriteLine("Depositing {0:C}", deposit);
      ba.Deposit(deposit);
      // Account balance
      Console.WriteLine("Account = {0}", ba.GetString());
      // Now add in a very small amount.
      double fractionalAddition = 0.002;
      Console.WriteLine("Adding {0:C}", fractionalAddition);
      ba.Deposit(fractionalAddition);
      // Resulting balance.
      Console.WriteLine("Resulting account = {0}", ba.GetString());
      // Wait for user to acknowledge the results.
      Console.WriteLine("Press Enter to terminate...");
      Console.Read();
    }
  }
  // BankAccount -- Define a class that represents a simple account.
  public class BankAccount
  {
    private static int _nextAccountNumber = 1000;
    private int _accountNumber;
    // Maintain the balance as a single decimal variable.
    private decimal _balance;
    // Init -- Initialize a bank account with the next
    //    account id and a balance of 0.
    public void InitBankAccount()
    {
      _accountNumber = ++_nextAccountNumber;
      _balance = 0;
    }
    // GetBalance -- Return the current balance.
    public double GetBalance()
    {
      return (double)_balance;
    }
    // AccountNumber
    public int GetAccountNumber()
    {
      return _accountNumber;
    }
    public void SetAccountNumber(int accountNumber)
    {
      this._accountNumber = accountNumber;
    }
    // Deposit -- Any positive deposit is allowed.
    public void Deposit(double amount)
    {
```

```
      if (amount > 0.0)
      {
        // Round off the double to the nearest cent before depositing.
        decimal temp = (decimal)amount;
        temp = Decimal.Round(temp, 2);
        _balance += temp;
      }
    }
    // Withdraw -- You can withdraw any amount up to the
    //    balance; return the amount withdrawn.
    public double Withdraw(double withdrawal)
    {
      // Convert to decimal and work with the decimal version.
      decimal decWithdrawal = (decimal)withdrawal;
      if (_balance <= decWithdrawal)
      {
        decWithdrawal = _balance;
      }
      _balance -= decWithdrawal;
      return (double)decWithdrawal;  // Return a double.
    }
    // GetString -- Return the account data as a string.
    public string GetString()
    {
      string s = String.Format("#{0} = {1:C}",
                          GetAccountNumber(), GetBalance());
      return s;
    }
  }
}
```


I've converted all internal representations to `decimal` values, a type better adapted to handling bank account balances than `double` in any case. The `Deposit()` method now uses the `Decimal.Round()` method to round the deposit amount to the nearest cent before making the deposit. The output from the program is now as expected:

```
Create a bank account object
Depositing $123.45
Account = #1001 = $123.45
Adding $0.00
Resulting account = #1001 = $123.45
Press Enter to terminate...
```

So what?

You could argue that I should have written the `BankAccount` program using `decimal` input arguments to begin with, and I probably would agree. But the point is that I didn't. Other applications were written using `double` as the form of storage. A problem arose. The `BankAccount` class was able to fix the problem internally and make no changes to the application software. (Notice that the class's public interface didn't change: `Balance()` and `Withdraw()` still return `double`s, and `Deposit()` and `Withdraw()` still take a `double` parameter.)

I repeat: Applications *using* class BankAccount didn't have to change.

In this case, the only calling method potentially affected was Main(), but the effects could have extended to dozens of methods that accessed bank accounts, and those methods could have been spread over hundreds of assemblies. None of those methods would have to change, because the fix was within the confines of the BankAccount class, whose *public interface* (its public methods) didn't outwardly change. This solution wouldn't have been possible if the internal members of the class had been exposed to external methods.

Internal changes to a class still require some retesting of other code, even though you didn't have to modify that code.

Defining Class Properties

The GetX() and SetX() methods demonstrated in the BankAccount programs in the previous section are *access methods,* or simply *accessors.* Although they signify good programming habits in theory, access methods can become clumsy in practice. For example, the following code line is necessary to increment _accountNumber by 1:

```
SetAccountNumber(GetAccountNumber() + 1);
```

C# defines a construct known as a *property,* which makes using access methods much easier than making them methods. The following code snippet defines a read-write property, AccountNumber (it's both a getter and a setter):

```
public int AccountNumber         // No parentheses here.
{
  get{ return _accountNumber; }  // The "read" part. Curly braces and semicolon.
  set{ _accountNumber = value; } // The "write" part. 'value' is a keyword.
}
```

The get section is called whenever the property is read, and the set section is invoked on the write. The following Balance property is read-only because only the get section is defined (using a less compact notation):

```
public double Balance
{
  get
  {
    return (double)_balance;
  }
}
```

In use, these properties appear as follows:

```
BankAccount ba = new BankAccount();
// Set the account number property.
ba.AccountNumber = 1001;
// Get both properties.
Console.WriteLine("#{0} = {1:C}", ba.AccountNumber, ba.Balance);
```

The properties `AccountNumber` and `Balance` look much like `public` data members, in both appearance and use. However, properties enable the class to protect internal members (`Balance` is a read-only property) and hide their implementation (the underlying `_balance` data member is `private`). Notice that `Balance` performs a conversion — it could have performed any number of calculations. Properties aren't necessarily one-liners.

By convention, the name of a property begins with a capital letter. Note that properties don't have parentheses: It's `Balance`, not `Balance()`.

Properties aren't necessarily inefficient. The C# compiler can optimize a simple accessor to the point that it generates no more machine code than accessing the data member directly. This concept is important, not only to an application program but also to C# itself. The C# library uses properties throughout, and you should too.

Use properties to access class data members, *even from methods in the same class.*

Static properties

A static (class) data member may be exposed through a static property, as shown in this simplistic example (note its compact layout):

```
public class BankAccount
{
  private static int _nextAccountNumber = 1000;
  public static int NextAccountNumber { get { return _nextAccountNumber; } }
  // . . .
}
```

The `NextAccountNumber` property is accessed through the class as follows because it isn't an instance property (it's declared *static*):

```
// Read the account number property.
int value = BankAccount.NextAccountNumber;
```

(In this example, `value` is outside the context of a property, so it isn't a reserved word.)

Properties with side effects

A `get` operation can perform extra work other than simply retrieving the associated property, as shown here:

```
public static int AccountNumber
{
  // Retrieve the property and set it up for the
  // next retrieval by incrementing it.
  get{ return ++_nextAccountNumber; }
}
```

This property increments the static account number member before returning the result. This action probably isn't a good idea, however, because the user of the property receives no clue that anything is happening other than the actual reading of the property. The incrementation is a *side effect*.

Like the accessor methods that they mimic, properties shouldn't change the state of the class other than, say, setting a data member's value. Both properties and methods generally should avoid side effects because they can lead to subtle bugs. Change a class as directly and explicitly as possible.

New feature: Letting the compiler write properties for you

Most properties described in the previous section are utterly routine, and writing them is tedious (though simple):

```
private string _name;  // An underlying data member for the property
public string Name { get { return _name; } set { _name = value; } }
```

Because you write this same boilerplate code repeatedly, the C# 3.0 compiler now does it for you. All you have to write for the previous property (including the private data member) is this line:

```
public string Name { get; set; }
```

This line is sort of equivalent to

```
private string <somename>;  // What's <somename>? Don't know or care.
public string Name { get { return <somename>; } set { <somename> = value; } }
```

The compiler creates a mysterious data member that shall be nameless along with the accessor boilerplate code. The `AccessorPropertyShortcuts` example on `csharp102.info` illustrates this usage. This style encourages using the property even inside other members of its containing class because the property name is all you know. For that reason, you must have both get and set. You can initialize such properties using the property syntax:

```
public int AnInt { get; set; } // Compiler provides a private variable.
. . .
AnInt = 2; // Initialize compiler-written instance variable via property.
```

Accessors with access levels

Accessor properties don't necessarily have to be declared public. You can declare them at any appropriate level, even private, if the accessor is used only inside its class. (The upcoming example marks the Name property internal.)

You can even adjust the access levels of the get and set portions of an accessor individually. Suppose that you don't want to expose the set accessor outside your class — it's for internal use only. You can write the property like this:

```
internal string Name { get; private set; }
```

The AccessorPropertyShortcuts example at csharp102.info illustrates this usage.

Getting Your Objects Off to a Good Start — Constructors

Controlling class access is only half the problem: *An object needs a good start in life if it is to grow.* A class can supply an initialization method that the application calls to get things started, but the application could forget to call the method. The class starts out with garbage, and the situation gets no better after that. If you want to hold the class accountable, you have to ensure that it has a chance to start out correctly.

C# solves that problem by calling the initialization method for you — for example:

```
MyObject mo = new MyObject();
```

In other words, this statement not only grabs an object from a special memory area, but it also initializes that object's members.

Keep the terms *class* and *object* separate in your mind. Cat is a class. My cat Striper is an object of class Cat.

The C#-Provided Constructor

C# keeps track of whether a variable has been initialized and doesn't allow you to use an uninitialized variable. For example, the following code chunk generates a compile-time error:

```
public static void Main(string[] args)
{
  int n;
  double d;
  double  calculatedValue = n + d;
}
```

C# tracks the fact that the *local variables* `n` and `d` haven't been assigned a value and doesn't allow them to be used in the expression. Compiling this tiny program generates these compiler errors:

```
Use of unassigned local variable 'n'
Use of unassigned local variable 'd'
```

By comparison, C# provides a *default constructor* that initializes the *data members* of an object to

- 0 for numbers
- `false` for Booleans
- `null` for object references

Consider the following simple program example:

```
using System;
namespace Test
{
  public class Program
  {
    public static void Main(string[] args)
    {
      // First create an object.
      MyObject localObject = new MyObject();
      Console.WriteLine("localObject.n is {0}", localObject.n);
      if (localObject.nextObject == null)
      {
        Console.WriteLine("localObject.nextObject is null");
      }
      // Wait for user to acknowledge the results.
      Console.WriteLine("Press Enter to terminate...");
      Console.Read();
    }
  }
  public class MyObject
  {
    internal int n;
    internal MyObject nextObject;
  }
}
```

This program defines a class `MyObject`, which contains both a simple data member `n` of type `int` and a reference to an object, `nextObject` (both declared `internal`). The `Main()` method creates a `MyObject` and then displays the initial contents of `n` and `nextObject`.

The output from executing the program appears this way:

```
localObject.n is 0
localObject.nextObject is null
Press Enter to terminate...
```

When the object is created, C# executes a small piece of code that the compiler provides to initialize the object and its members. Left to their own devices, the data members `localObject.n` and `nextObject` would contain random, garbage values.

The code that initializes values when they're created is the *default constructor.* It "constructs" the class, in the sense of initializing its members. Thus C# ensures that an object starts life in a known state: all zeros. This concept affects only data members of the class, not local variables in a method.

Replacing the Default Constructor

Although the compiler automatically initializes all instance variables to zeroes, for many classes (probably most classes), all zeroes isn't a valid state. Consider the following `BankAccount` class from earlier in this chapter:

```
public class BankAccount
{
  private int _accountNumber;
  private double _balance;
  // . . .other members
}
```

Although an initial balance of 0 is probably okay, an account number of 0 definitely isn't the hallmark of a valid bank account.

At this in the chapter, the `BankAccount` class includes the `InitBankAccount()` method to initialize the object. However, this approach puts too much responsibility on the application software using the class. If the application fails to invoke the `InitBankAccount()` method, the bank account methods may not work, through no fault of their own.

A class shouldn't rely on external methods such as `InitBankAccount()` to start the object in a valid state.

To work around this problem, you can have your class provide its own explicit *class constructor* that C# calls automatically when the object is created. The constructor could have been named `Init()`, `Start()`, or `Create()`, but C# *requires the constructor to carry the name of the class*. Thus a constructor for the `BankAccount` class appears this way:

```
public void Main(string[] args)
{
  BankAccount ba = new BankAccount();  // This invokes the constructor.
}
public class BankAccount
{
  // Bank accounts start at 1000 and increase sequentially.
  private static int _nextAccountNumber = 1000;
  // Maintain the account number and balance for each object.
  private int _accountNumber;
  private double _balance;
  // BankAccount constructor -- Here it is -- ta-da!
  public BankAccount()   // Parentheses, possible arguments, no return type
  {
    _accountNumber = ++_nextAccountNumber;
    _balance = 0.0;
  }
  // . . . other members . . .
}
```

The contents of the `BankAccount` constructor are the same as those of the original `Init...()` method. However, the way you declare and use the constructor differs:

- ✦ The constructor always carries the same name as the class.
- ✦ The constructor can take parameters (or not).
- ✦ The constructor never has a return type, not even `void`.
- ✦ `Main()` doesn't need to invoke any extra method to initialize the object when it's created; no `Init()` is necessary.

If you provide your own constructor, C# no longer supplies a default constructor. Your constructor replaces the default and becomes the only way to create an instance of your class.

Constructing something

Try out a constructor thingie. Consider the following program, `DemonstrateCustomConstructor`:

```
// DemonstrateCustomConstructor -- Demonstrate how you can replace the
//    C# default constructor with your own, custom constructor.
//    Creates a class with a constructor and then steps through a few scenarios.
using System;
namespace DemonstrateCustomConstructor
{
  // MyObject -- Create a class with a noisy custom constructor
```

```
  //    and an internal data object.
  public class MyObject
  {
    // This data member is a property of the class (it's static).
    private static MyOtherObject _staticObj = new MyOtherObject();
    // This data member is a property of each instance.
    private MyOtherObject _dynamicObj;
    // Constructor (a real chatterbox)
    public MyObject()
    {
      Console.WriteLine("MyObject constructor starting");
      Console.WriteLine("(Static data member constructed before " +
                        "this constructor)");
      Console.WriteLine("Now create nonstatic data member dynamically:");
      _dynamicObj = new MyOtherObject();
      Console.WriteLine("MyObject constructor ending");
    }
  }
  // MyOtherObject -- This class also has a noisy constructor but
  //    no internal members.
  public class MyOtherObject
  {
    public MyOtherObject()
    {
      Console.WriteLine("MyOtherObject constructing");
    }
  }
  public class Program
  {
    public static void Main(string[] args)
    {
      Console.WriteLine("Main() starting");
      Console.WriteLine("Creating a local MyObject in Main():");
      MyObject localObject = new MyObject();
      // Wait for user to acknowledge the results.
      Console.WriteLine("Press Enter to terminate...");
      Console.Read();
    }
  }
}
```


Executing this program generates the following output:

```
Main() starting
Creating a local MyObject in Main():
MyOtherObject constructing
MyObject constructor starting
(Static data member constructed before this constructor)
Now create nonstatic data member dynamically:
MyOtherObject constructing
MyObject constructor ending
Press Enter to terminate...
```

The following steps reconstruct what just happened:

1. The program starts, and `Main()` outputs the initial message and announces that it's about to create a local `MyObject`.
2. `Main()` creates a `localObject` of type `MyObject`.

3. `MyObject` contains a static member `_staticObj` of class `MyOtherObject`.

All static data members are initialized before the first `MyObject()` constructor runs. In this case, C# populates `_staticObj` with a newly created `MyOtherObject` before passing control to the `MyObject` constructor. This step accounts for the third line of output.

4. The constructor for `MyObject` is given control. It outputs the initial message, `MyObject constructor starting`, and then notes that the static member was already constructed before the `MyObject()` constructor began:

```
(Static data member constructed before this
   constructor).
```

5. After announcing its intention with `Now create nonstatic data member dynamically`, the `MyObject` constructor creates an object of class `MyOtherObject` using the `new` operator, generating the second `MyOtherObject constructing` message as the `MyOtherObject` constructor is called.

6. Control returns to the `MyObject` constructor, which returns to `Main()`.

Job well done!

Executing the constructor from the debugger

Executing the same program from the debugger is illuminating:

1. **Rebuild the program: Choose the command Build⇨Build DemonstrateCustomConstructor.**

2. **Before you start executing the program from the debugger, set a breakpoint at the `Console.WriteLine()` call in the `MyOtherObject` constructor.**

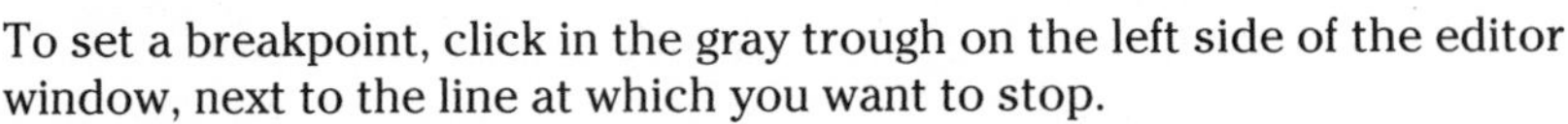

To set a breakpoint, click in the gray trough on the left side of the editor window, next to the line at which you want to stop.

Figure 5-1 shows my display with the breakpoint set: The dark ball is in the trough.

3. **Rather than choose Debug⇨Start Debugging, choose Debug⇨Step Into (or press F11).**

Your menus, toolbars, and windows should change a bit, and then a bright yellow highlight appears on the opening curly brace in `Main()`.

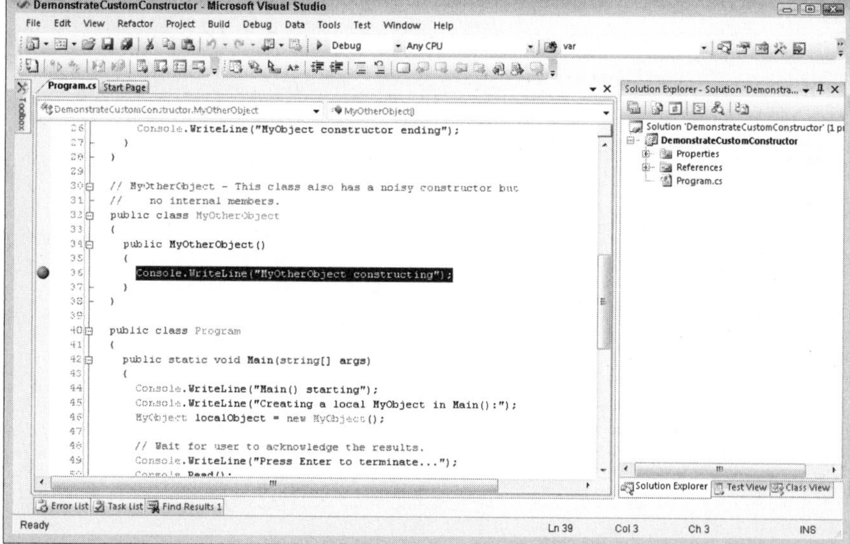

Figure 5-1: The highlighting in the `MyOther Object` constructor indicates the presence of a breakpoint.

4. **Press F11 three more times and lightly rest the mouse pointer on the `localObject` variable (without clicking).**

   You're about to call the `MyObject` constructor. Your display should now look like the one shown in Figure 5-2. You can see that `local Object` is currently `null` under the cursor. The Locals window shows the same thing. (If Locals isn't visible, choose Debug➪Windows➪Locals to display it.)

5. **Press F11 one more time.**

   The program executes to the breakpoint in `MyOtherObject`, as shown by the yellow bar shown in Figure 5-3. How did you reach this point? The last call in `Main()` invoked the constructor for `MyObject`. But before that constructor begins to execute, C# initializes the static data member in class `MyObject`. That data member is of type `MyOtherObject`, so initializing it means invoking *its* constructor — which lands you at the breakpoint. (Without the breakpoint, you wouldn't see the debugger stop there, although the constructor would indeed execute, as you could confirm by checking to ensure that the constructor's message shows up in the console window.)

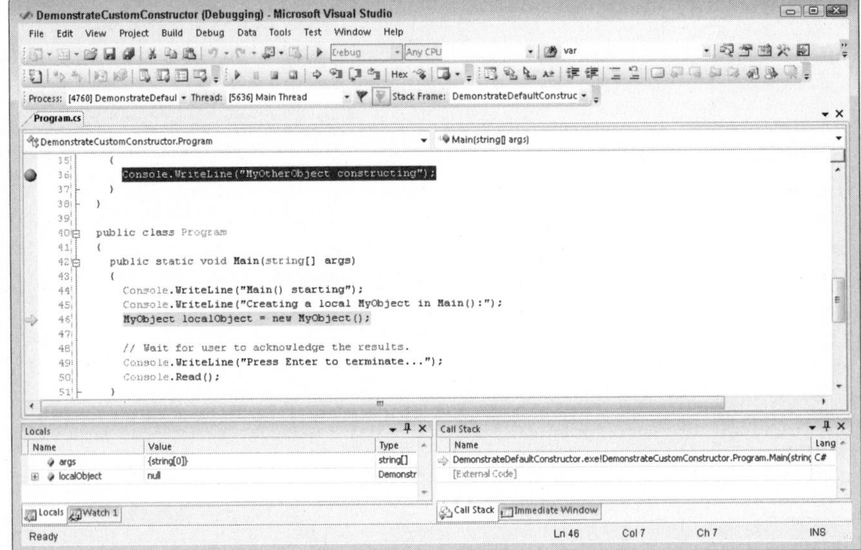

Figure 5-2: Just before you jump into Constructor Land, the Visual Studio debugger display looks like this.

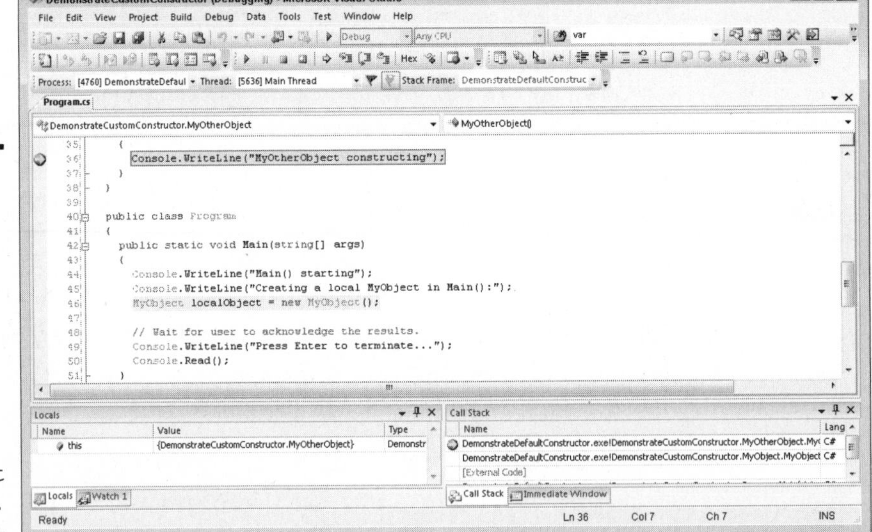

Figure 5-3: Control passes to the `MyOtherObject` constructor before heading into the `MyObject` constructor.

6. **Press F11 twice more, and you're stopped at the static data member, `_staticObj`, as shown in Figure 5-4.**

   It was that object's constructor you just stepped out of.

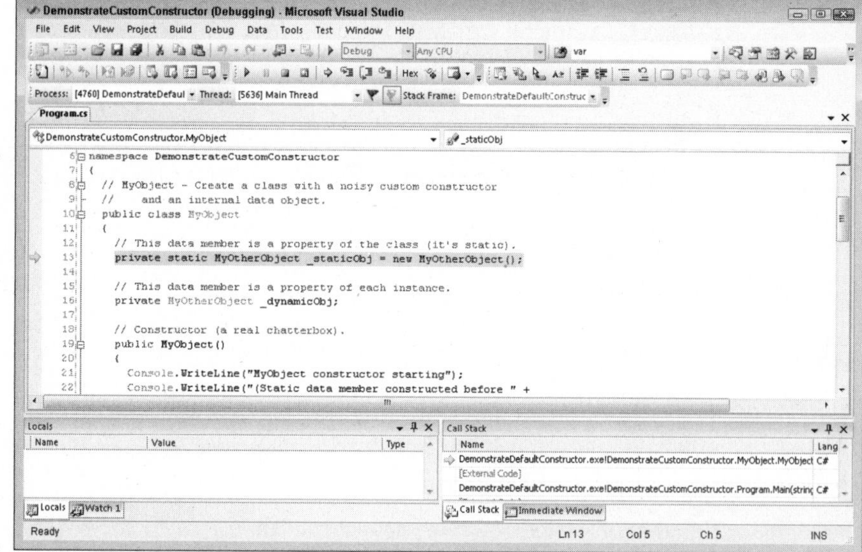

Figure 5-4: Having stepped through the `MyOther Object` constructor, you're back where the constructor was invoked.

7. **Continue pressing F11 as you walk through the program.**

   The first time you press F11, you stop at the beginning of the `MyObject` constructor, at last. Note that you step into the `MyOtherObject` constructor a second time when the `MyObject` constructor creates the other `MyObject` data member, `_dynamicObj` (the nonstatic one).

   Remember to continue the `Console.Read()` statement back in `Main()`. After viewing the console window, you can press Enter to close it.

Book IV gives you a thorough tour of the debugger.

Initializing an object directly with an initializer

Besides letting you initialize data members in a constructor, C# enables you to initialize data members directly by using *initializers*.

Thus I could have written the `BankAccount` class as follows:

```
public class BankAccount
{
  // Bank accounts start at 1000 and increase sequentially.
  private static int _nextAccountNumber = 1000;
  // Maintain the account number and balance for each object.
  private int _accountNumber = ++_nextAccountNumber;
  private double _balance = 0.0;
  // . . . other members . . .
}
```

Here's the initializer business. Both _accountNumber and _balance are assigned a value *as part of their declaration*, which has the same effect as a constructor but without having to do the work in it.

Be clear about exactly what's happening. You may think that this statement sets _balance to 0.0 right now. However, _balance exists only as a part of an object. Thus the assignment isn't executed until a BankAccount object is created. In fact, this assignment is executed every time an object is created.

Note that the static data member _nextAccountNumber is initialized the first time the BankAccount class is accessed — as your tour in the debugger showed, that's the first time you access any method or property of the object owning the static data member, including the constructor.

After the static member is initialized, it isn't reinitialized every time you construct a BankAccount instance. That's different from the nonstatic members.

Initializers are executed in the order of their appearance in the class declaration. If C# encounters both initializers and a constructor, the initializers are executed *before the body of the constructor*.

Seeing that construction stuff with initializers

In the DemonstrateCustomConstructor program, move the call new MyOtherObject() from the MyObject constructor to the declaration itself, as follows (see the bold text), modify the second WriteLine() statement as shown, and then rerun the program:

```
public class MyObject
{
  // This member is a property of the class (it's static).
  private static MyOtherObject _staticObj = new MyOtherObject();
  // This member is a property of each instance.
  private MyOtherObject _dynamicObj = new MyOtherObject();  // <- Here.
  public MyObject()
  {
    Console.WriteLine("MyObject constructor starting");
    Console.WriteLine(
      "Both data members initialized before this constructor)");
    // _dynamicObj construction was here, now moved up.
    Console.WriteLine("MyObject constructor ending");
  }
}
```

Compare the following output from this modified program with the output from its predecessor, DemonstrateCustomConstructor:

```
Main() starting
Creating a local MyObject in Main():
MyOtherObject constructing
MyOtherObject constructing
```

```
MyObject constructor starting
(Both data members initialized before this constructor)
MyObject constructor ending
Press Enter to terminate...
```

You can find the entire program (after these changes) on the Web site, under the illustrious name of `DemonstrateConstructorWithInitializer`.

New feature: Initializing an object without a constructor

Suppose that you have a little class to represent a `Student`:

```
public class Student
{
  public string Name { get; set; }
  public string Address { get; set; }
  public double GradePointAverage { get; set; }
}
```

A `Student` object has three public properties, `Name`, `Address`, and `GradePointAverage`, which specify the student's basic information.

Normally, when you create a new `Student` object, you have to initialize its `Name`, `Address`, and `GradePointAverage` properties like this:

```
Student randal = new Student();
randal.Name = "Randal Sphar";
randal.Address = "123 Elm Street, Truth or Consequences, NM 00000";
randal.GradePointAverage = 3.51;
```

(Yes, Virginia, there is a Truth or Consequences, New Mexico. My nephew Randal was born there.)

If `Student` had a constructor, you could do something like this:

```
Student randal = new Student
  ("Randal Sphar", "123 Elm Street, Truth or Consequences, NM, 00000", 3.51);
```

Sadly, however, `Student` lacks a constructor, other than the default one that C# supplies automatically — which takes no parameters.

In C# 3.0 and later, you can simplify that initialization with something that looks suspiciously like a constructor — well, sort of:

```
Student randal = new Student
  { Name = "Randal Sphar",
    Address = "123 Elm Street, Truth or Consequences, NM 00000",
    GradePointAverage = 3.51
  };
```

The last two examples are different in this respect: The first one, using a constructor, shows *parentheses* containing two strings and one `double` value separated by commas, and the second one, using the new object-initializer syntax, has instead *curly braces* containing three *assignments* separated by commas. The syntax works something like this:

```
new LatitudeLongitude
  { assignment to Latitude, assignment to Longitude  };
```

The new object-initializer syntax lets you assign to any accessible *set* properties of the `LatitudeLongitude` object in a code block (the curly braces). The block is designed to initialize the object. Note that you can set only accessible properties this way, not private ones, and you can't call any of the object's methods or do any other work in the initializer.

The new syntax is much more concise: one statement versus three. And, it simplifies the creation of initialized objects that don't let you do so through a constructor. (I broke the `Student` example into multiple lines only to fit it on the page — and that was only because the name Truth or Consequences is long. If you lived there, it would seem even longer.)

The new object-initializer syntax doesn't gain you much of anything besides convenience, but convenience when you're coding is high on any programmer's list. So is brevity. Besides, the feature becomes essential when you read about anonymous classes.

Use the new object-initializer syntax to your heart's content. I use it frequently myself throughout the rest of this book.

Look up the term *object initializer* in Help to find the lawyer-y language stuff concerning which kinds of properties it works with.

The `ObjectInitializers` program example on the Web site demonstrates object initializers.

Chapter 6: Inheritance: Is That All I Get?

In This Chapter

- **Defining one class in terms of another, more fundamental class**
- **Differentiating between *is a* and *has a***
- **Substituting one class object for another**
- **Constructing static or instance members**
- **Including constructors in an inheritance hierarchy**
- **Invoking the base class constructor specifically**

Object-oriented programming is based on four principles: the ability to control access (encapsulation), inherit from other classes, respond appropriately (polymorphism), and refer from one object to another indirectly (interfaces).

Inheritance is a common concept. I am a human, except when I first wake up. I inherit certain properties from the class `Human`, such as my ability to converse, more or less, and my dependence on air, food, and carbohydrate-based beverages with lots of caffeine. The class `Human` inherits its dependencies on air, water, and nourishment from the class `Mammal`, which inherits from the class `Animal`.

The ability to pass down properties is a powerful one. You can use it to describe items in an economical way. For example, if my son asks, "What's a duck?" I can say, "It's a bird that quacks." Despite what you may think, that answer conveys a considerable amount of information. My son knows what a bird is, and now he knows all those same characteristics about a duck plus the duck's additional property of "quackness."

Object-oriented languages express this inheritance relationship by allowing one class to inherit properties from another. This feature enables object-oriented languages to generate a model that's closer to the real world than the model generated by languages that don't support inheritance.

Class Inheritance

In the following InheritanceExample program, the class SubClass inherits from the class BaseClass:

```
// InheritanceExample -- Provide the simplest possible
//    demonstration of inheritance.
using System;
namespace InheritanceExample
{
  public class BaseClass
  {
    public int _dataMember;
    public void SomeMethod()
    {
      Console.WriteLine("SomeMethod()");
    }
  }
  public class SubClass : BaseClass
  {
    public void SomeOtherMethod()
    {
      Console.WriteLine("SomeOtherMethod()");
    }
  }
  public class Program
  {
    public static void Main(string[] args)
    {
      // Create a base class object.
      Console.WriteLine("Exercising a base class object:");
      BaseClass bc = new BaseClass();
      bc._dataMember = 1;
      bc.SomeMethod();
      // Now create a subclass object.
      Console.WriteLine("Exercising a subclass object:");
      SubClass sc = new SubClass();
      sc._dataMember = 2;
      sc.SomeMethod();
      sc.SomeOtherMethod();
      // Wait for user to acknowledge the results.
      Console.WriteLine("Press Enter to terminate...");
      Console.Read();
    }
  }
}
```

The class BaseClass is defined with a data member and the simple method SomeMethod(). Main() creates and exercises the BaseClass object bc.

The class SubClass inherits from that class by placing the name of the class, BaseClass, after a colon in the class definition:

```
public class SubClass : BaseClass
```

Inheritance is amazing

To make sense of their surroundings, humans build extensive taxonomies. For example, Fido is a special case of dog, which is a special case of canine, which is a special case of mammal — and so it goes. This ability to classify items shapes our human understanding of the world.

In an object-oriented language such as C#, you say that the class `Student` inherits from the class `Person`. You also say that `Person` is a base class of `Student` and that `Student` is a subclass of `Person`. Finally, you say that a `Student` IS_A `Person`. (Using all caps and an underscore is a common way of expressing this unique relationship — I didn't make up this concept.)

Notice that the IS_A property isn't reflexive: Although `Student` IS_A `Person`, the reverse isn't true. A `Person` IS_NOT_A `Student`. A statement such as this one always refers to the general case. A particular `Person` might be, in fact, a `Student` — but lots of people who are members of the class `Person` aren't members of the class `Student`. In addition, the class `Student` has properties that it doesn't share with the class `Person`. For example, `Student` has a grade-point average, but the ordinary `Person` quite happily does not.

The inheritance property is transitive. For example, if I define a new class `GraduateStudent` as a subclass of `Student`, `GraduateStudent` is also a `Person`. It must be that way: If a `GraduateStudent` IS_A `Student` and a `Student` IS_A `Person`, a `GraduateStudent` IS_A `Person`.

`SubClass` gets all members of `BaseClass` as its own, plus any members it may add to the pile. `Main()` demonstrates that `SubClass` now has a data member, `_dataMember`, and a member method, `SomeMethod()`, to join the brand-new member of the family, little method `SomeOtherMethod()` — and what a joy it is, too.

The program produces the following expected output (I'm usually sort of surprised whenever one of my programs works as expected):

```
Exercising a base class object:
SomeMethod()
Exercising a subclass object:
SomeMethod()
SomeOtherMethod()
Press Enter to terminate...
```

Why You Need Inheritance

Inheritance serves several important functions. You may think, for example, that inheritance reduces the amount of typing. In a way, it does — you don't need to repeat the properties of a `Person` when you're describing a `Student` class. A more important, related issue is the major buzzword *reuse.* Software scientists have known for some time that starting from scratch with each new project and rebuilding the same software components makes little sense.

Compare the situation in software development to that of other industries. Think about the number of car manufacturers that start out by building their own wrenches and screwdrivers before they construct a car. Of those who do that, estimate how many would start over completely and build all new tools for the next model. Practitioners in other industries have found that starting with existing screws, bolts, nuts, and even larger off-the-shelf components such as motors and compressors makes more sense than starting from scratch.

Inheritance enables you to tweak existing software components. You can adapt existing classes to new applications without making internal modifications. The existing class is inherited into — or, as programmers often say, *extended* by — a new subclass that contains the necessary additions and modifications. If someone else wrote the base class, you may not be able to modify it, so inheritance can save the day.

This capability carries with it a third benefit of inheritance. Suppose that you inherit from — extend — an existing class. Later, you find that the base class has a bug you must correct. If you modified the class to reuse it, you must manually check for, correct, and retest the bug in each application separately. If you inherited the class without changes, you can generally stick the updated class into the other application with little hassle.

But the biggest benefit of inheritance is that it describes the way life is. Items inherit properties from each other. There's no getting around it. (*Basta!* — as my Italian grandmother would say.)

Inheriting from a BankAccount Class (A More Complex Example)

A bank maintains several types of accounts. One type, the savings account, has all the properties of a simple bank account plus the ability to accumulate interest. The following `SimpleSavingsAccount` program models this relationship in C#.

The version of this program on the Web site includes some modifications from the next section of this chapter, so it's a bit different from the code listing shown here.

```
// SimpleSavingsAccount -- Implement SavingsAccount as a form of
//   bank account; use no virtual methods.
using System;
namespace SimpleSavingsAccount
{
```

```
// BankAccount -- Simulate a bank account, each of which
//    carries an account ID (which is assigned
//    on creation) and a balance.
public class BankAccount    // The base class
{
  // Bank accounts start at 1000 and increase sequentially.
  public static int _nextAccountNumber = 1000;
  // Maintain the account number and balance for each object.
  public int _accountNumber;
  public decimal _balance;
  // Init -- Initialize a bank account with the next account ID and the
  //    specified initial balance (default to zero).
  public void InitBankAccount()
  {
    InitBankAccount(0);
  }
  public void InitBankAccount(decimal initialBalance)
  {
    _accountNumber = ++_nextAccountNumber;
    _balance = initialBalance;
  }
  // Balance property.
  public decimal Balance
  {
    get { return _balance;}
  }
  // Deposit -- any positive deposit is allowed.
  public void Deposit(decimal amount)
  {
    if (amount > 0)
    {
      _balance += amount;
    }
  }
  // Withdraw -- You can withdraw any amount up to the
  //    balance; return the amount withdrawn.
  public decimal Withdraw(decimal withdrawal)
  {
    if (Balance <= withdrawal) // Use Balance property.
    {
      withdrawal = Balance;
    }
    _balance -= withdrawal;
    return withdrawal;
  }
  // ToString - Stringify the account.
  public string ToBankAccountString()
  {
    return String.Format("{0} - {1:C}",
      _accountNumber, Balance);
  }
}
// SavingsAccount -- A bank account that draws interest
public class SavingsAccount : BankAccount   // The subclass
{
  public decimal _interestRate;
  // InitSavingsAccount -- Input the rate expressed as a
  //    rate between 0 and 100.
  public void InitSavingsAccount(decimal interestRate)
  {
    InitSavingsAccount(0, interestRate);
  }
```

```
    public void InitSavingsAccount(decimal initialBalance, decimal interestRate)
    {
      InitBankAccount(initialBalance);  // Note call to base class.
      this._interestRate = interestRate / 100;
    }
    // AccumulateInterest -- Invoke once per period.
    public void AccumulateInterest()
    {
      _balance = Balance + (decimal)(Balance * _interestRate);
    }
    // ToString -- Stringify the account.
    public string ToSavingsAccountString()
    {
      return String.Format("{0} ({1}%)",
        ToBankAccountString(), _interestRate * 100);
    }
  }
  public class Program
  {
    public static void Main(string[] args)
    {
      // Create a bank account and display it.
      BankAccount ba = new BankAccount();
      ba.InitBankAccount(100M); // M suffix indicates decimal.
      ba.Deposit(100M);
      Console.WriteLine("Account {0}", ba.ToBankAccountString());
      // Now a savings account
      SavingsAccount sa = new SavingsAccount();
      sa.InitSavingsAccount(100M, 12.5M);
      sa.AccumulateInterest();
      Console.WriteLine("Account {0}", sa.ToSavingsAccountString());
      // Wait for user to acknowledge the results.
      Console.WriteLine("Press Enter to terminate...");
      Console.Read();
    }
  }
}
```

The `BankAccount` class is not unlike some that appear in other chapters of this book. It begins with an overloaded initialization method `InitBankAccount()`: one for accounts that start out with an initial balance and another for which an initial balance of zero will have to suffice. Notice that this version of `BankAccount` doesn't take advantage of the latest and greatest constructor advances. If you read this entire chapter and see that I clean up this topic in the final version of `BankAccount`, you can then see why I chose to "drop back" a little here.

The `Balance` property allows other people to read the balance without letting them modify it. The `Deposit()` method accepts any positive deposit. `Withdraw()` lets you take out as much as you want, as long as you have enough money in your account. (My bank's nice, but it isn't *that* nice.) `ToBankAccountString()` creates a `string` that describes the account.

The `SavingsAccount` class inherits all that good stuff from `BankAccount`. It also adds an interest rate and the ability to accumulate interest at regular intervals.

Main() does about as little as it can. It creates a BankAccount, displays the account, creates a SavingsAccount, accumulates one period of interest, and displays the result, with the interest rate in parentheses:

```
Account 1001 - $200.00
Account 1002 - $112.50 (12.500%)
Press Enter to terminate...
```

Notice that the InitSavingsAccount() method invokes InitBank Account(). It initializes the bank account–specific data members. The InitSavingsAccount() method could have initialized these members directly; however, a better practice is to allow BankAccount to initialize its own members. A class should be responsible for itself.

IS_A versus HAS_A — I'm So Confused_A

The relationship between SavingsAccount and BankAccount is the fundamental IS_A relationship in inheritance. In the following sections, I show you why, and then I show you what the alternative, the HAS_A relationship, would look like in comparison.

The IS_A relationship

The IS_A relationship between SavingsAccount and BankAccount is demonstrated by the modification to the class Program in the SimpleSavingsAccount program from the preceding section:

```
public class Program
{
  // Add this:
  // DirectDeposit -- Deposit my paycheck automatically.
  public static void DirectDeposit(BankAccount ba, decimal pay)
  {
    ba.Deposit(pay);
  }
  public static void Main(string[] args)
  {
    // Create a bank account and display it.
    BankAccount ba = new BankAccount();
    ba.InitBankAccount(100M);
    DirectDeposit(ba, 100M);
    Console.WriteLine("Account {0}", ba.ToBankAccountString());
    // Now a savings account
    SavingsAccount sa = new SavingsAccount();
    sa.InitSavingsAccount(12.5M);
    DirectDeposit(sa, 100M);
    sa.AccumulateInterest();
    Console.WriteLine("Account {0}", sa.ToSavingsAccountString());
    // Wait for user to acknowledge the results.
    Console.WriteLine("Press Enter to terminate...");
    Console.Read();
  }
}
```

In effect, nothing has changed. The only real difference is that all deposits are now being made through the local method DirectDeposit(), which isn't part of class BankAccount. The arguments to this method are the bank account and the amount to deposit.

Notice (here comes the good part) that Main() could pass either a bank account or a savings account to DirectDeposit() because a SavingsAccount IS_A BankAccount and is accorded all the same rights and privileges. Because SavingsAccount IS_A BankAccount, you can assign a SavingsAccount to a BankAccount-type variable or method argument.

Gaining access to BankAccount by using containment

The class SavingsAccount could have gained access to the members of BankAccount in a different way, as shown in the following code, where the key lines are shown in boldface:

```
// SavingsAccount -- A bank account that draws interest
public class SavingsAccount_    // Notice the underscore: this isn't
                                // the SavingsAccount class.
{
  public BankAccount _bankAccount;  // Notice this, the contained BankAccount.
  public decimal _interestRate;
  // InitSavingsAccount -- Input the rate expressed as a
  //    rate between 0 and 100.
  public void InitSavingsAccount(BankAccount bankAccount, decimal interestRate)
  {
    this._bankAccount = bankAccount;
    this._interestRate = interestRate / 100;
  }
  // AccumulateInterest -- Invoke once per period.
  public void AccumulateInterest()
  {
    _bankAccount._balance = _bankAccount.Balance
                 + (_bankAccount.Balance * interestRate);
  }
  // Deposit -- Any positive deposit is allowed.
  public void Deposit(decimal amount)
  {
    // Delegate to the contained BankAccount object.
    _bankAccount.Deposit(amount);
  }
  // Withdraw -- You can withdraw any amount up to the
  //    balance; return the amount withdrawn.
  public double Withdraw(decimal withdrawal)
  {
    return _bankAccount.Withdraw(withdrawal);
  }
}
```

In this case, the class SavingsAccount_ *contains* a data member _bankAccount (as opposed to inheriting from BankAccount). The _bankAccount object contains the balance and account number information needed by the savings account. The SavingsAccount_ class retains the data unique to a savings account and *delegates* to the contained BankAccount object as needed. That is, when the SavingsAccount needs, say, the balance, it asks the contained BankAccount for it.

In this case, you say that the SavingsAccount_ HAS_A BankAccount. Hard-core object-oriented jocks say that SavingsAccount *composes* a BankAccount. That is, SavingsAccount is partly *composed of* a BankAccount.

The HAS_A relationship

The HAS_A relationship is fundamentally different from the IS_A relationship. This difference doesn't seem so bad in the following application-code segment example:


```
// Create a new savings account.
BankAccount ba = new BankAccount()
SavingsAccount_ sa = new SavingsAccount_(); // HAS_A version of SavingsAccount
sa.InitSavingsAccount(ba, 5);
// And deposit 100 dollars into it.
sa.Deposit(100M);
// Now accumulate interest.
sa.AccumulateInterest();
```

The problem is that this modified SavingsAccount_ cannot be used as a BankAccount because it doesn't inherit from BankAccount. Instead, it *contains* a BankAccount — not the same concept. For example, this code example fails:

```
// DirectDeposit -- Deposit my paycheck automatically.
void DirectDeposit(BankAccount ba, int pay)
{
  ba.Deposit(pay);
}
void SomeMethod()
{
  // The following example fails.
  SavingsAccount_ sa = new SavingsAccount_();
  DirectDeposit(sa, 100);
  // . . . continue . . .
}
```

DirectDeposit() can't accept a SavingsAccount_ in lieu of a BankAccount. No obvious relationship between the two exists, as far as C# is concerned, because inheritance isn't involved. Don't think, though, that this situation makes containment a bad idea. You just have to approach the concept a bit differently in order to use it.

When to IS_A and When to HAS_A

The distinction between the IS_A and HAS_A relationships is more than just a matter of software convenience. This relationship has a corollary in the real world.

For example, a Ford Explorer IS_A car (when it's upright, that is). An Explorer HAS_A motor. If your friend says, "Come on over in your car" and you show up in an Explorer, he has no grounds for complaint. He may have a complaint if you show up carrying your Explorer's engine in your arms, however. (Or at least *you* will.)

The class `Explorer` should extend the class `Car`, not only to give `Explorer` access to the methods of a `Car` but also to express the fundamental relationship between the two.

Unfortunately, the beginning programmer may have `Car` inherit from `Motor`, as an easy way to give the `Car` class access to the members of `Motor`, which the `Car` needs in order to operate. For example, `Car` can inherit the method `Motor.Go()`. However, this example highlights a problem with this approach: Even though humans become sloppy in their speech, making a car go isn't the same thing as making a motor go. The car's "go" operation certainly relies on that of the motor's, but they aren't the same thing — you also have to put the transmission in gear, release the brake, and complete other tasks.

Perhaps even more than that, inheriting from `Motor` misstates the facts. A car simply isn't a type of motor.

Elegance in software is a goal worth achieving in its own right. It enhances understandability, reliability, and maintainability (and cures indigestion and gout).

Hard-core object-oriented jocks recommend preferring HAS_A over IS_A for simpler program designs. But use inheritance when it makes sense, as it probably does in the `BankAccount` hierarchy.

Other Features That Support Inheritance

C# implements a set of features designed to support inheritance. I discuss these features in the following sections.

Substitutable classes

A program can use a subclass object where a base class object is called for. In fact, you may have already seen this concept in one of my examples. `SomeMethod()` can pass a `SavingsAccount` object to the `DirectDeposit()` method, which expects a `BankAccount` object.

You can make this conversion more explicit:

```
BankAccount ba;
SavingsAccount sa = new SavingsAccount(); // The original, not SavingsAccount_
// OK:
ba = sa;                // Implicitly converting subclass to base class.
```

```
ba = (BankAccount)sa;     // But the explicit cast is preferred.
// Not OK:
sa = ba;                  // ERROR: Implicitly converting base class to subclass
sa = (SavingsAccount)ba; // An explicit cast is allowed, however.
```

The first line stores a `SavingsAccount` object into a `BankAccount` variable. C# converts the object for you. The second line uses a cast to explicitly convert the object.

The final two lines attempt to convert the `BankAccount` object back into `SavingsAccount`. You can complete this operation explicitly, but C# doesn't do it for you. It's like trying to convert a larger numeric type, such as `double`, to a smaller one, such as `float`. C# doesn't do it implicitly because the process involves a loss of data.

The IS_A property isn't reflexive. That is, even though an Explorer is a car, a car isn't necessarily an Explorer. Similarly, a `BankAccount` isn't necessarily a `SavingsAccount`, so the implicit conversion isn't allowed. The final line is allowed because the programmer has indicated her willingness to "chance it." She must know something.

Invalid casts at run time

Generally, casting an object from `BankAccount` to `SavingsAccount` is a dangerous operation. Consider this example:

```
public static void ProcessAmount(BankAccount bankAccount)
{
  // Deposit a large sum to the account.
  bankAccount.Deposit(10000.00M);
  // If the object is a SavingsAccount, collect interest now.
  SavingsAccount savingsAccount = (SavingsAccount)bankAccount;
  savingsAccount.AccumulateInterest();
}
public static void TestCast()
{
  SavingsAccount sa = new SavingsAccount();
  ProcessAmount(sa);
  BankAccount ba = new BankAccount();
  ProcessAmount(ba);
}
```

`ProcessAmount()` performs a few operations, including invoking the `AccumulateInterest()` method. The cast of `ba` to a `SavingsAccount` is necessary because the `bankAccount` parameter is declared to be a `BankAccount`. The program compiles properly because all type conversions are made by explicit cast.

All goes well with the first call to `ProcessAmount()` from within `TestCast()`. The `SavingsAccount` object `sa` is passed to the `ProcessAmount()` method. The cast from `BankAccount` to `SavingsAccount` causes no problem because the `ba` object was originally a `SavingsAccount`, anyway.

The second call to ProcessAmount() isn't as lucky, however. The cast to SavingsAccount cannot be allowed. The ba object doesn't have an AccumulateInterest() method.

An incorrect conversion generates an error during the execution of the program (a *runtime error*). Runtime errors are much more difficult to find and fix than compile-time errors. Worse, they can happen to a user other than you, which users tend not to appreciate.

Avoiding invalid conversions with the is operator

The ProcessAmount() method would work if it could ensure that the object passed to it is a SavingsAccount object before performing the conversion. C# provides two keywords for this purpose: is and as.

The is operator accepts an object on the left and a type on the right. The is operator returns true if the runtime type of the object on the left is compatible with the type on the right. *Use it to verify that a cast is legal before you attempt the cast.*

You can modify the example in the previous section to avoid the runtime error by using the is operator:

```
public static void ProcessAmount(BankAccount bankAccount)
{
  // Deposit a large sum to the account.
  bankAccount.Deposit(10000.00M);
  // If the object is a SavingsAccount . . .
  if (bankAccount is SavingsAccount)
  {
    // ...then collect interest now (cast is guaranteed to work).
    SavingsAccount savingsAccount = (SavingsAccount)bankAccount;
    savingsAccount.AccumulateInterest();
  }
  // Otherwise, don't do the cast -- but why is BankAccount not what
  // you expected? This could be an error situation.
}
public static void TestCast()
{
  SavingsAccount sa = new SavingsAccount();
  ProcessAmount(sa);
  BankAccount ba = new BankAccount();
  ProcessAmount(ba);
}
```

The added if statement checks the bankAccount object to ensure that it's of the class SavingsAccount. The is operator returns true when ProcessAmount() is called the first time. When passed a BankAccount object in the second call, however, the is operator returns false, avoiding the illegal cast. This version of the program doesn't generate a runtime error.

On one hand, I strongly recommend that you protect all casts with the `is` operator to avoid the possibility of a runtime error. On the other hand, you should avoid casts altogether, if possible. Read on.

Avoiding invalid conversions with the as operator

The `as` operator works a bit differently from `is`. Rather than return a `bool` if the cast *would* work, it converts the type on the left to the type on the right, but safely returns `null` if the conversion fails — rather than cause a runtime error. You should always use the result of casting with the `as` operator only if it isn't `null`. So, using `as` looks like this:

```
SavingsAccount savingsAccount = bankAccount as SavingsAccount;
if(savingsAccount != null)
{
  // Go ahead and use savingsAccount.
}
// Otherwise, don't use it: generate an error message yourself.
```

Generally, you should prefer `as` because it's more efficient. The conversion is already done with the `as` operator, whereas you must complete two steps when you use `is`: First test with `is` and then complete the cast with the cast operator.

Unfortunately, `as` doesn't work with value-type variables, so you can't use it with types such as `int`, `long`, or `double` or with `char`. When you're trying to convert a value-type object, prefer the `is` operator.

The object Class

Consider these related classes:

```
public class MyBaseClass {}
public class MySubClass : MyBaseClass {}
```

The relationship between the two classes enables the programmer to make the following runtime test:

```
public class Test
{
  public static void GenericMethod(MyBaseClass mc)
  {
    // If the object truly is a subclass . . .
    MySubClass msc = mc as MyBaseClass;
    if(msc != null)
    {
      // ...then handle as a subclass.
      // . . . continue . . .
    }
  }
}
```

In this case, the method `GenericMethod()` differentiates between subclasses of `MyBaseClass` using the `as` keyword.

To help you differentiate between seemingly unrelated classes using the same `as` operator, C# extends all classes from the common base class `object`. That is, any class that doesn't specifically inherit from another class inherits from the class `object`. Thus the following two statements declare classes with the same base class — `object` — and are equivalent:

```
class MyClass1 : object {}
class MyClass1 {}
```

Sharing the common base class of `object` provides for this generic method:

```
public class Test
{
  public static void GenericMethod(object o)
  {
    MyClass1 mc1 = o as MyClass1;
    if(mc1 != null)
    {
      // Use the converted object mc1.
      // . . .
    }
  }
}
```

`GenericMethod()` can be invoked with any type of object. The `as` keyword can dig the `MyClass1` pearls from the `object` oysters. (The *generic* I'm referring to isn't the kind covered in Book I.)

Inheritance and the Constructor

The `InheritanceExample` program described earlier in this chapter relies on those awful `Init...()` methods to initialize the `BankAccount` and `SavingsAccount` objects to a valid state. Outfitting these classes with constructors is definitely the right way to go, but it introduces some complexity. That's why I used those ugly `Init...()` methods earlier in this chapter until I could cover the features in this section.

Invoking the default base class constructor

The default base class constructor is invoked any time a subclass is constructed. The constructor for the subclass automatically invokes the constructor for the base class, as this simple program demonstrates:

```
// InheritingAConstructor -- Demonstrate that the base class
//    constructor is invoked automatically.
using System;
namespace InheritingAConstructor
{
```

```
  public class Program
  {
    public static void Main(string[] args)
    {
      Console.WriteLine("Creating a BaseClass object");
      BaseClass bc = new BaseClass();
      Console.WriteLine("\nnow creating a SubClass object");
      SubClass sc = new SubClass();
      // Wait for user to acknowledge.
      Console.WriteLine("Press Enter to terminate...");
      Console.Read();
    }
  }
  public class BaseClass
  {
    public BaseClass()
    {
      Console.WriteLine("Constructing BaseClass");
    }
  }
  public class SubClass : BaseClass
  {
    public SubClass()
    {
      Console.WriteLine("Constructing SubClass");
    }
  }
}
```


The constructors for `BaseClass` and `SubClass` do nothing more than output a message to the command line. Creating the `BaseClass` object invokes the default `BaseClass` constructor. Creating a `SubClass` object invokes the `BaseClass` constructor *before invoking its own constructor.*

Here's the output from this program:

```
Creating a BaseClass object
Constructing BaseClass

Now creating a SubClass object
Constructing BaseClass
Constructing SubClass
Press Enter to terminate...
```

A *hierarchy* of inherited classes is much like the floor layout of a building. Each class is built on the classes it extends, as upper floors build on lower ones, and for a clear reason: Each class is responsible for itself. A subclass shouldn't be held responsible for initializing the members of the base class. The `BaseClass` must be given the opportunity to construct its members before the `SubClass` members are given a chance to access them. You want the horse well out in front of the cart.

Passing arguments to the base class constructor — mama sang base

The subclass invokes the default constructor of the base class, unless specified otherwise — even from a subclass constructor other than the default. The following slightly updated example demonstrates this feature:

```
using System;
namespace Example
{
  public class Program
  {
    public static void Main(string[] args)
    {
      Console.WriteLine("Invoking SubClass() default");
      SubClass sc1 = new SubClass();
      Console.WriteLine("\nInvoking SubClass(int)");
      SubClass sc2 = new SubClass(0);
      // Wait for user to acknowledge.
      Console.WriteLine("Press Enter to terminate...");
      Console.Read();
    }
  }
  public class BaseClass
  {
    public BaseClass()
    {
      Console.WriteLine("Constructing BaseClass (default)");
    }
    public BaseClass(int i)
    {
      Console.WriteLine("Constructing BaseClass (int)");
    }
  }
  public class SubClass : BaseClass
  {
    public SubClass()
    {
      Console.WriteLine("Constructing SubClass (default)");
    }
    public SubClass(int i)
    {
      Console.WriteLine("Constructing SubClass (int)");
    }
  }
}
```

Executing this program generates the following result:

```
Invoking SubClass()
Constructing BaseClass (default)
Constructing SubClass (default)

Invoking SubClass(int)
Constructing BaseClass (default)
Constructing SubClass (int)
Press Enter to terminate...
```

The program first creates a default object. As expected, C# invokes the default SubClass constructor, which first passes control to the default BaseClass constructor. The program then creates an object, passing an integer argument. Again as expected, C# invokes the SubClass(int). This constructor invokes the default BaseClass constructor, just as in the earlier example, because it has no data to pass.

Getting specific with base

A subclass constructor can invoke a specific base class constructor using the keyword base.

This feature is similar to the way that one constructor invokes another within the same class by using the this keyword.

For example, consider this small program, InvokeBaseConstructor:

```
// InvokeBaseConstructor -- Demonstrate how a subclass can
//    invoke the base class constructor of its choice using
//    the base keyword.
using System;
namespace InvokeBaseConstructor
{
  public class BaseClass
  {
    public BaseClass()
    {
      Console.WriteLine("Constructing BaseClass (default)");
    }
    public BaseClass(int i)
    {
      Console.WriteLine("Constructing BaseClass({0})", i);
    }
  }
  public class SubClass : BaseClass
  {
    public SubClass()
    {
      Console.WriteLine("Constructing SubClass (default)");
    }
    public SubClass(int i1, int i2) : base(i1)
    {
      Console.WriteLine("Constructing SubClass({0}, {1})", i1,  i2);
    }
  }
  public class Program
  {
    public static void Main(string[] args)
    {
      Console.WriteLine("Invoking SubClass()");
      SubClass sc1 = new SubClass();

      Console.WriteLine("\ninvoking SubClass(1, 2)");
      SubClass sc2 = new SubClass(1, 2);

      // Wait for user to acknowledge.
      Console.WriteLine("Press Enter to terminate...");
```

```
      Console.Read();
    }
  }
}
```

The output from this program is

```
Invoking SubClass()
Constructing BaseClass (default)
Constructing SubClass (default)

Invoking SubClass(1, 2)
Constructing BaseClass(1)
Constructing SubClass(1, 2)
Press Enter to terminate...
```

This version begins the same as the previous examples, by creating a default `SubClass` object using the default constructor of both `BaseClass` and `SubClass`.

The second object is created with the expression `new SubClass(1, 2)`. C# invokes the `SubClass(int, int)` constructor, which uses the `base` keyword to pass one of the values to the `BaseClass(int)` constructor. `SubClass` passes the first argument to the base class for processing and then uses the second value itself.

The Updated BankAccount Class

The program `ConstructorSavingsAccount`, found on the Web site, is an updated version of the `SimpleBankAccount` program. In this version, however, the `SavingsAccount` constructor can pass information back to the `BankAccount` constructors. Only `Main()` and the constructors themselves are shown here:

```
// ConstructorSavingsAccount -- Implement a SavingsAccount as
//    a form of BankAccount; use no virtual methods, but
//    implement the constructors properly.
using System;
namespace ConstructorSavingsAccount
{
  // BankAccount -- Simulate a bank account, each of which carries an
  //    account ID (which is assigned upon creation) and a balance.
  public class BankAccount
  {
    // Bank accounts start at 1000 and increase sequentially.
    public static int _nextAccountNumber = 1000;
    // Maintain the account number and balance for each object.
    public int _accountNumber;
    public decimal _balance;
    // Constructors
    public BankAccount() : this(0)
    {
    }
    public BankAccount(decimal initialBalance)
    {
```

```
      _accountNumber = ++_nextAccountNumber;
      _balance = initialBalance;
    }
    public decimal Balance
    {
      get { return _balance; }
      // Protected setter lets subclass use Balance property to set.
      protected set { _balance = value; }
    }
    // Deposit -- Any positive deposit is allowed.
    public void Deposit(decimal amount)
    {
      if (amount > 0)
      {
        Balance += amount;
      }
    }
    // Withdraw -- You can withdraw any amount up to the
    //    balance; return the amount withdrawn.
    public decimal Withdraw(decimal withdrawal)
    {
      if (Balance <= withdrawal)
      {
        withdrawal = Balance;
      }
      Balance -= withdrawal;
      return withdrawal;
    }
    // ToString -- Stringify the account.
    public string ToBankAccountString()
    {
      return String.Format("{0} - {1:C}",
        _accountNumber, Balance);
    }
  }
  // SavingsAccount -- A bank account that draws interest
  public class SavingsAccount : BankAccount
  {
    public decimal _interestRate;
    // InitSavingsAccount -- Input the rate expressed as a
    //   rate between 0 and 100.
    public SavingsAccount(decimal interestRate) : this(interestRate, 0) { }
    public SavingsAccount(decimal interestRate, decimal initial) : base(initial)
    {
      this._interestRate = interestRate / 100;
    }
    // AccumulateInterest -- Invoke once per period.
    public void AccumulateInterest()
    {
      // Use protected setter and public getter via Balance property.
      Balance = Balance + (decimal)(Balance * _interestRate);
    }
    // ToString -- Stringify the account.
    public string ToSavingsAccountString()
    {
      return String.Format("{0} ({1}%)",
        ToBankAccountString(), interestRate * 100);
    }
  }
  public class Program
  {
    // DirectDeposit -- Deposit my paycheck automatically.
```

```
    public static void DirectDeposit(BankAccount ba, decimal pay)
    {
      ba.Deposit(pay);
    }
    public static void Main(string[] args)
    {
      // Create a bank account and display it.
      BankAccount ba = new BankAccount(100M);
      DirectDeposit(ba, 100M);
      Console.WriteLine("Account {0}", ba.ToBankAccountString());
      // Now a savings account
      SavingsAccount sa = new SavingsAccount(12.5M);
      DirectDeposit(sa, 100M);
      sa.AccumulateInterest();
      Console.WriteLine("Account {0}", sa.ToSavingsAccountString());
      // Wait for user to acknowledge the results.
      Console.WriteLine("Press Enter to terminate...");
      Console.Read();
    }
  }
}
```

`BankAccount` defines two constructors: one that accepts an initial account balance and the default constructor, which does not. To avoid duplicating code within the constructor, the default constructor invokes the `BankAccount(initial balance)` constructor using the `this` keyword.

The `SavingsAccount` class also provides two constructors. The `SavingsAccount(interest rate)` constructor invokes the `SavingsAccount(interest rate, initial balance)` constructor, passing an initial balance of 0. This most general constructor passes the initial balance to the `BankAccount(initial balance)` constructor using the `base` keyword, as shown in Figure 6-1.

Bank Account (0)
passes balance to base class
Savings Account (12.5%), 0)
defaults balance to 0
Savings Account (12.5%)

Figure 6-1: The path for constructing an object using the default constructor.

Garbage collection and the C# destructor

C# provides a method that's inverse to the constructor: the *destructor.* It carries the name of the class with a tilde (~) in front. For example, the `~BaseClass()` method is the destructor for `BaseClass`.

C# invokes the destructor when it is no longer using the object. The default destructor is the only destructor that can be created because the destructor cannot be invoked directly. In addition, the destructor is always virtual.

When an inheritance ladder of classes is involved, destructors are invoked in reverse order of constructors. That is, the destructor for the subclass is invoked before the destructor for the base class.

The destructor method in C# is much less useful than it is in other object-oriented languages, such as C++, because C# has *nondeterministic destruction.* Understanding what that term means — and why it's important — requires some explanation.

The memory for an object is borrowed from the heap when the program executes the `new` command, as in `new SubClass()`. This block of memory remains reserved as long as any valid references to that memory are used by any running programs. You may have several variables that reference the same object.

The memory is said to be *unreachable* when the last reference goes out of scope. In other words, no one can access that block of memory after no more references to it exist.

C# doesn't do anything in particular when a memory block first becomes unreachable. A low-priority system task executes in the background, looking for unreachable memory blocks. To avoid negatively affecting program performance, this "garbage collector" executes when little is happening in your program. As the garbage collector finds unreachable memory blocks, it returns them to the heap.

Normally, the garbage collector operates silently in the background. The garbage collector takes over control of the program for only a short period when heap memory begins to run out.

The C# destructor — for example, `~BaseClass()` — is nondeterministic because it isn't invoked until the object is garbage-collected, and that task can occur long after the object is no longer being used. In fact, if the program terminates before the object is found and returned to the heap, the destructor is never invoked. *Nondeterministic* means you can't predict when the object will be garbage-collected. It could be quite a while before the object is garbage-collected and its destructor called.

C# programmers seldom use the destructor. C# has other ways to return borrowed system resources when they're no longer needed, using a `Dispose()` method, a topic that's beyond the scope of this book. (You can search for the term *Dispose method* in Help.)

I've modified `Main()` to get rid of those infernal `Init...()` methods and replace them with constructors instead. The output from this program is the same.

Notice the `Balance` property in `BankAccount`, which has a `public` getter but a `protected` setter. Using `protected` here prevents use from outside of `BankAccount` but permits using the `protected` setter in subclasses, which occurs in `SavingsAccount.AccumulateInterest`, with `Balance` on the left side of the assignment operator. (Properties and the `protected` keyword are in Book I. You can look them up in this book's index.)

Chapter 7: Poly-what-ism?

In This Chapter

- Deciding whether to hide or override a base class method (so many choices!)
- Building abstract classes — are you for real?
- Declaring a method and the class that contains it to be abstract
- Using `ToString`, the class business card
- Sealing a class from being subclassed

In inheritance, one class "adopts" the members of another. Thus I can create a class `SavingsAccount` that inherits data members such as `account id` and methods such as `Deposit()` from a base class `BankAccount`. That's useful, but this definition of inheritance isn't sufficient to mimic what's going on out there in the business world.

See Chapter 6 of this minibook if you don't know (or remember) much about class inheritance.

A microwave oven is a type of oven, not because it looks like an oven but, rather, because it performs the same functions as an oven. A microwave oven may perform additional functions, but it performs, at the least, the base oven functions — most importantly, heating up my nachos when I say, "`StartCooking`." (I rely on my object of class `Refrigerator` to cool the beer.) I don't particularly care what the oven must do internally to make that happen, any more than I care what type of oven it is, who made it, or whether it was on sale when my wife bought it. (Hey, wait — I do care about that last one.)

From our human vantage point, the relationship between a microwave oven and a conventional oven doesn't seem like such a big deal, but consider the problem from the oven's point of view. The steps that a conventional oven performs internally are completely different from those that a microwave oven may take.

The power of inheritance lies in the fact that a subclass doesn't *have* to inherit every single method from the base class just the way it's written. A subclass can inherit the essence of the base class method while implementing the details differently.

Overloading an Inherited Method

As described in Chapter 3 of this minibook (look up *overloading* in the index), two or more methods can have the same name as long as the number or type of arguments differs (or as long as both differ).

It's a simple case of method overloading

Giving two methods the same name is *overloading,* as in "Keeping them straight is overloading my brain."

The arguments of a method become a part of its extended name, as this example demonstrates:

```
public class MyClass
{
  public static void AMethod()
  {
    // Do something.
  }
  public static void AMethod(int)
  {
    // Do something else.
  }
  public static void AMethod(double d)
  {
    // Do something even different.
  }
  public static void Main(string[] args)
  {
    AMethod();
    AMethod(1);
    AMethod(2.0);
}
```

C# can differentiate the methods by their arguments. Each of the calls within `Main()` accesses a different method.

The return type isn't part of the extended name. You can't have two methods that differ only in their return types.

Different class, different method

Not surprisingly, the class to which a method belongs is also a part of its extended name. Consider this code segment:

```
public class MyClass
{
  public static void AMethod1();
  public void AMethod2();
}
public class UrClass
{
```

```
  public static void AMethod1();
  public void AMethod2();
}
public class Program
{
  public static void Main(string[] args)
  {
    UrClass.AMethod1();  // Call static method.
    // Invoke the MyClass.AMethod2() instance method:
    MyClass mcObject = new MyClass();
    mcObject.AMethod2();
  }
}
```

The name of the class is a part of the extended name of the method. The method `MyClass.AMethod1()` has about as much to do with `UrClass.AMethod1()` as `YourCar.StartOnAColdMorning()` and `MyCar.StartOnAColdMorning()` — at least yours works.

Peek-a-boo — hiding a base class method

So a method in one class can overload another method in its own class by having different arguments. As it turns out, a method can also overload a method in its own base class. Overloading a base class method is known as *hiding* the method.

Suppose that your bank adopts a policy making savings account withdrawals different from other types of withdrawals. Suppose, just for the sake of argument, that withdrawing from a savings account costs $1.50.

Taking the procedural approach, you could implement this policy by setting a flag (variable) in the class to indicate whether the object is a `SavingsAccount` or just a simple `BankAccount`. Then the withdrawal method would have to check the flag to decide whether it needs to charge $1.50, as shown here:

```
public class BankAccount
{
  private decimal _balance;
  private bool _isSavingsAccount;  // The flag
  // Indicate the initial balance and whether the account
  // you're creating is a savings account.
  public BankAccount(decimal initialBalance, bool isSavingsAccount)
  {
    _balance = initialBalance;
    _isSavingsAccount = isSavingsAccount;
  }
  public decimal Withdraw(decimal amountToWithdraw)
  {
    // If the account is a savings account . . .
    if (_isSavingsAccount)
    {
      // ...then skim off $1.50.
      _balance -= 1.50M;
    }
```

```
    // Continue with the usual withdraw code:
    if (amountToWithdraw > _balance)
    {
      amountToWithdraw = _balance;
    }
    _balance -= amountToWithdraw;
    return amountToWithdraw;
  }
}
class MyClass
{
  public void SomeMethod()
  {
    // I want create a savings account:
    BankAccount ba = new BankAccount(0, true);
  }
}
```

Your method must tell the `BankAccount` whether it's a `SavingsAccount` in the constructor by passing a flag. The constructor saves that flag and uses it in the `Withdraw()` method to decide whether to charge the extra $1.50.

The more object-oriented approach hides the method `Withdraw()` in the base class `BankAccount` with a new method of the same name, height, and hair color in the `SavingsAccount` class:

```
// HidingWithdrawal -- Hide the withdraw method in the base
//    class with a method in the subclass of the same name.
using System;
namespace HidingWithdrawal
{
  // BankAccount -- A very basic bank account
  public class BankAccount
  {
    protected decimal _balance;
    public BankAccount(decimal initialBalance)
    {
      _balance = initialBalance;
    }
    public decimal Balance
    {
      get { return _balance; }
    }
    public decimal Withdraw(decimal amount)
    {
      // Good practice means avoiding modifying an input parameter.
      // Modify a copy.
      decimal amountToWithdraw = amount;
      if (amountToWithdraw > Balance)
      {
        amountToWithdraw = Balance;
      }
      _balance -= amountToWithdraw;
      return amountToWithdraw;
    }
  }
  // SavingsAccount -- A bank account that draws interest
  public class SavingsAccount : BankAccount
  {
```

```
      public decimal _interestRate;
      // SavingsAccount -- Input the rate expressed as a
      //    rate between 0 and 100.
      public SavingsAccount(decimal initialBalance, decimal interestRate)
      : base(initialBalance)
      {
        _interestRate = interestRate / 100;
      }
      // AccumulateInterest -- Invoke once per period.
      public void AccumulateInterest()
      {
        _balance = Balance + (Balance * _interestRate);
      }
      // Withdraw -- You can withdraw any amount up to the
      //    balance; return the amount withdrawn.
      public decimal Withdraw(decimal withdrawal)
      {
        // Take the $1.50 off the top.
        base.Withdraw(1.5M);
        // Now you can withdraw from what's left.
        return base.Withdraw(withdrawal);
      }
    }
    public class Program
    {
      public static void Main(string[] args)
      {
        BankAccount ba;
        SavingsAccount sa;
        // Create a bank account, withdraw $100, and
        // display the results.
        ba = new BankAccount(200M);
        ba.Withdraw(100M);
        // Try the same trick with a savings account.
        sa = new SavingsAccount(200M, 12);
        sa.Withdraw(100M);
        // Display the resulting balance.
        Console.WriteLine("When invoked directly:");
        Console.WriteLine("BankAccount balance is {0:C}", ba.Balance);
        Console.WriteLine("SavingsAccount balance is {0:C}", sa.Balance);
        // Wait for user to acknowledge the results.
        Console.WriteLine("Press Enter to terminate...");
        Console.Read();
      }
    }
  }
```


Main() in this case creates a BankAccount object with an initial balance of $200 and then withdraws $100. Main() repeats the trick with a SavingsAccount object. When Main() withdraws money from the base class, BankAccount.Withdraw() performs the withdraw function with great aplomb. When Main() then withdraws $100 from the savings account, the method SavingsAccount.Withdraw() tacks on the extra $1.50.

Notice that the SavingsAccount.Withdraw() method uses BankAccount.Withdraw() rather than manipulate the balance directly. If possible, let the base class maintain its own data members.

Making the hiding approach better than adding a simple test

On the surface, adding a flag to the `BankAccount.Withdraw()` method may seem simpler than all this method-hiding stuff. After all, it's just four little lines of code, two of which are nothing more than braces.

The problems are manifold. (I had to write several chapters just to be able to use that word.) One problem is that the `BankAccount` class has no business worrying about the details of `SavingsAccount`. More formally, it's known as "breaking the encapsulation of `SavingsAccount`." Base classes don't normally know about their subclasses, which leads to the real problem: Suppose that your bank subsequently decides to add a `CheckingAccount` or a `CDAccount` or a `TBillAccount`. All those likely additions have different withdrawal policies, each requiring its own flag. After adding three or four different types of accounts, the old `Withdraw()` method starts looking complicated. Each of those types of classes should worry about its own withdrawal policies and leave the poor old `BankAccount.Withdraw()` alone. Classes are responsible for themselves.

Accidentally hiding a base class method

Oddly enough, you can hide a base class method accidentally. For example, you may have a `Vehicle.TakeOff()` method that starts the vehicle rolling. Later, someone else extends your `Vehicle` class with an `Airplane` class. Its `TakeOff()` method is entirely different. In airplane lingo, "take off" means more than just "start moving." Clearly, this is a case of mistaken identity — the two methods have no similarity other than their identical name.

Fortunately, C# detects this problem.

C# generates an ominous-looking warning when it compiles the earlier `HidingWithdrawal` program example. The text of the warning message is long, but here's the important part:

```
'...SavingsAccount.Withdraw(decimal)' hides inherited member
  '...BankAccount.Withdraw(decimal)'.
  Use the new keyword if hiding was intended.
```

C# is trying to tell you that you've written a method in a subclass that has the same name as a method in the base class. Is that what you meant to do?

This message is just a warning — you don't even notice it unless you switch over to the Error List window to take a look. But you must sort out and fix all warnings. In almost every case, a warning is telling you about something that can bite you if you don't fix it.

Tell the C# compiler to treat warnings as errors, at least part of the time. To do so, choose Project⇨Properties. In the Build pane of your project's properties page, scroll down to Errors and Warnings. Set the Warning Level to 4, the highest level, which turns the compiler into more of a chatterbox. Also, in the Treat Warnings As Errors section, select All. (If a particular warning becomes annoying, you can list it in the Suppress Warnings box to keep it out of your face.) When you treat warnings as errors, you're forced to fix the warnings — just as you would be forced to fix real compiler errors. This practice makes for better code. Even if you don't enable the Treat Warnings As Errors option, leave the Warning Level at 4 and select the Error List window after each build.

The descriptor new, shown in the following sample code, tells C# that the hiding of methods is intentional and not the result of an oversight (and it makes the warning disappear):

```
// No withdraw() pains now.
new public decimal Withdraw(decimal withdrawal)
{
  // . . . no change internally . . .
}
```

This use of the keyword new has nothing to do with the same word new that's used to create an object. (C# even overloads itself!)

Calling back to base

Check out the SavingsAccount.Withdraw() method in the HidingWithdrawal example, shown earlier in this chapter. The call to BankAccount.Withdraw() from within this new method includes the new keyword base.

The following version of the method without the base keyword doesn't work:

```
new public decimal Withdraw(decimal withdrawal)
{
  decimal amountWithdrawn = Withdraw(withdrawal);
  amountWithdrawn += Withdraw(1.5);
  return amountWithdrawn;
}
```

This call has the same problem as this one:

```
void fn()
{
  fn(); // Call yourself.
}
```

The call to fn() from within fn() ends up calling itself *(recursing)* repeatedly. Similarly, a call to Withdraw() from within the method calls itself in a loop, chasing its tail until the program eventually crashes.

Somehow, you need to indicate to C# that the call from within SavingsAccount.Withdraw() is meant to invoke the base class BankAccount.Withdraw() method. One approach is to cast the this reference into an object of class BankAccount before making the call:

```
// Withdraw -- This version accesses the hidden method in the base
//    class by explicitly recasting the this object.
new public decimal Withdraw(decimal withdrawal)
{
  // Cast the this reference into an object of class BankAccount.
  BankAccount ba = (BankAccount)this;
  // Invoking Withdraw() using this BankAccount object
  // calls the method BankAccount.Withdraw().
  decimal amountWithdrawn = ba.Withdraw(withdrawal);
  amountWithdrawn += ba.Withdraw(1.5);
  return amountWithdrawn;
}
```

This solution works: The call `ba.Withdraw()` now invokes the `BankAccount` method, just as intended. The problem with this approach is the explicit reference to `BankAccount`. A future change to the program may rearrange the inheritance hierarchy so that `SavingsAccount` no longer inherits directly from `BankAccount`. This type of rearrangement breaks this method in a way that future programmers may not easily find. (Heck, I would never be able to find a bug like that one.)

You need a way to tell C# to call the `Withdraw()` method from "the class immediately above" in the hierarchy without naming it explicitly. That would be the class that `SavingsAccount` extends. C# provides the keyword `base` for this purpose.

This keyword `base` is the same one that a constructor uses to pass arguments to its base class constructor.

The C# keyword `base`, shown in the following chunk of code, is the same sort of beast as `this` but is automatically recast to the base class no matter what that class may be:

```
// Withdraw -- You can withdraw any amount up to the
//    balance; return the amount withdrawn.
new public decimal Withdraw(decimal withdrawal)
{
  // Take the $1.50 off the top.
  base.Withdraw(1.5M);
  // Now you can withdraw from what's left.
  return base.Withdraw(withdrawal);
}
```

The call `base.Withdraw()` now invokes the `BankAccount.Withdraw()` method, thereby avoiding the recursive "invoking itself" problem. In addition, this solution doesn't break if the inheritance hierarchy is changed.

Polymorphism

You can overload a method in a base class with a method in the subclass. As simple as this process sounds, it introduces considerable capability, and with capability comes danger.

Here's a thought experiment: Should you make the decision to call BankAccount.Withdraw() or SavingsAccount.Withdraw() at compile-time or at runtime?

To illustrate the difference, I change the previous HidingWithdrawal program in a seemingly innocuous way. I call this new version Hiding WithdrawalPolymorphically. (I've streamlined the listing by leaving out the stuff that doesn't change.) The new version is shown here:

```
// HidingWithdrawalPolymorphically -- Hide the Withdraw() method in the base
//    class with a method in the subclass of the same name.
public class Program
{
  public static void MakeAWithdrawal(BankAccount ba, decimal amount)
  {
    ba.Withdraw(amount);
  }
  public static void Main(string[] args)
  {
    BankAccount ba;
    SavingsAccount sa;

    // Create a bank account, withdraw $100, and
    // display the results.
    ba = new BankAccount(200M);
    MakeAWithdrawal(ba, 100M);

    // Try the same trick with a savings account.
    sa = new SavingsAccount(200M, 12);
    MakeAWithdrawal(sa, 100M);

    // Display the resulting balance.
    Console.WriteLine("When invoked through intermediary:");
    Console.WriteLine("BankAccount balance is {0:C}", ba.Balance);
    Console.WriteLine("SavingsAccount balance is {0:C}", sa.Balance);

    // Wait for user to acknowledge the results.
    Console.WriteLine("Press Enter to terminate...");
    Console.Read();
  }
}
```


The following output from this program may or may not be confusing, depending on what you expected:

```
When invoked through intermediary
BankAccount balance is $100.00
SavingsAccount balance is $100.00
Press Enter to terminate...
```

This time, rather than perform a withdrawal in Main(), the program passes the bank account object to the method MakeAWithdrawal().

The first question is fairly straightforward: Why does the MakeAWithdrawal() method even accept a SavingsAccount object when it clearly states that it's looking for a BankAccount? The answer is obvious: "Because a SavingsAccount IS_A BankAccount." (See Chapter 6 of this minibook.)

The second question is subtle. When passed a `BankAccount` object, `MakeAWithdrawal()` invokes `BankAccount.Withdraw()` — that's clear enough. But when passed a `SavingsAccount` object, `MakeAWithdrawal()` calls the same method. Shouldn't it invoke the `Withdraw()` method in the subclass?

The prosecution intends to show that the call `ba.Withdraw()` should invoke the method `BankAccount.Withdraw()`. Clearly, the `ba` object is a `BankAccount`. To do anything else would merely confuse the state. The defense has witnesses back in `Main()` to prove that although the `ba` object is declared `BankAccount`, it is in fact a `SavingsAccount`. The jury is deadlocked. Both arguments are equally valid.

In this case, C# comes down on the side of the prosecution: The safer of the two possibilities is to go with the declared type because it avoids any miscommunication. The object is declared to be a `BankAccount` and that's that. However, that may not be what you want.

Using the declared type every time (Is that so wrong?)

In some cases, you don't want to choose the declared type. What you want (or, "what you really, really want," to quote the popular Spice Girls song) is to make the call based on the *real type* — the runtime type — as opposed to the declared type. For example, you want to use the `SavingsAccount` stored in a `BankAccount` variable. This capability to *decide at runtime* is known as *polymorphism,* or *late binding.* Using the declared type every time is called *early binding* because it sounds like the opposite of *late binding.*

The ridiculous term *polymorphism* comes from the Greek language: *Poly* means "more than one," *morph* means "transform," and *ism* is a fairly useless Greek term. But we're stuck with it.

Polymorphism and late binding aren't exactly the same concept — but the difference is subtle:

✦ *Polymorphism* refers to the general ability to decide which method to invoke at runtime.

✦ *Late binding* refers to the specific way a language implements polymorphism.

Polymorphism is the key to the power of object-oriented (OO) programming. It's so important that languages that don't support it can't advertise themselves as OO languages. (I think it's an FDA regulation: You can't label a language that doesn't support it as OO unless you add a disclaimer from the surgeon general, or something like that.)

Languages that support classes but not polymorphism are *object-based languages.* Visual Basic 6.0 (not VB.NET) is an example of such a language.

Without polymorphism, inheritance has little meaning. Let me spring another example on you to show you why. Suppose that you had written a boffo program that uses a class named (just to pick a name out of the air) `Student`. After months of design, coding, and testing, you release this application to rave reviews from colleagues and critics alike. (You've even heard talk of starting a new Nobel Prize category for software, but you modestly brush such talk aside.)

Time passes and your boss asks you to add to this program the capability of handling graduate students, who are similar but not identical to undergraduate students. (The graduate students probably claim that they aren't similar in any way.) Suppose that the formula for calculating the tuition amount for a graduate student is completely different from the formula for an undergrad. Now, your boss doesn't know or care that, deep within the program, are numerous calls to the member method `CalcTuition()`. (A lot of things happen that your boss doesn't know or care about, by the way.) The following example shows one of those many calls to `CalcTuition()`:

```
void SomeMethod(Student s)  // Could be grad or undergrad
{
  // . . . whatever it might do . . .
  s.CalcTuition();
  // . . . continues on . . .
}
```

If C# didn't support late binding, you would need to edit `someMethod()` to check whether the `student` object passed to it is a `GraduateStudent` or a `Student`. The program would call `Student.CalcTuition()` when `s` is a `Student` and `GraduateStudent.CalcTuition()` when it's a graduate student.

Editing `someMethod()` doesn't seem so bad, except for two problems:

- ✦ You're assuming use by only one method. Suppose that `CalcTuition()` is called from many places.
- ✦ `CalcTuition()` might not be the only difference between the two classes. The chances aren't good that you'll find all items that need to be changed.

Using polymorphism, you can let C# decide which method to call.

Using `is` to access a hidden method polymorphically

C# provides one approach to manually solving the problem of making your program polymorphic, using the keyword `is`. (I introduce `is`, and its cousin `as`, in Chapter 6 of this minibook.) The expression `ba is SavingsAccount` returns `true` or `false` depending on the runtime class of the object. The declared type may be `BankAccount`, but which type is it really? The following code chunk uses `is` to access the `SavingsAccount` version of `Withdraw()` specifically:

```
public class Program
{
  public static void MakeAWithdrawal(BankAccount ba, decimal amount)
  {
    if(ba is SavingsAccount)
    {
      SavingsAccount sa = (SavingsAccount)ba;
      sa.Withdraw(amount);
    }
    else
    {
      ba.Withdraw(amount);
    }
  }
}
```

Now, when `Main()` passes the method a `SavingsAccount` object, `MakeAWithdrawal()` checks the runtime type of the `ba` object and invokes `SavingsAccount.Withdraw()`.

Just as an aside, the programmer could have performed the cast and the call in the following single line:

```
((SavingsAccount)ba).Withdraw(amount);  // Notice locations of parentheses.
```

I mention this technique only because you often see it in programs written by show-offs. (You can use it, but it's more difficult to read than when you use multiple lines. Anything written confusingly or cryptically tends to be more error-prone, too.)

The `is` approach works, but it's a bad idea. It requires `MakeAWithDrawal()` to be aware of all the different types of bank accounts and which of them is represented by different classes. That puts too much responsibility on poor old `MakeAWithdrawal()`. Right now, your application handles only two types of bank accounts, but suppose that your boss asks you to implement a new account type, `CheckingAccount`, and it has different `Withdraw()` requirements. Your program doesn't work properly if you don't search out and find every method that checks the runtime type of its argument.

Declaring a method virtual and overriding it

As the author of `MakeAWithdrawal()`, you don't want to know about all the different types of accounts. You want to leave to the programmers who use `MakeAWithdrawal()` the responsibility to know about their account types and just leave you alone. You want C# to make decisions about which methods to invoke based on the runtime type of the object.

You tell C# to make the runtime decision of the version of `Withdraw()` by marking the base class method with the keyword `virtual` and marking each subclass version of the method with the keyword `override`.

I used polymorphism to rewrite the program example from the previous section. I added output statements to the `Withdraw()` methods to prove that the proper methods are indeed being invoked. (I also cut out any duplicated information.) Here's the `PolymorphicInheritance` program:

```
// PolymorphicInheritance -- Hide a method in the
//    base class polymorphically. Show how to use
//    the virtual and override keywords.
using System;
namespace PolymorphicInheritance
{
  // BankAccount -- A basic bank account
  public class BankAccount
  {
    protected decimal _balance;
    public BankAccount(decimal initialBalance)
    {
      _balance = initialBalance;
    }
    public decimal Balance
    {
      get { return _balance; }
    }
    public virtual decimal Withdraw(decimal amount)
    {
      Console.WriteLine("In BankAccount.Withdraw() for ${0}...", amount);
      decimal amountToWithdraw = amount;
      if (amountToWithdraw > Balance)
      {
        amountToWithdraw = Balance;
      }
      _balance -= amountToWithdraw;
      return amountToWithdraw;
    }
  }
  // SavingsAccount -- A bank account that draws interest
  public class SavingsAccount : BankAccount
  {
    public decimal _interestRate;
    // SavingsAccount -- Input the rate expressed as a
    //    rate between 0 and 100.
    public SavingsAccount(decimal initialBalance, decimal interestRate)
                        : base(initialBalance)
    {
```

```
      _interestRate = interestRate / 100;
    }
    // AccumulateInterest -- Invoke once per period.
    public void AccumulateInterest()
    {
      _balance = Balance + (Balance * _interestRate);
    }
    // Withdraw -- You can withdraw any amount up to the
    //    balance; return the amount withdrawn.
    override public decimal Withdraw(decimal withdrawal)
    {
      Console.WriteLine("In SavingsAccount.Withdraw()...");
      Console.WriteLine("Invoking base-class Withdraw twice...");
      // Take the $1.50 off the top.
      base.Withdraw(1.5M);
      // Now you can withdraw from what's left.
      return base.Withdraw(withdrawal);
    }
  }
  public class Program
  {
    public static void MakeAWithdrawal(BankAccount ba, decimal amount)
    {
      ba.Withdraw(amount);
    }
    public static void Main(string[] args)
    {
      BankAccount ba;
      SavingsAccount sa;
      // Display the resulting balance.
      Console.WriteLine("Withdrawal: MakeAWithdrawal(ba, ...)");
      ba = new BankAccount(200M);
      MakeAWithdrawal(ba, 100M);
      Console.WriteLine("BankAccount balance is {0:C}", ba.Balance);
      Console.WriteLine("Withdrawal: MakeAWithdrawal(sa, ...)");
      sa = new SavingsAccount(200M, 12);
      MakeAWithdrawal(sa, 100M);
      Console.WriteLine("SavingsAccount balance is {0:C}", sa.Balance);
      // Wait for user to acknowledge the results.
      Console.WriteLine("Press Enter to terminate...");
      Console.Read();
    }
  }
}
```

The output from executing this program is shown here:

```
Withdrawal: MakeAWithdrawal(ba, ...)
In BankAccount.Withdraw() for $100...
BankAccount balance is $100.00
Withdrawal: MakeAWithdrawal(sa, ...)
In SavingsAccount.Withdraw()...
Invoking base-class Withdraw twice...
In BankAccount.Withdraw() for $1.5...
In BankAccount.Withdraw() for $100...
SavingsAccount balance is $98.50
Press Enter to terminate...
```

The `Withdraw()` method is flagged as `virtual` in the base class `BankAccount`, and the `Withdraw()` method in the subclass is flagged with the keyword `override`. The `MakeAWithdrawal()` method is unchanged, yet the output of the program is different because the call `ba.Withdraw()` is resolved based on the `ba` runtime type.

To get a good feel for how this works, step through the program in the Visual Studio 2005 debugger. Just build the program as normal and then repeatedly press F11 to watch the program walk through its paces. Watch the `Withdraw()` calls carefully. Watching the same call end up in two different methods at two different times is impressive.

Choose sparingly which methods to make virtual. Each one has a cost, so use the `virtual` keyword only when necessary. It's a trade-off between a class that's highly flexible and can be overridden (lots of virtual methods) and a class that isn't flexible enough (hardly any virtuals).

Getting the most benefit from polymorphism — the do-to-each trick

Much of the power of polymorphism springs from polymorphic objects sharing a common interface. For example, given a hierarchy of `Shape` objects — `Circles`, `Squares`, and `Triangles`, for example — you can count on all shapes having a `Draw()` method. Each object's `Draw()` method is implemented quite differently, of course. But the point is that, given a collection of these objects, you can freely use a `foreach` loop to call `Draw()` or any other method in the polymorphic interface on the objects. I call it the "do-to-each" trick.

The Class Business Card: ToString()

All classes inherit from a common base class that carries the clever name `Object`. However, it's worth mentioning here that `Object` includes a method, `ToString()`, that converts the contents of the object into a `string`. The idea is that each class should override the `ToString()` method to display itself in a meaningful way. I used the method `GetString()` until now because I didn't want to begin discussing inheritance issues until Chapter 6 of this minibook. After you understand inheritance, the `virtual` keyword, and overriding, we can describe `ToString()`. By overriding `ToString()` for each class, you give each class the ability to display itself in its own way. For example, a useful, appropriate `Student.ToString()` method may display the student's name and ID.

Most methods — even those built into the C# library — use the `ToString()` method to display objects. Thus overriding `ToString()` has the useful side effect of displaying the object in its own, unique format, no matter who does the displaying.

Always override `ToString()`.

C# During Its Abstract Period

The duck is a type of bird, I think. So are the cardinal and the hummingbird. In fact, every bird out there is a subtype of bird. The flip side of that argument is that no bird exists that *isn't* some subtype of `Bird`. That statement doesn't *sound* profound, but in a way, it is. The software equivalent of that statement is that all `bird` objects are instances of some subclass of `Bird` — there's never an instance of class `Bird`. What's a bird? It's always a robin or a grackle or another specific species.

Different types of birds share many properties (otherwise, they wouldn't be birds), yet no two types share every property. If they did, they wouldn't be different types. To pick a particularly gross example, not all birds `Fly()` the same way. Ducks have one style. The cardinal's style is similar but not identical. The hummingbird's style is completely different. (Don't even get me started about emus and ostriches or the rubber ducky in my tub.)

But if not all birds fly the same way and there's no such thing as a `Bird`, what the heck is `Bird.Fly()`? The subject of the following sections, that's what it is.

Class factoring

People generate taxonomies of objects by factoring out commonalities. To see how factoring works, consider the two classes `HighSchool` and `University`, shown in Figure 7-1. This figure uses the Unified Modeling Language (UML), a graphical language that describes a class along with the relationship of that class to others. UML has become universally popular with programmers and is worth learning (to a reasonable extent) in its own right.

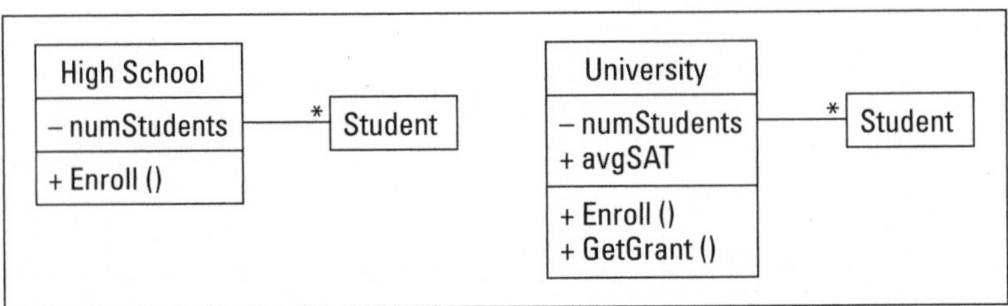

Figure 7-1: A UML description of the `High School` and `University` classes.

UML Lite

The Unified Modeling Language (UML) is an expressive language that's capable of clearly defining a great deal about the relationships of objects within a program. One advantage of UML is that you can ignore the more specific language features without losing its meaning entirely.

The most basic features of UML are described in this list:

- Classes are represented by a box divided vertically into three sections. The name of the class appears in the uppermost section.
- The data members of the class appear in the middle section, and the methods of the class in the bottom. You can omit either the middle or bottom section if the class has no data members or methods or if you want just a high-level classes-only view.
- Members with a plus sign (+) in front are public; those with a minus sign (–) are private. To provide protected and internal visibility, most people use the pound sign (#) — or should I say the "sharp" sign? — and the tilde (~), respectively.

  A private member is accessible only from other members of the same class. A public member is accessible to all classes. See Chapter 5.
- The label `{abstract}` next to a name indicates an abstract class or method.

  UML uses a different symbol for an abstract method, but I keep it simple. (It's UML *Lite.*) You can also just show abstract items in italics.
- An arrow between two classes represents a relationship between the two classes. A number above the line expresses cardinality — the number of items you can have at each end of the arrow. The asterisk symbol (*) means *any number.* If no number is present, the cardinality is assumed to be 1. Thus you can see that a single university has any number of students — a one-to-many relationship (refer to Figure 7-1).
- A line with a large, open arrowhead, or a triangular arrowhead, expresses the IS_A relationship (inheritance). The arrow points *up* the class hierarchy to the base class. Other types of relationships include the HAS_A relationship (a line with a filled diamond at the owning end).

To explore UML in depth, check out *UML 2 For Dummies,* by Michael Jesse Chonoles and James A. Schardt.

A Car IS_A Vehicle but a Car HAS_A Motor.

High schools and universities have several similar properties — many more than you may think (refer to Figure 7-1). Both schools offer a publicly available `Enroll()` method for adding `Student` objects to the school. In addition, both classes offer a private member `numStudents` that indicates the number of students attending the school. Another common feature is the relationship between students: One school can have any number of students — a student can attend only a single school at one time. Even high schools and most universities offer more than I describe, but one of each type of member is all I need for illustration.

In addition to the features of a high school, the university contains a method `GetGrant()` and a data member `avgSAT`. High schools have no SAT entrance requirements and receive no federal grants (unless I went to the wrong one).

Figure 7-1 is acceptable, as far as it goes, but lots of information is duplicated, and duplication in code (and UML diagrams) stinks. You can reduce the duplication by allowing the more complex class `University` to inherit from the simpler `HighSchool` class, as shown in Figure 7-2.

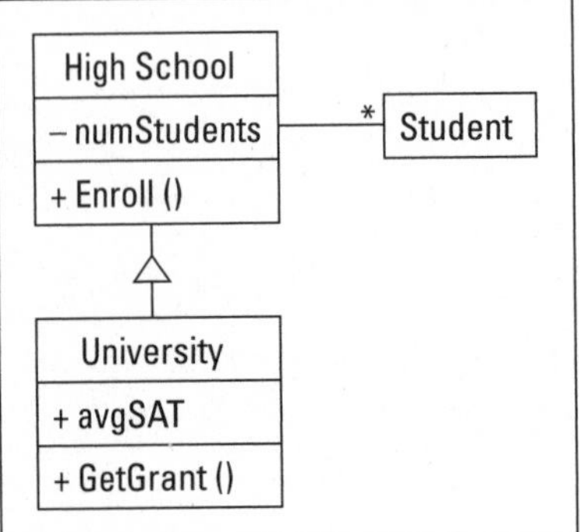

Figure 7-2: Inheriting `High School` simplifies the `University` class but introduces problems.

The `HighSchool` class is left unchanged, but the `University` class is easier to describe. You say that "a `University` is a `HighSchool` that also has an `avgSAT` and a `GetGrant()` method." But this solution has a fundamental problem: A university isn't a high school with special properties.

You say, "So what? Inheriting works, and it saves effort." True, but my reservations are more than stylistic trivialities. (My reservations are at some of the best restaurants in town — at least, that's what all the truckers say.) This type of misrepresentation is confusing to the programmer, both now and in the future. Someday, a programmer who is unfamiliar with your programming tricks will have to read and understand what your code does. Misleading representations are difficult to reconcile and understand.

In addition, this type of misrepresentation can lead to problems down the road. Suppose that the high school decides to name a "favorite" student at the prom — not that I would know anything about that sort of thing. The clever programmer adds the `NameFavorite()` method to the `HighSchool` class, which the application invokes to name the favorite `Student` object.

But now you have a problem: Most universities don't name a favorite anything, other than price. However, as long as `University` inherits from `HighSchool`, it inherits the `NameFavorite()` method. One extra method may not seem like a big deal. "Just ignore it," you say.

One extra method isn't a big deal, but it's just one more brick in the wall of confusion. Extra methods and properties accumulate over time, until the `University` class is carrying lots of extra baggage. Pity the poor software developer who has to understand which methods are "real" and which aren't.

"Inheritances of convenience" lead to another problem. The way it's written, Figure 7-2 implies that a `University` and a `HighSchool` have the same enrollment procedure. As unlikely as that statement sounds, assume that it's true. The program is developed, packaged up, and shipped off to the unwitting public — of course, I've embedded the requisite number of bugs so that they'll want to upgrade to Version 2.0 with all its bug fixes — for a small fee, of course.

Months pass before the school district decides to modify its enrollment procedure. It isn't obvious to anyone that modifying the high school enrollment procedure also modifies the sign-up procedure at the local college.

How can you avoid these problems? Not going to school is one way, but another is to fix the source of the problem: A university isn't a particular type of high school. A relationship exists between the two, but IS_A isn't the right one. (HAS_A doesn't work either. A university HAS_A high school? A high school HAS_A university? Come on!) Instead, both high schools and universities are special types of schools. That's what they have most in common.

Figure 7-3 describes a better relationship. The newly defined class `School` contains the common properties of both types of schools, including the relationship they both have with `Student` objects. `School` even contains the common `Enroll()` method, although it's abstract because `HighSchool` and `University` usually don't implement `Enroll()` the same way.

The classes `HighSchool` and `University` now inherit from a common base class. Each contains its unique members: `NameFavorite()` in the case of `HighSchool`, and `GetGrant()` for the `University`. In addition, both classes override the `Enroll()` method with a version that describes how that type of school enrolls students. In effect, I've extracted a superclass, or base class, from two similar classes, which now become subclasses.

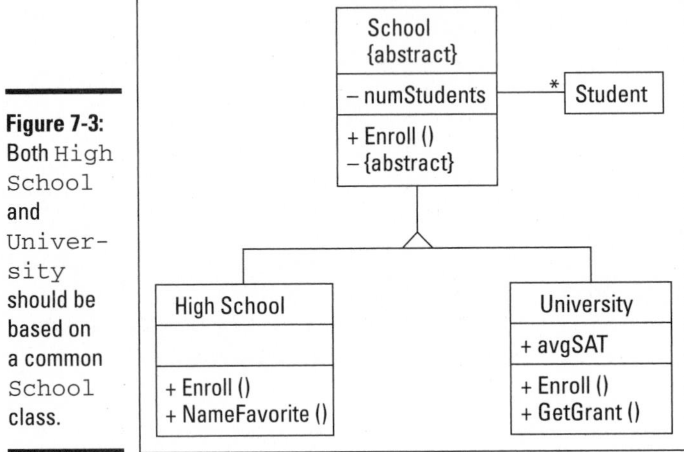

Figure 7-3: Both `High School` and `University` should be based on a common `School` class.

The introduction of the `School` class has at least two big advantages:

- **It corresponds with reality.** A `University` is a `School`, but it isn't a `HighSchool`. Matching reality is nice but not conclusive.
- **It isolates one class from changes or additions to the other.** When my boss inevitably requests later that I introduce the commencement exercise to the university, I can add the `CommencementSpeech()` method to the `University` class and not affect `HighSchool`.

This process of culling common properties from similar classes is known as *factoring.* This feature of object-oriented languages is important for the reasons described earlier in this minibook, plus one more: reducing redundancy. Let me repeat: Redundancy is bad.

Factoring is legitimate only if the inheritance relationship corresponds to reality. Factoring together a class `Mouse` and `Joystick` because they're both hardware pointing devices is legitimate. Factoring together a class `Mouse` and `Display` because they both make low-level operating-system calls is not.

Factoring can and usually does result in multiple levels of abstraction. For example, a program written for a more developed school hierarchy may have a class structure more like the one shown in Figure 7-4.

You can see that I have inserted a pair of new classes between `University` and `School`: `HigherLearning` and `LowerLevel`. For example, I've subdivided the new class `HigherLearning` into `College` and `University`. This type of multitiered class hierarchy is common and desirable when factoring out relationships. They correspond to reality, and they can teach you sometimes subtle features of your solution.

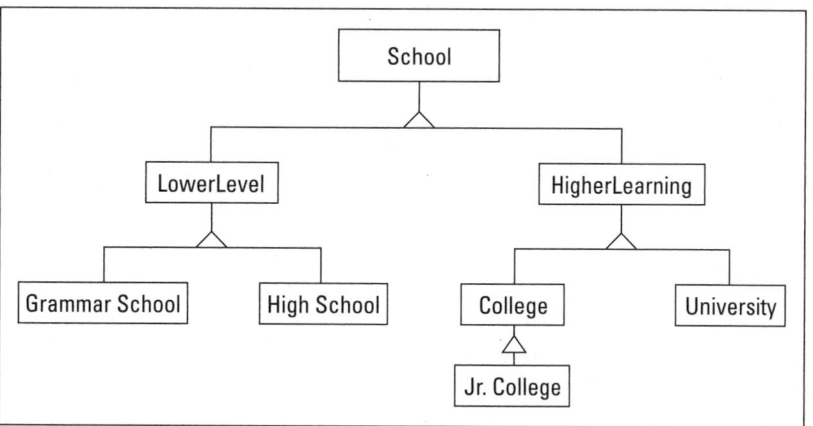

Figure 7-4: Class factoring can (and usually does) result in added layers of inheritance hierarchy.

Note, however, that no Unified Factoring Theory exists for any given set of classes. The relationship shown in Figure 7-4 seems natural, but suppose that an application cared more about differentiating types of schools that are administered by local politicians from those that aren't. This relationship, shown in Figure 7-5, is a more natural fit for that type of problem. No "correct" factoring exists: The proper way to break down the classes is partially a function of the problem being solved.

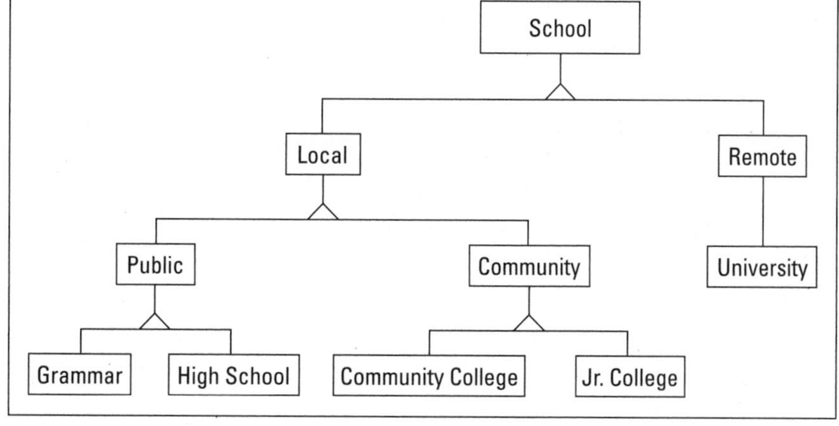

Figure 7-5: Breaking down classes is partially a function of the problem being solved.

The abstract class: Left with nothing but a concept

As intellectually satisfying as factoring is, it introduces a problem of its own. Visit (or revisit) `BankAccount`, introduced at the beginning of this chapter. Think about how you may go about defining the different member methods defined in `BankAccount`.

Most `BankAccount` member methods are no problem to refactor because both account types implement them in the same way. You should implement those common methods in `BankAccount`. `Withdraw()` is different, however. The rules for withdrawing from a savings account differ from those for withdrawing from a checking account. You have to implement `SavingsAccount.Withdraw()` differently from `CheckingAccount.Withdraw()`. But how are you supposed to implement `BankAccount.Withdraw()`?

Ask the bank manager for help. I imagine this conversation taking place:

> "What are the rules for making a withdrawal from an account?" you ask, expectantly.
>
> "Which type of account? Savings or checking?" comes the reply.
>
> "From an account," you say. "Just an account."
>
> [Blank look.] (You might say a "blank bank look." Then again, maybe not.)

The problem is that the question doesn't make sense. No such thing as "just an account" exists. All accounts (in this example) are either checking accounts or savings accounts. The concept of an account is *abstract:* It factors out properties common to the two concrete classes. It's incomplete because it lacks the critical property `Withdraw()`. (After you delve into the details, you may find other properties that a simple account lacks.)

The concept of a `BankAccount` is abstract.

How do you use an abstract class?

Abstract classes are used to describe abstract concepts.

An *abstract class* is a class with one or more abstract methods. (Oh, great. That helps a lot.) Okay, an abstract method is a method marked `abstract`. (We're moving now!) Let me try again: An abstract method has no implementation — now you're *really* confused.

Consider the following stripped-down demonstration program:

```
// AbstractInheritance -- The BankAccount class is abstract because
//    there is no single implementation for Withdraw.
namespace AbstractInheritance
{
  using System;
  // AbstractBaseClass -- Create an abstract base class with nothing
  //    but an Output() method. You can also say "public abstract."
  abstract public class AbstractBaseClass
  {
    // Output -- Abstract method that outputs a string
    abstract public void Output(string outputString);
  }
```

```
    // SubClass1 -- One concrete implementation of AbstractBaseClass
    public class SubClass1 : AbstractBaseClass
    {
      override public void Output(string source) // Or "public override"
      {
        string s = source.ToUpper();
        Console.WriteLine("Call to SubClass1.Output() from within {0}", s);
      }
    }
    // SubClass2 -- Another concrete implementation of AbstractBaseClass
    public class SubClass2 : AbstractBaseClass
    {
      public override void Output(string source)  // Or "override public"
      {
        string s = source.ToLower();
        Console.WriteLine("Call to SubClass2.Output() from within {0}", s);
      }
    }
    class Program
    {
      public static void Test(AbstractBaseClass ba)
      {
        ba.Output("Test");
      }
      public static void Main(string[] strings)
      {
        // You can't create an AbstractBaseClass object because it's
        // abstract -- duh. C# generates a compile-time error if you
        // uncomment the following line.
        // AbstractBaseClass ba = new AbstractBaseClass();
        // Now repeat the experiment with Subclass1.
        Console.WriteLine("\ncreating a SubClass1 object");
        SubClass1 sc1 = new SubClass1();
        Test(sc1);
        // And, finally, a Subclass2 object
        Console.WriteLine("\ncreating a SubClass2 object");
        SubClass2 sc2 = new SubClass2();
        Test(sc2);
        // Wait for user to acknowledge.
        Console.WriteLine("Press Enter to terminate... ");
        Console.Read();
      }
    }
  }
```


The program first defines the class `AbstractBaseClass` with a single abstract `Output()` method. Because it's declared `abstract`, `Output()` has no implementation — that is, no method body.

Two classes inherit from `AbstractBaseClass`: `SubClass1` and `SubClass2`. Both are concrete classes because they override the `Output()` method with "real" methods and contain no abstract methods themselves.

A class can be declared abstract whether it has abstract members or not; however, a class can be concrete only when all abstract methods in any base class above it have been overridden with full methods.

The two subclass `Output()` methods differ in a trivial way: Both accept input strings, which they regurgitate to users. However, one converts the string to all caps before output and the other converts it to all-lowercase characters.

The following output from this program demonstrates the polymorphic nature of `AbstractBaseClass`:

```
Creating a SubClass1 object
Call to SubClass1.Output() from within TEST

Creating a SubClass2 object
Call to SubClass2.Output() from within test
Press Enter to terminate...
```

An abstract method is automatically virtual, so you don't add the `virtual` keyword to an abstract method.

Creating an abstract object — not!

Notice something about the `AbstractInheritance` program: It isn't legal to create an `AbstractBaseClass` object, but the argument to `Test()` is declared to be an object of the class `AbstractBaseClass` *or one of its subclasses.* It's the "subclasses" clause that's critical here. The `SubClass1` and `SubClass2` objects can be passed because each one is a concrete subclass of `AbstractBaseClass`. The IS_A relationship applies. This powerful technique lets you write highly general methods.

Sealing a Class

You may decide that you don't want future generations of programmers to be able to extend a particular class. You can lock the class by using the keyword `sealed`.

A sealed class cannot be used as the base class for any other class.

Consider this code snippet:

```
using System;
public class BankAccount
{
  // Withdrawal -- You can withdraw any amount up to the
  //    balance; return the amount withdrawn
  virtual public void Withdraw(decimal withdrawal)
  {
    Console.WriteLine("invokes BankAccount.Withdraw()");
  }
}
public sealed class SavingsAccount : BankAccount
{
```

```
  override public void Withdraw(decimal withdrawal)
  {
    Console.WriteLine("invokes SavingsAccount.Withdraw()");
  }
}
public class SpecialSaleAccount : SavingsAccount  // Oops!
{
  override public void Withdraw(decimal withdrawal)
  {
    Console.WriteLine("invokes SpecialSaleAccount.Withdraw()");
  }
}
```

This snippet generates the following compiler error:

```
'SpecialSaleAccount' : cannot inherit from sealed class 'SavingsAccount'
```


You use the `sealed` keyword to protect your class from the prying methods of a subclass. For example, allowing a programmer to extend a class that implements system security enables someone to create a security back door.

Sealing a class prevents another program, possibly somewhere on the Internet, from using a modified version of your class. The remote program can use the class as is, or not, but it can't inherit bits and pieces of your class while overriding the rest.

Chapter 8: Interfacing with the Interface

In This Chapter

- **Beyond `IS_A` and `HAS_A`: The C# interface**
- **Creating your own interface or using one provided by .NET**
- **Unifying separate class hierarchies with interfaces**
- **Hiding part of your class's public interface behind an interface**
- **Managing software change — flexibility via interfaces**

A class can *contain* a reference to another class; this statement describes the simple `HAS_A` relationship. One class can *extend* another class by way of the marvel of inheritance — that's the `IS_A` relationship. The C# interface implements another, equally important association: the `CAN_BE_USED_AS` relationship.

This chapter introduces C# *interfaces* and shows some of the numerous ways they increase the power and flexibility of object-oriented programming.

Introducing CAN_BE_USED_AS

If you want to jot a note, you can scribble it with a pen, type it into your smartphone, or pound it out on your laptop's keyboard. You can fairly say that all three objects — pen, smartphone, and computer — implement the `TakeANote` operation. Suppose that you use the magic of inheritance to implement this concept in C#:

```
abstract class ThingsThatRecord          // The base class
{
  abstract public void TakeANote(string note);
}
public class Pen : ThingsThatRecord      // A subclass
{
  override public void TakeANote(string note)
  {
    // ... scribble a note with a pen ...
  }
```

```
}
public class PDA : ThingsThatRecord      // Another subclass
{
  override public void TakeANote(string note)
  {
    // ... stroke a note on the PDA ...
  }
}
public class LapTop : ThingsThatRecord  // A third subclass
{
  override public void TakeANote(string note)
  {
    // ... tap, tap, tap ...
  }
}
```

If the term *abstract* has you stumped, see Chapter 7 of this minibook and read the discussion later in this chapter. If the whole concept of inheritance is a mystery, check out Chapter 6 of this minibook.

The following simple method shows the inheritance approach working just fine:

```
void RecordTask(ThingsThatRecord recorder) // Parameter type is base class.
{
  // All classes that extend ThingsThatRecord have a TakeANote method.
  recorder.TakeANote("Shopping list");
  // ... and so on.
}
```

The parameter type is `ThingsThatRecord`, so you can pass any subclasses to this method, making the method quite general.

That might seem like a good solution, but it has two big drawbacks:

- **A fundamental problem:** Do `Pen`, `PDA`, and `LapTop` truly have an IS_A relationship? Are those three items all the same type in real life? I don't think so, do you? All I can say is that `ThingsThatRecord` makes a poor base class here.
- **A purely technical problem:** You might reasonably derive both `LapTop` and `PDA` as subclasses of `Computer`. But nobody would say that a `Pen` IS_A `Computer`. You have to characterize a pen as a type of `MechanicalWritingDevice` or `DeviceThatStainsYourShirt`. But a C# class can't inherit from two different base classes at the same time — a C# class can be only one type of item.

So the `Pen`, `PDA`, and `LapTop` classes have in common only the characteristic that they `CAN_BE_USED_AS` recording devices. Inheritance doesn't apply.

Knowing What an Interface Is

An *interface* in C# resembles a class with no data members and nothing but abstract methods, almost like an abstract class — almost:

```
interface IRecordable
{
  void TakeANote(string note);
}
```

The interface begins with the `interface` keyword. It contains nothing but abstract methods. It has no data members and no implemented methods.

Interfaces can contain a few other features, including properties (covered in Chapter 5 of this minibook), events (covered in Chapter 9 of this minibook), and indexers (covered at the end of Book I).

Among the elements that a C# interface *cannot* exhibit are

- Access specifiers, such as `public` or `private` (see Chapter 5 of this minibook)
- Keywords such as `virtual`, `override`, or `abstract` (see Chapter 7 of this minibook)
- Data members (see Chapter 2 of this minibook)
- Implemented methods — nonabstract methods with bodies

All members of a C# interface are public (you can't even mention access specifiers in defining interface methods), and a C# interface isn't involved in normal inheritance; hence, it has none of those keywords. (An interface itself can be `public`, `protected`, `internal`, or `private`.)

Unlike an abstract class, a C# interface isn't a class. It can't be subclassed, and none of the methods it contains can have bodies.

How to implement an interface

To put a C# interface to use, you *implement* it with one or more classes. The class heading looks like this:

```
class Pen : IRecordable  // Looks like inheritance, but isn't
```

A C# interface specifies that classes which implement the interface *must* provide specific implementations. They *must.* For example, any class that implements the `IRecordable` interface must provide an implementation for the `TakeANote` method. The method that implements `TakeANote` doesn't use the `override` keyword. Using an interface isn't like overriding a virtual method in classes.

Class Pen might look like this:

```
class Pen : IRecordable
{
  public void TakeANote(string note)     // Interface method implementations
  {                                      // MUST be declared public.
    // ... scribble a note with a pen ...
  }
}
```

This example fulfills two requirements: Note that the class implements `IRecordable`, and provide a method implementation for `TakeANote()`.

The syntax indicating that a class inherits a base class, such as `ThingsThatRecord`, is essentially no different from the syntax indicating that the class implements a C# interface such as `IRecordable`:

```
public class PDA : ThingsThatRecord ...
public class PDA : IRecordable ...
```

Visual Studio can help you implement an interface. Hover the mouse pointer over the interface name in the class heading. A little underline appears underneath the first character of the interface name. Move the mouse until a menu opens and choose Implement Interface *<name>*. Presto! A skeleton framework appears — you fill in the details.

How to name your interface

The .NET naming convention for interfaces precedes the name with the letter *I*. Interface names are typically adjectives, such as `IRecordable`.

Why C# includes interfaces

REMEMBER

The bottom line of interfaces is that an interface describes a capability, such as Swim Safety Training or Class A Driver's License. As a class, I earn my `IRecordable` badge when I implement the `TakeANote` ability.

More than that, an interface is a *contract*. If you agree to implement every method defined in the interface, you get to claim its capability. Not only that, but a client using your class in her program is guaranteed to be able to call those methods. Implementing an interface is a promise — enforced by the compiler. (Enforcing promises through the compiler reduces errors.)

Mixing inheritance and interface implementation

Unlike some languages, such as C++, C# doesn't allow *multiple inheritance* — a class inheriting from two or more base classes. Think of class `HouseBoat` inheriting from `House` and `Boat`. Just don't think of it in C#.

But although a class can inherit from only one base class, it can *in addition* implement as many interfaces as needed. After I treated *recordability* as an interface, a couple of the recording devices looked like this:

```
public class Pen : IRecordable          // Base class is Object.
{
  public void TakeANote(string note)
  {
    // Record the note with a pen.
  }
}
public class PDA : ElectronicDevice, IRecordable
{
  public void TakeANote(string note)
  {
    // Record the note with your thumbs or a stylus.
  }
}
```

Class PDA inherits from a base class *and* implements an interface.

And he-e-e-re's the payoff

To begin to see the usefulness of an interface such as IRecordable, consider this example:

```
public class Program
{
  static public void RecordShoppingList(IRecordable recorder)
  {
    // Jot it down, using whatever device was passed in.
    recorder.TakeANote(...);
  }
  public static void Main(string[] args)
  {
    PDA pda = new PDA();
    RecordShoppingList(pda);  // Oops, battery's low ...
    RecordShoppingList(pen);
  }
}
```

The IRecordable parameter is an instance of any class that implements the IRecordable interface. RecordShoppingList() makes no assumptions about the exact type of recording object. Whether the device is a PDA or a type of ElectronicDevice isn't important, as long as the device can record a note.

That concept is immensely powerful because it lets the RecordShopping List() method be highly general — and thus possibly reusable in other programs. The method is even more general than using a base class such as ElectronicDevice for the argument type, because the interface lets you pass almost arbitrary objects that don't necessarily have anything in common other than implementing the interface. They don't even have to come from the same class hierarchy, which truly simplifies the designing of hierarchies, for example.

Overworked word alert: Programmers use the term *interface* in more than one way. You can see the C# keyword `interface` and how it's used. People also talk about a class's *public interface*, or the public methods and properties that it exposes to the outside world. I keep the distinction clear by saying *C# interface* most of the time when that's what I mean, and saying *public interface* when I refer to a class's set of public methods.

C# structures can implement interfaces just as classes can.

Using an Interface

In addition to your being able to use a C# interface for a parameter type, an interface is useful as

- ✦ A method return type
- ✦ The base type of a highly general array or collection
- ✦ A more general kind of object reference for variable types

I explain the advantage of using a C# interface as a method parameter type in the previous section. Now I can tell you about other interfaces.

As a method return type

I like to farm out to a *factory method* the task of creating the key objects I need. Suppose that I have a variable like this one:

```
IRecordable recorder = null;  // Yes, you can have interface-type variables.
```

Somewhere, maybe in my constructor, I call a factory method to deliver a particular kind of `IRecordable` object:

```
recorder = MyClass.CreateRecorder("Pen");  // A factory method is often static.
```

where `CreateRecorder()` is a method, often on the same class, that returns not a reference to a `Pen` but, rather, an `IRecordable` reference:

```
static IRecordable CreateRecorder(string recorderType)
{
  if(recorderType == "Pen") return new Pen();
  ...
}
```

I say more about the factory idea later in this chapter. But note that the return type for `CreateRecorder()` is an interface type.

As the base type of an array or collection

Suppose that you have two classes, `Animal` and `Robot`, and that both are abstract. You want to set up an array to hold both `thisCat` (an `Animal`) and `thatRobot` (a cute droid). The only way is to fall back on type `Object`, the ultimate base class in C#, and the only base class that's common to both `Animal` and `Robot` as well as to their subclasses:

```
object[] things = new object[] { thisCat, thatRobot };
```

That's poor design for lots of reasons. But suppose that you're focused on the objects' movements. You can have each class implement an `IMovable` interface:

```
interface IMovable
{
  void Move(int direction, int speed, int distance);
}
```

and then set up an array of `IMovables` to manipulate your otherwise incompatible objects:

```
IMovable[] movables = { thisCat, thatRobot };
```

The interface gives you a commonality that you can exploit in collections.

As a more general type of object reference

The following variable declaration refers to a specific, physical, *concrete* object (see the later section "Abstract or concrete: When to use an abstract class and when to use an interface"):

```
Cat thisCat = new Cat();
```

One alternative is to use a C# interface for the reference:

```
IMovable thisMovableCat = (IMovable)new Cat();  // Note the required cast.
```

Now you can put any object into the variable that implements `IMovable`. This practice has wide, powerful uses in object-oriented programming, as you can see later in this chapter.

Using the C# Predefined Interface Types

Because interfaces are extremely useful, you find more interfaces in the .NET class library than gun racks at an NRA convention. I counted dozens in Help before I got tired and stopped. Among the dozen or more interfaces in the `System` namespace alone are `IComparable`, `IComparable<T>`, `IDisposable`, and `IFormattable`. The `System.Collections.Generics` namespace includes IEnumerable<T>, IList<T>, ICollection<T>, and IDictionary<TKey, TValue>. And there are many more. Those with the <T> notation are generic interfaces. I explain the <T> notation in the discussion of collection classes in Book I, Chapter 6.

The Help files show all the ISomething<T> types with little tick marks added (IList`1), but look for "IList<T>" in the Help index.

Two interfaces that are commonly used are IComparable and IEnumerable — largely superseded now by their generic versions IComparable<T> (read as "IComparable *of* T") and IEnumerable<T>.

I show you the IComparable<T> interface in this chapter. It makes possible a comparison of all sorts of objects, such as Students, to each other, and enables the Sort() method that all arrays and most collections supply. IEnumerable<T> makes the powerful foreach loop work — most collections implement IEnumerable<T>, so you can iterate the collections with foreach. You can find an additional major use for IEnumerable<T> in Book I, as the basis for the new C# 3.0 query expressions.

Looking at a Program That CAN_BE_USED_AS an Example

The following SortInterface program is a special offer. The capabilities brought to you by two different interfaces cannot be matched in any inheritance relationship. Interface implementations are standing by.

However, I want to break the SortInterface program into sections to demonstrate various principles. (Pfft! As though I have any principles. I just want to make sure that you can see exactly how the program works.)

Creating your own interface at home in your spare time

The following IDisplayable interface is satisfied by any class that contains a Display() method (and declares that it implements IDisplayable, of course). Display() returns a string representation of the object that can be displayed using WriteLine().

```
// IDisplayable -- Any object that implements the Display() method
interface IDisplayable
{
  // Return a description of yourself.
  string Display();
}
```

The following Student class implements IDisplayable:

```
class Student : IDisplayable
{
  public Student(string name, double grade)
  { Name = name; Grade = grade; }
  public string Name { get; private set; }
  public double Grade { get; private set; }
  public string Display()
  {
    string padName = Name.PadRight(9);
    return String.Format("{0}: {1:N0}", padName, Grade);
  }
}
```


Display() uses String's PadRight() and Format() methods, covered in Book I, Chapter 3, to return a neatly formatted string.

The following DisplayArray() method takes an array of any objects that implement the IDisplayable interface. Each of those objects is guaranteed (by the interface) to have its own Display() method (the entire program appears in the later section "Putting it all together"):

```
// DisplayArray -- Display an array of objects that implement
//   the IDisplayable interface.
public static void DisplayArray(IDisplayable[] displayables)
{
  foreach(IDisplayable disp in displayables)
  {
    Console.WriteLine("{0}, disp.Display());
  }
}
```

The following example shows the output from DisplayArray():

```
Homer    : 0
Marge    : 85
Bart     : 50
Lisa     : 100
Maggie   : 30
```

Implementing the incomparable IComparable<T> interface

C# defines the interface IComparable<T> this way:

```
interface IComparable<T>
{
  // Compare the current T object to the object 'item'; return a
  // 1 if larger, -1 if smaller, and 0 if the same.
  int CompareTo(T item);
}
```

A class implements the IComparable<T> interface by implementing a CompareTo() method. Notice that CompareTo() takes an argument of type T, a type you supply when you *instantiate the interface* for a particular data type — as in this example:

```
class SoAndSo : IComparable<SoAndSo>  // Make me comparable.
```

When you implement IComparable<T> for your class, its CompareTo() method should return 0 if the two items (of your class type) being compared are "equal" in a way that you define. If not, it should return 1 or –1, depending on which object is "greater."

It seems a little Darwinian, but you could say that one Student object is "greater than" another Student object if his grade-point average is higher. (Okay, either a better student or a better apple-polisher — it doesn't matter.)

Implementing the CompareTo() method implies that the objects have a sorting order. If one student is "greater than" another, you must be able to sort the students from "least" to "greatest." In fact, most collection classes (including arrays but not dictionaries) supply a Sort() method something like this:

```
void Sort(IComparable<T>[] objects);
```

This method sorts a collection of objects that implement the IComparable <T> interface. It doesn't even matter which class the objects belong to. For example, they could even be Student objects. Collection classes such as arrays or List<T> could even sort this version of Student:

```
// Student -- Description of a student with name and grade
class Student : IComparable<Student>, IDisplayable   // Instantiation
{
  // Constructor -- initialize a new student object.
  public Student(double grade)
  { Grade = grade; }
  public double Grade { get; private set; }
  // Implement the IComparable<T> interface:
  // CompareTo -- Compare another object (in this case, Student objects) and
  //    decide which one comes after the other in the sorted array.
  public int CompareTo(Student rightStudent)
  {
    // Compare the current Student (call her 'left') against the other
    // student (call her 'right').
    Student leftStudent = this;

    // Now generate a -1, 0 or 1 based on the Sort criteria (the student's
    // grade). I could use class Double's CompareTo() method instead).
    if (rightStudent.Grade < leftStudent.Grade)
    {
      return -1;
    }
```

```
      if (rightStudent.Grade > leftStudent.Grade)
      {
        return 1;
      }
      return 0;
    }
  }
```

Sorting an array of `Students` is reduced to this single call:

```
void MyMethod(Student[] students) // Where Student implements IComparable<T>
{
  Array.Sort(students); // Sort array of IComparable<Student>s
}
```

You provide the comparator (`CompareTo()`), and `Array` does all the work — sounds fair to me.

Putting it all together

This is the moment you've been waiting for: the complete `SortInterface` program that uses the features described earlier in this chapter:

```
// SortInterface -- Demonstrates how the interface concept can be used
//    to provide an enhanced degree of flexibility in factoring
//    and implementing classes.
using System;
namespace SortInterface
{
  // IDisplayable -- An object that can convert itself into a displayable
  //    string format (duplicates what you can do by overriding
  //    ToString(), but helps me make a point)
  interface IDisplayable
  {
    // Display -- return a string representation of yourself.
    string Display();
  }
  class Program
  {
    public static void Main(string[] args)
    {
      // Sort students by grade...
      Console.WriteLine("Sorting the list of students");
      // Get an unsorted array of students.
      Student[] students = Student.CreateStudentList();
      // Use the IComparable<T> interface to sort the array.
      Array.Sort(students);
      // Now the IDisplayable interface to display the results
      DisplayArray(students);

      // Now sort an array of birds by name using the same routines even
      // though the classes Bird and Student have no common base class.
      Console.WriteLine("\nsorting the list of birds");
      Bird[] birds = Bird.CreateBirdList();
      // Notice that it's not necessary to cast the objects explicitly
      // to an array of IDisplayables (and wasn't for Students, either) ...
```

```
      Array.Sort(birds);
      DisplayArray(birds);
      // Wait for user to acknowledge the results.
      Console.WriteLine("Press Enter to terminate...");
      Console.Read();
    }
    // DisplayArray -- Display an array of objects that
    //    implement the IDisplayable interface.
    public static void DisplayArray(IDisplayable[] displayables)
    {
      foreach(IDisplayable displayable in displayables)
      {
        Console.WriteLine("{0}", displayable.Display());
      }
    }
  }
  // ----------- Students -- Sort students by grade -------
  // Student -- Description of a student with name and grade
  class Student : IComparable<Student>, IDisplayable
  {
    // Constructor -- Initialize a new student object.
    public Student(string name, double grade)
    { Name = Name; Grade = grade; }
    // CreateStudentList -- To save space here, just create
    // a fixed list of students.
    static string[] names = {"Homer", "Marge", "Bart", "Lisa", "Maggie"};
    static double[] grades = {0, 85, 50, 100, 30};
    public static Student[] CreateStudentList()
    {
      Student[] students = new Student[names.Length];
      for (int i = 0; i < names.Length; i++)
      {
        students[i] = new Student(names[i], grades[i]);
      }
      return students;
    }
    // Access read-only properties.
    public string Name { get; private set; }
    public double Grade { get; private set; }
    // Implement the IComparable interface:
    // CompareTo -- Compare another object (in this case, Student objects)
    //    and decide which one comes after the other in the sorted array.
    public int CompareTo(Student rightStudent)
    {
      // Compare the current Student (call her 'left') against
      // the other student (call her 'right').
      Student leftStudent = this;
      // Now generate a -1, 0 or 1 based on the Sort criteria (the student's
      // grade). Double's CompareTo() method would work, too.
      if (rightStudent.Grade < leftStudent.Grade)
      {
        return -1;
      }
      if (rightStudent.Grade > leftStudent.Grade)
      {
        return 1;
      }
      return 0;
    }
    // Display -- Implement the IDisplayable interface:
```

```
    public string Display()
    {
      string padName = Name.PadRight(9);
      return String.Format("{0}: {1:N0}", padName, Grade);
    }
  }
  // -----------Birds -- Sort birds by their names--------
  // Bird -- Just an array of bird names.
  class Bird : IComparable<Bird>, IDisplayable
  {
    // Constructor -- initialize a new Bird object.
    public Bird(string name) { Name = name; }
    // CreateBirdList -- Return a list of birds to the caller;
    //    Use a canned list here to save space.
    static string[] birdNames =
       { "Oriole", "Hawk", "Robin", "Cardinal", "Bluejay", "Finch", "Sparrow"};
    public static Bird[] CreateBirdList()
    {
      Bird[] birds = new Bird[birdNames.Length];
      for(int i = 0; i < birds.Length; i++)
      {
        birds[i] = new Bird(birdNames[i]);
      }
      return birds;
    }
    public string Name { get; private set; }
    // Implement the IComparable interface:
    // CompareTo -- Compare the birds by name; use the
    //    built-in String class compare method.
    public int CompareTo(Bird rightBird)
    {
      // Compare the "current" bird to the "right hand object" bird.
      Bird leftBird = this;
      return String.Compare(leftBird.Name, rightBird.Name);
    }
    // Display -- Implement the IDisplayable interface.
    public string Display() { return Name; }
  }
}
```


The `Student` class (it's in the middle of the program listing) implements the `IComparable<T>` and `IDisplayable` interfaces, as described earlier. The `CompareTo()` method compares the students by grade, which results in the students being sorted by grade. `Student`'s `Display()` method returns the name and grade of the student.

The other methods of `Student` include the read-only `Name` and `Grade` properties, a simple constructor, and a `CreateStudentList()` method. This method just returns a fixed list of students for the code to work on.

The `Bird` class at the bottom of the listing also implements the interfaces `IComparable<T>` and `IDisplayable`. The class implements `CompareTo()` by comparing the names of the birds using `String.Compare()`. So one bird is greater than another if its name is greater. `Bird.CompareTo()` alphabetizes the list. `Bird`'s `Display()` method just returns the name of the bird.

Getting back to the Main() event

If you've followed along with us so far, you're set up for the good part, back in `Main()`. The `CreateStudentList()` method is used to return an unsorted list, which is stored in the array `students`.

You might think it necessary to cast the array of students into an array of `comparableObjects` so that you can pass the students to `Array`'s `Sort()` method:

```
IComparable<Student>[] comparables = (IComparable<Student>[])students;
```

But not so, my friend. `Sort()` sees that the array passed in consists of objects that implement `IComparable<something>` and simply calls `CompareTo()` on each `Student` object to sort them. Great, eh?

The sorted array of `Student` objects is then passed to the locally defined `DisplayArray()` method. `DisplayArray()` uses `foreach` to iterate through an array of objects that implement a `Display()` method (guaranteed by the objects' having implemented `IDisplayable`). In the loop, it calls `Display()` on each object and displays the result to the console using `WriteLine()`.

The program in `Main()` continues by sorting and displaying birds! I think we can agree that birds have nothing to do with students. Yet the same `Sort()` and `DisplayArray()` methods work on `Bird` as on `Student`.

The output from the program appears:

```
Sorting the list of students
Lisa      : 100
Marge     : 85
Bart      : 50
Maggie    : 30
Homer     : 0

Sorting the list of birds
Bluejay
Cardinal
Finch
Hawk
Oriole
Robin
Sparrow
Press Enter to terminate...
```

Unifying Class Hierarchies

Figure 8-1 shows the `Robot` and `Animal` hierarchies. Some, but not all, of the classes in each hierarchy not only inherit from the base classes, `Robot` or `Animal`, but they also implement the `IPet` interface (not all animals are pets, you see), as shown in the following code — I skipped lots of details:

```
// Two abstract base classes and one interface
abstract class Animal
{
  abstract public void Eat(string food);
  abstract public void Sleep(int hours);
  abstract public int NumberOfLegs { get; }
  public void Breathe() { ... } // Nonabstract, implementation not shown.
}
abstract class Robot
{
  public virtual void Speak(string whatToSay) { ... } // Impl not shown
  abstract public void LiftObject(object o);
  abstract public int NumberOfLegs { get; }
}
interface IPet
{
  void AskForStrokes();
  void DoTricks();
  int NumberOfLegs { get; }  // Properties in interfaces look like this.
  string Name { get; set; }  // get/set must be public in implementations.
}
// Cat -- This concrete class inherits (and partially implements)
//    class Animal and also implements interface IPet.
class Cat : Animal, IPet
{
  public Cat(string name) { Name = name; }
  // 1. Overrides and implements Animal members (not shown).
  // 2. Provides additional implementation for IPet.
  #region IPet Members
  public void AskForStrokes() ...
  public void DoTricks() ...
  public string Name { get; set; }
  // Inherits NumberOfLegs property from base class, thus meeting
  // IPet's requirement for a NumberOfLegs property.
  #endregion IPet Members
  public override string ToString() { return Name; }
}
class Cobra : Animal
{
  // 1. Inherits or overrides all Animal methods only (not shown).
}
class Robozilla : Robot    // Not IPet
{
  // 1. Override Speak.
  public override void Speak(string whatToSay)
  { Console.WriteLine("DESTROY ALL HUMANS!"); }
  // 2. Implement LiftObject and NumberOfLegs, not all shown.
  public override void LiftObject(object o) ...
  public override int NumberOfLegs { get { return 2; } }
}
class RoboCat : Robot, IPet
{
  public RoboCat(string name) { Name = name; }
  // 1. Override some Robot members, not all shown:
  #region IPet Members
  public void AskForStrokes() ...
  public void DoTricks() ...
  public string Name { get; set; }
  #endregion IPet Members
}
```

(Notice the properties in `IPet` — that's how you specify properties in interfaces. If you need both getter and setter, just add `set;` after `get;`.)

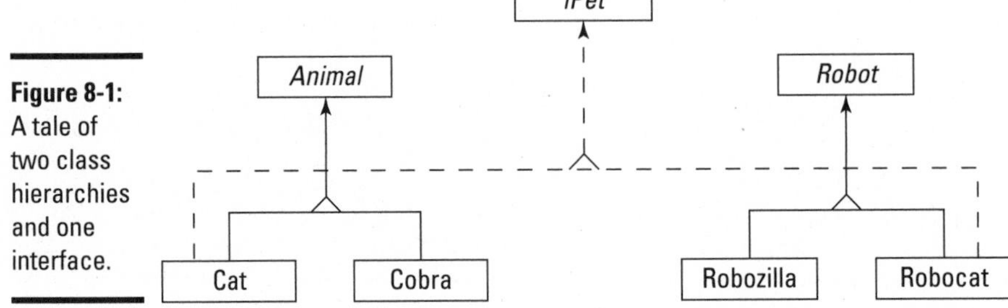

Figure 8-1: A tale of two class hierarchies and one interface.

I've shown you two concrete classes that inherit from `Animal` and two that inherit from `Robot`. However, you can see that neither class `Cobra` nor class `Robozilla` implements `IPet` — probably for good reasons. I have no plans to watch TV with my pet cobra beside me on the couch, and a robozilla sounds nasty too. Some of the classes in both hierarchies exhibit what you might call "petness" and some don't.

The `InterfacesBridgingHierarchies` example on this book's Web site puts these items through their paces.

The point of this section is that *any* class can implement an interface, as long as it provides the right methods and properties. `Robotcat` and `Robodog` can carry out the `AskForStrokes()` and `DoTricks()` actions and have the `NumberOfLegs` property, as can `Cat` and `Dog` in the `Animal` hierarchy — all while other classes in the same hierarchies don't implement `IPet`.

You can add support for an interface to any class — but only if you're free to modify the source code.

Hiding Behind an Interface

Often in this book, I discuss code that (a) you write but (b) someone else (a client) uses in her programs (you may be the client yourself, of course). Sometimes, you have a complex or tricky class for which you would truly rather not expose the whole public interface to clients. For various reasons, it includes some dangerous operations that nonetheless have to be public. Ideally, you would expose a safe subset of your class's public methods and properties and hide the dangerous ones. C# interfaces can do that too.

Here's a different Robozilla class, with several methods and properties that amateurs can use safely and enjoyably. But Robozilla also has some advanced features that can be, well, scary:

```
public class Robozilla  // Doesn't implement IPet!
{
  public void ClimbStairs();                     // Safe
  public void PetTheRobodog();                   // Safe? Might break it.
  public void Charge();                          // Maybe not safe
  public void SearchAndDestroy();                // Dangerous
  public void LaunchGlobalThermonuclearWar(); // Catastrophic
}
```


You want to expose only the two safer methods while hiding the last three dangerous ones. Here's how you can do that by using a C# interface:

1. Design a C# interface that exposes only the safe methods:

    ```
    public interface IRobozillaSafe
    {
      void ClimbStairs();
      void PetTheRobodog();
    }
    ```

2. Modify the Robozilla class to implement the interface. Because it already has implementations for the required methods, all you need is the `: IRobozillaSafe` notation on the class heading:

    ```
    public class Robozilla : IRobozillaSafe  ...
    ```

Now you can just keep Robozilla itself a secret from, say, everybody except Gandhi, Martin Luther King, and Mother Theresa and give most users the IRobozillaSafe interface. Give your clients a way to instantiate a new Robozilla, but return to them a reference to the interface (in this example, by using a static factory method added to class Robozilla):

```
// Creates a Robozilla but returns only an interface reference to it.
public static IRobozillaSafe CreateRobozilla(<parameter list>)
{
  return (IRobozillaSafe)new Robozilla(<parameter list>);
}
```

Clients then use Robozilla like this:

```
IRobozillaSafe myZilla = Robozilla.CreateRobozilla(...);
myZilla.ClimbStairs();
myZilla.PetTheRobodog();
```

It's that simple. Using the interface, they can call the Robozilla methods that it specifies — but not any other Robozilla methods.

Programmers (I think I can guess which ones) can defeat my little ploy with a simple cast:

```
Robozilla myKillaZilla = (Robozilla)myZilla;
```

Doing so is usually a bad idea, though. The interface has a purpose. Bill Wagner says, "Programmers who go to that much work to create bugs get what they deserve."

In real life, programmers sometimes use this hand-out-an-interface technique with the complex `DataSet` class used in ADO.NET to interact with databases. A `DataSet` can return a set of database tables loaded with records — such as a table of `Customers` and a table of `Orders`. (Modern relational databases, such as Oracle and SQL Server, contain tables linked by various relationships. Each table contains lots of records, where each record might be, for example, the name, rank, and serial number of a `Customer`.)

Unfortunately, if you hand a client a `DataSet` reference (even through a read-only property's `get` clause), he can easily muddle the situation by reaching into the `DataSet` and modifying elements that you don't want modified. One way to prevent such mischief is to return a `DataView` object, which is read-only. Alternatively, you can create a C# interface to expose a safe subset of the operations available on the `DataSet`. Then you can subclass `DataSet` and have the subclass (call it `MyDataSet`) implement the interface. Finally, give clients a way to obtain an interface reference to a live `MyDataSet` object and let them have at it in relative safety — through the interface.

You usually shouldn't return a reference to a collection, either, because it lets anyone alter the collection outside the class that created it. Remember that the reference you hand out can still point to the original collection inside your class. That's why `List<T>`, for instance, provides an `AsReadOnly()` method. This method returns a collection that can't be altered:

```
private List<string> _readWriteNames = ...  // A modifiable data member
...
ReadonlyCollection<string> readonlyNames = _readWriteNames.AsReadOnly();
return readonlyNames; // Safer to return this than _readWriteNames.
```

Although it doesn't qualify as using an interface, the purpose is the same.

The `HidingBehindAnInterface` example on this book's Web site shows the `Robozilla` code in this section.

Inheriting an Interface

A C# interface can "inherit" the methods of another interface. I use quotes around the word *inherit* because it's not true inheritance, no matter how it may appear. The following interface code lists a *base interface*, much like a base class, in its heading:

```
interface IRobozillaSafe : IPet   // Base interface
{
  // Methods not shown here ...
}
```

By having IRobozillaSafe "inherit" IPet, you can let this subset of Robozilla implement its own "petness" without trying to impose petness inappropriately on all of Robozilla:

```
class PetRobo : Robozilla, IRobozillaSafe // (also an IPet by inheritance)
{
  // Implement Robozilla operations.
  // Implement IRobozillaSafe operations, then ...
  // Implement IPet operations too (required by the inherited IPet interface).
}
...
// Hand out only a safe reference, not one to PetRobo itself.
IPet myPetRobo = (IPet)new PetRobo();
// ... now call IPet methods on the object.
```

The IRobozillaSafe interface inherits from IPet. Classes that implement IRobozillaSafe must therefore also implement IPet to make their implementation of IRobozillaSafe complete.

This type of inheritance isn't the same concept as class inheritance. For instance, class PetRobo in the previous example, can have a constructor, but no equivalent of a base-class constructor exists for IRobozillaSafe or IPet. Interfaces don't have constructors. More important, polymorphism doesn't work the same way with interfaces. Though you can call a method of a subclass through a reference to the base class (class polymorphism), the parallel operation involving interfaces (interface polymorphism) doesn't work: You can't call a method of the derived interface (IRobozillaSafe) through a base interface reference (IPet).

Although interface inheritance isn't polymorphic in the same way that class inheritance is, you *can* pass an object of a derived interface type (IRobozillasafe) through a parameter of its base interface type (IPet). Therefore, you can also put IRobozillasafe objects into a collection of IPet objects. The PassInterface example on this book's Web site demonstrates the ideas in this section.

Using Interfaces to Manage Change in Object-Oriented Programs

Interfaces are the key to object-oriented programs that bend flexibly with the winds of change. Your code will laugh in the face of new requirements.

You've no doubt heard it said, "Change is a constant." When you hand a new program to a bunch of users, they soon start requesting changes. Add this feature, please. Fix that problem, please. The RoboWarrior has feature X, so why doesn't Robozilla? Many programs have a long shelf life — thousands of programs, especially old Fortran and Cobol programs, have been in service for 20 or 30 years or longer. They undergo lots of *maintenance* in that extended time span, *which makes planning and designing for change one of your highest priorities.*

Here's an example: In the `Robot` class hierarchy, suppose that all robots can move in one way or another. `Robocat`s *saunter.* `Robozilla`s *charge* — at least when operated by a power (hungry) user. And `Robosnake`s *slither.* One way to implement these different modes of travel involves inheritance: Give the base class, `Robot`, an abstract `Move()` method. Then each subclass overrides the `Move()` method to implement it differently:

```
abstract public class Robot
{
  abstract public void Move(int direction, int speed);
  // ...
}
public class Robosnake : Robot
{
  public override void Move(int direction, int speed)
  {
    // A real Move() implementation here: slithering.
    ... some real code that computes angles and changes
    snake's location relative to a coordinate system, say ...
  }
}
```

But suppose that you often receive requests to add new types of movement to existing `Robot` subclasses. "Please make `Robosnake` *undulate* rather than *slither,*" maybe. (Don't ask me what the difference is.) Now you have to open up the `Robosnake` class and modify its `Move()` method directly.

After the `Move()` method is working correctly for *slithering*, most programmers would prefer not to meddle with it. Implementing slithering is difficult, and changing the implementation can introduce brand-new bugs. If it ain't broke, don't fix it.

The code just given illustrates the problem. The StrategyExample program on this book's Web site illustrates the solution, discussed in the next several sections. The solution has the advantage of allowing the old, slithering code to flourish for some applications while providing the new, undulating movement in newer applications. Everybody's happy.

Making flexible dependencies through interfaces

There must be a way to implement Move() that doesn't require you to open a can of worms every time a client wants *wriggling* instead. You can use interfaces, of course!

Look at the following code that uses HAS_A, a now-familiar relationship between two classes in which one class *contains* the other:

```
public class Robot
{
  // This object is used to implement motion.
  protected Motor _motor = new Motor(); // Refers to Motor by name
  // ...
}
internal class Motor { ... }
```

The point about this example is that the contained object is of type Motor, where Motor is a concrete object. (That is, it represents a real item, not an abstraction.) HAS_A sets up a *dependency* between classes Robot and Motor: Robot *depends on* the concrete class Motor. A class with concrete dependencies is *tightly coupled* to them: When you need to replace Motor with something else, code that depends directly on Motor like this has to change too. Instead, insulate your code by relying only on the public interface of dependencies, which you can do with interfaces. You can depend on dependent objects in a, er, *less dependent* way.

Depend on abstractions, not on concrete classes. I show you how.

Abstract or concrete: When to use an abstract class and when to use an interface

In Chapter 7 of this minibook, in my little discourse about birds, I say, "Every bird out there is a subtype of Bird." In other words, a duck is an instance of a subclass Duck. You never see an instance of Bird itself — Bird is an *abstraction*. Instead, you always see *concrete*, physical ducks, sparrows, or hummingbirds. Abstractions are concepts. As living creatures, ducks are real, concrete objects. And, concrete objects are instances of concrete classes. (A *concrete* class is a class that you can instantiate. It lacks the abstract keyword, and it implements all methods.)

You can represent abstractions in two ways in C#: with abstract classes or with C# interfaces. The two have differences that can affect your choice of which one to use:

- **Use an abstract class** when you can profitably share an implementation with subclasses — the abstract base class can contribute real code that its subclasses can use by inheritance. For instance, maybe class `Robot` can handle part of the robot's tasks, just not movement.

  An abstract class doesn't have to be completely abstract. Though it has to have at least one abstract, unimplemented method or property, some can provide implementations (bodies). Using an abstract class to provide an implementation for its subclasses to inherit prevents duplication of code. That's always a good thing.

- **Use an interface** when you can't share any implementation or your implementing class already has a base class.

  C# interfaces are purely, totally abstract. A C# interface supplies no implementation of any of its methods. Yet it can also add flexibility that isn't otherwise possible. The abstract class option may not be available because you want to add a capability to a class that already has a base class (that you can't modify). For example, class `Robot` may already have a base class in a library that you didn't write and therefore can't alter. Interfaces are especially helpful for representing completely abstract capabilities, such as movability or displayability, that you want to add to multiple classes that may otherwise have nothing in common — for example, being in the same class hierarchy.

Doing HAS_A with interfaces

I mention earlier in this chapter that you can use interfaces as a more general reference type. The containing class can refer to the contained class not with a reference to a concrete class but, rather, with a reference to an abstraction — either an abstract class or a C# interface will work:

```
  AbstractDependentClass dependency1 = ...;
  ISomeInterface dependency2 = ...;
```

Suppose that you have an `IPropulsion` interface:

```
interface IPropulsion
{
  void Movement(int direction, int speed);
}
```

Class `Robot` can contain a data member of type `IPropulsion` instead of the concrete type `Motor`:

```
public class Robot
{
  private IPropulsion _propel;     //<--Notice the interface type here.
  // Somehow, you supply a concrete propulsion object at runtime ...
  // Other stuff and then:
  public void Move(int speed, int direction)
  {
    // Use whatever concrete propulsion device is installed in _propel.
    _propel.Movement(speed, direction); // Delegate to its methods.
  }
}
```

Robot's Move() method delegates the real work to the object referred to through the interface. Be sure to provide a way to install a concrete Motor or Engine or another implementer of IPropulsion in the data member. Programmers often install that concrete object — "inject the dependency" — by passing it to a constructor:

```
Robot r = new Robosnake(someConcreteMotor);  // Type IPropulsion
```

or by assigning it via a setter property:

```
r.PropulsionDevice = someConcreteMotor;      // Invokes the set clause
```

Another approach to dependency injection is to use a *factory method* (which I discuss earlier in this chapter, in the section "As a method return type," and illustrate in the section "Hiding Behind an Interface"):

```
IPropulsion _propel = CreatePropulsion();    // A factory method
```

Chapter 9: Delegating Those Important Events

In This Chapter

- Using delegates to solve the callback problem
- Using delegates to customize a method
- Implementing delegates by using anonymous methods
- Using C# events to notify the world when interesting events happen

This chapter looks into a corner of C# that has been around since the birth of the language, but one that I've avoided because it's challenging stuff. However, if you can bear with me — and I try to go as easy on you as possible — the payoff is well worth it.

E.T., Phone Home — The Callback Problem

If you've seen the Steven Spielberg movie *E.T., the Extraterrestrial* (1982), you watched the cute but ugly little alien stranded on Earth try to build an apparatus from old toy parts with which he could "phone home." He needed his ship to pick him up.

It's a big jump from *E.T.* to C#, but code sometimes needs to phone home, too. For example, you may have wondered how the Windows progress bar works. It's the horizontal "bar" that gradually fills up with coloring to show progress during a lengthy operation, such as copying files. (On my machine, of course, good old Murphy's law — "Whatever can go wrong will go wrong" — seems to fill it up well before the task is finished. Figure 9-1 shows a green progress bar (though it isn't easy being green in a black-and-white book).

The progress bar is based on a lengthy operation's periodic pause to "phone home." In programmerese, it's a *callback*. Usually, the lengthy operation estimates how long its task should take and then checks frequently to see how far it has progressed. Periodically, the progress bar sends a signal by calling a *callback method* back on the mother ship — the class that kicked off the long operation. The mother ship can then update its progress bar.

The trick is that you have to supply this callback method for the long operation to use.

That callback method may be on the same class as the lengthy operation — such as phoning your sister on the other side of the house. Or, more often, it's on another class that knows about the progress bar — such as phoning Aunt Maxie in Minnesota. Somehow, at its start, the lengthy operation has been handed a mechanism for phoning home — sort of like giving your kid a cellphone so that she can call you at 10 p.m.

This chapter talks about how your code can set up this callback mechanism and then invoke it to phone home when needed.

Callbacks are used a lot in Windows programming, typically for a piece of code, down in your program's guts, to notify a higher-level module that the task has finished, to ask for needed data, or to let that module take a useful action, such as write a log entry or update a progress bar.

Figure 9-1: Making progress with the Windows ProgressBar control.

Defining a Delegate

C# provides *delegates* for making callbacks — and a number of other tasks. Delegates are the C# way (the .NET way, really, because any .NET language can use them) for you to *pass around methods as though they were data.*

You're saying, "Here, execute this method when you need it" (and then handing over the method to execute).

This chapter helps you get a handle on that concept, see its usefulness, and start using it yourself.

You may be an experienced coder who will recognize immediately that delegates are similar to C/C++ function pointers — only much, much better. But I'm assuming in this section that you aren't and you don't.

Think of a delegate as a vehicle for passing a callback method to a "workhorse" method that needs to call you back or needs help with that action, as in doing the same action to each element of a collection. Because the collection doesn't know about your custom action, you need a way to provide the action for the collection to carry out. Figure 9-2 shows how the parts of this scheme fit together.

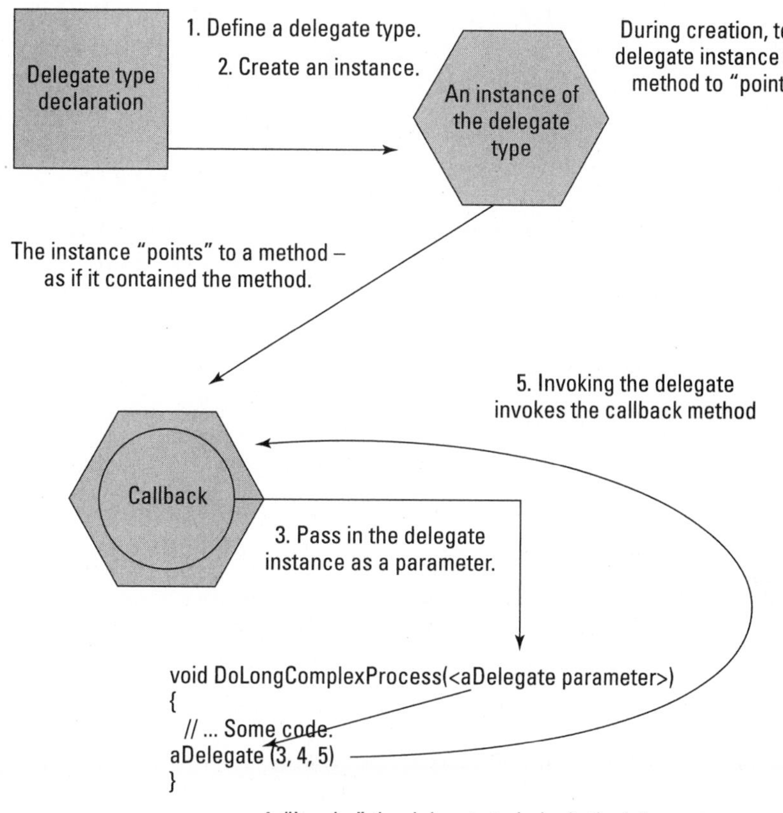

Figure 9-2: Sending your delegate to the bungee-jump on your behalf.

A delegate is a data type, similar to a class. As with a class, you create an instance of the delegate type in order to use the delegate. Figure 9-2 shows the sequence of events in the delegate's life cycle as you complete these steps:

1. Define the delegate type (in much the same way as you would define a class).

   Sometimes, C# has already defined a delegate you can use. Much of the time, though, you need to define your own, custom delegates.

Under the surface, a delegate *is* a class, derived from the class `System.MulticastDelegate`, which knows how to store one or more "pointers" to methods and invoke them for you. Relax: The compiler writes the class part of it for you.

2. Create an instance of the delegate type — such as instantiating a class.

   During creation, you hand the new delegate instance the name of a method that you want it to use as a callback or an action method.

3. Pass the delegate instance to a workhorse method, *which has a parameter of the delegate type*. That's the doorway through which you insert the delegate instance into the workhorse method.

   It's like smuggling a candy bar into a movie theater — except that in this example, the movie theater expects, even invites, the contraband candy.

4. When the workhorse method is ready — for example, when it's time to update the progress bar — the workhorse "invokes" the delegate, passing it any expected arguments.

5. Invoking the delegate in turn invokes (calls) the callback method that the delegate "points" to. Using the delegate, the workhorse phones home. (Older readers may remember Mr. Ed: "A horse is a horse. . . .")

This fundamental mechanism solves the callback problem — and it has other uses too.

Delegate types can also be generic, allowing you to use the same delegate for different data types, much as you can instantiate a `List<T>` collection for `string` or `int`. Book I covers this in detail.

Pass Me the Code, Please — Examples

Let's jump right into a couple of examples — and solve the callback problem discussed at the beginning of this chapter.

I delegated the example to Igor

In this section, I walk you through two examples of using a callback — a delegate instance phoning home to the object that created it, like *E.T.* But first take a look at some common variations on what you can use a callback delegate for:

- **To notify the delegate's home base of an event:** A lengthy operation has finished or made some progress or perhaps run into an error. "Mother, this is E.T. Can you come get me at Elliot's house?"
- **To call back to home base to ask for the necessary data to complete a task:** "Honey, I'm at the store. Should I get white bread or wheat?"

✦ **More generally, to customize a method:** The method you're customizing provides a framework, and its caller supplies a delegate to do the work. "Honey, take this grocery list to the store and follow it exactly." The delegate method carries out a task that the customized method needs done (but can't handle by itself). The customized method is responsible for invoking the delegate at the appropriate moment.

First, a simple example

The `SimpleDelegateExample` program on the Web site demonstrates a simple delegate:

```
// SimpleDelegateExample -- Demonstrate a simple delegate callback.
using System;
namespace SimpleDelegateExample
{
  class Program
  {
    delegate int MyDelType(string name);  // Inside class or inside namespace

    static void Main(string[] args)
    {
      // Create a delegate instance pointing to the CallBackMethod below.
      // Note that the callback method is static, so you prefix the name
      // with the class name, Program.
      MyDelType del = new MyDelType(Program.CallBackMethod);
      // Call a method that will invoke the delegate.
      UseTheDel(del, "hello");
      // Wait for user to acknowledge results.
      Console.WriteLine("Press Enter to terminate...");
      Console.Read();
    }
    // UseTheDel -- A "workhorse" method that takes a MyDelType delegate
    //    argument and invokes the delegate. arg is a string I want to pass
    //    to the delegate invocation.
    private static void UseTheDel(MyDelType del, string arg)
    {
      if (del == null) return; // Don't invoke a null delegate!
      // Here's where you invoke the delegate.
      // What's written here? A number representing the length of arg.
     Console.WriteLine("UseTheDel writes {0}", del(arg));
    }
    // CallBackMethod -- A method that conforms to the MyDelType
    //    delegate signature (takes a string, returns an int).
    //    The delegate will call this method.
    public static int CallBackMethod(string stringPassed)
    {
      // Leave tracks to show you were here.
      // What's written here? stringPassed.
      Console.WriteLine("CallBackMethod writes: {0}", stringPassed);
      // Return an int.
      return stringPassed.Length;  // Delegate requires an int return.
    }
  }
}
```

The delegate-related parts of this example are highlighted in boldface.

First you see the delegate definition. `MyDelType` defines a *signature* — you can pass any method with the delegate; such a method must take a `string` argument and return an `int`. Second, the `CallBackMethod()`, defined at the bottom of the listing, matches that signature. Third, `Main()` creates an instance of the delegate, called `del`, and then passes the delegate instance to a "workhorse" method, `UseTheDel()`, along with some string data, `"hello"`, that the delegate requires.

In that setup, here's the sequence of events:

1. `UseTheDel()` takes two arguments, a `MyDelType` delegate, and a `string` that it calls `arg`. So, when `Main()` calls `UseTheDel`, it passes my delegate instance to be used inside the method. When I created the delegate instance, `del`, in `Main()`, I passed the *name* of the `CallBackMethod()` as the method to be called. Because `CallBackMethod()` is static, I had to prefix the name with the class name, `Program`. I tell you more about it later in this chapter.
2. Inside `UseTheDel()`, the method ensures that the delegate isn't `null` and then starts a `WriteLine()` call. Within that call, before it finishes, the method invokes the delegate by calling `del(arg)`. `arg` is just something you can pass to the delegate, which causes the `CallBackMethod()` to be called.
3. Inside `CallBackMethod()`, the method writes its own message, including the string that was passed when `UseTheDel()` invoked the delegate. Then `CallBackMethod()` returns the length of the string it was passed, and that length is written out as the last part of the `WriteLine()` in `UseTheDel()`.

The output looks like this:

```
CallBackMethod writes: hello
UseTheDel writes 5
Press Enter to terminate...
```

`UseTheDel()` phones home and `CallBackMethod()` answers the call.

A More Real-World Example

For a more realistic example than `SimpleDelegateExample`, I show you how to write a little app that puts up a progress bar and updates it every time a lengthy method invokes a delegate.

Getting an overview of the bigger example

The `SimpleProgress` example on the Web site demonstrates the Windows Forms `ProgressBar` control that I discuss at the top of this chapter. (By the way, this example of Windows *graphical* programming is the only one in this book — even if it's simple-minded — so I step through it carefully. I urge you to complete the steps as I provide them.)

The example displays a small dialog-box-style window with two buttons and a progress bar (refer to Figure 9-1). When you load the solution example into Visual Studio and then build it, run it, and click the upper button, marked Click to Start, the progress bar runs for a few seconds. You see it gradually fill up, one-tenth of its length at a time. When it's completely full, you can click the Close button to end the program or click Click to Start again.

Putting the app together

To create the sample app on your own, rather than just load it from the Web site example — and experience a bit of Windows graphical programming — follow these steps, working first in *design mode*, where you're just laying out the appearance of your app.

First create the project and position the necessary controls on your "window":

1. **Choose File⇨New Project and select Windows on the left, under C#, but this time select Windows Forms Application on the right instead of the usual Console Application. Name your project SimpleProgress.**

   The first thing you see is the *form*: a window that you lay out yourself using several *controls*.

2. **Choose View⇨Toolbox, and from the Toolbox window's Common Controls group, drag a `ProgressBar` control to the form and drop it. Then drag two `Button`s onto the form.**

3. **Position the buttons and the `ProgressBar` so that they look somewhat like the one shown in Figure 9-1. Note the handy guide lines that help with positioning.**

Next, set properties for these controls: Choose View⇨Properties, select a control on the form, and set the control's properties:

1. **For the progress bar — named `progressBar1` in the code — make sure that the `Minimum` property is 0, the `Maximum` property is 100, the `Step` property is 10, and the `Value` property is 0.**

2. **For the upper button, change the** `Text` **property to** `"Click to Start"` **and drag the sizing handles on the button image until it looks right and shows all its text.**

3. **For the lower button, change the** `Text` **property to** `"Close"` **and adjust the button's size to your liking.**

In this simple example, you're putting all code in the *form* class. (The form is your window; its class — here, named `Form1` — is responsible for all things graphical.) Generally, you should put all "business" code — the code that does your calculations, data access, and other important work — in other classes. Reserve the form class for code that's intimately involved with displaying elements on the form and responding to its controls. I break that rule here — but the delegate works no matter where its callback method is.

Now, still in design mode, add a *handler method* for each button:

1. **On the form, double-click the new Close button.**

   This action generates a method in the "code behind the form" (or, simply, "the code-behind") — the code that makes the form work. It looks like this — you add the boldfaced code:

   ```
   private void button2_Click(object sender, EventArgs e)
   {
     this.Close();  // 'this' refers to the Form1 class.
   }
   ```

   To toggle between the form's code and its image, choose View⇨Code or View⇨Designer.

2. **Double-click the new Click to Start button to generate its handler method, which looks like the following in the code-behind:**

   ```
   private void button1_Click(object sender, EventArgs e)
   {
     UpdateProgressCallback callback = UpdateProgressCallback(this.
        DoUpdate);
     // Do something that needs periodic progress reports.
     // This passes a delegate instance that knows how to update the bar.
     DoSomethingLengthy(callback);
     // Clear the bar so that it can be used again.
     progressBar1.Value = 0;
   }
   ```

3. **Add the following callback method to the form class:**

   ```
   private void DoUpdate()
   {
     progressBar1.PerformStep(); // Tells progress bar to update itself
   }
   ```

I walk you through the remaining code, all of it on the form class, in the next section. Later in the chapter, I show you other variations on the delegate that's passed.

Looking at the code

The remaining bits of code tucked into the `Form1` class consist of the parts of the delegate life cycle, covered earlier in this chapter. I show you the class and then show you where the parts are. The boldfaced lines are new code that you add beyond the items you added in the previous section:

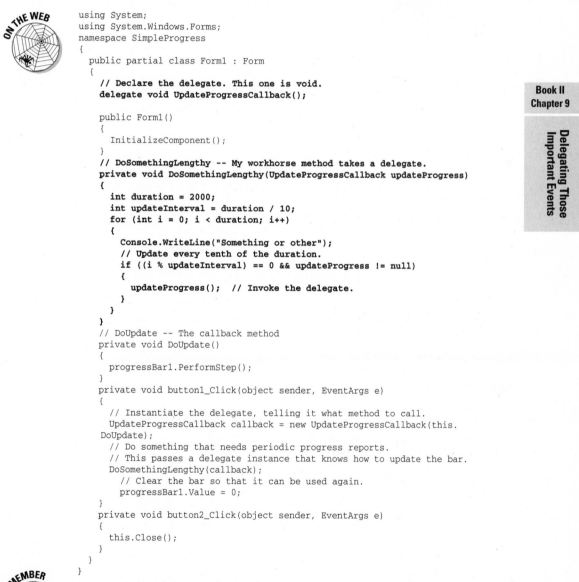

```
using System;
using System.Windows.Forms;
namespace SimpleProgress
{
  public partial class Form1 : Form
  {
    // Declare the delegate. This one is void.
    delegate void UpdateProgressCallback();

    public Form1()
    {
      InitializeComponent();
    }
    // DoSomethingLengthy -- My workhorse method takes a delegate.
    private void DoSomethingLengthy(UpdateProgressCallback updateProgress)
    {
      int duration = 2000;
      int updateInterval = duration / 10;
      for (int i = 0; i < duration; i++)
      {
        Console.WriteLine("Something or other");
        // Update every tenth of the duration.
        if ((i % updateInterval) == 0 && updateProgress != null)
        {
          updateProgress();  // Invoke the delegate.
        }
      }
    }
    // DoUpdate -- The callback method
    private void DoUpdate()
    {
      progressBar1.PerformStep();
    }
    private void button1_Click(object sender, EventArgs e)
    {
      // Instantiate the delegate, telling it what method to call.
      UpdateProgressCallback callback = new UpdateProgressCallback(this.
    DoUpdate);
      // Do something that needs periodic progress reports.
      // This passes a delegate instance that knows how to update the bar.
      DoSomethingLengthy(callback);
        // Clear the bar so that it can be used again.
        progressBar1.Value = 0;
    }
    private void button2_Click(object sender, EventArgs e)
    {
      this.Close();
    }
  }
}
```

The class declaration is interesting as an aside:

```
public partial class Form1 : Form
```

The `partial` keyword indicates that this line is only part of the full class. The rest can be found in the `Form1.Designer.cs` file listed in Solution Explorer. (Take a look at it.) Later in this chapter, I revisit that file to show you a couple of things about "events." Partial classes, which were introduced in C# 2.0, let you split a class between two or more files. The compiler generates the `Form1.Designer.cs` file, so don't modify its code directly. You can modify it indirectly, however, by changing elements on the form. `Form1.cs` is *your* part.

Tracking the delegate life cycle

Look at the example through the parts of the delegate life cycle:

1. **You define the `UpdateProgressCallback` delegate near the top of the class:**

   ```
   delegate void UpdateProgressCallback();
   ```

   Methods that this delegate can "point" to will be `void`, with no parameters. After the `delegate` keyword, the rest defines the *signature* of any method that the delegate can point to: its return type and the number, order, and types of its parameters. Delegates don't have to be `void` — you can write delegates that return any type and take any arguments.

   Defining a delegate defines a *type*, just as `class Student {...}` does. You can declare your delegate `public`, `internal`, `protected`, or even `private`, as needed.

   It's considered good form to append the name `Callback` to the name of a delegate type that defines a callback method, though C# couldn't care less.

2. **You instantiate the delegate and then pass the instance to the `DoSomethingLengthy()` method in the `button1_Click()` method:**

   ```
   UpdateProgressCallback callback =
     new UpdateProgressCallback(this.DoUpdate); // Instantiate the delegate.
   DoSomethingLengthy(callback); // Pass the delegate instance to a method.
   ```

   This delegate "points" to a method on `this` class (and `this` is optional). To point to a method on another class, you need an instance of that class (if the method is an instance method), and you pass the method like this:

   ```
   SomeClass sc = new SomeClass();
   UpdateProgressCallback callback =
     new UpdateProgressCallback(sc.DoUpdate);
   ```

   But if the method is a `static` method (located anywhere), pass it like this:

   ```
   UpdateProgressCallback callback =
     new UpdateProgressCallback(SomeClass.DoUpdate);
   ```

What you're passing in the instantiation is just the method's *name*, no parameters. What you pass to `DoSomethingLengthy()` is the delegate instance, `callback` (which points to the method).

3. **Your `DoSomethingLengthy()` method does some "lengthy processing" and periodically pauses to call back to the form so that it can update its progress bar.**

   Invoking the delegate inside `DoSomethingLengthy()` looks like calling a method, complete with parameters, if any:

```
updateProgress();  // Invoke the delegate instance passed in.
```

   `DoSomethingLengthy()` looks like this:

```
private void DoSomethingLengthy(UpdateProgressCallback updateProgress)
{
  int duration = 2000;
  int updateInterval = duration / 10; // Every 200 milliseconds
  for (int i = 0; i < duration; i++)
  {
    Console.WriteLine("Something or other");
    // Update the form periodically.
    if ((i % updateInterval) == 0 && updateProgress != null)
    {
      updateProgress();  // Invoke the delegate.
    }
  }
}
```


   The "lengthy process" doesn't do much. It sets the `duration` variable to 2,000 loop iterations — a few seconds at runtime, which is more than enough for this demo. Next, the method computes an "update interval" of 200 iterations by dividing the overall duration into tenths. Then the `for` loop ticks off those 2,000 iterations. For each one, it checks whether it's time to update the user interface, or UI. Most times through the loop, no update occurs. But whenever the `if` condition is true, the method invokes the `UpdateProgressCallback` instance that was passed to its `updateProgress` parameter. That modulo expression, `i % updateInterval`, comes out only with a 0 remainder, thus satisfying the `if` condition, once every 200 iterations.

   Always check a newly instantiated delegate for `null` before invoking it.

4. **When `DoSomethingLengthy()` invokes the delegate, the delegate in turn invokes the method you pointed it at — in this case, the `DoUpdate()` method on the `Form1` class.**

5. **When called via the delegate, `DoUpdate()` carries out the update by calling a method on the `ProgressBar` class named `PerformStep()`:**

```
private void DoUpdate()
{
  progressBar1.PerformStep();
}
```

`PerformStep()`, in turn, fills another 10 percent increment of the bar with green, the amount dictated by its `Step` property, set to 10 at the outset. Watch the last step closely — it's just a flicker.

6. **Finally, control returns to `DoSomethingLengthy()`, which continues looping. When the loop runs its course, `DoSomethingLengthy()` exits, returning control to the `button1_Click()` method. That method then clears the `ProgressBar` by setting its `Value` property to 0. And the app settles down to wait for another click on one of its buttons (or its Close box).**

And there you have it. Using the delegate to implement a callback, the program keeps its progress bar up to date. See the list of uses for delegates in the section "I delegated the example to Igor." For more delegate examples, see the `DelegateExamples` program on the Web site.

Write a *custom* delegate when you need to define a type for delegate-type parameters so that you can implement a callback. Use *predefined* delegates for events and the collection classes' `Find()` and `ForEach()` methods.

Shh! Keep It Quiet — Anonymous Methods

After you have the gist of using delegates, take a quick look at Microsoft's *first* cut at simplifying delegates in C# 2.0 a couple of years ago.

To cut out some of the delegate rigamarole, you can use an anonymous method. Anonymous methods are just written in more traditional notation. Although the syntax and a few details are different, the effect is essentially the same whether you use a "raw" delegate, an anonymous method, or a lambda expression. You can find out more about lambda expressions on this book's companions Web site.

An anonymous method creates the delegate instance and the method it "points" to at the same time — right in place, on the fly, *tout de suite*. Here are the guts of the `DoSomethingLengthy()` method again, this time rewritten to use an anonymous method (boldfaced):

```
private void DoSomethingLengthy()  // No arguments needed this time.
{
  ...
  for (int i = 0; i < duration; i++)
  {
    if ((i % updateInterval) == 0)
    {
      UpdateProgressCallback anon = delegate() // Create delegate instance.
      {
        progressBar1.PerformStep();            // Method 'pointed' to
      };
      if(anon != null) anon();                 // Invoke the delegate.
    }
  }
}
```

The code looks like the delegate instantiations I describe, except that after the = sign, you see the `delegate` keyword, any parameters to the anonymous method in parentheses (or empty parentheses if none), and the method body. The code that used to be in a separate `DoUpdate()` method — the method that the delegate "points" to — has moved inside the anonymous method — no more pointing. And this method is utterly nameless.

You still need the `UpdateProgressCallback` delegate type definition, and you're still invoking a delegate instance, named `anon` in this example.

Needless to say, this description doesn't cover everything there is to know about anonymous methods, but it's a start. Look up the term *anonymous method* in Help to see more anonymous method examples in the DelegateExamples program on the Web site. My parting advice is to keep your anonymous methods short.

Stuff Happens — C# Events

One more application of delegates deserves discussion in this section: the C# *event*, which is implemented with delegates. An event is a variation on a callback but provides a simpler mechanism for alerting "interested observers" whenever an important event occurs. An event is especially useful when more than one anxious relative is waiting for a callback. Events are widely used in C#, especially for connecting the objects in the user interface to the code that makes them work. The buttons in the `SimpleProgress` example, presented earlier in this chapter, illustrate this use.

The Observer design pattern

It's extremely common in programming for various objects in the running program — those anxious relatives I mentioned — to be "interested in" events that occur on other objects. For example, when the user clicks a button, the form that contains the button "wants" to know about it. Events provide the standard mechanism in C# and .NET for notifying any interested parties of important actions.

The event pattern is so common that it has a name: the Observer design pattern. It's one of many common *design patterns* that people have published for anyone to use in their own code. To begin learning about other design patterns, you can consult *Design Patterns For Dummies*, by Steve Holzner.

The Observer pattern consists of an Observable object — the object with interesting events (sometimes called the Subject, though that confuses me) — and any number of Observer objects: those interested in a particular event. The observers register themselves with the Observable in some way and, when events of interest occur, the Observable notifies all registered observers. You can implement this pattern in numerous ways without events (such as callbacks and interfaces), but the C# way is to use events.

An alternative name for *observers* that you may encounter is *listeners*. Listeners "listen" for events. And that's not the last of the alternatives.

What's an event? Publish/Subscribe

One analogy for events is your local newspaper. You and many other people contact the paper to subscribe, and then the paper delivers current newspapers to you, typically soaked in a rain puddle. The newspaper company is the Publisher, and its customers are Subscribers, so this variation of Observer is often called *Publish/Subscribe*. That's the analogy I stick to in this chapter, but keep in mind that the Observer pattern *is* the Publish/Subscribe pattern with different terminology. Observers are subscribers, and the Observable object that they observe is a publisher.

In C#, when you have a class on which interesting events arise, you advertise the availability of notifications to any classes that may have an interest in knowing about such events by providing an *event object* (usually public).

The term *event* has two meanings in C#. You can think of the word *event* as meaning both "an interesting occurrence" and a specific kind of C# object. The former is the real-world concept, and the latter is the way it's set up in C#, using the `event` keyword.

How a publisher advertises its events

To advertise for subscribers, a class declares a delegate and a corresponding event, something like this:

```
public class PublisherOfInterestingEvents
{
  // A delegate type on which to base the event.
  // Should be declared 'internal' if all subscribers are in the same assembly.
  public delegate void NewEditionEventHandler(object sender,
                                              NewEditionEventArgs e);
  // The event:
  public event NewEditionEventHandler NewEdition;
  // ... other code.
}
```

The delegate and event definitions announce to the world: "Subscribers welcome!" You can think of the `NewEdition` event as similar to a variable of the `NewEditionEventHandler` delegate type. (So far, no events have been sent. This is just the infrastructure for them.)

It's considered good practice to append `EventHandler` to the name of a delegate type that is the basis for events.

A common example, which you can see in the SimpleProgress code example, discussed earlier in this chapter, is a Button advertising its various events, including a Click event. In C#, class Button exposes this event as

```
event _dispCommandBarControlEvents_ClickEventHandler Click;
```

where the second, lo-o-ong item is a delegate defined somewhere in .NET.

Because events are used so commonly, .NET defines two event-related delegate types for you, named EventHandler and EventHandler<TEventArgs>. You can change NewEditionEventHandler in the previous code to EventHandler or to the generic EventHandler<TEventArgs>, and you don't need your own delegate type. Throughout the rest of this chapter, I pretend that I used the built-in EventHandler<TEventArgs> delegate type mentioned earlier, not EventHandler or my custom type, NewEdition EventHandler. You should prefer this form, too:


```
event EventHandler<NewEditonEventArgs> NewEdition;
```

The NewspaperEvents example on the Web site demonstrates correctly setting up your event and handling it in various subscribers. (A second sample program, NewspaperEventsNongeneric, avoids the generic stuff if you get <ahem> code feet. If so, you can mentally omit the <eventhandler-args> information in the following section.)

How subscribers subscribe to an event

To receive a particular event, subscribers sign up something like this:

```
publisher.EventName +=
  new EventHandler<some EventArgs type here >(some method name here);
```

where publisher is an instance of the publisher class, EventName is the event name, and EventHandler<TEventArgs> is the delegate underneath the event. More specifically, the code in the previous example might be:

```
myPublisher.NewEdition += new EventHandler<NewEditionEventArgs>(MyPubHandler);
```

Because an event object is a delegate under its little hood, the += syntax is adding a method to the list of methods that the delegate will call when you invoke it.

Any number of objects can subscribe this way (and the delegate will hold a list of all subscribed "handler" methods) — even the object on which the event was defined can subscribe, if you like. (And yes, this example shows that a delegate can "point" to more than one method.)

In the SimpleProgress program, look in the Form1.Designer.cs file for how the form class registers itself as a subscriber to the buttons' Click events.

How to publish an event

When the publisher decides that something worthy of publishing to all subscribers has occurred, it *raises* (sends) the event. This situation is analogous to a real newspaper putting out the Sunday edition.

To publish the event, the publisher would have code like this in one of its methods (but see the later section "A recommended way to raise your events"):

```
NewEditionEventArgs e = new NewEditionEventArgs(<args to constructor here>);
NewEdition(this, e);  // Raise the event -- 'this' is the publisher object.
```

Or for the Button example, though this is hidden in class Button:

```
EventArgs e = new EventArgs();  // See next section for more on this topic.
Click(this, e);                 // Raise the event.
```

In each of these examples, you set up the necessary arguments — which differ from event to event; some events need to pass along a lot of info. Then you raise the event by "calling" its name (like invoking a delegate!):

```
eventName(<argumentlist>); // Raising an event (distributing the newspaper)
NewEdition(this, e);
```

Events can be based on different delegates with different signatures, that have different parameters, as in the earlier NewEditionEventHandler example, but providing the sender and e parameters is conventional for events. The built-in EventHandler and EventHandler<TEventArgs> delegate types define them for you.

Passing along a reference to the event's sender (the object that raises the event) is useful if the event-handling method needs to get more information from it. Thus a particular Button object, button1, can pass a reference to the Form class the button is a part of. The button's Click event handler resides in a Form class, so the sender is the form: You would pass this.

You can "raise" an event in any method on the publishing class. *But when?* Raise it whenever appropriate. I have a bit more to say about raising events after the next section.

How to pass extra information to an event handler

The e parameter to an event handler method is a custom subclass of the System.EventArgs class. You can write your own NewEditionEventArgs class to carry whatever information you need to convey:

```
public class NewEditionEventArgs : EventArgs
{
  public NewEditionEventArgs(DateTime date, string majorHeadline)
  { PubDate = date; Head = majorHeadline; }
  public DateTime PubDate { get; private set; }  // Compiler creates details.
  public string Head { get; private set; }  //
}
```

You should implement this class's members as properties, as shown in the previous code example. The constructor uses the private setter clauses on the properties.

Often, your event doesn't require any extra arguments and you can just fall back on the `EventArgs` base class, as shown in the next section.

If you don't need a special `EventArgs`-derived object for your event, just pass:

```
NewEdition(this, EventArgs.Empty);  // Raise the event.
```

A recommended way to raise your events

The earlier section "How to publish an event" shows the bare bones of raising an event. However, I recommend that you always define a special "event raiser" method, like this:

```
protected virtual void OnNewEdition(NewEditionEventArgs e)
{
  EventHandler<NewEditionEventArgs> temp = NewEdition;
  if(temp != null)
  {
    temp(this, e);
  }
}
```

Providing this method ensures that you always remember to complete two steps:

1. **Store the event in a temporary variable.**

   This step makes your event more usable in situations where multiple "threads" try to use it at the same time — threads divide your program into a foreground task and one or more background tasks, which run simultaneously (concurrently). I don't cover how to write multithreaded programs in this book; just follow this guideline.

2. **Check the event for `null` before you try to raise it.**

   If it's `null`, trying to raise it causes an error. Besides, `null` also means that no other objects have shown an interest in your event (none is subscribed), so why bother raising it? *Always* check the event for `null`, regardless of whether you write this On*SomeEvent* method.

Making the method protected and virtual allows subclasses to override it. That's optional.

After you have that method, which always takes the same form (making it easy to write quickly), you call the method when you need to raise the event:

```
void SomeMethod()
{
  // Do stuff here and then:
  NewEditionEventArgs e =
    new NewEditionEventArgs(DateTime.Today, "Peace Breaks Out!");
  OnNewEdition(e);
}
```

How observers "handle" an event

The subscribing object specifies the name of a *handler method* when it subscribes — it's the argument to the constructor (boldfaced):

```
button1.Click += new EventHandler<EventArgs>(button1_Click);
```

This line sort of says, "Send my paper to this address, please." Here's a handler for the NewEdition event:

```
myPublisher.NewEdition += new EventHandler<NewEditionEventArgs>(NewEdHandler);
...
void NewEdHandler(object sender, NewEditionEventArgs e)
{
  // Do something in response to the event.
}
```

For example, a BankAccount class can raise a custom TransactionAlert event when anything occurs in a BankAccount object, such as a deposit, withdrawal, or transfer or even an error. A Logger observer object can subscribe and log these events to a file or a database as an audit trail.

When to delegate, when to event, when to go on the lambda

Events: Use events when you may have multiple subscribers or when communicating with client software that uses your classes.

Delegates: Use delegates or anonymous methods when you need a callback or need to customize an operation.

Lambdas: There is an article about lambdas on this book's companion Web site. A lambda expression is, in essence, just a short way to specify the method you're passing to a delegate. You can use lambdas instead of anonymous methods.

When you create a button handler in Visual Studio (by double-clicking the button on your form), Visual Studio generates the subscription code in the `Form1.Designer.cs` file. You shouldn't edit the subscription, but you can delete it and replace it with the same code written in your half of the partial form class. Thereafter, the form designer knows nothing about it.

In your subscriber's handler method, you do whatever is supposed to happen when your class learns of this kind of event. To help you write that code, you can cast the `sender` parameter to the type you know it to be:

```
Button theButton = (Button)sender;
```

and then call methods and properties of that object as needed. Because you have a reference to the sending object, you can ask the subscriber questions and carry out operations on it if you need to — like the person who delivers your newspaper knocking on your door to collect the monthly subscription fees. And, you can extract information from the `e` parameter by getting at its properties in the same way:

```
Console.WriteLine(e.HatSize);
```

You don't always need to use the parameters, but they can be handy.

Chapter 10: Can I Use Your Namespace in the Library?

In This Chapter

- **Dealing with separately compiled assemblies**
- **Writing a class library**
- **More access-control keywords: `protected`, `internal`, `protected internal`**
- **Working with namespaces**

C# gives you a variety of ways to break code into meaningful, workable units.

You can use a *method* to divide a long string of code into separate, maintainable units. Use the *class structure* to group both data and methods in meaningful ways to further reduce the complexity of the program. Programs are complex already, and we simple humans become confused easily, so we need all the help we can get.

C# provides another level of grouping: You can group similar classes into a separate library. Beyond writing your own libraries, you can use anybody's libraries in your programs. These programs contain multiple modules known as *assemblies.* I describe libraries and assemblies in this chapter.

Meanwhile, the access-control story in Chapter 5 of this minibook leaves a few untidy loose ends — the `protected`, `internal`, and `protected internal` keywords — and is slightly complicated further by the use of *namespaces*, another way to group similar classes and allow the use of duplicate names in two parts of a program. I cover namespaces in this chapter as well.

The program examples mentioned in this chapter are part of the chapter download. You can also download them separately on the Example Code page of the Web site at `csharp102.info` or `csharpfordummies.net`.

Dividing a Single Program into Multiple Source Files

The programs in this book are only for demonstration purposes. Each program is no more than a few dozen lines long and contains no more than a few classes. An industrial-strength program, complete with all the necessary bells and whistles, can include hundreds of thousands of lines of code, spread over a hundred or more classes.

Consider an airline ticketing system: You have the interface to the reservations agent whom you call on the phone, another interface to the person behind the gate counter, the Internet (in addition to the part that controls aircraft seat inventory plus the part that calculates fares, including taxes); the list goes on and on. A program such as this one grows *huge* before it's all over.

Putting all those classes into one big `Program.cs` source file quickly becomes impractical. It's unreasonable, for these reasons:

- **You have to keep the classes straight.** A single source file can become extremely difficult to understand. Getting a grip on modules such as these, for example, is much easier:

  ```
  Aircraft.cs
  Fare.cs
  GateAgent.cs
  GateAgentInterface.cs
  ResAgent.cs
  ResAgentInterface.cs
  ```

  They also make the task of finding things easier.

- **The work of creating large programs is usually spread among numerous programmers.** Two programmers can't edit the same file at the same time — each programmer needs her own source file or files. You may have 20 or 30 programmers working on a large project at one time. One file would limit 24 programmers to one hour of editing a day, around the clock. If you break the program into 24 files, you could, with difficulty, have each programmer edit at the same time. If you break up the program so that each class has its own file, orchestrating the same 24 programmers becomes much easier.

- **Compiling a large file may take a considerable length of time.** You can draw out a coffee break for only so long before the boss starts getting suspicious.

You certainly wouldn't want to rebuild all the instructions that make up a big system just because a programmer changed a single line. Visual Studio 2010 can rebuild the single modified file in a multifile program and then stack all the object files together.

For these reasons, the smart C# programmer divides a program into multiple `.cs` source files, which are compiled and built together into a single executable `.exe` file.

A *project file* contains the instructions about which files should be used together and how they're combined.

You can combine project files to generate combinations of programs that depend on the same user-defined classes. For example, you may want to couple a write program with its corresponding read program. That way, if one changes, the other is rebuilt automatically. One project would describe the write program while another describes the read program. A set of project files is known as a *solution.* (I could have handled the `FileRead` and `FileWrite` programs covered in Book III as a single combined solution, but I didn't.)

Visual C# programmers use the Visual Studio Solution Explorer to combine multiple C# source files into projects within the Visual Studio 2008 environment. I describe Solution Explorer in Book IV.

Dividing a Single Program into Multiple Assemblies

In Visual Studio, and in C#, Visual Basic .NET, and the other .NET languages, one project equals one compiled *module* — otherwise known as an *assembly* in .NET.

The words *module* and *assembly* have somewhat different technical meanings, but only to advanced programmers. In this book, you can just equate the two terms.

Executable or library?

C# can produce two basic assembly types:

- **Executable (`.EXE`):** A program in its own right that contains a `Main()` method. You can double-click a `.EXE` file in Windows Explorer, for example, and cause it to run. This book is full of executables in the form of console applications. Executable assemblies often use supporting code from libraries in other assemblies.

✦ **Class library (.DLL):** A compiled library of functionality that can be used by other programs. All programs in this book also use libraries. For example, the `System` namespace (the home of classes such as `String`, `Console`, `Exception`, `Math`, and `Object`) exists in a set of library assemblies. Every program needs `System` classes. Libraries are housed in DLL assemblies.

Libraries aren't executable — you can't make them run directly. Instead, you must call their code from an executable or another library. The Common Language Runtime (CLR), which runs C# programs, loads library assemblies into memory as needed.

The important concept to know is that you can easily write your own class libraries. I show you how in the later section "Putting Your Classes into Class Libraries."

Assemblies

Assemblies, which are the compiled versions of individual projects, contain the project's code in a special format, along with a bunch of *metadata,* or detailed information about the classes in the assembly.

I introduce assemblies in this section because they round out your understanding of the C# build process — and they come into play in my discussion of namespaces and access keywords such as `protected` and `internal`. (I cover namespaces and these two access keywords later in this chapter.) Assemblies also play a big part in understanding class libraries. It's all covered in the later section "Putting Your Classes into Class Libraries."

The C# compiler converts the project's C# code to Common Intermediate Language (usually called IL) that's stored in the appropriate type of assembly file. IL resembles assembly language (one step beyond the 1s and 0s used in machine language) that hardcore programmers have used for decades to get down "close to the metal" because their higher-level languages couldn't do what they needed or the compilers couldn't produce the most efficient code possible.

One major consequence of compiling from .NET to IL, regardless of language, is that a program can use assemblies written in different languages. For example, a C# program can call methods in an assembly originally written in Visual Basic or C++ or the C# program can subclass a VB class.

You can take a look at some IL by running the `Ildasm.exe` tool in the .NET Software Development Kit (SDK) or the Reflector tool that I point you to at `csharp102.info`. Select a `.EXE` or `.DLL` assembly file to view its code as IL. A Visual Studio solution can contain any number of projects.

Executables

You can run executable assemblies in a variety of ways:

- ✦ Run them in Visual Studio: Choose Debug➪Start Debugging (F5) or Debug➪Start without Debugging (Ctrl+F5).
- ✦ Double-click the assembly file (.EXE) in Windows Explorer.
- ✦ Right-click the file in Windows Explorer and choose Run or Open from the pop-up menu.
- ✦ Type the assembly's name (and path) into a console window.
- ✦ If the program takes arguments, such as filenames, from the command line, drag the files to the executable file in Windows Explorer. I show you this process in the article "Passing Arguments to a Program" at csharp102.info; click the Articles tab and look in the section "C# Techniques."

A solution in Visual Studio can contain multiple projects — some .DLL and some .EXE. If a solution contains more than one .EXE project, you must tell Visual Studio which project is the *start-up project*: That one runs from the Debug menu. To specify a start-up project, right-click that project in Solution Explorer and choose Set As Startup Project. The start-up project's name appears in boldface in Solution Explorer.

Think of a solution containing two .EXE assemblies as two separate programs that happen to use the same library assemblies. For example, you might have in a solution a console executable and a Windows Forms executable plus some libraries. If you make the console app the start-up project and compile the code, you produce a console app. If you make the Windows Forms app the start-up — well, you get the idea.

Class libraries

A *class library* contains one or more classes, usually ones that work together in some way. Often, the classes in a library are in their own namespaces. (I explain namespaces later in this chapter.) You may build a library of math routines, a library of string-handling routines, and a library of input/output routines, for example.

Sometimes, you even build a whole solution that is nothing but a class library, rather than a program that can be executed on its own. (Typically, while developing this type of library, you also build an accompanying .EXE project, or *driver,* with which to test your library during development. But when you release the library for programmers to use, you release just the .DLL [not the .EXE] — and documentation for it that's generated by the XML comments are described in Book IV, which is all about Visual Studio.)

The next section shows you how to write your own class libraries (and drivers).

Putting Your Classes into Class Libraries

The simplest definition of a *class library project* is one whose classes contain no `Main()` method. Can that definition be correct? It can and is. The existence of `Main()` distinguishes a class library from an executable. C# libraries are much easier to write and use than similar libraries were in C or C++.

The following sections explain the basic concepts involved in creating your own class libraries. Don't worry: C# does the heavy lifting. Your end of it is quite simple.

Even the free Visual C# 2010 Express Edition can now create class libraries. It used to require a small hack to make it work.

Creating the projects for a class library

You can create the files for a new class library project and its driver in either of two ways:

- **Create the class library project first and then add the driver project to its solution.** You might take this approach if you were writing a stand-alone class library assembly. I describe how to create the class library project in the next section.
- **Create a driver program first and then add one or more library projects to its solution.** Thus you might first create the driver program as a console application or a graphical Windows Forms (or Windows Presentation Foundation) application. Then you would add class library projects to that solution.

  This approach is the one to take if you want to add a supporting library to an ongoing application. In that case, the "driver" could be either the ongoing program or a special driver project added to the solution just to test the library. For testing, you set the driver project as the start-up project as described in the earlier section "Executables."

Creating a stand-alone class library

If your whole purpose is to develop a stand-alone class library that can be used in various other programs, you can create a solution that contains a class library project from scratch — here's how simple it is:

1. Create a new project.
2. When you pick the template to base it on in the New Project dialog box, select Class Library (rather than, say, Console Application).

   Figure 10-1 shows what Solution Explorer looks like at this point.

After you have a class library project, you can add a driver project (or a unit test project or both) using the approach described in the next section.

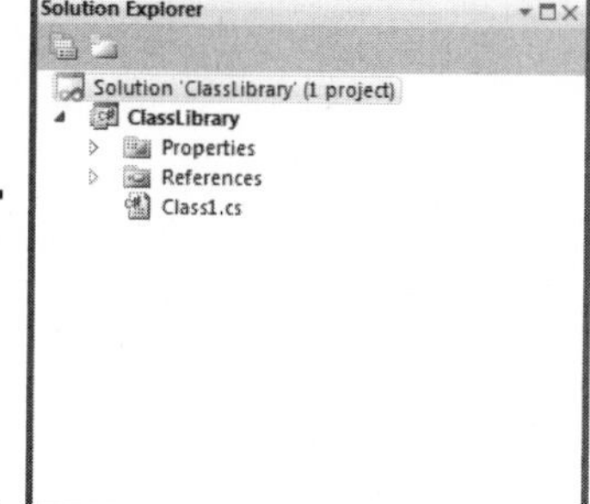

Figure 10-1: A new library in Solution Explorer.

Adding a second project to an existing solution

If you have an existing solution — whether it's an ongoing application or a class library project such as the one described in the previous section — you can easily add a second project to your solution: either a class library project or an executable project, such as a driver. Follow these steps:

1. **After your existing solution is open in Visual Studio, right-click the solution node (the top node) in Solution Explorer.**
2. **From the pop-up menu, choose Add⇨New Project.**
3. **In the New Project dialog box, select the type of project you want to add.**

   Select a class library, a console application, a Windows Forms application, or another available type on the right side of the dialog box.
4. **Use the Location box to navigate to the folder where you want the project.**

   The location you navigate to depends on how you want to organize your solution. You can put the new project's folder in either of two places:

   - *All-in-one-folder:* Navigate into the main project folder, making the added project a subfolder. (See Figure 10-2.)
   - *Side-by-side:* Navigate to the folder that contains the main project folder so that the two projects are at the same level. (See Figure 10-3.)
5. **Name your project and click OK.**

   If the new project is a library project, choose its name carefully — it will become the name of the library's `.DLL` file and the name of the namespace containing the project's classes.

If you need to give the library project the same name as another project or even the main project, you can distinguish it by appending the suffix `Lib`, as in `MyConversionLib`.

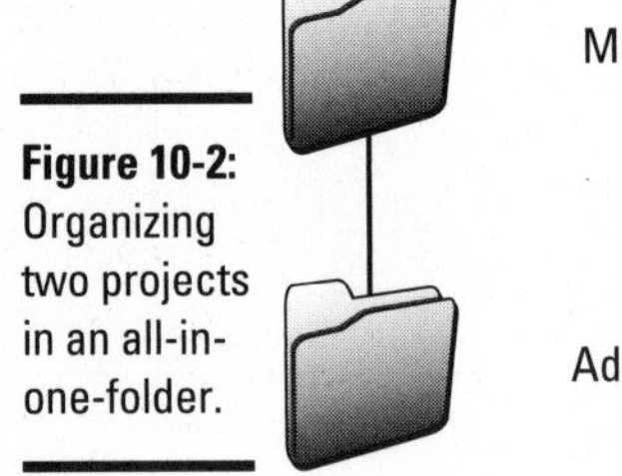

Figure 10-2: Organizing two projects in an all-in-one-folder.

If the project you're adding is intended to stand on its own and be usable in other programs, use the side-by-side approach.

The `ClassLibrary` example in this section (like most examples in this book) takes the all-in-one-folder approach. The point is that although the folders don't have to be in the same place, putting them there can be convenient.

The task of selecting the location is independent of adding the new project directly to the `ClassLibrary` *solution*. The two project folders can be in the same solution while still being located in different places.

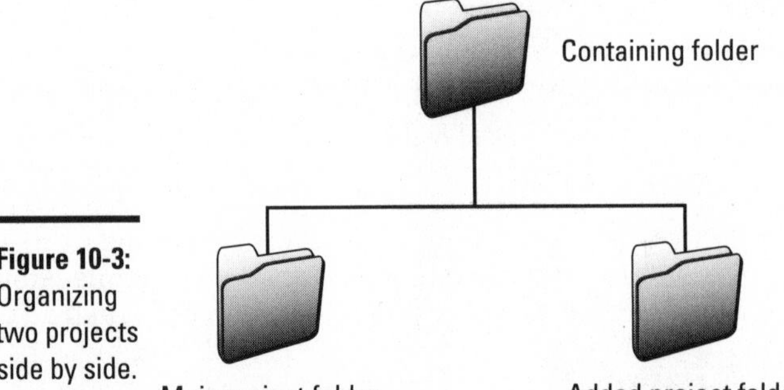

Figure 10-3: Organizing two projects side by side.

Creating classes for the library

After you have a class library project, create the classes that make up the library. The following `ClassLibrary` example shows a simple class library — I show you some driver code for it after the example:

```
// ClassLibrary -- in a Class Library project

// File: Program.cs in ClassLibraryDriver project
// ClassLibrary -- A simple class library and its driver program
using System;
namespace ClassLibrary
{
  public class MyLibrary
  {
    public void LibraryFunction1()
    {
      Console.WriteLine("This is LibraryFunction1()");
    }
    public static int LibraryFunction2(int input)
    {
      Console.WriteLine("This is LibraryFunction2(), returning {0}", input);
      return input;  // Just parrot the input.
    }
  }
}
```


Libraries can contain any C# type: class, structure, delegate, interface, and enumeration. I cover structures (`structs`) in Book I, delegates in Chapter 9 of this minibook, interfaces in Chapter 8 of this minibook, and enumerations (`enums`) in the article "Enumerating the Charms of the Enum" on `csharp102.info`.

In class library code, you normally shouldn't catch exceptions. Let them bubble up from the library to the client code that's calling into the library. Clients need to know about these exceptions and handle them in their own ways. I cover exceptions in Book II.

Using a driver program to test a library

By itself, the class library doesn't do anything, so you need a *driver* program, a small executable program that "drives" the library to test it during development by calling its methods.

In other words, write a program that uses classes and methods from the library. You see this behavior in the `NamespaceUse` program example later in this chapter (and other programs in this book) — for example, when you call the `WriteLine()` method of class `Console` from the .NET Framework class libraries. (`Console` is in the `System` namespace, in the library file `mscorlib.dll`.)

The following chunk of code continues the previous code listing. This one adds a new project with one class that contains a `Main()` method, and you can write code to exercise your library inside `Main()`:

```
// ClassLibrary driver program

// In a separate Console Application project:
```

```
// File: Program.cs in ClassLibraryDriver project
using System;
using ClassLibrary;
namespace ClassLibraryExample
{
  class Program
  {
    static void Main(string[] args)
    {
      // Create a library object and use its methods.
      MyLibrary ml = new MyLibrary();
      ml.LibraryFunction1();
      // Call its static methods through the class.
      int result = MyLibrary.LibraryFunction2(27);
      Console.WriteLine(result.ToString());
      // Wait for user to acknowledge the results.
      Console.WriteLine("Press Enter to terminate...");
      Console.Read();
    }
  }
}
```

To run and test the library through the driver, add a reference to the library in the driver project references, mark the driver project as the start-up project (as described earlier, in the "Executables" section), and run the program the same as you run all console applications in this book.

You can test your library in another, even better way, too — using the unit testing features of Visual Studio. In Book IV, and a little in Book V, I cover testing using the unit testing framework of Visual Studio.

Here's the output from the test driver:

```
This is LibraryMethod1()
This is LibraryMethod2(), returning 27
27
Press Enter to terminate...
```

Libraries often provide only `static` methods. In that case, you don't need to instantiate the library object. Just call the methods through the class.

Using a class library from a program

From any program you ever write, just include `using` directives for your class library's namespaces and add a reference to the `.DLL` file that contains the library (providing a path to wherever it lives). Then use the classes in the library in your program. This strategy is exactly how other programs in this book use classes from the .NET Framework libraries. Note that the compiler copies the libraries into your project's build directories.

Going Beyond Public and Private: More Access Keywords

Dividing a program into multiple assemblies, as discussed in the previous sections, has a bearing on which code in `AssemblyB` you can access from `AssemblyA`.

The access control examples in Chapter 5 of this minibook do a good job (I hope) of illustrating the `public` and `private` keywords. But that chapter doesn't say a lot about the other access keywords: `protected`, `internal`, and the combination `protected internal`. I rectify that situation in this section, assuming that you understand inheritance and method overriding as well as `public` and `private`.

To ensure that this section makes sense, you might need to read (or reread) Chapter 5.

Internal: Eyes only at the CIA

Suppose that a program has these two projects:

- `InternalLimitsAccess`: An executable whose class `Congress` contains the `Main()` method that kicks off program execution. (No law requires the `Main()` class to be named *Program.*)
- `CIAAssembly`: The class library project.

You can see this setup in the `InternalLimitsAccess` example on the Web.

In real life, the U.S. Congress has the annoying habit of expecting the Central Intelligence Agency (CIA) to reveal its secrets — just to members of Congress and senators, of course. ("We won't leak your secrets — honest.") Meanwhile, those overly secretive spooks at the CIA have secrets they would prefer to hang on to. (Maybe they know the secret formula for Coca-Cola or Colonel Sanders's secret herbs and spices or a more sinister entity.) Exactly what Secret X is doesn't matter here, but the CIA wants to keep Secret X, well, secret.

There's a problem, though. Everybody at the CIA needs to know Secret X. In the `InternalLimitsAccess` example, the CIA is divided into several classes — class `GroupA` and class `GroupB`, for example. Think of them as sections of the CIA that (sometimes) communicate and share with each other. Suppose that `GroupA` is the holder of Secret X, so the group marked it `private`. The code looks something like this:

```
// In assembly InternalLimitsAccess:
class Congress
{
  static void Main(...)
  {
    // Code to oversee CIA
  }
}

// In assembly CIAAssembly:
public class GroupA
{
  private string _secretFormulaForCocaCola; // Secret X
}
public class GroupB
{
  public void DoSomethingWithSecretX()
  {
    // Do something with Secret X, if only you could access it.
  }
}
```

Now GroupB can't see Secret X, but suppose that it has a legitimate need to know it. GroupA can, of course, bump Secret X to public status, but if it does, the secret isn't much of a secret any more. If GroupB can see the secret, so can those snoops over in Congress. Even worse, CNN knows it too, not to mention Fox, ABC, and other networks. And you know how well those folks keep secrets. Oh, right — Russia can see Secret X too.

Luckily, C# also has the internal keyword. Using internal is just one step down from public and well above private. If you mark the GroupA class and its "public" methods — the ones that are visible outside the class — with the internal keyword instead, everybody at the CIA can see and access Secret X — as long as you either mark the secret itself (a data member) as internal or provide an internal property to get it with, as shown in this version:

```
// In assembly CIAAssembly:
internal class GroupA
{
  private string _secretFormulaForCocaCola; // Secret X
  internal string SecretX { get { return _secretFormulaForCocaCola; } }
}
public class GroupB
{
  public void DoSomethingWithSecretX()
  {
    // Do something with Secret X, now that we can see it:
    Console.WriteLine("I know Secret X, which is {0} characters long, but " +
    "I'm not telling.", GroupA.SecretX.Length);
  }
}
```

Now class GroupB has the access it needs — and it isn't giving up the secret (even under threat of waterboarding). All it tells Congress, over in Main(), is that it knows secret X and secret X has 11 characters. Here's that chunk of code:

```
class Congress
{
  static void Main(string[] args)
  {
    // Code to oversee CIA
    // The following line doesn't compile because GroupA isn't accessible
    // outside CIAAssembly. Congress can't get at GroupA over at CIA.

    // CIAAssembly.GroupA groupA = new CIAAssembly.GroupA();

    // Class Congress can access GroupB because it's declared public.
    // GroupB is willing to admit to knowing the secret, but it's
    // not telling -- except for a small hint.
    GroupB groupB = new GroupB();
    groupB.DoSomethingWithSecretX();

    // Wait for user to acknowledge results.
    Console.WriteLine("Press Enter to terminate...");
    Console.Read();
  }
}
```

From Main(), GroupA is now invisible, so an attempt to construct an instance of it doesn't compile. But because GroupB is public, Main() can access it and call its public method DoSomethingWithSecretX().

Wait! CIA does have to talk to Congress about certain topics, I'm happy to report — but on a need-to-know basis, limited to selected members of Congress and senators, of course. They can do so already, via GroupB, as long as they present the proper credentials, although you need to add them to the code:

```
public string DoSomethingWithSecretXUsingCredentials(string credentials)
{
   if (credentials == "congressman with approved access")
   {
     return GroupA.SecretX;
   }
   return string.Empty;
}
```

The internal keyword makes classes and their members accessible only inside their own assembly. But within the assembly, the internal items are effectively "public" to all local classes.

You can mark a method inside an `internal` class as `public`, though it isn't truly public. A class member can't be more accessible than its class, so the so-called "public" member is just `internal`.

CIA can still keep its deepest, darkest secrets ultra-hush-hush by declaring them private inside their owning class. That strategy makes them accessible only in that class.

Protected: Sharing with subclasses

The main purpose of `private` is to hide information. In particular, `private` hides a class's internal implementation details. (Classes who know classes too intimately aren't the luckiest classes in the world. In fact, they're the unluckiest.) Classes with a lot of implementation details are said to be "too tightly coupled" with the classes they know too much about. If class `A` is aware of the internal workings of class `B`, `A` can come to rely too much on those details. If they ever change, you end up having to modify both classes.

The less the other classes — and assemblies — know about *how* class `B` performs its magic, the better. In Chapter 5 of this minibook, I use the example of a `BankAccount` class. The bank doesn't want forgetful folks like me — or forgetful classes such as class `A` — to be able to change a balance directly. That balance is properly part of the `BankAccount` class's implementation. It's private. `BankAccount` provides access to the balance — but only through a carefully controlled public interface. In the `BankAccount` class, the public interface consists of three public methods:

- `Balance`: Provides a read-only way to find out the current balance. You can't use `Balance` to modify the underlying balance.
- `Deposit()`: Lets someone outside the class add to the balance in a controlled way.
- `Withdraw()`:Lets someone (presumably the account owner) subtract from the balance, but within carefully controlled limits. `Withdraw()` enforces the *business rule* that you can't withdraw more than you have.

Access control considerations other than `private` and `public` arise in programming. I explain in the previous section how the `internal` keyword opens a class — but only to other classes in its own assembly.

However, suppose that the `BankAccount` class has a subclass, `SavingsAccount`. Methods in `SavingsAccount` need access to that balance defined in the base class, of course, although other classes, even in the same assembly, probably don't. Luckily, `SavingsAccount` can use the same public interface, the same access, as outsiders: using `Balance`, `Deposit()`, and `Withdraw()`.

Sometimes, though, the base class doesn't supply such access methods for its subclasses (and others) to use. What if the _balance data member in BankAccount is private and the class doesn't provide the Balance property?

Enter the protected keyword: If the _balance instance variable in the base class is declared protected rather than private, outsiders can't see it — it's effectively private to them. But subclasses can see it just fine.

An even better solution is to mark _balance private in BankAccount as before and then provide a Balance property marked protected. Subclasses such as SavingsAccount can access _balance by using the Balance property. But the balance is invisible to outsiders, which protects the BankAccount implementation even from its subclasses.

If the balance does indeed need to be accessible (read-only) to outsiders, you should, of course, provide the public Balance property to *get* the balance (read-only). However, you may still need to *set* the balance from inside SavingsAccount itself. To do that, you can give the set accessor of Balance protected access — accessible from SavingsAccount and other subclasses but inaccessible to outsiders. The discussion of properties in Chapter 5 of this minibook shows how to do it, and here's what the code looks like:

```
// In BankAccount:
public decimal Balance
{
  get { return _balance; }              // Public
  protected set { _balance = value; }  // Not public
}
```

The ProtectedLimitsAccess example on the Web illustrates using the protected keyword as just described.

You can even subclass BankAccount in a *different assembly* and the subclass has access to anything declared protected in BankAccount. The ProtectedLimitsAccess example also illustrates this process.

The example has two subclasses of BankAccount: one in the same assembly as BankAccount and one in a different assembly. What's interesting with respect to protected is that *either* BankAccount subclass can access any item in BankAccount marked protected. The subclass doesn't have to be in the same assembly as its base class.

The ability to extend (subclass) a class *from outside the base class's assembly* has implications for security, which is why many classes should be marked sealed. Sealing a class prevents outsiders from gaining access by subclassing it. That's why you're advised to make classes extendable (nonsealed)

only if they *need* to be subclassable. One way to give other code in the same assembly access to a base class's members — including a subclass in the same assembly — is to mark those members internal rather than protected. That way, you gain the desired level of access from a local subclass while preventing access from an external subclass. Of course, access is then allowed from other classes in the assembly. This solution may not be ideal, but it should be more secure — if that's a consideration.

Protected internal: Being a more generous protector

Making items in the `BankAccount` base class `protected internal`, rather than just `protected`, simply adds a new dimension to the accessibility of those items in your program. Using `protected` alone allows a subclass (in any assembly in the program) to access `protected` items in the base class. Adding `internal` extends the items' accessibility to any class, as long as it's in the same assembly as `BankAccount` or at least a subclass in some other assembly.

In the `ProtectedInternalLimitsAccess` example on `csharp102.info`, you can see this effect. The class `AnotherClass` that's defined within `BankAccount`'s own assembly can access the `protected internal set` accessor in the `Balance` property. However, the nearly identical `AnotherClass` in a different assembly cannot access `Balance`'s `set` accessor to set the balance.

Make items as *inaccessible* as possible. Start with `private`. If some parts of your code need more access than that, increase it selectively. Maybe just `protected` will work (that's all a subclass needs). Maybe other classes in the same assembly truly do need access. If so, increase it to `internal`. If subclasses and other classes in the same assembly need access, use `protected internal`. Use `public` only for classes (and their members) that should be accessible to every class in the program, regardless of assembly.

The same advice that applies to whole classes also applies to class members: Keep them as inaccessible as possible. Little *helper classes*, or classes that support the implementation of more public classes, can be limited to no more than `internal`.

If a class or other type needs to be `private`, `protected`, or `protected internal`, nest it, if you can, inside the class that needs access to it.

Putting Classes into Namespaces

Namespaces exist to put related classes in one bag and to reduce collisions between names used in different places. For example, you may compile all math-related classes into a `MathRoutines` namespace.

A single file can be (but isn't commonly) divided into multiple namespaces:

```
// In file A.cs:
namespace One
{
}
namespace Two
{
}
```

More commonly, you group multiple files. For example, the file `Point.cs` may contain the class `Point`, and the file `ThreeDSpace.cs` contains class `ThreeDSpace` to describe the properties of a Euclidean space (like a cube). You can combine `Point.cs` and `ThreeDSpace.cs` and other C# source files into the `MathRoutines` namespace (and, possibly, a `MathRoutines` library assembly). Each file would wrap its code in the same namespace. (It's the classes in those files, rather than the files themselves, that make up the namespace. Which files the classes are in is irrelevant for namespaces. Nor does it matter which assembly they're in: A namespace can span multiple assemblies.)


```
// In file Point.cs:
namespace MathRoutines
{
  class Point { }
}
// In file ThreeDSpace.cs:
namespace MathRoutines
{
  class ThreeDSpace { }
}
```

If you don't wrap your classes in a namespace, C# puts them in the *global namespace*, the base (unnamed) namespace for all other namespaces. A better practice, though, is to use a specific namespace.

The namespace serves these purposes:

- **A namespace puts oranges with oranges, not with apples.** As an application programmer, you can reasonably assume that the classes that comprise the `MathRoutines` namespace are all math related. By the same token, when looking for just the perfect math method, you first would look in the classes that make up the `MathRoutines` namespace.
- **Namespaces avoid the possibility of name conflicts.** For example, a file input/output library may contain a class `Convert` that converts the representation in one file type to that of another. At the same time, a translation library may contain a class of the same name. Assigning the namespaces `FileIO` and `TranslationLibrary` to the two sets of classes avoids the problem: The class `FileIO.Convert` clearly differs from the class `TranslationLibrary.Convert`.

Declaring a namespace

You declare a namespace using the keyword namespace followed by a name and an open and closed curly-braces block. The classes (and other types) within that block are part of the namespace:

```
namespace MyStuff
{
  class MyClass {}
  class UrClass {}
}
```

In this example, both MyClass and UrClass are part of the MyStuff namespace.

Namespaces are implicitly public, and you can't use access specifiers on namespaces, not even public.

Besides classes, namespaces can contain other types, including these:

- delegate
- enum
- interface
- struct

A namespace can also contain *nested namespaces*, to any depth of nesting. You may have Namespace2 nested inside Namespace1, as in this example:

```
namespace Namespace1
{
  // Classes in Namespace1 here ...
  // Then the nested namespace:
  namespace Namespace2
  {
    // Classes in Namespace2
    public class Class2
    {
      public void AMethod() { }
    }
  }
}
```

To call a method in Class2, inside Namespace2, from somewhere outside Namespace1, you specify this line:

```
Namespace1.Namespace2.Class2.AMethod();
```

Imagine these namespaces strung together with dots as a sort of logical path to the desired item.

"Dotted names" such as `System.IO` look like nested namespaces, but they name only one namespace. So `System.Data` is a complete namespace name, not the name of a `Data` namespace nested inside `System`. This convention makes it easier to have several related namespaces, such as `System.IO`, `System.Data`, and `System.Text` and make the family resemblance obvious. In practice, nested namespaces and namespaces with dotted names are indistinguishable.

Prefixing all namespaces in a program with your company name is conventional — making the company name the front part of multiple segments separated by dots: `MyCompany.MathRoutines`. (That statement is true if you have a company name; you can also use just your own name. I could use either `CMSCo.MathRoutines` or `Sphar.MathRoutines`.) Adding a company name prevents name clashes if your code uses two third-party code libraries that happen to use the same basic namespace name, such as `MathRoutines`.

The Visual Studio New Project dialog box runs an Application Wizard that puts all code it generates in namespaces. The wizard names these namespaces after the project directory it creates. Look at any of the programs in this book, each of which was created by the Application Wizard. For example, the `AlignOutput` program is created in the `AlignOutput` folder. The name of the source file is `Program.cs`, which matches the name of the default class. The name of the namespace containing `Program.cs` is the same as that of the folder: `AlignOutput`.

(You can change any of those names, though. Just do it carefully and thoroughly. You can change the overall namespace name for a project in the project's Properties window. Rather than try to rename everything, I sometimes create a new program using the correct names and then import the class files from the original program — after which I scrap the original.)

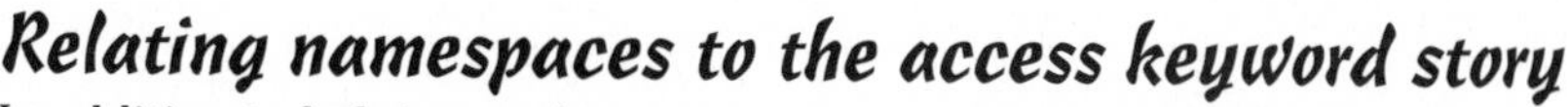

Relating namespaces to the access keyword story

In addition to helping package your code into a more usable form, namespaces extend the notion of access control presented in Chapter 5 of this minibook (which introduces the `public`, `private`, `protected`, `internal`, and `protected internal` keywords). Namespaces extend access control by further limiting which members of a class you can access from where.

However, namespaces affect *visibility* more than *accessibility*. By default, classes and methods in `NamespaceA` are invisible to classes in `NamespaceB`, regardless of their access-control specifiers. But you can make one namespace's classes and methods visible to another namespace in a couple of ways. The bottom line is that you can access only what's visible to you *and* "public enough."

I define "public enough" as having a strong enough access specifier from the viewpoint of `Class1`, the caller. This issue involves access control, extended earlier in this chapter and covered in the discussion of access specifiers in Chapter 5 of this minibook.

Determining whether the class and method you need are visible and accessible to you

To determine whether `Class1` in `NamespaceA` can call `NamespaceB.Class2.AMethod()`, consider these two questions:

- **Is `Class2` over in `NamespaceB` *visible* to the calling class, `Class1`?**

  This issue involves namespace visibility, discussed at the end of this list.

- **If the answer to the first question is True, are `Class2` and its `AMethod()` also "public enough" for `Class1` to access?**

  If `Class2` is in a different assembly from `Class1`, it must be `public` for `Class1` to access its members. `Class2`, it's in the same assembly, needs to be declared at least `internal`. Classes can only be `public`, `protected`, `internal`, or `private`.

  Likewise, the `Class2` method must have at least a certain level of access in each of those situations. Methods add the `protected internal` option to the list of access specifiers that classes have. Chapter 5 in this minibook and the earlier section "Going Beyond Public and Private: More Access Keywords" supply the gory details.

You need to answer Yes to both questions before `Class1` can call the `Class2` method.

Making classes and methods in another namespace visible

C# provides two ways to make items in `NamespaceB` visible in `NamespaceA`:

- ***Fully qualify* names from `NamespaceB` wherever you use them in `NamespaceA`.** This method results in code such as the following line, which starts with the namespace name and then adds the class and lists the method:

  ```
  System.Console.WriteLine("my string");
  ```

- **Eliminate the need for fully qualified names in `NamespaceA` by giving the namespace files a *using directive* for `NamespaceB`:**

  ```
  using System;
  using NamespaceB;
  ```

Programs throughout this book make items in NamespaceB visible in NamespaceA with the using directive. I discuss full qualification and using directives in the next two sections.

If the items in NamespaceB are in other assemblies, choose Project⇨Add Reference and add a reference for those assemblies.

Using fully qualified names

The namespace of a class is a part of the extended class name, which leads to the first way to make classes in one namespace visible in another. This example doesn't have any using directives to simplify referring to classes in other namespaces:


```
namespace MathRoutines  // Broken into two segments -- see below.
{
  class Sort
  {
    public void SomeMethod(){}
  }
}
namespace Paint
{
  public class PaintColor
  {
    public PaintColor(int nRed, int nGreen, int nBlue) {}
    public void Paint() {}
    public static void StaticPaint() {}
  }
}
namespace MathRoutines  // Another piece of this namespace
{
  public class Test
  {
    static public void Main(string[] args)
    {
      // Create an object of type Sort from the same namespace
      // we're in and invoke a method.
      Sort obj = new Sort();
      obj.SomeMethod();
      // Create an object in another namespace -- notice that the
      // namespace name must be included explicitly in every
      // class reference.
      Paint.PaintColor black = new Paint.PaintColor(0, 0, 0);
      black.Paint();
      Paint.PaintColor.StaticPaint();
    }
  }
}
```

In this case, the two classes Sort and Test are contained within the same namespace, MathRoutines, even though they appear in different declarations within the file (or in different files). That namespace is broken into two parts.

Normally, `Sort` and `Test` would be in different C# source files that you build together into one program.

The method `Test.Main()` can reference the `Sort` class without specifying the namespace because the two classes are in the same namespace. However, `Main()` must specify the `Paint` namespace when referring to `PaintColor`, as in the call to `Paint.PaintColor.StaticPaint()`. This process is known as *fully qualifying* the name.

Notice that you don't need to take any special steps when referring to `black.Paint()`, because the class of the `black` object is specified, namespace and all, in the `black` declaration.

Book III

Designing for C#

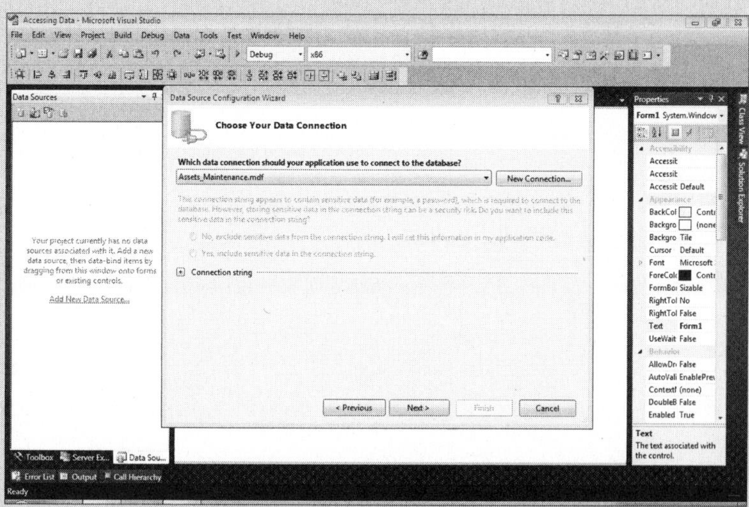

Using the Data Source Configuration Wizard

Contents at a Glance

Chapter 1: Writing Secure Code

In This Chapter

- **Designing for security**
- **Building secure Windows and Web applications**
- **Digging into `System.Security`**

Security is a big topic. Ignoring for a moment all the buzzwords surrounding security, I'm sure you realize that you need to protect your application from being used by people who shouldn't use it. You also need to prevent your application from being used for things it shouldn't be used for.

At the beginning of the electronic age, security was usually performed by *obfuscation.* If you had an application that you didn't want people peeking at, you just hid it, and no one would know where to find it. Thus, it would be secure. (Remember *War Games,* the movie in which the military assumed that no one would find the phone number needed to connect to its mainframes — but Matthew Broderick's character did?)

That obviously doesn't cut it anymore; now you need to consider security as an integral requirement of every system that you write. Your application might not contain sensitive data, but can it be used to get to other information on the machine? Can it be used to gain access to a network that it shouldn't? The answers to these questions matter.

The two main parts to security are authentication and authorization. *Authentication* is the process of making sure a user is authentic — that the user is who he claims to be. The most common method of authentication is to require the use of a username and password, though other ways exist, such as thumbprint scans. *Authorization* is the act of ensuring that a user has the authority to do what he asks to do. File permissions are a good example of this — users can't delete system-only files, for instance.

The silent partner of security makes sure that your system can't be fooled into believing a user is authentic or authorized. Because of this requirement, there is more to security than inserting username and password text boxes in your program. In this chapter, I tell you what tools are available in the .NET Framework to help you make sure that your applications are secure.

Designing Secure Software

Security takes a fair amount of work to accurately design. If you break the process into pieces, you find that it's a lot easier to accomplish. The Patterns and Practices team (a group of software architects at Microsoft who devise programming best practices) have created a systematic approach to designing secure programs that I think you will find straightforward, so I describe it in the following sections.

Determining what to protect

Different applications have different artifacts that need protection, but all applications share something that needs protection. If you have a database in your application, that is the most important item to protect. If your application is a server-based application, the server should rate fairly high when you're determining what to protect.

Even if your program is just a little single-user application, the software should do no wrong — an outsider shouldn't be able to use the application to break into the user's computer.

Documenting the components of the program

If you think this section's title sounds similar to part of the design process, you're right. A lot of threat modeling is just understanding how the application works and describing it well.

First, describe what the application does. This description becomes a functional overview. If you follow the commonly accepted Software Development Life Cycle (SDLC), and then the use cases, requirements, or user stories document (depending on your personal methodology) should give you a good starting point.

Next, describe how the application accomplishes all those tasks at the highest level. A Software Architecture Overview (SAO) diagram is a useful way to do it. This diagram shows which machines and services do what in your software.

If you happen to be using Visual Studio Team System, building a diagram in the Enterprise Architect version is the ultimate SAO diagram and is a good model.

Sometimes the SAO is a simple diagram — if you have a standalone Windows Forms program like a game, that's all there is! A standalone program has no network connection, and no communication between software parts. Therefore, the software architecture diagram contains only one instance.

Decomposing components into functions

After you create a document that describes what the software is doing and how, you need to break out the individual functional pieces of the software. If you have set up your software in a component fashion, the classes and methods show the functional decomposition. It's simpler than it sounds.

The end result of breaking the software into individual pieces is having a decent matrix of which components need to be protected, which parts of the software interact with each component, which parts of the network and hardware system interact with each component, and which functions of the software do what with each component.

Identifying potential threats in functions

After you create the list of components that you need to protect, you tackle the tough part: Put two and two together. Identifying threats is the process that gets the security consultants the big bucks, and it's almost entirely a factor of experience.

For instance, if your application connects to a database, you have to imagine that the connection could be intercepted by a third party. If you use a file to store sensitive information, the file could, theoretically, be compromised.

To create a threat model, you need to categorize the potential threats to your software. An easy way to remember the different categories of threats is as the acronym STRIDE:

- ***S*poofing identity:** Users pretend that they are someone who they are not.
- ***T*ampering with data or files:** Users edit something that shouldn't be edited.
- ***R*epudiation of action:** Users have the opportunity to say they didn't do something that they actually did do.
- ***I*nformation disclosure:** Users see something that shouldn't be seen.
- ***D*enial of service:** Users prevent legitimate users from accessing the system.
- ***E*levation of privilege:** Users get access to something that they shouldn't have access to.

All these threats must be documented in an outline under the functions that expose the threat. This strategy not only gives you a good, discrete list of threats but also focuses your security hardening on those parts of the application that pose the greatest security risk.

Rating the risk

The final step in the process is to rate the risks. Microsoft uses the DREAD model to assess risk to its applications. The acronym DREAD represents five key attributes used to measure each vulnerability:

- ***D*amage potential:** The dollar cost to the company for a breach
- ***R*eproducibility:** Special conditions to the breach that might make it harder or easier to find
- ***E*xploitability:** A measure of how far into a corporate system a hacker can get
- ***A*ffected users:** The number of users who are affected and who they are
- ***D*iscoverability:** The ease with which you can find the potential breach

You can research the DREAD model at `msdn.microsoft.com/security`, or position your threat model to consider those attributes. The key is to determine which threats are most likely to cause problems and then mitigate them.

Building Secure Windows Applications

The framework lives in a tightly controlled sandbox when running on a client computer. Because of the realities of this sandbox, the configuration of security policy for your application becomes important.

The first place you need to look for security in writing Windows applications is in the world of authentication and authorization. *Authentication* confirms the identity of a user, and *authorization* determines what she can and can't do within an application.

When you are threat modeling, you can easily consider all of the possible authentication and authorization threats using the STRIDE acronym. (See the earlier section "Identifying potential threats in functions," for more about STRIDE.)

Authentication using Windows login

To be straightforward, the best way for an application to authorize a user is to make use of the Windows login. A host of arguments take place about this strategy and others, but the key is simplicity: Simple things are more secure.

For much of the software developed with Visual Studio, the application will be used in an office by users who have different roles in the company; for example, some users might be in the Sales or Accounting department. In many environments, the most privileged users are managers or administrators — yet another set of roles. In most offices, each employee has her own user account, and each user is assigned to the Windows groups that are appropriate for the roles she plays in the company.

Using Windows security works only if the Windows environment is set up correctly. You can't effectively build a secure application in a workspace with a bunch of Windows XP machines on which everyone logs on as the administrator, because you can't tell who is in what role.

Building a Windows application to take advantage of Windows security is straightforward. The goal is to check to see who is logged on (authentication) and then check that user's role (authorization).

The following steps show you how to create an application that protects the menu system for each user by showing and hiding buttons:

1. **Start a new Windows Forms Application project by choosing File➪New Project and giving your project a descriptive name.**

   This would work for Windows Presentation Foundation (WPF) too, but it's easier to show in Windows Forms. (Book V is all about WPF.) I named my project Windows Security.

2. **Add three buttons to your form — one for Sales Menu, one for Accounting Menu, and one for Manager's Menu.**

   My example is shown in Figure 1-1.

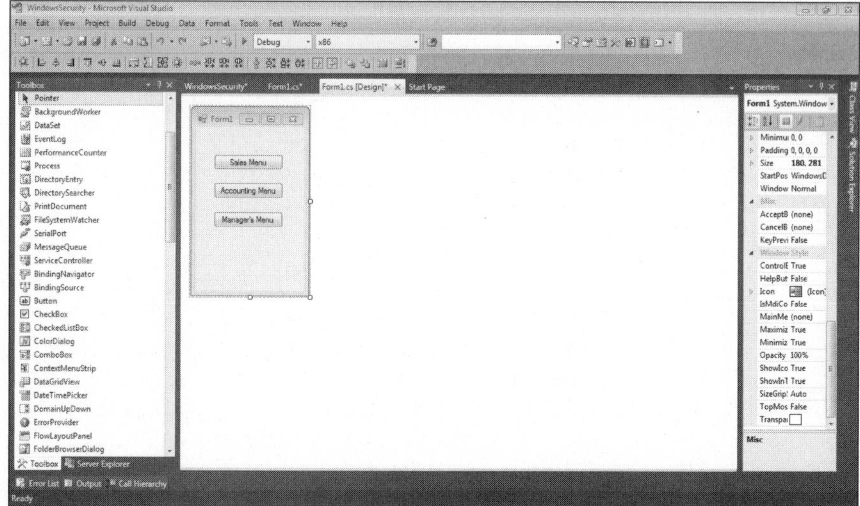

Figure 1-1: The Windows Security application sample.

3. **Set every button's visible properties to** `False` **so that they aren't shown on the form by default.**
4. **Double-click the form to reach the** `Form1_Load` **event handler.**
5. **Above the** `Namespace` **statement, import the** `System.Security.Principal` **namespace this way:**

   ```
   using System.Security.Principal;
   ```

6. **In the** `Form1_Load` **event handler, instantiate a new** `Identity` **object that represents the current user with the** `GetCurrent` **method of the** `WindowsIdentity` **object by adding this bit of code:**

   ```
   WindowsIdentity myIdentity = WindowsIdentity.
       GetCurrent();
   ```

7. **Get a reference to this identity with the** `WindowsPrincipal` **class:**

   ```
   WindowsPrincipal myPrincipal = new
       WindowsPrincipal(myIdentity);
   ```

8. **Finally, also in the** `Form1_Load` **subroutine, code a little** `If/Then` **statement to determine which button to show. The code is shown in Listing 1-1.**

Listing 1-1: The Windows Security Application Code

```
using System;
using System.Collections.Generic;
using System.ComponentModel;
using System.Data;
using System.Drawing;
using System.Linq;
using System.Text;
using System.Windows.Forms;
using System.Security.Principal;

namespace WindowsSecurity
{
    public partial class Form1 : Form
    {

        public Form1()
        {
            InitializeComponent();
        }

        private void Form1_Load(object sender, EventArgs e)
        {
            WindowsIdentity myIdentity = WindowsIdentity.GetCurrent();
            WindowsPrincipal myPrincipal = new WindowsPrincipal(myIdentity);
            if(myPrincipal.IsInRole("Accounting"))
            {
                AccountingButton.Visible=true;
            }
            else if (myPrincipal.IsInRole("Sales"))
            {
```

```
                SalesButton.Visible = true;
            }
            else if (myPrincipal.IsInRole("Management"))
            {
                ManagerButton.Visible = true;
            }
        }
    }
}
```

To successfully run this code, you must have an environment that has Accounting, Sales, and Management NT user groups.

In some cases, you don't need this kind of role diversification. Sometimes you just need to know whether the user is in a standard role, which `System.Security` provides for. Using the `WindowsBuiltInRole` enumerator, you describe actions that should take place when, for example, the administrator is logged on:

```
if (myPrincipal.IsInRole(WindowsBuiltInRole.Administrator))
      {
          //Do something
      }
```

Encrypting information

Encryption is, at its core, an insanely sophisticated process. Five namespaces are devoted to different algorithms. Because encryption is so complex, I don't get into the details in this book.

Nonetheless, it is important that you understand one cryptographic element for a key element of security — encrypting files. When you work with a file in a Windows Forms application, you risk someone loading it up in a text editor and looking at it, unless you have encrypted the program.

The common encryption scheme Data Encryption Standard (DES) is implemented in .NET. It isn't the strongest encryption in these days of 64-bit desktop machines, but it's strong enough to encrypt the data files for a Windows application. You can find the methods to encrypt for DES in the `DESCryptoServiceProvider` in the `System.Security.Cryptography` namespace.

Deployment security

If you deploy your application using `ClickOnce`, you need to define the access to the PC that the application will request. `ClickOnce` is a Web server–based deployment strategy that allows users to run Windows Forms applications from a Web browser by using the WindowsSecurity tab in the My Project configuration file, shown in Figure 1-2.

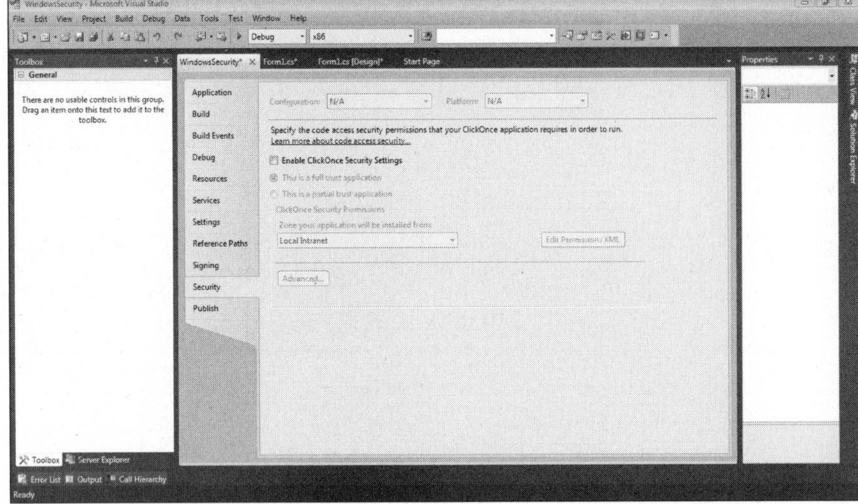

Figure 1-2: The Windows Security tab of the My Project configuration file.

Getting to the My Project configuration file is straightforward:

1. **From an open project, go the Solution Explorer by pressing Ctrl+Alt+L.**
2. **Double-click the My Project file.**
3. **Click the WindowsSecurity tab.**

Here, you can define the features that your application uses, so that the user installing it receives a warning at installation rather than a security error when running the application.

Building Secure Web Forms Applications

Web Forms applications are disconnected, loosely coupled programs that expose a server to potential attacks through the exposed ports used by the applications. By *loosely coupled,* I mean they have a transact-and-wait relationship with the server.

Because of this coupling, building for security becomes more important than ever with a Web Forms application. A side effect is that your application can become less functional.

When building Web-based applications, you spend less time worrying about authentication (especially if your application is made publicly available) and more time worrying about crackers. Because you are making a server — usually something you keep private — available to the public, your programs are subject to a whole new set of security rules.

The key to protecting a public server is honesty. You have to be honest with yourself about the weaknesses of the system. Don't think, "Well, a cracker could figure out the password by doing XYZ, but no one would ever do that." Trust me, someone will figure it out.

The two main types of attacks to be concerned about for a Web Forms application are SQL Injection attacks and script exploits.

SQL Injection attacks

A *SQL Injection attack* happens when a hacker enters a line of SQL code into an input field used to query a database in a form on a Web page (such as the username and password text boxes in a login form). Malicious SQL code causes the database to act in an unexpected way or to allow the hacker to gain access to, alter, or damage the database.

Understanding SQL Injection

The best way to understand how a hacker uses a SQL Injection is to see an example. For instance, a Web page has code that accepts a Product ID from the user in a text box and returns product details based on the Product ID the user entered. The code on the server might look like this:

```
//Get productId from user
string ProductId = TextBox1.Text;
//Get information from the database
string SelectString = "SELECT * FROM Items WHERE ProductId =
    '" + ProductId + "';";
SqlCommand cmd = new SqlCommand(SelectString, conn);
conn.Open();
SqlDataReader myReader = cmd.ExecuteReader();
//Process results
myReader.Close();
conn.Close();
```


Normally, a user enters the appropriate information into the text box. But a cracker attempting a SQL Injection attack would enter the following string into `textBox1`:

```
"FOOBAR';DELETE FROM Items;--"
```

The SQL code that would be run by your code would look like this:

```
SELECT * FROM Items WHERE ProductID = 'FOOBAR';DELETE FROM
   Items;--'
```

The SQL Server executes some code you didn't expect; in this case, the code deleted everything in the Items table.

Preventing SQL Injection

The easiest way to prevent SQL Injection is to never use string concatenation to generate SQL. Use a stored procedure and SQL parameters. You can read more about that in Chapter 2 of this minibook.

Script exploits

A *script exploit* is a security flaw that takes advantage of the JavaScript engine in a user's Web browser. Script exploits take advantage of one of the more common features of public Web Forms applications — enabling interaction among users. For instance, a Web Forms application may enable a user to post a comment that other users of the site can view, or it may allow a user to fill out an online profile.

Understanding script exploits

If a malicious user were to put some script code in his or her profile or comment, that hacker could take over the browser of the next user who comes to the site. Several outcomes are possible, and none of them are good.

For instance, the cookies collection is available to JavaScript when a user comes to your site. A malicious user would put some script code in his or her profile that could copy the cookie for your site to a remote server. This could give the malicious user access to the current user's session because the session identifier is stored as a cookie. The malicious user would then be able to spoof the current user's identity.

Preventing script exploits

Fortunately, ASP.NET prevents users from typing most script code into a form field and posting it to the server. Try it with a basic Web Forms project by following these steps (you see the error shown in Figure 1-3):

1. **Create a new Web Forms project.**
2. **Add a text box and a button to the default page.**
3. **Run the project.**
4. **Type** <script>msgbox()</script> **into the text box.**
5. **Click the button.**

Additionally, you can use the `Server.HTMLEncode` method to encode anything that the Web Forms application sends to the screen — this will make script code appear in real text rather than in HTML.

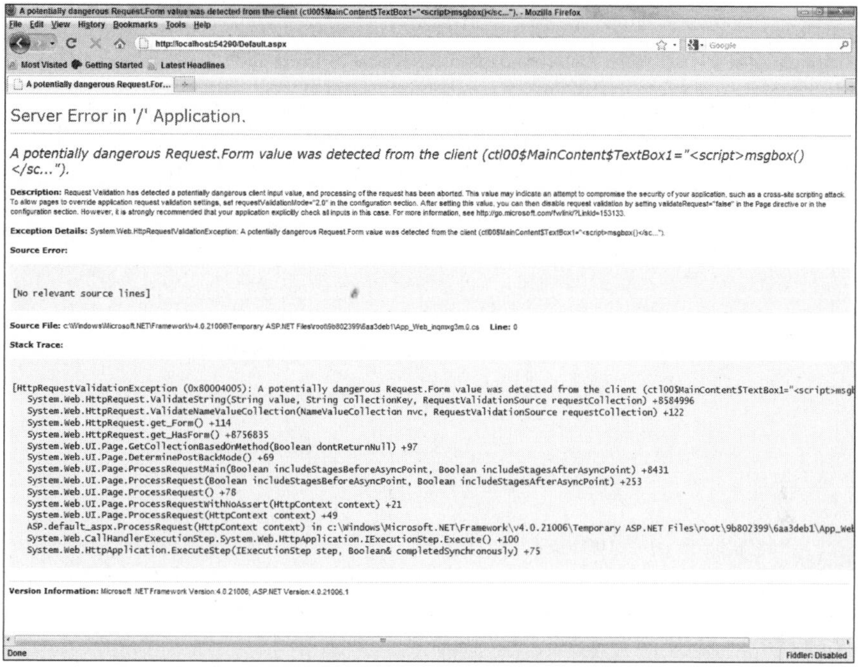

Figure 1-3: Script exploits are blocked by default.

Best practices for securing Web Forms applications

Aside from make sure that your Web Forms application will prevent SQL Injection attacks and script exploits, you should keep in mind some good practices for securing your Web applications.

The following list runs down some of the most important practices for securing your Web applications:

- ✦ Keep your IIS box up to date.
- ✦ Back up everything.
- ✦ Avoid using a `Querystring` variable.
- ✦ Don't leave HTML comments in place. Any user can view the HTML code and see your comments by choosing View➪Source in a browser.
- ✦ Don't depend on client-side validation for security — it can be faked.
- ✦ Use strong passwords.
- ✦ Don't assume what the user sent you came from your form and is safe. It is easy to fake a form post.
- ✦ Make sure that error messages don't give the user any information about your application. E-mail yourself the error messages instead of displaying them to the user.

- Use Secure Sockets Layer.
- Don't store anything useful in a cookie.
- Close all unused ports on your Web server.
- Turn off SMTP on IIS unless you need it.
- Run a virus checker if you allow uploads.
- Don't run your application as Administrator.
- Use temporary cookies, if possible, by setting the expiration date to a past date. The cookie will stay alive only for the length of the session.
- Put a size limit on file uploads. You can do it in the `Web.Config` file:

```
<configuration>
   <system.web>
        <httpRuntime maxRequestLength="4096" />
   </system.web>
</configuration>
```

- Remember that the `ViewState` of Web Forms is easily viewable.

Using System.Security

Although many of the security tools are built into the classes that use them, some classes defy description or classification. For that reason, `System.Security` is the holding pot for stuff that doesn't fit anywhere else.

The more common namespaces for `System.Security` are described in Table 1-1. I show how to use the `Security.Principal` namespace in the earlier section "Authentication using Windows login."

Table 1-1 Common Namespaces in System.Security

Namespace	*Description*	*Common Classes*
`Security`	Base classes for security	`CodeAccessPermission`, `SecureString`
`AccessControl`	Sophisticated control for authorization	`AccessRule`, `AuditRule`
`Authorization`	Enumerations that describe the security of an application	`CipherAlgorithmType`

Namespace	*Description*	*Common Classes*
`Cryptography`	Contains several namespaces that help with encryption	`CryptoConfig`, `DESCryptoServiceProvider`
`Permissions`	Controls access to resources	`PrincipalPermission`, `SecurityPermission`
`Policy`	Defends repudiation with classes for evidence	`Evidence`, `Site`, `Url`
`Principal`	Defines the object that represents the current user context	`WindowsIdentity`, `WindowsPrincipal`

Chapter 2: Accessing Data

In This Chapter

- Understanding the **`System.Data`** namespace
- Connecting to a data source
- Working with data from databases

Not to predispose you to the contents of this chapter, but you will probably find that data access is the most important part of your use of the .NET Framework. You likely will use the various features of the `System.Data` namespace more than any other namespace.

Unquestionably, one of the most common uses of Visual Studio is the creation of business applications. Business applications are about data. This is the black and white of development with Visual Studio. While understanding a little of everything is important, complete understanding of the `System.Data` namespace is essential when you're building business applications.

Until the .NET Framework became popular in the 2003 timeframe, most business applications built using Microsoft products used FoxPro or Visual Basic. C# has unquestionably replaced those languages as the business programmer's language of choice over the past several years.

You can look at the data tools in C# in three ways:

- **Database connectivity:** Getting information out of and into a database is a primary part of the `System.Data` namespace.
- **Holding data in containers within your programs:** The `DataSet`, `DataView`, and `DataTable` containers are useful mechanisms for accomplishing the holding of data. If you are a Visual Basic 6 or ASP programmer, you remember Recordsets, which have been replaced by the new constructs.

The Language Integrated Query enables you to get the data out of the data containers using Structured Language Queries (SQL) rather than complicated object-oriented language (OOL).

+ **Integration with data controls:** The `System.Web` and `System.Windows` namespaces function to integrate with the data controls. Data control integration uses database connectivity and data containers extensively. This makes data controls a great target for your reading in this chapter.

Getting to Know System.Data

Data in .NET is different from data in any other Microsoft platform. Microsoft has and continues to change the way data is manipulated in the .NET Framework. ADO.NET, whose implementation is contained in the new data library `System.Data`, provides yet another new way to think about data from a development perspective:

+ **Disconnected:** After you get data from a data source, your program is no longer connected to that data source. You have a copy of the data. This cures one problem and causes another:
  - You no longer have a row-locking problem. Because you have a copy of the data, you don't have to constrain the database from making changes.
  - You have the *last in wins* problem. If two instances of a program get the same data, and they both update it, the last one back to the database overwrites the changes made by the first program.
+ **XML driven:** The data copy that's collected from the data source is XML under the hood. It might be moved around in a custom format when Microsoft deems it necessary for performance, but it is just XML either way, making movement between platforms or applications or databases much easier.
+ **Database-generic containers:** The containers don't depend on the type of database at all — they can be used to store data from anywhere.
+ **Database-specific adapters:** Connections to the database are specific to the database platform, so if you want to connect to a specific database, you need the components that work with that database.

The process for getting data has changed a little, too. You used to have a connection and a command, which returned a Recordset. Now, you have an adapter, which uses a connection and a command to fill a `DataSet` container. What has changed is the way the user interface helps you get the job done.

`System.Data` has the classes to help you connect to a lot of different databases and other types of data. These classes are broken up into the namespaces in Table 2-1.

Table 2-1 The System.Data Namespaces

Namespace	*Purpose*	*Most Used Classes*
`System.Data`	Classes common to all of ADO.NET	The containers `DataSet`, `DataView`, `DataTable`, `DataRow`
`System.Data.Common`	Utility classes used by database-specific classes	`DbCommand`, `DbConnection`
`System.Data.ODBC`	Classes for connections to ODBC databases such as dBASE	`OdbcCommand`, `OdbcAdapter`
`System.Data.OleDb`	Classes for connections to OleDb databases such as Access	`OleDbCommand`, `OleDbAdapter`
`System.Data.OracleClient`	Classes for connections to Oracle	`OracleCommand`, `OracleAdapter`
`System.Data.SqlClient`	Classes for connections to Microsoft SQL Server	`SqlCommand`, `SqlDataAdapter`
`System.Data.SqlTypes`	For referencing the native types common to SQL Server	`SqlDateTime`

Though there is a lot to the `System.Data` namespace and related tools, I focus on the way Visual Studio implements these tools. In previous versions of the development software of all makes and models, the visual tools just made things harder because of the black box problem.

The *black box problem* is that of having a development environment do some things for you over which you have no control. Sometimes it's nice to have things done for you, but when the development environment doesn't build them exactly how you need them, code is generated that isn't useful.

Fortunately, that isn't the case anymore. Visual Studio now generates completely open and sensible C# code when you use the visual data tools. I think you will be pleased with the results.

How the Data Classes Fit into the Framework

The data classes are all about information storage. In Book I, I talk about collections, which are for storage of information while an application is running. Hashtables are another example of storing information. *Collections* hold lists of objects, and *hashtables* hold name and value pairs.

The data containers hold data in larger amounts and help you manipulate that data. Here are the data containers:

- `DataSet`: Kind of the granddaddy of them all, the `DataSet` container is an in-memory representation of an entire database.
- `DataTable`: A single table of data stored in memory, the `DataTable` container is the closest thing you can find to a Recordset, if you are a VB 6 programmer and are looking. `DataSet` containers are made up of `DataTable` containers.
- `DataRow`: Unsurprisingly, a row in a `DataTable` container.
- `DataView`: A copy of a `DataTable` that can be used to sort and filter data for viewing purposes.
- `DataReader`: A read-only, forward-only stream of data used for one-time processes such as filling up list boxes. Usually called a *fire hose*.

Getting to Your Data

Everything in the `System.Data` namespace revolves around getting data from a database such as Microsoft SQL Server and filling these data containers. You can get to this data manually. Generally speaking, the process goes something like this:

1. You create an adapter.
2. You tell the adapter how to get information from the database (the connection).
3. The adapter connects to the database.
4. You tell the adapter which information to get from the database (the command).
5. The adapter fills the `DataSet` container with data.
6. The connection between the adapter and the database is closed.
7. You now have a disconnected copy of the data in your program.

Not to put too fine a point on it, but you shouldn't have to go through that process at all. Visual Studio does a lot of the data management for you if you let it, and I recommend that you do.

Using the System.Data Namespace

The `System.Data` namespace is another namespace that gets mixed up between the code world and the visual tools world. Though it is more of a relationship between the form controls and the `Data` namespace, it often seems like the data lives right inside the controls, especially when you're dealing with Windows Forms.

In the following sections, you deal primarily with the visual tools, which are as much a part of the C# experience as the code. First, I go over connecting to data sources, and then I show you how to write a quick application using one of those connections. Finally, I go over a little of the code side.

To make all this work, you need to have some kind of schema set up in your database. It can be a local project of your own creation or a sample schema. The next section tells you how.

Setting up a sample database schema

To get started, direct your browser to `www.microsoft.com/sqlserver/2005/en/us/express-starter-schemas.aspx`. If this URL doesn't work, search the Web for *SQL Server 2008 sample schema* and find the nearest Microsoft link. It should get you there.

This page offers two sample listings — sample applications and sample schemas. The sample applications are full-blown applications that show complete end-to-end implementation of data-driven software built using .NET. Some are in C#, some are in Visual Basic. The sample schemas are databases only and are designed for database administrators to practice getting experience in handling the system.

Any of the sample schemas will work. If you want exactly the same one as I use in the examples here, choose the Asset Management schema. Other options may be a better fit for the work you're doing. They include

- ✦ Assets Maintenance
- ✦ Contact Management
- ✦ Customers and Orders
- ✦ Document Management
- ✦ e-Commerce
- ✦ Helpdesk
- ✦ Issue Tracking Software
- ✦ Retail Inventory Control
- ✦ Not for Profits
- ✦ Product Catalogs

To install, follow these steps:

1. **Click the Install link to display the familiar Internet Explorer download dialog box. Agree to run the software, and you see a confirmation for the installation. Click Yes to that confirmation, and then agree to the EULA.**

   Gotta do the licensing bit!

2. **Pick a destination for the database files. I used `c:\databases`. Agree to create the folder and acknowledge that you did business with Microsoft, and then you should be golden.**

   The expanded folder includes four items in the following order: the license that you agreed to, a picture of the database schema, the SQL files for the schema themselves, and an `*.mdf` file with the schema and the database within.

If you are familiar with SQL Server, you can add a database to your local install and point to it there. In the case that you aren't a DBA, it is also possible to point a data provider directly to a file. That's the angle I take for the rest of this chapter.

Connecting to a data source

There is more to connecting to a database than establishing a simple connection to Microsoft Access these days. Visual Basic developers have to connect to mainframes, text files, unusual databases, Web services, and other programs. All these disparate systems get integrated into windows and Web screens, with update, add, and delete functionality to boot.

Getting to these data sources is mostly dependent on the `Adapter` classes of the individualized database namespaces. Oracle has its own, as does SQL Server. Databases that are ODBC (Open Database Connectivity) compliant (such as Microsoft Access) have their own `Adapter` classes; the newer OLEDB (Object Linking and Embedding Database) protocol has one, too.

Fortunately, a wizard handles most of this. The Data Source Configuration Wizard is accessible from the Data Sources panel, where you spend much of your time when working with data. To get started with the Data Source Configuration Wizard, follow these steps:

1. **Start a new Windows Application project by clicking the New Project icon in the Start page. Select a C# Windows Forms Application and give it an appropriate name.**

   For this example, I named the Windows Application project `Accessing Data`.

2. **To open the Data Sources panel, choose Data⇨Show Data Sources, or press Shift+Alt+D.**

   It should tell you that you have no data sources, as shown in Figure 2-1.

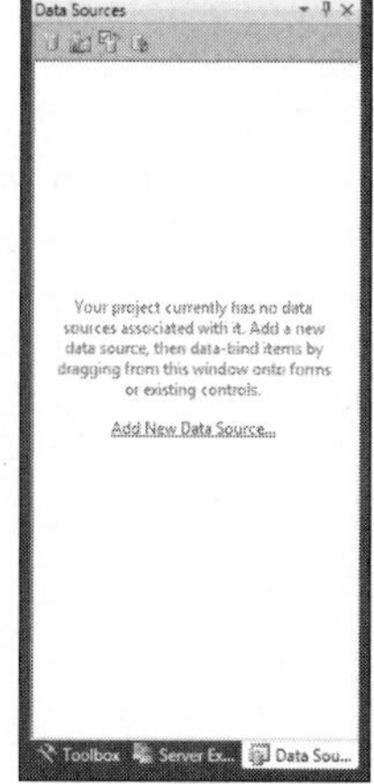

Figure 2-1: The Data Sources panel.

3. **Click the Add New Data Source link in the Data Sources panel.**

   This brings up the Data Source Configuration Wizard. The wizard has a variety of data source types that you can choose from. The most interesting of these is the Object source, which gives you access to an object in an assembly to bind your controls to.

4. **Click the Object source type to see the options there, as shown in Figure 2-2. Then click the Previous button to go back to the preceding screen.**

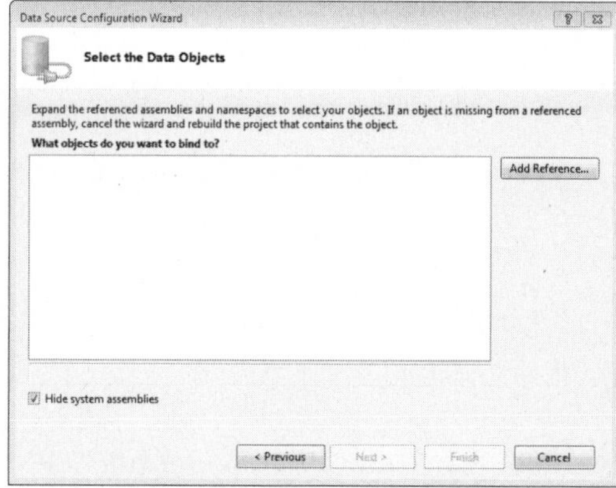

Figure 2-2: Using an object for a data source.

You can pick a Web service to connect to a function on another computer. I cover Web service creation and consumption in Book V, but this functionality sets you up to have a data source along with the Web service reference. It's cool. An example of the blank screen is shown in Figure 2-3.

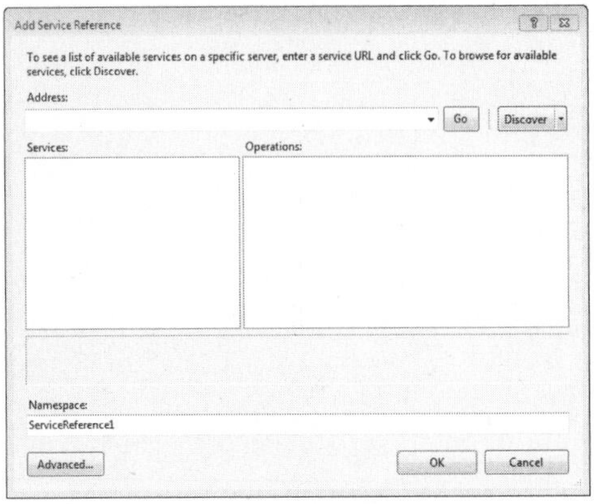

Figure 2-3: Using a Web service for a data source.

When you finish looking around, click the Cancel button to return.

5. **Click the Database data source type to be taken to the Choose Your Database Model screen.**

   For this example, I just used a DataSet. The next part of the wizard is the Choose Your Data Connection screen, as shown in Figure 2-4.

   The most common point of access is a database.

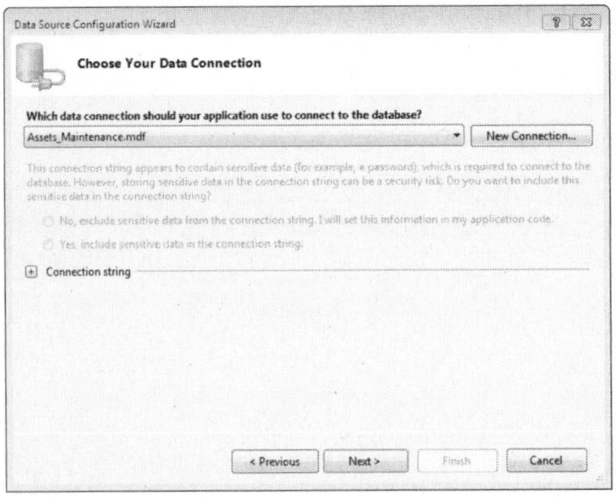

Figure 2-4: Choosing your data connection.

6. **If you have an existing data connection, it appears in the drop-down list. Otherwise, you need to click the New Connection button to bring up the Add Connection dialog box, as shown in Figure 2-5.**

   For this example, I click the New Connection button and select Northwind, the Microsoft sample database.

Figure 2-5: The Add Connection dialog box.

The Add Connection dialog box assumes that you are going to connect to a SQL server. If that isn't the case, click the Change button to select a different database from the Change Data Source dialog box, as shown in Figure 2-6. For this example, I chose Microsoft SQL Server Database File and clicked OK.

Figure 2-6: The Change Data Source dialog box.

If you do use a database file, Visual Studio will copy pertinent files to your project. If you are working through this book in an isolated project, that's fine. If you are on a development effort with others, check to make sure it is appropriate to your life cycle methodology.

7. **Click the Next button to save the connection string to the application configuration file.**
8. **Accept the defaults by clicking Next.**

   You see the Choose Your Database Objects screen. You can choose the tables, views, or stored procedures that you want to use.

9. **Under Tables, select Parts and Part_Faults (as shown in Figure 2-7), and click Next.**

Figure 2-7: Selecting data objects.

You're done! If you look at the Data Sources panel, you find that the new data connection was added, as shown in Figure 2-8.

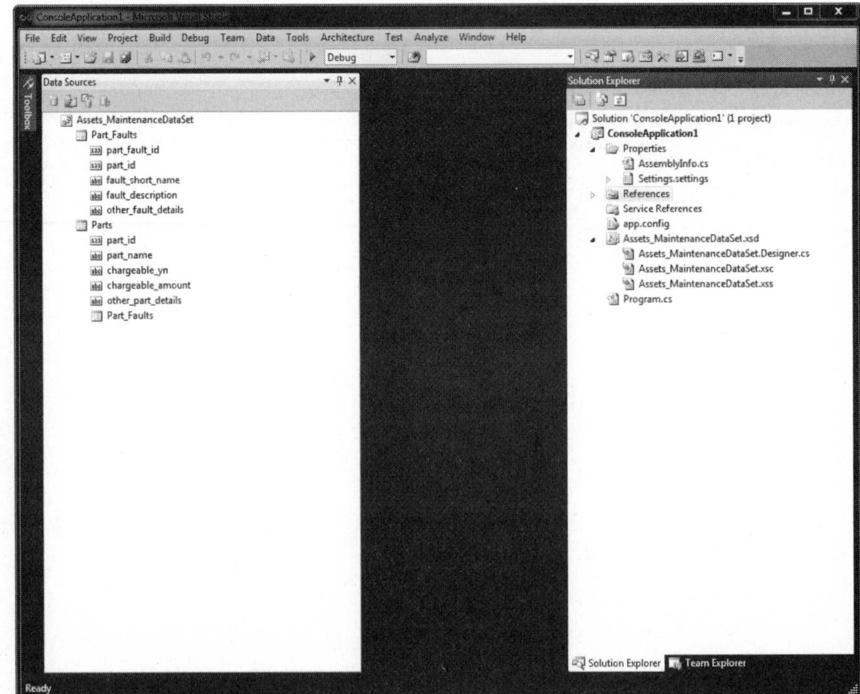

Figure 2-8: New data connections appear in the Data Sources panel to the left.

Note that the Data Sources panel has the Parts tables, and the Data Connections panel has all the tables. This is because the `DataSet` container that you built in the wizard just has the Parts table and related tables in it. The Data Connections panel shows everything in the database.

By following the preceding steps, you create two significant entities in Visual Studio:

- ✦ You create a connection to the database, shown in the Database Explorer. You find that it sticks around — it's specific to this installation of Visual Studio.
- ✦ You also create a project data source, which is specific to this project and won't be there if you start another project.

Both of them are important, and they provide different functionality. In this chapter, I focus on the project-specific data source displayed in the Data Sources panel.

Working with the visual tools

The Rapid Application Development (RAD) data tools for Visual Basic are a massive improvement over what Microsoft previously provided. The RAD data tools in Visual Studio are usable and do what you need, and they write decent code for you.

You need to know that I would *never* show this kind of black magic if it weren't a best practice. In the past, tools that did something you couldn't see often did their job poorly. Using the tools, in the long run, made your program worse. The new tools, though, are a good way to build software. People may tell you that I am wrong, but it really isn't bad. Try it!

If you click a table in the Data Sources panel, a drop-down arrow appears, as shown in Figure 2-9. Click it and you see something interesting: A drop-down list appears, and you can then choose how that table is integrated into Windows Forms.

Change the Parts table to Details View. It's used to create a detail type form — one that easily enables users to view and change data. Then drag the table to the form, and Details View is created for you, as shown in Figure 2-10.

A whole lot of things happened when you dropped the table on your form:

- ✦ The fields and the field names were added.
- ✦ The fields are in the most appropriate format.
- ✦ The field name is a label.
- ✦ Visual Studio automatically adds a space where the case changes.

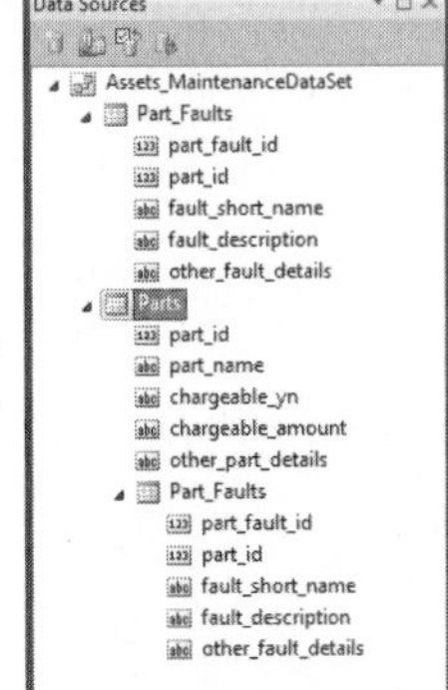

Figure 2-9: Table Options drop-down list.

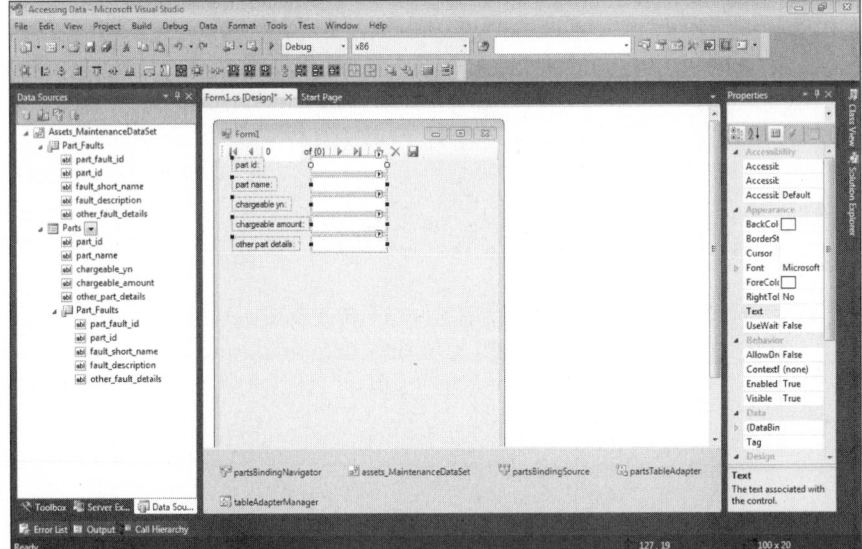

Figure 2-10: Creating a Parts Detail data form.

Note that each field gets a SmartTag that enables you to specify a query for the values in the text box. You can also preset the control that's used by changing the values in the Data Sources panel (refer to Figure 2-10).

Also, a VCR Bar (technically called the `BindingNavigator`) is added to the top of the page. When you run the application, you can use the VCR Bar to cycle among the records in the table.

Finally, four completely code-based objects are added in the Component Tray at the bottom of the page: the `DataSet`, the `BindingSource`, the `DataAdapter`, and the `BindingNavigator` objects.

Click the Play button and you can see the VCR Bar work. You can walk through the items in the database with no problems, as shown in Figure 2-11. It's just like working in Access or FoxPro, but with enterprise quality!

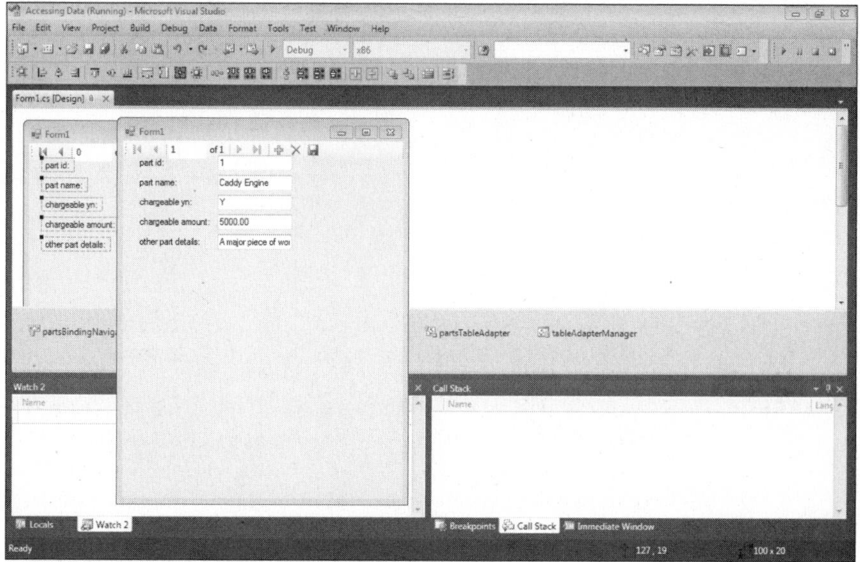

Figure 2-11: Running the example.

It gets better. Follow these steps to create a child table interface:

1. **Open the Parts table in the Data Sources panel by clicking the plus sign (+) next to the table.**
2. **Scroll down until you see the Part FaultsParts table nested in the Orders table.**

   Note that this table is in there twice. You want the one under Parts.
3. **Drag that instance of the table over to the form and place it under the Parts fields you placed on the form earlier in this section (refer to Figure 2-10).**
4. **Click the Play button to run the example, as shown in Figure 2-12.**

You have a running, easy-to-use parent/child form, with parts and part faults. Creating this form would have required you to write a hundred lines of code in other environments. With the capability to choose an assembly for a data source that C# gives you, the form is even nearly enterprise ready. It's slick stuff.

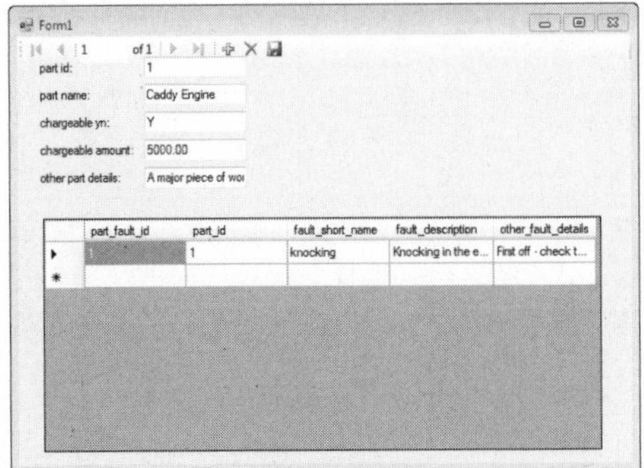

Figure 2-12: A complete edit form.

Writing data code

In most enterprise development environments, however, you won't be using the visual tools to build data access software. Generally, an infrastructure is already in place.

The reason for this is that often, enterprise software has specific requirements, and the easiest way to manage those specifications is with unique and customized code. In short, some organizations don't want things done the way Microsoft does them.

Output of the visual tools

The reason that the visual tools often aren't used in enterprise environments is that the code the tools put out is rather sophisticated. If you switch to Code View and right-click an instance of an object (such as the `PartsTableAdapter` object) and select Go to Definition, you see the code behind the designer.

Figure 2-13 shows what you see when you first get in there. The box marking the region near the top of the code window is marked as `Windows Form Designer generated code`, and you can't help but notice that the line number before that section is in the twenties and the number after that is in the four hundreds. That's a lot of generated code.

Nothing is wrong with this code, but it is purposely generic to support anything that anyone might want to do with it. Enterprise customers often want to make sure that everything is done the same way. For this reason, they often define a specific data code format and expect their software developers to use that, rather than the visual tools.

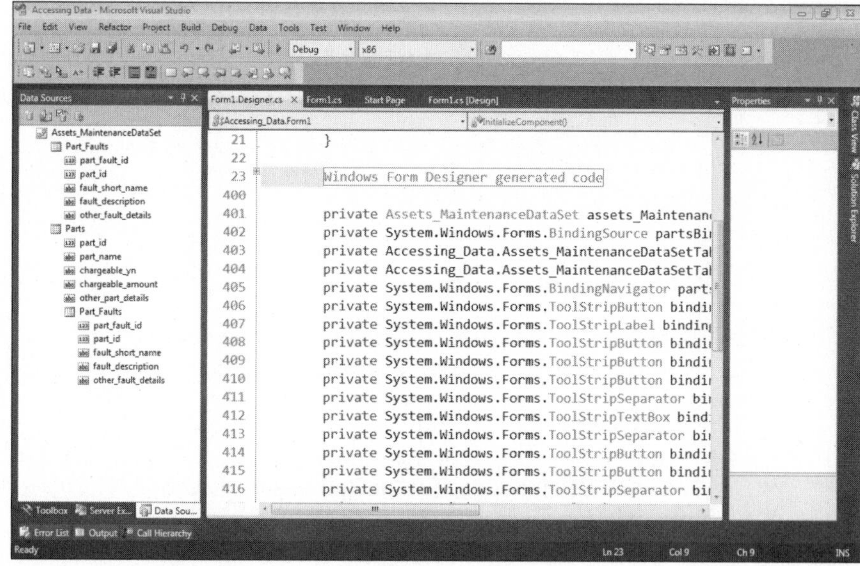

Figure 2-13: Generated code. Huh?

Basic data code

The code of the sample project is simple:

```
using System;
using System.Collections.Generic;
using System.ComponentModel;
using System.Data;
using System.Drawing;
using System.Linq;
using System.Text;
using System.Windows.Forms;

namespace Accessing_Data
{
    public partial class Form1 : Form
    {
        public Form1()
        {
            InitializeComponent();
        }

        private void partsBindingNavigatorSaveItem_Click(object sender, EventArgs
    e)
        {
            this.Validate();
            this.partsBindingSource.EndEdit();
            this.tableAdapterManager.UpdateAll(this.assets_MaintenanceDataSet);

        }
```

```
        private void Form1_Load(object sender, EventArgs e)
        {
            // TODO: This line of code loads data into the 'assets_
    MaintenanceDataSet.Part_Faults' table. You can move, or remove it, as needed.
            this.part_FaultsTableAdapter.Fill(this.assets_MaintenanceDataSet.
    Part_Faults);
            // TODO: This line of code loads data into the 'assets_
    MaintenanceDataSet.Parts' table. You can move, or remove it, as needed.
            this.partsTableAdapter.Fill(this.assets_MaintenanceDataSet.Parts);

        }
    }
}
```

While this is fairly straightforward, it obviously isn't everything that you need. The rest of the code is in the file that generates the visual form itself, supporting the visual components.

The time may come when you want to connect to a database without using visual tools. I discuss the steps in the earlier section "How the Data Classes Fit into the Framework," and here I show the code to go with it:

```
1. SqlConnection mainConnection = new SqlConnection();
2. mainConnection.ConnectionString = "server=(local);database=Assets_
    Maintenance;Trusted_Connection=True"
3. SqlDataAdapter partsAdapter = new SqlDataAdapter("SELECT * FROM
    Parts", mainConnection)
4. DataSet partsDataSet = new DataSet();
5. mainConnection.Open();
6. partsAdapter.Fill(partsDataSet);
7. mainConnection.Close();
```

This becomes useful especially when you want to build a Web service or a class library — though it should be noted that you can still use the visual tools in those project types.

Let's talk about this a line at a time. Line one sets up a new data connection, and line two populates it with the connection string. You can get this from your DBA or from the properties panel for the data connection.

Line three has a SQL Query in it. In Chapter 1, I talk about how this is a bad deal, and you should use Stored Procedures. That's true. Don't use inline SQL for production systems. I could have just as easily put a stored procedure name in there.

Line four builds a new dataset. This is where the schema of the returned data is held and what I would use to navigate the data.

Lines 5, 6, and 7 perform the magic: Open the connection, contact the database. Fill the dataset using the adapter, and then close the database. It's all straightforward in this simple example. More complex examples make for more complex code.

After running this code, you would have the Parts table in a `DataSet` container, just as you did in the visual tools in the earlier section, "How the Data Classes Fit into the Framework." To access the information, you set the value of a text box to the value of a cell in the `DataSet` container, like this:

```
TextBox1.Text = myDataSet.Tables[0].Rows[0]["part_name"]
```

To change to the next record, you need to write code that changes the `Rows[0]` to `Rows[1]` in the next example. As you can see, it would be a fair amount of code.

That's why few people use the basic data code to get the databases. Either you use the visual tools or you use a data broker of some sort.

Using the Entity Framework

I don't want to get into much programming philosophy here, but object models (which I discuss in much of this book) and databases just don't go together. They're two different ways of thinking of the same information.

The problem mostly lies in inheritance, which I discuss in Book II. If you have a class called `ScheduledEvent`, which has certain properties, and a bunch of classes that inherit from it, like `Courses`, `Conferences`, and `Parties`, there just isn't a good way to show this in a relational type of database.

If you make a big table for `ScheduledEvents` with all possible types of properties, and just make a `Type` property so you can tell the `Courses` from the `Parties`, and then you will have a lot of empty cells. If you make a table for just the properties that are in `ScheduledEvents`, and then separate tables for `Courses` and `Parties`, you make the database remarkably complex.

To address this problem, Microsoft created the Entity Framework. It's the latest edition of a product that Microsoft and everyone else has tried to create since the popularity of relational databases and object-oriented programming made object role modelers necessary.

Object Role Modelers try and take the whole shootin' match and turn it on its head. The goal is to design the database first (which I recommend anyway), and then make an object model to work with it automatically. Then, keep it up to date.

The Entity Framework does an acceptable job at that process. It generates a context for you that you can use to communicate with your data in a way that looks more like an object model than it does a database.

Generating the entity model

To get started, you need the model itself. Just follow these steps to generate the entity model:

1. **Create a new project (I used a Windows Forms project again, called Entity Framework).**
2. **Right-click the project and click Add New in the context menu. Select ADO.NET Entity Data Model. Name it** PartsDatabase.
3. **Choose Generate from Database Option in the Choose Model Contents window.**
4. **Select the** `Assets_Database.mdf` **from the Connection drop-down list. If it isn't there, see "Connecting to a data source."**
5. **If you get a message asking if you would like to copy the database into the project, select No. Copying the database is usually a bad practice, especially if you are on a shared project. If you are building a stand-alone project, and are working alone, it is an acceptable solution.**
6. **Select the Asset_Parts, Assets, Part_Faults, and Parts tables, just for fun. (See Figure 2-14.) Keep the default name.**

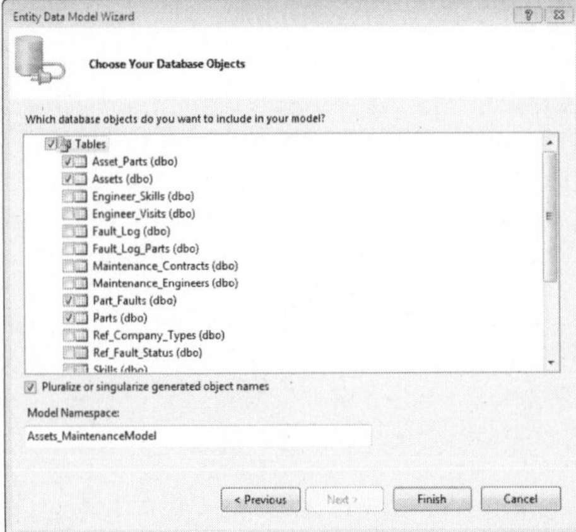

Figure 2-14: Select a few tables.

The next thing you see is the designer canvas for the Class Designer. A sample diagram is shown in Figure 2-15. It's just a class diagram, like the ones in Book II.

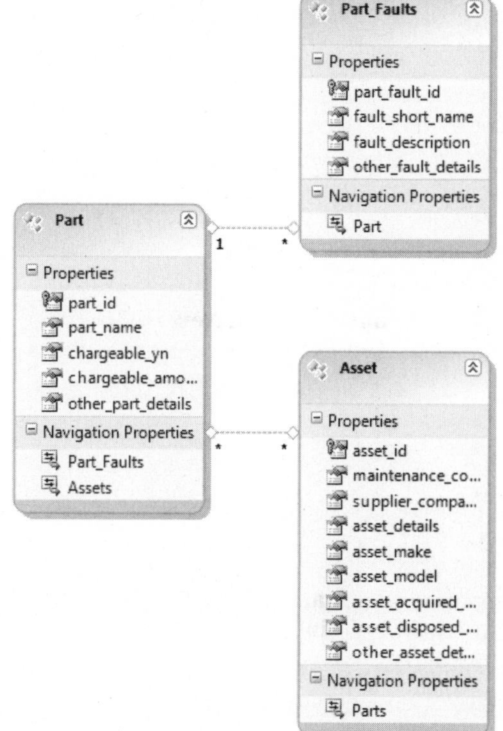

Figure 2-15: Looks like a class model, walks like a database.

Notice something missing? The `Asset_Parts` table is gone; it's been abstracted into the model for you because the table was there only to link the Assets and Parts tables in a many-to-many relationship. Slick, isn't it?

Writing code for the entity model

After you have an interesting addition to your coding environment and the database is meshed nicely into the C# object model, you can code with the objects provided in this new entity model. To start, follow these steps:

1. **Go back to the window designer and double-click on the window to go to Code View.**
2. **In the** `window.load` **event handler, type** Part part = new Part();.
3. **In the next line, type** part. **and check out the IntelliSense. It contains all columns in the Parts table as properties to the class.**

What you now have is a context to work against. No complex Linq queries — they're all done under the covers. No inline SQL. No stored procedures. You can do it all with a scoped object.

Chapter 3: Fishing the FileStream

In This Chapter

- Reading and writing data files
- Using the `Stream` classes
- Using the `using` statement
- Dealing with input/output errors

I once caught two trout on a single hook, in a lovely mountain stream in my native Colorado — quite a thrill for an 11-year-old. Fishing the "file stream" with C# isn't quite so thrilling, but it's one of those indispensable programming skills.

File access refers to the storage and retrieval of data on the disk. I cover basic text-file input/output in this chapter. Reading and writing data from databases is covered in Chapter 2 of this minibook, and reading and writing information to the Internet is covered in Chapter 4.

Going Where the Fish Are: The File Stream

The console application programs in this book mostly take their input from, and send their output to, the console. Programs outside this chapter have better — or at least different — things to bore you with than file manipulation. I don't want to confuse their message with the extra baggage of involved input/output (I/O). However, console applications that don't perform file I/O are about as common as Sierra Club banners at a paper mill.

The I/O classes are defined in the `System.IO` namespace. The basic file I/O class is `FileStream`. In days past, the programmer would open a file. The `open` command would prepare the file and return a *handle*. Usually, this handle was nothing more than a number, like the one they give you when you place an order at a Burger Whop. Every time you wanted to read from or write to the file, you presented this ID.

Streams

C# uses a more intuitive approach, associating each file with an object of class `FileStream`. The constructor for `FileStream` opens the file and manages the underlying handle. The methods of `FileStream` perform the file I/O.

`FileStream` isn't the only class that can perform file I/O. However, it represents your good ol' basic file that covers 90 percent of your file I/O needs. This primary class is the one described in this chapter. If it's good enough for C#, it's good enough for me.

The *stream* concept is fundamental to C# I/O. Think of a parade, which "streams" by you, first the clowns, and then the floats, and then a band or two, some horses, a troupe of `Customer` objects, a `BankAccount`, and so on. Viewing a file as a stream of bytes (or characters or strings) is much like a parade. You "stream" the data in and out of your program.

The .NET classes used in C# include an abstract `Stream` base class and several subclasses, for working with files on the disk, over a network, or already sitting as chunks of data in memory. Some stream classes specialize in encrypting and decrypting data, some are provided to help speed up I/O operations that might be slow using one of the other streams, and you're free to extend class `Stream` with your own subclass if you come up with a great idea for a new stream (although I warn you that extending `Stream` is arduous). I give you a tour of the stream classes in the later section "Exploring More Streams than Lewis and Clark."

Readers and writers

`FileStream`, the stream class you'll probably use the most, is a basic class. Open a file, close a file, read a block of bytes, and write a block — that's about all you have. But reading and writing files down at the byte level is a lot of work, something I eschew studiously. Fortunately, the .NET class library introduces the notion of "readers" and "writers." Objects of these types greatly simplify file (and other) I/O.

When you create a new *reader* (of one of several available types), you associate a stream object with it. It's immaterial to the reader whether the stream connects to a file, a block of memory, a network location, or the Mississippi. The reader requests input from the stream, which gets it from — well, wherever. Using *writers* is quite similar, except that you're sending output to the stream rather than asking for input. The stream sends it to a specified destination. Often that's a file, but not always.

The `System.IO` namespace contains classes that wrap around `FileStream` (or other streams) to give you easier access and that warm fuzzy feeling:

✦ **`TextReader/TextWriter`:** A pair of abstract classes for reading characters (text). These classes are the base for two flavors of subclasses: `StringReader/StringWriter` and `StreamReader/StreamWriter`.

Because `TextReader` and `TextWriter` are abstract, you'll use one of their subclass pairs, usually `StreamReader/StreamWriter`, to do actual work. I explain abstract classes in Book II.

✦ **`StreamReader/StreamWriter`:** A more sophisticated text reader and writer for the more discriminating palate — not to mention that they aren't abstract, so you can even read and write with them. For example, `StreamWriter` has a `WriteLine()` method much like that in the `Console` class. `StreamReader` has a corresponding `ReadLine()` method and a handy `ReadToEnd()` method that grabs the whole text file in one gulp, returning the characters read as a `string` — which you could then use with a `StringReader` (discussed later), a `foreach` loop, the `String.Split()` method, and so on. Check out the various constructors for these classes in Help.

  You see `StreamReader` and `StreamWriter` in action in the next two sections.

One nice thing about reader/writer classes such as `StreamReader` and `StreamWriter` is that you can use them with any kind of stream. This makes reading from and writing to a `MemoryStream` no harder than reading from and writing to the kind of `FileStream` discussed in earlier sections of this chapter. (I cover `MemoryStream` later in the chapter.)

See the later section "More Readers and writers" for additional reader/writer pairs.

The following sections provide the `FileWrite` and `FileRead` programs, which demonstrate ways to use these classes for text I/O the C# way.

Asynchronous I/O: Is it worth waiting for?

Normally, a program waits for a file I/O request to complete before continuing. Call a `read()` method, and you generally don't get control back until the file data is safely in the boat. This is known as *synchronous I/O.* Think of *synchronous* as meaning "while you wait."

The C# `System.IO` classes also support *asynchronous* I/O. Using asynchronous I/O, the `read()` call returns immediately to allow the program to continue doing something else while the I/O request is completed in the background. The program can check a "done" flag at its leisure to decide when the I/O has completed.

This is sort of like cooking hamburgers. Using synchronous I/O, you put the meat in the pan on the stovetop and stand there watching it until the meat has completely cooked before you go off and start cutting the onions that go on the burgers.

Using asynchronous I/O, you can start cutting up the onions while the hamburger patties are cooking. Every once in a while, you peek over to see whether the meat is done. When it is, you stop cutting, take the meat off the grill, and slap it on the buns.

Asynchronous I/O can substantially improve performance of the program, but it adds another level of complexity. I don't discuss it further in this minibook.

StreamWriting for Old Walter

In the movie *On Golden Pond,* Henry Fonda spent his retirement years trying to catch a monster trout that he named Old Walter. You aren't out to drag in the big fish, but you should at least cast a line into the stream. This section covers writing to files.

Programs generate two kinds of output:

- Some programs write blocks of data as bytes in pure binary format. This type of output is useful for storing objects in an efficient way — for example, a file of `Student` objects that you need to *persist* (keep on disk in a permanent file).

  See the later section "More Readers and Writers" for the `BinaryReader` and `BinaryWriter` classes.

  A sophisticated example of binary I/O is the persistence of groups of objects that refer to each other (using the HAS_A relationship). Writing an object to disk involves writing identifying information (so its type can be reconstructed when you read the object back in), and then each of its data members, some of which may be references to connected objects, each with its own identifying information and data members. Persisting objects this way is called *serialization.* You can look it up in Help when you're ready; I don't cover it here. Sophistication is out of my league.

- Most programs read and write human-readable text: you know, letters, numbers, and punctuation, like Notepad. The human-friendly `StreamWriter` and `StreamReader` classes are the most flexible ways to work with the stream classes. For some details, see the earlier section "Readers and writers."

  Human-readable data was formerly known as ASCII or, slightly later, ANSI, text. These two monikers refer to the standards organization that defined them. However, ANSI encoding doesn't provide the alphabets east of Austria and west of Hawaii; it can handle only Roman letters, like those used in English. It has no characters for Russian, Hebrew, Arabic, Hindi, or any other language using a non-Roman alphabet, including Asian languages such as Chinese, Japanese, and Korean. The modern, more flexible Unicode file format is "backward-compatible" — including the familiar ANSI characters at the beginning of its character set, but still providing a large number of other alphabets, including everything you need for all the languages I just listed. Unicode comes in several variations, called *encodings;* however, UTF8 is the default format for C#. (You can find out more about encodings and how to use them in the article "Converting between Byte and Char Arrays" at `csharp102.info`.)

Using the stream: An example

The following `FileWrite` program reads lines of data from the console and writes them to a file of the user's choosing. This is pseudocode — it isn't meant to compile. I used it only as an example.

```
// FileWrite -- Write input from the Console into a text file.
using System;
using System.IO;

namespace FileWrite
{
  public class Program
  {
    public static void Main(string[] args)
    {
      // Get a filename from the user -- the while loop lets you
      // keep trying with different filenames until you succeed.
      StreamWriter sw = null;
      string fileName = "";
      while(true)
      {
        try
        {
          // Enter output filename (simply hit Enter to quit).
          Console.Write("Enter filename "
                      + "(Enter blank filename to quit):");
          fileName = Console.ReadLine();
          if (fileName.Length == 0)
          {
            // No filename -- this jumps beyond the while
            // loop to safety. You're done.
            break;
          }

          // I factored out these tasks to simplify the loops a bit.

          // Call a method (below) to set up the StreamWriter.
          sw = PrepareTheStreamWriter(fileName);
          // Read one string at a time, outputting each to the
          // FileStream open for writing.
          ReadAndWriteLines(sw);

          // Done writing, so close the file you just created.
          sw.Close(); // A very important step. Closes the file too.
          sw = null;  // Give it to the garbage collector.
        }
        catch (IOException ioErr)
        {
          // Ooops -- Error occurred during the processing of the
          // file -- tell the user the full name of the file:
          // Tack the name of the default directory to the filename.
          string dir = Directory.GetCurrentDirectory();  // Directory class
          string path = Path.Combine(dir, fileName); // System.IO.Path class
          Console.WriteLine("Error on file {0}", path);

          // Now output the error message in the exception.
          Console.WriteLine(ioErr.Message);
        }
      }
```

```
      // Wait for user to acknowledge the results.
      Console.WriteLine("Press Enter to terminate...");
      Console.Read();
    }

    // GetWriterForFile -- Create a StreamWriter set up to write
    //    to the specified file.
    private static StreamWriter GetWriterForFile(string fileName)
    {
      StreamWriter sw;
      // Open file for writing in one of these modes:
      //   FileMode.CreateNew to create a file if it
      //      doesn't already exist or throw an
      //      exception if file exists.
      //   FileMode.Append to append to an existing file
      //      or create a new file if it doesn't exist.
      //   FileMode.Create to create a new file or
      //      truncate an existing file.

      //   FileAccess possibilities are:
      //      FileAccess.Read,
      //      FileAccess.Write,
      //      FileAccess.ReadWrite.
      FileStream fs = File.Open(fileName,
                                FileMode.CreateNew,
                                FileAccess.Write);

      // Generate a file stream with UTF8 characters.
      // Second parameter defaults to UTF8, so can be omitted.
      sw = new StreamWriter(fs, System.Text.Encoding.UTF8);
      return sw;
    }

    // WriteFileFromConsole -- Read lines of text from the console
    //    and spit them back out to the file.
    private static void WriteFileFromConsole(StreamWriter sw)
    {
      Console.WriteLine("Enter text; enter blank line to stop");
      while (true)
      {
        // Read next line from Console; quit if line is blank.
        string input = Console.ReadLine();
        if (input.Length == 0)
        {
          break;
        }
        // Write the line just read to output file.
        sw.WriteLine(input);
        // Loop back up to get another line and write it.
      }
    }
  }
}
```

`FileWrite` uses the `System.IO` namespace as well as `System`. `System.IO` contains the file I/O classes.

Revving up a new outboard StreamWriter

The FileWrite program starts in Main() with a while loop containing a try block. This is common for a file-manipulation program.

Encase all file I/O activity in a try block. File I/O can be prone to errors, such as missing files or directories, bad paths, and so on. See Book I for more on exception handling.

The while loop serves two functions:

- It allows the program to go back and retry in the event of an I/O failure. For example, if the program can't find a file that the user wants to read, the program can ask for the filename again before blowing off the user.
- Executing a break command from within the program breezes you right past the try block and dumps you off at the end of the loop. This is a convenient mechanism for exiting a method or program. Keep in mind that break only gets you out of the loop it's called in. (Chapter 4 covers loops and break.)

The FileWrite program reads the name of the file to create from the console. The program terminates by breaking out of the while loop if the user enters an empty filename. The key to the program occurs in the call to a GetWriterForFile() method; you can find the method below Main(). The key lines in GetWriterForFile() are

```
FileStream fs = File.Open(fileName, FileMode.CreateNew, FileAccess.Write);
// ...
sw = new StreamWriter(fs, System.Text.Encoding.UTF8);
```

In the first line, the program creates a FileStream object that represents the output file on the disk. The FileStream constructor used here takes three arguments:

- **The filename:** This is clearly the name of the file to open. A simple name like filename.txt is assumed to be in the current directory (for FileWrite, working inside Visual Studio, that's the \bin\Debug subdirectory of the project directory; it's the directory containing the .EXE file after you build the program). A filename that starts with a backslash, like *some directory*\filename.txt, is assumed to be the full path on the local machine. Filenames that start with two slashes — for example, *your machine**some directory*\filename.txt — are resident on other machines on your network. The filename encoding gets rapidly more complicated from here and is beyond the scope of this minibook.

- **The file mode:** This argument specifies what you want to do to the file. The basic write modes are create (`CreateNew`), append (`Append`), and overwrite (`Create`). `CreateNew` creates a new file but throws an `IOException` if the file already exists. `Create` mode creates the file if it doesn't exist but overwrites ("truncates") the file if it exists. Just like it sounds, `Append` adds to the end of an existing file or creates the file if it doesn't exist.
- **The access type:** A file can be opened for reading, writing, or both.

`FileStream` has numerous constructors, each of which defaults one or both of the mode and access arguments. However, in my humble opinion, you should specify these arguments explicitly because they have a strong effect on the program's clarity. That's good advice in general. Defaults can be convenient for the programmer but confusing for anyone reading the code.

In the second noncomment line of the `GetWriterForFile()` method, the program "wraps" the newly opened `FileStream` object in a `StreamWriter` object, `sw`. The `StreamWriter` class wraps around the `FileStream` object to provide a set of text-friendly methods. This `StreamWriter` is what the method returns.

The first argument to the `StreamWriter` constructor is the `FileStream` object. There's the wrapping. The second argument specifies the encoding to use. The default encoding is UTF8.

You don't need to specify the encoding when *reading* a file. `StreamWriter` writes out the encoding type in the first three bytes of the file. The `StreamReader` reads these three bytes when the file is opened to determine the encoding. Hiding this kind of detail is an advantage that good software libraries provide.

Finally, we're writing!

After setting up its `StreamWriter`, the `FileWrite` program begins reading lines of string input from the console (this code is in the `WriteFileFromConsole()` method, called from `Main()`). The program quits reading when the user enters a blank line; until then, it gobbles up whatever it's given and spits it into the `StreamWriter sw` using that class's `WriteLine()` method.

The similarity between `StreamWriter.WriteLine()` and `Console.WriteLine()` is more than a coincidence.

Finally, the stream is closed with the `sw.Close()` expression. This is important to do, because it also closes the file. (I have more to say about closing things in the next section.)

Wrap my fish in newspaper

This kind of wrapping one class around another is a useful software pattern — the `StreamWriter` "wraps" (contains a reference to) another class, `FileStream`, and extends the `FileStream`'s interface with some nice amenities. The `StreamWriter` methods *delegate* to (call) the methods of the inner `FileStream` object. This is the HAS_A relationship discussed in Book II, so anytime you use HAS_A, you're wrapping. Thus, in effect, you tell the `StreamWriter`, the wrapper, what to do, and it translates your simple instructions into the more complex ones needed by the wrapped `FileStream`. `StreamWriter` hands these translated instructions to the `FileStream` for action.

Wrapping is a powerful, frequently used technique in programming. A `Wrapper` class looks like this:

```
class Wrapper
{
  private Wrapped _wrapped;
  public Wrapper(Wrapped w)
  {
    _w = w; // Now Wrapper has a
          reference to Wrapped.
  }
}
```

In this example, I used class `Wrapper`'s constructor to install the wrapped object, letting the caller provide the wrapped object. You might install it through a `SetWrapped()` method or by some other means, such as creating the wrapped object inside a constructor.

You can also wrap one *method* around another, like so:

```
void WrapperMethod()
{
  _wrapped.DoSomething();
}
```

In this example, `WrapperMethod()`'s class HAS_A reference to whatever the `_wrapped` object is. In other words, the class wraps that object. `WrapperMethod()` delegates all or part of the evening chores to the `DoSomething()` method on the `_wrapped` object.

Think of wrapping as a way to translate one model into another. The wrapped item may be complicated, so that you want to provide a simpler version, or the wrapped item may have an inconvenient interface that you want to make over into a more convenient one. Generally speaking, wrapping illustrates the Adapter design pattern (which you can find using your favorite search engine). You can see it in the relationship between `StreamWriter` and `FileStream`.

In many cases, you can wrap one stream around another stream in order to convert one kind of stream into another.

Notice that the program nulls the `sw` reference after closing `StreamWriter`. A file object is useless after the file has been closed. It is good programming practice to null a reference after it becomes invalid so that you won't try to use it again. (If you do, your code will throw an exception, letting you know about it!) Closing the file and nulling the reference lets the garbage collector claim it (see Book II to meet the friendly collector on your route) and leaves the file available for other programs to open.

The catch block is like a soccer goalie: It's there to catch any file error that may have occurred in the program. The catch outputs an error message, including the name of the errant file. But it doesn't output just a simple filename — it outputs the entire filename, including the path, for your reading pleasure. It does this by using the Path.Combine() method to tack the current directory name, obtained through the Directory class, onto the front of the filename you entered. (Path is a class designed to manipulate path information. Directory provides properties and methods for working with directories.) Book I gives you the goods on exceptions, including the exceptions to exceptions, the exceptions to those — I give up.

The *path* is the full name of the file folder. For example, in the filename c:\user\temp directory\text.txt, the path is c:\user\temp directory.

The Combine() method is smart enough to realize that for a file like c:\test.txt, the path isn't in the current directory. Path.Combine() is also the safest way to ensure that the two path segments being combined will combine correctly, including a path separator character between them. (In Windows, the path separator character is \. You can obtain the correct separator for whatever operating system your code is running on, whether it's Windows or some brand of Unix, say, with Path.DirectorySeparatorChar. The .NET Framework library is full of features like that, clearly aimed at writing C# programs that run on multiple operating systems, such as Mono for Linux and Unix, which I discuss in this book's Introduction.)

Upon encountering the end of the while loop, either by completing the try block or by being vectored through the catch, the program returns to the top of the while loop to allow the user to write to another file.

A few sample runs of the program appear as follows. My input is boldfaced:

```
Enter filename (Enter blank filename to quit):TestFile1.txt
Enter text; enter blank line to stop
This is some stuff
So is this
As is this

Enter filename (Enter blank filename to quit):TestFile1.txt
Error on file C:\C#Programs\FileWrite\bin\Debug\TestFile1.txt
The file 'C:\C#Programs\FileWrite\bin\Debug\TestFile1.txt' already exists.

Enter filename (Enter blank filename to quit):TestFile2.txt
Enter text; enter blank line to stop
I messed up back there. I should have called it
TestFile2.

Enter filename (Enter blank filename to quit):
Press Enter to terminate...
```

Everything goes smoothly when I enter some random text into `TestFile1.txt`. When I try to open `TestFile1.txt` again, however, the program spits out a message, the gist of which is `The file already exists`, with the filename attached. The path to the file is tortured because the "current directory" is the directory in which Visual Studio put the executable file. Correcting my mistake, I enter an acceptable filename — such as `TestFile2.txt` — without complaint.

Using some better fishing gear: The using statement

Now that you've seen `FileStream` and `StreamWriter` in action, I should point out the more usual way to do stream writing in C# — inside a `using` statement:

```
using(<someresource>)
{
  // Use the resource.
}
```

The `using` statement is a construct that automates the process of cleaning up after using a stream. On encountering the closing curly brace of the `using` block, C# manages "flushing" the stream and closing it for you. (To *flush* a stream is to push any last bytes left over in the stream's buffer out to the associated file before it gets closed. Think of pushing a handle to drain the last water out of your . . . trout stream.) Using `using` eliminates the common error of forgetting to flush and close a file after writing to it. Don't leave open files lying around.

Without `using`, you'd need to write:

```
Stream fileStream = null;
TextWriter writer = null;
try
{
  // Create and use the stream, then ...
}
finally
{
  stream.Flush();
  stream.Close();
  stream = null;
}
```

Note how I declared the stream and writer above the `try` block (so they're visible throughout the method). I also declared the `fileStream` and `writer` variables using abstract base classes rather than the concrete types `FileStream` and `StreamWriter`. That's a good practice. I set them to `null` so the compiler won't complain about uninitialized variables.

The preferred way to write the key I/O code in the FileWrite example looks more like this:

```
// Prepare the file stream.
FileStream fs = File.Open(fileName,
                          FileMode.CreateNew,
                          FileAccess.Write);
// Pass the fs variable to the StreamWriter constructor in the using statement.
using (StreamWriter sw = new StreamWriter(fs))
{
  // sw exists only within the using block, which is a local scope.

  // Read one string at a time from the console, outputting each to the
  // FileStream open for writing.
  Console.WriteLine("Enter text; enter blank line to stop");
  while (true)
  {
    // Read next line from Console; quit if line is blank.
    string input = Console.ReadLine();
    if (input.Length == 0)
    {
      break;
    }
    // Write the line just read to output file via the stream.
    sw.WriteLine(input);
    // Loop back up to get another line and write it.
  }
} // sw goes away here, and fs is now closed. So ...
fs = null;  // Make sure you can't try to access fs again.
```

The items in parentheses after the using keyword are its "resource acquisition" section, where you allocate one or more resources such as streams, readers/writers, fonts, and so on. (If you allocate more than one resource, they have to be of the same type.) Following that section is the enclosing block, bounded by the outer curly braces.

The using statement's *block* is not a loop. The block only defines a local scope, like the try block or a method's block. (Variables defined within the block, including its head, don't exist outside the block. Thus the StreamWriter sw isn't visible outside the using block.) I discuss scope in Book I.

At the top of the preceding example, in the resource-acquisition section, you set up a resource — in this case, create a new StreamWriter wrapped around the already-existing FileStream. Inside the block is where you carry out all your I/O code for the file.

At the end of the using block, C# automatically flushes the StreamWriter, closes it, and closes the FileStream, also flushing any bytes it still contains to the file on disk. Ending the using block also *disposes* the StreamWriter object — see the warning and the technical discussion coming up.

It's a good practice to wrap most work with streams in `using` statements. Wrapping the `StreamWriter` or `StreamReader` in a `using` statement, for example, has the same effect as putting the use of the writer or reader in a `try/finally` exception-handling block. (See Book I for exceptions.) In fact, the compiler translates the `using` block into the same code it uses for a `try/finally`, which guarantees that the resources get cleaned up:

```
try
{
  // Allocate the resource and use it here.
}
finally
{
  // Close and dispose of the resource here.
}
```

After the `using` block, the `StreamWriter` no longer exists, and the `FileStream` object can no longer be accessed. The `fs` *variable* still exists, assuming that you created the stream outside the `using` statement, rather than on the fly like this:

```
using(StreamWriter sw = new StreamWriter(new FileStream(...)) ...
```

Flushing and closing the writer has flushed and closed the stream as well. If you try to carry out operations on the stream, you get an exception telling you that you can't access a closed object. Notice that in the `FileWrite` code earlier in this section I nulled the `FileStream` object, `fs`, after the `using` block to ensure that I won't try to use `fs` again. After that, the `FileStream` object is handed off to the garbage collector.

Book III Chapter 3

Fishing the FileStream

Of course, the file you wrote to disk exists. Create and open a new file stream to the file if you need to work with it again.

Specifically, `using` is aimed at managing cleanup of objects that implement the `IDisposable` interface (see Book II for information on interfaces). The `using` statement ensures that the object's `Dispose()` method gets called. Classes that implement `IDisposable` guarantee that they have a `Dispose()` method. `IDisposable` is mainly about disposing non-.NET resources, mainly stuff in the outside world of the Windows operating system, such as file handles and graphics resources. `FileStream`, for example, wraps a Windows file handle that must be released, which is why I mention `IDisposable` here. (Many classes and `structs` implement `IDisposable`; your classes can too, if necessary.)

I don't go into `IDisposable` in this book, but you should plan to become more familiar with it as your C# powers grow. Implementing it correctly has to do with the kind of indeterminate garbage disposal that I mention briefly in Book II and can be complex. So `using` is for use with classes and `structs` that implement `IDisposable`, something that you can check in Help. *It won't help you with just any old kind of object.* ***Note:*** The intrinsic C# types — `int`, `double`, `char`, and such — do *not* implement `IDisposable`. Class `TextWriter`, the base class for `StreamWriter`, does implement the interface. In Help, that looks like this:

```
public abstract class TextWriter : MarshalByRefObject, IDisposable
```

When in doubt, check Help to see if the classes or `structs` you plan to use implement `IDisposable`.

You can examine a rewritten version of `FileWrite` in the `FileWriteWithUsing` example on the Web. Note that in the rewrite, I had to un-factor the two methods that `Main()` calls, pulling their code back into `Main()` — *inlining* it — before I could introduce the `using` block.

Pulling Them Out of the Stream: Using StreamReader

Writing to a file is cool, but it's sort of worthless if you can't read the file back later. The following `FileRead` program puts the *input* back into the phrase *file I/O.* This program reads a text file like the ones created by `FileWrite` or by Notepad — it's sort of `FileWrite` in reverse (note that I don't use `using` in this one):

```
// FileRead -- Read a text file and write it out to the Console.
using System;
using System.IO;

namespace FileRead
{
  public class Program
  {
    public static void Main(string[] args)
    {
      // You need a file reader object.
      StreamReader sr = null;
      string fileName = "";

      try
      {
        // Get a filename from the user.
        sr = GetReaderForFile(fileName);

        // Read the contents of the file.
        ReadFileToConsole(sr);
      }
      catch (IOException ioErr)
      {
        //TODO: Before release, replace this with a more user friendly message.
        Console.WriteLine("{0}\n\n", ioErr.Message);
      }
      finally  // Clean up.
      {
```

```
      if (sr != null) // Guard against trying to Close()a null object.
      {
        sr.Close();   // Takes care of flush as well
        sr = null;
      }
    }

    // Wait for user to acknowledge the results.
    Console.WriteLine("Press Enter to terminate...");
    Console.Read();
  }

  // GetReaderForFile -- Open the file and return a StreamReader for it.
  private static StreamReader GetReaderForFile(string fileName)
  {
    StreamReader sr;
    // Enter input filename.
    Console.Write("Enter the name of a text file to read:");
    fileName = Console.ReadLine();

    // User didn't enter anything; throw an exception
    // to indicate that this is not acceptable.
    if (fileName.Length == 0)
    {
      throw new IOException("You need to enter a filename.");
    }

    // Got a name -- open a file stream for reading; don't create the
    // file if it doesn't already exist.
    FileStream fs = File.Open(fileName, FileMode.Open, FileAccess.Read);

    // Wrap a StreamReader around the stream -- this will use
    // the first three bytes of the file to indicate the
    // encoding used (but not the language).
    sr = new StreamReader(fs, true);
    return sr;
  }

  // ReadFileToConsole -- Read lines from the file represented
  //    by sr and write them out to the console.
  private static void ReadFileToConsole(StreamReader sr)
  {
    Console.WriteLine("\nContents of file:");
            // Read one line at a time.
            while(true)
            {
              // Read a line.
              string input = sr.ReadLine();

              // Quit when you don't get anything back.
              if (input == null)
              {
                break;
              }

              // Write whatever you read to the console.
              Console.WriteLine(input);
            }
  }
 }
}
```

Recall that the current directory that FileRead uses is the \bin\Debug subdirectory under your FileRead project (not the \bin\Debug directory under the FileWrite program's directory, which is where you used FileWrite to create some test files in the preceding section). Before you run FileRead to try it out, place any plain text file (.TXT extension) in FileRead's \bin\Debug directory and note its name so you can open it. A copy of the TestFile1.txt file created in the FileWrite example would be good.

In FileRead, the user reads one and only one file. The user must enter a valid filename for the program to output. No second chances. After the program has read the file, it quits. If the user wants to peek into a second file, she'll have to run the program again. That's a design choice you might make differently.

The program starts out with all of its serious code wrapped in an exception handler. In the try block, this handler tries to call two methods, first to get a StreamReader for the file and then to read the file and dump its lines to the console. In the event of an exception, the catch block writes the exception message. Finally, whether the exception occurred or not, the finally block makes sure the stream and its file are closed and the variable sr is nulled so the garbage collector can reclaim it (see Book II). I/O exceptions could occur in either method called from the try block. These percolate up to Main() looking for a handler. (No need for exception handlers in the methods.)

Note the //TODO: comment in the catch block. This is a reminder to make the message more user-friendly before releasing the program. Comments marked this way appear in the Visual Studio Task List window. In that window, select Comments from the drop-down list at the upper left. Double-click an item there to open the editor to that comment in the code.

Because the variable sr is used inside an exception block, you have to set it to null initially — otherwise, the compiler complains about using an uninitialized variable in the exception block. Likewise, check whether sr is already (or still) null before trying to call its Close() method. Better still, convert the program to use using.

Within the GetReaderForFile() method, the program gives the user one chance to enter a filename. If the name of the file entered at the console is nothing but a blank, the program throws its own error message: You need to enter a filename. If the filename isn't empty, it's used to open a FileStream object in read mode. The File.Open() call here is the same as the one used in FileWrite:

- The first argument is the name of the file.
- The second argument is the file mode. The mode FileMode.Open says, "Open the file if it exists, and throw an exception if it doesn't." The other option is OpenNew, which creates a zero-length file if the file doesn't exist. Personally, I never saw the need for that mode (who wants to read from an empty file?), but each to his own is what I say.

✦ The final argument indicates that I want to read from this `FileStream`. The other alternatives are `Write` and `ReadWrite`. (It would also seem a bit odd to open a file with `FileRead` using the `Write` mode, don't you think?)

The resulting `FileStream` object `fs` is then wrapped in a `StreamReader` object `sr` to provide convenient methods for accessing the text file. The `StreamReader` is finally passed back to `Main()` for use.

When the file-open process is done, the `FileRead` program calls the `ReadFileToConsole()` method, which loops through the file reading lines of text using the `ReadLine()` call. The program echoes each line to the console with the ubiquitous `Console.WriteLine()` call before heading back up to the top of the loop to read another line of text. The `ReadLine()` call returns a `null` when the program reaches the end of the file. When this happens, the method breaks out of the `read` loop and then returns. `Main()` then closes the object and terminates. (You might say that the reading part of this reader program is wrapped within a `while` loop inside a method that's in a `try` block wrapped in an enigma.)

The `catch` block in `Main()` exists to keep the exception from propagating up the food chain and aborting the program. If the program throws an exception, I have the `catch` block write a message and then simply swallow (ignore) the error. You're in `Main()`, so there's nowhere to rethrow the exception to and nothing to do but close the stream and close up shop. The `catch` is there to let the user know why the program failed and to prevent an unhandled exception. You could have the program loop back up and ask for a different filename, but this program is so small that it's simpler to let the user run it again.

Providing an exception handler with a `catch` block that swallows the exception keeps a program from aborting over an unimportant error. However, use this technique and swallow the exception only if an error would be truly, no fake, nondamaging. See the more extensive discussion in Book II.

Here are a few sample runs:

```
Enter the name of a text file to read:yourfile.txt
Could not find file 'C:\C#Programs\FileRead\bin\Debug\yourfile.txt'.

Press Enter to terminate...

Enter the name of a text file to read:
You need to enter a filename.

Pres Enter to terminate...

Enter the name of a text file to read:myfile.txt

Contents of file:
Dave?
What are you doing, Dave?
Press Enter to terminate...
```

For an example of reading arbitrary *bytes* from a file — which could be either binary or text — see the `LoopThroughFiles` example in Book I, Chapter 7. The program actually loops through all files in a target directory, reading each file and dumping its contents to the console, so it gets tedious if there are lots of files. Feel free to terminate it by pressing Ctrl+C or by clicking the console window's close box. See the discussion of `BinaryReader` in the next section.

More Readers and Writers

Earlier in this chapter, I show you the `StreamReader` and `StreamWriter` classes that you'll probably use for the bulk of your I/O needs. However, .NET also makes several other reader/writer pairs available:

- **`BinaryReader/BinaryWriter`:** A pair of stream classes that contain methods for reading and writing each value type: `ReadChar()`, `WriteChar()`, `ReadByte()`, `WriteByte()`, and so on. (These classes are a little more primitive: They don't offer `ReadLine()`/`WriteLine()` methods.) The classes are useful for reading or writing an object in binary (nonhuman-readable) format, as opposed to text. You can use an array of `byte`s to work with the binary data as raw bytes. For example, you may need to read or write the bytes that make up a bitmap graphics file.

  Experiment: Open a file with a .EXE extension using Notepad. You may see some readable text in the window, but most of it looks like some sort of garbage. That's binary data.

  The article "Converting Between Byte and Char Arrays" on my Web site gives you a brief tour of working with arrays of `byte`s or `char`s. Book II includes an example, mentioned earlier, that reads binary data. The example uses a `BinaryReader` with a `FileStream` object to read chunks of bytes from a file and then writes out the data on the console in hexadecimal (base 16) notation, which I explain in that chapter. Although it wraps a `FileStream` in the more convenient `BinaryReader`, that example could just as easily have used the `FileStream` itself. The reads are identical. While the `BinaryReader` brings nothing to the table in that example, I used it there to provide an example of this reader. The example does illustrate reading raw bytes into a *buffer* (an array big enough to hold the bytes read).

- **`StringReader/StringWriter`:** And now for something a little more exotic: simple reader and writer classes that are limited to reading and writing `string`s. They let you treat a `string` like a file, an alternative to accessing a `string`'s characters in the usual ways, such as with a `foreach` loop

  ```
  foreach(char c in someString) { Console.Write(c); }
  ```

  or with array-style bracket notation (`[ ]`)

  ```
  char c = someString[3];
  ```

or with String methods like Split(), Concatenate(), and IndexOf(). With StringReader/StringWriter, you read from and write to a string much as you would to a file. This technique is useful for long strings with hundreds or thousands of characters that you want to process in bunches, and it provides a handy way to work with a StringBuilder.

When you create a StringReader, you initialize it with a string to read. When you create a StringWriter, you can pass a StringBuilder object to it or create it empty. Internally, the StringWriter stores a StringBuilder — either the one you passed to its constructor or a new, empty one. You can get at the internal StringBuilder's contents by calling StringWriter's ToString() method.

Each time you read from the string (or write to it), the "file pointer" advances to the next available character past the read or write. Thus, as with file I/O, you have the notion of a "current position." When you read, say, 10 characters from a 1,000-character string, the position is set to the eleventh character after the read.

The methods in these classes parallel those described earlier for the StreamReader and StreamWriter classes. If you can use those, you can use these.

The StringReadingAndWriting example on the Web illustrates using StringReader and StringWriter, including a few quirks to watch for.

Exploring More Streams than Lewis and Clark

I should mention, before meandering on, that file streams are not the only kinds of Stream classes available. The flood of Stream classes includes (but probably is not limited to) those in the following list. Note that unless I specify otherwise, these stream classes all live in the System.IO namespace.

- **FileStream:** For reading and writing files on a disk.

- **MemoryStream:** Manages reading and writing data to a block of memory. I use this technique sometimes in unit tests, to avoid actually interacting with the (slow, possibly troublesome) file system. In this way, I can "fake" a file when testing code that reads and writes. See my Web site for an illustration of this technique. (I'll leave a breadcrumb there.) And see some brief notes on MemoryStream on the Web, in the MemoryStreamSpike example.

  Note that the StringReader/StringWriter classes discussed in the preceding section can be useful in unit testing in much the same way as with MemoryStream. I prefer StringReader/StringWriter for that purpose. The StringReadingAndWriting example on the Web illustrates the technique with some simple unit tests.

- **`BufferedStream`:** *Buffering* is a technique for speeding up input/output operations by reading or writing bigger chunks of data at a time. Lots of small reads or writes mean lots of slow disk access — but if you read a much bigger chunk than you need now, you can then continue to read your small chunks out of the buffer — which is far faster than reading the disk. When a `BufferedStream`'s underlying buffer runs out of data, it reads in another big chunk — maybe even the whole file. Buffered writing is similar.

  Class `FileStream` automatically buffers its operations, so `BufferedStream` is for special cases, such as working with a `NetworkStream` to read and write bytes over a network. In this case, you wrap the `BufferedStream` around the `NetworkStream`, effectively "chaining" streams. When you write to the `BufferedStream`, it writes to the underlying `NetworkStream`, and so on.

  When you're wrapping one stream around another, you're *composing streams.* (You can look it up in the Help index for more information.) I discuss wrapping in the earlier sidebar "Wrap my fish in newspaper."

- **`NetworkStream`:** Manages reading and writing data over a network. See `BufferedStream` for a simplified discussion of using it. `NetworkStream` is in the `System.Net.Sockets` namespace because it uses a technology called *sockets* to make connections across a network.

- **`UnmanagedMemoryStream`:** Lets you read and write data in "unmanaged" blocks of memory. *Unmanaged* means, basically, "not .NET" and not managed by the .NET runtime and its garbage collector. This is advanced stuff, dealing with interaction between .NET code and code written under the Windows operating system.

- **`CryptoStream`:** Located in the `System.Security.Cryptography` namespace, this stream class lets you pass data to and from an encryption or decryption transformation. I'm sure you'll use it daily. I know I do.

Chapter 4: Accessing the Internet

In This Chapter

- **Taking a tour of the `System.Net` namespace**
- **Using built-in tools to access the network**
- **Making the network tools work for you**

In my opinion, the reason that Microsoft had to create the .NET Framework in the first place was the lack of Internet interoperability within the existing infrastructure. COM just couldn't handle the Internet. The Internet works differently than most platforms, such as PCs. The Internet is based on *protocols* — carefully defined and agreed upon ways to get things like mail and file transfers working. Microsoft's environment before 2002 distinctly didn't handle those as well.

As you can see throughout this book, the .NET Framework is designed from the ground up to take the Internet and networking in general into consideration. Not surprisingly, that is nowhere more clear than it is in the `System.Net` namespace. The Internet takes first chair here, with Web tools taking up nine of the classes in the namespace.

In this fourth version of the framework, even more Internet functionality is baked in. Although in version one the focus was on tools used to build other tools (low-level functions), now it contains features that are useful to you, such as Web, mail, and File Transfer Protocol (FTP). Secure Sockets Layer — the Internet's transport security — is much easier to use in this version, as are FTP and mail, which previously required other, harder-to-use classes.

`System.Net` is a big, meaty namespace, and finding your way around it can be difficult. My goal for this chapter is to take things that you do often and show the basics, and then give you the tools to research the more complex features of the classes.

Networking is a big part of the .NET Framework, and all the functionality is in this namespace — a whole book can be (and has been) written on the subject. For the purposes of this introduction to networking with C#, I show you these features:

- Getting a file from the network
- Sending e-mail

- Logging transfers
- Checking the status of the network around your running application

Keep in mind that I am not saying that sockets and IPv6 and other advanced Internet protocols aren't important. This chapter talks about the parts of the namespace that you will use every day. As always, there is more to learn about `System.Net`.

Getting to Know System.Net

The `System.Net` namespace is full of classes that are confusing if viewed in the documentation but make a lot of sense when used in an application. The namespace removes all the complexity of dealing with the various protocols used on the Internet.

There are more than 2,000 RFCs for Internet protocols (an *RFC* is a Request For Comments, a document that is sent to a standards body for review by peers before it becomes a standard), and if you have to learn all of them separately, you will never complete your project. The `System.Net` namespace is about making it less painful.

`System.Net` is not just for Web projects. Like everything else in the base class library, you can use `System.Net` with all kinds of projects. You can

- Get information from Web pages on the Internet and use them on your programs.
- Move files via the Internet using FTPs.
- Send e-mail easily.
- Use more advanced network structures.
- Secure communications over the Internet using the SSL protocol.

If you need to check on the connectivity of a computer from a Windows application, you can use `System.Net`. If you need to build a class that will download a file from a Web site, `System.Net` is the namespace you need. Just because most classes relate to the Internet doesn't mean that only Web applications can use it. That's the magic of `System.Net`. Any application can be a connected application. While some parts of the namespace function to make the development of Web applications easier, the namespace in general is designed to make any application work with the Web.

How Net Classes Fit into the Framework

The System.Net namespace contains 62 classes and six smaller namespaces. Even as I write this, I am overwhelmed. However, if you look closely, you can see patterns.

If you need help using classes, you can find more information in Book II.

The classes are well named, and you will note that a few protocols get a number of classes each. After you translate, you can narrow down what you need based on the way the protocol is named:

- `Authentication` and `Authorization`: These classes provide security.
- `Cookie`: This class manages cookies from Web browsers and usually is used in ASP.NET pages.
- `DNS` (Domain Name Services): These classes help to resolve domain names into IP addresses.
- `Download`: This class is used to get files from servers.
- `EndPoint`: This class helps to define a network node.
- `FileWeb`: This brilliant set of classes describes network file servers as local classes.
- `FtpWeb`: This class is a simple File Transfer Protocol implementation.
- `Http` (HyperText Transfer Protocol): This class is the Web protocol.
- `IP` (Internet Protocol): This class helps to define network endpoints that are specifically Internet related.
- `IrDA`: This class is an infrared endpoint. Infrared ports are networks too!
- `NetworkCredential`: This class is another security implementation.
- `Service`: This class helps manage network connections.
- `Socket`: This class deals with the most primitive of network connections.
- `Upload`: This set of classes helps you upload information to the Internet.
- `Web`: These classes help with the World Wide Web — largely implementations of the `http` classes that are more task oriented.

This list is extensive because the classes build on each other. The `EndPoint` classes are used by the `socket` classes to define certain network specifics, and the `IP` classes make them specific to the Internet. The `Web` classes are specific to the World Wide Web. You will rarely use highest-level classes, but it's often tough to see what is needed when.

Most of the functions that you use every day, though, are encapsulated within seven mostly new namespaces under the `System.Net` namespace:

- `Cache`: This function has a lot of enumerators that manage the browser and network caching functions built into the namespace.
- `Configuration`: This function grants access to the properties that you need to set to make many of the other `System.Net` classes work.
- `Mail`: This function takes over for `System.Web.Mail` to facilitate the sending of Internet e-mail.
- `Mime`: This function bundles file attachments with the `Mail` namespace.
- `NetworkInformation`: This function gets details about the network around your application.
- `Security`: This function implements the network security managed by many classes of `System.Net`.
- `Sockets`: This function utilizes the most basic network connections available to Windows.

Using the System.Net Namespace

The `System.Net` namespace is *code-oriented,* which means that few implementations are specifically for user interfaces. Most everything that you do with these classes is behind the scenes. You have few drag-and-drop user controls — the `System.Net` namespace is used in the Code View.

To demonstrate this, in the rest of this chapter, I go over building a Windows Forms application that has the following requirements:

- Check the network status.
- Get a specific file from the Internet.
- E-mail it to a specific e-mail address.
- Log the whole transaction.

This is not an insignificant set of requirements. In fact, even in the 1.0 and 1.1 versions of C#, this would be difficult. One of the main goals of the `System.Net` namespace in this version is to make common tasks much easier. You can start by loading the sample code or by starting a new project and following the steps in the following sections.

Checking the network status

First, you need to inform the user about network connectivity by following these steps:

1. **Create a new Windows Forms Application project in Visual Studio.**

   I called mine `NetworkTools`.

2. **Add a `StatusStrip` control to the form by dragging it from the Toolbox.**

3. **Select the SmartTag that appears and add a `StatusLabel`.**

4. **Double-click the form to get the `Form_Load` event handler and move to Code View.**

5. **Reference the `System.Net` namespace by adding the line `using System.NET.NetworkInformation;` to the top of the code.**

6. **Add the code in bold from the following listing to test whether the network is available and display it on the status bar:**

```
using System;
using System.Collections.Generic;
using System.ComponentModel;
using System.Data;
using System.Drawing;
using System.Linq;
using System.Text;
using System.Windows.Forms;
using System.Net.NetworkInformation;

namespace NetworkTools
{
    public partial class Form1 : Form
    {
        public Form1()
        {
            InitializeComponent();
        }

        private void Form1_Load(object sender, EventArgs e)
        {
            if (NetworkInterface.GetIsNetworkAvailable())
            {
                toolStripStatusLabel1.Text = "Connected";
            }
            else
            {
                toolStripStatusLabel1.Text = "Disconnected";
            }

        }
    }
}
```

That's all there is to it. The `NetworkInformation` class contains a bunch of information about the status of the network, current IP addresses, the gateway being used by the current machine, and more.

Keep in mind that the `NetworkInformation` class will work only on a local machine. If you use this class in an ASP.NET Web Forms application, you will get information about the server.

Downloading a file from the Internet

You can get a file from the Internet in one of several ways, and one of the most common is by using FTP. The lightweight FTP protocol is favored because it's secure and supported on many systems.

To build an application that uses FTP, follow these steps:

1. **Drag a button onto the form from the Toolbox.**
2. **Double-click the button to get the** `Click` **event handler.**
3. **Add the required imports,** `System.Net`**,** `System.Net.Mail`**, and** `System.IO` **to the top of the code.**
4. **Create a new subroutine called** `Download File` **that accepts a remote filename and a local filename as strings.**
5. **In the new subroutine, create a new** `FileStream` **(called** `local FileStream`**) and** `FTPWebRequest` **(called** `ftpRequest`**), as shown in Listing 4-1.**

   The `FileStream` references a local file and accepts the local file that is passed into the subroutine. The `FtpWebRequest` is the same thing for the remote file.
6. **Set the** `Method` **parameter of the** `FtpWebRequest` **to** `WebRequest Methods.Ftp.Downloadfile`**.**
7. **Set the** `Credentials` **property of the** `FtpWebRequest` **to a new** `NetworkCredential` **with anonymous information, like I did in Listing 4-1.**
8. **Create a new** `WebResponse` **object from the** `ftpRequest` **method. This gets the statement back from the FTP server about how your request will be handled.**
9. **Get the** `Stream` **from the** `Response` **object.**
10. **Read the file into a 1024-byte buffer, one block at a time, using a** `While` **loop, as shown at the end of Listing 4-1.**

11. **Call the** `DownloadFile` **method from the** `Button1_Click` **event handler, like I show in this chunk of code:**

```
private void button1_Click(object sender, EventArgs e)
    DownloadFile(@"ftp://ftp.csharpfordummies.net/sampleFile.bmp", @"c:\
    sampleFile.bmp");
End Sub
```

Listing 4-1: The DownloadFile Method

```
private void DownLoadFile(string remoteFile, string localFile)
{
    FileStream localFileStream = new FileStream(localFile, FileMode.
OpenOrCreate);
    FtpWebRequest ftpRequest = (FtpWebRequest)WebRequest.
Create(remoteFile);
    ftpRequest.Method = WebRequestMethods.Ftp.DownloadFile;
    ftpRequest.Credentials = new NetworkCredential("Anonymous", "bill@
sempf.net");
    WebResponse ftpResponse = ftpRequest.GetResponse();
    Stream ftpResponseStream = ftpResponse.GetResponseStream();
    byte[] buffer = new byte[1024];
    int bytesRead = ftpResponseStream.Read(buffer, 0, 1024);
    while (bytesRead > 0)
    {
        localFileStream.Write(buffer, 0, bytesRead);
        bytesRead = ftpResponseStream.Read(buffer, 0, 1024);
    }
    localFileStream.Close();
    ftpResponseStream.Close();
}
```


This FTP example is watered down, but it makes my point. The `WebRequest` and `WebResponse` classes in the `System.Net` namespace are fully utilized to create the more complete `FtpWebRequest`, for instance. Properties like the `Method` of download and `Credentials` make it an easy call.

In fact, the toughest part of this process is dealing with a `FileStream` object, which is still the best way to move files and not specific to the `System.Net` namespace. Streams are discussed in Chapter 3 of this minibook, which covers the `System.IO` namespace, but they have significance to the network classes too. Streams represent a flow of data of some kind, and a flow of information from the Internet qualifies.

That's what you are doing when you get a Web page or a file from the Internet — gathering a flow of data. If you think about it, it makes sense that this is a flow, because the status bar in an application shows a percentage of completion. Just like pouring water into a glass, the flow of data is a stream, so the concept is named `Stream`.

This concept holds true for getting a file from the World Wide Web, as well. HTTP, the Web protocol, is just another protocol that defines how a document is moved from a server on the Internet to your local machine. In fact, the code looks strikingly similar to the FTP example, as you can see in the following bit of code. The same stream is recovered; only the formatting is different.

```
private void DownLoadWebFile(string remoteFile, string localFile)
{
    FileStream localFileStream = new FileStream(localFile, FileMode.
    OpenOrCreate);
    WebRequest webRequest = WebRequest.Create(remoteFile);
    webRequest.Method = WebRequestMethods.Http.Get;
    WebResponse webResponse = webRequest.GetResponse();
    Stream webResponseStream = webResponse.GetResponseStream();
    byte[] buffer = new byte[1024];
    int bytesRead = webResponseStream.Read(buffer, 0, 1024);
    while (bytesRead > 0)
    {
        localFileStream.Write(buffer, 0, bytesRead);
        bytesRead = webResponseStream.Read(buffer, 0, 1024);
    }
    localFileStream.Close();
    webResponseStream.Close();
}
```

You need to pass in a Web address, so your subroutine call looks like this:

```
DownloadWebFile(@"http://www.csharpfordummies.net/sampleFile.bmp", @"c:\
    sampleFile.bmp");
```

Note the changes, marked as bold. `webRequest` is now a `WebRequest` rather than an `FtpWebRequest`. Also, the `Method` property of `webRequest` has been changed to `WebRequestMethods.Http.Get`. Finally, the `Credentials` property has been removed because the credentials are no longer required.

E-mailing a status report

E-mail is a common requirement of networked systems. If you are working in an enterprise environment, you are going to write a larger scale application to handle all e-mail requirements, rather than make each individual application e-mail-aware.

However, if you are writing a standalone product, it might require e-mail support. Because I happen to be writing a standalone application, that is exactly what I'm going to do.

E-mail is a server-based operation, so if you don't have an e-mail server that you can use to send from, this might be hard. Many ISPs no longer allow *relaying,* which is sending an outgoing message without first having an account and logging in. Therefore, you might have trouble running this part of the sample.

If you are in a corporate environment, however, you can usually talk to your e-mail administrator and get permission to use the e-mail server. Because outgoing requests are usually only harnessed inside the firewall, relaying is often available. To build your e-mail function, follow these steps:

1. **Add a text box to the default form in Design View, and then change to Code View.**

   At the top of Code View, make sure that you have referenced the `System.Net.Mail` namespace.

2. **Create a new subroutine called** `SendEmail`**.**

   It should accept the from e-mail address, the to e-mail address, the subject of the e-mail, and the body of the e-mail.

3. **Declare a new** `MailMessage` **and pass in the** `fromAddress`**,** `toAddress`**,** `subject`**, and** `body` **parameters, like this:**

   ```
   MailMessage message = New MailMessage(fromAddress,
       toAddress, subject, body);
   ```

4. **Declare a new** `SmtpClient` **and pass in the address of your mail server.**

   This can be an IP address, machine name, or URL.

5. **Use the** `Send` **method of the** `SmtpClient` **object you created to send the** `MailMessage`**, which is passed in as a parameter.**

6. **When you're finished, make sure that you set the values of the** `MailMessage` **and** `SmtpClient` **to** `Nothing`**, because they do take up resources.**

Listing 4-2 shows the completed subroutine.

Listing 4-2: The SendEmail Subroutine

```
private void SendEmail(string fromAddress, string toAddress, string subject,
    string body)
{
    MailMessage message = new MailMessage(fromAddress, toAddress, subject, body);
    SmtpClient mailClient = new SmtpClient("localhost");
    mailClient.Send(message);
    message = null;
    mailClient = null;
}
```

Notice that I used `localhost` as the e-mail server name. If you have an e-mail server software installed locally, even IIS 6.0 with SMTP, this will work. Most of the time, you will have to put another e-mail server name in the `SmtpClient` constructor. The e-mail server name can often be found in your Outlook preferences.

After you have written your method, you need to call it after the file is downloaded in the `Button1_Click` event handler. Change the code of that subroutine to the following to call that method:

```
private void button1_Click(object sender, EventArgs e)
{
    DownloadFile(@"ftp://ftp.csharpfordummies.net/sampleFile.bmp", @"c:\
    sampleFile.bmp");
    SendEmail(textBox1.Text, textBox1.Text, "FTP Successful", "FTP Successfully
    downloaded");
}
```

Notice that I sent in the value of the text box twice: once for the to address, and once for the from address. This isn't always necessary, because you may have a situation where you want the e-mail to come only from a Webmaster address or to go only to your address.

You should have enough code in place to run the application now. Press F5 to launch the application in debug mode and give it a try.

When you click the button, the application should download the file to the local drive and then e-mail you to inform you that the download is complete. A host of things can go wrong with network applications, though, and you should be aware of them. Here are a few:

- For most network activity, the machine running the software must be connected to a network. This isn't a problem for you as the developer, but you need to be conscious of the end users, who may need connectivity to have access to the features they want to use. Use of the network status code can help inform users about the availability of those features.
- Firewalls and other network appliances sometimes block network traffic from legitimate applications. Some examples of this include:
    - FTP is often blocked from corporate networks.
    - Network analysis features of .NET are often blocked on corporate servers. If the server is available to the public, these openings can cause holes for hackers to crawl through.
    - Speaking of hackers, make sure that if you use incoming network features in your application, you have adequately secured your application. More on this can be found in the excellent book *Writing Secure Code,* Second Edition, by Michael Howard and David C. LeBlanc (published by Microsoft Press).
    - E-mail is especially fragile. Often, Internet service providers will block e-mail from an address that is not registered on a mail server. This means that if you are using your localhost server (like in the example in Listing 4-2), your ISP might block the e-mail.

✦ Network traffic is notoriously hard to debug. For instance, if the sample application works, but you never receive an e-mail from the `SmtpServer` you coded, what went wrong? You may never know. XML Web services (covered in Book VII) have a similar problem — it's spectacularly tough to see the actual code in the *SOAP envelope* (markup added around requests for Web services) to tell what went wrong.

Logging network activity

This brings you to the next topic, which is network logging. Because network activity problems are so hard to debug and reproduce, Microsoft has built in several tools for the management of tracing network activity.

What's more, like the ASP.NET tracing available, the `System.Net` namespace tracing is completely managed using the configuration files. To be able to use the functions, therefore, you don't need to change and recompile your code. In fact, with a little management, you can even show debug information to the user by managing the `config` files your application uses.

Each kind of application has a different kind of configuration file. For Windows Forms applications, which you are using here, the file is called `app.config` and is stored in the development project directory. When you compile, the name of the file is changed to the name of the application, and it's copied into the `bin` directory for running.

If you open your `app.config` file now, you see that it already contains some diagnostic information, as shown in Listing 4-3. You will add some information to it.

Listing 4-3: The Default app.config File

```
<?xml version="1.0" encoding="utf-8" ?>
<configuration>
    <system.diagnostics>
        <sources>
            <!-- This section defines the logging configuration for
    My.Application.Log in Windows Forms projects.-->
            <source name="Microsoft.VisualBasic.Logging.Log.WindowsFormsSource"
    switchName="DefaultSwitch">
                <listeners>
                    <add name="FileLog"/>
                    <!-- Uncomment the below section to write to the Application
    Event Log -->
                    <!--<add name="EventLog"/>-->
                </listeners>
            </source>
        </sources>
        <switches>
            <add name="DefaultSwitch" value="Information" />
        </switches>
```

```
        <sharedListeners>
            <add name="FileLog"
                 type="Microsoft.VisualBasic.Logging.FileLogTraceListener,
    Microsoft.VisualBasic, Version=8.0.0.0, Culture=neutral, PublicKeyToken=b03f
    5f7f11d50a3a, processorArchitecture=MSIL"
                 initializeData="FileLogWriter"/>
            <!-- Uncomment the below section and replace APPLICATION_NAME with
    the name of your application to write to the Application Event Log -->
            <!--<add name="EventLog" type="System.Diagnostics.
    EventLogTraceListener" initializeData="APPLICATION_NAME"/> -->
        </sharedListeners>
    </system.diagnostics>
</configuration>
```

First, you need to add a new source for the `System.Net` namespace. Next, you add a switch to the `Switches` section for the source you added. Finally, you add a `SharedListener` to that section and set the file to flush the tracing information automatically.

The finished `app.config` file, with the adds in bold, is shown in Listing 4-4. It's also in the sample code on this book's companion Web site.

Listing 4-4: The Finished app.config File

```
<?xml version="1.0" encoding="utf-8" ?>
<configuration>
    <system.diagnostics>
        <sources>
            <source name="Microsoft.VisualBasic.Logging.Log.WindowsFormsSource"
    switchName="DefaultSwitch">
                <listeners>
                    <add name="FileLog"/>
                </listeners>
            </source>
            <source name="System.Net">
                <listeners>
                    <add name="System.Net"/>
                </listeners>
            </source>
        </sources>
        <switches>
            <add name="DefaultSwitch" value="Information" />
            <add name="System.Net" value="Verbose" />
        </switches>
        <sharedListeners>
            <add name="FileLog"
                 type="Microsoft.VisualBasic.Logging.FileLogTraceListener,
    Microsoft.VisualBasic, Version=8.0.0.0, Culture=neutral, PublicKeyToken=b03f
    5f7f11d50a3a, processorArchitecture=MSIL"
                 initializeData="FileLogWriter"/>
            <add name="System.Net"
                 type="System.Diagnostics.TextWriterTraceListener"
                 initializeData="my.log"/>
        </sharedListeners>
        <trace autoflush="true" />
    </system.diagnostics>
</configuration>
```

Run the application again and watch the Output window. Advanced logging information is shown there because of your changes to the configuration file. Additionally, a log file was written. In the development environment, this is in the bin/debug directory of your project. You might have to click the Show All Files button at the top of the Solution Explorer to see it.

In that folder, you should see the file named `my.log`, where the `Shared Listener` you added to the `app.config` file directed the logging information. My copy of that file is shown in Listing 4-5 — your mileage may vary.

Listing 4-5: The Log Information

```
System.Net Information: 0 : WebRequest::Create(ftp://ftp.csharpfordummies.net/
    sample.bmp)
System.Net Information: 0 : Exiting WebRequest::Create() ->
    FtpWebRequest#37460558
System.Net Information: 0 : FtpWebRequest#37460558::GetResponse()
System.Net Information: 0 : Exiting FtpWebRequest#37460558::GetResponse()
System.Net Information: 0 : Associating Message#59487907 with
    HeaderCollection#23085090
System.Net Information: 0 : HeaderCollection#23085090::Set(mime-version=1.0)
System.Net Information: 0 : Associating MailMessage#6964596 with Message#59487907
System.Net Information: 0 : SmtpClient::.ctor(host=24.123.157.3)
System.Net Information: 0 : Associating SmtpClient#17113003 with
    SmtpTransport#30544512
System.Net Information: 0 : Exiting SmtpClient::.ctor()        ->
    SmtpClient#17113003
System.Net Information: 0 : SmtpClient#17113003::Send(MailMessage#6964596)
System.Net Information: 0 : SmtpClient#17113003::Send(DeliveryMethod=Network)
System.Net Information: 0 : Associating SmtpClient#17113003 with
    MailMessage#6964596
System.Net Information: 0 : Associating SmtpTransport#30544512 with
    SmtpConnection#44365459
System.Net Information: 0 : Associating SmtpConnection#44365459 with
    ServicePoint#7044526
System.Net Information: 0 : Associating SmtpConnection#44365459 with
    SmtpPooledStream#20390146
System.Net Information: 0 : HeaderCollection#30689639::Set(content-transfer-
    encoding=base64)
System.Net Information: 0 : HeaderCollection#30689639::Set(content-transfer-
    encoding=quoted-printable)
System.Net Information: 0 : HeaderCollection#23085090::Remove(x-receiver)
System.Net Information: 0 : HeaderCollection#23085090::Set(from=bill@sempf.net)
System.Net Information: 0 : HeaderCollection#23085090::Set(to=bill@sempf.net)
System.Net Information: 0 : HeaderCollection#23085090::Set(date=1 Apr 2010
    16:32:32 -0500)
System.Net Information: 0 : HeaderCollection#23085090::Set(subject=FTP
    Successful)
System.Net Information: 0 : HeaderCollection#23085090::Get(mime-version)
System.Net Information: 0 : HeaderCollection#23085090::Get(from)
System.Net Information: 0 : HeaderCollection#23085090::Get(to)
System.Net Information: 0 : HeaderCollection#23085090::Get(date)
System.Net Information: 0 : HeaderCollection#23085090::Get(subject)
System.Net Information: 0 : HeaderCollection#30689639::Get(content-type)
System.Net Information: 0 : HeaderCollection#30689639::Get(content-transfer-
    encoding)
System.Net Information: 0 : Exiting SmtpClient#17113003::Send()
```

Reading this file, you can see that the reference numbers that match the requests on the server all appear, dramatically improving the ease of debugging. Also, because everything is in order of action, finding out exactly where the error occurred in the process is much easier.

Chapter 5: Creating Images

In This Chapter

- **Understanding the `System.Drawing` namespace**
- **Finding out how the drawing classes fit into the .NET Framework**
- **Using `System.Drawing` to create a simple game application**

No one is going to write the next edition of *Bioshock* using C#. It just isn't the kind of language you use to write graphics-intensive applications like shoot-'em-up games.

Still, C# packs a fair amount of power into the `System.Drawing` classes. Though these classes are somewhat primitive in some areas, and using them might cause you to have to write a few more lines of code than you should, there isn't much that these classes can't do with sufficient work.

The drawing capability provided by the .NET Framework is divided into four logical areas by the namespace design provided by Microsoft. All the general drawing capability is in the `System.Drawing` namespace. Then there are some specialized namespaces:

- `System.Drawing.2D` has advanced vector drawing functionality.
- `System.Drawing.Imaging` is mostly about using bitmap graphic formats, like `.bmp` and `.jpg` files.
- `System.Drawing.Text` deals with advanced typography.

In this chapter, I focus on the base namespace and cover only the basics of drawing in C#. (Discussing every aspect of drawing could easily fill an entire book.)

Getting to Know System.Drawing

Even at the highest level, graphics programming consists of drawing polygons, filling them with color, and labeling them with text — all on a canvas of some sort. Unsurprisingly, this leaves you with four objects that form the core of the graphics code you write: graphics, pens, brushes, and text.

Graphics

Generally speaking, the `Graphics` class creates an object that is your palette. It's the canvas. All the methods and properties of the `Graphics` object are designed to make the area you draw upon more appropriate for your needs.

Also, most of the graphics- and image-related methods of other classes in the framework provide the `Graphics` object as output. For instance, you can call the `System.Web.Forms.Control.CreateGraphics` method from a Windows Forms application and get a `Graphics` object back that enables you to draw in a form control in your project. You can also handle the `Paint` event of a form, and check out the `Graphics` property of the event.

`Graphics` objects use pens and brushes (discussed later in this chapter, in the "Pens" and "Brushes" sections) to draw and fill. Graphics objects have methods such as these:

- `DrawRectangle`
- `FillRectangle`
- `DrawCircle`
- `FillCircle`
- `DrawBezier`
- `DrawLine`

These methods accept pens and brushes as parameters. You might think, "How can a circle help me?" but you must remember that even complex graphic objects such as the Covenant in *Halo 3* are made up of circles and rectangles — thousands of them. The trick to useful art is using math to put together lots of circles and squares until you have a complete image. The sample application described later in this chapter is a simple example of just that.

Pens

You use pens to draw lines and curves. Complex graphics are made up of polygons, and those polygons are made of lines, and those lines are generated by pens. Pens have properties such as

- `Color`
- `DashStyle`
- `EndCap`
- `Width`

You get the idea: You use pens to draw things. These properties are used by the pens to determine how things are drawn.

Brushes

Brushes paint the insides of polygons. Though you use the pens to draw the shapes, you use brushes to fill in the shapes with gradients, patterns, or colors. Brushes are usually passed in as parameters to a `Draw`*`Whatever`* method of the pen objects. When the pen draws the shape it was asked to draw, it uses the brush to fill in the shape — just as you did in kindergarten with crayons and coloring books. (The brush object always stays inside the lines, though.)

Don't look for the `Brush` class, however. It's a holding area for the real brushes, which have kind of strange names. Brushes are made to be customized, but you can do a lot with the brushes that come with the framework as is. Some of the brushes include

- `SolidBrush`
- `TextureBrush`
- `HatchBrush`
- `PathGradientBrush`

Although the pens are used to pass into the `Draw` methods of the `Graphics` object, brushes are used to pass into the `Fill` methods that form polygons.

Text

Text is painted with a combination of fonts and brushes. Just like pens, the `Font` class uses brushes to fill in the lines of a text operation.

`System.Drawing.Text` has collections of all the fonts installed in the system running your program, or installed as part of your application. `System.Drawing.Font` has all the properties of the typography, such as

- Bold
- Size
- Style
- Underline

The `Graphics` object, again, provides the writing of the text on the palette.

Printing a form

In VB6, and earlier, one of the most common ways to get information to paper was to print a form. This functionality was lacking in .NET but came back in a Power Pack and now is built into Visual Studio 2008. It's available to all languages, but VB programmers miss it the most.

If you need to build a report, you should use Microsoft Report Viewer, which isn't covered in this book. If you just want to get some text and images to the user's printer, though, the `PrintForm` component should do the trick.

To use the `PrintForm` component, drag it from the Toolbox onto your form in Design View. It will appear in the component tray. In the event handler for your print function (the `MenuItem.Click` function, for instance), set up the Form property of the component, the Print Action, and then call the Print command. It looks like this:

```
using PrintForm printForm = new PrintForm
    .Form =TheFormIWantPrinted
    .PrintAction = PrintToPrinter
    .Print()
end using
```

The form will be sent to the windows Print function, just as though you had used the Print dialog box to print a file.

How the Drawing Classes Fit into the Framework

The `System.Drawing` namespace breaks drawing into two steps:

1. Create a System.Drawing.Graphics object.
2. Use the tools in the System.Drawing namespace to draw on it.

It seems straightforward, and it is. The first step is to get a `Graphics` object. `Graphics` objects come from two main places — existing images and Windows Forms.

To get a `Graphics` object from an existing image, look at the `Bitmap` object. The `Bitmap` object is a great tool that enables you to create an object using an existing image file. This gives you a new palette that is based on a bitmap image (a JPEG file, for example) that is already on your hard drive. It's a convenient tool, especially for Web images.

```
Bitmap currentBitmap = new Bitmap(@"c:\images\myImage.jpg");
Graphics palette = Graphics.FromImage(currentBitmap);
```

Now the object `myPalette` is a `Graphics` object whose height and width are based on the image in `myBitmap`. What's more, the base of the `myPalette` image looks exactly like the image referenced in the `myBitmap` object.

You can use the pens, brushes, and fonts in the `Graphics` class to draw directly on that image, as though it were a blank canvas. I use it to put text on images before I show them on Web pages and to modify the format of images on the fly, too.

Another way to get a `Graphics` object is to get it from Windows Forms. The method you want is `System.Windows.Forms.Control.CreateGraphics`. This method gives you a new palette that is based on the drawing surface of the control being referenced. If it's a form, it inherits the height and width of the form and has the form background color. You can use pens and brushes to draw right on the form.

When you have a `Graphics` object, the options are endless. Sophisticated drawing isn't out of the question, though you would have to do a ton of work to create graphics like you see in *Halo 2* using Visual Studio. (There isn't a Master Chief class that you can just generate automatically.)

Nonetheless, even the most complex 3D graphics are just colored polygons, and you can make those with the `System.Drawing` class. In the following sections, I build a cribbage board with a `Graphics` object, pens, brushes, and fonts.

Using the System.Drawing Namespace

Good applications come from strange places. Gabrielle (my wife) and I enjoy games, and one of our favorites is the card game cribbage. We were on vacation in Disney World when she had the urge to play, but we didn't have a cribbage board. We had cards, but not the board.

However, I did have my laptop, Visual Studio, and the `System.Drawing` namespace. After just an hour or two of work, I built an application that serves as a working cribbage board!

It's shocking, I know, but somehow she still wanted to play me after watching me program for two hours!

This application is fairly complete, and I don't have enough pages to walk you through it step by step. Load the application from this book's Web site, and follow along with the rest of this chapter. This application isn't complex, but it's long.

Getting started

Cribbage is a card game where hands are counted up into points, and the first player to score 121 points wins. It's up to the players to count up the points, and the score is kept on a board.

Cribbage boards are made up of two lines of holes for pegs, usually totaling 120, but sometimes 60 holes are used and you play through twice. Figure 5-1 shows a typical cribbage board. Cribbage boards come in a bunch of styles — check out `www.cribbage.org` if you're curious; it has a great gallery of almost 100 boards, from basic to whimsical.

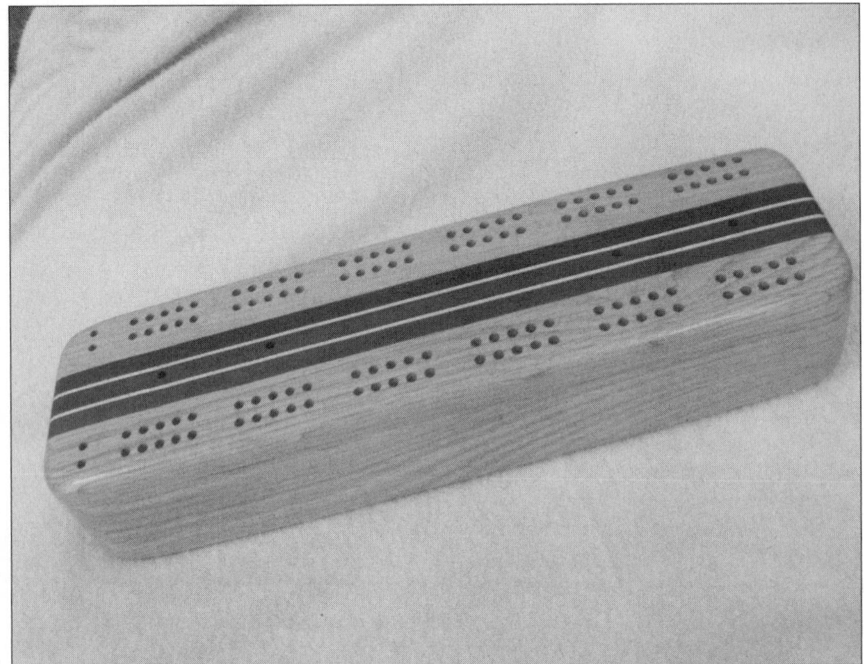

Figure 5-1: A traditional cribbage board.

For this example, I create the board image for an application that keeps score of a cribbage game — but it wouldn't be beyond C# to write the cards into the game too!

So the board for this application has 40 holes on each of three pairs of lines, which is the standard board setup for two players playing to 120, as shown in Figure 5-2. The first task is to draw the board, and then to draw the pegs as the players' scores — entered in text boxes — change.

The premise is this: The players play a hand and enter the resulting scores in the text box below their respective names (refer to Figure 5-2). When the score for each hand is entered, the score next to the player's name is updated, and the peg is moved on the board. The next time that same player scores a hand, the peg is moved forward, and the back peg is moved into its place. Did I mention the back peg? Oh, yes, the inventor of cribbage was paranoid of cheating — if you're unfamiliar with cribbage, you may want to check out the rules at www.cribbage.org.

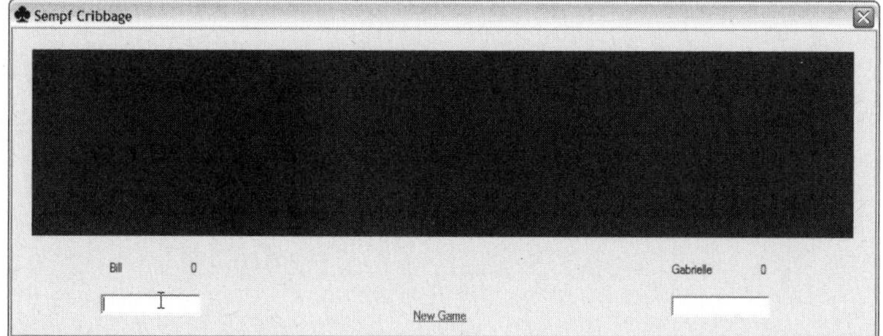

Figure 5-2: The digital cribbage board.

Setting up the project

To begin, create a playing surface. I set up the board shown in Figure 5-2 without drawing the board itself — I show you how to paint it on later with System.Drawing. My board looked a lot like Figure 5-3 when I was ready to start with the business rules.

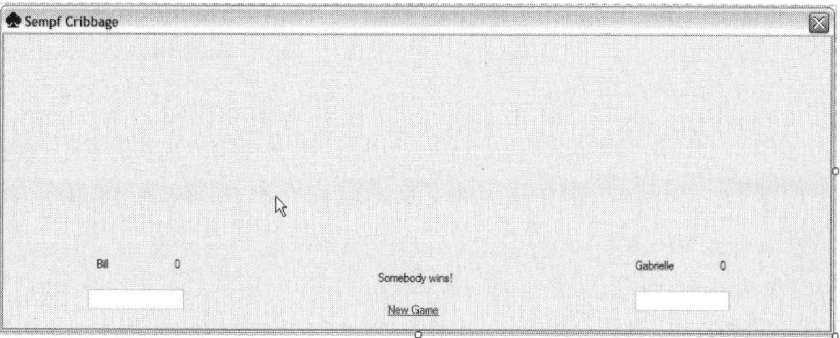

Figure 5-3: The basic board.

I used a little subroutine to handle score changes by calling it from the two text boxes' OnChange events. Here's the code that calls the subroutine:

```
private void HandleScore(TextBox scoreBox, Label points, Label otherPlayer)
{
    try {
        if (0 > (int)scoreBox.Text | (int)scoreBox.Text > 27) {
            ScoreCheck.SetError(scoreBox, "Score must be between 0 and 27");
            scoreBox.Focus();
        }
```

```
        else {
            ScoreCheck.SetError(scoreBox, "");
            //Add the score written to the points
            points.Text = (int)points.Text + (int)scoreBox.Text;
        }
    }
    catch (System.InvalidCastException ext) {
        //Something other than a number
        if (scoreBox.Text.Length > 0) {
            ScoreCheck.SetError(scoreBox, "Score must be a number");
        }
    }
    catch (Exception ex) {
        //Eek!
        MessageBox.Show("Something went wrong!  " + ex.Message);
    }
    //Check the score
    if ((int)points.Text > 120) {
        if ((int)points.Text / (int)otherPlayer.Text > 1.5) {
            WinMessage.Text = scoreBox.Name.Substring(0, scoreBox.Name.Length -
    6) + " Skunked 'em!!!";
        }
        else {
            WinMessage.Text = scoreBox.Name.Substring(0, scoreBox.Name.Length -
    6) + " Won!!";
        }
        WinMessage.Visible = true;
    }
}
```

All this changing of screen values causes the `Paint` event of the form to fire — every time C# needs to change the look of a form for any reason, this event fires — so I just tossed a little code in that event handler that would draw my board for me:

```
private void CribbageBoard_Paint(object sender, PaintEventArgs e)
{
    PaintBoard(BillsPoints, GabriellesPoints);
}
```

From that point on, my largest concern is drawing the board itself.

Drawing the board

I need to paint right on a form to create the image of the board for my cribbage application, so I use the `CreateGraphics` method of the form control. From there, I need to complete these tasks:

- Paint the board brown using a brush.
- Draw six rows of little circles using a pen.
- Fill in the hole if that is the right score.
- Clean up my supplies.

To that end, I came up with the `PaintBoard` method, which accepts the labels that contain the standing scores for both players. It's shown in Listing 5-1.

Listing 5-1: The PaintBoard Method

```
private void PaintBoard(ref Label Bill, ref Label Gabrielle)
{
    Graphics palette = this.CreateGraphics;
    SolidBrush brownBrush = new SolidBrush(Color.Brown);
    palette.FillRectangle(brownBrush, new Rectangle(20, 20, 820, 180));
    //OK, now I need to paint the little holes.
    //There are 244 little holes in the board.
    //Three rows of 40 times two, with the little starts and stops on either end.
    //Let's start with the 240.
    int rows = 0;
    int columns = 0;
    int scoreBeingDrawn = 0;
    Pen blackPen = new Pen(System.Drawing.Color.Black, 1);
    SolidBrush blackBrush = new SolidBrush(Color.Black);
    SolidBrush redBrush = new SolidBrush(Color.Red);

    //There are 6 rows, then, at 24 and 40, 80 and 100, then 140 and 160.
    for (rows = 40; rows <= 160; rows += 60) {
        //There are 40 columns. They are every 20
        for (columns = 40; columns <= 820; columns += 20) {
            //Calculate score being drawn
            scoreBeingDrawn = ((columns - 20) / 20) + ((((rows + 20) / 60) - 1) *
    40);
            //Draw Bill
            //If score being drawn = bill fill, otherwise draw
            if (scoreBeingDrawn == (int)Bill.Text) {
                palette.FillEllipse(blackBrush, columns - 2, rows - 2, 6, 6);
            }
            else if (scoreBeingDrawn == BillsLastTotal) {
                palette.FillEllipse(redBrush, columns - 2, rows - 2, 6, 6);
            }
            else {
                palette.DrawEllipse(blackPen, columns - 2, rows - 2, 4, 4);
            }
            //Draw Gabrielle
            //If score being drawn = Gabrielle fill, otherwise draw
            if (scoreBeingDrawn == (int)Gabrielle.Text) {
                palette.FillEllipse(blackBrush, columns - 2, rows + 16, 6, 6);
            }
            else if (scoreBeingDrawn == GabriellesLastTotal) {
                palette.FillEllipse(redBrush, columns - 2, rows + 16, 6, 6);
            }
            else {
                palette.DrawEllipse(blackPen, columns - 2, rows + 16, 4, 4);
            }
        }
    }
    palette.Dispose();
    brownBrush.Dispose();
    blackPen.Dispose();
}
```

Aside from the math, note the decision making. If the score being drawn is the score in the label, fill in the hole with a red peg. If it's the last score drawn, fill in the hole with a black peg. Otherwise, well, just draw a circle.

It's tough to fathom, but this is exactly how large-scale games are written. Admittedly, big graphics engines make many more If-Then decisions, but the premise is the same.

Also, large games use bitmap images sometimes, rather than drawing all the time. For the cribbage scoring application, for example, you could use a bitmap image of a peg rather than fill an ellipse with a black or red brush!

Book IV

A Tour of Visual Studio

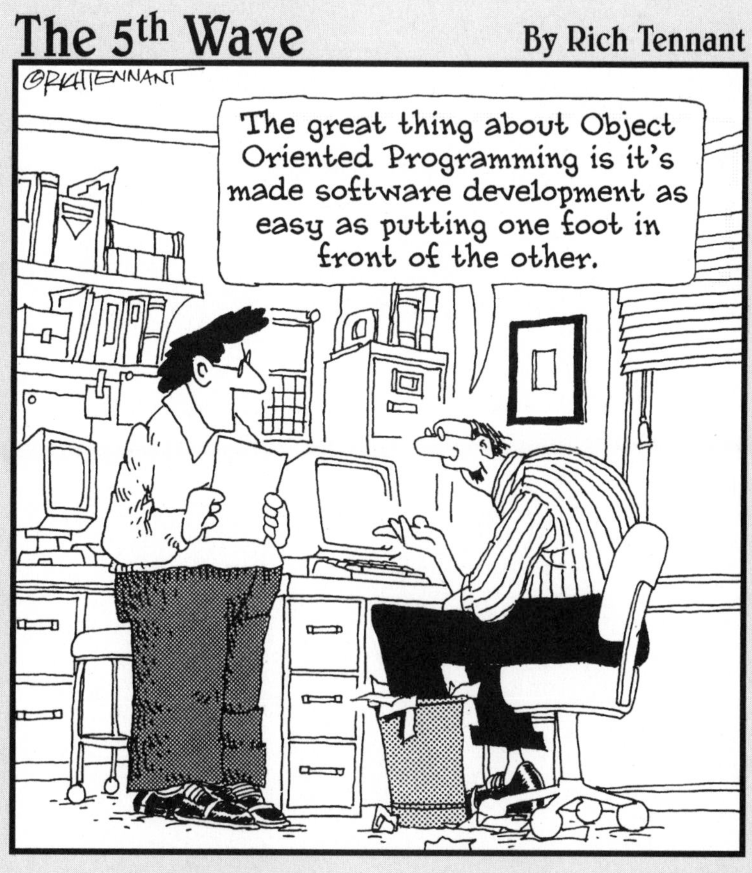

Contents at a Glance

Chapter 1: Getting Started with Visual Studio

In This Chapter

- **Surveying the available versions**
- **Installing Visual Studio**
- **Understanding projects and solutions**
- **Exploring the different types of projects**

Much that you most likely have discovered about C# can be run using a command prompt and `cs.exe`. Fact is, that's a less-than-wonderful way to program. It's unforgiving and slow, and it's hard to remember the specifics of the language. An Integrated Development Environment (IDE) is a program that provides a platform for development. It helps make development easier.

Programmers who are used to starting with a blank screen and a command line often dismiss an IDE as a slow, bogged-down waste of time. However, I have never failed to see any of those coders change their tune after working in Visual Studio. It's quick, easy to use, agile, and smart.

It's true that you don't have to use an IDE to program, but if you're going to use one, it should be Visual Studio. It was purposely built to write C# code, and it's made to construct Windows programs. (Sales pitch over — Microsoft, I'll take my 20 bucks now.)

Seriously, ever since I did a deep dive to write *Effective Visual Studio .NET,* I have been a fan of Visual Studio. It truly makes writing software easier. It doesn't replace knowing the language or understanding object-oriented programming or the .NET Framework, but it sure makes life a little smoother.

This chapter introduces you to the various versions of Visual Studio and discusses the C# projects available to you.

Versioning the Versions

Visual Studio has lots of different versions (a metric ton of them — a bushel and a peck, even).

The reason is its famous licensing problem. If they just sold the whole package for what it was worth, only the Fortune 50 could afford it, and they would cut out about 99 percent of their audience. If they make a lot of different versions, and try to incorporate the features that different groups of people use, they can capture nearly 100 percent of the audience.

This book focuses on the Professional Edition, as I mention in the introduction. However, much of the sample code works in any version — though the step lists are different.

In this chapter I run down the features and benefits of all the major editions. At the end of the section, a grid shows the major features and what each edition includes.

Express

Express is the free version of Visual Studio.

Yes, I said *free,* as in "without cost."

Express is made for hobbyists, but many professional programmers I know use it as their "home" edition, for small personal projects, or for working on open source projects.

Although Express is significantly less functional than the Professional Edition, nearly every code sample in this book can be compiled in Express. It has the power of the .NET Framework, which is also free, and gives you a significant means of learning C#.

Express edition is not designed for making production software. It lacks several project types and many of the tools for team development. Nonetheless, it runs C# as well as anything else — remember that C# is just a language.

Express has a number of different subeditions. They split the main technologies of .NET into parts. You can't build packaged software for sale using these editions, but you sure can learn with it. The different subeditions are described in this list:

- **Visual C# Express:** This edition provides much of the power of C# in a free package. Most of the project types are available, including WPF, Windows Forms, Web Forms, and service applications. The only kicker — you can't deploy. You can't deploy for production anyway, without breaking the license agreement.

This version is great for learning the language and for participating in open source application projects, though. Open source projects (in which you just contribute code, not a whole project for pay) are a good use for Express editions. I recommend that you get started here if you have nothing else. Much of the material in Books I and II work in Express.

- **Visual Basic Express:** Like C# Express, Visual Basic Express is a free implementation of the language. It isn't for production use, though you can learn the language and participate in open source projects. Most of the project types are available.
- **Visual Web Developer:** VWD is an interesting free edition of Visual Studio. It's designed around the creation of Web pages using ASP.NET or Silverlight. Because those languages aren't compiled, you can write production software for free. All the better for you and me.

  Both VB and C# are supported as of this writing, and most of the functionality of the Web projects in Visual Studio is available. Find out more at `www.microsoft.com/express/vwd`.

Professional

Professional Edition is designed for professional programmers. This edition of Visual Studio is the one I use daily. It's made to generate standalone programs that solve specific problems.

Microsoft is on the ball, with three goals for its Professional Edition:

- Enable emerging trends
- Inspire developer delight
- Ride the next-generation platform wave

That hits the nail on the head. This is the edition that the entire book is built on, and what I recommend for the production of most programs.

As good as it is, Professional doesn't have every feature that Microsoft has to offer. The comprehensive team management features, reporting, check-in, and testing features are reserved for the pricy version: Team System.

Team System

Visual Studio Team System, usually referred to as VSTS, is the grand poohbah of the Microsoft platform. It connects to Team Foundation Server (a Microsoft product that provides team metrics for software development), which provides a plethora of software creation metrics when teams are involved in the development.

Figure 1-1 shows a little of what I'm talking about. Build statistics and development details can be gathered using the dashboard provided in SharePoint.

Facts are facts — Team System is cool software, but it just doesn't work without a big enterprise environment around you. It needs SharePoint, Exchange, and SQL Server to work right.

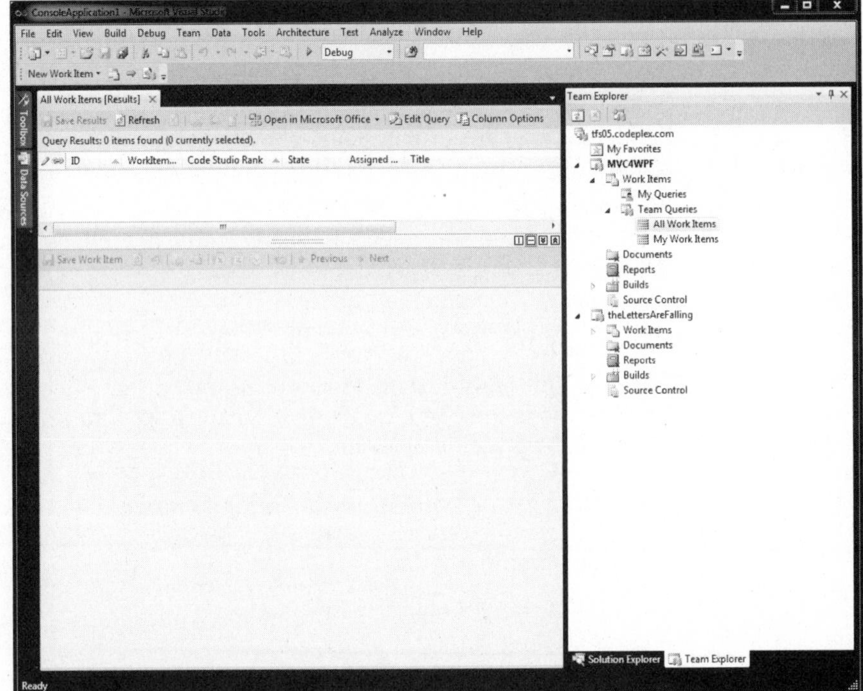

Figure 1-1: Managing software development with Team Foundation Server.

MSDN

The Microsoft Developer Network (MSDN) subscription is by far the best way to get Microsoft products. It seems like setting up a development environment to develop anything of significance would be impossibly expensive. This is not necessarily the case.

The MSDN subscription is exactly what it sounds like — a subscription to a majority of the Microsoft products that matter. For around a thousand dollars a year, you get access to everything you need. This isn't actually an edition of Visual Studio.

That sounds like a lot, but think about it this way — even if you do only one project a year on your own time, your investment will pay off.

Considering the fact that Visual Studio alone is half of that, and it gets a revision every two years or so, it's a bargain. Along with Visual Studio Professional, you also get subscriptions to

- Microsoft Office
- Windows client platforms
- Windows Server platforms
- SQL Server
- Neat middleware like SharePoint and BizTalk
- Weird bits that you never used before (but will now)

Basically how it works is this — you go to Amazon or elsewhere and buy an MSDN license code. Then you go to `msdn.microsoft.com` and register the code with your Live account. From there, depending on your license level, you can download the software for development use only.

That point is an important one. The products you get from MSDN are for development purpose. So, yes, you get SQL Server (for instance). No, you can't put up your new Widget store on the Internet using the MSDN license.

So the operating system in the MSDN license is for development only. That's okay. This is a development book. If you can get MSDN, get it.

Academic

If you can't afford MSDN but you're a school student or an instructor, buy the Academic edition of Visual Studio, intended just for learning institutions. It's less expensive than MSDN, but is even more limited from the licensing perspective.

The Academic edition now costs only a hundred bucks or so. That means it costs more than the free Express edition, but it has all the features of Professional. If you're just in it to learn, it's a helpful option. If you want to deploy production software, though, you have to look elsewhere. This product isn't licensed for it.

Students, teachers, head over to the school bookstore. If they don't have Visual Studio Academic, tell them they should get it.

An edition breakdown

Table 1-1 describes the big features that Microsoft sees and the features in different versions. I use it every time I recommend software to a client, and I hope you find it just as useful.

Table 1-1 Visual Studio Versions

Visual Studio 2010	*VS 2010 Professional with MSDN*	*VS 2010 Premium with MSDN*	*VS 2010 Ultimate with MSDN*
Team Foundation Server	****	****	****
Development Platform Support	****	****	****
Testing	*	***	****
Database Development		****	****
Debugging and Diagnostics	**	***	****
Architecture and Modeling		*	****
Lab Management			***

Installing Visual Studio

Visual Studio Professional, the edition that I use for most of this book, installs much like any other Windows program. First, assure yourself that your machine can run Visual Studio. Then you run the setup program (or it automatically runs from the DVD) and make a few decisions.

Then you wait. Visual Studio is big. It takes a while.

The official requirements for Visual Studio are shown in this list:

- **Operating system:**
  - Windows® XP Professional with Service Pack 2 installed, Windows Server 2003, or Windows Vista in 32 bit
  - Microsoft Windows Server® 2003 with SP1, Standard x64 Edition (WOW)
  - Microsoft Windows Server 2003 with SP1, Enterprise x64 Edition (WOW)
  - Microsoft Windows Server 2003 with SP1, Datacenter x64 Edition (WOW)
  - Microsoft Windows Server 2003 R2, Standard x64 Edition (WOW)
  - Microsoft Windows Server 2003 R2, Enterprise x64 Edition (WOW)
  - Microsoft Windows Server 2003 R2, Datacenter x64 Edition (WOW)

- Microsoft Windows XP Professional x64 Edition (WOW)
- Windows Vista

✦ **Client software:**

- Internet Explorer® 6.0 with Service Pack 1,
- Microsoft Office 2003 with Service Pack 1 or
- Microsoft Office 2007, MDAC 9.0, .NET Framework 2.0

✦ **Hardware:**

- *Minimum:* 2.0 GHz CPU, 512MB RAM, 8GB HDD
- *Recommended:* 2.6 GHz CPU, 1GB RAM, 20GB HDD

You can run on this configuration — I have tried it and it works. It's not pretty. Visual Studio 2010 is all written in WPF, which can (with this size of an application) be a resource hog.

Seeing how that is the case, I am sure you aren't surprised to find that I have a collection of suggestions for installing Visual Studio.

First, here is what I consider to be a realistic base configuration for Visual Studio:

✦ 2.4 GHz 64 bit dual core processor

✦ 64-bit Windows 7 with 8GB of RAM

✦ 250GB of available HDD space

✦ Dual monitors (or a laptop with an external monitor)

Seems excessive? It isn't. First, I recommend that you use a virtual machine for any project that does anything to your base install of Windows. Virtual PC is free, and you can usually get a 180-day trial of Windows 7 without a problem. Change the settings on Virtual PC to run only the clock while the machine is running, and you have a perfect test bed.

To find Virtual PC, search for Virtual PC on `download.microsoft.com`. To find the hack to change the clock on virtual PCs, go to the Virtual PC Guy's blog at `www.virtualpcguy.com` and search for "clock only while active."

This plan takes power, though. You must have 4GB of RAM so that you can give 2GB of it to the virtual machine. The virtual hard drives are usually around 13GB, so you need space. Two monitors make it possible to easily see the host operating system while still running the virtual machine full screen.

Even if you aren't going to run in a virtual PC (but I recommend that you do), you still want a solid, dual core processor and lots of RAM. Why skimp? Hardware is cheap. Your time isn't!

Breaking Down the Projects

All there is left to do after you have run the setup program and set your default settings is to start on a project and get your fingers dirty. All the project types (expect maybe one or two) in the first two minibooks were Console applications, meaning they are meant to be run at the command prompt. There are a lot more projects available.

Notice three main kinds of projects in the Visual Studio New Project dialog box.

- **Windows projects** are rich client applications that compile into . EXEs and run right on your computer. Microsoft Word is a Windows application.
- **Web projects** make Web sites and require a Web server to run. (A Web server is included with Visual Studio for development purposes.) Microsoft.com is an example of a Web application.
- **Special projects** include things like setup projects (projects that build setup programs) and database projects (projects that give a framework for databases). They usually are used with a Windows or Web application. The Setup.exe program you run in the preceding section to install Visual Studio is an example of one of these special project — a setup project.

Exploring the New Project dialog box

Let's start with a breakdown of the New Project dialog box, shown in Figure 1-2. This screen is an important part of the usability of Visual Studio. You open it by clicking the New Project link on the setup page.

The section of the dialog box to the far left is a tree-view selector, similar to the one in Outlook. You have three options — Recent Templates, Installed Templates, and Online templates. Installed Templates is selected. These templates, as Visual Studio calls them, are project types.

Within the selector is a WPF style tree viewer. Instead of maples and oaks, this tree viewer has all the project categories described in upcoming sections of this chapter.

If you click, for example, the Visual C# option in the tree view, all the projects for Visual C# appear in the window just to the right. If you click one of the suboptions, just those project types — for Visual C# —appear.

To specify the version of the .NET Framework you would like to develop for, you can use the drop-down list just above the project list that currently says .NET Framework 4.0. To change the sorting options, use the Sort By: drop-down list directly to the right. One more step to the right and you can change your view options.

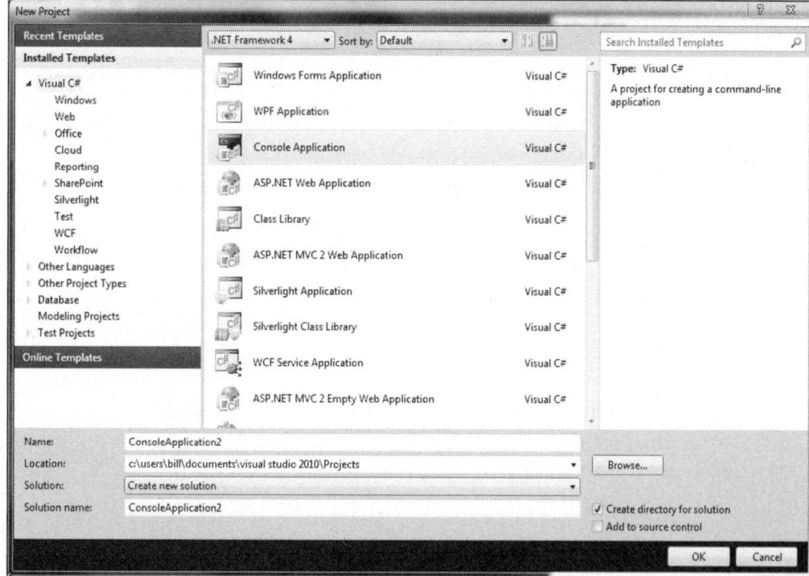

Figure 1-2: So many (project) options!

In the upper-right corner is a search box, which isn't as silly as it sounds given the large number of templates now in Visual Studio. Just below the search box is the description panel, where you can see a text description of the selected project type.

At the bottom are three important text boxes:

- **Name:** The name of this project.
- **Location:** The path to the project file.
- **Solution:** The name of the solution. Solutions are collections of projects.

For more about solutions and projects, see the next section.

Understanding solutions and projects

Visual Studio project files, and the solutions that love them, are a constant topic of interest to Microsoft developers. You work on one solution at a time, with a number of projects within. How you organize your solutions and their projects will make or break you when it comes time to find something.

You can think of solutions as folders that hold projects. They're just folders with special properties. In fact, note the check box shown earlier, in Figure 1-2. It's the one labeled Create Directory for Solution. That's what I mean — the solution is really an organizational "folder" for the projects.

Projects are where you put the code files for your programs. They store all kinds of things, like references to the .NET Framework, resources like graphics or files, and what file should be used to start the project.

Solutions do the same thing for projects that projects do for files. They keep the projects in a folder, and store certain properties. For instance, they store which project should be started when debugging starts.

Neither the project nor the solutions have much to do with a finished program. They are just simple organizational structures for Visual Studio. The installation of finished program is determined by the setup project. The solution itself is just a logical storage mechanism for the source files.

In reality, the solution is more than a folder. It's a file in a folder that is used by Visual Studio to manage the developer experience. So, inside the folder for the solution is a file describing the projects within, and then a bunch of folders with the projects themselves.

There are files for the projects, too — files that describe the resources and references for the project. They are all XML files that contain text references to the values that you set using Visual Studio.

When developing in Visual Studio, you shouldn't worry about that. In 14 years of working in various versions of Visual Studio, I have had to look at a solution or project file only a few times, and only in special situations. Knowing how they work, however, will help you design your project structure.

The way I work is to look at what I want to be a finished program and consider it a solution. Above that, I have a client folder. The result looks like Figure 1-3.

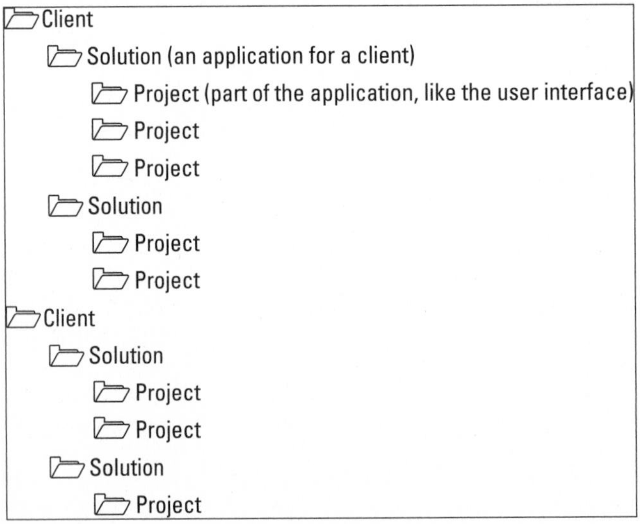

```
Client
    Solution (an application for a client)
        Project (part of the application, like the user interface)
        Project
        Project
    Solution
        Project
        Project
Client
    Solution
        Project
        Project
    Solution
        Project
```

Figure 1-3: My preferred project structure.

This strategy keeps me much more organized and works with the Visual Studio model. All I have to do is use the Browse button to change the location of the project and solution. It also helps to make the main project of a solution first (like the user interface) before the rest of the solution.

A brief survey of the available project categories

The following list describes the project types listed in the New Project dialog box in Visual Studio. These kinds of finished programs are ones you can make using the installed templates.

- **Windows Projects:** Windows projects in Visual C# are programs that compile into a running program, like Microsoft Word, or Visual Studio itself. The projects include
  - *Windows Forms Application:* The classic "program." Compiles into a program that runs with its own window and with a red close box (with the little X in it) to exit. This is the original Windows Program style, gradually being replaced by Windows Presentation Foundation.
  - *Class Library:* Makes a DLL when you're all done. This is the basis of the .NET Framework, and COM before that. It's used to make blocks of reusable code.
  - *WPF Application:* The new "program." Also compiles into an EXE, but uses a new user interface format called Windows Presentation Foundation. I cover this in depth in Book V.
  - *WPF Browser Application:* Just like a WPF application but runs in Internet Explorer. This is *not* a Silverlight application; it's an XBAP application, short for XML Browser Application. It has a smaller set of available user interface toys but is still powerful.
  - *Console application:* These EXEs are designed to be run from a command prompt.
  - *WPF Custom Control Library:* This is a way to make actual controls that appear in the toolbox that you can use in your WPF applications.
  - *Empty Project:* Just what it sounds like — a project that's empty, poetic. It's used to build a program for which you don't have a template.

  - *Windows Services:* These programs appear in the Services control panel. Didn't know you could make those with .NET? You aren't alone. It's a powerful feature that few people know about. Windows Services are essentially terminate-and-stay-resident, or TSR, programs. (Remember those from your DOS days? They stay in memory.) Check out the article on the topic at `csharpfordummies.net`.

- *WPF User Control Library:* The finished product of this looser control format doesn't appear in the toolbox but is much easier to build because it doesn't require coding the whole thing in C#.
- *Windows Forms control library:* Like the WPF control library but for Windows Forms. It helps to build a control that you can use from the toolbox.

✦ **Web Projects:** Web projects are programs that require a server to run (well, usually) and are used from the browser. They render HTML to the browser, rather than fancy formats like Silverlight. Projects include

- *ASP.NET Web Application:* This is the centerpiece of the Web development space. It creates an application that can be run on IIS, which presents a Web page to the user.
- *ASP.NET Web Service Application:* This is a class library for service-oriented applications. If you're going to distribute applications over several machines, or provide broadly distributed applications, this project type will provide a standards-based implementation for your service offerings.
- *ASP.NET AJAX Server Control:* Asynchronous JavaScript And XML is a development style that provides a significant quantity of user interactions within the Web browser. This allows you to build controls that support this pattern.
- *WCF Service Application:* This project belongs in the Communication Foundation section. It's like the ASP.NET Web Service Application, except it provides a number of different standards-based implementations for your service offerings. ASP.NET Web services only provide one.
- *ASP.NET Server Control:* This Web control would appear in the toolbox, enabling you to drag the selected functionality right onto the Web page in development.
- *ASP.NET AJAX Server Control Extender:* This control extends the functionality of another AJAX control. It targets a control and adds a feature.
- *Dynamic Data Linq to SQL Web Application:* This is an ASP.NET Web application that uses Linq to make a data-active Web page.
- *Dynamic Data Entities Web Application:* This ASP.NET Web application uses ADO.NET Data Entities to make a data-active Web page.

✦ **Office Projects:** Office projects are part of the Visual Studio Tools for Office package, and use Office as a platform instead of Windows or a Web browser. To find out more, look at the book I coauthored with Peter Jaunovich, *Office Development For Dummies.* Office Projects include

- *Excel 2007 Workbook:* Has a Microsoft Excel Workbook (a collection of Excel worksheets) as an output.

- *Word 2007 Template:* Has a Microsoft Word 2007 template (a `.dot` file) as an output.
- *Project 2007 Add-in:* Creates an add-in for Microsoft Project.
- *Visio 2007 Add-in:* Creates an add-in for Microsoft Visio.
- *Word 2007 Add-in:* Creates an add-in for Microsoft Word.
- *Excel 2007 Add-in:* Creates an add-in for Microsoft Excel.
- *Outlook 2007 Add-in:* Creates an add-in for Microsoft Outlook.
- *Word 2007 Document:* Has a Microsoft Word 2007 document as an output.
- *Excel 2007 Template:* Has a Microsoft Excel 2007 template (an `.xlt` file) as an output.
- *InfoPath 2007 Add-in:* Creates an add-in for Microsoft Infopath.
- *PowerPoint 2007 Add-in:* Creates an add-in for Microsoft PowerPoint.

✦ **Communication Foundation Projects:** Windows Communication Foundation is Microsoft's way to provide a mechanism for programs to speak with one another:

- *Syndication Service Library:* Creates a syndicated feed service (RSS) that speaks either ATOM or RSS.
- *WCF Service Library:* A class library for Communication Foundation.
- *Declarative Flowchart Service Library:* Makes a set of services that use a flowchart-style workflow to provide services.
- *Declarative Sequential Service library:* Makes a set of services that use a sequential-style workflow to provide services.

✦ **Workflow Projects:** Workflow Foundation is the standard library for creating workflows in Microsoft programs. You can set up standard approvals, movement of documents, and the like:

- *Activity Designer Library:* This project assists you with creating a user interface for creating activities.
- *Activity Library:* If you aren't in the mood to create user interfaces for the creation of activities, you can create an activity.
- *Flowchart Workflow Console application:* This project, and the sequential project, provides a way to test WF workflows in a safe environment.
- *Sequential Workflow Console Application:* This is just like the flowchart WF project, but for sequential workflows.

- **Special Projects:** Refers to anything that doesn't fit into the preceding bullets:
  - *Test Project:* If you're working in Visual Studio, right-click a method, and select Create Unit Test, you will get this kind of project. In the case where you want to make a test project manually, this is your project.
  - *Silverlight:* Admittedly, Microsoft Expression would be your best choice for Silverlight. If you want to use Visual Studio, however, you can use this project.
  - *SQL Server Project:* Again, I would rather use Microsoft SQL Server Management Studio to make database projects. If you have to use Visual Studio for some reason, this is your project.
  - *Reports Application:* You can include reports right in your Windows or Web application. If you're deploying directly to Reporting Services, this project does the job.
- **Other kinds of projects:** It's easy to make a project type for Visual Studio, and there are a bunch of them out there. Some of them are patterns, some of them are languages, and some of them are new project outputs. Here are a few of my favorites:
  - *ASP.NET MVC:* Model View Controller (MVC), a project type that allows for a separation of duties between development teams. This project type allows you to make ASP.NET applications using MVC. Search MSDN for more information.
  - *MVC4WPF:* Allows for Model View Controller development for Windows Presentation Foundation. It has automation and templates just like regular WPF applications. Check it out at `www.mvc4wpf.com`.
  - *IRONRuby:* An implementation of Ruby in Visual Studio.
  - *IRONPython:* An implementation of Python in Visual Studio.

Chapter 2: Using the Interface

In This Chapter

- Using the Designer
- Exploring Solution Explorer
- Coding with Code View
- Using the Tools menu

Integrated Development Environments, or IDEs, are the Swiss army knife of the programmer's toolkit. IDEs provide a mechanism for storing program code, organizing and building it, and looking at finished products with design editors. IDEs make things happen, and in the bargain, cut hours from a task.

Visual Studio is becoming truly globally recognized as the cream of the crop of IDEs, even by Microsoft detractors. I know Python programmers who will rail on Windows all day while surfing their Linux box and then switch to a Windows partition to use Visual Studio to code with IRONPython in Visual Studio.

Visual Studio is impressive; it is massive. I wrote a book with David Deloveh at the turn of the century (heh!) that attempted to cover all Visual Studio features. It was 600 pages. The major complaint by readers: too short. Didn't cover enough. Visual Studio is twice as large now. It's far too big for a single chapter.

So, rather than try to cover everything, I give you the chance to experience only the features of Visual Studio that I use every day. I don't want to try and cover anything up, and I hope that you continue exploring the IDE and discovering new stuff — don't just stop with what I tell you about. This is only a brief overview of some of the astonishing features in the tool.

Designing in the Designer

One thing that is integrated into an Integrated Development Environment is a way to edit files graphically, sometimes called a Graphic Development Environment or *designer*. Visual Studio allows you to graphically edit five different types of code bases and provides adjunct tools for the further management of said code bases.

In short, the designer is the drag-and-drop element of the Visual Studio world. It isn't always the best way to develop a program, but it sure can help sometimes.

For each major type of project that Visual Studio maintains, there is a designer. The designer handles the What You See Is What You Get portion of the experience and usually the behind-the-scenes markup code.

The problem is that because of the necessities of the software development world we live in, different designers all work a little differently. A significant difference exists between HTML and XAML, for example, so the Web designer and the WPF designer don't look or act the same.

Visual Studio gives you several visual designers to help develop applications, including these:

- Class Designer
- Data View
- Web Forms
- Windows Forms
- Windows Presentation Foundation

Windows Presentation Foundation (WPF)

Windows Presentation Foundation is covered in some depth in Book V, but for now you should know that it is the future of Microsoft's Windows development experience. Book V talks all about WPF, so you can read more about it there.

The core of the user interface design experience is a language called XAML, which (unsurprisingly) is an XML-derived domain-specific markup language for the creation of user interfaces. In the Designer, shown in Figure 2-1, the design is in the top frame, and the underlying code is in the bottom frame.

You can click in the design in the designer and move things around, if you want, or use the designer to select things and edit the properties in the Properties panel (which I cover in the upcoming section "Paneling the Studio"). Additionally, if you change something in the code area, you'll see the change in the design. It's a good system.

There are a few small but significant features in the WPF designer that should be pointed out. You can see them all in Figure 2-1.

Near the upper-left corner is a zoom bar. You can click at the bottom of it and Zoom To Fit, or move the slider. This is invaluable for working on an application that is bigger than your screen, or lightening things just so.

At the left side of the dividing line between the Design and XAML frames is a little double-arrow icon. Clicking this icon changes whatever is in the bottom frame to be in the top frame, and vice versa.

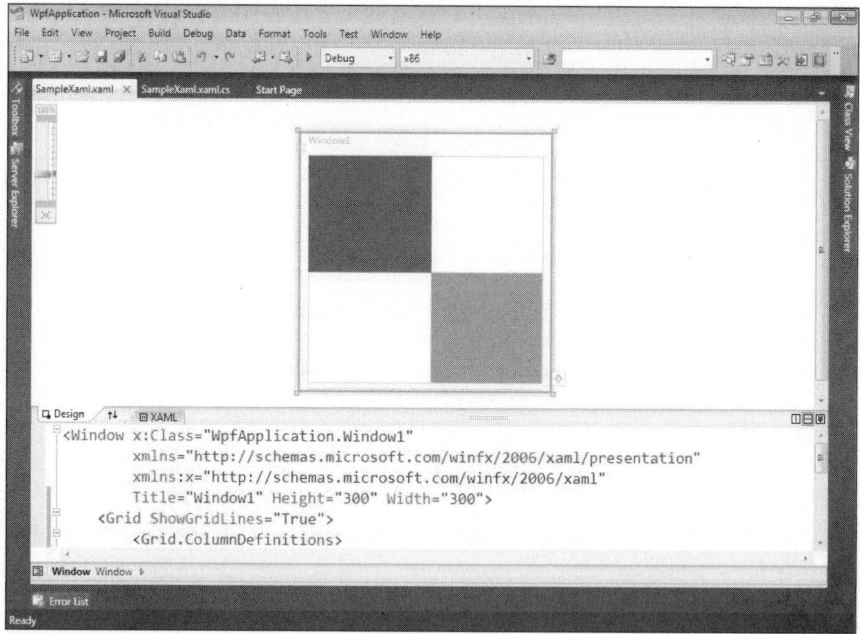

Figure 2-1: The WPF Designer.

On the right side of the same dividing line are three buttons that determine the kind of split you have — a vertical split, a horizontal split (which is default), or no split.

A few cool point-and-click adjustment tools are in the designer itself. Here's just one: Click in the red area of the table in the window in the designer. Put your mouse right above where the "146" size designation appears.

See the little floating box that appears, with an asterisk, a hash, and the word *Auto?* That's just one of the many little helpers that you find in the WPF designer. The hash sets the column width to a set number (as it is by default). The asterisk sets it to a percentage of the table — useful for resizing. The word *Auto* sizes the column based on the contents.

These little features make changes only to the XAML in the frame below the designer. If you click the word *Auto* in the floating table designer, you will change this line of code:

```
<ColumnDefinition Width="146" />
```

to this line of code in the XAML frame:

```
<ColumnDefinition Width="Auto" />
```

Some people like the code. Some people like the designer. Some people (like me) prefer a strange mixture of the two. You determine how you want to use the tools.

Windows Forms

The main difference between the Windows Forms designer and the WPF designer is the lack of a code panel in Windows Forms. Although there is code (of sorts) backing up Windows Forms, you don't get to edit it. So there.

The topic of Windows Forms isn't covered in this book. Though it's still an active development platform, I had to make the tough call to cover WPF instead. It performs the same programming duties as Windows Forms but is the newer technology. The Windows Forms designer is shown in Figure 2-2.

In truth, there is little to say about the Windows Forms designer itself. The individual controls have some nice designer features, but the designer itself doesn't do much.

It should be said, though, that I don't do much with Windows Forms in this book. First, this isn't a Windows programming book; it is a C# book. Second, Windows Forms is on its way out. WPF is the future of Windows programming. Window Forms is just there for backward compatibility.

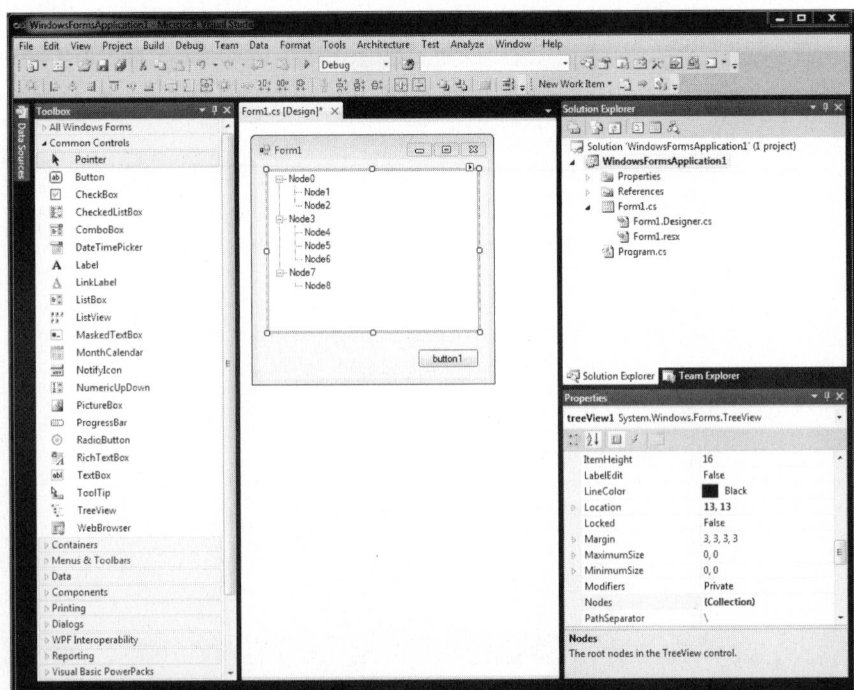

Figure 2-2: The Windows Forms designer.

Web Forms

Web programming resembles WPF programming more than it resembles Windows Forms programming, but it's run from a Web server and viewed in a browser. (Book VI is all about Web forms.) Because the designer has a back-end code element, you can see a split view, as shown in Figure 2-3.

Getting around in the HTML designer is easy. I want to point out two features in particular about the HTML designer. These features can be found in a menu strip along the bottom of the designer view:

✦ **The view change buttons, which read Source, Design, and Split:** Source shows only the HTML code. Design shows only the visual designer. Split, unsurprisingly, shows both in two panels, just like the WPF designer.

Interestingly, the two frames do not stay in sync. If you change the HTML, the design frame shows a message that says "Design view is out of sync with Source view. Click here to synchronize views." Here's hoping they fix that before they release to manufacturing.

✦ **The small document tree next to the view change buttons:** This shows you where in the hierarchal tree your cursor is and its relationship to the rest of the HTML document.

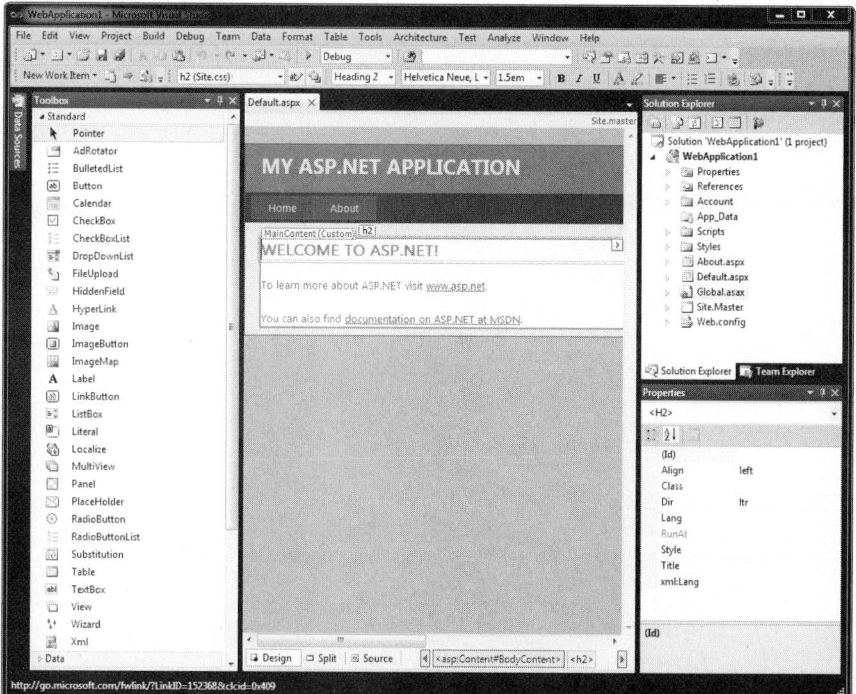

Figure 2-3: Back to code with Web projects.

Class Designer

You can make a Class Designer from any project, but I used a Class Library project for my next example, shown in Figure 2-4:

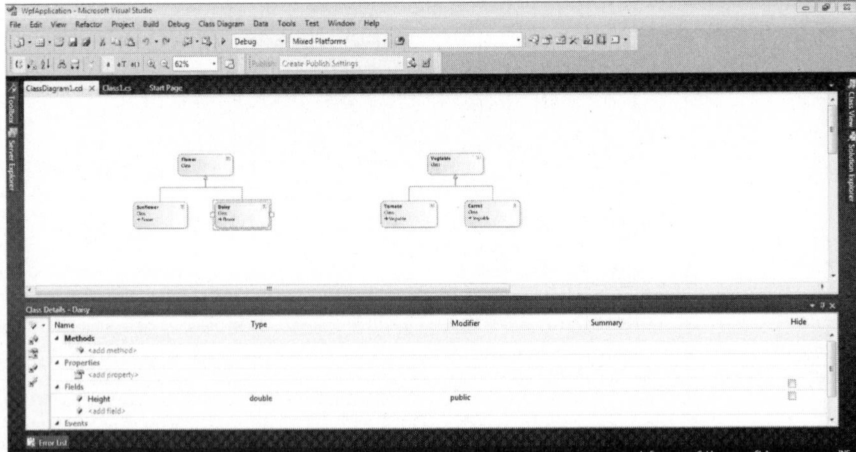

Figure 2-4: My garden, in digital form.

The class designer gives you a visual interface into a class library. You can easily see the inheritance, and the members are visible and editable. Here is the class library I used for Figure 2-4:

```
namespace MyGarden
{
    public class Flower
    {
        public string Color;
    }
    public class Vegetable
    {
        public bool Yummy;
    }
    public class Daisy : Flower
    {
        public double Height;
    }
    public class Sunflower : Flower
    {
        public bool Harvested;
    }
    public class Tomato: Vegetable
    {
```

```
        public double StakeHeight;
    }
    public class Carrot : Vegetable
    {
        public double Depth;
    }
}
```

To create a class library like this, follow these steps:

1. **Create a new Class Library project.**
2. **Replace the default code with a listing of your own.**

   You can use the one in this section, if you want.
3. **Build the class library by pressing Ctrl + Shift + B.**
4. **Right-click on the project and select View Class Diagram.**

   Visual Studio creates a new file called `ClassDiagram1.cd`. This is your Class Diagram file.
5. **Save your project.**

You can add methods to your new class as well. Click on the Methods of the `Flower` class and add a `Water` method by typing **Water** under name **Void** under type, and **Public** under modifier. If you change back to the library view, you'll find that there has been a method added to the code under that class.

To aid in documentation of projects, you can right-click anywhere in the designer pane and select Export This Diagram as an Image, and then save it off as a `.PNG` file. I find this immensely useful when I am creating documentation for a project. It is a lot more useful than Visio because its integrated with your code, included in Visual Studio, and it's free!

Data View

Data View is usually used with the Server Explorer and is part of an in-studio representation of SQL Management Studio. You can view and edit data tables in the SQL Server (and other) database management system right inside Visual Studio. An example is shown in Figure 2-5.

There is a remarkable amount of power here, and there just isn't enough space to cover it all. Again, this isn't a database book, so I recommend reading over the MSDN entries for the Data Connections feature of SQL Explorer for more details.

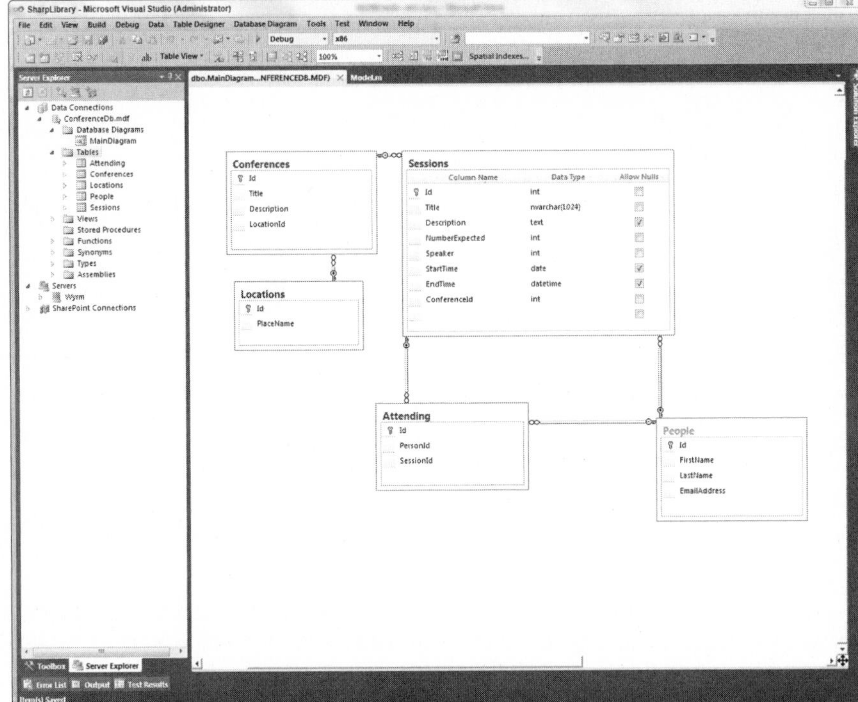

Figure 2-5: When you use Data View, who needs SQL Management Studio?

Paneling the Studio

Paneling: That's just *so* very seventies.

To be as flexible as it needs to, Visual Studio has a large collection of modular windows that are called **panels.** These panels do everything that isn't involved with directly editing a design or code. They manage files, manage objects, show feedback, show properties, all sorts of stuff.

Visual Studio has something like 23 panels. I don't have room to discuss them all here, so I cover only 5 — the ones you use every day. The rest you can find on the View menu.

Solution Explorer

Solution Explorer (see Figure 2-6) manages solutions, projects, and files. Despite my claim earlier that solutions are just a matter of files and folders, it is a somewhat more complex operation than it seems at first blush.

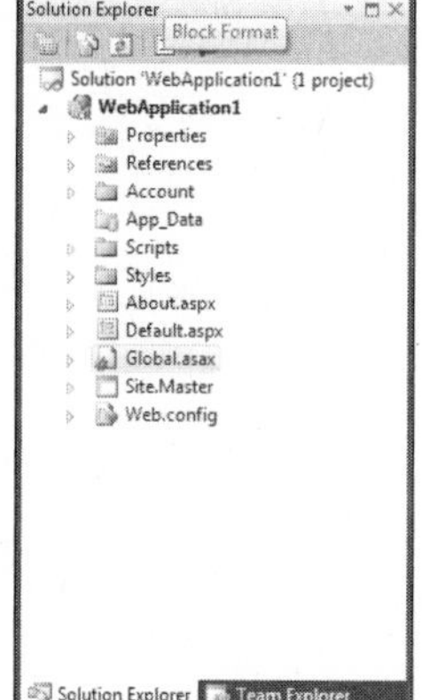

Figure 2-6: The explorer of solutions.

Solutions

For solutions themselves, Solution Explorer provides a number of important tools, including the following:

- **Configuration Manager** provides a useful interface for what is basically a settings file in the solution itself. You can specify whether Release or Debug compilation is desired for your build here, if you want all debugging information stored with your file. You can tell the compiler whether you want the software built for 32-bit systems or 64-bit systems too.
- **Project Dependencies** shows how your projects are interrelated and describes the way in which your projects depend on each other. It has a tab for the build order, too. When you are getting weird "referenced member not available in object" errors, check here first.
- **Property Pages** determine which project should start on debug and where source files are kept, among other things.

Additionally, Solution Explorer is a repository for projects. Each appears in a tree view.

Projects

Projects are the individual compiled units and are divided by type. You can find more about projects in Chapter 1 of this minibook.

Solution Explorer brings to projects the capability to add and remove files, make references and services, set up a class diagram, open the representative Windows Explorer folder, and set properties.

All this information is saved in the Project file. The project file is just an XML file. There are a few key characteristics of the file:

- ✦ It includes a PropertyGroup for each build type. This is because you can set different properties for each type of executable.
- ✦ It contains an ItemGroup that has all the references in it, including required Framework versions, and another set of ItemGroups that have the project load details.
- ✦ The file includes the import of the project general details and the Target collections. You can actually edit the file manually to make a custom build environment.

You likely won't modify your Project file, but I think it's important that you know it can be done, and that Microsoft has inline comments. They expect the file to get hacked.

Files

Files are a lot less exciting. They are pretty much exactly what you expect. They host the source code of the program being developed. Nothing hidden here.

Solution Explorer manages the files in the project basically like Windows Explorer does. Solution Explorer lists the files and folders and allows them to be opened in the designer or the code editor.

Solution Explorer also knows what files to show. If the file isn't in the project, but happens to be sitting in the folder for the project, it won't show in the Explorer. If you can't find a file, try clicking the Show All Files button in the gray button bar at the top of the Explorer. The hidden files will show up grayed out, but still won't compile into the project.

Properties

The Properties panel (see Figure 2-7) is a simple, flexible tool that allows you to update those endless lists of details about everything in development projects. The panel is basically a window with a two-column-wide datagrid. It reads properties in key/value pairs and allows for easy view and edit.

When I say it shows endless lists of details about everything, I mean *everything.* If you click on nearly anything in Visual Studio, press F4 to bring up the Property Panel (refer to Figure 2-7), you will get properties. Try it with these fun selections:

- ✦ Files in Solution Explorer
- ✦ Database connections
- ✦ A textbox in a WPF project

- An XML tree node
- An item in Class Explorer

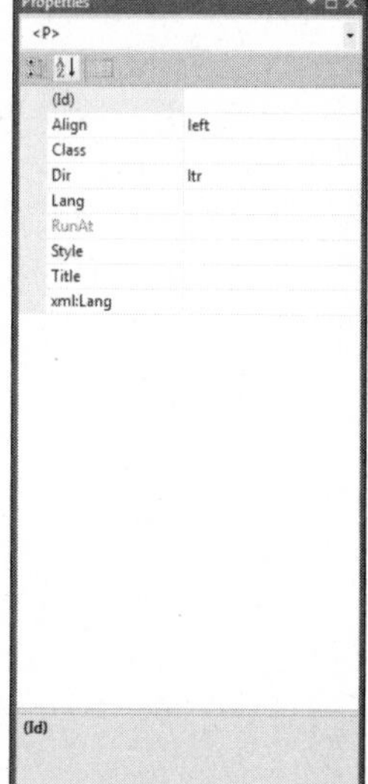

Figure 2-7: Paneling your property.

If there is any meta-data about something, the properties are in the Property Panel. It's a great tool.

The Toolbox

One of the great misunderstood tools is the Toolbox. (See Figure 2-8.) On the surface it seems so simple. The design-time controls for a given file type are available to drag and drop. Still, there is one important thing you need to remember about the Toolbox. Wait, I'll get out my Remember icon.

The Toolbox displays only controls that are appropriate to the file in focus.

So, if you are running a Windows Form in the designer, you won't see a database table available to drop. Trust me; if you expect to see a certain control, and it isn't there, the Toolbox probably isn't messed up. If there isn't a file open, the Toolbox is empty. That's by design.

I can't tell you how many times I have been expecting to see something in the Toolbox only to find it blank. Then I spend ten minutes tracking down the problem, only to realize that the problem is mine — I didn't have a file open. I once actually *called Microsoft* because I couldn't find a `maskedtextbox` for my Web Forms project.

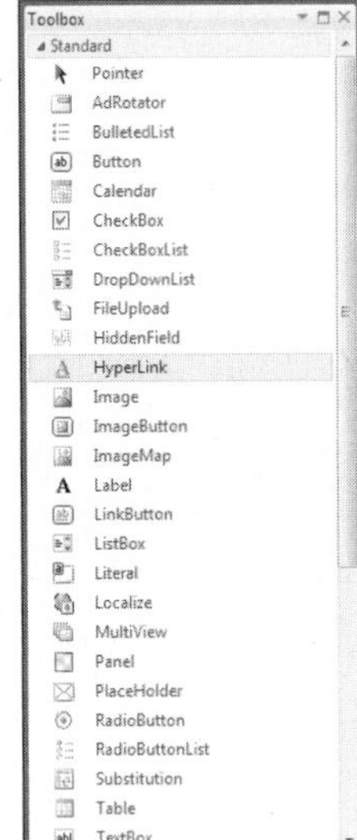

Figure 2-8: The Toolbox, with tools.

There is no `maskedtextbox` for Web Forms projects.

So keep it in mind that the Toolbox is context-sensitive. It works only when it wants to.

There is one other interesting property of the Toolbox: It can be used to store text clippings, which can be useful for demonstrations and presentations. It is also handy for storing often-used pieces of code, but snippets (covered in Chapter 3) are even better. To do so, follow these steps:

1. **Open a code file.**

   Anything will do, `.cs` file, `.xaml` file, whatever.

2. **Highlight a piece of code.**
3. **Make sure the Toolbox is open. Then drag the selected code to the General section of the Textbox.**

   The copied code becomes a tool.

4. **Open up another blank code file.**
5. **Drag the new tool into the code.**

   The copied code now appears in the code file.

Server Explorer

Server Explorer (see Figure 2-9) isn't in every version of Visual Studio. At the time this book was printed, it was included only in the Professional Edition and later.

Server Explorer enables developers to access important services on a remote machine. These could be anything from SharePoint to MSMQ but generally include two types of services:

- ✦ Managed services
- ✦ Database connections

Managed services

Managed services are things like Event Viewer and Microsoft Message Queue: things that you would need to look at to test parts of your application. Internet Information Services, for example, is a managed service that would show up in the list.

To get a server into Server Explorer, follow these steps:

1. **Right-click on Servers.**
2. **Click the Add Server button.**
3. **Type the machine name or IP number of the server you want to add.**
4. **If you want to use different credentials than you used to log in (for a different account, for instance), click Connect Using a Different User Name and enter the new credentials.**
5. **Click OK.**

Play around with the services you see. There are a lot of features in this panel that I don't have space to get into here.

Data connections

Above the Services in Figure 2-9 are the data connections. These are data connections that have been made on previous projects, which Visual Studio keeps around in case you need them for any other projects. Although keeping these connections around seems like a bit of a security risk, it sure as heck is convenient.

The goal is to reduce the dependency on SQL Management Console (the old method for managing the database for developers), and it does a darn good job. The key issue is access to the data model (table names and columns) and stored procedures; developing a program without access to the database is tough.

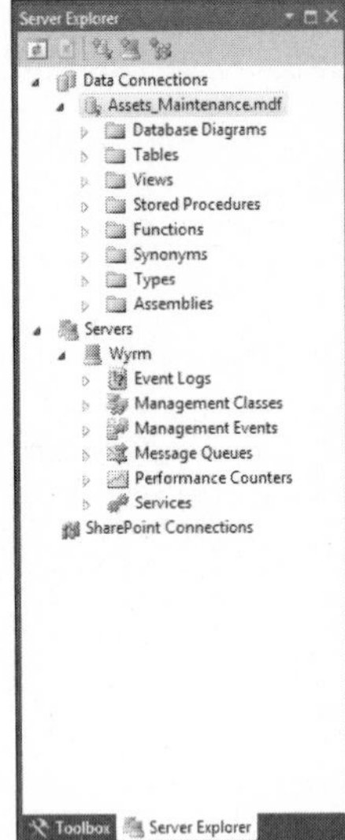

Figure 2-9: Server Explorer.

In a new connection, these database objects are given default folders:

- ✦ Database diagrams
- ✦ Tables
- ✦ Views
- ✦ Stored Procedures
- ✦ Functions
- ✦ Types
- ✦ Synonyms
- ✦ Assemblies

The key thing I want you to try is opening a Stored Procedure (you can do this by double-clicking it in the Data Sources panel). When you do so, you can easily edit SQL code, with indenting and colorization, right in Visual Studio. Use this. It's really neat.

Class View

The last of the five main panels is Class View. As I discuss throughout Books I and II, everything in the .NET Framework is an object. The classes that make up the framework — all derivatives of Object — are viewable in a tree view.

The Class Viewer is the home for that tree view. (See Figure 2-10.)

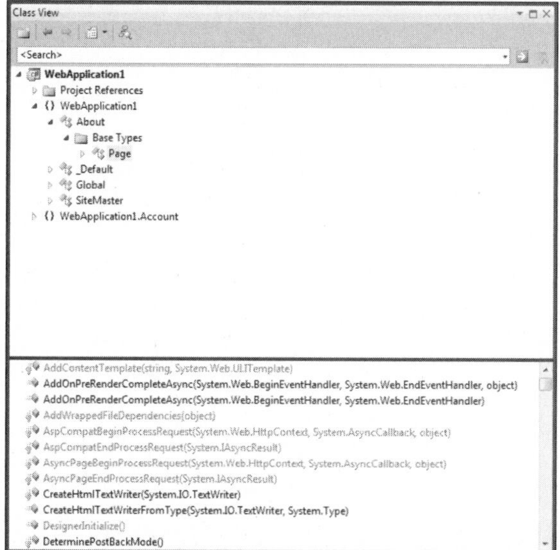

Figure 2-10: A viewer with Class.

From the Class View, you can look at all the members of a class and access the inline documentation, which gives you an overview of the framework and custom classes that make up your project.

Coding in Code View

Really, what else would you do in Code View? Nothing, that's what!

There is a lot to the Code Viewer in Visual Studio. Fact is, this is where you will spend 75 percent of your time, and boy, will you be glad that it works well.

Code Viewer has two primary tools:

- **The Code Viewer itself:** The first is the screen on which you edit the code — the Code Viewer.
- **Auxiliary windows:** The second are the little auxiliary windows that do a lot of useful things that don't directly relate to the code.

Exercising the Code Viewer

The Code Viewer is where you edit code. Doesn't matter what type of code, all of it is edited here. (See Figure 2-11.)

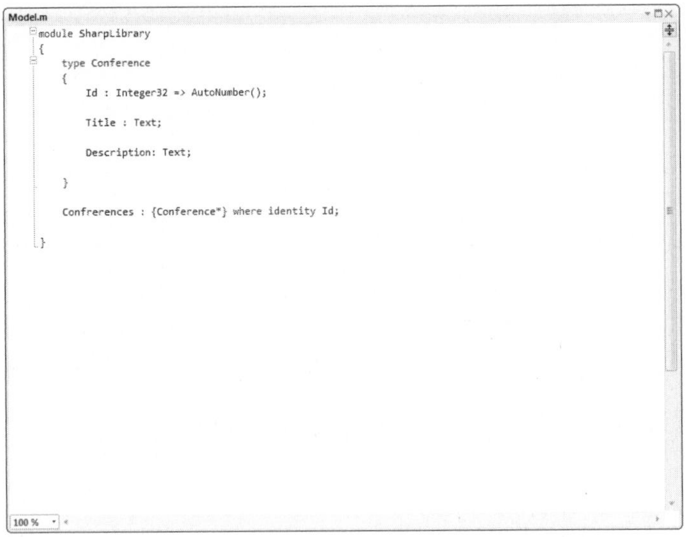

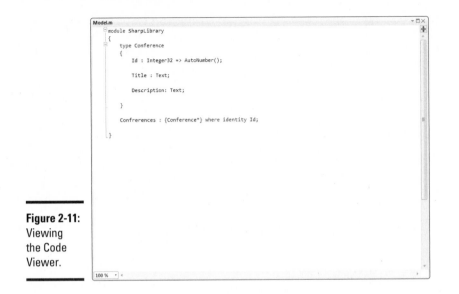

```
Model.m
module SharpLibrary
{
    type Conference
    {
        Id : Integer32 => AutoNumber();

        Title : Text;

        Description: Text;

    }

    Confrerences : {Conference*} where identity Id;

}
100 %
```

Figure 2-11: Viewing the Code Viewer.

It is a smart tool, however. If you are in XML, it works like an XML editor. In C++, it helps with the tabbing.

You can get to a code file in the Code Viewer a few ways. The most common way is to double-click on a code-driven file in Solution Explorer, and it will open in Code Viewer.

If you are viewing something in the designer, you can get to the code-behind related to the file in question by any of three methods:

- Click the View Code button in Solution Explorer.
- Right-click on the design surface and select View Code.
- Double-click on a control in the designer to generate an event for that control, and be moved to Code View.

You'll find yourself using all three over time. Note that you can get directly to the code-behind files by clicking the little triangle next to a designer file and then double-clicking the code files nested within.

Autocompleting with IntelliSense

IntelliSense is Microsoft's autocompletion feature, and it's a prominent part of the Code Viewer. You find IntelliSense no matter whether you want to. In Code View, click inside a class and press Ctrl+spacebar. Everything you are allowed to type there shows up in a big list.

The nice thing is, it is context-sensitive. Type **Console** and press the dot (`.`). All available members of Console appear. IntelliSense keeps you honest and prevents having to remember the two-million-odd members of the .NET Framework on a day-by-day basis.

IntelliSense helps with method signatures, too. Continue the line you started earlier by adding **WriteLine** — in other words, type (`Console.WriteLine(` — then check out the IntelliSense. It will tell you all the overloads for the member in question. Use the up and down arrows to move between them. It's slick.

Outlining

Visual Studio will auto-outline your code for you. Notice the little box with a minus sign (–) next to every namespace, class, and method? (See Figure 2-12.) Those are close-up sections of the code for readability. Doesn't seem like much now, but when you have 2,200 lines of code in there, you will be glad.

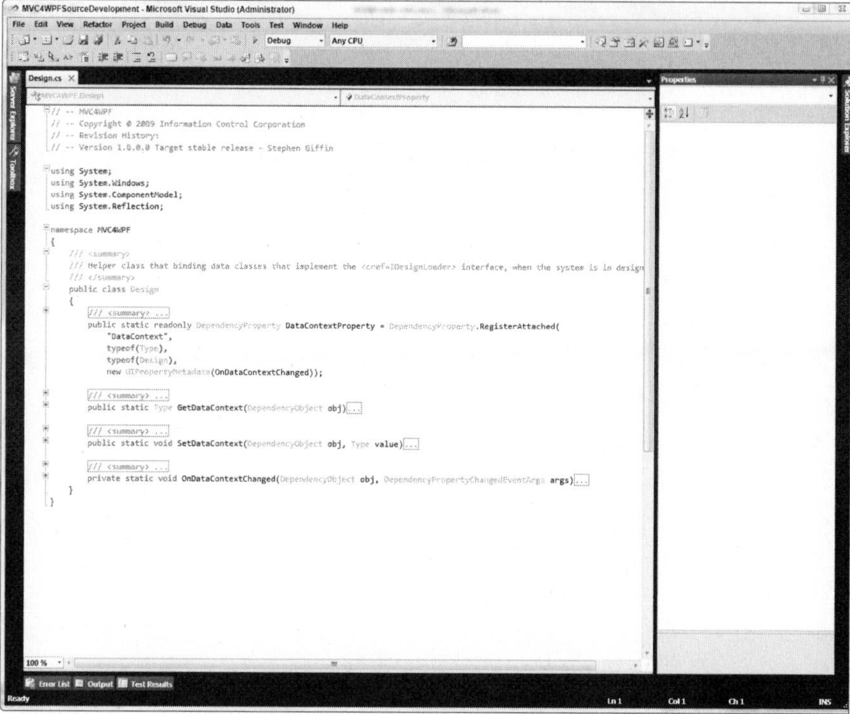

Figure 2-12: Teeny little outline marks.

You can create your own outlining, too. Preceding a section that you want to outline, put **#region** on a new line. After that section, put **#endregion**. This newly defined section — regardless of whether it's at an existing outline point — will get a new outline mark.

If there is a comment added after a `region` statement, it will show in the collapsed outline — as you can see in Figure 2-12.

Exploring the auxiliary windows

A number of windows affect text input and output in order to solve certain problems. As a group, they don't really have a name, so I call them auxiliary windows. I cover four of them here.

✦ **The Output window:** I use the Output window regularly for two things:

  • *Build logging:* Every time you build, the Output window tracks all of the linking and compiling that goes on under the sheets and shows any errors that might come up.

    By default, the Output window shows when you build. You can set it to not show the Visual Studio Options dialog box, after choosing General⇨Projects and Solutions.

    Errors listed in the Output windows can be used to navigate the code. The buttons in the Output box assist with getting around the code based on the messages in the window.

  • *Debug statements:* The second use of the Output window is Standard Out (for all you C++ people). If you use a `Debug.Write` statement in your code, the Output window is where it will go. Additionally, if you use `Console.Write`, but are running a Windows Forms application, for instance, the text will go to the Output window.

✦ **The Immediate window:** This window does exactly what one would expect it to do — it does something immediately. In debug mode, you can use the Immediate window to send commands to the program as it is running, to change the state, or evaluate operations. Try this to see what I mean:

1. **Open a Windows Forms project.**

   The one in the sample code for this chapter on this book's companion Web site is fine — you just need a default project template.

2. **Put a breakpoint on** `form.load`**. Do this by clicking in the grey bar running down the side of Code View.**

   A red dot should appear.

3. **Debug the program.**

   The program should stop on the `load` method.

4. **Open the Immediate window.**

   You should be able to do this in the Debug window, or by pressing Ctrl+D, I.

5. **Type** `?this.`

   See the IntelliSense menu?

6. **After the dot, type** WindowPosition.

   The question mark in Step 5 means Print. This command prints the window position to the screen.

   The response should be `windowDefaultLocation`.

That's what the Immediate window is for. You can do more than print values, too. You can change variable values and modify the execution of your program. It is a powerful part of your debugging toolbox.

✦ **The Breakpoints window:** Wait! Don't change anything in Visual Studio after trying the last example. Press Ctrl+D, B. The Breakpoints window appears, and the breakpoint you just added will be in it. (See Figure 2-13.)

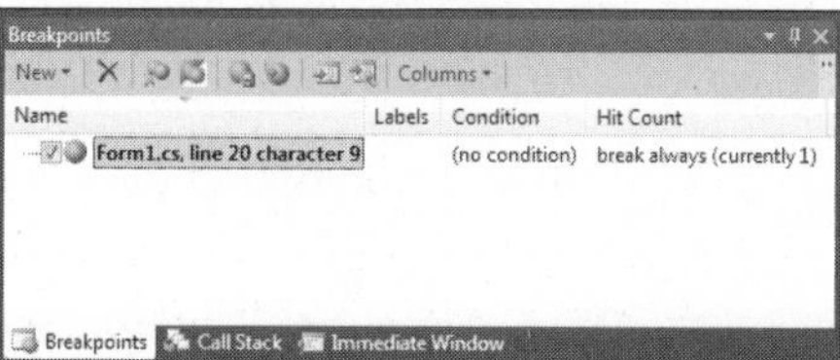

Figure 2-13: The Breakpoints window, which isn't called the Bookmark window.

What's cool here is that you can right-click on any breakpoint and completely alter the properties of that breakpoint. Try it — the important options are described in this list:

- *Location:* Specifies the location of the line of code that should host the breakpoint. This is convenient if you have filters set and you find you need to shift a line back.
- *Condition:* You can teach the breakpoint to stop at this line only if a certain variable is a specific value.
- *Hit Count:* Stop here only after the *x*th time it is hit.

   - *Filter:* It's similar to Condition, except that you can use system values such as `MachineName`, `ProcessName`, `ProcessId`, `ThreadName`, and `ThreadId`. It's useful for multiprocessor development, among other things.
   - *WhenHit:* You can do more than just stop on a breakpoint — instead, you can do something like print a value to the Output window, or even run a test script.

- **The Tasks window:** While coding, have you ever wanted to tell the developer working after you that something still needs to be done? Maybe you make a comment, maybe call it `//TODO:`.

  Well, if you do that, it appears in a task in the Tasks window. Isn't that just cool?

Using the Tools of the Trade

There are always a few things in any overview chapter that just don't fit in any category. In this one, there are a double handful of tools that I want to at least mention.

The Tools menu

I am sure you are shocked to find that the Tools menu is a great place to find tools that don't fit anywhere else, including the following:

- **Attach to Process:** For debugging, this tool enables you to connect to another running program on a machine and debug your code in that service.
- **Connect to Database:** See the "Server Explorer" section, earlier in this chapter.
- **Connect to Server:** Discussed in the "Server Explorer" section.
- **Code Snippets Manager:** I chat about snippets in Chapter 3.
- **Choose Toolbox Items:** This tool helps you manage the items in the Toolbox.
- **Add-in Manager:** Manages Visual Studio Add-ins. Add, remove, enable, and disable.
- **Macros:** You can group these commands or instructions as a single command to accomplish a task automatically. They're generally used to automate repetitive actions. Macros are covered in Chapter 4.
- **Create GUID:** Funny that this is here. This tool literally creates a Globally Unique ID (GUID), one of those 25 character codes that are supposed to be unique over the next 2,500 years or something. Make a new one and sell it on eBay.

- **Dotfuscator Community Edition:** This is a free code obfuscator for .NET.
- **WCF Service Configuration Manager:** Graphic interface for the WCF `config` files. Services are covered in Book VI.
- **External Tools:** This tool enables you to separate `.EXE` files that add functionality to Visual Studio.
- **Import and Export Settings:** This tools helps you move projects between development tools.
- **Customize:** This tool enables you to alter the look and feel of Visual Studio.
- **Options:** With these, you can alter the way Visual Studio works. Options are covered in some depth in Chapter 3.

Building and Debugging

I'm sure by now you have gotten the basics of building and debugging. A few other options in the Build and Debug menus deserve at least a small explanation, including the following:

- **Rebuild:** This checks all the references throughout the project before compiling the project. It's useful if your development computer has changed configuration since your last build.
- **Clean:** This actually deletes not only the components created as part of your project, but also all DLLs that were copied into your project by references that were set to that mode.
- **Batch Build:** This enables you to build release and debug versions (for instance), or 32 and 64 bit (as another example) at the same time.
- **Configuration Manager:** Use this to set the order and mode in which you build your projects.

Refactor menu

Refactoring is the practice of reorganizing code that might have become scattered during development or debugging. The Refactoring menu in Visual Studio provides a few tools that help with refactoring in C#, including these:

- **Rename:** Rename is simple — anytime you rename a symbol (a named object such as a variable, a method, a property, or an enum, for example), you can change the name throughout the project. After you change the name of something, you should see a smart tag appear near the end of the symbol name that has Rename as an option.

  Rename changes all other symbols with that same name in the project (not the solution). Rename with Preview shows you each change before it is performed.

✦ **Extract Method:** Perhaps you've written a block of code and then thought "oh boy, I am going to need this over there." If so, Extract Method is for you. It will take a highlighted block of code, move it to a method, extract all the variables, make them parameters, and then you'll be ready for code reuse.

✦ **Encapsulate Field:** In a similar vein as extracting a method, Encapsulate Field takes a private variable and makes it a public field. For instance, take a line of code like private string `_theValue`; highlight it in code designer and select Encapsulate Field from the Refactor menu.

Visual Studio asks you to name the new property and create a new property based on your selections:

```
public string TheValue
{
  get { return _theValue; }
  set { _theValue = value; }
}
```

✦ **Extract Interface:** Extract Interface takes a set of method signatures and makes an interface for you. Interfaces are vital to contract driven development.

If you are working a project that suddenly has more than one programmer (as in, they got you help!), extracting interfaces to common classes in your project decreases barriers to the new folks' entry pattern.

✦ **Remove Parameters:** This is the safe way to get excess parameters out of methods. In all honesty, I use this refactoring tool the least.

✦ **Reorder Parameters:** Being able to change the order of parameters is significantly handier. Sometimes, you just need to switch the order of two parameters. If you do this, all the places where you call that method must have the parameter order changed, or they will send in the wrong stuff.

This simple tool enables you to change the parameter order and then finds all places that call the method in question, and switch the parameter order sent in.

Chapter 3: Customizing Visual Studio

In This Chapter

- **Setting environment options**
- **Changing menus and commands**
- **Making and accessing snippets**
- **Hacking project templates**

You have seen how to install Visual Studio and make a new project. You have seen the bits that the user interface gives you. The fun's over. Now you get to make it work for you.

Then again, maybe the fun is just starting.

Visual Studio offers a dizzying array of options for customization. Used poorly, these options have the real potential to make the lives of you and your coworkers miserable. Used correctly, they have the potential to double your velocity.

I am after the doubling part.

At its most basic, customization involves setting options to better match your environment, style, and work patterns. These options include everything from your code visibility to source control. The idea is to configure Visual Studio's options to your exact specifications.

The next step is to improve the usability of the application to match your day-to-day operations. One of the best overall ways to accomplish this is to change the button tape and the menus to make what you use every day more available. Another great way to do this is to manage or create snippets that automate generation of code.

Finally, you take a short deep dive (just hold your breath, you'll be fine) into the Project and File templates of Visual Studio. Did you know that when you create a new XAML file (for example) or C# Class file that the contents of that file are controlled by a template and are editable? No? Well, do I have a surprise for you!

All these things put together amount to a rather flexible Integrated Development Environment (IDE). Although the flexibility is nice, the goal is to set a configuration that matches your style. I can't tell you what that configuration is. All I can do is tell you what the software can do and give you the tools to make the changes.

I learned a new phrase yesterday at DevLink: *convention over configuration.* You build software the way most people use it, rather than provide 10,000 options to change the way it works. I think Visual Studio gives you some of each, but you have to push the balance to the convention side yourself.

Setting Options

The Options dialog box can be found by choosing the Tools⇨Options menu item, and looks a whole lot like Figure 3-1. It is generally designed to set Boolean type options like Show This or Provide That or to change paths to resources where Visual Studio will store certain files.

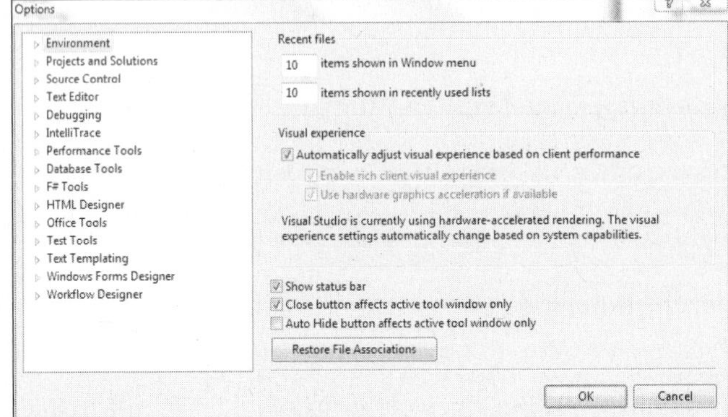

Figure 3-1: The default Options screen.

Those details are all well and good, but my goal is to introduce the other things that the options provide. I start with adjustments to your environment and then describe the remarkable language options, and then I explore some neat stuff.

Environment

The Environment section is where you begin in the Options dialog box. Sections here include the font details of code-editing screens, key mappings, and the RSS feed settings for the Start page.

The Font and Colors settings will probably be of interest only when you need them for a presentation. Sixteen points is the size of choice for most speakers, including myself. There are a number of "code friendly" fonts out there, and this is where you select them.

Defining the Start Page

The *start page* is the first page you see when you start Visual Studio. It consumes an RSS feed from Microsoft with news related to the kind of development you do, as you told Visual Studio when you first installed the software. Often, people change roles and the RSS feed no longer applies to their work. This is a problem.

The solution is the Start Page News Channel field. You can pick any RSS feed you are interested in using for your Start Page content. If you like Microsoft Developer content, you can choose Scott Hanselman's feed for your Start Page. If you are interested in security, you can use Exotic Liability's blog. If you like silliness, you can use the feed at `www.sempf.net`. Alternatively, you can set it to show nothing. You're in charge.

Keyboard commands

The most useful settings in the Options dialog box are the Keyboard settings. This is where you make Visual Studio feel like Emacs through the use of keyboard mappings.

Keyboard mappings are key combinations you set to run commands you usually run by clicking your mouse. For example, one commonly used mapping is Ctrl+C, which copies material in the same way that clicking the Edit menu and then clicking Copy does. Many developers feel that using keyboard mapped commands makes the development experience faster and easier.

The keyboard settings essentially enable you to set keyboard commands for any menu selection in Visual Studio. The Apply the Following Additional Keyboard Mapping Scheme drop-down list enables the key mappings to be different, if you happen to like the mappings of other development environments.

Language

By *language,* I don't mean the Internationalization setting that enables you to change the display language of Visual Studio if you have additional language packs installed (although that is neat). I am talking about the *programming* languages you work in with Visual Studio. The Languages option is where you can provide settings for each of these programming languages.

The Text Editor options change the way the Code Editor behaves. All the languages that Visual Studio supports out of the box appear in the tree view under the main heading and allow you to alter general options, tabbing, formatting, sometimes advanced options, and miscellaneous features of the text editor.

For instance, look at C#. To open the C# view, click where it says C# with the little triangle in the Options tree view (that's a WPF tree view — you'll get used to it). The first view in the Options panel is the General view. Here you can change the default options for statement completion, various behavior settings, and what the Code Editor should display aside from the code.

After you click the little triangle next to the C# node, you see the General panel (which is the default view) and then the other panels you can use:

- **Tabs:** This section is for people who are obsessive about the tabbing of their source code. The Tabs panel determines how many spaces make up a tab, and whether Visual Studio should insert them automatically.
- **Advanced:** This section should probably be called *Miscellaneous*. Everything that doesn't fit into other categories is here. In this section, handling comments, interface implementation, and refactoring details all have a checkbox that basically says "If you don't like it when Visual Studio does this, click here."
- **Formatting:** Formatting in C# is very in-depth. Generally, C# coders are a little persnickety about the look of their code. Visual Studio does a lot of work to help make your code look the way you want it, but you have to tell it what to do. Options for formatting include:
  - Automatic formatting
  - Indentation
  - Newlines
  - Spacing
  - Wrapping
- **IntelliSense:** The most interesting field is the list of characters that "commit" an IntelliSense selection. By typing one of these characters, you select the highlighted IntelliSense member. Usually, I just use space or dot (`.`) but there are many more options, and I had no idea!

Neat stuff

I provide a canonical list of the options that I always forget are in here, but that I have to use frequently. Right now, they probably won't make a lot of sense, but you may remember them when you need them later.

- To implement a new source control provider, first install the package (for instance, Turtle for CodePlex's SVN implementation, or Team System) and then go to Source Control in Options to pick the one you want to use. Just one at a time!
- Many people recommend that you store your projects in a short file path, like `c:\Projects`. You can change where you store projects in the Projects and Solutions section in the options dialog box.

- Specify which browser you are coding your HTML for in the Text Editor / HTML / Validation section of the Options dialog box.
- Set up automatic Windows Forms data binding in the Designer for custom controls (that you have bought or built) in the Windows Forms Designer / Data UI Customization section of the Options dialog box.
- If you are one of those crazy people who think table names should not be pluralized, you can turn off that behavior in the Data Designer in the Database Tools / O/R Designer section of the Options dialog box.
- You can teach Visual Studio to open a file with a given extension in a certain file editor using the Text Editor / File Extension section of the Options panel.

Using Snippets

Snippets are little bits of pre-coded logic that are meant to help you remember how to perform some standard code functions in various languages. In VB, for instance, you might not remember how to read from a file, so there is a snippet for that. In C#, you may want implement a property getter and setter, so you use a shortcut to get the snippet in place.

Using snippets

You can use a snippet in a few different ways, most of which are somewhat slow. The fastest way is through the use of key commands. To use a snippet this way, type its shortcut code and press Tab twice. For instance, try these steps:

1. **Open Visual Studio and start a new Class Library project in C#.**
2. **In the new class that is created, place the cursor inside the curly braces.**
3. **Type** prop.
4. **Press Tab twice. Your results should look like the ones shown in Figure 3-2.**

   See the template that is put into place? `Int` is highlighted. You can type over it.
5. **Type** string **and press Tab twice. Now** `MyProperty` **is highlighted.**
6. **Type** FirstName **and press Enter twice.**

   Now you have a finished automatically implemented property. It should look like this:

   ```
   public string FirstName {get; set; }
   ```

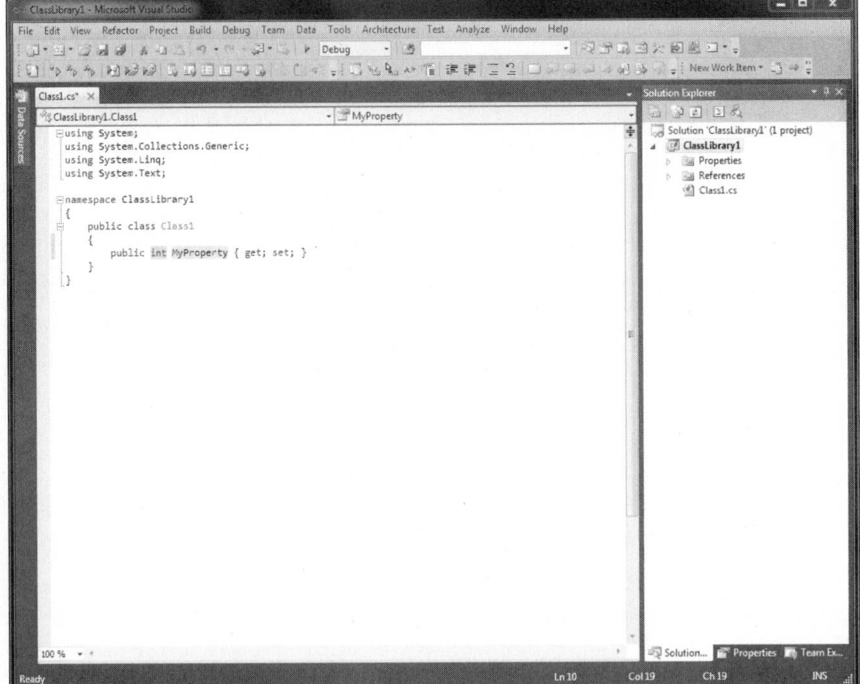

Figure 3-2: The automatically generated property snippet.

You can get to a snippet in other ways, including this one:

1. **Right-click at the insertion point.**

   You have the option to select Insert Snippet.

2. **Click Insert Snippet.**

   The full list of all the installed snippets appears at the insertion point.

3. **Click an item in the list, and the contents of that folder appear.**

   Continue selecting categories (the menu extends to the right) until you have selected the snippet you were looking for.

4. **Double-click the snippet to insert it.**

After they're inserted, populating the variables works just like the shortcut version.

Using surround snippets

Surround snippets are very cool. Have you ever written a few lines of code, and then realized that you should probably try and catch errors? You have to add a little code at the beginning, and then add a little code at the end, and then make sure the middle is in the right place. It's a pain.

Surround snippets are designed to solve that problem. They are normal snippets with a bit of logic in them that says "This part goes above the selection, and this part goes below the selection." If you want to handle errors for a section, you highlight that section, and the snippet will put the `try` before the selection and the `catch` at the end. To use a surround snippet, follow these steps:

1. **Highlight some code in the Code Designer.**
2. **Press Ctrl+K,S to open the snippets menu.**
3. **Select the appropriate snippet from the menu.** You can choose the snippet that is right for whatever you are coding. Try `prop` for a property getter and setter.
4. **Set the various variables that Visual Studio prompts you.**

The snippet will appear appropriately above and below the selected text. For instance, if I had this chunk of code:

```
for (int loopcounter = 1; loopcounter <= 10; loopcounter++)
{
     Console.WriteLine(string.Format("The number is {0}.",
   loopcounter));
}
```

and I felt that I needed a `try ... catch` block around it, I could highlight that code and do the preceding steps. If I select `try` from the menu, I will get this:

```
try
{
    for (int loopcounter = 1; loopcounter <= 10;
   loopcounter++)
    {
        Console.WriteLine(string.Format("The number is {0}.",
   loopcounter));
    }
}
catch (Exception)
{
     throw;
}
```

Exception is highlighted in green; I can tab to that and add the exception type I am expecting. It's a slick system.

Making snippets

Snippets are XML files that follow a format understood by Visual Studio. They include a Header and Snippet element. The Header includes a title, which is how the snippet is referred. The Snippet element, where all the work is done, includes a Code element, which has the code to be inserted.

The best way to make a new snippet is to modify an existing one. Snippets can be found in your Visual Studio install directory, which should be `C:\Program Files (x86)\Microsoft Visual Studio 10.0\VC#\Snippets\1033` if you are on a 64-bit operating system (otherwise you can drop the x86).

In the folder referenced in the preceding paragraph, let's look at a simple example: `cw.snippet` is a `Console.Writeline` command. Right-click the file to open it. Here's the code:

```
<?xml version="1.0" encoding="utf-8" ?>
<CodeSnippets xmlns="http://schemas.microsoft.com/VisualStudio/2005/CodeSnippet">
   <CodeSnippet Format="1.0.0">
    <Header>
         <Title>cw</Title>
         <Shortcut>cw</Shortcut>
         <Description>Code snippet for Console.WriteLine</Description>
         <Author>Microsoft Corporation</Author>
         <SnippetTypes>
            <SnippetType>Expansion</SnippetType>
         </SnippetTypes>
      </Header>
      <Snippet>
         <Declarations>
            <Literal Editable="false">
               <ID>SystemConsole</ID>
               <Function>SimpleTypeName(global::System.Console)</Function>
            </Literal>
         </Declarations>
         <Code Language="csharp">
            <![CDATA[$SystemConsole$.WriteLine($end$);]]>
         </Code>
      </Snippet>
   </CodeSnippet>
</CodeSnippets>
```

This list describes what's in the Header element:

- **Title:** Shows up on the context menu.
- **Shortcut:** The key combination you can type for IntelliSense.
- **Description and Author:** Show up in the tooltip when you mouse over the snippet in Visual Studio.
- **SnippetType:** Defines which menus the snippet appears on. The most common types are Expansion and SurroundsWith. *Expansion* means that it inserts the text. SurroundsWith means that it's placed above and below the selection.

The Snippet element is where the work is done. In the `cw.snippet` example there are two elements in Snippet: Declarations and Code. Declarations declares the variables, and Code is what gets inserted. Within these, these statements are true:

- ✦ The Literal element describes a variable that will be used in the creation of the snippet.
- ✦ In this case, Function tries to get the simplest version of the `System.Console` namespace given the current constraints, and ID names it `SystemConsole`.
- ✦ The Code element specifies the language and then puts the actual code in place.

If you want to make your own snippet, I suggest that you start with one of the samples provided in the Visual Studio install. You can just start from scratch too — if you wish, you can create an XML file and give it a `.snippet` file extension — but I think these things are best done iteratively.

Deploying snippets

To deploy a snippet of your own, use the Code Snippets Manager. The manager is found on the Tools menu and looks like the one shown in Figure 3-3.

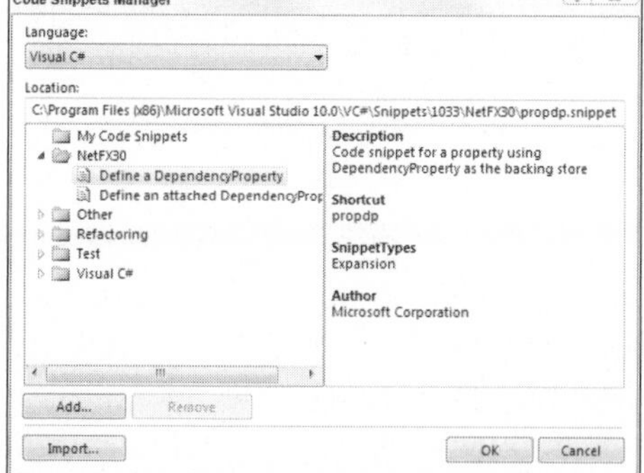

Figure 3-3: The Code Snippets Manager.

Adding a new snippet this way is fairly simple. After you create your snippets file, click the Import button, and select the `.snippet` file. It's placed in the selected folder, so make sure you have the snippet folder highlighted.

The Add and Remove buttons in the Manager refer to directories, not files. Use them to make new snippet folders. The Search Online feature just searches Help for IntelliSense Code Snippets.

Sharing snippets

Sharing a snippet is a more complicated act than it should be. One would think that you could just create a `.snippet` file, send it to someone, and that would be that. It isn't so.

I should amend that — it is so if you are just sending it to a friend — then it is just a matter of using the Manager. On the other hand, if you are making a package of snippets for a group to install, you get to the nitty-gritty.

A snippet sharing escapade has three components:

- **The `.snippet` file itself:** This topic is discussed in the preceding section.
- **The `.vscontent` file that lists the snippets (even if there is only one):** The `.vscontent` file is one with a listing of snippets in a package. It consists of multiple Content elements that describe the various files in the package. For instance, here is the `.vscontent` file that would be used for the previous `Console.Writeline` example.

  ```
  <VSContent xmlns="http://schemas.microsoft.com/
      developer/vscontent/2010">
       <Content>
           <FileName>cw.snippet</FileName>
           <DisplayName>cw</DisplayName>
           <Description>Console.Writeline</Description>
           <FileContentType>Code Snippet</FileContentType>
           <ContentVersion>3.0</ContentVersion>
           <Attributes>
               <Attribute name="lang" value="csharp"/>
           </Attributes>
       </Content>
  </VSContent>
  ```

  This gives you two files in the package — the snippet and the content file. These need to be packaged in a `.vsi` file, and then distributed.

- **The `.vsi` file to package it all together:** The `.vsi` file is a Zip file with a new extension. To make it, literally zip your folder of snippets with the `vscontent` file and change the file extension from `.zip` to `.vsi`.

  Visual Studio users can double-click `.vsi` files in order to have the `vstudio` installer handle them. The command line can also be used for more in-depth installs. The complexity of the system on the snippet developer side makes sense when you consider that the end user ends up with a better experience.

Hacking the Project Types

Throughout the book, I recommend that you not start with a blank screen. Click New Project and select a project type in order to get some basic set of code to start with. In `C:\Program Files (x86)\Microsoft Visual Studio 10.0\Common7\IDE`, you find the files that make all the magic project types work.

Hacking Project templates

The first, most obvious target for hacking are the project types because they are text based and have a lot of useful information in them. Found in the IDE folder referenced in the preceding paragraph, the ProjectTemplates folder follows the hierarchy of the New Project tree view. (See Figure 3-4.)

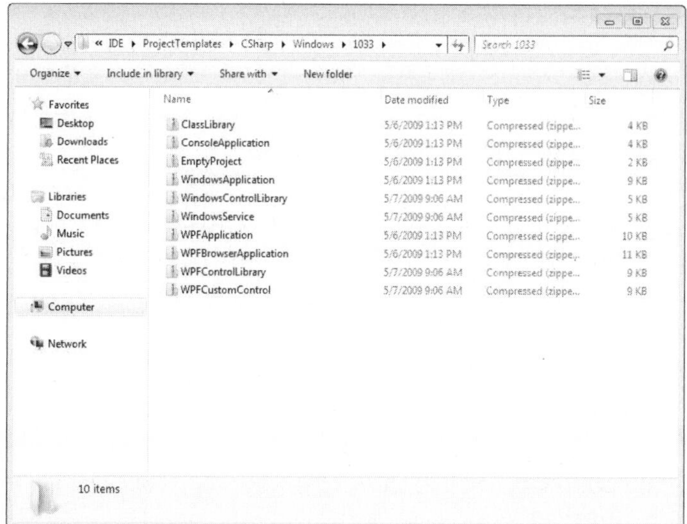

Figure 3-4: A bunch of project-type Zips.

I focus on the `CSharp` directory tree because this book is about C#. To keep examples to a minimum, open the `Windows/1033` folder, in order to view Windows project types. In a default install, that looks something like this:

- ClassLibrary
- ConsoleApplication
- EmptyProject
- WindowsApplication

- WindowsControlLibrary
- WindowsService
- WPFApplication
- WPFBrowserApplication
- WPFControlLibrary
- WPFCustomControl

The explorer should look like Figure 3-4. The files are Zip files and should stay that way. The setup process for the development environment reads right from the Zips.

The ConsoleApplication is about the simplest project type, and it is a great place to begin creating your own. Open the `ConsoleApplication zip` and take a look at the four files it includes:

- `assemblyinfo.cs`: This file goes directly into the project. Take a look at the code; it is the exact code that is in the `assemblyinfo` file in a project, except there are project-specific variables surrounded by dollar signs.
- `consoleapplication.csproj`: This is the actual project file; the name will be replaced by the new project-creation process. As with the other included files, there are variable names within the XML of the file.
- `csConsoleApplication.vstemplate`: This is the magic file that tells the project-creation process how to build the new project. The important part is the TemplateContent element, which contains the name of the ProjectFile and the ProjectItems that go into the finished product. This is clearly where you would put new files if you needed them.
- `program.cs`: This is the default file for the application. This is where you begin when you start coding. Take a look at the code — it should look familiar.

So where does that leave you? You can change the projects. Try these steps:

1. **Copy the** `ConsoleApplication.zip` **from** `C:\Program Files\Microsoft Visual Studio 10.0\Common7\IDE\ProjectTemplates\CSharp\Windows\1033`.
2. **Paste the file back into the folder — it should make** `ConsoleApplication - Copy.zip`.
3. **Rename that file** ConsoleAndClass.zip.
4. **Drag the new class to your desktop temporarily.**
5. **Right-click and select Extract All from the menu. Select the defaults.**

   A new `ConsoleAndClass` folder is created.

6. **Delete the** `ConsoleAndClass.zip` **file from your desktop.**
7. **Open** `C:\Program Files\Microsoft Visual Studio 10.0\Common7\IDE\ProjectTemplates\CSharp\Windows\1033\ClassLibrary.zip`.
8. **Copy the** `class1.cs` **file from that compressed folder.**
9. **Paste it back into the new** `ConsoleAndClass` **folder on your desktop.**
10. **Right-click** `csConsoleApplication.vstemplate` **and select Edit from the menu to open the file in Notepad.**
11. **In the file, change each instance of** `ConsoleApplication` to `ConsoleClassApplication`.
12. **Add the bolded line to the file, in order to reference the new file.**

```
<?xml version="1.0" encoding="utf-8"?>
<VSTemplate Version="3.0.0" Type="Project" xmlns="http://schemas.
    microsoft.com/developer/vstemplate/2005">
  <TemplateData>
    <Name Package="{FAE04EC1-301F-11d3-BF4B-00C04F79EFBC}" ID="2320" />
    <Description Package="{FAE04EC1-301F-11d3-BF4B-00C04F79EFBC}"
    ID="2321" />
    <Icon Package="{FAE04EC1-301F-11d3-BF4B-00C04F79EFBC}" ID="4548" />
    <TemplateID>Microsoft.CSharp.ConsoleClassApplication</TemplateID>
    <ProjectType>CSharp</ProjectType>
    <RequiredFrameworkVersion>2.0</RequiredFrameworkVersion>
    <SortOrder>70</SortOrder>
    <NumberOfParentCategoriesToRollUp>1</
    NumberOfParentCategoriesToRollUp>
    <CreateNewFolder>true</CreateNewFolder>
    <DefaultName>ConsoleClassApplication</DefaultName>
    <ProvideDefaultName>true</ProvideDefaultName>
  </TemplateData>
  <TemplateContent>
    <Project File="ConsoleClassApplication.csproj"
    ReplaceParameters="true">
      <ProjectItem ReplaceParameters="true" TargetFileName="Properties\
    AssemblyInfo.cs">AssemblyInfo.cs</ProjectItem>
      <ProjectItem ReplaceParameters="true" OpenInEditor="true">Program.
    cs</ProjectItem>
      <ProjectItem ReplaceParameters="true" OpenInEditor="true">Class1.
    cs</ProjectItem>
    </Project>
  </TemplateContent>
</VSTemplate>
```

13. **Save and close** `csConsoleApplication.vstemplate`.
14. **Rename** `consoleapplication.csproj` **to** `consoleclassapplication.csproj`.
15. **Close the folder, right-click its icon on your desktop, and click Send To / Compressed folder from the resulting menu in order to make a new** `ConsoleAndClass.zip` **folder.**
16. **Copy the Zip file back to the original folder.**

17. **Close Visual Studio if it is open.**

18. **Open the Visual Studio Command Prompt as Administrator.**

    (It is in the All Programs folder in the Start Bar, under Visual Studio 2010 / Visual Studio tools.)

19. **Run** `devenv /setup`.

Now, when you open Visual Studio and click New Project, there should be a new project type, called Console And Class. Create a new project based on this type, and it will make you a Console `.cs` file and a class `.cs` file.

Hacking item templates

Items work the same way. Check into `C:\Program Files\Microsoft Visual Studio 10.0\Common7\IDE\ItemTemplates\CSharp` and you'll see the same set of items types that show in the Add New Item dialog box:

- Code
- Data
- General
- Office
- Reporting
- Silverlight
- Web
- Windows Forms
- Workflow
- WPF

If you dig into a directory through the Code/1033 folder, you will find more or less the same kinds of things you saw in the project templates in the preceding section. The templates are in Zip files (and have to stay that way). These files include a `.vstemplate` file that has the details Visual Studio needs. The files that go into the project are in there, too.

Yes, some of these item templates are duplicates of the items in the project templates. I don't like that, but I can't see any way around it.

Look in the Code/1033 folder. There is a Class.zip file that maintains the Class template, if you were to right-click a project name and select Add New Class. Suppose that you want to put the default comment block in here too. Here's what to do:

1. **Extract the Class.zip onto your desktop temporarily.**
2. **Open the class1.cs file in Visual Studio.**
3. **Add the bold lines to the file.**

   The file in the project group looks like the following listing. To edit it, you just make a new line before the class declaration and type ///.

```
using System;
using System.Collections.Generic;
$if$ ($targetframeworkversion$ >= 3.5)using System.Linq;
$endif$using System.Text;


namespace $rootnamespace$
{
    /// <summary>
    ///
    /// </summary>
   class $safeitemrootname$
   {
   }
}
```

4. **Save the file and close Visual Studio.**
5. **Zip the folder on your desktop by right-clicking the folder and choosing Send To/Compressed Folder from the resulting menu.**
6. **Put the file back in** C:\Program Files\Microsoft Visual Studio 10.0\Common7\IDE\ItemTemplates\CSharp\Code\1033.
7. **Open Visual Studio and make a new Class project.**
8. **Right-click the project name and select Add⇨Class.**

   Keep the default name.

   Visual Studio makes a new file with the comment block, as shown in Figure 3-5.

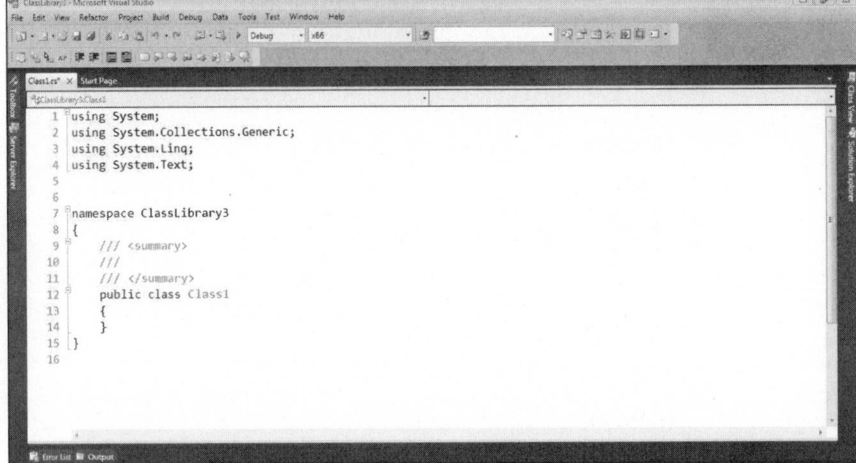

Figure 3-5: You've changed Visual Studio behavior — again!

Chapter 4: Transforming Text Templates

In This Chapter

- ✔ **Discovering where templating for Visual Studio originated**
- ✔ **Figuring out when to use T4**
- ✔ **Getting your environment ready for T4 use**
- ✔ **Using some basic T4 directives**

T4 (Text Template Transformation Toolkit) is a code generation toolkit built into Visual Studio. It is a built in language used to make the default ASP.NET and Windows Forms files in C# or VB, for example, when you use the Add New Item feature.

Scott Hanselman, from Microsoft, said it best: "Now's the time to introduce code generation to your company." I wholeheartedly agree. Code generation increases developer productivity, decreases bugs in final versions, and makes people happy.

Lars Corneliussen, a Microsoft MVP, said, "T4 in VS is the equivalent to `index.php` in Apache," and he isn't far from the truth. T4 is a starting point for a project, providing seamless redirection and logical formatting of what the user (in this case, the developer) actually sees. It is the template, just as the name suggests.

T4 is a big topic, like so many others in this book, but you should be able to get started creating code generation from the material here. Getting your environment ready and understanding the concepts are the most important steps.

Getting to Know T4

In this chapter, I look at T4 as a code-generation tool. It is a lot more than that. Really, it is a tool for the management of metadata around Domain Specific Languages. If that makes no sense to you, join the club.

Many things about computer science are elegant, and the current drive toward meta-programming and the use of higher and higher level languages to solve tougher and tougher problems is one of them. I am a second-generation kind of guy, though. I let the early adopters try something out first and see whether it works. If it works, then I use it.

For code generation, T4 works.

At its most complex, T4 can review information about the kind of projects you build and determine what kind of templates you need to get the job done. That's cool, but let's stick with our analysis and just let T4 do the dirty work.

Looking back at the DSL Tools

One of the first ways that Microsoft tried to implement code generation back in the day (and it is still around) was through the Environment Design Time Environment (EnvDTE), and by giving developers access to the code files themselves.

This bare-bones approach provided by EnvDTE isn't really what they were after, though. The goal of templating was to provide a language of languages, which developers could use to model their own development style. The code generation is almost secondary.

Microsoft's next shot to solving the code-generation problem was the Domain-Specific Language Tools. The idea here was to use the EnvDTE and other markup languages to describe a very high-level idea in a project — for example, a new ASPX page. Not any specific ASPX page: *any* ASPX page.

That description can then become the starter code that you see when you ask for a new ASPX page. See what I mean? When you describe a higher-level concept like requesting a new ASPX page, the DLS implements a concrete version, which you then can edit.

Looking ahead to what it became

To put it in REAL general terms, the DSL Tools split into two things: code generation and modeling tools. The modeling tools are Oslo and M. The code generation is T4.

Because T4 is designed to generate anything, it can emit any kind of file. If you think about it, it all makes sense. If an entity in your domain model is a product Web site, then T4 would have to emit HTML, CSS, and JavaScript when a new product is added to the database.

The same thing applies to the language that is emitted as part of the project. T4 doesn't care what code you are emitting. It just wants to stamp out what matches the model you define for it. If you set up the model to use C#, that's fine. VB? Fine. T4 is just generating and giving text an extension.

Additionally, you can write your code inside the T4 file in C# or VB.NET. This is the code that makes any decisions about the output, accesses data sources that might be needed to generate the code, and so on. It follows the same .NET rules.

Even though T4 was developed as an addition to Visual Studio 2008 and is baked into version 2010, you can use it in all previous versions back to 2005.

Figuring Out When to Use T4

Now that it is more or less clear what T4 is designed to do, the next step is figuring out when to use it. There are two main applications, as well as many lesser ones out there — the following sections are not all-inclusive. The main ones are replacing repetitive coding and building code based on outside data.

Replacing repetitive coding

Like snippets do at the class level, T4 can replace repetitive coding at the file level. If you think about it, you realize that there is a whole host of code that you shouldn't have to write over and over and over, but nonetheless you do.

Take something simple, like an HTML page. Every page must have certain elements, by the HTML 4.0 Transitional standard:

```
<!DOCTYPE html PUBLIC "-//W3C//DTD XHTML 1.0 Transitional//
   EN" "http://www.w3.org/TR/xhtml1/DTD/xhtml1-transitional.
   dtd">

<html xmlns="http://www.w3.org/1999/xhtml">
<head>
  <title></title>
</head>
<body>

</body>
</html>
```

Those are required elements! Can't they just be . . . *assumed?* As it turns out, no, they can't, because some of the elements must have data inserted inside them. This is just the starting point — exactly what T4 is good at providing.

Building code based on outside data

The more powerful use of T4 is to reference outside data to set up code templates. This can be metadata about a project like supporting files that need to be referenced, or direct data like the previous product Web site example.

Let's look at project metadata for a moment. MVC4WOF is an open source project that I participate in, and it uses metadata in the form of contract files to generate code. (Check it out at `www.mvc4wpf.com`.)

In a classic example of an automation pattern, MVC4WPF's New File dialog box (see Figure 4-1) checks with the user to get the contract (in the form of an interface) that is being referenced for the given Model, View, or Controller being generated.

This allows T4 to parse through the interface, grab pertinent information, and add it to the resultant file.

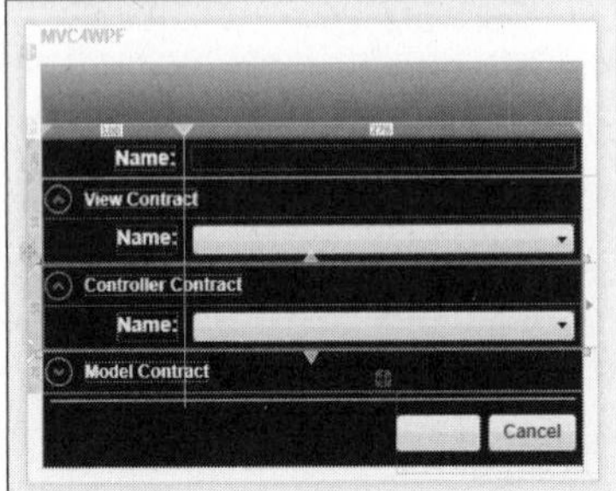

Figure 4-1: Selecting controller interfaces.

Setting Up the Environment

You need to know a few details relating to the environment.

Changing the security settings

You can relax the security requirements for T4. If you write T4 documents and don't sign them (which is often the case), you will receive a dialog box warning you that you might be generating some dangerous code. You can see that message in Figure 4-2.

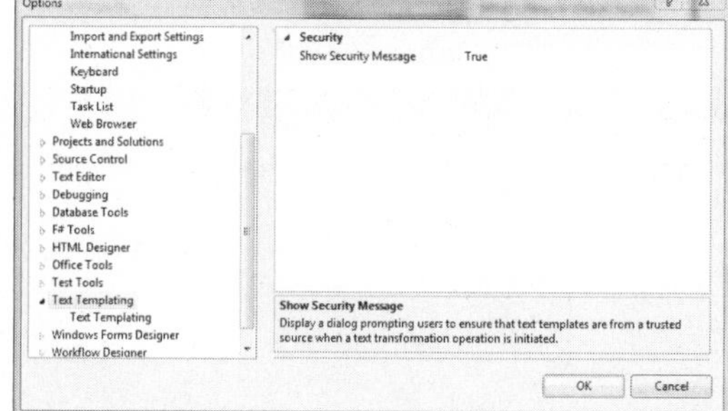

Figure 4-2: The security setting in the Tools/ Options box.

As T4 files are essentially macros, this warning makes sense. It is possible for someone to write malicious code and execute it on your development workstation. I advise that you turn off the security during development of the template and back on when you are back to your daily scheduled programming.

Creating a template from a text file

The simplest TT file is just a text file, edited in Notepad, with some basic commands in it called Directives. Follow these steps to create a template from that basic text file:

1. **Open Notepad.**
2. **In the new file, add the following lines of code.**

   ```
   <#@ output extension=".cs" #>

   public class TestClass
   {
   }
   ```

   The lines are cryptic, I know, but they will make sense in a second.
3. **Save the file in your Documents folder as** `GenerateClass.tt`**.**

   It should look like Figure 4-3.

4. **Create a new class library in Visual Studio.**

5. **Right-click on the project file, select Add, and then Existing File.**

   You'll see a file selection dialog box.

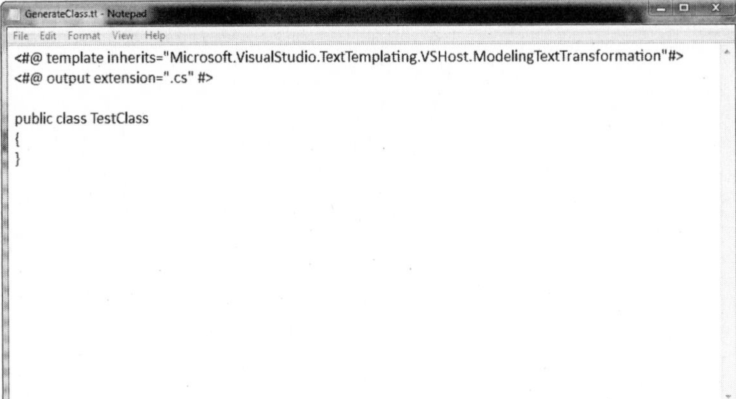

Figure 4-3: The world's simplest TT file.

6. **Select the `GenerateClass.tt` file you created in Step 3.** You might have to select All Files from the Files of Type drop-down menu if `.tt` isn't one of the file types available.

7. **Click OK.**

   You get the security warning discussed in the section "Changing the security settings," earlier in this chapter, shown in Figure 4-4. Click OK to that, too.

   Notice that in the file tree in Solution Explorer, under the TT file, there is now a CS file with your code in it, as shown in Figure 4-5.

Security Warning

Running this text template can potentially harm your computer. Do not run it if you obtained it from an untrusted source.

Click OK to run the template.
Click Cancel to stop the process.

Do not show this message again

OK Cancel

Figure 4-4: The vaunted security message.

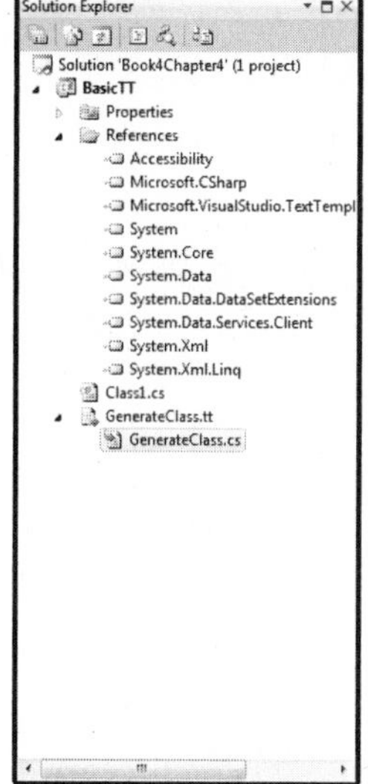

Figure 4-5: The generated code file.

Using Some of the T4 Directives

Clearly this is a very Hello World example. The magic of T4 is complex, and I had to spend a lot of time (believe it or not) making the simplest example.

One of the things that makes T4 work well are the directives built into the language. These commands are just like shell commands. They have parameters and perform certain tasks on the file.

Setting the output

The first directive you see in the example in the earlier section "Creating a template from a text file" is the `output` directive. I wanted a C# file, so I used the `.cs` extension. You could emit anything, though — text, HTML, VB, or even a custom format that you need for your project, such as

```
<#@ output extension=".bill" #>
```

Another parameter for output is Encoding, which is exactly what it sounds like. Options include

- Default
- ASCII

- BigEndianUnicode
- Unicode
- UTF32
- UTF7
- UTF8

If you need to represent special characters in your files, you need to specify your encoding.

Configuring a template

`Template` is a directive that specifies the various properties of the T4 text itself. The goal is to affect how the parsing engine interprets the code in the template itself. The options include

- **language:** This is the language for the code that does the work. You can emit anything, but the code in the template has to be VB or C#.
- **inherits:** This is a class that derives from TextTransformation to be used as the base class.
- **culture:** This sets the System.Globalization culture. You know, like en-US or en-GB.
- **debug:** Just like the ASP.NET debugger, this sets the return of debug symbols.
- **hostspecific:** This is for use with custom hosts — you'll run into it if you are writing for custom hosts.

Including includes

Includes are nice and easy.

Remember ASP classic? No, I don't mean ASP.NET pre-MVC. I mean the *old* ASP, with VB script, pre-.NET. This is like that. (If you don't, that's okay; I explain it in the next section.)

If you want to include the contents of a file somewhere in your template, just drop the `include` directive in there and the name of the file in a file attribute.

```
<#@ include file="c:\specialsource.cs" #>
```

That's all there is to it.

Importing items and assemblies

The `import` and `assembly` directives assist with writing code in a template. In the example earlier in this chapter, I emitted text, but in the real examples that you find in MSDN, you write C# or VB code to modify the text.

If you want that code to use .NET Framework constructs, you need to reference the `assembly` and `import` the namespace. For instance, if you are going to get values from a file in your template, you need the `System.IO` library.

First you need to reference the `assembly`, unless you are certain the `assembly` will be referenced in the project. Then you should `import` the namespace so you don't have to reference items via fully qualified names, as like this:

```
<#@ assembly name="System.IO.DLL" #>
<#@ import namespace="System.IO" #>
```

Then, you can reference the file maintenance classes inside the code of the template. You reference code using the `<#` and `#>` statements.

Book V

Windows Development with WPF

A Stack Panel

Contents at a Glance

Chapter 1: Introducing WPF

In This Chapter

- ✓ **Taking a first look at WPF and what it can do for you**
- ✓ **Working with XAML**
- ✓ **Building your first WPF application**
- ✓ **Comparing XAML to C#**

WPF, or Windows Presentation Foundation, is a graphical system for rendering user interfaces. It provides great flexibility in how you can lay out and interact with your applications. With Common Language Runtime (CLR) at its core, you can use C# or any other CLR language to communicate with user interface elements and develop application logic. The advantages of WPF for your application are its rich data binding and visualization support and its design flexibility and styling.

WPF enables you to create an application that is more usable to your audience. It gives you the power to design an application that would previously take extremely long development cycles and a calculus genius to implement. Now you can implement difficult things like graphics and animations in as few as three lines of code!

This chapter introduces you to key WPF concepts as well as common application patterns used in the software industry today.

Understanding What WPF Can Do

WPF's graphics capabilities make it the perfect choice for data visualization. Take, for instance, the standard drop-down list (or combo box). Its current use is to enable the user to choose a single item from a list of items. For this example, suppose we want the user to select a car model for purchase.

The standard way of displaying this choice is to display a drop-down list of car model names from which users can choose. There is a fundamental usability problem with this common solution: Users are given only a single piece of information from which to base their decision — the text that is used to represent the item in the list.

For the power user (or car fanatic) this may not be an issue, but other users need more than just a model name to make an educated decision on the car they wish to purchase. This is where WPF and its data visualization capabilities come into play.

A template can be provided to define how each item in the drop-down list is rendered. The template can contain any visual element, such as images, labels, text boxes, tooltips, drop shadows, and more!

Figure 1-1 shows a typical display of a combo box. This control has limitations: It can relay to the user only a single piece of information, the text used to represent the car model. Work can be done to display images of the car models in a separate control based on the selection in the list, but this still mandates users to make their selection before seeing exactly what it is they are choosing. In contrast, WPF has the flexibility to display many pieces of information in each combo box item, like a one-stop shop for all the information the user will need to make their decision (see Figure 1-2 for a WPF combo box).

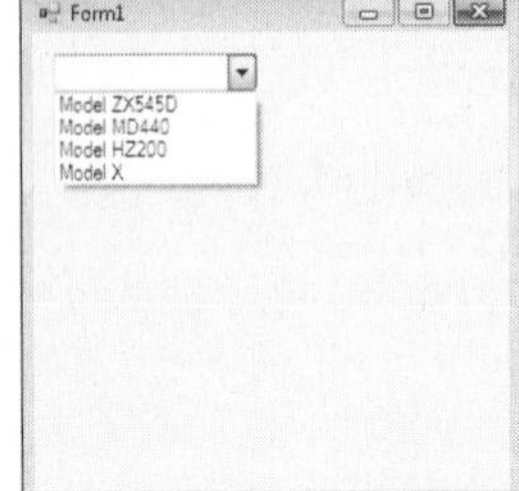

Figure 1-1: A typical combo box.

Figure 1-2 shows a sample combo box in WPF. The way the combo box item is rendered is defined using a data template. (I cover Data Templates in Chapter 3 of this minibook.) Each item in this combo box is rendered to provide the user a visual cue along with multiple data fields. Displaying all this information enables users to make an educated decision about the choice they are making.

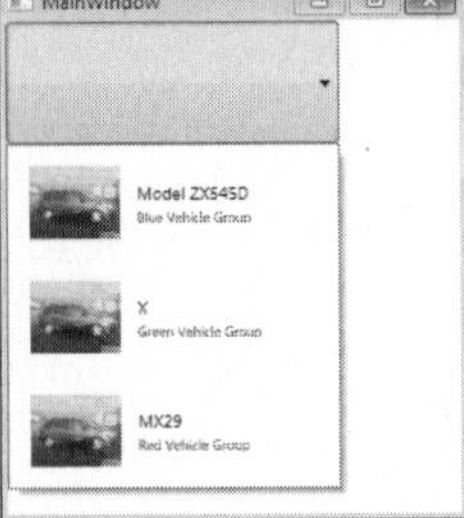

Figure 1-2: Visualizing data — a WPF combo box.

Introducing XAML

WPF enables you to build user interfaces declaratively. XAML (hint: it rhymes with *camel*) forms the foundation of WPF. XAML is similar to HTML in the sense that interface elements are defined using a tag-based syntax.

TECHNICAL STUFF

XAML is XML-based and as such it must be well formed, meaning all opening tags require closing tags, and all elements and attributes contained in the document must validate strictly against the specified schemas.

By default, when creating a WPF application in Visual Studio 2010, the following schemas are represented in generated XAML files:

- `http://schemas.microsoft.com/winfx/2006/xaml/presentation`: This schema represents the default Windows Presentation Framework namespace.
- `http://schemas.microsoft.com/winfx/2006/xaml`: This schema represents a set of classes that map to CLR objects.

Most CLR objects can be expressed as XAML elements (with the exception of abstract base classes and some other nonabstract base classes used strictly for inheritance purposes in the CLR). XAML elements are mapped to classes; attributes are mapped to properties or events.

At runtime when a XAML element is processed, the default constructor for its underlying class is called, and the object is instantiated; its properties and events are set based on the attribute values specified in XAML.

I'm a firm believer that the best way to become comfortable using WPF and XAML is to jump right in and give it a try. The next section reviews more XAML basics and gets you started on the path of WPF application development.

Diving In! Creating Your First WPF Application

Now it's time to get comfortable, stop for a moment, go grab a caffeinated beverage, sit in a comfortable chair, pull up to your computer, and get ready to go!

To create your first project, follow these steps:

1. **Open Visual Studio 2010.**
2. **Create a new project by choosing File➪New Project.**
3. **In the Installed Templates region under the "Visual C#" section in the tree, click on the Windows item.**
4. **Select WPF Application from the list box of templates located in the center of the window.**

5. **In the Name text box, enter** MyFirstWPFApplication **(this also sets the name of the solution to the same value, which is okay). (See Figure 1-3.)**

6. **Click OK.**

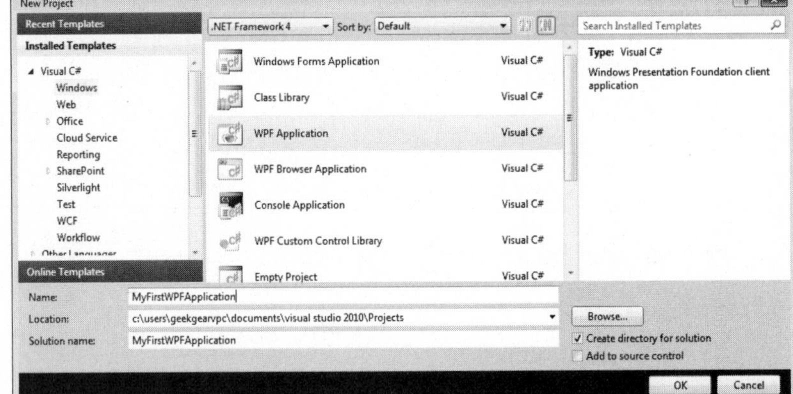

Figure 1-3: Creating a project in the New Project dialog box.

Visual Studio now does its thing, creating the solution structure of the application. By default, as shown in Figure 1-4, the WPF Application template creates two XAML files along with their respective code-behind files: `App.xaml` (`App.xaml.cs`) and `MainWindow.xaml` (`MainWindow.xaml.cs`). (See Figure 1-4.)

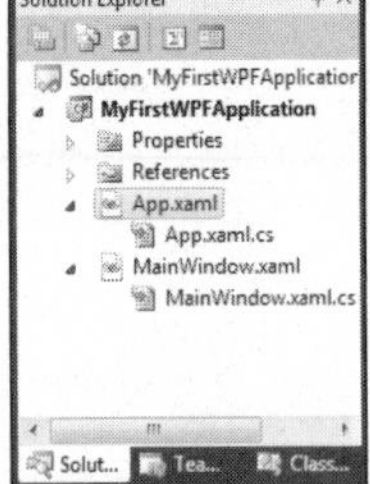

Figure 1-4: WPF Application solution structure

`App.xaml` represents the entry-point of the application. This is where application-wide (globally scoped) resources and the startup window are defined. (See Listing 1-1.)

Resources are a keyed collection of reusable objects. Resources can be created and retrieved using both XAML and C#. Resources can be anything — data templates, arrays of strings, or brushes used to color the background of text boxes. Resources are also *scoped,* meaning they can be available to the entire Application (global), to the Window, to the User Control, or even to only a specific control.

Listing 1-1: App.xaml

```
<Application x:Class="MyFirstWPFApplication.App"
             xmlns="http://schemas.microsoft.com/winfx/2006/xaml/presentation"
             xmlns:x="http://schemas.microsoft.com/winfx/2006/xaml"
             StartupUri="MainWindow.xaml">
    <Application.Resources>

    </Application.Resources>
</Application>
```

Listing 1-1 displays the XAML that was generated by the WPF Application template in Visual Studio. Note that the WPF namespaces are defined. The namespace that represents the CLR objects will be distinguished in the XAML file with the `.x` prefix.

The `StartupUri` value defines the window that will be displayed after the application is executed. In this case, the `MainWindow.xaml` window will be displayed.

The `x:Class` attribute defines the C# code-behind file of this XAML file. If you open `App.xaml.cs`, you see that its class name is `App` and it inherits from the `Application` class (which is the root element of the XAML file).

C# uses namespaces to organize and locate classes. In order to create objects from a specific namespace, you use the "using" syntax at the top of your class definitions. Similar to C#, XAML also requires you to declare which namespaces are used in the document. Namespaces are typically defined as an attribute within the root element of the document, the root element is the first XML tag in the XAML document. XAML uses XML syntax to define a namespace — "xmlns" means "XML namespace," and it's typically followed by a colon (:) and then an alias. This alias is the shorthand reference to the namespace throughout the XAML document; it's what you use to instantiate an object from a class in that namespace.

For instance, if you want to add the namespace **MyTemplates.DataTemplates** from the assembly `MyTemplates.dll`, you could define the namespace as:

```
xmlns:myDTs="clr-namespace:MyTemplates.DataTemplates;assembly=MyTemplates.dll"
```

You will then be able to instantiate an object from the **MyTemplates.DataTemplates** namespace as follows:

```
<myDTs:myClass></myDTs:myClass>
```

Declaring an application-scoped resource

To demonstrate the creation and use of a global application-scoped resource, in this section we create a resource that holds a string used in our application. An application-scoped resource is available to all Windows and user controls defined in the project. Follow these steps:

1. **Add the** `System` **namespace located in the** `mscorlib.dll` **assembly.**

   This is where the `String` class is located.

2. **To do this, add the following namespace to the** `App.xaml` **root element:**

   ```
   xmlns:sys="clr-namespace:System;assembly=mscorlib"
   ```

   The `String` class is now available for use throughout the `App.xaml` document.

3. **Create the resource between the** `Application.Resource` **tags, add the following** `String` **class element:**

   ```
   <sys:String x:Key="Purpose">Hello WPF World!</sys:String>
   ```

   This element instantiates an object of type `String`, initialized to the value `Hello WPF World!`, and keyed off of the key `Purpose`. This resource is now available throughout the `MyFirstWPFApplication` application by requesting the resource "Purpose." (See Listing 1-2.)

Listing 1-2: Updated App.xaml with Resource and System Namespace Defined

```
<Application x:Class="MyFirstWPFApplication.App"
             xmlns="http://schemas.microsoft.com/winfx/2006/xaml/presentation"
             xmlns:x="http://schemas.microsoft.com/winfx/2006/xaml"
             xmlns:sys="clr-namespace:System;assembly=mscorlib"
             StartupUri="MainWindow.xaml">
    <Application.Resources>
        <sys:String x:Key="Purpose">Hello WPF World!</sys:String>
    </Application.Resources>
</Application>
```

You may observe the `Application.Resource` tag looks kind of odd. `Application.Resources` does not define a class as most XAML elements do. It is actually assigning a value to the Resources property of its containing Application object.

This type of tag is called a *Property Element,* an XML element that represents a property (or attribute) of an object. Property Elements are used when complex objects are assigned to a property of an object that can't be expressed as a simple string value. Property Elements must be contained within the tags of the parent element — in this case, within the Application tags.

Making the application do something

If you run the application as is, not much happens beyond the display of an empty window. The empty window is the one defined in `MainWindow.xaml`.

App.xaml is the entry point of the WPF application. Within App.xaml, the StartupUri value defines the window displayed on application startup. In this case, the StartupUri value is MainWindow.xaml.

Let's add a label to MainWindow.xaml that displays the purpose of the String we defined in our Resources. Just follow these steps:

1. **Open** MainWindow.xaml.
2. **Between the Grid tags, define a grid with a single row and single column by adding the following XAML markup:**

```
<Grid.ColumnDefinitions>
    <ColumnDefinition></ColumnDefinition>
</Grid.ColumnDefinitions>
<Grid.RowDefinitions>
    <RowDefinition></RowDefinition>
</Grid.RowDefinitions>
```

   Each column and row is defined by the ColumnDefinition and RowDefinition element contained within the Grid.ColumnDefinitions and Grid.RowDefinitions properties, respectively. If you want to add more columns, you simply add another ColumnDefinition element to the Grid.ColumnDefinitions Property Entity. The same goes for adding rows: You add an additional RowDefinition element to the Grid.RowDefinitions Property Entity.

3. **Directly below the** Grid.RowDefinitions **Property entity, create a label using the following XAML:**

```
<Label x:Name="lblPurpose" Content="{StaticResource Purpose}"
    FontSize="25" Grid.Row="0" Grid.Column="0" />
```

   This markup instantiates a WPF Label object accessible to the code-behind file (MainWindow.xaml.cs) using the variable lblPurpose. The Content attribute contains the text that is to be displayed in the label; in this case, we will use the Application Resource that we defined in the preceding section by retrieving it using its key value, which is Purpose. The label text is rendered with a font size of 25 units and is to be located in the grid in the first row and first column.

WOW! That line of XAML really packs quite the punch! Let's review some of what is going on in there:

- x:Name: This attribute assigns a variable name to the object being created by the XAML tag. This enables you to access the object from the code-behind file. In this case, the variable name of the label object being instantiated is lblPurpose.
- Content: The value assigned to this attribute can be of any type. By default, you can assign it a string value and it will render as you would think a standard label would render. In the WPF reality, Content can be composed of anything: a string, an image, an instance of a user control, a text box, and so forth. For more info, see Chapter 2 of this minibook.

- `FontSize`: The size of the font of the label. It is important to note that the size is not denoted in points; it is expressed in Device Independent Units. WPF gets away from the concepts of pixels and points and moves to a universal sizing strategy. Think of Device Independent Units as more of a ratio than a pixel. For instance, if the containing element of the label were 100 units by 100 units, the label would render as ¼ of that size.
- `Grid.Row`: Identifies the grid row in which to render the label. Grid row collections are zero-based, meaning the first row is row 0, the second row is row 1, and so on. You should also note that the Label class does not contain a property named Grid. What you see here is the concept of Attached Properties. Attached Properties are a way to assign the context of a current control relative to the properties of an ancestor control. In this case, we assign the label to appear in the first row (row index 0) of its containing grid. Also observe that the label is located within the Grid tags; this is how the ancestor Grid element is located.
- `Grid.Column`: Similar to `Grid.Row`, this attached property identifies the grid column in which to render the label. Together with `Grid.Row`, both properties identify the cell where the label is located. In this case, we are assigning the label to render in the first column of its containing grid. Grid column collections are also zero-based.

Go ahead and run your application, you will now see Hello World displayed in the label on your Window. Congratulations, you have just created your first WPF application!

The complete solution is available at `www.csharpfordummies.net` in the chapter downloads.

Whatever XAML Can Do, C# Can Do Better!

Anything that you can implement using XAML can be implemented in C#. This is not true in reverse; not everything you can do in C# can be done in XAML. C# is the obvious choice for performing business logic tasks with procedural code that can't be expressed in XAML. Let's create an identical WPF application to the one we've just created, this time using C# to implement its functionality. Here's all you have to do:

1. **Create a new project by choosing File ➪New Project.**
2. **Under Visual C#, select Windows.**
3. **Select WPF Application.**
4. **Name the application** MyFirstCodeOnlyWPFApplication.
5. **Click OK.**

   Visual Studio creates the Solution and Project structure.

6. **Open** `App.xaml.cs`**.**
7. **Override the** `OnStartup` **method to include the creation of the Purpose application resource by adding the following code to the App class:**

```
protected override void OnStartup(StartupEventArgs e)
{
    //create and add the Purpose application resource
   string purpose = "Hello WPF World, in C#";
   this.Resources.Add("Purpose", purpose);

   base.OnStartup(e);
}
```

8. **Open** `MainWindow.xaml`**, and give the** `Grid` **element a name by adding the following attribute:**

```
x:Name="gridLayout"
```

9. **Open** `MainWindow.xaml.cs`**, and in the default constructor, after the** `InitializeComponents` **method call, add the following code:**

```
//define grid column and row
this.gridLayout.ColumnDefinitions.Add(new ColumnDefinition());
this.gridLayout.RowDefinitions.Add(new RowDefinition());

//obtain label content from the application resource, Purpose
string purpose = this.TryFindResource("Purpose") as string;
Label lblPurpose = new Label();
lblPurpose.Content = purpose;
lblPurpose.FontSize = 25;

//add label to the grid
this.gridLayout.Children.Add(lblPurpose);

//assign attached property values
Grid.SetColumn(lblPurpose, 0);
Grid.SetRow(lblPurpose, 0);
```

Run the application and observe the resulting product is similar to that obtained in the section "Diving In! Creating Your First WPF Application," earlier in this chapter.

The complete solution is available at the `www.csharpfordummies.net` Web site chapter downloads.

Chapter 2: Understanding the Basics of WPF

In This Chapter

- **Laying out applications**
- **Using layout panels**
- **Working with the grid**
- **Implementing display-only, input, and list-based controls**

As Chapter 1 explains, WPF brings not only a dramatic shift to the look and feel of Windows applications but also changes the manner of development. The days of dragging and dropping controls from the toolbox onto a form are long gone. Even though it is still possible to drag and drop in WPF, you will find yourself better off and much happier if you work in XAML directly.

What was once difficult is now relatively simple. For example, in traditional Windows applications, when the user changes the size of the form, the controls typically stay huddled in their corner and a large area of empty canvas is displayed. The only cure for this was a lot of custom code or expensive third-party controls. WPF brings the concept of *flow layout* from the Web into the Windows world.

In the GDI/GDI+ world of WinForms, modifying a control's style or building complex looks was a Herculean feat. WPF has completely redefined the control paradigm, giving you, the developer, the freedom to make a control do unimaginable tasks — including playing a video on a button face. However, keep in mind that just because you *can* do something doesn't mean you *should!*

In this chapter, we work with WPF's layout process to control the layout of your application and introduce you to the various WPF controls.

Using WPF to Lay Out Your Application

Traditional Windows Forms development deals in absolutes. Position and size for controls are decided at design time and are based on the resolution of the developer's machine. When applications are deployed to users, the form that looked great on the developer's machine could now look very different (and possibly be downright unusable) because of hardware resolution differences.

New tech, new terms

It seems every time Microsoft introduces a new technology, we have to learn new a whole new set of terms. WPF is no different! At the root of the change are what we referred to as Forms and Controls in Windows Forms (WinForms). Here are some of the new terms:

- A *Form* in WinForms is referred to as a *Window* in WPF.
- Anything placed on a WinForms Form is called a *control*, whereas items placed on a WPF Window are referred to as *UIElements.*
- *Panels* are WPF UIElements used for layout.
- A *Control* in WPF is a UIElement that can receive focus and respond to user events.
- A Content control in WPF can contain only a single item, which can in turn be other UIElements.
- The WPF Window class is a specialized Content control.

Instead of depending on screen resolution, WPF measures UI Elements in Device Independent Units (DIUs) that are based on the *system DPI.* This enables a consistent look between many different hardware configurations.

WPF layout is based on *relative* values and is adjusted at runtime. When you place controls in a layout container (see the next section), the rendering engine considers the height and width only as "suggested" values. Location is defined in relation to other controls or the container. Actual rendering is a two-step process that starts with measuring all controls (and querying them for their preferred dimensions) and then arranging them accordingly. If controls could speak, the conversation might go something like this:

> Layout Engine: "Control, how much space would you like to have?"
>
> *<This is the Measure Stage>*
>
> Control: "I would like 50 DIUs for height, 100 DIUs for width, and a margin of 3 DIUs in the containing Grid cell."
>
> *Layout Engine asks all other controls and layout containers.*
>
> Layout Engine: "Sorry, you can have only 40 DIUs for height, but I can grant the rest of your requests."
>
> *<This is the Arrange Stage>*

Arranging Elements with Layout Panels

Designing a Window begins with a Layout control, or Panel. Panels are different than Content controls in that they can hold multiple items, and depending on the Panel, a significant amount of plumbing is taken care of for you.

Panels control how UIElements relate to each other and to their containing UIElement and do not dictate absolute positioning. Most application Windows require some combination of Panels to achieve the required user interface, so it's important to understand them all. WPF ships with six core Panels:

- Stack Panel
- Wrap Panel
- Dock Panel
- Canvas
- Uniform Grid
- Grid

The Stack Panel

Stack Panels place UIElements in — wait for it — *stacks.* Items are placed in either a vertical pile (the default), like a stack of DVDs, or a horizontal arrangement, like books on a shelf. It is important to understand that the order items appear in the XAML is the order they appear in the Panel — the first UIElement in the XAML appears at the top (vertical) or on the far left (horizontal). Figures 2-1 and 2-2 show the same set of buttons in both orientations. Listing 2-1 contains the XAML for the Vertical Stack Panel shown in Figure 2-1.

The code for these samples can be found at `csharpfordummies.net`.

Figure 2-1: Vertical Stack Panel.

Listing 2-1: Vertical Stack Panel XAML

```
<StackPanel Name="pnlStack" Grid.Row="0"
   Orientation="Vertical">
    <Button Content="A Button"/>
    <Button Content="Another Button"/>
    <TextBlock Text="This is a text block"/>
    <Button Content="Short"/>
    <Button Content="Really Long Button Label"/>
</StackPanel>
```

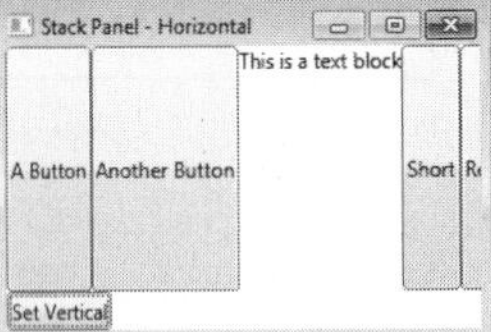

Figure 2-2: Horizontal Stack Panel.

Remember the conversation between the rendering Engine and the Control at the beginning of this chapter? The horizontal layout illustrates the clipping that can take place when the sum of the preferred sizes of controls in a container is larger than the container can hold.

Orientation (as well as all other properties) can be changed at runtime, as illustrated by Listing 2-2. The Button at the bottom of the Window changes the orientation, the button label, and the Window Title in the click event. Chapter 4 shows a better way of coding Button click events.

Listing 2-2: Changing Stack Panel Orientation in Code

```
private void cmdOrientation_Click(object sender,
   RoutedEventArgs e)
{
    Button button = sender as Button;
    if (button.Content.ToString() == "Set Vertical")
    {
        pnlStack.Orientation = Orientation.Vertical;
        button.Content = "Set Horizontal";
        Title = "Stack Panel - Vertical";
    }
    else
    {
        pnlStack.Orientation = Orientation.Horizontal;
        button.Content = "Set Vertical";
        Title = "Stack Panel - Horizontal";
    }
}
```

The Wrap Panel

The Wrap Panel automatically wraps overflow content onto the next line(s). This is different than how a typical toolbar works, where overflow items are hidden when there isn't enough real estate to show them. Figures 2-3 and 2-4 show the same content controls from the Stack Panel (a mixture of buttons and a text block) in a Wrap Panel. The first Window has enough room to show all the UIElements, and the second shows the wrapping of elements because of a lack of room. The XAML for the Wrap Panel sample is in Listing 2-3.

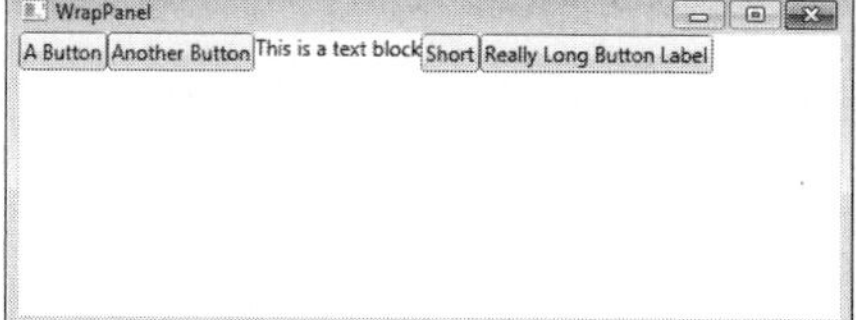

Figure 2-3: Wrap Panel (wide form).

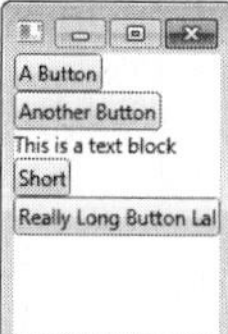

Figure 2-4: Wrap Panel (narrow form).

Note that even with the Wrap Panel, if the container can't hold the widest item (the last button in the example), some clipping will take place.

Listing 2-3: Wrap Panel XAML

```
<WrapPanel>
    <Button Content="A Button"/>
    <Button Content="Another Button"/>
    <TextBlock Text="This is a text block"/>
    <Button Content="Short"/>
    <Button Content="Really Long Button Label"/>
</WrapPanel>
```

The Dock Panel

The Dock Panel uses attached properties (introduced in Chapter 1 of this minibook) to "dock" child UIElements. (See Figure 2-5 and Listing 2-4.) An important thing to remember is that child elements are docked in XAML order, which means if you have two items assigned to the left side (through `DockPanel.Dock="left"`), the first UIElement *as it appears in the XAML* gets the far left wall of the Panel, followed by the next item.

The Dock Panel also has a setting called `LastChildFill`. If this is true, the last element in XAML will fill the remaining real estate. Elements (prior to the last XAML element) that do not have a Dock setting specified will default to `DockPanel.Dock="Left"`.

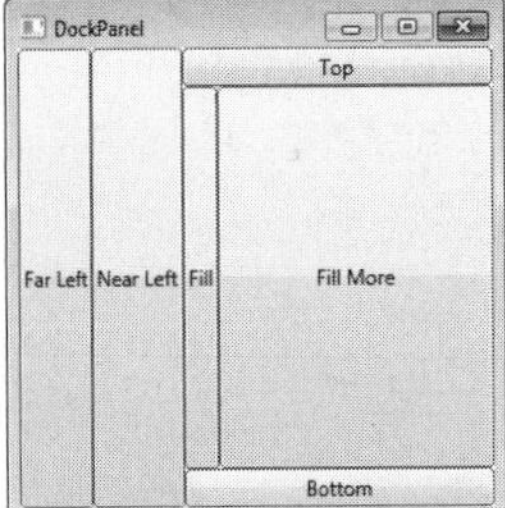

Figure 2-5: Dock Panel.

Listing 2-4: Dock Panel XAML

```
<DockPanel LastChildFill="True">
    <Button DockPanel.Dock="Left" Content="Far Left"/>
    <Button DockPanel.Dock="Left" Content="Near Left"/>
    <Button DockPanel.Dock="Top" Content="Top"/>
    <Button DockPanel.Dock="Bottom" Content="Bottom"/>
    <Button Content="Fill"/>
    <Button Content="Fill More"/>
</DockPanel>
```

Canvas

The Canvas is a bit of an anomaly in WPF, since it doesn't use flow layout, but goes back to fix position layout rendering. "What?!" you say. "I thought flow layout was the way of the future!"

Well, it is . . . most of the time. In some cases, part of your application needs to be laid out the "old way." A graphical application used to design floor plans is a perfect example.

Items are placed (or drawn) on the canvas relative to any side, and layering is handled through z-order. (See Figure 2-6 and Listing 2-5.)

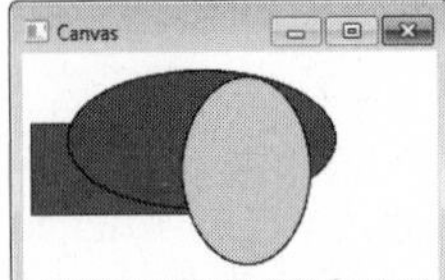

Figure 2-6: Canvas sample.

Listing 2-5: Canvas XAML

```
<Canvas>
    <Rectangle Canvas.Left="40" Canvas.Top="40"
   Height="53" Name="rectangle1" Stroke="Black" Width="96"
   Fill="#FFE22323" />
    <Ellipse Canvas.Left="28" Canvas.Top="142"
   Height="80" Name="ellipse1" Stroke="Black" Width="161"
   Fill="#FF0000FA" />
    <Ellipse Canvas.Left="96" Canvas.Top="14" Height="108"
   Name="ellipse2" Stroke="Black" Width="78" Fill="#FFE5D620"
   />
</Canvas>
```

The Uniform Grid

The Uniform Grid divides the layout area into equally sized cells. (See Figure 2-7 and Listing 2-6.) The number of Rows and Columns are defined in the `UniformGrid` XAML tag. As discussed in Chapter 1, cell contents are positioned using the `Grid.Row` and `Grid.Column` attached properties. Note that the Rows and Columns are zero-based.

The Uniform Grid is not as versatile as the Grid (see the next section), but if you need a very quick checkerboard pattern, it can be an effective Panel. In order to highlight the borders of the cells, I've added Borders. For more on Borders, see the section "Exploring Common XAML Controls," later in this chapter.

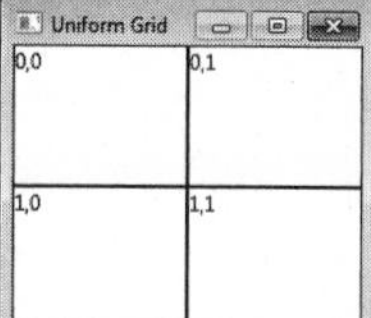

Figure 2-7: Uniform Grid.

Listing 2-6: Uniform Grid XAML

```
<UniformGrid Rows="2" Columns="2">
    <Border Grid.Row="0" Grid.Column="0" BorderBrush="Black"
   BorderThickness="1" HorizontalAlignment="Stretch"
   VerticalAlignment="Stretch">
        <TextBlock Text="0,0"/>
    </Border>
    <Border Grid.Row="0" Grid.Column="1" BorderBrush="Black"
   BorderThickness="1" HorizontalAlignment="Stretch"
   VerticalAlignment="Stretch">
        <TextBlock Text="0,1"/>
```

(continued)

Listing 2-6 *(continued)*

```
    </Border>
    <Border Grid.Row="1" Grid.Column="0" BorderBrush="Black"
   BorderThickness="1" HorizontalAlignment="Stretch"
   VerticalAlignment="Stretch">
        <TextBlock Text="1,0"/>
    </Border>
    <Border Grid.Row="1" Grid.Column="1" BorderBrush="Black"
   BorderThickness="1" HorizontalAlignment="Stretch"
   VerticalAlignment="Stretch">
        <TextBlock Text="1,1"/>
    </Border>
</UniformGrid>
```

The Grid

Chapter 1 introduced the Grid, which is the most common starting point to screen design. The Grid is in fact the default panel in a Window when you add a new WPF Window to your project.

The Grid divides the layout area with rows (`RowDefinitions`) and columns (`ColumnDefinitions`). The difference between the Grid and the Uniform Grid is that the Grid allows for sizing of the cells by defining `RowDefinition Height` and `ColumnDefinition Width`.

Definitions for Rows and Columns are specified with the `Grid.RowDefinitions` and `Grid.ColumnDefinitions` tags (see Listing 2-7).

Listing 2-7: XAML Grid RowDefinitions and ColumnDefinitions

```
<Grid>
    <Grid.RowDefinitions>
        <RowDefinition Height="2*" />
        <RowDefinition Height="3*" />
    </Grid.RowDefinitions>
    <Grid.ColumnDefinitions>
        <ColumnDefinition Width="*"/>
    </Grid.ColumnDefinitions>
</Grid>
```

Sizing Rows and Columns

There are three `GridUnitTypes` used for defining Heights and Widths:

- `Pixel`: Fixed size in Device Independent Units.

  You define a fixed height or width based on DIUs by specifying a number in the definition. This goes against the Flow Layout grain, but there are certainly valid reasons to do this, such as when a graphic image on a Window doesn't scale well (up or down) and needs to be a fixed size. Fixed sizing should be used with caution, as it can limit the effectiveness of the user interface. If the content is dynamic or needs to be localized, the controls could clip the content or wind up leaving a lot of wasted space.

✦ `Auto`: Size is based on the preferred size of the contents.

  The Auto definition allows the Row or Column to determine how large (or small) it can be based on its content. This is decided during the measure stage of the layout process.

✦ `Star`: Size uses all remaining space.

  The Star tells the rendering engine, "Give me all you've got! I'll take it all!" Each star defined gets an equal portion of what's left after all other sizing options have been computed. To achieve proportional sizing, multipliers can be added. For example, in Figure 2-8 (and in Listing 2-8), the first row uses 40 percent (2/5) of the available space and the second row uses the remaining 60 percent (3/5).

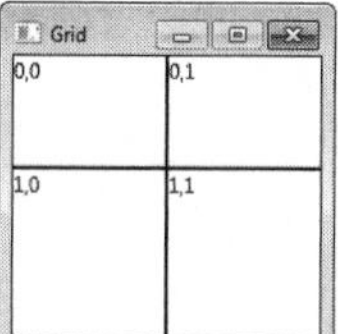

Figure 2-8: Basic Grid with proportional (*) row heights.

Listing 2-8: Basic Grid XAML

```
<Grid>
    <Grid.RowDefinitions>
        <RowDefinition Height="2*" />
        <RowDefinition Height="3*" />
    </Grid.RowDefinitions>
    <Grid.ColumnDefinitions>
        <ColumnDefinition Width="*"/>
        <ColumnDefinition Width="*"/>
    </Grid.ColumnDefinitions>
    <Border Grid.Row="0" Grid.Column="0" BorderBrush="Black"
   BorderThickness="1" HorizontalAlignment="Stretch"
   VerticalAlignment="Stretch">
        <TextBlock Text="0,0"/>
    </Border>
    <Border Grid.Row="0" Grid.Column="1" BorderBrush="Black"
   BorderThickness="1" HorizontalAlignment="Stretch"
   VerticalAlignment="Stretch">
        <TextBlock Text="0,1"/>
    </Border>
```

(continued)

Listing 2-8 *(continued)*

```
    <Border Grid.Row="1" Grid.Column="0" BorderBrush="Black"
   BorderThickness="1" HorizontalAlignment="Stretch"
   VerticalAlignment="Stretch">
        <TextBlock Text="1,0"/>
    </Border>
    <Border Grid.Row="1" Grid.Column="1" BorderBrush="Black"
   BorderThickness="1" HorizontalAlignment="Stretch"
   VerticalAlignment="Stretch">
        <TextBlock Text="1,1"/>
    </Border>
</Grid>
```

RowSpan and ColumnSpan

Similar to HTML tables, content in a Grid can span rows or columns by using the `Grid.RowSpan` and `Grid.ColumnSpan` attached properties. Figure 2-9 (and Listing 2-9) shows a Grid layout with the Border controls spanning both columns in the first row and spanning the next two rows in the first column.

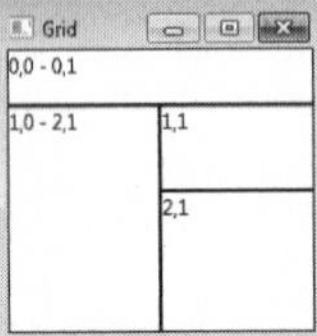

Figure 2-9: Grid with row and column spans.

Listing 2-9: Column and Row Span XAML

```
<Grid>
    <Grid.RowDefinitions>
        <RowDefinition Height="2*" />
        <RowDefinition Height="3*" />
        <RowDefinition Height="5*" />
    </Grid.RowDefinitions>
    <Grid.ColumnDefinitions>
        <ColumnDefinition Width="*"/>
        <ColumnDefinition Width="*"/>
    </Grid.ColumnDefinitions>
    <Border Grid.Row="0" Grid.Column="0" Grid.
   ColumnSpan="2"  BorderBrush="Black" BorderThickness="1"
   HorizontalAlignment="Stretch" VerticalAlignment="Stretch">
        <TextBlock Text="0,0 - 0,1"/>
    </Border>
    <Border Grid.Row="1" Grid.Column="0" Grid.
   RowSpan="2" BorderBrush="Black" BorderThickness="1"
   HorizontalAlignment="Stretch" VerticalAlignment="Stretch">
        <TextBlock Text="1,0 - 2,1"/>
```

```
    </Border>
    <Border Grid.Row="1" Grid.Column="1" BorderBrush="Black"
   BorderThickness="1" HorizontalAlignment="Stretch"
   VerticalAlignment="Stretch">
        <TextBlock Text="1,1"/>
    </Border>
    <Border Grid.Row="2" Grid.Column="1" BorderBrush="Black"
   BorderThickness="1" HorizontalAlignment="Stretch"
   VerticalAlignment="Stretch">
        <TextBlock Text="2,1"/>
    </Border>
</Grid>
```

Horizontal and vertical alignment within parent container's layout slot

You align an element within a container's layout slot by setting the `VerticalAlignment` and `HorizontalAlignment` properties (see the `Border` element in Listing 2-9 for an example). Horizontal settings are `Center`, `Left`, `Right`, and `Stretch`. Vertical options are `Center`, `Top`, `Bottom`, and `Stretch`. `Stretch` specifies the element to fill all available space. Explicit sizing of elements overrides the `Stretch` setting.

Content alignment within Content Controls

The same options can be used for setting the alignment of the Content within a Content Control by using the `HorizontalContentAlignment` and `VerticalContentAlignment` properties in the control.

Margin versus padding

Margins create space around a UIElement and its parent container. Margin values start with the left and rotate clockwise (which is different than CSS, just to keep you on your toes). You can also use some abbreviations. Setting the value as one number makes a uniform margin; setting the value to two numbers (comma separated) sets the left and right margins to the first number and the top and bottom margins to the second.

```
<Button Margin="2,4,2,4" Content="Push Me" /> <!--L,T,R,B-->
<Button Margin="2,4" Content="Push Me" /> <!--LR,TB-->
<Button Margin="2" Content="Push Me" /> <!--LTRB-->
```

Shared size groups

Most complex Windows require multiple Panels to achieve the desire User Experience. This can introduce erratic Windows if size of the content in one Grid is different than that of the other. Figure 2-10 illustrates the problem.

Fortunately, there is a simple solution. By setting the `Grid.IsSharedSizeScope` attached property on the *parent* Grid, all the child Grids can define Rows and Columns that subscribe to a `SharedSizeGroup`, and the rendering engine will ensure that they are sized correctly. Figure 2-11 illustrates the effects of setting these properties. The abbreviated XAML is shown in Listing 2-10.

Listing 2-10: Shared Size Groups

```
<Grid Grid.IsSharedSizeScope="False">
    <Grid Grid.Row="1" Grid.Column="0">
        <Grid.RowDefinitions>
            <RowDefinition Height="Auto" />
            <RowDefinition Height="Auto" />
        </Grid.RowDefinitions>
        <Grid.ColumnDefinitions>
            <ColumnDefinition Width="Auto"
   SharedSizeGroup="Header" />
            <ColumnDefinition Width="*" />
        </Grid.ColumnDefinitions>
    </Grid>
    <Grid Grid.Row="3" Grid.Column="0">
        <Grid.RowDefinitions>
            <RowDefinition Height="Auto"/>
            <RowDefinition Height="Auto"/>
        </Grid.RowDefinitions>
        <Grid.ColumnDefinitions>
            <ColumnDefinition Width="Auto"
   SharedSizeGroup="Header"/>
            <ColumnDefinition Width="*" />
        </Grid.ColumnDefinitions>
    </Grid>
</Grid>
```


Figure 2-10: Multiple Grids without shared sizing.

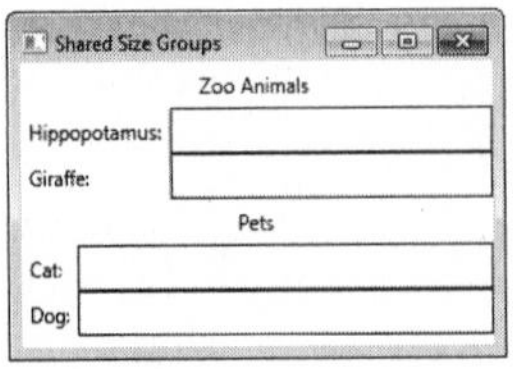

Figure 2-11: Multiple Grids with shared sizing.

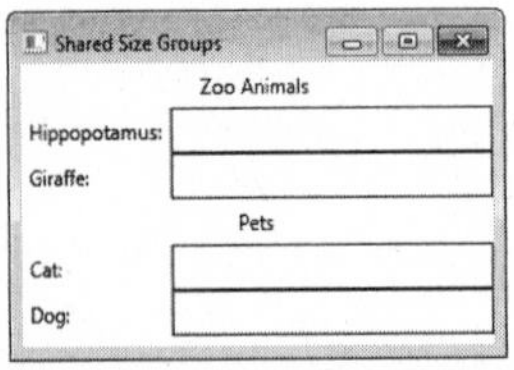

Putting it all together with a simple data entry form

For complex data entry forms, the DataGrid is most appropriate (for more information, see the section "Exploring Common XAML Controls," later in this chapter). The data entry form in this example uses multiple Grids to achieve the desired look. The text boxes are contained in columns with Star sizing so they will grow and shrink with the form. Also notice how the buttons stay in the same relative position as the form size changes.

Listing 2-11 shows the XAML required to build the Window shown in Figures 2-12 and 2-13.

Listing 2-11: Simple Data Entry Form XAML

```
<Grid Background="FloralWhite">
    <Grid.RowDefinitions>
        <RowDefinition Height="Auto"/>
        <RowDefinition Height="Auto"/>
        <RowDefinition Height="Auto"/>
        <RowDefinition Height="Auto"/>
        <RowDefinition Height="Auto"/>
        <RowDefinition Height="10"/>
        <RowDefinition Height="Auto"/>
    </Grid.RowDefinitions>
    <Grid.ColumnDefinitions>
        <ColumnDefinition Width="Auto" />
        <ColumnDefinition Width="Auto" />
        <ColumnDefinition Width="*" />
        <ColumnDefinition Width="Auto" />
    </Grid.ColumnDefinitions>
    <Label  Grid.Row="0" Grid.Column="0" Grid.RowSpan="2"
   Content="Name"
            HorizontalAlignment="Stretch" HorizontalContentAl
   ignment="Center">
        <Label.LayoutTransform>
            <RotateTransform Angle="-90"/>
        </Label.LayoutTransform>
    </Label>
    <Label Grid.Row="0" Grid.Column="1" Content="First:"
            HorizontalAlignment="Stretch" HorizontalContentAl
   ignment="Right"/>
    <TextBox Grid.Row="0" Grid.Column="2"
   HorizontalAlignment="Stretch" />
    <Label Grid.Row="1" Grid.Column="1" Content="Last:"
            HorizontalAlignment="Stretch" HorizontalContentAl
   ignment="Right"/>
    <TextBox Grid.Row="1" Grid.Column="2"
   HorizontalAlignment="Stretch" />
    <Label Grid.Row="2" Grid.Column="1" Content="Address:"
            HorizontalAlignment="Stretch" HorizontalContentAl
   ignment="Right"/>
```

(continued)

Listing 2-11 *(continued)*

```
    <TextBox Grid.Row="2" Grid.Column="2"
   HorizontalAlignment="Stretch" />
    <Label Grid.Row="3" Grid.Column="1" Content="City:"
           HorizontalAlignment="Stretch" HorizontalContentAl
   ignment="Right"/>
    <TextBox Grid.Row="3" Grid.Column="2"
   HorizontalAlignment="Stretch" />
    <Button Grid.Row="3" Grid.Column="3" Content="Lookup"
   Margin="3,0,3,0"/>
    <Label Grid.Row="4" Grid.Column="1" Content="State:"
           HorizontalAlignment="Stretch" HorizontalContentAl
   ignment="Right"/>
    <Grid Grid.Row="4" Grid.Column="2">
        <Grid.RowDefinitions>
            <RowDefinition Height="*"/>
        </Grid.RowDefinitions>
        <Grid.ColumnDefinitions>
            <ColumnDefinition Width="*"/>
            <ColumnDefinition Width="Auto"/>
            <ColumnDefinition Width="2*"/>
        </Grid.ColumnDefinitions>
        <TextBox Grid.Row="0" Grid.Column="0"
   HorizontalAlignment="Stretch" />
        <Label Grid.Row="0" Grid.Column="1" Content="Zip:"
   HorizontalAlignment="Right" />
        <TextBox Grid.Row="0" Grid.Column="2"
   HorizontalAlignment="Stretch" />
    </Grid>
    <Grid Grid.Row="6" Grid.Column="0" Grid.ColumnSpan="3">
        <Grid.RowDefinitions>
            <RowDefinition Height="Auto"/>
        </Grid.RowDefinitions>
        <Grid.ColumnDefinitions>
            <ColumnDefinition Width="*"/>
            <ColumnDefinition Width="Auto"/>
            <ColumnDefinition Width="Auto"/>
        </Grid.ColumnDefinitions>
        <Button Grid.Row="0" Grid.Column="1" Content="Save"
   Margin="3,0"/>
        <Button Grid.Row="0" Grid.Column="2" Content="Close"
   Margin="3,0"/>
    </Grid>
</Grid>
```

And yes, that's a *lot* of XAML! One of the many great things about WPF is the flexibility to be able to create just about any look and feel you can dream up. But, sometimes (well, most of the time) it will take a lot of angle brackets.

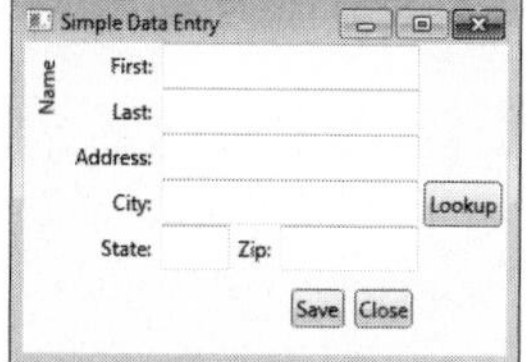

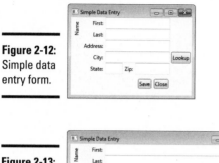

Figure 2-12: Simple data entry form.

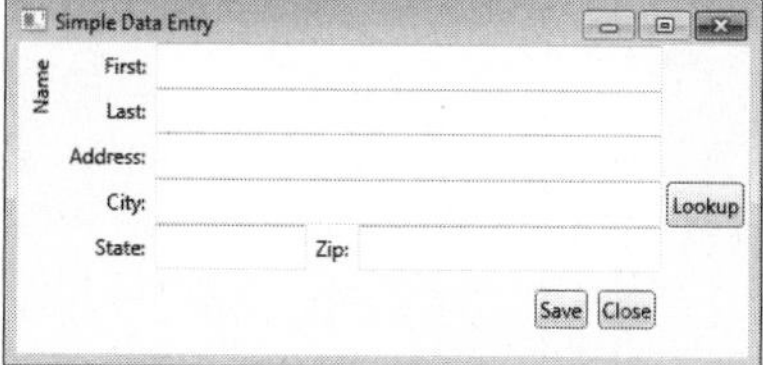

Figure 2-13: Simple data entry form widened.

In addition to using XAML for layout, all the examples shown can be done exclusively in code. "Shenanigans!" you say? No, it's true. Even Row/Column sizing.

Fixed sizing is specified by assigning a number to the Width property of the `ColumnDefinition` or `RowDefinition`. Assigning `Auto` or `*` is more complicated, since the `Width` property is of type `GridLength`. (See Listing 2-12.)

Listing 2-12: Setting Auto and Star Sizing in Code

```
//Set to Auto sizing
column1 = new ColumnDefinition();
column1.Width = new GridLength(1, GridUnitType.Auto);
//Set to Star sizing
column2 = new ColumnDefinition();
column2.Width = new GridLength(1, GridUnitType.Star);
```

For the full example (and many more), refer to the MSDN Documentation found here: `http://msdn.microsoft.com/en-us/library/system.windows.gridunittype.aspx`

Panels of honorable mention

In addition to the Panels already discussed, there are four additional specialized Layout Panels. As they are extremely specialized, I won't cover them in any great detail:

- **`TabPanel`:** Handles the layout of items on a TabControl.
- **`ToolbarPanel`:** Handles the layout of items in a Toolbar.

- **ToolbarOverflowPanel:** Handles the layout of the controls that overflow from a Toolbar.
- **VirtualizingStackPanel:** Used for large amounts of data binding scenarios. Renders only the visible items in the data collection.
- **InkCanvas:** Canvas panel that accepts digital ink input. Used for scenarios like collection of signatures with Tablet PCs.

Exploring Common XAML Controls

A significant number of controls ship out of the box with Visual Studio 2010 (and more and more vendor-supplied controls are available for purchase). This section covers the more commonly used controls. I prefer to divide the available controls into three categories:

- Display-only controls
- Basic input controls
- List- based controls

All the controls in this section are bindable to data (see Chapter 3 in this minibook) and modifiable through code.

Display only controls

Four main controls focus on displaying information to the user:

- `Image`: The `Image` control display images (of type `.bmp`, `.gif`, `.ico`, `.jpg`, `.png`, `.wdp`, and `.tiff`). To preserve the image's aspect ratio, set the `Width` *or* `Height`, but not both. Additionally, the `DecodePixelWidth` should be set to the same size as the `Width`. This will cause the rendering engine to scale the image appropriately, potentially saving a significant amount of memory.

  Listing 2-13 shows the XAML to load an image that shows a color wheel. Only the `Width` and `DecodePixelWidth` are set. The resulting Window is shown in Figure 2-14.

Listing 2-13: Image Control

```
<Image Grid.Row="0" Grid.Column="0" Width="256" >
    <Image.Source>
        <BitmapImage DecodePixelWidth="256" UriSource="/
    Images/1460_PaintPalette_256x256.png"/>
    </Image.Source>
</Image>
```

Figure 2-14: Image control.

- TextBlock and Label: Both the TextBlock and the Label controls are designed to provide text or other content to the user with a few distinctions. The TextBlock control is designed to be the light-weight "little brother" to the Label, deriving directly from UIElement.

  The Label control provides access modifier capability and also derives from ContentControl, which opens up additional possibilities. Placing an underscore (_) before a letter enables the access modifiers. To provide an underscore in the Label, use a double underscore. In XAML, since it is essentially XML, the underscore is used because an ampersand would break the XAML. The Target attribute specifies the control to receive focus when the access modifier is keyed. You have to use a Binding expression, which is covered in Chapter 3.

  Both the TextBlock and Label controls are illustrated in Listing 2-14 and Figure 2-15.

Listing 2-14: TextBlock and Label

```
<TextBlock Grid.Row="0" Grid.Column="0" Margin="5,0"
   HorizontalAlignment="Right" Text="Text_Block:"/>
<TextBox Grid.Row="0" Grid.Column="1" Margin="5,0"
   HorizontalAlignment="Stretch"/>
<Label Grid.Row="1" Grid.Column="0" Margin="5,0"
   HorizontalAlignment="Stretch"
       HorizontalContentAlignment="Right" Content="_Label__
   Content:" Target="{Binding ElementName=SampleTextBox}"/>
<TextBox Name="SampleTextBox" Grid.Row="1" Grid.Column="1"
   Margin="5,0" HorizontalAlignment="Stretch" />
```

In the sample, the "L" in the Label content is the access modifier and the double underscore adds an underscore character to the rendered output.

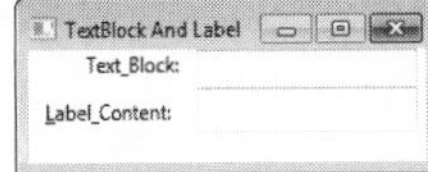

Figure 2-15: TextBlock and Label controls.

- `ProgressBar`: The final display-only control is the Progress Bar. Although technically a descendant of the `RangeBase` class, it does not enable user input like the Slider (see the next section). Figure 2-16 shows a progress bar sample. To have the bar in perpetual motion, set the `IsIndeterminate` property to True (although in Visual Studio 2010 Beta 2, this is not functioning properly — I'm sure it will be fixed by the final release of Visual Studio 2010 and .NET 4).

Figure 2-16: Progress Bar at 50 percent.

Basic input controls

The workhorses of line of business applications are the basic input controls. You will find some of these on every Window you create, and they are very straightforward. Figure 2-17 shows all these controls on a single Window. Here are the basic input controls:

- `TextBox` and `PasswordBox`: The `TextBox` and `PasswordBox` both allow for the input of standard text into the Window. The `PasswordBox` obfuscates the characters typed (using either the default system password character or a developer-specified character) and is used for collection of sensitive information. The `TextBox` exposes its contents through the `Text` property, the `PasswordBox` through the `Password` property.

  ```
  <TextBox Text="Some Text"/>
  ```

  ```
  <PasswordBox PasswordChar="X" Password="Some Text"/>
  ```

- `CheckBox`: Check boxes represent Boolean values through the `IsChecked` property. The `IsChecked` property is nullable, which provides for three-state display (True, False, Unknown).

  ```
  <CheckBox IsChecked="True" Content="True"/>
  <CheckBox IsChecked="False" Content="False"/>
  <CheckBox IsChecked="{x:Null}" Content="Null"/>
  ```

- `RadioButton`: Radio buttons allow for a single selection within a range of choices. The choices are determined by the `GroupName` property. After one of the radio buttons is selected, the group can only be entirely unselected programmatically.

```
<RadioButton GroupName="RBSample" IsChecked="True" Content="Red"/>
<RadioButton GroupName="RBSample" Content="White"/>
<RadioButton GroupName="RBSample" Content="Blue"/>
```

- `Slider`: The slider control is a ranged input control. Similar to the `ProgressBar`, the control takes `Minimum`, `Maximum`, and `Interval` values. Additionally, you can specify to show Ticks, the location, and the Tick frequency. Ticks? Those are the value lines that show on sliders.

```
<Slider Interval="1" Minimum="1" Maximum="10" IsSnapToTickEnabled="True"
    TickPlacement="BottomRight" TickFrequency="1"/>
```

- `DatePicker`: New in Visual Studio 2010, the `DatePicker` control provides a concise method for getting (or displaying) date information by combining a `TextBox` with a `Calendar` control. Included in the many options is the capability to select multiple dates for a range of dates.

```
<DatePicker />
```

- `Calendar`: Also new in Visual Studio 2010 is the `Calendar` Control. The difference between the `Calendar` and the `DatePicker` is the `Calendar` control is always in full display mode whereas the `DatePicker`'s default look is similar to a text box.

```
<Calendar />
```

- `Button`: Okay, you caught me. The `Button` control doesn't really fit in with the other controls in this section, because it's more of an action control. Buttons respond to a user's click. The following code shows the Button implemented with an event handler in the Window's code-behind file. In Chapter 4, you find out how to use Commands to gain much more control of Buttons, but for now clicking the button merely displays `"Hello World."`

```
<Button Content="Click Me" Click="Button_Click"/>
private void Button_Click(object sender, RoutedEventArgs e)
{
    MessageBox.Show("Hello World");
}
```

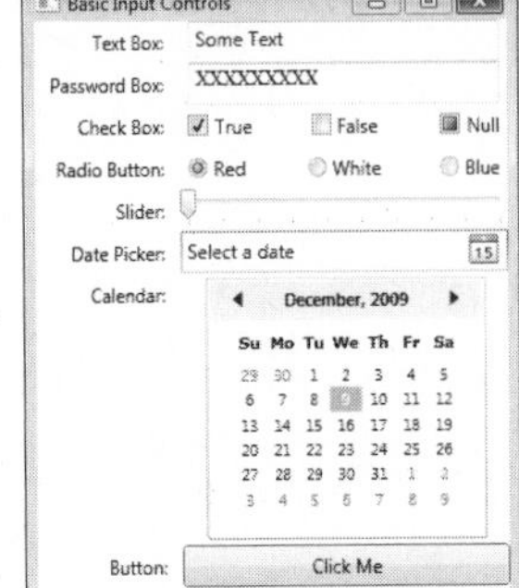

Figure 2-17: All the basic input controls.

List-based controls

The list-based controls (also referred to as Item controls) add an incredible amount of flexibility. As I discuss in Chapter 1, the list based controls no longer have to rely on data tricks or other magic to make the content meaningful to the user but can be templated to show greater details about the Items contained.

Data binding is covered in great detail in Chapter 3, but the controls don't do anything unless you have something to show. The `ComboBox`, `ListBox`, and `DataGrid` control samples will be bound to a class that represents a Person. `IList<Person>`. See the Person class:

```
public class Person
{
    public string Name { get; set; }
    public string Address { get; set; }
    public string City { get; set; }
    public string State { get; set; }
    public string Zip { get; set; }
}
```

Here are the list based controls:

- `ComboBox` and `ListBox`: The `ListBox` and the `ComboBox` in the sample below use a `DataTemplate` to create the display for the contained Items. The main difference between the two controls is that the `ComboBox` displays a single item with a drop-down selector (see Figure 2-18) and the `ListBox` shows the entire list of items up to the allowed space and scrolls the rest (see Figure 2-19). The `ComboBox` can be set up to enable selecting items that are NOT in the list, as well as editing the items in the list.

  Both the `ComboBox` and `ListBox` shown in Figures 2-18 and 2-19 use the exact same XAML between the `DataTemplate` tags, so only the `ComboBox` XAML is shown in Listing 2-15.

Listing 2-15: ComboBox XAML

```
<ComboBox Margin="5,0" HorizontalAlignment="Stretch" Hori
   zontalContentAlignment="Stretch" ItemsSource="{Binding
   Path=People}">
  <ComboBox.ItemTemplate>
    <DataTemplate>
      <Border HorizontalAlignment="Stretch"
   BorderBrush="AliceBlue" BorderThickness="1">
        <Grid HorizontalAlignment="Stretch">
          <Grid.RowDefinitions>
            <RowDefinition Height="Auto"/>
            <RowDefinition Height="Auto"/>
            <RowDefinition Height="Auto"/>
          </Grid.RowDefinitions>
          <Grid.ColumnDefinitions>
            <ColumnDefinition Width="Auto"/>
            <ColumnDefinition Width="Auto"/>
            <ColumnDefinition Width="*"/>
          </Grid.ColumnDefinitions>
          <TextBlock Grid.Row="0" Grid.Column="0" Grid.
   ColumnSpan="3" Margin="5,0" Text="{Binding Name}"/>
          <TextBlock Grid.Row="1" Grid.Column="0" Grid.
   ColumnSpan="3" Margin="5,0" Text="{Binding Address}"/>
          <TextBlock Grid.Row="2" Grid.Column="0"
   Margin="5,0" Text="{Binding City}"/>
          <TextBlock Grid.Row="2" Grid.Column="1"
   Margin="5,0" Text="{Binding State}"/>
          <TextBlock Grid.Row="2" Grid.Column="2"
   Margin="5,0" Text="{Binding Zip}"/>
        </Grid>
      </Border>
    </DataTemplate>
  </ComboBox.ItemTemplate>
</ComboBox>
```

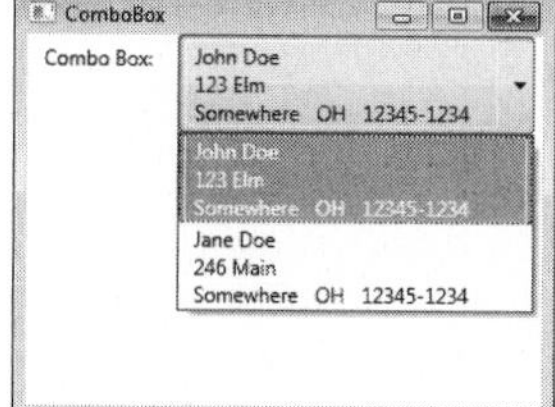

Figure 2-18: The ComboBox.

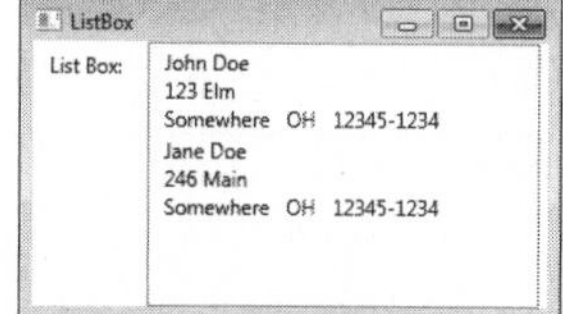

Figure 2-19: The ListBox.

✦ `TreeView`: The `TreeView` is a hierarchical `ItemsControl` much like Windows Explorer. The nodes (or branches) can be expanded or contracted, giving a nice user interface into any multilevel data. (See Figure 2-20.)

The sample shown in Listing 2-16 (taken from MSDN) uses hard-coded data, but with a simple hierarchical template tree views can be bound just like any other control.

Listing 2-16: The TreeView XAML

```
<TreeView Name="myTreeViewEvent" >
    <TreeViewItem Header="Employee1" IsSelected="True">
        <TreeViewItem Header="Jesper Aaberg"/>
        <TreeViewItem Header="Employee Number">
            <TreeViewItem Header="12345"/>
        </TreeViewItem>
        <TreeViewItem Header="Work Days">
            <TreeViewItem Header="Monday"/>
            <TreeViewItem Header="Tuesday"/>
            <TreeViewItem Header="Thursday"/>
        </TreeViewItem>
    </TreeViewItem>
    <TreeViewItem Header="Employee2">
        <TreeViewItem Header="Dominik Paiha"/>
        <TreeViewItem Header="Employee Number">
            <TreeViewItem Header="98765"/>
        </TreeViewItem>
        <TreeViewItem Header="Work Days">
            <TreeViewItem Header="Tuesday"/>
            <TreeViewItem Header="Wednesday"/>
            <TreeViewItem Header="Friday"/>
        </TreeViewItem>
    </TreeViewItem>
</TreeView>
```

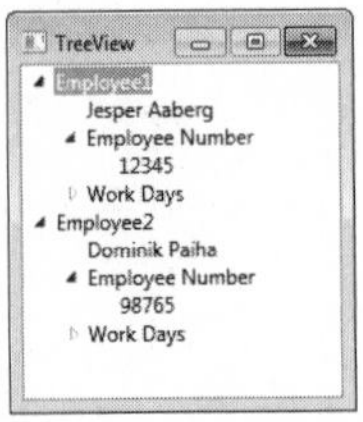

Figure 2-20: The TreeView.

- `DataGrid`: Also new in the .NET 4 (along with the DatePicker and Calendar controls) is the `DataGrid`. (See Figure 2-21.) Conspicuously absent from the earlier versions of WPF, this control was part of the WPF Toolkit, an out-of-band release available from `www.codeplex.com/wpf` (still a great resource for WPF information).

  The `DataGrid` has five base columns:

  - *`DataGridTextColumn`:* For Text
  - *`DataGridCheckBoxColumn`:* For Boolean
  - *`DataGridComboBoxColumn`:* For ListItems
  - *`DataGridHyperlinkColumn`:* For displaying Links
  - *`DataGridTemplateColumn`:* For designing custom columns

  The `DataGrid` can be set to `AutoGenerate` the columns based on the data it is bound to (as in the sample). It then uses reflection to determine the best column type based on the data.

```
<DataGrid HorizontalAlignment="Stretch"
   VerticalAlignment="Stretch"
   AutoGenerateColumns="True" ItemsSource="{Binding
   People}">
</DataGrid>
```

Name	Address	City	State	Zip
John Doe	123 Elm	Somewhere	OH	12345-1234
Jane Doe	246 Main	Somewhere	OH	12345-1234

Figure 2-21: A simple Data Grid.

Chapter 3: Data Binding in WPF

In This Chapter

- Understanding dependency properties
- Understanding binding modes
- Defining an example binding object
- Editing, converting, and visualizing data

Data binding allows data from your application objects (the binding source) to be displayed in your user interface elements (the binding target). What this means is that you can bind a Textbox's Text property (for example) to the Name property of an instance of your Car class. Depending on the binding mode used when setting up the relationship, changes in the Text property value of the Textbox can automatically update the underlying Name property of your Car object (and vice versa) without requiring any additional code.

It's no mystery these days that most applications deal with data. As a WPF developer, you have full creative reign on how data is presented, and how information entered by your user can be validated and used to update your underlying objects. One of WPF's strengths is its rich data binding support. This chapter walks you through the details.

Getting to Know Dependency Properties

Data binding happens when you set up a relationship between a binding source property with a binding target property. The binding target object must be a `DependencyObject`, and the target property must be a `DependencyProperty`.

Understanding dependency properties is crucial to obtaining a firm grasp on WPF technology. Dependency properties are found in objects that inherit from `DependencyObject`. At its root, a dependency property extends the functionality of a regular property that already exists on a CLR object by adding a set of services that is also known as the WPF Property System (together, `DependencyObject` and `DependencyProperty` make up this property system). Dependency properties can have their values determined by multiple input sources, meaning that their values can be obtained through a Style or a data binding expression. Dependency properties act like regular properties, but they allow you to set values based on the following:

✦ **A default value:** These are pre-defined on the property.

✦ **A calculated expression (similar to CSS expressions in the Web world):** This can be a data binding expression or a reference to resources defined in the application.

✦ **Data binding:** This actually is built upon the preceding bullet using binding expressions on the binding source object.

✦ **Property value inheritance:** Not to be confused with object inheritance, property value inheritance allows values set on parent properties to be propagated down to its children. For instance, if you set `FontSize` values on the `Window` element (the root element), child elements such as `TextBlock` and `Label` automatically inherit those font property values. You can see another example of this by reviewing the concept of Attached Properties introduced in Chapter 1.

✦ **Styling:** Each style typically contains setters to set one or more property values.

The WPF property system also provides built-in property value change notification and property value validation functionality, which I review in more detail in this chapter.

At the end of the day, dependency properties give the developer the capability to set property values directly in XAML as well as in code. The advantage to this is that you can keep your code clean and leave initializing object property values to XAML.

Exploring the Binding Modes

You have full control over how the binding relationship you create behaves. Multiple types of binding modes are available to you in WPF. These include the following:

✦ **The OneTime binding mode** is used when you want the source property to only initially set the target property value. Subsequent changes to the source property are not reflected in the target property. Similarly, changes to the target property are not reflected in the source property.

✦ **The OneWay binding mode** is typically used for read-only behaving properties. In this binding mode, data from the source property sets the initial value of the target property. Subsequent changes to the source property will automatically update the binding target property value. Conversely, any subsequent changes made to the target property value are not reflected in the source property.

- **The OneWayToSource binding mode** is essentially the opposite of the OneWay binding mode. In this binding mode, data from the source property initializes the target property value. Subsequent changes to the source property value will not update the target property. However, updates to the target property value will automatically update the source property value.
- **The TwoWay binding mode** merges the functionality of the OneWay and OneWayToSource binding modes. In this binding mode, the source property value initializes the target property value. Subsequent changes to the source property value update the target property value. Similarly, updates to the target property value will update the source property value.

Investigating the Binding Object

Bindings can be defined using code or XAML. Here we begin with the XAML version. In order to see how to bind data to your UI elements, we first define a test set of data to work with.

The complete solution is available at `www.csharpfordummies.net` in the chapter downloads under BindingSample1

Defining a binding with XAML

Just follow these steps to create a binding with XAML:

1. **Create a new WPF Application project, name it** BindingSample1,
2. **Define a simple Car class by adding a new Class to your solution named** `Car.cs`**. Code it as follows:**

```
using System;
using System.Collections.Generic;
using System.Linq;
using System.Text;

namespace BindingSample1
{
   public class Car
   {
        private string _make;

        public string Make
        {
```

```
                get { return _make; }
                set { _make = value; }
            }
            private string _model;

            public string Model
            {
                get { return _model; }
                set { _model = value; }
            }

            public Car() { }
        }
    }
```

3. **In** `MainWindow.xaml`**, replace the grid with one that defines a double column and single row grid. Then add a label in each grid cell, like this:**

```
<Grid>
    <Grid.ColumnDefinitions>
        <ColumnDefinition></ColumnDefinition>
        <ColumnDefinition></ColumnDefinition>
    </Grid.ColumnDefinitions>
    <Grid.RowDefinitions>
        <RowDefinition></RowDefinition>
    </Grid.RowDefinitions>
    <Label x:Name="lblCarMake" Grid.Row="0" Grid.Column="0"
           Content="{Binding Path=Make, Mode=OneTime}" />
    <Label x:Name="lblCarModel" Grid.Row="0" Grid.Column="1"
           Content="{Binding Path=Model, Mode=OneTime}" />
 </Grid>
```

   Take a look at the `Content` dependency property value. The information contained within the curly braces defines the binding for the content to be displayed in the labels. I describe what this Binding expression means in just a moment, but first, let's get some data to bind to!

4. **Open the** `MainWindow.xaml.cs` **code-behind file, and create a method called** `GenerateData` **that instantiates a Car object and assigns it to the** `DataContext` **of the window, like this:**

```
private void GenerateData()
{
    Car car1 = new Car() { Make = "Athlon", Model = "XYZ" };
    this.DataContext = car1;
}
```

   `DataContext` defines the root object relative to which all child elements obtain their values (as long as the `DataContext` value on the child elements is not directly set via XAML or code — this property is an example of property value inheritance; its value is obtained from its parent element unless otherwise specified).

5. **Call the** `GenerateData()` **method in the** MainWindow **constructor method (public MainWindow()), immediately following** `InitializeComponents()` **call.**

   Now, looking back to the XAML file (MainWindow.xaml), the first label `lblCarMake` will bind to the `DataContext`'s `Make` property. The value is retrieved from the property specified in the binding's `Path` component. Similarly, the second label lblCarModel will bind to the DataContext's Model property as specified in the binding expression's Path property. Each of these bindings is using a OneWay mode, which means the label content will be bound only once, regardless if the underlying object property being bound to changes.

The Path component of the XAML Binding expression simply tells the XAML processor to take its value from a specific property of its DataContext. The Path value can also express properties that are nested, such as in the case of nested complex objects. In these cases, you use dot notation to reach the desired property, such as Property.SomeObject.SomeOtherProperty.

6. **Run the application.**

   You can see that the labels now display the Make and Model of the Car object that was assigned to the DataContext of the window. (See Figure 3-1.)

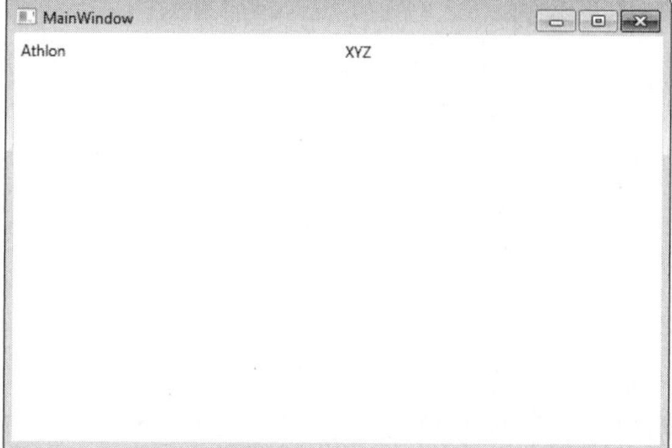

Figure 3-1: Data binding to properties of a DataContext.

Defining a binding with C#

Defining bindings can also be done using C#. To demonstrate this, remove the Content attribute entirely from both labels in the XAML file. The label markup should now resemble the following:

```
<Label x:Name="lblCarMake" Grid.Row="0" Grid.Column="0" />
<Label x:Name="lblCarModel" Grid.Row="0" Grid.Column="1" />
```

Modify the GenerateData() method in MainWindow.xaml.cs to implement the Binding definitions in code. To do this, you must instantiate Binding objects directly. The constructor of the Binding object takes in the string Path value. Use the BindingOperations class to apply the Binding to the Content dependency property of your labels.

BindingOperations is a helper class provided to you by WPF. It has static methods that give you the power to add and clear data binding definitions on application elements.

The following code shows you how to define the Binding objects, and assign the binding to the Content of the labels:

```
private void GenerateData()
{
    Car car1 = new Car() { Make = "Athlon", Model = "XYZ" };

    Binding makeBinding = new Binding("Make");
    makeBinding.Mode = BindingMode.OneTime;
    BindingOperations.SetBinding(lblCarMake,
              Label.ContentProperty, makeBinding);

    Binding modelBinding = new Binding("Model");
    modelBinding.Mode = BindingMode.OneTime;
    BindingOperations.SetBinding(lblCarModel,
                    Label.ContentProperty, modelBinding);

    this.DataContext = car1;
}
```

Run the application and observe that it runs the same way as when the bindings were defined using XAML.

Dependency properties are typically defined with the suffix "Property," but you only see them this way navigating MSDN documentation and accessing them through code. In XAML, you specify dependency property attributes by dropping the "Property" suffix on the name.

Editing, Validating, Converting, and Visualizing Your Data

In the preceding section, you got a taste of binding syntax and saw data appear on the screen. This section builds on this knowledge and shows you a simple example of updating data, from user interface elements as well as updating the user interface with changes happening to objects behind the scenes.

The complete solution is available on the Web in the BindingSample2 project.

To do this, follow these steps:

1. **Create a new WPF Application project and name it** BindingSample2.

   Let's reuse the Car class that we created in `BindingSample1` (Note: If copying and pasting this class, ensure you change the namespace of the class to `BindingSample2`.)

In this example, you will display the make and model of a Car object (the DataContext) in TextBox controls. This enables you to edit the values of the Car properties. You will also use a TwoWay data binding mode so that changes made from the user interface will be reflected in the underlying Car object, and any changes made to the Car object from code-behind will be reflected in the user interface.

2. **Define two buttons, one that shows a message box containing the current value of the** `DataContext`**, the other that forces changes to the** `DataContext` **through code-behind.**

   In `MainWindow.xaml`, replace the Grid content with this:

```
<Grid>
    <Grid.ColumnDefinitions>
        <ColumnDefinition></ColumnDefinition>
        <ColumnDefinition></ColumnDefinition>
    </Grid.ColumnDefinitions>
    <Grid.RowDefinitions>
        <RowDefinition></RowDefinition>
        <RowDefinition></RowDefinition>
    </Grid.RowDefinitions>

    <StackPanel Orientation="Horizontal" Grid.Row="0" Grid.
Column="0">
        <Label Content="Make" />
        <TextBox x:Name="lblCarMake"  VerticalAlignment="Top"
           Text="{Binding Path=Make, Mode=TwoWay}"
           Width="200" Height="25" />
    </StackPanel>

    <StackPanel Orientation="Horizontal" Grid.Row="0" Grid.Column="1"
>
        <Label Content="Model" />
        <TextBox x:Name="lblCarModel"  VerticalAlignment="Top"
           Text="{Binding Path=Model, Mode=TwoWay}"
           Width="200" Height="25" />
    </StackPanel>

    <Button x:Name="btnShowDataContextValue"
            Click="btnShowDataContextValue_Click"
            Content="Show Current Data Context Value"
            Grid.Row="1" Grid.Column="0"/>

    <Button x:Name="btnChangeDataContextValue"
            Click="btnChangeDataContextValue_Click"
            Content="Change Data Context Value with Code-Behind"
            Grid.Row="1" Grid.Column="1" />

</Grid>
```

3. **In the code-behind file,** `MainWindow.xaml.cs`**, add the following methods:**

```
private void GenerateData()
{
    Car car1 = new Car() { Make = "Athlon", Model = "XYZ" };
    this.DataContext = car1;
}
```

```
private void btnShowDataContextValue_Click(object sender,
                                        RoutedEventArgs e)
{
    Car dc = this.DataContext as Car;
    MessageBox.Show("Car Make: " + dc.Make + "\nCar Model: "
                + dc.Model);
}

private void btnChangeDataContextValue_Click(object sender,
                                        RoutedEventArgs e)
{
    Car dc = this.DataContext as Car;
    dc.Make = "Changed Make";
    dc.Model = "Changed Model";
}
```

4. **In the constructor for** `MainWindow()`**, ensure that you call the** `GenerateData()` **method immediately following the** `InitializeComponents()` **call.**

5. **Run this application.**

   You will see that the values from the DataContext display properly in the TextBox controls. Feel free to change the values in the TextBox controls. For instance, change the Make value to `Athlon X`, and the model to `ABC`. When you are finished with your edits, click the Show Current Data Context Value button. The changes you made to the values in the TextBox are now reflected in the underlying DataContext object. (See Figure 3-2.)

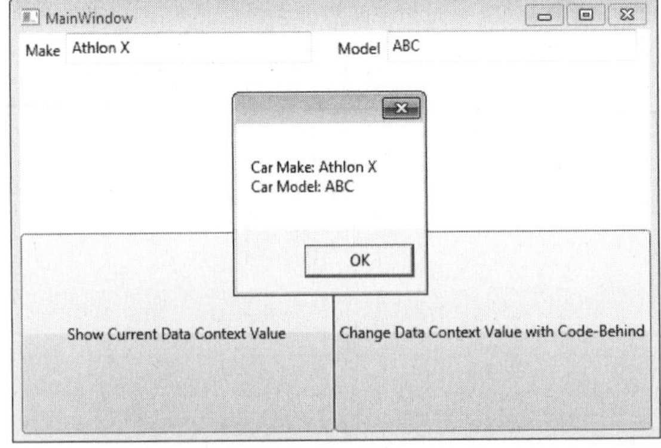

Figure 3-2: Editing data using a TwoWay binding mode.

6. **Click the OK button to get rid of the message box.**

   If you look in the Click event handler of the Change Data Context Value With Code-Behind button (`btnChangeDataContextValue_Click`), you will note that the `DataContext Car` object properties will be changed to and `Changed Model`, respectively.

7. **Click the Change Data Context Value With Code-Behind button.**

   Hmmm. Nothing is happening. What is up with that? If you click on the Show Current Data Context Value button, you will see the properties have in fact been changed. Because you're using a TwoWay binding, your settings should automatically update your UI, right? Wrong! This is where another feature of WPF, the concept of `INotifyPropertyChanged`, comes into play.

   `INotifyPropertyChanged` is a simple interface that allows your objects to raise an event that notifies its subscribers (namely your application) that a property value on the object has changed. Client applications subscribe to these events and update the user interface with the new values only when changes occur.

   A similar interface exists for collections as well — the `INotifyCollectionChanged` interface. WPF also provides a generic class called `ObservableCollection`<T> that already implements `INotifyCollectionChanged` for you. When creating an `ObservableCollection` or your own collection that implements `INotifyCollectionChanged`, you need to ensure that the objects that will be contained within the collection also implement `INotifyPropertyChanged` interface.

   The `INotifyPropertyChanged` interface contains a single event that must be implemented. This event is called `PropertyChanged`, and its parameters are the object that owns the property that has changed (the sender), and the string name of the property that has changed.

8. **Open your Car class, and have it implement the** `INotifyPropertyChanged` **interface.**

   The interface is located in the `System.ComponentModel` namespace (add using System.ComponentModel to the top of your class) Implementing this interface adds the following event to the `Car` class:

   ```
   public event PropertyChangedEventHandler PropertyChanged;
   ```

   In order for the application to be notified of the changes that occur in `Car` objects, the `PropertyChanged` event must be fired each time a property value has changed.

9. **To implement this in the** `Car` **class, create a helper method called** `NotifyPropertyChanged` **that takes in a string property name and fires the** `PropertyChanged` **event for the object instance and the name of the property that has changed, like this:**

   ```
   private void NotifyPropertyChanged(string propertyName)
   {
       if (PropertyChanged != null)
       {
           this.PropertyChanged(this,
                 new PropertyChangedEventArgs(propertyName));
       }
   }
   ```

Checking to see if `PropertyChanged` is not null essentially means we are checking to see if anyone is listening (subscribed) to the `PropertyChanged` event.

10. **Now you need to modify the Set methods in each of the public properties on the `Car` object to call the `NotifyPropertyChanged` helper method each time the property value has changed. Edit the public properties like this:**

```
public string Make
{
    get { return _make; }
    set {
        if (_make != value)
        {
            _make = value;
            NotifyPropertyChanged("Make");
        }
    }
}

public string Model
{
    get { return _model; }
    set {
        if (_model != value)
        {
            _model = value;
            NotifyPropertyChanged("Model");
        }
    }
}
```

11. **Run the application again.**

    Now when you click the Change Data Context Value with Code-Behind button, the changed values get reflected automatically in the TextBox elements. This is due to the combination of the TwoWay binding mode as well as the implementation of `INotifyPropertyChanged`. (See Figure 3-3.)

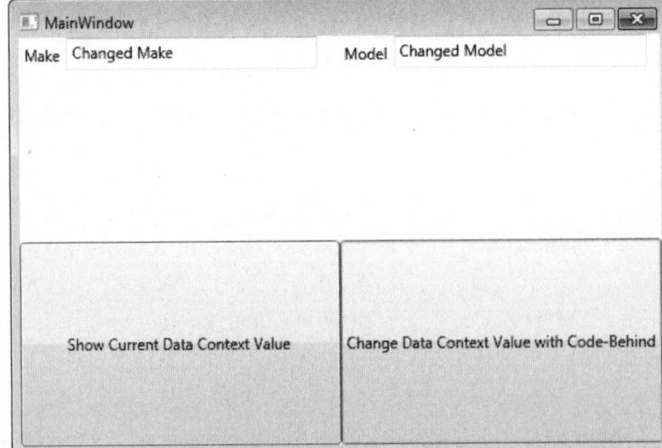

Figure 3-3: TwoWay Data Binding with INotify-Property-Changed.

Element binding

In this chapter, we bind `Label` and `TextBox` controls to properties of underlying objects. You are not limited to this scenario; you can bind to just about anything from primitive variables to property values gleaned from other UIElements. Element binding in particular has its own component in the `Binding` expression. For instance, suppose you have a `TextBox` and `Label` control in your window. You would like to have the `Content` of the `Label` automatically update with the changing value of the `Text` property of the `TextBox`. The XAML code to accomplish Element Binding between the `TextBox` and the `Label` looks similar to:

```
<Label x:Name="lblCarMake"
      Content="{Binding
ElementName=txtCarMake,
Path=Text}" />
  <TextBox x:Name="txtCarMake"
Width="200" Height="25" />
```

The C# code to define this binding looks similar to:

```
  Binding b = new
Binding("Text");
  b.ElementName = "txtCarMake";
  BindingOperations.
SetBinding(lblCarMake, Label.
ContentProperty, b);
```

Validating data

It is good practice to validate any input provided to you from the user. People aren't perfect, and some people can be downright malicious. WPF provides a built-in framework for data validation and error notification. It is available to you through the implementation of the `IDataErrorInfo` interface on your classes.

Let's add validation to the `Car` class you already created in `BindingSample2` from the preceding section.

The complete solution is available on the Web in the `BindingSample2 Validation` project.

Just follow these steps to add validation to your `Car` class:

1. **Open the `Car.cs` file, and edit the class to also implement the `IDataErrorInfo` interface, like this:**

    ```
    public class Car : INotifyPropertyChanged, IDataErrorInfo
    ```

    Implementing this interface adds the following methods to the Car class:

    ```
    public string Error
    {
        get { throw new NotImplementedException(); }
    }
    ```

```
public string this[string columnName]
{
    get { throw new NotImplementedException(); }
}
```

2. **Edit the** `Get` **method of the** `Error` **property to return null.**

   Now it's time to add some validation rules to the properties of the `Car` object. The `Car Make` and `Model` properties should enforce the rule that they must always be at least three characters in length. The `public string this[string columnName]` method is used by the `DataBinding` engine to validate the properties of the object as they are changed, based on the name of the property (which is what they mean by `columnName` in the method signature). This method returns any error messages related to the property being edited.

3. **To define and enforce these rules, edit the** `public string this[string columnName]` **method like this:**

```
public string this[string columnName]
{
    get {
        string retvalue = null;
        if (columnName == "Make")
        {
            if (String.IsNullOrEmpty(this._make)
                    || this._make.Length < 3)
            {
                retvalue = "Car Make must be at least 3 " +
                           "characters in length";
            }
        }

        if (columnName == "Model")
        {
            if (String.IsNullOrEmpty(this._model)
                     || this._model.Length < 3)
            {
                retvalue = "Car Model must be at least 3 "+
                              "characters in length";
            }
        }

        return retvalue;
    }
}
```

4. **In** `MainWindow.xaml`**, the** `Make` **and** `Model` **properties are bound to** `TextBox` **controls in the user interface. To enable the text being entered into the TextBoxes to be validated against the constraints defined on the underlying property, edit the binding expressions in each TextBox like this:**

```
<TextBox x:Name="txtCarMake"  VerticalAlignment="Top"
         Text="{Binding Path=Make, Mode=TwoWay,
               UpdateSourceTrigger=PropertyChanged,
               ValidatesOnDataErrors=True,
```

```
                ValidatesOnExceptions=True}"
        Width="200" Height="25" />

    <TextBox x:Name="txtCarModel"  VerticalAlignment="Top"
        Text="{Binding Path=Model, Mode=TwoWay,
                UpdateSourceTrigger=PropertyChanged,
                ValidatesOnDataErrors=True,
                ValidatesOnExceptions=True}"
        Width="200" Height="25" />
```

`UpdateSourceTrigger` identifies when the validation calls take place. In this example, validations occur as the text is changing, and is fired off when the underlying object property fires the `PropertyChanged` event.

`ValidatesOnDataErrors` is what enables the `IDataErrorInfo` validation method to be called on the property.

`ValidatesOnExceptions` will invalidate the TextBox if the underlying data source throws an exception, like when, for instance, you have an integer property and the user enters a string — WPF automatically throws the exception that the input string was not in the correct format.

5. **Run the Sample, and remove all text from the `Make` and `Model` `TextBox` controls. You will see the `TextBox` controls are now rendered in red; as you enter text back into the TextBox, as soon as you reach three characters, the red stroke disappears Figure 3-4 shows the Make text box in an invalid state.**

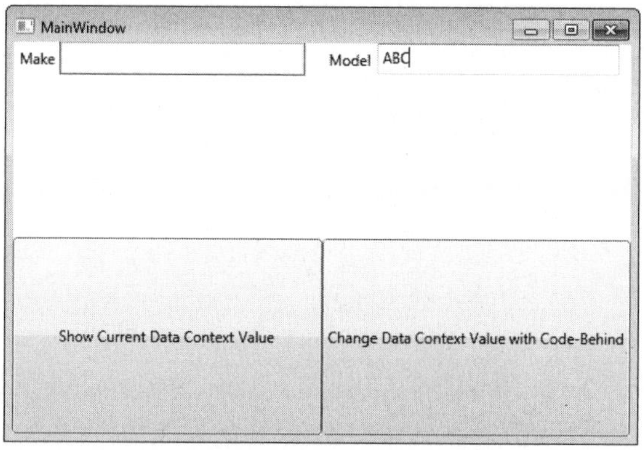

Figure 3-4: Simple Data Validation using the IDataErrorInfo interface.

6. **The red stroke is sufficient enough to indicate that an error has occurred, but it's of little use to the users as they are not informed of the details of the error. A simple way to display the error is to add a tooltip on the `TextBox`. Do this by adding a Style resource to your Window that defines a style that will trigger the tooltip when the**

data is in an invalid state. Add the following XAML directly below the Window tag at the top of MainWindow.xaml, like this.

```
<Window.Resources>
    <Style x:Key="errorAwareTextBox" TargetType="{x:Type TextBox}">
        <Style.Triggers>
            <Trigger Property="Validation.HasError" Value="true">
                <Setter Property="ToolTip"
            Value="{Binding RelativeSource={x:Static RelativeSource.
Self},
            Path=(Validation.Errors)[0].ErrorContent}"/>
            </Trigger>
        </Style.Triggers>
    </Style>
</Window.Resources>
```

7. **Add a `Style` attribute to your `TextBox` `Style`, like this:**

```
Style="{StaticResource ResourceKey=errorAwareTextBox}"
```

Now when you run the application and remove the text out of the TextBox controls, the TextBox displays a tooltip with the actual error message. (See Figure 3-5.)

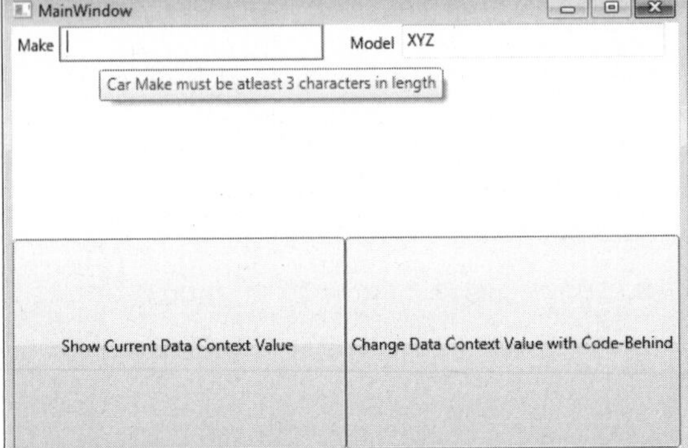

Figure 3-5: Displaying error messages using Styles.

Converting your data

WPF provides you the capability to cater your user interface to be intuitive for the user. Sometimes this means allowing them to enter data in different formats that make sense to them, giving you the responsibility of translating their data entry into a format allowable by your data source. The same is true vice versa; you will want to translate data from your data source into a more intuitive form for the user. A popular use-case for this type of conversion is the string representation of a date value, or if you want to display a red or green circle instead of the values True or False.

WPF makes converting data easy by providing a simple interface to implement called `IValueConverter`. This interface contains two methods:

- **Convert:** This method obtains values from the data source and molds them to the form to be displayed to the user onscreen.
- **ConvertBack:** This method does the opposite — it takes the value from the user interface and molds it into a form that the data source expects.

It is important to note that with these methods you are not held to the same data type as the value being bound. For instance, your data source property being bound can be a Date data type and the `Convert` method can still return a string value to the user interface.

To demonstrate this feature, create a new WPF application project called `BindingSample3`. This project is a dashboard application that can show the status of servers on the network. In this project, you implement two user controls, `RedX` and `GreenCheck`. You also create a value converter named `BooleanToIconConverter` that converts a Boolean False value to display the `RedX` control and converts a True value to display the `GreenCheck` control. These values indicate whether the server is available.

A user control is a collection of reusable XAML. It can be made up of any number of elements and is implemented with the same rules as when you implement a normal Window (for instance, you can have only one root element). You can also define properties (including dependency properties!!) on user controls.

Project is available on the Web under `BindingSample3`.

Follow these steps to create your Sample:

1. **Create a new WPF application named** BindingSample3.
2. **Add a new User Control to the project; name it** GreenCheck.xaml.
3. **Replace the XAML found in** `GreenCheck.xaml` **with this XAML:**

```
<UserControl x:Class="BindingSample3.GreenCheck"
             xmlns="http://schemas.microsoft.com/winfx/2006/xaml/
    presentation"
             xmlns:x="http://schemas.microsoft.com/winfx/2006/xaml"
             xmlns:mc="http://schemas.openxmlformats.org/markup-
    compatibility/2006"
             xmlns:d="http://schemas.microsoft.com/expression/blend/2008"
             mc:Ignorable="d"
             d:DesignHeight="50" d:DesignWidth="50">

        <Canvas x:Name="CheckCanvas" Width="50.4845" Height="49.6377"
                Canvas.Left="0" Canvas.Top="0">

                <Path x:Name="CheckPath" Width="43.4167" Height="45.6667"
                   Canvas.Left="0" Canvas.Top="1.3113e-006"
                  Stretch="Fill" Fill="#FF006432"
                  Data="F1 M 19.0833,45.6667L 43.4167,2.16667L 38,
                         1.3113e-006L 19.0833,42.5833L 2.41667,25.3333L
    0,
                        27.9167L 17.4167,44.25"/>
        </Canvas>
</UserControl>
```

You are not expected to come up with things like the `CheckPath` off the top of your head. (The path is what describes how the check mark is drawn.) In the Expression Suite, you find designer tools that allow you to draw items in a graphics program and export your final graphics in a XAML format. Expression Design was the tool used to create the user controls in this example.

4. **Add another user control to the project; name it** `RedX.xaml`.
5. **Replace the XAML in the** `RedX.xaml` **file with this XAML:**

```
<UserControl x:Class="BindingSample3.RedX"
             xmlns="http://schemas.microsoft.com/winfx/2006/xaml/
    presentation"
             xmlns:x="http://schemas.microsoft.com/winfx/2006/xaml"
             xmlns:mc="http://schemas.openxmlformats.org/markup-
    compatibility/2006"
             xmlns:d="http://schemas.microsoft.com/expression/blend/2008"
             mc:Ignorable="d"
             d:DesignHeight="50" d:DesignWidth="50">

        <Canvas Width="44.625" Height="45.9394">

            <Path x:Name="Line1Path" Width="44.625" Height="44.375"
                  Canvas.Left="0" Canvas.Top="0" Stretch="Fill"
                   Fill="#FFDE0909"
                  Data="F1 M 0,3.5L 3.5,0L 44.625,41L 42.125,44.375"/>

            <Path x:Name="Line2Path" Width="43.5772" Height="45.3813"
                  Canvas.Left="0.201177" Canvas.Top="0.55809"
    Stretch="Fill"
                  Fill="#FFDE0909" Data="F1 M 3.7719,45.9394L 0.201177,
                  42.5115L 40.353,0.55809L 43.7784,2.98867"/>

        </Canvas>
</UserControl>
```

6. **Add a new class called** `BooleanToIconConverter.cs`.
7. **Add the following using statement to your class:**

```
using System.Windows.Data;
```

8. **Have the** `BooleanToIconConverter` **inherit the** `IValueConverter` **interface. In the** `Convert` **method, if the value passed in is True, have it return a new instance of the** `GreenCheck` **user control. If the value passed in is False, have the** `Convert` **method return an instance of the RedX user control. Here's the code for the** `BooleanToIconConverter` **class:**

```
using System;
using System.Collections.Generic;
using System.Linq;
using System.Text;
using System.Windows.Data;

namespace BindingSample3
{
    public class BooleanToIconConverter : IValueConverter
    {
        public object Convert(object value, Type targetType,
```

```
                              object parameter,
                               System.Globalization.CultureInfo culture)
        {
            if (value != null)
            {
                bool boolValue = (bool)value;
                if (boolValue)
                    return new GreenCheck();
                else
                    return new RedX();
            }

            return value;
        }

        public object ConvertBack(object value, Type targetType,
                                 object parameter,
                                 System.Globalization.CultureInfo
    culture)
        {
            throw new NotImplementedException();
        }
}
```

9. **Add a new class called** `ServerStatus.cs` **that has three properties: the Server name, a Boolean indicator if the server is up, and a number of currently connected users. This will be the data class used in the application. Here is the code for** `ServerStatus.cs`**:**

```
public class ServerStatus
{
    private string _serverName;

    public string ServerName
    {
        get { return _serverName; }
        set { _serverName = value; }
    }
    private bool _isServerUp;

    public bool IsServerUp
    {
        get { return _isServerUp; }
        set { _isServerUp = value; }
    }
    private int _numberOfConnectedUsers;

    public int NumberOfConnectedUsers
    {
        get { return _numberOfConnectedUsers; }
        set { _numberOfConnectedUsers = value; }
    }

    public ServerStatus() { }
}
```

10. **In** `MainWindow.xaml.cs`**, create a** `GenerateData()` **method (call it immediately following the** `InitializeComponent()` **method in the** `Window` **constructor) that will initialize a list of a few** `ServerStatus`

objects and make that list the `DataContext` of the `Window`. Here's the code:

```
private void GenerateData()
{
    ServerStatus ss = new ServerStatus() {
        ServerName = "HeadquartersApplicationServer1",
        NumberOfConnectedUsers = 983,
        IsServerUp = true
    };

    ServerStatus ss2 = new ServerStatus()
    {
        ServerName = "HeadquartersFileServer1",
        NumberOfConnectedUsers = 0,
        IsServerUp = false
    };

    ServerStatus ss3 = new ServerStatus()
    {
        ServerName = "HeadquartersWebServer1",
        NumberOfConnectedUsers = 0,
        IsServerUp = false
    };

    ServerStatus ss4 = new ServerStatus()
    {
        ServerName = "HQDomainControllerServer1",
        NumberOfConnectedUsers = 10235,
        IsServerUp = true
    };

    List<ServerStatus> serverList = new List<ServerStatus>();
    serverList.Add(ss);
    serverList.Add(ss2);
    serverList.Add(ss3);
    serverList.Add(ss4);

    this.DataContext = serverList;
}
```

11. **Save and build your application — this is done so that the user control classes that you have defined are available to your XAML files.**

12. **In `MainWindow.xaml`, replace the XAML with the XAML found in the following code segment.** I describe the details of this markup in a moment.

```
<Window x:Class="BindingSample3.MainWindow"
        xmlns="http://schemas.microsoft.com/winfx/2006/xaml/presentation"
        xmlns:x="http://schemas.microsoft.com/winfx/2006/xaml"
        xmlns:local="clr-namespace:BindingSample3"
        Title="MainWindow" Height="400" Width="525">
    <Window.Resources>
        <local:BooleanToIconConverter x:Key="BooleanToIconConverter" />

         <DataTemplate x:Key="ServerTemplate">
            <Border BorderBrush="Blue" Margin="3" Padding="3"
                    BorderThickness="2" CornerRadius="5"
    Background="Beige">
```

```
            <StackPanel Orientation="Horizontal">

                <Label Content="{Binding
                     Path=IsServerUp,
                     Converter={StaticResource
    BooleanToIconConverter}}" />

                <StackPanel Orientation="Vertical"
                       VerticalAlignment="Center">

                    <TextBlock FontSize="25" Foreground="Goldenrod"
                       Text="{Binding Path=ServerName}" />

                     <TextBlock FontSize="18" Foreground="BlueViolet"
                       Text="{Binding Path=NumberOfConnectedUsers}"
    />
                </StackPanel>

            </StackPanel>
        </Border>
    </DataTemplate>

    </Window.Resources>
    <Grid>
        <Grid.ColumnDefinitions>
            <ColumnDefinition />
        </Grid.ColumnDefinitions>
        <Grid.RowDefinitions>
            <RowDefinition />
        </Grid.RowDefinitions>

         <ListBox x:Name="lstServers" Width="490" Height="350"
                 ItemsSource="{Binding}" Grid.Row="0" Grid.Column="0"
                 ItemTemplate="{StaticResource
    ResourceKey=ServerTemplate}" />
    </Grid>
</Window>
```

The first thing to note in `MainWindow.xaml` is that the namespace for the local assembly (`BindingSample3`) was added to the `Window` (identified by the namespace definition in the Window tag with the prefix `local`). This enables you to instantiate classes that are defined in the current assembly in XAML.

In the `Window` resources, we initialized an instance of our `BooleanToIconConverter`, which is available to you through the local namespace.

```
<local:BooleanToIconConverter x:Key="BooleanToIconConverter" />
```

The next Window resource that is defined is a data template. This data template provides a way to look at the data associated with a server's current status. The data template is defined as follows:

```
<DataTemplate x:Key="ServerTemplate">
   <Border BorderBrush="Blue" Margin="3" Padding="3"
           BorderThickness="2" CornerRadius="5" Background="Beige">
```

```
            <StackPanel Orientation="Horizontal">

                 <Label Content="{Binding
                      Path=IsServerUp,
                      Converter={StaticResource BooleanToIconConverter}}" />

                 <StackPanel Orientation="Vertical"
                         VerticalAlignment="Center">

                     <TextBlock FontSize="25" Foreground="Goldenrod"
                         Text="{Binding Path=ServerName}" />

                      <TextBlock FontSize="18" Foreground="BlueViolet"
                         Text="{Binding Path=NumberOfConnectedUsers}" />
                 </StackPanel>

             </StackPanel>
         </Border>
     </DataTemplate>
```

In Chapter 1, I state that one of the main reasons to adopt WPF as a user interface technology is its data visualization flexibility. Data templates enable you to represent data contained in an object using any number of XAML elements. The world is your oyster, and you can get as creative as you want to relay application information to your user in the most usable, intuitive fashion using data templates.

Let's analyze the `ServerTemplate` data template. This data template represents the display of an instance of a `ServerStatus` object. Look at the `Label` element in the data template:

```
<Label Content="{Binding Path=IsServerUp,
                Converter={StaticResource BooleanToIconConverter}}" />
```

The `Content` property of the label is bound to the Boolean `IsServerUp` property of the `ServerStatus` object. You'll also notice that there is another component to the binding expression, called `Converter`. This is where the Boolean value (`IsServerUp`) gets passed into the `BooleanToIconConverter` and is rendered as the `RedX` or the `GreenCheck` user control, depending on its value.

The rest of the data template simply outputs the server name of the `ServerStatus` object in yellow, and the number of connected users in blue-violet.

Within the Grid on the Window, a `ListBox` control is defined that displays a list of servers on the network. Let's look at the definition of the `ListBox`:

```
<ListBox x:Name="lstServers" Width="490" Height="350"
         Grid.Row="0" Grid.Column="0"
         ItemsSource="{Binding}"
         ItemTemplate="{StaticResource ResourceKey=ServerTemplate}" />
```

WPF provides a number of controls called `ItemsControls` that allow you to bind collections of objects to them. Examples of `ItemsControls` are `ListBox` and `ComboBox` (among others). Collections are bound to an `ItemsControl` through the `ItemsSource` attribute. A data template can also be applied to each object being bound through the `ItemsControl` `ItemTemplate` attribute.

Through Property Value inheritance, the `ItemsSource` of the `ListBox` is defaulted to the `DataContext` of `Window`. The empty `{Binding}` element simply states that it will use the current binding of its parent, which uses recursion up the element tree until it reaches a place where a binding is set. Remember that in the `GenerateData` we are setting the `Data Context` binding to the list of Servers to the `Window` itself, so the `ListBox` will inherit that list as its `ItemSource`.

The data template that was defined in resources to describe a `ServerStatus` object will be used to render each object being bound. You see this through the `ItemTemplate` attribute that uses the `StaticResource` that points to the `ServerTemplate` that was defined in resources.

Now when you run the application, you will see the ServerStatus data presented in a visually pleasing way! (See Figure 3-6.)

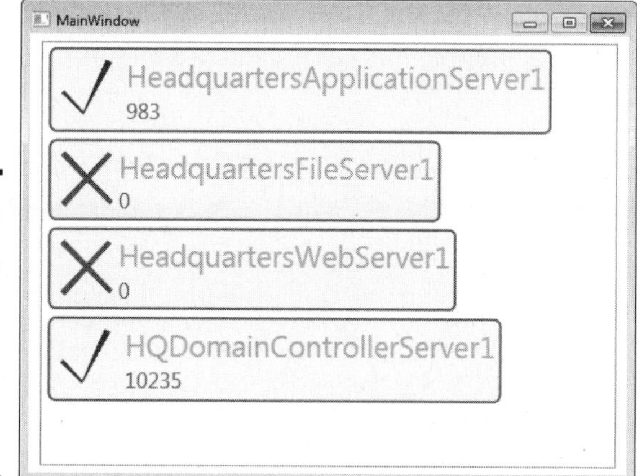

Figure 3-6: Rendering a collection of data using a value converter and data templates.

Finding Out More about WPF Data Binding

This chapter is not meant to be inclusive of all functionality possible through WPF's amazing data binding support. Other aspects of WPF data templates worth looking into include these concepts:

- **`DataTemplateSelector`:** This is a base class that allows you to render a data template based on some logical condition.

- **Using data templates as a means to provide data adding/editing capabilities to the user.**
- **Switching a data template at runtime at the preference of the user.** This allows users to switch a data template at will. For instance, in a `ListBox`, you may only display summary information; however, you can provide a button in your data template that will enable users to switch between the summary template and a more detailed template on demand.

Chapter 4: Practical WPF

In This Chapter

- **Commanding attention**
- **Getting your ViewModel on**

Even though WPF still supports the direct event handler wire up (for example, through the OnClick event), WPF introduces a much better mechanism for responding to user events. It significantly reduces the amount of code you have to write and adds testability to your application. Traditional event handling is all contained in the code-behind for your form, which is extremely difficult to test in an automated fashion.

Software patterns have been around for a long time, first brought to the forefront by the classic tome *Design Patterns: Elements of Reusable Object-Oriented Software* by Erich Gamma, Richard Helm, Ralph Johnson, and John Vissides — commonly referred to as the "Gang of Four." Software has evolved and many new patterns have been developed over the years. One of the most effective user interface patterns developed for WPF is the Model-View-View Model pattern (commonly referred to as ViewModel). Using the ViewModel pattern in your WPF applications will improve software reuse, testability, readability, maintainability, and most of the other "ilities" as well.

Commanding Attention

The Command Pattern has been around since, well, forever, and you most likely use it every day. Copy and Paste commands are example implementations of the pattern built into Windows and most Windows applications. WPF provides a significant number of built-in commands and also allows for completely customized commands!

Traditional handling of user events (and still supported in WPF) is through an event handler. When the button on the Window is clicked, the code in the event handler (which has to be in the code-behind file) will execute. By placing this code in the code-behind event handler, the business logic is now mixed with the user interface code, mixing concerns. To be fair, nothing in the framework *makes* one put the code in the code-behind; it just seems to always end up there.

This gets compounded when additional UIElements are added to the Window that needs to execute the same code. The common fix for this situation is to refactor the code in the original event handler out into a separate method and have the event handlers for the related UIElements call the new method. The new method can even be moved into the Business Layer, separating concerns and allowing for testability.

The other issue is one of user experience. Often, menus and buttons need to be actively enabled or disabled based on the condition of the data (or some other condition/user action) in the Window. If the user has the option, they tend to click "active" items repeatedly, wondering why nothing is happening. They are, after all, trained at birth to find holes in your application.

The command pattern as implemented in WPF cleanly and easily resolves both issues.

ICommand

ICommand (which is the base interface for all commands discussed here) defines two event handlers and one event. See Listing 4-1.

Listing 4-1: ICommand Interface

```
bool CanExecute(object parameter);
void Execute(object parameter);
event EventHandler CanExecuteChanged
```

Perhaps the most powerful feature of WPF commands is the capability to determine at runtime if the controls they are bound to are able to execute (see the next section for a detailed discussion). `CanExecute` is run by the CommandManager whenever Focus changes, the PropertyChanged or CollectionChanged events are raised, or on demand through code. If the event handler returns false, all UIElements bound to that command are disabled.

The Execute event handler contains the code that gets executed when the user action is processed or the command is executed through code.

The CanExecuteChanged event provides a mechanism to tie into the INotifyCollectionChanged and INotifyPropertyChanged event handlers to determine when CanExecute needs to be requeried.

Routed commands

The ICommand interface doesn't provide the entire goodness of commands in WPF. The `RoutedCommand` class (and its first descendant, the `RoutedUICommand`) take advantage of Event Routing to provide additional power.

The CanExecute event handler raises the PreviewCanExecute event and the Execute event handler raises the PreviewExecuted event. These events are raised just prior to the CanExecute and Execute handlers, and bubble up the element tree until an element with the correct Command Binding is located. This is useful for allowing control of commands at a higher level while the fine-grained elements still control the CanExecute and the Execute event handlers.

RoutedCommand versus RoutedUICommand

The only difference between the Routed Command and the RoutedUICommand is that the RouteUICommand adds a `Text` property used to decorate the bound controls content uniformly. `MenuItems` picks up this property automatically, and assigns it to the Header property. Buttons (and other UIElements) need a bit of binding kung fu, such as the following XAML snippet, to get the `Text` into the `Content` property.

```
Content="{Binding
          RelativeSource={RelativeSource
          Mode=Self}, Path=Command.Text}"
```

Routed Commands also expose a collection of InputGestures — keystrokes or other gestures that will fire the Execute event handler. This allows assigning hot key combinations to the commands, such as Control+S for saving (as in most Windows applications).

Built-in commands

WPF provides a number of built-in commands that you can use with very little (sometimes no) code. The most common set used by line of business developers is wrapped up in the ApplicationCommands Library. The advantage of using the built-in commands is that all the plumbing is taken care of for you. For example, the CanExecute and Execute event handlers are already implemented. All you have to do is bind them to UIElements through XAML.

The full list of built-in commands is available online at `http://msdn.microsoft.com/en-us/library/system.windows.input.aspx`.

The sample shown in Listing 4-2 and Figure 4-1 uses the ApplicationsCommand.Copy and ApplicationsCommand.Paste commands to facilitate clipboard manipulation in your application. When the UIElement with focus supports the clipboard Paste action *and* there is data in the clipboard that is supportable by the element with focus, any elements bound to the Paste command are enabled. When the UIElement with focus supports the clipboard Copy action *and* there are items selected that can be copied to the clipboard, then any elements bound to the Copy command are enabled. As a side note, WPF allows you to abbreviate the built-in commands by dropping the container name (ApplicationCommands), so Copy and Paste are legitimate abbreviations for the command bindings ApplicationCommands.Copy and ApplicationCommands.Paste. For readability, I prefer to fully qualify the names.

The full code for the Command samples is in the project Chapter4Commands and Chapter4CommandsTests in the Chapter4 Solution.

Listing 4-2: Built-in Commands in XAML

```
<Menu Grid.Row="0" Grid.Column="0" HorizontalAlignment="Left"
    Name="menu1">
     <MenuItem Command="ApplicationCommands.Copy"/>
     <MenuItem Command="ApplicationCommands.Paste"/>
</Menu>
<TextBox Grid.Row="1" Grid.Column="0"
    HorizontalAlignment="Stretch"/>
<TextBox Grid.Row="2" Grid.Column="0"
    HorizontalAlignment="Stretch"/>
```

Figures 4-1 through 4-3 show the Window produced by the XAML in Listing 4-2 in different states. When there is text selected in a text box, the Copy menu is enabled. When there is data in the clipboard that can be pasted into a text box, the Paste menu becomes enabled. This is all done without a single line of code!

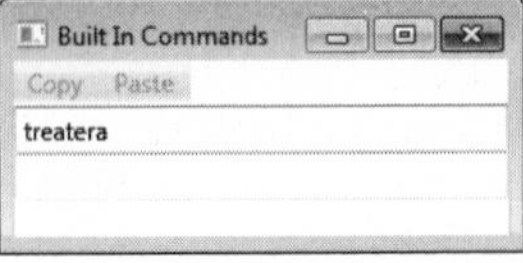

Figure 4-1: Built-in commands (with empty clipboard and no selections).

Figure 4-2: Built-in commands (with empty clipboard and text selection).

Figure 4-3: Built-in commands (with clipboard data and no text selection).

Focus!

I know the question you're dying to ask: If the user clicks on a menu item, doesn't that menu item then have focus? The answer is a confusing "No!" That's because menus in WPF work a little bit of magic to determine what UIElement has focus *just before* a menu item is clicked.

Unfortunately, this doesn't apply to standard buttons and other command bindable controls. Even though the menu items in Figure 4-4 are enabled, the buttons are not. There are two fixes for this problem. The first is by binding the `CommandTarget` property in addition to the command to the UIElement. This is a single element solution, though. To resolve the issue for all UIElements, the `FocusManager.IsSharedScope` property needs to be set to True in the parent container.

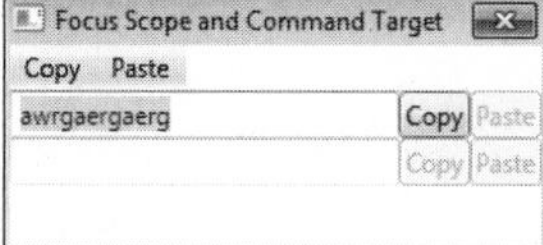

Figure 4-4: Built-in controls with buttons.

Custom commands

Creating a custom command requires either instantiation of a new Routed[UI]Command or coding a new command based on the ICommand interface. Well, okay, you are correct — there are other methods as well. The two most popular are what I discuss here.

Custom routed UI commands

Creating a new RoutedUICommand is a simple instantiation, as the code in Listing 4-3 shows.

Listing 4-3: Creating a Custom RoutedUICommand

```
public static RoutedUICommand SaveCommand =
   new RoutedUICommand("Save","SaveCommand",
    typeof(UIElement) );
```

The first parameter in the constructor populates the `Text` property, the second parameter is the name used in serialization of the command (I usually append Command to the text from the first parameter), and the last parameter is the UIParent. (In this example, the code states *any* UIElement can be the parent.) There is a fourth parameter in another Constructor (not shown here) that is a list of InputGestures.

Custom RoutedUICommands are usually created as static variables so there is only once instance (and it makes binding simpler). Yes, it's still in the code-behind file, so we don't yet have Separation of Concerns, but we're getting there!

Command bindings

Unlike the built-in commands (which are part of the framework and automatically wired into the CommandManager and the binding system), custom commands are not. Three changes need to be made in the XAML to support custom commands:

- Add the namespace for the command to the namespace declaration.
- Change the command assignment to a binding expression.
- Add the command to the bindings collection of the container.

As Chapter 1 explains, you can add custom namespace declarations to the Window to allow XAML access to custom classes and namespaces. The namespace for the custom command (which is the same namespace as the Window if the command is a static variable in the code-behind) needs to be added to the Window tag. Listing 4-4 shows an example namespace declaration. The bolded text is what has changed from the default namespace declarations that are in the standard WPF Window.

Listing 4-4: Updated XAML for Custom RoutedUICommand

```
<Window x:Class="Chapter4.Commands.CommandBindingSample"
    xmlns="http://schemas.microsoft.com/winfx/2006/xaml/
    presentation"
   xmlns:x="http://schemas.microsoft.com/winfx/2006/xaml"
   xmlns:Commands="clr-namespace:Chapter4.Commands"
   Title="Command Binding" Height="122" Width="261">
```

After the namespace is brought into the Window, the command must be inserted into the Window.CommandBindings collection. Three main properties need to be set and are shown in Listing 4-5:

- Command: The binding to the command object
- CanExecute: Event handler for testing execution status
- Executed: Event handler for the execution of the command

With built-in commands, a simple string assigned the command to the UIElement. With custom commands, you have to use a binding expression (as discussed in Chapter 3). The format for a static command binding is

```
{x:Static NamespaceReference:Class.CommandVariableName}.
```

The NamespaceReference is the nickname assigned in the Window tag. Interestingly, the `CanExecute` and `Executed` properties are set to the name of the methods — no funky binding required!

Listing 4-5: Window CommandBindings XAML

```
<Window.CommandBindings>
  <CommandBinding Command="{x:Static
   Commands:CommandBindingSample.SaveCommand}"
   CanExecute="Save_CanExecute"
   Executed="Save_Executed"/>
</Window.CommandBindings>
```

The `Command` property of the CommandBinding and UIElements use the same binding expressions as shown in Listing 4-6. When a UIElement has a command bound to it, the framework looks for the first match in the CommandBindings section up the element tree. When one is located, the UIElement uses the assigned event handlers CanExecute and Execute.

Listing 4-6: Command Assignment to MenuItem and Button

```
<MenuItem Command="{x:Static
   Commands:CommandBindingSample.SaveCommand}"/>
<Button Command="{x:Static
   Commands:CommandBindingSample.SaveCommand}"
   Content="{Binding RelativeSource={RelativeSource
   Mode=Self}, Path=Command.Text}"/>
```

The CanExecute event handler for a Routed[UI]Command uses the `CanExecuteRoutedEventArgs` instead of returning True or False. Setting `e.CanExecute` to True (can run) or False (cannot run) will enable or disable the command (and any associated UIElements).

If the command is enabled, the Executed event handler gets executed when the UIElement triggers the command (for example, when a button is clicked).

Command parameters

The `CanExecuteRoutedEventArgs` and `ExecutedRoutedEventArgs` contain a `Parameter` property that provides a mechanism for passing objects from the Window into the CanExecute and Executed event handlers. For the example in Figure 4-5, the text of the TextBox is being passed as the parameter. The `CanExecute` property of the `CanExecuteRoutedEventArgs` in the CanExecute event handler is set to False if the string is empty or null, and the Executed event handler displays it back to the user in a message box. Okay, not a realistic example, but it's a demo!

Listings 4-7 and 4-8 show passing a parameter into the command through XAML and then using that parameter in the C# implementation of the events.

Listing 4-7: Updated XAML to Include Command Parameter

```
<Button Command="{x:Static
   Commands:CommandBindingSample.SaveCommand}"
   CommandParameter="{Binding ElementName=txtField,
    Path=Text}"
   Content="{Binding RelativeSource={RelativeSource
    Mode=Self}, Path=Command.Text}"/>
```

Listing 4-8: Updated C# to Display Parameter to User

```
private void Save_CanExecute(object sender,
    CanExecuteRoutedEventArgs e)
{
  e.CanExecute = !String.IsNullOrEmpty(e.Parameter as
    string);
}
private void Save_Executed(object sender,
    ExecutedRoutedEventArgs e)
{
  MessageBox.Show(e.Parameter.ToString());
}
```

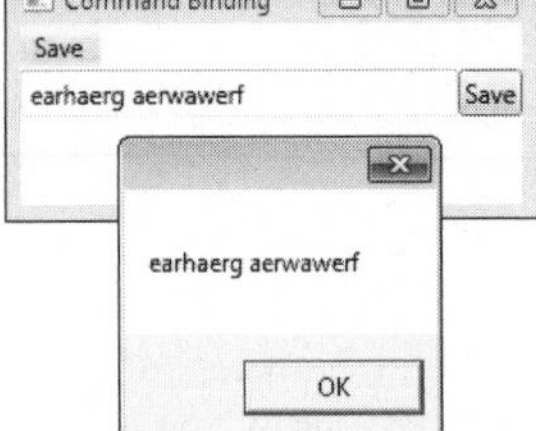

Figure 4-5: Custom routed UI command.

Custom commands with ICommand

Custom RoutedUICommands solve the problem of getting rid of all those nasty OnClick event handlers, consolidating execution code into one event handler and bringing along the goodness of the CanExecute event handler to enable a more dynamic and intuitive user interface.

To truly achieve Separation of Concerns by removing the implementation from the code behind, implement the commands from the ground up starting with the ICommand interface. The interface for ICommand contains the CanExecute and the Executed event handlers as well as the CanExecuteChanged event.

The code in Listing 4-9 shows an example custom Save command. There are some differences to consider:

- ✦ The sender and CanExecuteRoutedEventArgs/ExecuteRoutedEventArgs parameters are not in the signature for the event handlers. In their place is a single parameter of type object. This is the "parameter" object passed in from the UIElement.
- ✦ The CanExecute event handler returns a bool. The return value is the mechanism for enabling/disabling commands (instead of setting the `CanExecute` property of the event argument).
- ✦ The command does not get set in the CommandBindings XAML, but instead uses the CanExecuteChanged event to tie into the CommandManager system. To enable the correct handling of the custom command by the Command subsystem, the RequerySuggested events get hooked into the CanExecuteChanged event.
- ✦ The ICommand interface doesn't have a `Text` property. This is only necessary if your code uses binding to populate the labels for MenuItems and Buttons bound to the command. The sample code adds a `Text` property to enable this, but since it is a simple property and not tied into the Dependency or RoutedEvent subsystems, MenuItems will *not* automatically populate the Header.

Listing 4-9: CustomSaveCommand

```
public class CustomSaveCommand : ICommand
{
    public string Text { get; set; }
    public CustomSaveCommand(string text)
    {
        Text = text;
    }
    public void Execute(object parameter)
    {
        //Insert Actual "Save" code here
        //Display feedback message to user
        MessageBox.Show(parameter.ToString());
    }

    public bool CanExecute(object parameter)
    {
        return !String.IsNullOrEmpty(parameter as string);
    }

    public event EventHandler CanExecuteChanged
    {
        add { CommandManager.RequerySuggested += value; }
        remove { CommandManager.RequerySuggested -= value; }
    }
}
```

Unit testing

Unit testing is an important piece of software development. There are many great resources on getting started with unit testing and test-driven development, including Kent Beck's classic tome, *Test-Driven Development: By Example.*

The popular convention for setting up test projects is to create one for each Line of Business project and name the projects <ProjectToTestName>Tests. The project in the sample code for this chapter is named Chapter4Commands; therefore, the Test Project is named Chapter4CommandsTests.

Each test should exercise a distinct Unit of Code (in C#, this translates to a method), have a meaningful name that describes the test scenario, and be composed of three parts:

- Arrange: Sets up any objects or data required for the test
- Act: Executes the Unit of Code
- Assert: Validates the results

The unit tests in this chapter are by no means extensive, but they illustrate the capabilities gained by adhering to the principle of Separation of Concerns.

In the sample, the custom command is instantiated through a static property in the code-behind the same way the custom RoutedUICommand was in the preceding example. The next section details a much better way to handle exposing the commands to the XAML.

Separation of Concerns and testability

The end result for the Window with the custom SaveCommand has the same look and features as the preceding example. The difference between the two is that the business logic is now in a wholly self-contained class that is independent of the display mechanism (in this case, WPF).

This allows for execution of the code in the custom command class without having to work (some would say "fight") with the CommandManager subsystem or the WPF rendering engine. It also allows for the command to be reused for more than one Window.

The unit tests in this chapter use MbUnit, which is part of Gallio. Any test framework will work (including NUnit, XUnit, MSTest, and so forth). Gallio can be found at `http://www.gallio.org`.

First unit test

The first unit test verifies that the `Text` property of the instantiated command gets populated in the constructor. The complete unit test is shown in Listing 4-10. The Arrange, Act, and Assert comments are not usually included in the unit tests. They are included in Listing 4-10 to demonstrate the structure of a unit test.

To execute the test, run Gallio Icarus — the GUI test runner that ships with Gallio. Click on Add Files, navigate to your compiled test project, and then click on Start to run the tests.

Listing 4-10: Unit Testing the Constructor Setting the Text Property

```
[Test]
public void Should_Set_Text_Property_In_The_Constructor()
{
    //Arrange
    CustomSaveCommand command;
    //Act
    string expectedValue = "Save";
    command = new CustomSaveCommand(expectedValue);
    //Assert
    Assert.AreEqual(expectedValue, command.Text);
}
```

Test positive and negative conditions

When writing unit tests, it's important to test success as well as failure conditions. For the `CanExecute` method of the custom Save command, that means tests must cover when the parameter is null or empty in addition to having a string value. These tests are shown in Listing 4-11.

Listing 4-11: Testing the CanExecute Event Handler

```
[Test]
public void Should_Not_Execute_If_Parameter_Is_Null()
{
    ICommand command = new CustomSaveCommand("Save");
    bool canExecute = command.CanExecute(null);
    Assert.IsFalse(canExecute);
}
[Test]
public void Should_Not_Execute_If_Parameter_Is_Empty_String()
{
    ICommand command = new CustomSaveCommand("Save");
    bool canExecute = command.CanExecute(string.Empty);
    Assert.IsFalse(canExecute);
}
[Test]
public void Should_Execute_If_Parameter_Is_Not_Empty_String()
{
    ICommand command = new CustomSaveCommand("Save");
    bool canExecute = command.CanExecute("Test");
    Assert.IsTrue(canExecute);
}
```

Get Your ViewModel On

Design patterns have been around for quite some time. Over time, some of the older patterns lose relevance, and new ones get created to fill needs of current development. One new pattern that has gained significant traction with WPF and Silverlight is the Model-View-View Model pattern. Commonly referred to as "ViewModel" (although this is still very much in flux, even within the walls of Microsoft), this pattern is very similar to Martin Fowler's Presentation Model Pattern.

You can read Martin Fowler's paper on the Presentation Model pattern at `http://martinfowler.com/eaaDev/PresentationModel.html`.

Who cares?

I know what you're thinking. "Why can't I just sit down and start coding up a WPF application using all the goodies I've learned so far?" The short answer is that you can. But should you? That debate still rages on among those who like to sit around and debate these things. Using a user interface pattern (such as ViewModel) that promotes separation of concerns, cuts down on repeated code, increases testability, and reduces complexity can't hurt.

"Won't it take longer to develop an application using one of these patterns?" That is a common question, and the answer is a very definite, "It depends." Once developers fully understand the objectives and techniques, velocity (the amount of work accomplished by a team in a given period of time) starts ratcheting up. Getting to that level of understanding (especially if several variations are attempted) can take time and usually involves a bit of thrashing along the way.

MVVM? ViewModel? Who's on first?

Several versions of this pattern are floating around, and an equal number of "frameworks." They all seem to have slightly different names and implementations. This is largely because MVVM is a recently created pattern (as patterns go), and there are quite a few people trying to make "their" name stick. In the end, the name doesn't matter as much as the benefit received. This book uses the name ViewModel because that is where the dart hit the wall.

My best recommendation is to look at all the different flavors of user interface patterns, take the parts that work best in your situation, and throw out the parts that don't make sense. Patterns are meant to spark critical thought, not be considered as absolutes.

The ViewModel pattern presented in this book has been working extremely well for my customers in both large and small applications and is not meant to be an exact blueprint.

When there is a change request (users call them "bugs," but I prefer a different nomenclature), if you are using a presentation pattern that ensures separation of concerns, it is clear where to go in the codebase to resolve the issue. Traditional development styles (like those techniques commonly used in Windows Forms) make it all too easy to place business code into event handlers and code-behind files, mixing concerns and dependencies.

Tradition!

To fully understand why the ViewModel pattern helps, you need to understand the parts of a "traditional" application architecture.

Data Access Layer (DAL)

The DAL is the set of classes and methods that get the data out of the data store (such as SQL Server) and populate the Model (see next item). It is also responsible for persisting any changes to the data back to the data store.

Model

The Model is the data that composes your application — not the data store itself (for example, the database), but the object graph that represents the data for your application. In a sales application, example objects could be classes like `Customer`, `SalesRegion`, and `SalesPerson`.

Business Layer (BL)

The BL is the implementation of the business rules for the application. This layer ensures that the data in the Model adheres to the law of the land.

View

The View represents the pieces of the application that interact with the user. For WPF, this is the collection of Windows that compose the application.

The biggest gap with displaying an object graph (Model) in a View is that applications seldom display only one type of object at a time. If the Window allows for editing a customer, then it probably needs to display the sales regions, sales people, and so forth.

Combining multiple objects into a data object clouds the Model, and placing all that code into the view places too much knowledge in the View — not to mention a total testability fail. The compilation of the required parts of the object graph should not detract from any other part of the application.

The Command Objects are another consideration. There isn't a tidy place in the traditional application layers to place the custom commands. The code contained in the commands is (typically) Business Logic, but the Window needs to bind to the commands, and is therefore specific to the View.

Introducing the ViewModel

The ViewModel fills that gap. It is designed to be a single class that pulls in all the necessary data points and commands into a one-stop shop for a particular view. Each view typically has its own ViewModel, but that is entirely dependent on your particular application.

As Chapter 3 discusses, WPF automatically monitors any class that implements either INotifyPropertyChanged (for items bound to a property of a class) and/or INotifyCollectionChanged (for items bound to a collection of items). These interfaces should be implemented in one of two camps — the ViewModel or the Model.

Implementing those two interfaces in the ViewModel is the more academic, textbook implementation. This is because it separates user interface code from the Model. It also requires a lot of additional work, because it entails recoding all the properties and collections of your Model to include raising the proper events.

Implementing in the Model reduces work, because it merely entails adding a few lines of code into properties already being implemented in the classes. A main argument against Model implementation revolves around code reuse. For example, if the Model is also used by an ASP.NET application, those events are still raised but no one is listening. This could potentially present a performance issue. Of course, if you use the same model for WPF and non-WPF Views, then a simple flag passed into the constructor of the `Model` classes indicating whether the events should be raised or not resolves that issue.

Both ways are valid implementations. Your application and specific situation will most likely dictate where those interfaces are implemented.

In Chapter 3, you discover that if a control doesn't have an explicit DataContext, it is inherited from the closest parent in the control tree that does have a DataContext explicitly assigned.

When developing WPF applications using the ViewModel pattern, the instantiated ViewModel becomes the Window's (or user control's) DataContext.

Show me the code!

The full code for the ViewModel samples is in the project Chapter4View Models and Chapter4ViewModelsTests in the Chapter4 Solution.

Just what are we building?

The Window (or View, to use "architecture speak") is a simple customer maintenance form. The user can select a customer and edit his name and sales region. Clicking the Add Customer button will add a customer to the list. You're right — not very realistic, but it demonstrates the ViewModel principles. Figure 4-6 shows the completed sample user interface.

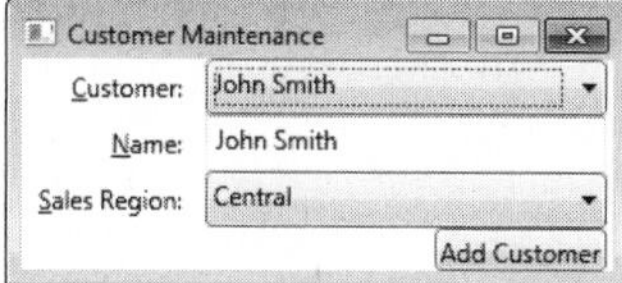

Figure 4-6: The Customer Maintenance Window.

The model

Okay, enough talk. For the sample ViewModel, we need to define a Model.

Listing 4-12 shows the base class from which all the Model classes will derive. The base class implements the INotifyPropertyChanged interface as well as the IsDirty property.

Listing 4-12: ModelBase

```
public class ModelBase : INotifyPropertyChanged
{
    public bool IsDirty { get; private set; }
    public event PropertyChangedEventHandler PropertyChanged;
    internal void NotifyPropertyChanged(object sender, string
   propertyName)
    {
        if (PropertyChanged != null)
        {
            PropertyChanged(sender, new PropertyChangedEventA
   rgs(propertyName));
        }
        IsDirty = true;
    }
}
```

Listings 4-13 and 4-14 show the `Customer` and `SalesRegion` classes that will populate the View. For each property in the class (except for the primary key and the collection properties), there is a check to see if the value of the property is being set to a new value. If it is new, then the PropertyChanged event is raised. The `NotifyPropertyChanged` method also sets the IsDirty flag to True to indicate that the model has changes that need to be persisted.

Why "internal"?

The `NotifyPropertyChanged` method is marked with the internal access modifier instead of protected for one main reason — testing. Protected methods can be accessed only from derived classes, whereas internal methods can be accessed by any sibling class in the same assembly.

The assembly level attribute InternalsVisibleTo specifies what *other* assemblies have access to the internal methods and classes of the assembly decorated with the attribute. Adding this attribute to the Chapter4ViewModels project (usually placed in the `assemblyinfo.cs` class) and specifying the test project (Chapter4ViewModelsTests) grants access for your tests to the internals.

The primary key (in this example) is being set by the data store, so it will never change in the view. Because the property changed event will never need to be raised, the property can be coded as an automatic property.

Listing 4-13: The Customer Model Class

```
public class Customer : ModelBase
{
    private string _name;
    private SalesRegion _region;
    public int ID { get; set; }
    public string Name
    {
        get { return _name; }
        set
        {
            if (value == _name)
            {
                return;
            }
            _name = value;
            NotifyPropertyChanged(this, "Name");
        }
    }
    public SalesRegion SalesRegion
    {
        get { return _region; }
        set
        {
            if (value == _region)
            {
                return;
```

```
                }
                _region = value;
                NotifyPropertyChanged(this, "SalesRegion");
            }
        }
}
```

Listing 4-14: The SalesRegion Model Class

```
public class SalesRegion:ModelBase
{
    private string _name;
    public int ID {get; set;}
    public string Name
    {
        get { return _name; }
        set
        {
            if (value == _name)
            {
                return;
            }
            _name = value;
            NotifyPropertyChanged(this, "Name");
        }
    }
}
```

Model unit tests

There isn't much to test in the model. You don't typically write tests against the .NET Framework itself — one has to assume that it works! The only real logic in this sample is setting of the IsDirty and the raising of the PropertyChanged event when something changes.

The first test is to verify that the IsDirty flag gets set when a property changes, and it is very straightforward. We create a new Customer, assert that the IsDirty flag is False, make a change, and then assert that the IsDirty flag is True. This test is shown in Listing 4-15.

Listing 4-15: Testing the IsDirty Flag

```
[Test]
public void Should_Set_Is_Dirty_On_Property_Change()
{
    var sut = new Customer();
    Assert.IsFalse(sut.IsDirty);
    sut.Name="New Name";
    Assert.IsTrue(sut.IsDirty);
}
```

Why "SUT"?

The variable name stands for "System Under Test" and is a common convention in unit testing. It clearly delineates what is being tested from other objects that are required for the test. Why don't the earlier examples use this? Ah, grasshopper — gradual introduction is in play so you aren't drinking from a fire hose!

The second test is much more involved, because it tests the raising of the PropertyChanged event. We have to create a subscriber to listen for this event. Windows (and the WPF rendering engine) automatically attach to this event, but we don't want to re-create the rendering engine just to test one method. To test the event, create a subscriber, raise the event, and then assert that the handler of the event was executed.

Tests of this type are typically done with a mocking framework, such as RhinoMocks (the tool used in the samples). Mocking frameworks allow tests for behavior in addition to state, and since the test needs to validate that an event was raised, RhinoMocks is the perfect fit. A deep dive into mocking and behavior testing is beyond the scope of this book. Look at the code, digest it, and tinker with it. It's a great way to expand your testing knowledge!

Mocking frameworks create proxy objects based on interfaces. For the single event, create an interface (shown in Listing 4-16) that has the required signature for the event handler — in this case, the PropertyChanged event.

Listing 4-16: The Event Subscriber

```
public interface IPropertyChangedSubscriber
{
    void Handler(object sender, PropertyChangedEventArgs e);
}
```

The test starts off by creating a mock of the subscriber and registering the PropertyChanged event with the handler. The test acts on the Customer object by changing the name and then asserts that the handler was called. The `Arg<object>.Is.Anything` syntax tells RhinoMocks to not test the arguments for equality. Again, the test is just verifying that the event is raised when a property on the Customer object is updated. See the code in Listing 4-17.

Listing 4-17: Testing an Event Was Raised

```
[Test]
public void Should_Raise_Property_Changed_Event_On_Property_
    Change()
{
     var sut = new Customer();
     var eventArgs = new PropertyChangedEventArgs(string.
    Empty);
     var subscriber = MockRepository.GenerateMock<IPropertyCha
    ngedSubscriber>();
     sut.PropertyChanged += subscriber.Handler;
     sut.Name = "New Name";
     subscriber.AssertWasCalled(x => x.Handler(Arg<object>.
    Is.Anything, Arg<PropertyChangedEventArgs>.Is.Anything));
}
```

The RhinoMocks tool can be found on the Web at `http://ayende.com/projects/rhino-mocks/downloads.aspx`. For a good description of mocks versus stubs, see Martin Fowler's paper "Mocks Aren't Stubs," located at `http://martinfowler.com/articles/mocksArentStubs.html`.

Model repositories

The repository pattern is commonly used for Line of Business applications to move data between the data store and the model classes. For the sample ViewModel, I've included a very simple interface (shown in Listing 4-18) that has a `GetAll` method and an `Update` method (not even remotely a complete repository, but all that we need for the examples). Note the use of generics to enforce strong typing in the repositories that implement this interface.

Listing 4-18: The Repository Interface

```
public interface IRepository<T>
{
    IList<T> GetAll();
    bool Update(T model);
}
```

The repositories in the samples return hard-coded values instead of connecting to a data store. It's common practice to create classes that are used only for testing or prototyping. The convention I prefer is to call them out by appending Fake to the name (as shown in Listing 4-19) so other developers have no doubt about their intended purpose. Additionally, the examples don't implement the `Update` methods because they aren't used for the ViewModel samples shown.

State versus behavior testing

State-based testing tests the values of an object (for example, whether the IsDirty flag is set). Behavior testing is used to test actions and interactions of objects. To test that a particular method was called or an event was raised becomes much more trivial with the more advanced frameworks like RhinoMocks.

Listing 4-19: Fake SalesRegion Repository

```
public class SalesRegionRepositoryFake :
   IRepository<SalesRegion>
{
    public IList<SalesRegion> GetAll()
    {
        var list = new ObservableCollection<SalesRegion>
        {
            new SalesRegion {ID = 1, Name = "East"},
            new SalesRegion {ID = 2, Name = "Central"},
            new SalesRegion {ID = 3, Name = "West"}
        };
        return list;
    }

    public bool Update(SalesRegion region)
    {
        throw new NotImplementedException();
    }
}
```

To create a customer, a list of Sales Regions must be available, so the Customer Repository Fake (as shown in Listing 4-20) uses Constructor Injection to insert the allowable values into the repository. It could have created its own list, but that would have thrown off the binding in XAML since the objects would be different.

Listing 4-20: Fake Customer Repository

```
public class CustomerRepositoryFake : IRepository<Customer>
{
    readonly IList<SalesRegion> _salesRegions;

    public CustomerRepositoryFake(IList<SalesRegion>
   salesRegions)
    {
        _salesRegions = salesRegions;
    }
```

```
    public IList<Customer> GetAll()
    {
        var list = new ObservableCollection<Customer>();
        var customer = new Customer {Name = "Jane Doe", ID=1,
    SalesRegion = _salesRegions[0]};
        list.Add(customer);
        customer = new Customer {Name = "John Smith", ID=2,
    SalesRegion = _salesRegions[1]};
        list.Add(customer);
        customer = new Customer { Name = "John Doe", ID = 3,
    SalesRegion = _salesRegions[2] };
        list.Add(customer);
        return list;
    }
    public bool Update(Customer customer)
    {
        throw new NotImplementedException();
    }
}
```

The Add Customer command

Interestingly enough, using the ViewModel pattern, the commands can be developed prior to the view, enabling Test Driven Development for the commands. Using the same approach discussed in the "Commanding Attention" section earlier in this chapter, a `CommandBase` class (shown in Listing 4-21) is extracted to hold the common properties and the CanExecuteChanged event.

Listing 4-21: CommandBase Class

```
public abstract class CommandBase : ICommand
{
    public string Text { get; internal set; }
    public abstract void Execute(object parameter);
    public abstract bool CanExecute(object parameter);
    public event EventHandler CanExecuteChanged
    {
        add { CommandManager.RequerySuggested += value; }
        remove { CommandManager.RequerySuggested -= value; }
    }
}
```

The AddCustomerCommand (shown in Listing 4-22) will take the Customer list as a parameter and add another customer to the list. In this example, it's a hard-coded set of values, but in reality you would probably have another Window (or some data entry mechanism) to gather the required information.

Defensive programming or try-catch?

Is it better to code extra lines to prevent exceptions, or just wrap the code in a try-catch block? Exceptions are expensive and generally should not be considered flow-of-control devices. Just like their name, exceptions should be, well, exceptional. It is better to code defensively *and* wrap your code in try-catch blocks to handle those pesky conditions users have such a knack for finding.

Why don't these samples have try-catch blocks? Merely for brevity. Logging and error handling are musts in any real code, but take a significant amount of space and could send the reader down a rabbit hole that would detract from the concepts of the current section.

The CanExecute event handler checks that the parameter is a List<Customer>. There is an additional check in the `Execute` method. It is essentially redundant — the command should never execute if the parameter is not an IList<Customer>. However, defensive programming kicks in, and I always check again to avoid the possibility of throwing an error.

Listing 4-22: AddCustomerCommand

```
public class AddCustomerCommand : CommandBase
{
    public AddCustomerCommand()
    {
        Text = "Add Customer";
    }
    public override void Execute(object parameter)
    {
        var list = parameter as IList<Customer>;
        if (list == null)
        {
            return;
        }
        list.Add(new Customer { ID = 4, Name = "New Customer"
   });
    }
    public override bool CanExecute(object parameter)
    {
        return parameter is IList<Customer>;
    }
}
```

The Add Customer Command unit tests

The tests for the AddCustomerCommand are similar to the tests from the "Commanding Attention" section, earlier in this chapter. In the code in Listing 4-23, the first three tests validate the CanExecute event handler; the last test validates the Executed event handler.

Listing 4-23: The AddCustomerCommand Unit Tests

```
[Test]
public void Should_Not_Execute_If_Parameter_Is_Null()
{
    var cmd = new AddCustomerCommand();
    var canExecute = cmd.CanExecute(null);
    Assert.IsFalse(canExecute);
}
[Test]
public void Should_Not_Execute_If_Parameter_Is_Not_List_
   Customer()
{
    var cmd = new AddCustomerCommand();
    var canExecute = cmd.CanExecute("test");
    Assert.IsFalse(canExecute);
}
[Test]
public void Should_Execute_If_Parameter_Is_List_Customer()
{
    var cmd = new AddCustomerCommand();
    var canExecute = cmd.CanExecute(new List<Customer>());
    Assert.IsTrue(canExecute);
}

[Test]
public void Should_Add_Customer_To_List_On_Execute()
{
    var cmd = new AddCustomerCommand();
    var customers = new List<Customer>();
    var count = customers.Count;
    cmd.Execute(customers);
    Assert.AreEqual(count+1, customers.Count);

}
```

The ViewModel

So, you're thinking to yourself at this point, "There's been a lot of code slung so far. And we haven't even touched the ViewModel yet?" And you're right. However, as you will soon see, the ViewModel becomes a rather trivial exercise because of the setup that we have already done. There are just three properties in the ViewModel and two lines of code that need to be run in the constructor (and one of them is required by the XAML rendering engine). Yep. That's it.

The image in Figure 4-6 contains two combo boxes that need to be populated. One of the tenants of the ViewModel pattern is to provide a one-stop shop for the View. In addition to the main data (Customers), this includes any reference data (Sales Regions). The ViewModel (shown in Listing 4-24) contains these IList<T> as properties that can be bound to in the view and (in this example) are populated in the constructor.

The Window also contains a single Button that needs to be bound to the AddCustomerCommand. Commands require a bit more plumbing, because they must be instantiated prior to use. The technique shown in this sample is *just in time* instantiation and is meant to cut down on resource consumption. If the button never gets clicked, why create the command in memory?

Listing 4-24: The ViewModel

```
public class CustomerMaintenanceViewModel
{
    ICommand _addCustomerCmd;

    public CustomerMaintenanceViewModel()
    {
        Regions = new SalesRegionRepositoryFake().GetAll();
        Customers = new CustomerRepositoryFake(Regions).
   GetAll();
    }
    public IList<Customer> Customers { get; set;}
    public IList<SalesRegion> Regions { get; set;}

    public ICommand AddCustomerCmd
    {
        get { return _addCustomerCmd ?? (_addCustomerCmd =
   new AddCustomerCommand()); }
        set { _addCustomerCmd = value; }
    }

}
```

Testing the ViewModel

There's actually nothing to test in this ViewModel, because it's all been tested elsewhere. But if there was code in a ViewModel that needed testing, it can be tested like any other class library.

The View

There are a couple of items worth mentioning when it comes to the view. First and foremost, the constructor for the view needs to assign its DataContext to an instance of the ViewModel (see the bolded line in Listing 4-25).

Dependency Injection (DI)

The ViewModel in this example *depends* on getting customer and sales region data. But hard-coding the fake repositories isn't a very good idea in the wild. More than once have I released a piece of software with a test value still in the code! "I'll change that back before I release" tends to be forgotten in the release two-step.

Dependency Injection is a technique that *injects* required dependencies into the class that needs them. This helps prevent just such a scenario. A common tool for DI with WPF is Unity, but several other high-quality open source tools exist, such as NInject. Well beyond the scope of this book, DI is an extremely valuable pattern in software development.

Listing 4-25: The View Code-Behind

```
public partial class CustomerMaintenance : Window
{
    public CustomerMaintenance()
    {
        InitializeComponent();
        DataContext = new CustomerMaintenanceViewModel();
    }
}
```

Wait! Didn't I say we want to remove all code from the code-behind? No, not *all* code. *Almost* all code. Event handlers stuffed with business logic, definitely. But you have to have two lines in the constructor: `InitializeComponent()`, which renders all the XAML, and the DataContext assignment. You might have cases for additional code living in the code-behind, and those cases might be perfectly valid. Just use critical thought before you start adding code in places where it can't be tested or reused.

The Command Binding expressions become very different using the ViewModel pattern. They actually become quite a bit easier as shown in Listing 4-26. Since the base class hooks the Command into the CommandManager, the need for the Windows.CommandBindings section is eliminated.

Listing 4-26: The Add Customer Button XAML

```
<Button HorizontalAlignment="Right" Margin="3,0,3,0"
   Command="{Binding Path=AddCustomerCmd}"
   CommandParameter="{Binding Path=Customers}"
Content="{Binding RelativeSource={RelativeSource
   Mode=Self},Path=Command.Text}"
/>
```

The Content hasn't changed from the earlier examples, but the Command and CommandParameter assignments have. The DataContext for all controls roll up the element tree looking for the first DataContext. Because the only DataContext is set at the Window level (in the constructor), all elements have as their DataContext the ViewModel. So binding is reduced to setting the Path to the property of the ViewModel (in this case, the AddCustomerCmd for the Command, and the Customers property for the Command Parameter).

Likewise, ComboBoxes bind their `ItemsSource` property to the IList<T> properties in the ViewModel. Listing 4-27 shows the XAML for the two ComboBoxes on the Window.

Listing 4-27: ComboBoxes XAML with ViewModel

```
<ComboBox ItemsSource="{Binding Path=Customers}"
   DisplayMemberPath="Name"/>
<ComboBox ItemsSource="{Binding Path=Regions}"
   DisplayMemberPath="Name"
   SelectedItem="{Binding ElementName=CustomerList,Path=Selec
    tedItem.SalesRegion}"
/>
```

The second ComboBox shows the power of WPF data binding. The SelectedItem should be set to the value of the `SalesRegion` property for the Customer. To do this through binding, the item is set to the SelectedItem of the CustomerList. This returns a Customer object, allowing any property on that Customer to be selected in the Path (in this case, the `SalesRegion` property).

Wrap up

I was asked recently if using the ViewModel pattern is worth it since it "seems like a lot of extra work." This is a common theme among WPF developers currently, and it isn't surprising considering the newness of the pattern, all the current variations in the wild, and conflicting opinions on the subject.

In short, it ***is*** absolutely worth it. The biggest benefit the ViewModel brings to the table is true separation of concerns with a side of testability. Any time you can reduce the dependence on manual user testing and increase automatic test coverage, it's a win. Increased code isolation, improved capabilities for code reuse, and reduced complexities all come with the package. And there isn't "more" code developed — it's just moved out of the code-behind files for the Windows.

Book VI

Web Development with ASP.NET

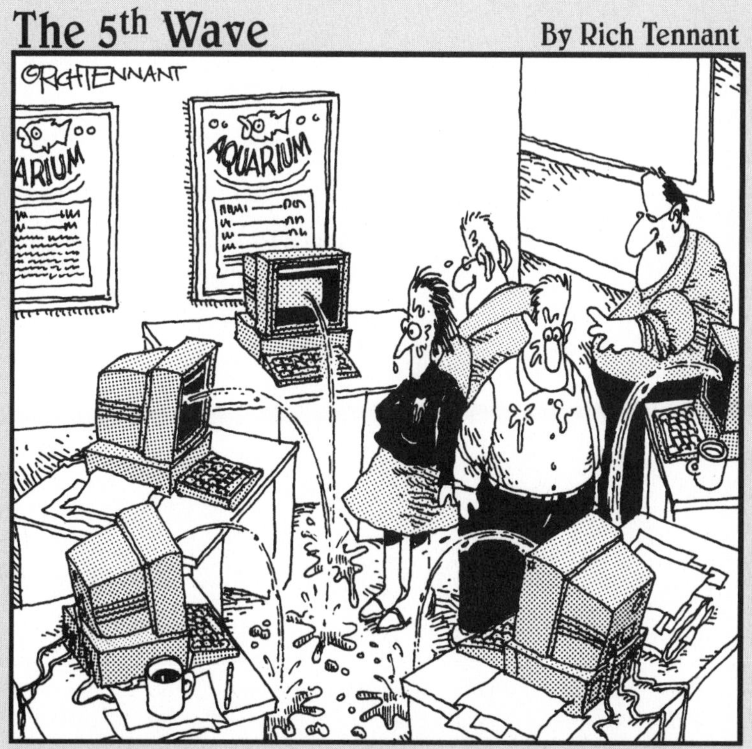

"Okay, I think I forgot to mention this, but we now have a Web management function that automatically alerts us when there's a broken link on The Aquarium's Web site."

Contents at a Glance

Chapter 1: Looking at How ASP.NET Works with C#

In This Chapter

- **Getting to know Web applications**
- **Conferring with the client**
- **Working with Web servers**

When I first started writing about World Wide Web applications, I had to describe the Web first. There were still a significant number of programmers who didn't know what it was, or thought it was CompuServe.

I don't really have that problem anymore.

The World Wide Web is now ubiquitous. Programmers of all stripes use the Web for research and communication. Providers use it for product updates and documentation. It is everywhere.

All the more reason to know how to code in the Web environment. Problem is that there are so many so-called frameworks for development that it is nearly impossible to decide which to use with a reasonable methodology. You almost have the draw straws.

If you are working in a Microsoft environment, and if you are writing a non-exceptional program, I recommend that you use plain, vanilla ASP.NET. Why? Sempf's Fourth Law: Simplicity above all. ASP.NET is a straightforward platform for Web creation.

ASP.NET has its share of problems, most of which involve writing Google (or some other really big complicated program). You probably aren't writing Google, so don't worry about it. If your site gets famous, you can get some venture capital and rewrite it into some custom framework. For now, just get your site written.

That's what ASP.NET enables you to do — get the job done. With ASP.NET, you can write a good Web site quickly, one that can be hosted just about anywhere. No one can ask for much more than that.

This chapter delves into the details of using ASP.NET with C#.

Breaking Down Web Applications

A Web application is a computer program that uses a very light client interface communicating with a server over the Internet in a stateless manner. *Stateless* means that the computer browsing the site and the server providing the site don't maintain a connection. You can see this process at a high level in Figure 1-1.

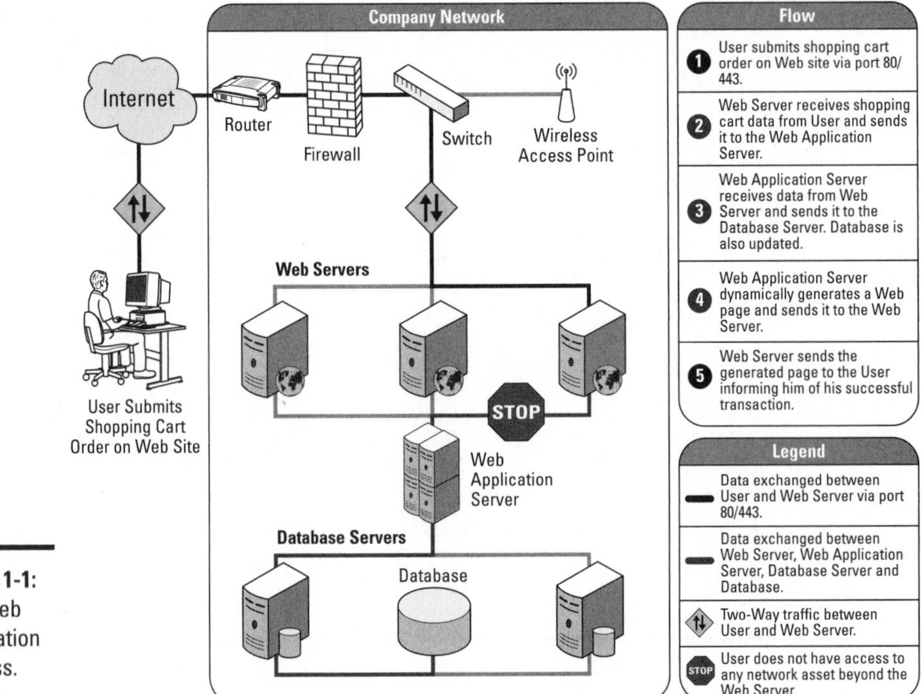

Figure 1-1: The Web application process.

The client requests a document from the server, and the server sends the document when it gets around to it. The document, usually a combination of Hypertext Markup Language (HTML), Cascading Style Sheets (CSS), and JavaScript, contains standardized elements which make up the interface of the application.

Why do we need this? If there is just a set of documents on the server and the client is just requesting one after another, what's the point of that? Of course, getting a document is a good thing, but where does the application part come in?

The answer is within Web applications. Web applications are powerful because the server can construct the document on the fly whenever it receives a request. This server process is what makes Web applications work. (See Figure 1-2.)

Don't get me wrong, the light client interface — called the *Web browser* or just the *browser* — provides some important functionality. It handles the user interface and can do things independently of the server.

The server is largely where it's at, though. Because the server can remember things from moment to moment, and because it is assumed that the client forgets everything from page to page, the server is where the long-running communications all reside.

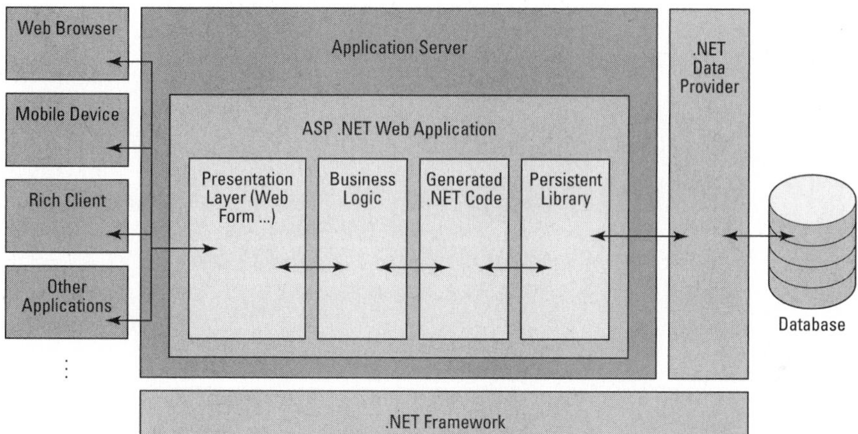

Figure 1-2: ASP.NET deconstructed.

ASP.NET is a library of controls and processing logic that makes constructing the server side of things much easier. You construct "server pages," but they end up transformed into the documents that the client uses to show you the user interface. ASP.NET is classified as a Web Application Framework, not a programming language.

The programming language, for our purposes, is C#. However, you can code for ASP.NET in any .NET language — it is just another set of tools in the framework.

C# is the language that you use to tell the server how to organize the ASP. NET pieces and send them to the client. The clients will never see any C# code; they won't even know that you coded it in C#.

This gets into the same discussion that we have several times throughout the book regarding the difference between the library and the language. ASP.NET is a library of tools, and that library is language independent. You orchestrate the functionality of the parts of the library using the language.

There are a few little caveats to Web development, however. The client — which doesn't care a whit that you are coding in C# — needs some care and feeding. There is no state in Web applications, so you need to think a little differently. The client does a lot automatically for you in Web development. The server has some security concerns.

Before we dig into the details of using C# with ASP.NET, I'd like to take a tour through the details of Web development and point out some things you need to keep in mind. So here we go.

Questioning the Client

When you are writing a Windows Form, WPF, or console application, your platform for the client is a Windows computer. When you are writing a Web application, you have no idea what the platform for your client is. It could be a Mac, any one of 12 Windows operating systems, or Linux. It could be a phone, a tablet, or a netbook. It could be a television, a gaming device, or a refrigerator (really: see Figure 1-3).

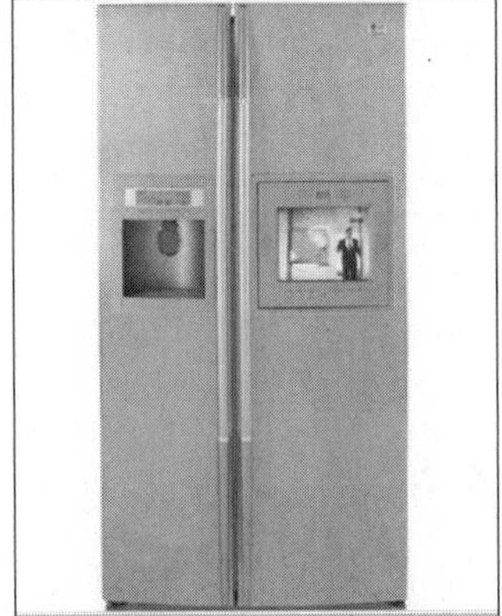

Figure 1-3: Yes, a refrigerator.

The point is that you don't know what you are writing for, so you have a very different development experience for a Web browser than you do for a Windows client. You don't know what size the screen is, you don't know what language the machine is set to, you don't know how fast the connection to the Internet is. You know nothing about your client.

You have to question the client. You can't assume much about the browser, so you have to make certain design decisions differently than you usually would.

You can depend on the browser to do some things for you that you might be used to having to do for yourself. The programming details are explained in Chapter 4, but it is important to get a good overview now.

First, the client browser has a built-in scripting system called ECMAScript. Second, the browser can tell you some subset of details about itself, its host machine, and the user that is using it.

Scripting the client

By now you get the idea that communication with the browser occurs via the network, and that the client and browser are disconnected. Although that is true, the client isn't completely out in the fog when it comes to interacting with the user.

You can send a script along with your HTML document. This script references objects on the screen — just like your C# code would — and makes things happen for the user.

Usually this script is in the JavaScript language. Why not C#? Well, C# isn't a scripting language. C# needs to be compiled, and JavaScript isn't compiled. It just sits there, in text, waiting for the browser to run it.

The fact that it is in text means you have to be careful not to put secure information in a script. Right-click on any Web page in your browser and click View Source to see that page's script code.

A lot of the script that your pages need will be generated by ASP.NET. This book is about C#, not JavaScript, so we focus on the server features, not the client features. For now, you should just know that "things are happening" on the client side, however.

Getting information back from the client

When a browser makes a request to a server, a lot of useful information about the client gets sent along with the page name that is requested. You can reference this in the backwardly named `ServerVariables` collection.

This is about as good as learning about the client gets. These details will, however, help you get the most out of your communication with the client. Here some examples of the values available:

- **`AUTH_USER`:** The logged-in user.
- **`REMOTE_USER`:** The same as AUTH_USER.

- **CONTENT_LENGTH:** Size of the request. This is useful if a file is uploaded.
- **HTTP_USER_AGENT:** Which browser the client is using.
- **REMOTE_ADDR:** The IP number of the client computer.
- **QUERY_STRING:** All the stuff after the question mark in the request. Check out the Address bar of a browser in many Web applications to see what I mean.
- **ALL_HTTP:** Every *header variable* (request details made available to the server) sent by the client.

In total, there are usually 63 variables in the header. The most commonly accessed of them are in the `System.Web.HttpRequest` class. You'll also find the collection of `ServerVariables` there. More on getting to that class in Chapter 4. Search MSDN for ServerVariables to get the complete list.

Understanding the weaknesses of the browser

As you can imagine, there are a few weaknesses to the browser-as-client model. At this point in the book, you should know that the more layers you stack on, the more problems you are going to encounter. Not even letting the programmer know what computer the user has is another.

Here are a few of these weaknesses:

- **Changing window sizes:** The most basic difficulty in using a browser as a client is changing window sizes. In a Windows program, you have at least some control over how large the window is — if it gets too small, you can change it programmatically. In a Web application, however, you have very little control over the window size. For all you know, the user could be using a cellphone, right? That's a small window!

  Because of this, every form you develop using ASP.NET has to be size-agnostic to the best of your ability. Especially when your form is destined for the public Internet — you just can't make assumptions about the size of the user's screen.
- **Sporadic communication:** When the client wants something from the server, the client requests it from the server. It is the server's responsibility to get the client what it wants, and then wait. And wait. And wait some more.

  Even if the server wants an acknowledgement from the client, it might never get one. The user might have closed the browser.

  Communication from the client to the server is sporadic. Secure transactions are nearly impossible because the server can't be sure that the client will communicate any information back. Because of the loosely coupled nature of the Internet, you just can't make any assumptions about communication time.

✦ **Distrusted input:** Browser documents are sent as a package of text and images (and sounds and fonts and Flash movies, if needed) to the client from the server. The requests are sent back to the server from the client in a similar way — text.

With all this text, you would think that someone would find a way to fake a request. Oh wait, they have. Lots of them. And it is easy, and free.

Take a look at Fiddler, a free tool that lets you completely alter the requests sent from a browser. (See Figure 1-4.) Fiddler gives you the capability to view a request — including the results from a form (even a login form) — alter the text directly, then send it on its merry way.

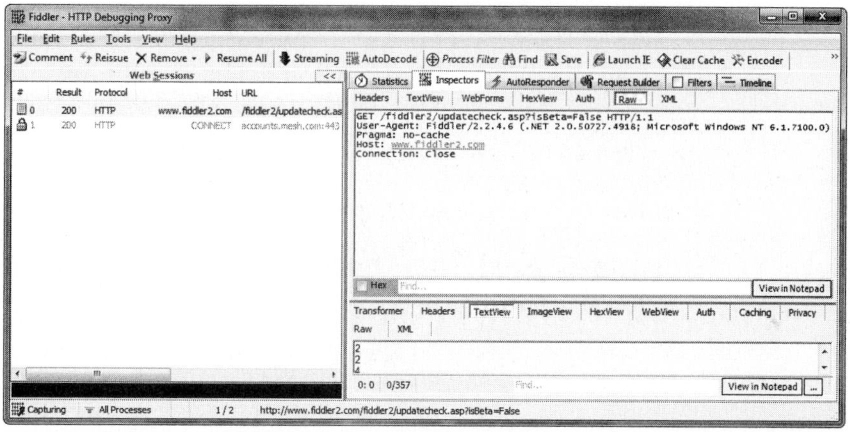

Figure 1-4: Fiddler (`www.fiddlertool.com`).

Security risk? You betcha. You need to distrust every character sent to you from the client. Validate everything in the server code. We look at this in Chapters 2 and 3.

✦ **Random implementations:** When you are writing a WPF application in C#, you know the application will be running on Windows. You might not know which edition, but you have a good idea about how it will work. When you write an ASP.NET system, on the other hand, you know that the client might or might not follow a set of standards, but that's about it. You don't know how the browser will behave.

The more significant impact of this is in positioning, as it turns out. The technology that specified most of the positioning and styling in browsers, called Cascading Style Sheets (CSS), is rife with misimplementation.

That means that not only do you not know how your application will behave out there, but also that it might not look right, either! Yea for the Web! Seriously, scripting is another piece of the puzzle that isn't the same across browsers. ECMAScript is another standard, and it is implemented differently by different browser companies.

The only way around all of this is to test, test, test. If all else fails, take the simplest road. And don't get tremendously picky about a pixel here and there.

Dealing with Web Servers

The other side of this client/server equation is the server. For those of us writing in ASP.NET, the server will be Internet Information Server fully 99.5 percent of the time. Other servers implement ASP.NET in one fashion or another, but you almost never see them.

The role of the Web server is to accept requests from clients, do whatever processing is required, and then pass back a browser-viewable page. This means that the ASP.NET code we write will be turned into HTML and JavaScript by the Web server. You have less control over what is happening than you might think.

Getting a PostBack (Hint: It's not a returned package)

A PostBack isn't a returned package from the post office. It is how ASP.NET handles communication between the client and the server so you don't have to.

The first time users request a page in ASP.NET in a given session, they usually type the URL into the address bar, or click a link like `www.csharpfordummies.com`. The next page loaded, however, is a carefully controlled communication with the server, called a PostBack.

A PostBack is a JavaScript function used in place of the built-in POST function to send information about the data on the page back to the server. It looks like this to the client:

```
javascript:WebForm_DoPostBackWithOptions(new WebForm_PostBackOptions(&quot;ctl
    00$cphAdmin$btnSave&quot;, &quot;&quot;, true, &quot;&quot;, &quot;&quot;,
    false, false))
```

Quite a change from a URL, huh? To make what I mean more clear, let's go back in time.

Looking back to how things used to be

Back in the day, Web servers supported GETs and POSTs. What's more, they still support GETs and POSTs.

A GET is a request for a page, using just the URL. You can send data in the URI (after a question mark in the link of text) but that's all you are sending — nothing from the page itself goes back. A GET request looks like this:

```
GET /fiddler2/updatecheck.asp?isBeta=False HTTP/1.1
User-Agent: Fiddler/2.2.4.6 (.NET 2.0.50727.4918; Microsoft Windows NT
    6.1.7100.0)
Pragma: no-cache
Host: www.fiddler2.com
Connection: Close
```


A POST sends values from a form on the page. The form can be invisible, but it has to be there. POSTs are a lot bigger than GETs and have a set format that is hard to navigate at times. Here is an example POST:

```
POST /feedbackAction.asp HTTP/1.1
Accept: application/x-ms-application, image/jpeg, application/xaml+xml, image/
    gif, image/pjpeg, application/x-ms-xbap, application/vnd.ms-excel,
    application/vnd.ms-powerpoint, application/msword, application/x-shockwave-
    flash, */*
Referer: http://www.grovecity.com/feedback.asp
Accept-Language: en-US
User-Agent: Mozilla/4.0 (compatible; MSIE 8.0; Windows NT 6.1; WOW64;
    Trident/4.0; SLCC2; .NET CLR 2.0.50727; .NET CLR 3.5.30729; .NET
    CLR 3.0.30729; Media Center PC 6.0; .NET CLR 1.1.4322; InfoPath.2;
    OfficeLiveConnector.1.3; OfficeLivePatch.0.0)
Content-Type: application/x-www-form-urlencoded
Accept-Encoding: gzip, deflate
Host: www.grovecity.com
Content-Length: 69
Connection: Keep-Alive
Pragma: no-cache
Cookie: ASPSESSIONIDAATQCRCA=MJEFOIFACGPONMOBADPIDLKH

user=Bill&email=bill@sempf.net&subject=Test&comment=This+is+a+POST%21
```

All the header variables are there, and then the contents of the form are all linked together at the end of the request.

From the past to the PostBack

Having to handle the header had a lot of problems when it came to the sophisticated Web forms that ASP.NET provides, so Microsoft used JavaScript to short-circuit the process. They created a special method that would be on every page that ASP.NET generates.

This method formats the information in order to better manage the communication with the server. A PostBack looks like this:

```
POST /admin/Pages/Add_entry.aspx?id=e387aab8-1292-4c75-985f-5f8e5db3089a HTTP/1.1
Accept: application/x-ms-application, image/jpeg, application/xaml+xml, image/
    gif, image/pjpeg, application/x-ms-xbap, application/vnd.ms-excel,
    application/vnd.ms-powerpoint, application/msword, application/x-shockwave-
    flash, */*
Referer: http://www.sempf.net/admin/Pages/Add_entry.aspx?id=e387ccb8-1292-4c75-
    985f-5f8e5db3089a
Accept-Language: en-US
User-Agent: Mozilla/4.0 (compatible; MSIE 7.0; Windows NT 6.1; WOW64;
    Trident/4.0; SLCC2; .NET CLR 2.0.50727; .NET CLR 3.5.30729; .NET
    CLR 3.0.30729; Media Center PC 6.0; .NET CLR 1.1.4322; InfoPath.2;
    OfficeLiveConnector.1.3; OfficeLivePatch.0.0)
Content-Type: multipart/form-data; boundary=---------------------------
    7d922c323b0016
Accept-Encoding: gzip, deflate
Host: www.sempf.net
Content-Length: 9399
Connection: Keep-Alive
Pragma: no-cache

-----------------------------7d922c323b0016
Content-Disposition: form-data; name="__LASTFOCUS"


-----------------------------7d922c323b0016
Content-Disposition: form-data; name="ctl00$cphAdmin$txtTitle"

C# 4.0 at CONDG
-----------------------------7d922c323b0016
Content-Disposition: form-data; name="ctl00$cphAdmin$ddlAuthor"

Admin
-----------------------------7d922c323b0016
Content-Disposition: form-data; name="ctl00$cphAdmin$txtDate"

2009-09-08 22:21
-----------------------------7d922c323b0016
Content-Disposition: form-data; name="ctl00$cphAdmin$txtContent$TinyMCE1$txtCont
    ent"

<p>I was very pleased to be able to give my C# 4.0 talk at the <a href="http://
    www.condg.org/">Central Ohio .NET Developers Group</a> last month.</p>
-----------------------------7d922c323b0016
Content-Disposition: form-data; name="ctl00$cphAdmin$txtUploadImage"; filename=""
Content-Type: application/octet-stream


-----------------------------7d922c323b0016
Content-Disposition: form-data; name="ctl00$cphAdmin$txtUploadFile"; filename=""
Content-Type: application/octet-stream


-----------------------------7d922c323b0016
Content-Disposition: form-data; name="ctl00$cphAdmin$txtSlug"

C-40-at-CONDG
-----------------------------7d922c323b0016
```

Notice the nice layout of the data, with the form field name, and the data and everything all nice to read? Fortunately, you don't have to worry about any of this. ASP.NET gets it for you.

When you create an event handler for an object — a button, for instance — a PostBack will be used for that communication. This is how ASP.NET changes your interface with the server and client. It makes Web programming look like Windows programming, at least as far as events are concerned.

It's a matter of state

The other major piece of the puzzle in Web server usage is state. No, I don't mean that field in the Address database. I mean that the server should know the state of the application at any given time.

Web servers don't do a very good job of remembering state because of one of the problems with Web browsers — inconsistency of communications. Because the server doesn't know if you are going to send anything from one minute to the next, they can't depend on getting it.

For this reason, the server tries to remember certain things about your session by putting values in the form that they can use later. The server uses a `ViewState` value for that. The `ViewState` is an encrypted string that the server can use to remember who you are from POST to POST.

Even with these values, maintaining session state has its problems. For instance, in a secure application you might need to maintain a transaction for a database function. This is nearly impossible in a Web application, because you can't be sure you will get the return acknowledgment. Because of this, nearly all the data processing happens on the server — I cover this in more detail in Chapter 5.

Chapter 2: Building Web Applications

In This Chapter

- **Working in Visual Studio**
- **Developing with Style**
- **Modeling the View Controller**

There is a lot to Web development. People used to ask me what language I programmed in. I told them I was a Web developer.

"No, really, what language do you program in?" they would ask.

"Web. It's seven languages. Seven that I have to know. Criminy, is it really seven?"

At the time, it was seven. I needed to know SQL, VBScript, XML, Visual Basic, HTML, CSS, and JavaScript. At least it is a little better now. You can get by without C++, which was once required. Oh, and C# can replace Visual Basic. The rest ...

With Visual Studio in the mix, things are a little easier than they once were. You have two considerations when you choose Visual Studio to be your tool of choice to build a Web application. The first is the tool itself. The second is the way you are going to use the tool, or your *methodology*.

If you've been working with the samples in this book, working in Visual Studio is going to feel very familiar. There is a design view for the user interface. Code View works just like the Code View in all the other environments. The only caveat is the unusual file types that you will see occasionally in Web applications. You'll get used to those. I did.

The methodology debate — that is, which methodology works better — is harder to get used to because it is a religious war. People will tell you to use one or the other for this reason and that. I do the same thing here. Feel free to ignore me. Just don't use something only because it is new and shiny. Do the research, try things, and build software that works. In this chapter, you see how to build an application in one methodology, using Visual Studio as your tool.

Working in Visual Studio

You already know the basics of working in Visual Studio in C#; we have been working in Visual Studio all along. Working with Visual Studio in the Web world is a little different, but not much. Using Visual Studio to build a Web application is a lot like WPF actually, because Web applications have a code element to the design view — the HTML document, in an ASPX file. Then there is a code element, in an ASPX.CS file.

A lot of other files make Web pages work, too. There are images and style sheets and script files. All of them have editors in Visual Studio. None of them have a darn thing to do with C#, though, so I won't talk about them much here. For more on those files, see the upcoming section, "Recognizing the other file types," or refer to *ASP.NET 3.5 For Dummies* by Ken Cox.

Let's set up a simple site in Visual Studio. You'll use it to look at all of Visual Studio's cool Web features. Then you can begin looking at more complex sites. Here's all you need to do to set up your simple site:

1. **Open Visual Studio, and click on Projects, and then New Project.**
2. **In the New Project dialog box, select Visual C# in the treeview to the left, then Web, and choose ASP.NET Web application in the right-side window.**

   I named mine **AspNetFirstSample**.
3. **Click OK.**

   Visual Studio makes a project.

Hey, that's it. It runs a lot like all the other projects that you have done, making all the files that you need to make a Web project work. To run the project, press <F5>. When you do so, Visual Studio launches Cassini, the Web Server that comes with Visual Studio. Your Web browser launches, and your project launches.

Now let's make it complicated. Web applications have a lot of moving parts, which can be hard to manage. Visual Studio makes it as easy as anything I have worked with in 17 years of Web development to manage a Web application.

Handling the Designer

Visual Studio launches the Web project in the designer. The only problem is that the designer shows a Code View of sorts. That's not going to help us build this application right away, is it?

Back in the day, visual interfaces were developed using a *black box* architecture. A black box architecture is a way of designing a component so that the user has no idea how it works. You used a visual designer to place objects on a page, and the locations and such were stored in a custom binary format. Nothing about the "document," the form itself, was really editable without the designer. HTML, and now XAML, changes all that. Forms are now at least laid out using standards-based, well-understood markup language.

To view a form designer, click the Design tab. You'll get a blank view there. That's okay for now. You are going to add stuff.

Click the Toolbox tab all the way to the left. I have used the toolbox for Windows Forms and other applications. Now it has the controls for Web applications. Open the Standard tree view.

The Standard tree view has the main HTML controls that are part of the standard library with an ASP.NET twist. Drag a Label control and a Button control onto the Web form. It should look like Figure 2-1.

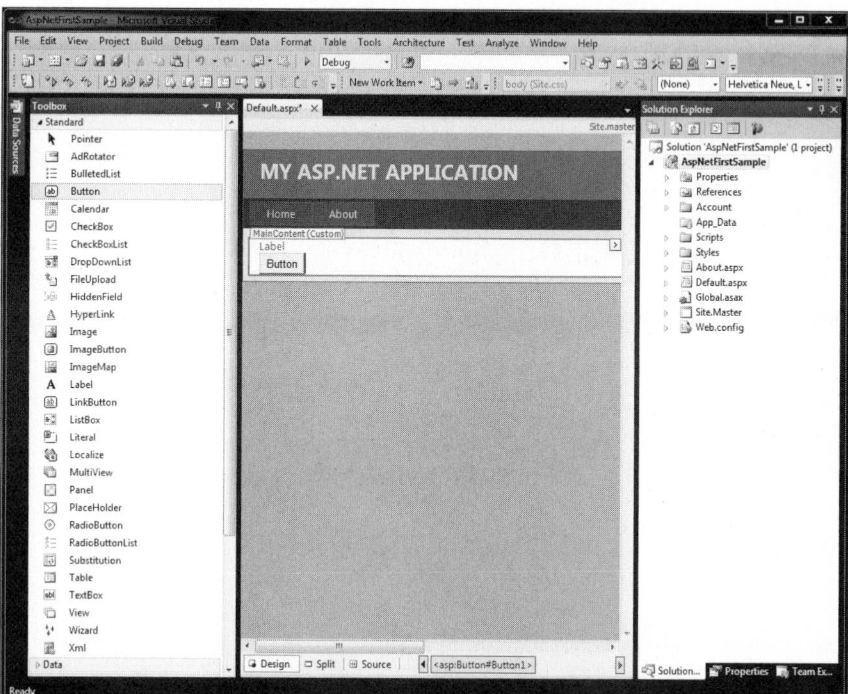

Figure 2-1: Getting started is simple.

What have you done here? Well, you have added a Label control which becomes a `<SPAN>` tag with some text in it, and a Button control that will effectively be an `<INPUT>` tag when you are done.

Change to the Source view, back where you started. Check out the designer source and I'll break down the ASP.NET code from the HTML code a little bit. Here is the code after the controls are added:

```
<%@ Page Language="C#" AutoEventWireup="true" CodeBehind="Default.aspx.cs"
    Inherits="AspNetFirstSample._Default" %>

<!DOCTYPE html PUBLIC "-//W3C//DTD XHTML 1.0 Transitional//EN" "http://www.
    w3.org/TR/xhtml1/DTD/xhtml1-transitional.dtd">

<html xmlns="http://www.w3.org/1999/xhtml" >
<head runat="server">
  <title></title>
</head>
<body>
  <form id="form1" runat="server">
  <div>

    <asp:Label ID="Label1" runat="server" Text="Label"></asp:Label>

  </div>
  <p>
    <asp:Button ID="Button1" runat="server" Text="Button" />
  </p>
  </form>
</body>
</html>
```

If you have any experience with HTML, you recognize 90 percent of what is on the screen. `<html>`, `<head>`, `<body>`, and `<form>` are all common HTML tags that you can find on any Web page. The two tags that begin with `<asp` are ASP.NET Server controls, and that is what I am talking about here.

To see what these control do, press <F5>. Cassini launches, your Web browser launches, and your new page appears. (See Figure 2-2.)

Looks a lot like the designer. There are some differences under the sheets. Remember that Web browsers don't speak ASP.NET; they speak HTML. Your Web server must translate our ASP.NET code into something that the Web browser can use. Here is that translation:

```
<!DOCTYPE html PUBLIC "-//W3C//DTD XHTML 1.0 Transitional//EN" "http://www.
    w3.org/TR/xhtml1/DTD/xhtml1-transitional.dtd">

<html xmlns="http://www.w3.org/1999/xhtml" >
<head><title>

</title></head>
<body>
    <form name="form1" method="post" action="Default.aspx" id="form1">
<div>
<input type="hidden" name="__VIEWSTATE" id="__VIEWSTATE" value="/
    wEPDwUKMTI2NTY4ODI3MWRkf5c0g2jxUkjj5CIoHCiRot7EU38=" />
</div>
```

```
<div>

     <input type="hidden" name="__EVENTVALIDATION" id="__EVENTVALIDATION" value="/
     wEWAgKZydGJAwKM54rGBjN10vDX6YoBChZcj2JzWRrR7tJR" />
</div>
    <div>

        <span id="Label1">Label</span>

    </div>
    <p>
        <input type="submit" name="Button1" value="Button" id="Button1" />
    </p>
    </form>
</body>
</html>
```


As promised, the ASP.NET Label control became a `<span>`, and the ASP.NET Button control becomes an `<input>` control. All that the designer is doing is helping you write markup code. There is no magic here.

All the controls that were just added have their default values. In order to have clean code, you need to intelligently name your controls. Additionally, you may have other values you need to set on those controls. There might even be things you didn't even know the control could do that you can set.

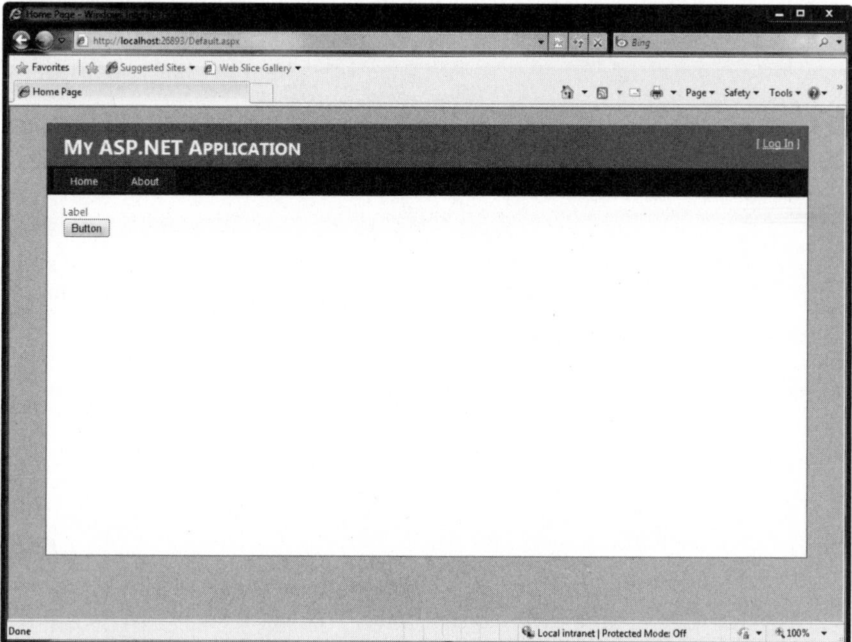

Figure 2-2: Your artistic new Web application.

The trick to doing this is in the Properties panel, which was introduced in Book IV, Chapter 2. The Properties panel handles the properties of ASP.NET controls just as well as it does anything else. For instance, to rename the controls from the preceding example, follow these steps:

1. **Open the project you were working on earlier, if it isn't already open.**
2. **Double-click on Default.aspx in the Solution Explorer.**
3. **Change to Design view.**
4. **Press the <F4> key to bring up the Properties panel.**
5. **In the Designer, click on the Label you added.**
6. **Notice that the Properties panel changes to look like Figure 2-3. Change the Text Property to** This is The Text to Change.

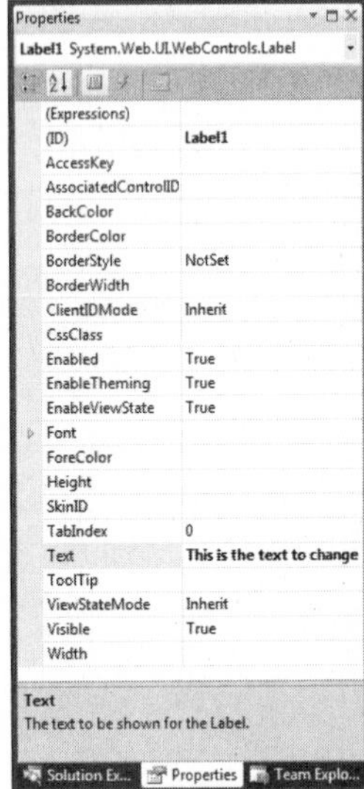

Figure 2-3: Properties look like this!

7. **Open the Font tree view by clicking the little triangle next to the word Font.**
8. **Change the Size property to 14.**

   See the label change in the designer?
9. **Change the (ID) to** TextToChange.
10. **Change the Text to** Text to Change.

11. **Click the Button in the designer.**

    The Properties panel changes to show the button's properties.

12. **Change the Text property to** Click Me.

13. **Change the (ID) to** ChangeText.

Now change back to Source view and note the changes in the code:

```
<%@ Page Language="VB" AutoEventWireup="false"
   CodeFile="Default.aspx.cs" Inherits="_Default" %>

<!DOCTYPE html PUBLIC "-//W3C//DTD XHTML 1.0 Transitional//
   EN" "http://www.w3.org/TR/xhtml1/DTD/xhtml1-transitional.
   dtd">

<html xmlns="http://www.w3.org/1999/xhtml">
<head runat="server">
    <title></title>
</head>
<body>
    <form id="form1" runat="server">
    <div>

        <asp:Label ID="TextToChange" runat="server" Font-
   Size="14pt" Text="Label">Text to change</asp:Label>
        <br />
        <asp:Button ID="ChangeText" runat="server"
   Text="Click Me" />

    </div>
    </form>
</body>
</html>
```

So the management of your code is what the designer does for you. Now, some people don't like Visual Studio messing with their code. Some people don't like to remember all the ins and outs of ASP.NET. It's all up to you; you can use it or not.

This isn't where the magic is, though. This is a C# book, and if you are working in a big shop your ASP.NET code is probably being written for you anyway. You want to play with the server code, and I don't blame you.

Coding in Code View

If you go back to the design view and double-click on the Button control you dragged over, you will see something a little more familiar than all of this crazy markup. Usually called the code-behind, this is the C# code that makes the form manageable by the server. This code should look like this:

```
using System;
using System.Collections.Generic;
using System.Linq;
using System.Web;
using System.Web.UI;
using System.Web.UI.WebControls;

public partial class _Default : System.Web.UI.Page
{
    protected void Page_Load(object sender, EventArgs e)
    {

    }
    protected void ChangeText_Click(object sender, EventArgs
   e)
    {

    }
}
```

Let's break this down a little. I know you've seen a class before, and that's all this is, but there are a few things that I want to point out:

- **This is a partial class.** Partial classes are covered in Book II. The rest of this class is built-in Web functionality, and it used to appear in this file. Fact is, no one ever needed to edit it, so Microsoft took it out. I'm glad they did. This is a lot easier to look at.
- **The class inherits from `System.Web.UI.Page`.** The `Page` class provides all the tools you need to keep a collection of the controls in the page together. This is very important for some Web applications, but it's a little beyond the scope of this book. Read the documentation for the `Page` class. It's an important part of ASP.NET.
- **There is an event handler for `Page.Load`.** Remember the ASP.NET load sequence in Chapter 1? This is why it is important. You can do pre-setup operations in this handler.
- **There is an event handler for the `Button.Click` event.** Hey, how did *this* get there? Oh yeah, you double-clicked on the control to get the default event handler, just like I talk about in Book I.

Depending on your background, you might find this feels either very familiar, or very foreign. This is *not* like the classic Active Server Pages days, or like modern PHP with inline scripting. Although inline scripting is a way you can code with ASP.NET, it isn't the default way.

If you are a Windows programmer, you will probably feel very comfortable with Web forms. They work in a similar fashion. However, as I mention in Chapter 1, there is no real state management on these controls — it is all faked by the `ViewState` variable in the HTML, and if you overuse the `ViewState`, you will have a slow application.

Adding some functionality using C#

Let's start by making the form do something. Code View basically allows the developer to write code that does something useful with the Web form. Here I keep it simple, but it can get much more complex.

There is already an event handler for the `Button.Click` event so I suggest you use that method to change the text of the Label. This is a common operation in Web applications. The label ID was `TextToChange`, so you need to add this code:


```
TextToChange.Text = "It has changed!";
```

That was simple. You need to know that this will be the simplest event handler that you will ever write, however. They get harder.

Run the application by pressing <F5>. (If neither of us made a mistake, it should build.) Then launch the Cassini server, and then your browser should launch. Click the Click Me button, and your screen should look like the one in Figure 2-4.

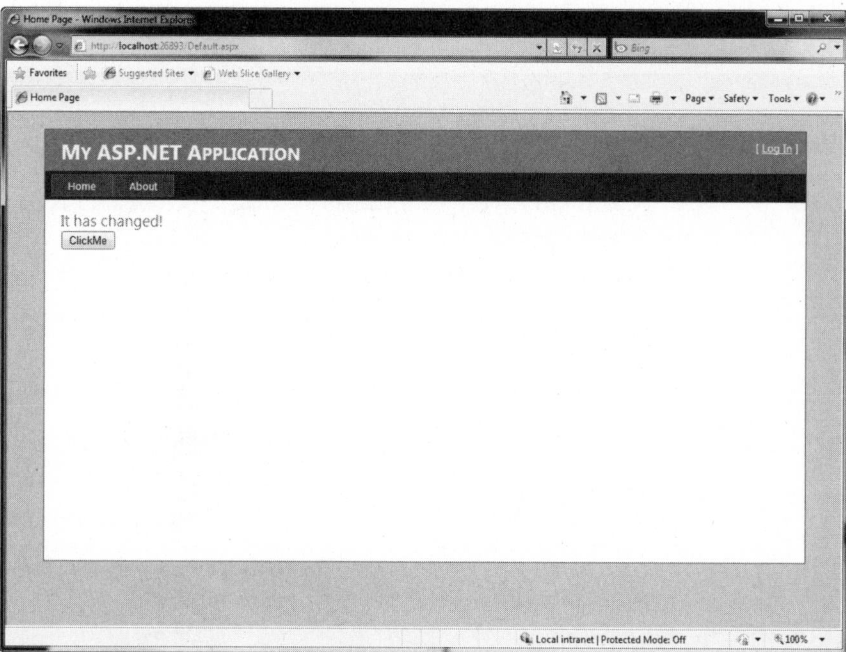

Figure 2-4: Hey, it worked!

The first time you run the Web form in the debugger, you get a message telling you that if you want to debug this project you need to change the Web config. For the purposes of this book, say Yes and move on. However, remember that when you go to production, you will need to review the config and change this setting. I cover it in Chapter 5.

You can do even more in Code View — a lot more (and more than I can cover here). The next three chapters include tips and tricks that you can absorb.

Using Page.Load to add even more functionality

Now let's say the client wants something to happen when the page loads. Pretend that this "something" is dynamic. It isn't gonna be dynamic for this example, but it could be.

Because of the nature of ASP.NET, and programming in general for Windows, you can't always code properties in the design time controller — especially for events. Sometimes you need to manually write an event handler to deal with an event. That is what you are going to do — from the Code View out this time. Last time you used the designer. Just follow these steps to write the event handler:

1. **Start by writing an event handler in Code View.**

   ```
    protected void ChangeTheColor(object sender,
   EventArgs e)
    {
        TextToChange.BackColor = System.Drawing.Color.
   Red;
    }
   ```

   No event arguments are required in C# 4.0, if you aren't planning on using them. If you want the forms designer to work properly, however, include them.

2. **Change back to Design view and select the** TextToChange **label.**
3. **Open the Properties panel and click the lightning bolt in the button bar at the top.**

   This changes the Properties panel into an Event panel of sorts.

4. **Click on the Load event under the Misc header.**

   You should see a little drop-down icon as shown in Figure 2-5.

5. **Pick the** ChangeTheColor **method you created in Step 1.**
6. **Run the application again. The background color of the label should be set to red.**

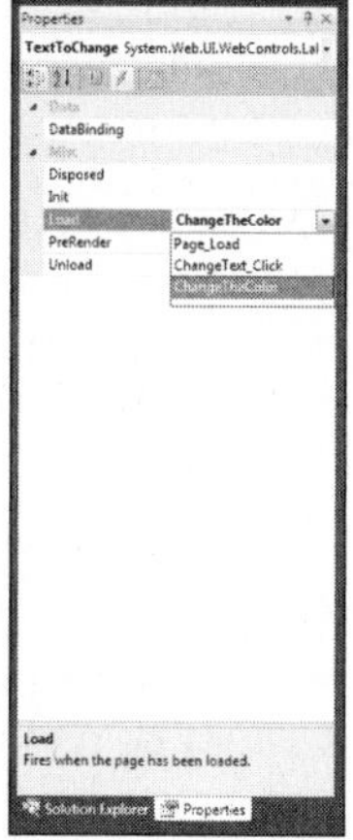

Figure 2-5: The Event panel.

Recognizing the other file types

I am sure you get the idea at this point on the ASPX markup file. There are ASPX files that have markup, and there are ASPX.CS files that have C# code. That's the core of the ASP.NET model.

If you have done any Web development before, you know that there are other files that get used. Lots of other files get used, in fact.

Visual Studio has a place for nearly all those other files. Table 2-1 is a breakdown of some of those files, what they are for, and how they are accessed.

Table 2-1 Web Application File Types

File Type	*What It Does*	*How Visual Studio Handles It*
Stylesheets (.css files, usually)	Controls how the page looks. For more on CSS, check out *HTML and CSS For Dummies.*	Visual Studio has a fantastic CSS handler. I like it more than the supposedly better ones from Blend.
JavaScript Files	Handles client-side interactivity.	Now that Microsoft supports AJAX, JavaScript (the J in AJAX) is suddenly a lot more important. IntelliSense is supported now, as well as real debugging.

(continued)

Table 2-1 *(continued)*

File Type	*What It Does*	*How Visual Studio Handles It*
Images (GIFs, JPEGs, and PNGs)	Making pretties.	Don't depend on Visual Studio to edit your images. Use Photoshop, or a merged product or suite like Expression Blend.
User Controls (ASCX)	I deal with these in Chapter 4, but basically they are a way to combine the Toolbox controls to do something specific.	Perfect support, and always has been. Visual Studio *wants* you to reuse code, so do it!

Developing with Style

There are a number of different flavors of ASP.NET development. These flavors include inline scripting and regular Web forms, and also MVC, *n*-tier, three-tier, and forms over data. I am not sure why there are so many patterns for the development of ASP.NET applications, but there are.

Keep in mind, none of this has much to do with how the application runs. These are just different ways to do the same thing. Each way has pros and cons. Look into them carefully before making your decisions.

You'll find that many of the options here have a lot to do with where to put the code. This falls into the arena of application architecture or software patterns. I translate the following ASP.NET patterns into the traditional names as closely as possible, so you can translate what others say to what you learn here.

This is just high-level software design principles. Nothing you see here will matter to the end users — they see HTML. Nothing you see here will change the way ASP.NET works. There is still HTML markup with ASP.NET controls, and C# code to manage those controls.

Your style of application will be dictated by several different things. The project type is first and foremost, and your team is second. In this section I go over a few of the more popular styles, and how these variables fit.

Coding behind

The default condition for creating ASP.NET applications is with a code-behind file. Just as you saw in the first example, Visual Studio creates an ASPX file for the markup code and an ASPX.CS file for the C# code. If diagrammed, it would look like Figure 2-6.

Figure 2-6: The structure of a code-behind style project.

There are a few benefits to this, and they are fairly important.

- **Division of labor:** First, it separates the C# server code from the ASP.NET and HTML template code. Although it doesn't do a perfect job, it's a lot better than scripting languages like Active Server Pages and PHP that have everything merged together. It just makes things easier to keep track of.
- **Speed and security:** Using this pattern, Microsoft compiles the C# code into a DLL, just like the class libraries Book II delves into. This makes the application much faster and protects the application somewhat from criminals.
- **Legacy-based:** This pattern mimics Windows Forms development, going back to Visual Basic 3. It is easy for people to pick up if they already have experience. I know that history isn't always the best to mimic, but it can't hurt.

Scripting the experience

Using the code-behind isn't the only way to skin this digital cat, though. If you want to take a trip back to the nineties, you can code your C# right into an ASPX file, with your controls in your HTML.

However, if you can't tell, I am not in favor of this method. It compiles at runtime, rather than at design time, so it is slower. The code is all junked together, making it hard to find anything.

Nonetheless, sometimes you have to do this. I once deployed a Web project to a hosting company that wouldn't let me upload a `.DLL` file. I had to rewrite the whole app into inline script so that it would run. Knowing how to do this is important.

Let me give you an example. Let's start with the project you were editing earlier. From there, follow these steps:

1. **Right-click on the project and select Add New Item.**
2. **In the dialog box that comes up, select Web Form, as shown in Figure 2-7.**

   See the red box (added) at the bottom of Figure 2-7? By default, it is checked.

3. **Uncheck the box in Step 2 so that you don't build a code-behind file.**
4. **Name your file and press OK.**

   I named mine **InlineCode**.

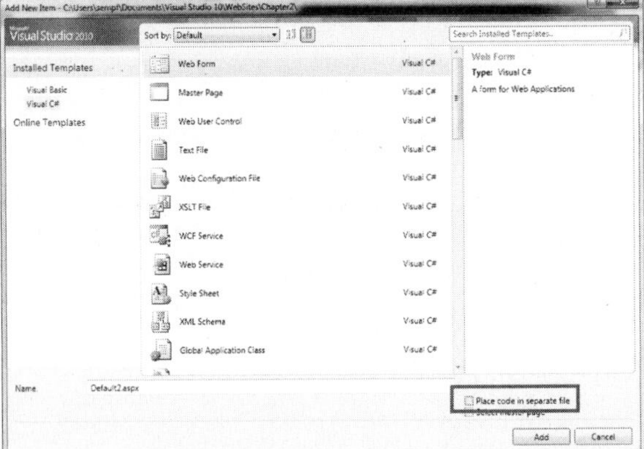

Figure 2-7: Adding inline code.

That's all there is to it, one check box.

What you have now is practically the same thing as the code-behind version, except no ASPX.CS file. Instead you have a `<script>` block in the markup code, which looks like this:

```
<%@ Page Language="C#" %>

<!DOCTYPE html PUBLIC "-//W3C//DTD XHTML 1.0 Transitional//
   EN" "http://www.w3.org/TR/xhtml1/DTD/xhtml1-transitional.
   dtd">

<script runat="server">

</script>

<html xmlns="http://www.w3.org/1999/xhtml">
<head runat="server">
    <title></title>
</head>
<body>
    <form id="form1" runat="server">
    <div>

    </div>
    </form>
</body>
</html>
```

Note also that there is a language declaration at the top of the page rather than an `InheritsFrom`. This is because you are no longer building a DLL file but are just interpreting this all at runtime.

Go back to Design view, add a button, and double-click on it in the designer. You return to Source view rather than Code View, because there is no Code View. The event handler is now in the `<script>` block, as shown:

```
<%@ Page Language="C#" %>

<!DOCTYPE html PUBLIC "-//W3C//DTD XHTML 1.0 Transitional//
   EN" "http://www.w3.org/TR/xhtml1/DTD/xhtml1-transitional.
   dtd">

<script runat="server">

    protected void Button1_Click(object sender, EventArgs e)
    {

    }
</script>

<html xmlns="http://www.w3.org/1999/xhtml">
<head runat="server">
    <title></title>
</head>
<body>
    <form id="form1" runat="server">
    <div>

        <asp:Button ID="Button1" runat="server"
   onclick="Button1_Click" Text="Button" />

    </div>
    </form>
</body>
</html>
```

That's really about it. It looks and works a lot like Active Server Pages. Sometimes you might need to use it so it is valuable to understand how to do it.

Building in n-tier

Going the opposite direction from inline code, I have what used to be called n-tier code, but now it's called a hundred different things. At the essence here, I am talking about purposefully dividing the code of the application up into DLLs, instead of just having Visual Studio do it for you.

To show what I mean in pictures, Figure 2-8 shows a normal code-behind style ASP.NET application. Now, say you put all the data access code — code that talks to the database — in one class project. Then you put all the business logic — math and validation and stuff — in another class project.

Figure 2-8: Structure of n-tier code.

All the code in the code-behind layer, then, would be stuff that makes the markup work, right? Yup. That's the idea. Layering your application like this makes debugging easier, separates concerns even more, and provides for code reuse. If you have a cellphone application that uses the same data model, then you can use the same database code if you break it out.

Implementing n-tier is simple. Just make a class project for every logical division in your code. Something so simple can sometimes be demanding, however. Determining where to put what and how to hook everything together is non-trivial — but also beyond the scope of this book. recommend getting some of the Wrox Professional ASP.NET titles to learn more about Web application architecture.

Modeling the View Controller

ASP.NET MVC takes the idea of n-tier a step further by formalizing it. The tough decisions I mention related to deciding where everything goes are largely made for you in ASP.NET MVC.

MVC stands for Model View Controller. In a nutshell, the idea is that your markup goes in the View, your business logic goes in the Controller, and your database connection code goes in the Model. Sounds like n-tier to you, too, huh? I understand. The differences are mostly theoretical.

The big benefit to MVC over other kinds of Web forms apps is that the user interface code is much more testable with automated tests. In fact, when you start an ASP.NET MVC project, it asks you to create a test project along with it.

Another difference from n-tier is some formalization to the implementation of MVC. It is a project type, and rather than having to figure out how things hook up, MVC does some of the work for you.

MVC is a big topic that I just can't cover here in any detail. If you have a large project for which you need to divide up the work among developers with varying skill sets, it's cool. Read more in *Professional ASP.NET* by Wrox Press.

Chapter 3: Controlling Your Development Experience

In This Chapter

- **Showing stuff to the user**
- **Getting some input from the user**
- **Binding**
- **Styling with the best**
- **Making sure the site is accessible**
- **Constructing user controls**
- **Adding custom controls**

ASP.NET is a rendering engine. It takes preset batches of functionality and renders it into HTML. For instance, ASP.NET can take a database table and a little bit of layout information and make a nice, dynamic HTML table.

Rendering engines are a good idea in the W world. With a bunch of different implementations and versions, your rendering engine can produce different user markup out of the same effective code base.

ASP.NET does this well. You can tell it to make mobile-device markup and text-only markup and rich Internet Explorer markup from the same ASP.NET file, and it will do an okay job.

This is possible because of *Web controls.* Web controls are controls that ASP.NET renders into client-side markup, like HTML, CSS, and JavaScript. Well-programmed controls protect the developer from the implementation details but can still do what is needed to be done when the time comes.

Web controls aren't anything special. Basically, they show a pretty text box in the designer pane of Visual Studio, and then emit text — an `<input>` tag — when called upon to do so.

ASP.NET has a lot of included controls, many other controls are available from third-party providers, and you can even build your own and base them on existing controls. It's a good system.

Showing Stuff to the User

Web surfers want to look at stuff. For them to look at it, you have to show it. Most of the controls in the ASP.NET control library are about showing things to the user.

Although there are a lot of controls, only some of them apply to the subject matter of this book — C#. This doesn't mean you shouldn't use them, but they are more about the HTML and less about the code on the server. So I am just going to cover a few controls. For more, please pick up *ASP.NET For Dummies*.

Labels versus plain old text

The most basic item on an average Web page is text. Take a look at a normal site, like Microsoft.com. You find a text box, maybe two; a handful of images also. Most of what is there is text.

Text comes in a few flavors in ASP.NET. The two I want to talk about are Label text and, well, *text* text. Label text is text inside a named span that you can change with C# code. Then there is just normal text on the page. This text is static — downloaded to the client just as you typed it.

To see what I mean, start a new Web project. Just follow these steps:

1. **Click the New Project button and select C# ASP.NET project.**

   I called mine **Chapter 3**.

2. **Make a new ASP.NET page called `Text.aspx`.**
3. **Change to Design view.**

   There will be a default `div` that you saw in Chapter 2. Put your cursor between the `<div>` and the `</div>` and then type something innovative, like **This is new text**. Then press Enter.

4. **On the new line, drag a Label from the Toolbox.**

   Your finished product should look like Figure 3-1.

5. **Double-click elsewhere on the form to get to the code-behind.**
6. **Change the value of the label in the `Page.Load` event handler by setting the `Text` property. The new handler should look like this:**

```
using System;
using System.Collections.Generic;
using System.Linq;
using System.Web;
using System.Web.UI;
using System.Web.UI.WebControls;
```

```
namespace Chapter_3
{
    public partial class Text : System.Web.UI.Page
    {
        protected void Page_Load(object sender, EventArgs e)
        {
            Label1.Text = "This is some text from the codebehind.";
        }
    }
}
```

7. **Press <F5> to launch the application.**

   You'll see that the label text was set by the C# code.

How to decide between labels and text? It's usually easy. Use a label if the text will need to change based on input from the user or the server. Use text if the text is static. A description of an item that is loaded from a database? That's a label. Your CEO's bio? That's text.

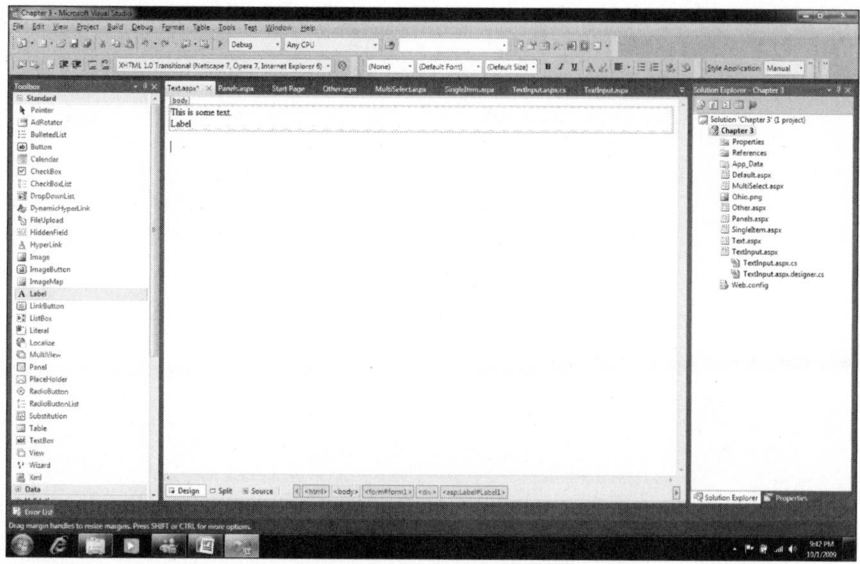

Figure 3-1: There is text, and there is text.

Images

Images are next to text in the realm of standard Web site fare. It's a complex topic because few programmers are graphic artists, and making nice images that fit together and look good is hard.

Nonetheless, sometimes you just want to show a picture on a page. Just as with text, there are two ways you can go about this. (Okay, there are more than two.) You can use the HTML `<img>` tag, or you can use the ASP.NET `Image` control.

Differences? Same as the text: If you need an image that you can manage from the C# side of things, use an image control: a product image, for example. If it is just a static image, like the picture of your CEO, then use the HTML tag.

Just follow these steps to add an image with ASP.NET's `Image` control:

1. **Add two images to your project by right-clicking the project and choosing Add⇨Existing Item.**

   You can find two images, or download some. I used a drum and a tuba. (It's college football!)

2. **Add a new page called `Images.aspx`.**
3. **Drag one of the pictures right into the box that denotes the div.**

   You'll get the Accessibility Properties dialog box, and then the picture will just show right up. Press Enter a few times to make some space.

4. **Drag an Image control from the Toolbox onto the page where the cursor is sitting.**

   It should appear as a broken image. That's okay.

5. **Double-click elsewhere on the page to get the `Page.Load` event handler and switch to Code View.**
6. **Just like we did in the Text example, set the visible property of the control. In this case, it is `ImageUrl`. The new code should look like this:**

```
using System;
using System.Collections.Generic;
using System.Linq;
using System.Web;
using System.Web.UI;
using System.Web.UI.WebControls;

namespace Chapter_3
{
    public partial class Images : System.Web.UI.Page
    {
        protected void Page_Load(object sender, EventArgs e)
        {
            Image1.ImageUrl = "tuba.gif";
        }
    }
}
```

7. **Right-click the `Images.aspx` page in the Solution Explorer and select Set as Start Page from the context menu.**
8. **Press <F5> to see it run.**

You are probably getting the idea by this point. You can use HTML and set static values, or you can use the ASP.NET controls and set dynamic values. In the examples here, we are obviously just setting "static" dynamic values, but we could be reading from a Web service, a database, or even calculating the values. Images can be listed from a directory. Text could be generated and read into a table. The options are endless.

Panels and multiviews

Managing all these text blocks and images can be rough. ASP.NET provides a number of tools that help, including the two following tools.

- **Panels** are just divs that you can manage in code-behind. Just like the text and images we added earlier, panels can be named and controlled in C#. The server will process changes before it sends the HTML to the browser. This helps to break the content into manageable groups.
- **Multiviews** are essentially containers that hold a lot of panels. You can use them for wizards and tag groupings. They help to manage the panels, which help manage the content. For more information, search MSDN for ASP.NET Multiview.

From the client's perspective, panels and multiviews are effectively the same structure, but they provide developers with a few options. For instance, the multiview shows one view only of itself by default, whereas you have to hide panels that are not in use.

Tables

Tables work like other Web controls. In HTML, you have the basic `<table>`, `<tr>`, and `<td>` tags. In ASP.NET there is a Table control, with TableRows and TableCells. If you add an ASP.NET table, it looks like this:

```
<%@ Page Language="C#" AutoEventWireup="true" CodeBehind="Tables.aspx.cs"
    Inherits="Chapter_3.Tables" %>

<!DOCTYPE html PUBLIC "-//W3C//DTD XHTML 1.0 Transitional//EN" "http://www.
    w3.org/TR/xhtml1/DTD/xhtml1-transitional.dtd">

<html xmlns="http://www.w3.org/1999/xhtml" >
<head runat="server">
    <title></title>
</head>
<body>
    <form id="form1" runat="server">
    <div>

        <asp:Table ID="Table1" runat="server">
            <asp:TableRow runat="server">
                <asp:TableCell runat="server"></asp:TableCell>
                <asp:TableCell runat="server"></asp:TableCell>
                <asp:TableCell runat="server"></asp:TableCell>
            </asp:TableRow>
            <asp:TableRow runat="server">
                <asp:TableCell runat="server"></asp:TableCell>
                <asp:TableCell runat="server"></asp:TableCell>
                <asp:TableCell runat="server"></asp:TableCell>
            </asp:TableRow>
```

```
            <asp:TableRow runat="server">
                <asp:TableCell runat="server"></asp:TableCell>
                <asp:TableCell runat="server"></asp:TableCell>
                <asp:TableCell runat="server"></asp:TableCell>
            </asp:TableRow>
        </asp:Table>

    </div>
    </form>
</body>
</html>
```

So what's the point of creating tables this way? Well, you can name those rows and cells, and then manage then in the code-behind using C#. In all honesty, though, that's not how I recommend doing things.

Tables are good for two things — layout and tabular data. Layout has been superseded by CSS. I recommend you use CSS to lay things out.

For tabular data, tables still work. However, there is a more interesting solution. The GridView (found in the Data section of the Toolbox) is just as functional — and it is bindable. We chat more about that in the Binding section later.

Getting Some Input from the User

Acquiring input from the user is one of the most significant processes that Web developers do. Data-active Web is all about interactivity; Web 2.0 is all about interactivity. Getting information from a user is job one.

You can do a lot of things to get input from the user, but there is a subset of the controls that is generally considered to be "User Input." You'll use those controls a lot.

Using text input controls

The most obvious form of collecting data from a user is the text input boxes, as shown in Figure 3-2. In HTML there are three defined controls: the `textbox`, the `password`, and the `textarea`. The `TextBox` ASP.NET control handles all of those. A `TextMode` property tells IIS how to render the control.

To use the `TextBox` control, drag it into the designer from the Toolbox. We can change the property of the control instance — the only other significant element — in the ASP.NET markup, the property panel, or the C# code.

The properties that we are the most interested in include:

- **ID:** The name that you use to reference the control in the C# code. This needs to be set first, before you can use the control.

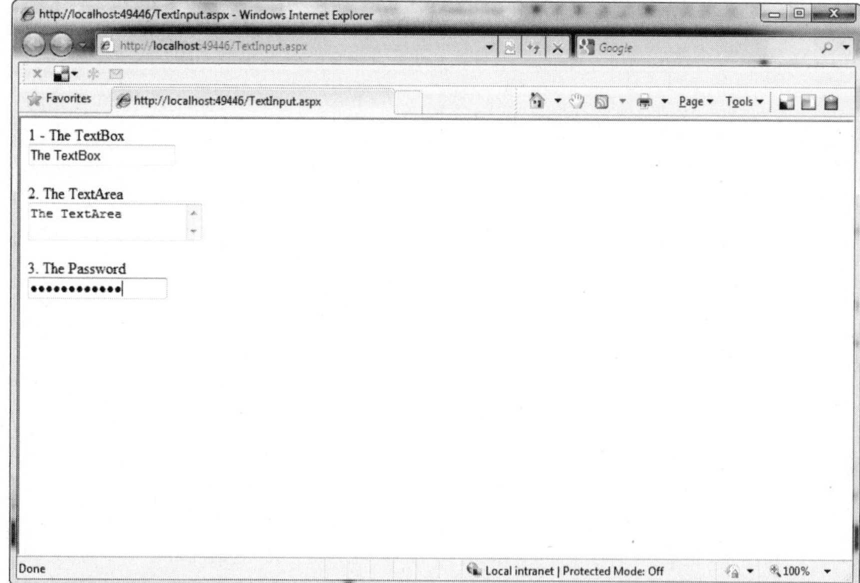

Figure 3-2: The three text inputs, all in a row.

- **TextMode:** This determines the type of text box that gets rendered, as I mentioned.
- **MaxLength:** The maximum number of characters that the user can type in the field. Note that this doesn't work when the TextMode is defined as TextArea.
- **Height and Width:** The size that the text box appears on the page.
- **CssClass:** The style sheet class that the control will be rendered to use. Must be used in conjunction with a style sheet.
- **Enabled:** Marks if the field can be typed in by the user.

In the example in Figure 3-1, I just dragged the `TextBox` control onto the designer three times and set each to the three different `TextModes`. Here is the resultant ASP.NET markup:

```
<%@ Page Language="C#" AutoEventWireup="true" CodeBehind="TextInput.aspx.cs"
    Inherits="Chapter_3.WebForm1" %>

<!DOCTYPE html PUBLIC "-//W3C//DTD XHTML 1.0 Transitional//EN" "http://www.
    w3.org/TR/xhtml1/DTD/xhtml1-transitional.dtd">

<html xmlns="http://www.w3.org/1999/xhtml" >
<head runat="server">
    <title></title>
</head>
<body>
    <form id="form1" runat="server">
    <div>
```

```
        1 - The TextBox<br />
        <asp:TextBox ID="TextBox1" runat="server">The TextBox</asp:TextBox>
        <br />
        <br />
        2. The TextArea<br />
        <asp:TextBox ID="TextBox2" runat="server" TextMode="MultiLine">The
    TextArea</asp:TextBox>
        <br />
        <br />
        3. The Password<br />
        <asp:TextBox ID="TextBox3" runat="server" TextMode="Password">The
    Password</asp:TextBox>

    </div>
    </form>
</body>
</html>
```

In order to set properties in the C# code, I would refer to the ID, as set in the property panel. If you use the defaults (don't do this in real code, make real names for controls), configuring the first text box might look something like this:

```
public partial class WebForm1 : System.Web.UI.Page
{
    protected void Page_Load(object sender, EventArgs e)
    {
        TextBox1.MaxLength = 20;
        TextBox1.Height = 22;
        TextBox1.Width = 135;
        TextBox1.Enabled = true;
    }
}
```

Using single-item selection controls

After collecting text, the next most common user-input gathering operation is asking them to choose an item from a list. In HTML, you can do this with check boxes, radio buttons, or drop-down lists. (See Figure 3-3.)

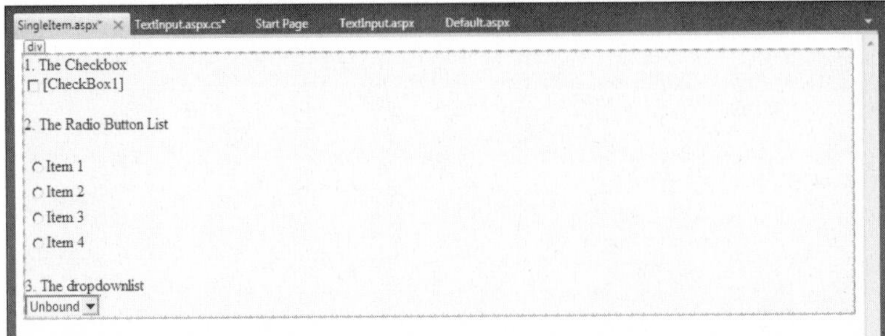

Figure 3-3: The single selectors.

ASP.NET provides for all of these items:

- **The Boolean check box:** This is just one single check box where the answer is Yes or No. This is still considered a single item selection even though there is only one item to select from and is usually used to represent a Boolean or bit in the C# code. It is represented by the `checkbox` control.
- **The radio button list:** Radio buttons are nice because they prevent the user from selecting more than one option while seeing all the options. Lists are an interesting beast, because they can be bound to collections. We cover that in the next section, "Binding." This control is `radiobuttonlist`.
- **The drop-down list:** Represented by the `dropdownlist` control, this type of list allows the user to click to see the list, and then click one item, which then closes the list. It can also be bound to a collection.

Here is the code for all three. Note that both the `dropdownlist` and the `radiobuttonlist` use the `listitem` control to render the list items.

```
<%@ Page Language="C#" AutoEventWireup="true" CodeBehind="SingleItem.aspx.cs"
    Inherits="Chapter_3.SingleItem" %>

<!DOCTYPE html PUBLIC "-//W3C//DTD XHTML 1.0 Transitional//EN" "http://www.
    w3.org/TR/xhtml1/DTD/xhtml1-transitional.dtd">

<html xmlns="http://www.w3.org/1999/xhtml" >
<head runat="server">
    <title></title>
</head>
<body>
    <form id="form1" runat="server">
    <div>

        1. The Checkbox<br />
        <asp:CheckBox ID="CheckBox1" runat="server" />
        <br />
        <br />
        2. The Radio Button List<br />
        <asp:RadioButtonList ID="RadioButtonList1" runat="server">
            <asp:ListItem>Item 1</asp:ListItem>
            <asp:ListItem>Item 2</asp:ListItem>
            <asp:ListItem>Item 3</asp:ListItem>
            <asp:ListItem>Item 4</asp:ListItem>
        </asp:RadioButtonList>
        <br />
        3. The dropdownlist<br />
        <asp:DropDownList ID="DropDownList1" runat="server">
            <asp:ListItem>Item 1</asp:ListItem>
            <asp:ListItem>Item 2</asp:ListItem>
            <asp:ListItem>Item 3</asp:ListItem>
            <asp:ListItem>Item 4</asp:ListItem>
        </asp:DropDownList>

    </div>
    </form>
</body>
</html>
```

Using multiple-item selection controls

Sometimes you want the user to be able to choose more than one of the items available in a list. HTML has two controls that handle that: the `listbox` and the `checkbox list`. (See Figure 3-4.)

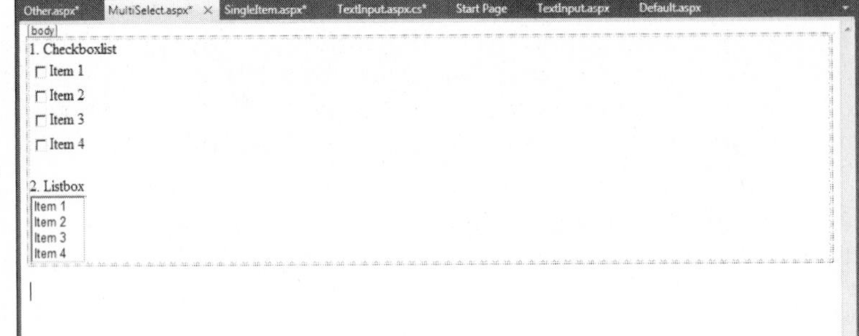

Figure 3-4: Controls for multiple selections.

ASP.NET replicates these, like this:

- **The `listbox`:** This list is a lot like a `dropdownlist`, except there is no expansion required — you see the expanded list right away, scroll bar and all. To select more than one item, the user is usually required to hold down the control or command key while clicking.
- **The `checkboxlist`:** This is exactly what it sounds like: a list of check boxes. It looks just like a radio button list, except with check boxes. You can see what I mean in Figure 3-4.

Here is the code for these. As with the `dropdownlist`, the `listitem` is used to show the items. If it were databound, the `listitems` would not be there — they would just be rendered from the data source at runtime.

```
<html xmlns="http://www.w3.org/1999/xhtml" >
<head runat="server">
    <title></title>
</head>
<body>
    <form id="form1" runat="server">
    <div>

        1. Checkboxlist<br />
        <asp:CheckBoxList ID="CheckBoxList1" runat="server">
            <asp:ListItem>Item 1</asp:ListItem>
            <asp:ListItem>Item 2</asp:ListItem>
            <asp:ListItem>Item 3</asp:ListItem>
            <asp:ListItem>Item 4</asp:ListItem>
        </asp:CheckBoxList>
        <br />
```

```
        2. Listbox<br />
        <asp:ListBox ID="ListBox1" runat="server">
            <asp:ListItem>Item 1</asp:ListItem>
            <asp:ListItem>Item 2</asp:ListItem>
            <asp:ListItem>Item 3</asp:ListItem>
            <asp:ListItem>Item 4</asp:ListItem>
        </asp:ListBox>

    </div>
    </form>
</body>
</html>
```

Using other kinds of input controls

ASP.NET provides a number of other input types that are combinations of the above, or are nontraditional inputs. (See Figure 3-5.) They are all special-use controls, but they need to be in your toolbox so you can use them when the need arises.

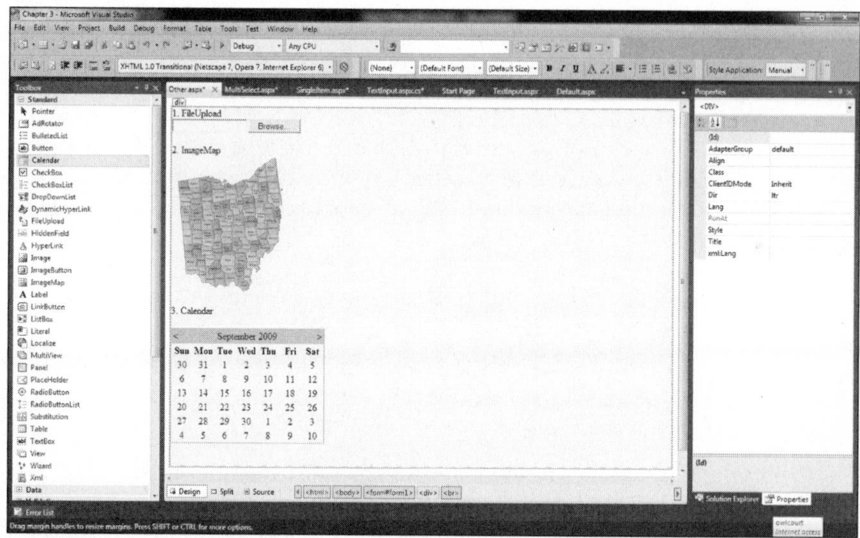

Figure 3-5: The stragglers.

They include the following input types:

- **FileUpload:** The FileUpload does exactly what it says. It creates an HTML input of type `File` and makes the form *enctype* (encoding type) into multipart form-data. This allows the Web server to accept a long stream of binary data, which you can then capture with a streamreader.
- **Imagemaps:** Imagemaps are nearly relics of a bygone era. Essentially, they allow you to mark off pixel by pixel maps on top of images and then assign regions within those maps to URLs or other actions.

This control assists you by giving you the framework. You still have to provide the map. Now, usually people use separate images.

✦ **Calendars:** The calendar control is just a textbox that helps the user format dates properly. It works well. There are a ton of formatting options, too — check them out in the property panel.

There are others. I might have covered all the things you will see in the ToolBox, but there is a lot more out there. What you need to remember are the basics — they are visible controls with ASP.NET implementations and HTML output. You can use the property panel, the markup, or the C# code to change the properties. And you can bind them to objects in your code — which we discuss later in this chapter.

Submitting input with Submit buttons

After you get all this input into a form, you need the user to send it to you. The basic way to do this is through the Submit button.

In Chapter 1, I talk about the PostBack event, and how Microsoft used JavaScript to change the way the posting of forms back to the server works. The Submit button is how one does this.

Let's be clear — *any* control can cause a postback. If you set an event handler for an event in a control, it will cause a postback. You can save off the form data at any point once it gets back to the server. We use the Submit button because it is what the user is used to.

The ASP.NET default controls have three buttons.

✦ `Button` is just what it says — an input of type submitted in HTML.

✦ `ImageButton` is a button control that has a built-in src property for images.

✦ `LinkButton` just shows an HTML anchor and treats it like a button.

We use one of these for nearly every page where we accept user input. Most of the time, the users expect it.

Data Binding

Getting the data into a control in a Web page isn't enough. There needs to be some way to *persist* (save for reuse) that information after the data is entered. Data binding is the answer.

Data binding tells a control what member of the underlying class to get its data from. For instance, if you have a collection of `Apple` objects with a property of `Color` that you want to show in a text box, you can bind the value `Apple.Color` to the `Text` property.

But things get more interesting than that. Let's say that you want to provide a list of colors and allow the user to select the color of the object in question. You can do that by binding the list of a collection and the selected value to the `SelectedItem` property of the list control. If you want to show the color itself, you can bind to the `FontColor` property of a text control.

Setting up your markup for binding

Back in the Active Server Page days, you put all your data on the page by simply printing it there. Sounds simple but it had a lot of problems. Foremost, your form had to have a lot of knowledge about the data it was showing. This is a bad thing. Anyway, the format for doing it was

```
<%= ThisIsWhatIWantToPrint %>
```

If you needed a list, you looped in the surrounding code. If you needed a method result, you just put the method right in there. What you saw was what you got.

Data binding is the more enlightened form of getting data on the screen. The controls that are built into ASP.NET know how to handle data on their own, so long as that data meets some basic specifics.

Data binding is accomplished by setting a property of a control to a member of the underlying class. For a single control, like a text box, you just set the property in question, like this:

```
<asp:Label ID="Label1" runat="server" Text='<%#
   IAmBindingToThisVariable %>' />
```

If you are binding to a repeating control, like a Grid or a ListBox, then you set the DataSource property. I show you how to do that in the next section, "Bindings in code."

The variables you are binding to need to be in the code-behind, and be public. If they aren't, you will get runtime errors. That's also why binding in the code is a good idea, which we do in the next section.

Right now, let's talk binding in the markup. Here's all you need to do to set up your markup for binding:

1. **In the Chapter 3 Web project that we have been adding pages with controls to, right-click and choose Add New and then Class.**

   I named my class Show.

2. **Click OK, and then put this simple data class in there.** This class is just for example — it could be a database or a data class or an Entity Framework model.

```
using System;

namespace Chapter_3
{
    public class Show
    {
        public int ID { get; set; }
        public String ShowTitle { get; set; }
        public String EpisodeTitle { get; set; }
        public DateTime ScheduledTime { get; set; }
        public int Channel { get; set; }
    }
}
```

3. **Open the `Text.aspx` file in the Chapter 3 project.**

4. **Double-click the design surface to get to the code-behind.**

   If any code already appears in the `Page.Load`, you can delete it.

5. **Add code to the `Page.Load` to make a mock Show object.**

   In a real project, you would get this object from the database or the service layer. For this example, I just use mock code:

```
        Show show = new Show { ID = 1, Channel = 5,
EpisodeTitle = "ASP.NET Databinding", ScheduledTime
= new DateTime(2009, 4, 12, 12, 0, 0), ShowTitle =
"The C# Show" };
```

6. **We need to tell the page that we are going to be data binding. Add a `Page.DataBind()` call at the end of the Page_Load.**

   The finished method looks like this:

```
    protected void Page_Load(object sender, EventArgs e)
    {
        Show show = new Show { ID = 1, Channel = 5, EpisodeTitle =
"ASP.NET Databinding", ScheduledTime = new DateTime(2009, 4, 12, 12,
0, 0), ShowTitle = "The C# Show" };
        Page.DataBind();
    }
```

7. **Change to the markup in the designer.**

8. **The Text field gets the markup for the binding. We can just give it the property, like this:**

```
<asp:Label ID="Label1" runat="server" Text='<%# show.EpisodeTitle %>'></
    asp:Label>
```

This isn't the interesting way to bind things. It is nice because you can edit the binding without recompiling but the interesting way is in the C# code. Doing it in the C# code is much more readable and manageable. There are times to use each, but this is a C# book. The least we can do is to focus on the code-behind, right?

Data binding using the code-behind

Rather than set a property directly in the markup, we can set it equal to a value in the code-behind. For a repeating control, we can set a `DataSource` property in the C# code for the control. Then, when we bind the page, it uses that value to load in the right value or values from the code-behind.

Keep in mind, though, that with the `Text` property of a Label (for instance) this just simple data binding. I am just setting a value.

Let's try it with the earlier example. Just follow these steps:

1. **Keep the label text simple — just drop the `Text` property, like this:**

```
<%@ Page Language="C#" AutoEventWireup="true" CodeBehind="Text.aspx.cs"
    Inherits="Chapter_3.Text" %>

<!DOCTYPE html PUBLIC "-//W3C//DTD XHTML 1.0 Transitional//EN" "http://
    www.w3.org/TR/xhtml1/DTD/xhtml1-transitional.dtd">

<html xmlns="http://www.w3.org/1999/xhtml" >
<head runat="server">
    <title></title>
</head>
<body>
    <form id="form1" runat="server">
    <div>

        This is some text.<br />
        <asp:Label ID="Label1" runat="server" />

    </div>
    </form>
</body>
</html>
```

2. **In the code-behind, set the `Text` property equal to the property on the control that you want to bind to.**

   Notice that there is no `DataBind` command for the page:

```
using System;
using System.Collections.Generic;
using System.Linq;
using System.Web;
using System.Web.UI;
using System.Web.UI.WebControls;
```

```
namespace Chapter_3
{
    public partial class Text : System.Web.UI.Page
    {
        public Show show;
        protected void Page_Load(object sender, EventArgs e)
        {
            show = new Show { ID = 1, Channel = 5, EpisodeTitle = "ASP.
NET Databinding", ScheduledTime = new DateTime(2009, 4, 12, 12, 0,
0), ShowTitle = "The C# Show" };
            Label1.Text = show.EpisodeTitle;
        }
    }
}
```

3. **Run the application to see the value get set.**

This works well, but remember, this is only simple data binding. It's just setting values. Full data binding is for controls with repeating properties.

Using commonly bound controls

After all this label stuff, let's talk about what data binding is really good for — collections. Data binding is great for dealing with groups of items, bound to repeating structures in HTML.

The typical example of data binding is the DataGrid control. If everything is set up correctly, you have remarkable control over how the grid looks. If things aren't named correctly, you still have the option to show all of the data in a default style. So let's get started. To create a databound grid, follow these steps:

1. **Add a new ASPX file to the projects called** `Grid.aspx`**.**
2. **Change to design view.**
3. **Open the Data section of the Toolbox and drag a GridView onto the design surface.**
4. **Double-click the design surface to change to Code View and get a page load event handler.**
5. **Make a mock collection of** `Shows` **in the page load event handler. I used a generic list of** `Show`**.**

```
List<Show> shows = new List<Show>();
protected void Page_Load(object sender, EventArgs e)
        {
            shows.Add(new Show { ID = 1, Channel = 5, EpisodeTitle =
"ASP.NET Databinding", ScheduledTime = new DateTime(2009, 4, 12, 12,
0, 0), ShowTitle = "The C# Show" });
            shows.Add(new Show { ID = 2, Channel = 5, EpisodeTitle =
"ASP.NET Styling", ScheduledTime = new DateTime(2009, 4, 12, 13, 0,
0), ShowTitle = "The C# Show" });
            shows.Add(new Show { ID = 3, Channel = 8, EpisodeTitle =
"Inheritance", ScheduledTime = new DateTime(2009, 4, 16, 9, 0, 0),
ShowTitle = "Learning C#" });
```

```
        shows.Add(new Show { ID = 4, Channel = 8, EpisodeTitle =
"Partial Classes", ScheduledTime = new DateTime(2009, 4, 17, 9, 0,
0), ShowTitle = "Learning C#" });
        shows.Add(new Show { ID = 5, Channel = 8, EpisodeTitle =
"Operator Overloading", ScheduledTime = new DateTime(2009, 4, 18, 9,
0, 0), ShowTitle = "Learning C#" });
    }
```

6. **Add the datasource and the databind commands at the bottom of the page load.**

   I have bolded the lines that I added in the code:

```
    List<Show> shows = new List<Show>();
    protected void Page_Load(object sender, EventArgs e)
    {
        shows.Add(new Show { ID = 1, Channel = 5, EpisodeTitle =
"ASP.NET Databinding", ScheduledTime = new DateTime(2009, 4, 12, 12,
0, 0), ShowTitle = "The C# Show" });
        shows.Add(new Show { ID = 2, Channel = 5, EpisodeTitle =
"ASP.NET Styling", ScheduledTime = new DateTime(2009, 4, 12, 13, 0,
0), ShowTitle = "The C# Show" });
        shows.Add(new Show { ID = 3, Channel = 8, EpisodeTitle =
"Inheritance", ScheduledTime = new DateTime(2009, 4, 16, 9, 0, 0),
ShowTitle = "Learning C#" });
        shows.Add(new Show { ID = 4, Channel = 8, EpisodeTitle =
"Partial Classes", ScheduledTime = new DateTime(2009, 4, 17, 9, 0,
0), ShowTitle = "Learning C#" });
        shows.Add(new Show { ID = 5, Channel = 8, EpisodeTitle =
"Operator Overloading", ScheduledTime = new DateTime(2009, 4, 18, 9,
0, 0), ShowTitle = "Learning C#" });

        GridView1.DataSource = shows;
        Page.DataBind();
    }
```

7. **Press <F5> to see the application run.**

   As you can see in Figure 3-6, the columns from the database are all automatically bound to the HTML grid.

That's all well and good, but what if you don't want to show the ID, or want to put the columns someplace more to your liking? You can do that, too; it just takes a little more effort.

The capability of the gridview to automatically show all columns in a table is handled by a property: `AutoGenerateColumns`. The first thing we need to do is set that to `False`. This tells ASP.NET that we are going to set all of the columns by hand.

Next, we have to tell C# what columns we are using. This can be done in the ASP.NET code, but this is a C# book. Let's do it in the C# code.

We need to add two columns to the grid — let's say Channel and Episode. In order to do this, we need to define and set up two `BoundColumn` objects. Then we need to add them to the grid. That's what happens under the sheets when we add a `datacolumn` tag in the markup.

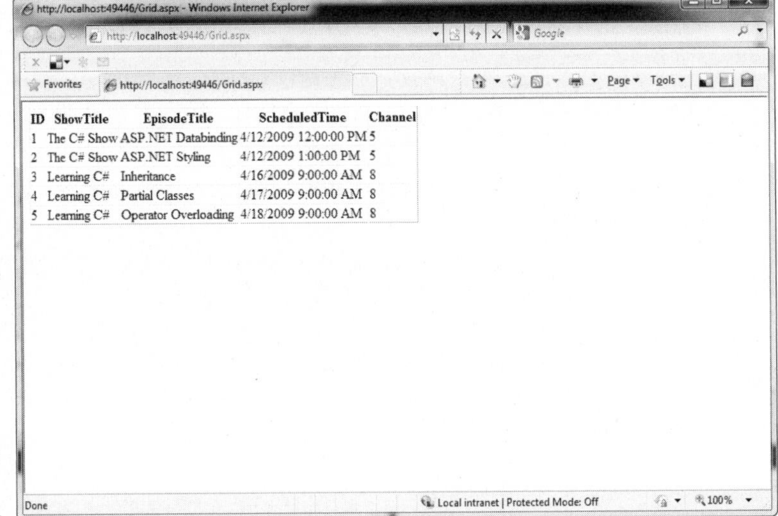

Figure 3-6: The TV schedule! Columns here are bound to the grid.

Here's the resulting markup. I bolded the lines of code that I added to the page load event handler:

```
List<Show> shows = new List<Show>();
protected void Page_Load(object sender, EventArgs e)
{
    shows.Add(new Show { ID = 1, Channel = 5, EpisodeTitle = "ASP.NET 
Databinding", ScheduledTime = new DateTime(2009, 4, 12, 12, 0, 0), ShowTitle 
= "The C# Show" });
    shows.Add(new Show { ID = 2, Channel = 5, EpisodeTitle = "ASP.NET 
Styling", ScheduledTime = new DateTime(2009, 4, 12, 13, 0, 0), ShowTitle = 
"The C# Show" });
    shows.Add(new Show { ID = 3, Channel = 8, EpisodeTitle = 
"Inheritance", ScheduledTime = new DateTime(2009, 4, 16, 9, 0, 0), ShowTitle 
= "Learning C#" });
    shows.Add(new Show { ID = 4, Channel = 8, EpisodeTitle = "Partial 
Classes", ScheduledTime = new DateTime(2009, 4, 17, 9, 0, 0), ShowTitle = 
"Learning C#" });
    shows.Add(new Show { ID = 5, Channel = 8, EpisodeTitle = "Operator 
Overloading", ScheduledTime = new DateTime(2009, 4, 18, 9, 0, 0), ShowTitle 
= "Learning C#" });

    GridView1.DataSource = shows;
    GridView1.AutoGenerateColumns = false;

    BoundField channelColumn = new BoundField();
    channelColumn.DataField = "Channel";
    channelColumn.HeaderText = "Channel";
    GridView1.Columns.Add(channelColumn);

    BoundField episodeColumn = new BoundField();
    episodeColumn.DataField = "EpisodeTitle";
    episodeColumn.HeaderText = "Episode";
    GridView1.Columns.Add(episodeColumn);

    Page.DataBind();
}
```

Styling Your Controls

When you have the data in your controls, you need to get the control looking a certain way. There are a lot of options here. All the controls come with properties that can be set at design time and at runtime, or bound to cascading style sheets (CSS).

Being able to style is necessary; being able to manage the styles at runtime with C# is darn near magic. Using a combination of the three methods makes it possible to create dynamic applications that give the user the best experiences.

Setting control properties

By far, the simplest way to set style on a control is to use the built-in properties. It is straightforward, you know exactly what you are applying a look to, and IntelliSense helps you do so.

Notice I didn't say it was the "best" way to do styles. I said it was the simplest.

Setting control properties has a host of problems. If you have more than one control to set up, you have to set the properties on each of them — even if they are the same. The runtime has to handle a lot of extra stuff. Also, it makes your code messy.

Sometimes, though, you need to set a style this way. The best way to see them all is to check out the Properties panel. Set it to Categorized, and look the bottom, as shown in Figure 3-7. If you actually set properties here, they will be in the markup like the below example, not the code-behind, but you can at least find the names here.

```
<asp:GridView ID="GridView1" runat="server"
     onselectedindexchanged="GridView1_SelectedIndexChanged">
    <RowStyle BackColor="#FF6666" />
</asp:GridView>
```

After you get the name of something you want to set, you just set it like any other property:

```
GridView1.RowStyle.BackColor = System.Drawing.Color.Red;
```

The roughest part is discovering what framework element that the style will want as a value. The easiest way to determine this is to type the part to the left of the equal sign, and then mouse over the property to see how it is declared. `BackColor`, for instance, requires a `System.Drawing.Color` element. When I discovered that, I knew where to go to get the value.

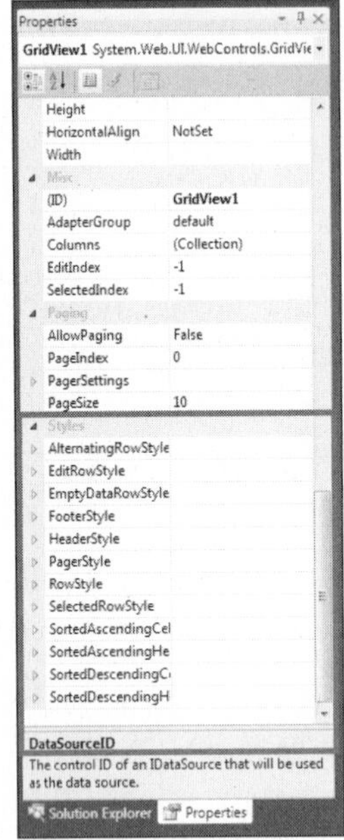

Figure 3-7: Styles in the Properties panel.

Binding styles with CSS

Because we are in a Web application, using Cascading Style Sheets (CSS) seems like a good approach to handle our styles. Nearly every control in ASP.NET has a property — `CssClass` — that takes advantage of the styles loaded as part of the project.

To get started, you need a few CSS classes, which are not the same as .NET classes. A class in CSS is a collection of styles that can be connected to a collection of markup, so as to match the properties that can be matched between them. To bind styles with CSS, follow these steps:

1. **Right-click the project and select Add New.**
2. **Select Style Sheet from the dialog box.**

   I named mine **Chapter3.css**.
3. **When the style sheet comes up, right-click the CSS Outline and select Add Style Rule.**
4. **In the element dialog box, select Class Name and type** GridViews **in the text box.**
5. **Click the right arrow button as shown in Figure 3-8.**
6. **Press OK, and notice the new entry in the style sheet.**

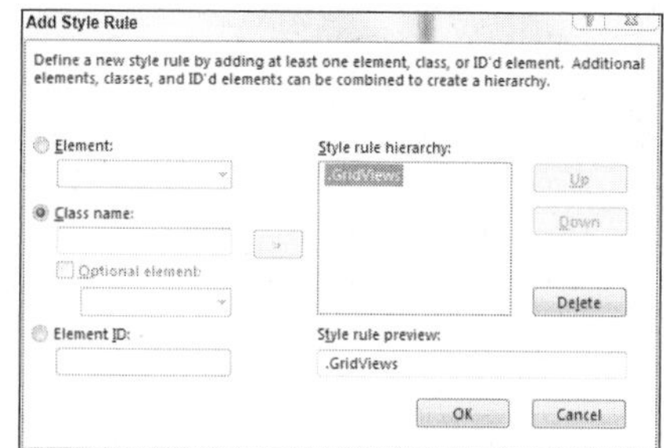

Figure 3-8: Adding a style sheet class.

Just for demonstration, I added a few things to the style sheet.

```
body
{
}
.GridView
{
   font-family:French Script MT;
   background-color: Fuchsia;
}
```

To bind this to the control, we use the `CssStyle` property, which accepts the class in the CSS file. Link the CSS file to the page in question in the page markup first, using the "link" snippet in the ASP.NET markup (remember to put it in the `<head>` tag section).

In the code-behind, just set the CssStyle property like you would any other property, like this:

```
GridView1.CssStyle = "GridViews";
```

Making Sure the Site Is Accessible

When I say *accessible* here, I am not talking about the server being up. I am talking about making sure the controls you use are available to people who have disabilities, such as diminished senses of sight, hearing, or touch. Such people have a different browsing experience than you or I.

Microsoft has made a significant investment in accessible Web browsing, and you'll be pleased to find that most of the controls make good decisions about accessibility right out of the box. Understanding how to use them for this purpose takes a little effort, however.

If you are building Web sites for large enterprises or the government, Section 508 (an amendment to the Rehabilitation Act) makes this very important. Check out `www.section508.gov` for more information.

Control features for accessibility

Most ASP.NET controls, where applicable, fit a certain feature list for accessibility. The goal is to make coding for accessibility easy for the programmer and functional for the user.

- Any element that isn't made of text should have an alternate text option. For instance, all image tags support an `AlternateText` property, which populates the HTML `alt` tag. Web-to-text readers will "speak" the contents of this tag in place of the image. If you add an Image to a Web page, Visual Studio even prompts you for the alternate text.
- Controls don't require the use of style sheets or color dependency. If you wish, it is easy to strip all style information from a page for simplicity of use by a reader or a low-sight version of the application.
- All input controls in Getting Input from the User support a `TabIndex` property, which allows users to tab from control to control. For those not using a mouse, this is optimum.
- Setting which part of the form has the cursor by default (called *default focus*) is easy in ASP.NET with the DefaultFocus property. Changing it is easy with the `SetFocus` method.
- Buttons can get keyboard equivalents using the `AccessKey` property.
- Labels and input controls can be associated, which many Web readers depend on.

Design considerations

The principle design consideration for accessibility is to use the features. Set the alternate text. Use the tab indexing. Set a default focus. Make your application easy to use for everyone.

There is a new feature in Visual Studio 2010 called Check Page for Accessibility, which checks WCAG and Section 508 errors. If you use this feature, warnings will actually be posted to your build process.

Constructing User Controls

Have you ever been to a site with a three-part U.S. phone number shown as three textboxes? You can usually automatically tab between them, and this structure makes sure you have exactly the right number of digits in each text box. That's something that you might very well use on every page of many applications, right?

That phone number control consists of things that we already have around us: text box controls, client-side scripting, and validation. All that you need is to put them together.

The technology that you use to combine existing controls in useful ways is called a User Control, or ASCX. ASCX is encapsulated, easy to create, and easier to use.

Making a new phone number user control

To show you what I mean, here I show you how to make my favorite user control, the Phone Number control. In this incarnation, it is only good for U.S. format, but that's okay. It gets the point across. Just follow these steps to create a phone number control:

1. **In the Web project we have been using in this chapter, right-click the project file, and choose Add⇨New Item.**
2. **Select Web User Control. (See Figure 3-9.)**

   I named it PhoneNumber.ascx.

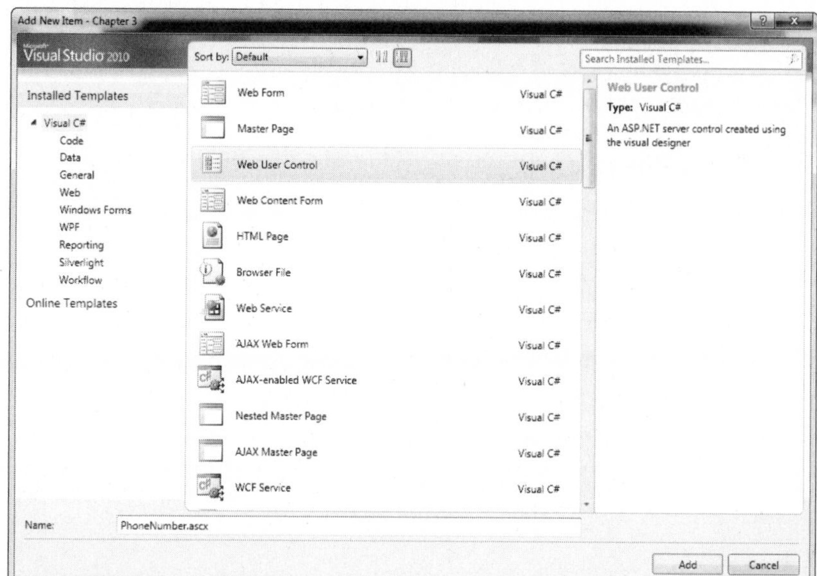

Figure 3-9: Adding the Phone Number control.

3. **Switch to Design view.**
4. **Drag three text boxes to the designer, next to one another. If you want to get fancy, put hyphens between them.**
5. **In the Properties panel, set the MaxLength for the first two text boxes to 3 and the last one to 4. This prevents the user from putting too many characters in a field.**

6. **Right-click the designer and select View Code.**
7. **Add a property to the code-behind that allows a page using the control to get to the phone number.**

   The goal is to get all the content from the controls, patch it together, format it, and deliver it as a public property. Here is the code:

   ```
   private string _phoneNumber;
   public string PhoneNumberValue
   {
       get
       {
           _phoneNumber = string.Format("({0}){1}-{2}");
           return _phoneNumber;
       }
   }
   ```

So now we have a control — just like the controls in the Toolbox — that accepts a phone number in pieces and formats it nicely. Let's play with it.

Using your new control

You'll love using this control. It really does work just like a Toolbox control. Follow these steps to see how it works:

1. **Right-click on the project, and add a new Web file.**

   I named mine **UseThePhoneNumber.aspx**.
2. **Change to the design view.**
3. **Drag the ascx control right from the Solution Explorer onto the design surface.**

   Ta da! The control shows up just like a plain text box would, but it is just like we formatted it. Check out Figure 3-10.

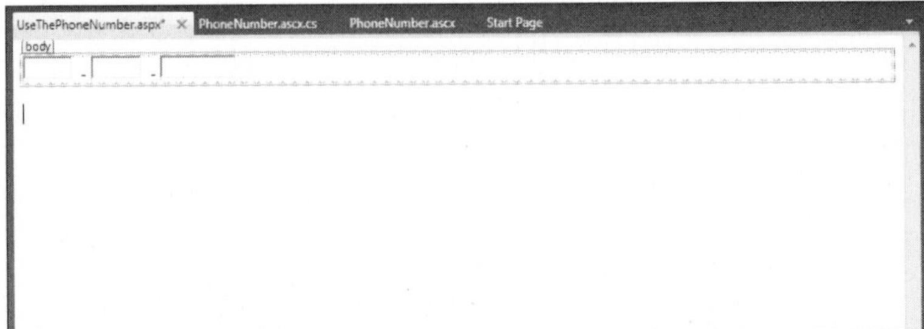

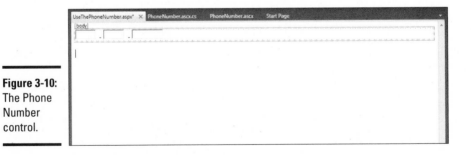

Figure 3-10: The Phone Number control.

4. **Add a label and a button to the form. Try to fill out the control, click the button, and see the formatted phone number.**

5. **Double-click the button to get an event handler for the click event. Add some code to populate the label on the button click, like this:**

```
using System;
using System.Collections.Generic;
using System.Linq;
using System.Web;
using System.Web.UI;
using System.Web.UI.WebControls;

namespace Chapter_3
{
    public partial class UseThePhoneNumber : System.Web.UI.Page
    {
        protected void Button1_Click(object sender, EventArgs e)
        {
            Label1.Text = PhoneNumber1.PhoneNumberValue;
        }
    }
}
```

6. **Right-click on the ASPX page and set it as the start page.**
7. **Press <F5> and run the application. Enter a phone number in the control and click the button.**

   The formatted phone number should appear in the label.

This is a boring example, but you can see how this can be used to collect commonly used fields together for reuse in an application. Order details, addresses, and map coordinates, among other types of information, all are usually grouped together and make great user controls. In a travel application I recently worked on, the start city and date and the end city and date became user controls. It's a great way to solve simple reuse problems.

Adding Custom Controls

Beyond the scope of a user control is a control that — perhaps — no one has thought of before. Maybe your company makes a device with a pressure gauge that you need to replicate in code. Or perhaps you need to display a unique set of patient statistics on a monitor, or demonstrate the running of some data engine.

Those kinds of controls call for the next level: *custom controls,* sometimes called *server controls.* A custom control is a Web control built using essentially the same tools that Microsoft used to build the controls that we have used throughout this chapter.

I won't fool you — building a server control is nontrivial. To get one started, you need a whole new project, not just a new file. The project type is a Server Control project, and it gives us a whole battery of code to start with, much like this:

```
using System;
using System.Collections.Generic;
using System.ComponentModel;
using System.Linq;
using System.Text;
using System.Web;
using System.Web.UI;
using System.Web.UI.WebControls;

namespace NewServerControl
{
    [DefaultProperty("Text")]
    [ToolboxData("<{0}:ServerControl1 runat=server></{0}:ServerControl1>")]
    public class ServerControl1 : WebControl
    {
        [Bindable(true)]
        [Category("Appearance")]
        [DefaultValue("")]
        [Localizable(true)]
        public string Text
        {
            get
            {
                String s = (String)ViewState["Text"];
                return ((s == null) ? "[" + this.ID + "]" : s);
            }

            set
            {
                ViewState["Text"] = value;
            }
        }

        protected override void RenderContents(HtmlTextWriter output)
        {
            output.Write(Text);
        }
    }
}
```

One property and one method appear in the default configuration. A server control is basically just text output to the screen. It causes markup, just like a Label control emits a set of `<span>` tags. If you want this control to emit a set of `<div>` tags, you just change the property `get` statement.

For more information about making good controls, search for Server Control in MSDN. There are a number of good articles, and anything from ASP.NET 2.0 or later works just fine.

Chapter 4: Leveraging the .NET Framework

In This Chapter

- **Working with the .NET Framework**
- **Dealing with requests**
- **Using ASP.NET security**
- **Using site maps**
- **Managing files and cookies**
- **Tracing and debugging**

Let's be clear about ASP.NET and the .NET Framework. They are different. ASP.NET has a dependency on the .NET Framework, but it is really defined as the collection of controls that are in Chapter 3, plus others. The .NET Framework brings a different set of tools.

The controls that are in ASP.NET are user experience focused — they focus on the way the user views the application. The tools that are in the Framework are transport focused — focused on passing information back and forth between client and the server. If you look at the `System.Web` namespace (which is where most of these bits are stored), you'll quickly see that most of the classes within start with "Http." There is a reason for that: HTTP is the transport protocol.

This is important because manipulating the information that goes back and forth between the client and the server is the first and best way to do anything off-trail in a Web application. Whenever the default condition of the control or the server or the client isn't exactly what you need, the first place you turn is the classes of the `System.Web` namespace.

Controls in ASP.NET and controls in the .NET Framework overlap quite a bit, but each group is distinct. You should always keep in mind which tools are at your disposal and how best to use them.

Surfing Web Streams

At its core, ASP.NET is about the sending and receiving of streams of text. The client sends requests in, and the server sends HTML out. Sometimes our application is the client, and sometimes it is the server. Classes in the `System.Web` namespace handle all these cases.

Note that these solutions, along with many others within the `System.Web` namespace, aren't exclusively related to ASP.NET Web sites. Other applications can sometimes make use of the goodness provided by `System.Web`, so consider carefully!

Intercepting the request

In a sudden fit of reasonable naming, Microsoft decided to name the object that has all the data from the client request: "Request." That person has since been fired.

There are a few different ways to look at a request, but we are concerned here with the current request, or the context request. Fortunately this is the default request in the ASP.NET space. You can "intercept" that request with ASP.NET. But let's back up.

Digging up the request data

Every time a user types in a URL or clicks a button, a request is issued. Requests are processed by the server, and you can access them through the current context.

Don't let the language fool you: All I mean by "current context" is the object set that ASP.NET gives you just for being there when the request is processed. In short, the class is called `HttpRequest`, and ASP.NET makes an instance and calls it `Request`. It is an instance of the `HttpRequest` class and is the `HttpContext.Request` property.

To create an environment to show you what I mean, set up a project with these steps:

1. **Create a new ASP.NET project.**

   I called mine **Chapter4**.
2. **Add a page called Request.aspx.**
3. **Right-click on the new Request.aspx page and set it as the start page.**
4. **Drag a button control onto the page in the designer.**
5. **Double-click the new button to get the Click event handler.**

6. **In the new `Button1_Click` method, add some code to flip through the Request object.**

```
protected void Button1_Click(object sender, EventArgs e)
{
    foreach (String requestInfo in Request.Form)
    {
        Debug.WriteLine(requestInfo);
    }
}
```

What we are doing here is just looking at the context returned by the request. It is just somewhere for us to put the debugger, really.

7. **Right-click on the `Debug` statement and resolve the System.Diagnostics reference.**

8. **In `Page_Load`, add more or less the same code, so we can see the difference between the original request and the postback.**

Notice the check for the postback statement.

```
protected void Page_Load(object sender, EventArgs e)
{
    if (!(Page.IsPostBack))
    {
        foreach (String requestInfo in Request.Form)
        {
            Debug.WriteLine(requestInfo);
        }
    }
}
```

9. **Put breakpoints next to the two `foreach` statements.**
10. **Press <F5> to run the application.**

When you run, before the Web application appears, the application breaks on the `foreach` in the `Page_Load` method. Put your mouse over the `Request` object there, and you'll see something like Figure 4-1. Notice that the `ContentLength` is 0 and the `HttpMethod` is GET. This is an initial URL-based request for a page.

Now press <F10> until the `Page_Load` event is over the Visual Studio returns control to your Web browser. Notice that the `Debug.WriteLine` statement is never called. Why? `ContentLength` is 0. There is no Form. (Kinda like "There is no spoon.") The content is empty, because it is an initial request. The Form collection is empty. Nothing is there except the basic request information.

Press the button when the browser comes back. Visual Studio breaks again on the other `foreach` statement in the `Button1_Click` method. Put your mouse over the `Request` object again. Note the Form collection, shown in Figure 4-2. There are three items in it, the two hidden fields added by ASP. NET and the button that we added, Button1.

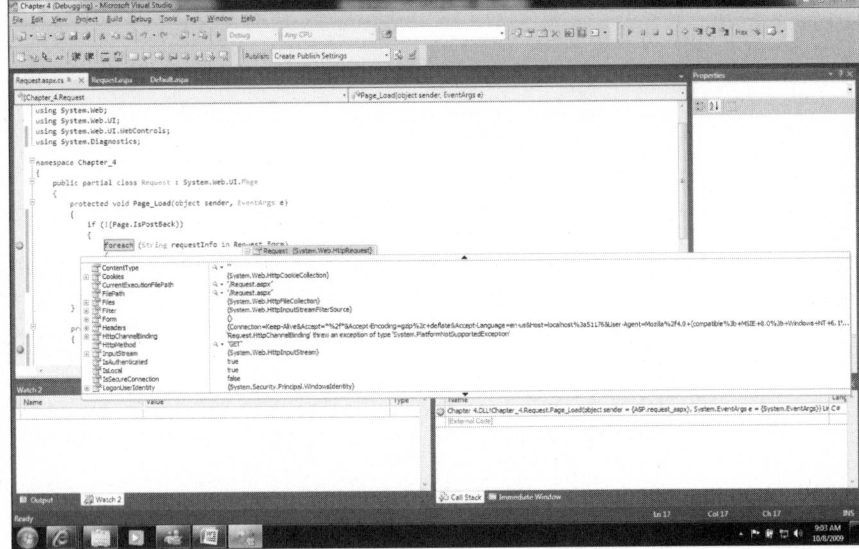

Figure 4-1: The initial request.

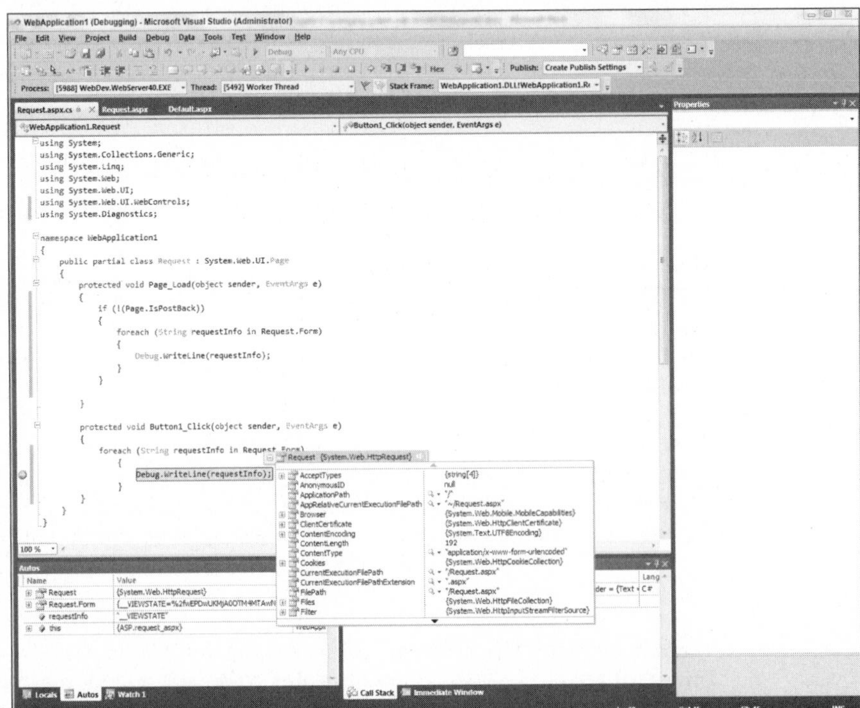

Figure 4-2: The form request.

This is the second type of request — the POST. It is in response to a form. This is where a lot useful information can be found.

Using information from requests

The request is a place that you can collect information about the user's needs, and use it. Especially on postback (though not just then), there is a lot of information that you can use, including the following:

- **The content of the request.** The type (ContentType) of the request tells us if it has data or just text. I can learn if it is ISO or Unicode (ContentEncoding). I also know how long the request is (ContentLength).
- **The text of the request itself.** For instance, I have all the text of the URL (Url) and the request before this one (UrlReferrer). If I just want the querystring (the part after the question mark), I can get it with QueryString.
- **Whether the user is logged into a domain (IsAuthenticated) and if so, who the user is (LogonUserIdentity).**
- **Access to the Cookies collection (Cookies).**

When you have access to the request, you can make decisions about content. If you need to know about their login information, you have it. Check a cookie — no problem. Confirm the querystring. Whatever needs to be done. You get information to the business layer, get what you need back, compose the new page of controls, and then need to modify the response. That's when you need the `HttpResponse` class.

Altering content sent to clients

ASP.NET and IIS do a good job of setting up markup for a client browser. You can even tell Visual Studio that you are targeting a certain browser (say, in a workgroup environment), and it will tweak the HTML it sends to the client to make it closer to the exact implementation of the HTML standard that browser supports.

You sometimes need to change the way the page is rendered on the client. More often, you need to change the way the metadata about the page is handed to the client. An HTML page has a lot more than the values you see on the screen. `HttpResponse` helps you to manage what you can and can't see.

Sending the user somewhere else

One of the most common uses of the `Response` object is to send the user somewhere else entirely. If you look at the request headers and realize (for instance) that the user isn't logged into a Windows domain account (using `HttpRequest.IsAuthenticated`), you can redirect the user to a login screen:

```
If(!Request.IsAuthenticated){
  Response.Redirect("login.aspx");
}
```

On the other hand, sometimes you need to tell the user that this isn't the right place to be at all. Especially useful if you have to change the structure of your Web site, `RedirectPermanently` tells search engine spiders "nope, this isn't here anymore. Go over there and change your index."

For instance, say you have a product line that was moved to a whole new URL. You could check the `QueryString` for the product line statement, and if you find it, redirect the link permanently.

```
If(Request.Querystring("ProductLineId")==4){
  Response.RedirectPermanently("http://newproduct.com")
}
```

Changing the request or response directly

Sometimes you just want to change things directly.

`Response.Write`, `Response.WriteFile`, and `Response.WriteSubstitution` all are designed to allow you to do just that. In the old days (before debugging), we had to use `Response.Write` to put errors into the HTML that we could view with ViewSource. If you are using MVC, there is still a place for that.

In today's development, `Response.Write` is mostly used to do something that you want to do on every page that meets a certain criteria, no matter who coded it. You can add it to the code-behind of the master page (more on that in Chapter 5) and know that the output stream of the site will be altered directly.

Securing with ASP.NET

Book III covers security, and there is a whole book on security that you should read — *Code Complete* by Steve McConnell. I'm only covering security in this chapter because the `AspNetHostingPermission` is in the `System.Web` namespace, and I want to give it a little airtime.

ASP.NET security is a complex topic. Because visitors to a Web site are anonymous, bypassing the Windows security system occurs often. That bypassing — called *impersonation* — allows IIS to do things on behalf of the user even if the user isn't really known to Windows. Remember, just because you have put in a username and password doesn't mean that Windows is okay with your credentials.

So ASP.NET Web sites are run most often with whatever permissions the IIS service is running with. Under normal conditions, this service is a fairly restricted account called Network Service. The fact is, however, that you really have no idea what the permissions will be because a hosting company most likely will be managing that. Your users can have administrative permissions for all you know.

You can purposefully restrict the permissions of your users in your code. This prevents someone from finding a way through your code logic to call a method you don't want them to be able to call.

Believe me, it happens.

The general idea is to trust no one, which I harp on in the Security chapter in Book III. You want to pretend that most people who are going to run your code are the enemy. I realize that isn't any fun. But it is necessary today. There are pre-built scripts to break into Web pages — there doesn't even have to be a real person there to bust in.

The MSDN documentation states this:

"It is recommended that you set the level attribute of the trust configuration element to High for sites that are trusted. For sites that are not trusted, such as a Web server that hosts sites that run code from an external customer, it is recommended that you set the level attribute of the trust configuration element to Medium."

For the record, sites without a permission level set default to Full, which is obviously higher than either of those.

Changing trusts

To change the trust of a class, you want to decorate the class in the ASP.NET application with the hosting permission, like this:

```
using System;
using System.Web;
using System.Security.Permissions;

[AspNetHostingPermission(SecurityAction.Demand, Level=AspNetHostingPermissionLe
    vel.High)]
public class ApplicationClass
{
   //My Code is here.
}
```

So this code uses the High level. The others are None, Minimal, Low, Medium, and Unrestricted. Table 4-1 shows the general breakdown.

Table 4-1	ASP.NET Permission Levels
AspNetHostingPermissionLevel	*Description*
None	Can't get anywhere. Don't ask.
Minimal	The code can execute but it can't DO anything.
Low	You have read-only access to some restricted information, like the Request itself. Very rough.
Medium	More or less can look at anything — database, network, whatever. No write access.
High	Read/Write for any managed code, but can't run unmanaged (native) code.
Unrestricted	Full run of the box.

Fixing problems

The most common problem is the use of None or Minimal as a permission level. I don't even know why Microsoft offers these choices. If you set the class to Minimal, nothing can get to anything so far as I have been able to figure out. Stick to High for trusted environments, and Medium for shared servers.

Navigating with Site Maps

A *site map* is an XML file that assists Web design tools in formulating dynamic navigation. There has been a more interesting use for them recently, however. They are used by search engines for indexing your site better.

`Webmasters.bing.com` is a new Microsoft product that makes your suite more available to users of Bing. It uses the site map file to make your site more indexable. Check it out!

Search Engine Optimization is a big topic these days, and sitemaps can make your life a lot easier. Search engines have set up readers that check for the site map, and then use it to walk the file structure and make sure the links to the site are accurate.

Adding a site map

To make a site map, follow these steps:

1. **Right-click on the project and select Add New ... Item.**

2. **Select Site Map from the context menu, as shown in Figure 4-3.**

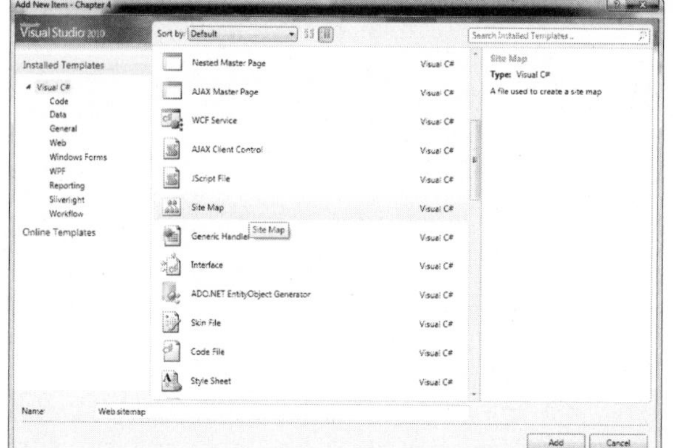

Figure 4-3: Adding a site map.

3. **Accept the default name, Web.SiteMap.**

   Visual Studio builds a template site map. Here is the default code:

```
<?xml version="1.0" encoding="utf-8" ?>
<siteMap xmlns="http://schemas.microsoft.com/AspNet/SiteMap-File-1.0" >
    <siteMapNode url="" title="" description="">
        <siteMapNode url="" title="" description="" />
        <siteMapNode url="" title="" description="" />
    </siteMapNode>
</siteMap>
```

   The template file shows you a guideline for adding the navigation of a site. If you have a number of files inside an About section, you make a SiteMapNode of About, and then inside it (before the closing **</sitemap-node>**), you add the pages in that section, like Contact Us or Our Story.

   For our example, though, there are no sectional divisions to the site. There are in Chapter 5. In this current case, we make it flat and play with that.

4. **Set up the site map for our three-page, flat structure, like this:**

```
<?xml version="1.0" encoding="utf-8" ?>
<siteMap xmlns="http://schemas.microsoft.com/AspNet/SiteMap-File-1.0" >
  <siteMapNode>
    <siteMapNode url="" title="" description="" />
    <siteMapNode url="" title="" description="" />
    <siteMapNode url="" title="" description="" />
  </siteMapNode>
</siteMap>
```

   Note that the SiteMapNode must be two layers deep, by specification.

5. **Add in the three page names and URLs, like this:**

```
<?xml version="1.0" encoding="utf-8" ?>
<siteMap xmlns="http://schemas.microsoft.com/AspNet/SiteMap-File-1.0" >
  <siteMapNode>
    <siteMapNode url="Cookies.aspx" title="Cookies"  description="Learn
     all about Cookies" />
    <siteMapNode url="Default.aspx" title="Home"  description="The main
     page" />
    <siteMapNode url="Request.aspx" title="Request"  description="Coding
     for the Request" />
  </siteMapNode>
</siteMap>
```

Navigating a site with SiteMap

With the `web.sitemap` file installed safely in the application, IIS now has a SiteMap collection that includes the XML file we made right there in memory. If you need to figure out what other pages are related to the page the user is viewing, you can do that. Follow these steps:

1. **Open up the Default.aspx page in the current project.**
2. **Drag an empty ListBox control into the page.**
3. **Go to Code View.**
4. **Loop through the items in the SiteMap collection, and add items to the listbox.**

```
using System;
using System.Collections.Generic;
using System.Linq;
using System.Web;
using System.Web.UI;
using System.Web.UI.WebControls;

namespace Chapter_4
{
    public partial class _Default : System.Web.UI.Page
    {
        protected void Page_Load(object sender, EventArgs e)
        {
            // Reference the parent node to keep the object model happy.
            string baseNode = SiteMap.CurrentNode.Title;

            // Check to make sure there are subpages.
            if (SiteMap.CurrentNode.HasChildNodes)
            {
                foreach (SiteMapNode sitemapKids in SiteMap.CurrentNode.
    ChildNodes)
                {
                    // Put the node name in the listbox.
                    ListBox1.Items.Add( new ListItem(sitemapKids.Title));
                }
            }

        }
    }
}
```

If you get interested, put a debugger in the loop, and check out that `SiteMap` object. It's a nice collection of the pages that have been referenced in the `Web.sitemap` file. Though this technology won't cure every navigational problem on every site, it is a nice, underused part of System.Web.

Managing Files

The forms collection contains all the data being sent back from the client. That includes any file that is being uploaded, using the multipart-data format.

ASP.NET uses a two-part plan to get file data to you. Keep in mind, you can do this all by hand, but this all goes back to the idea behind the ASP.NET model. Controls on the front end, System.Web stuff on the back end.

Let's start with the design view. All the user must do is select a local file and the browser handles encoding the file and sending it up to the server. The file encoding standard is built into the protocol, like HTML itself. Follow these steps to set up the upload:

1. **Create a new Web form in our Chapter 4 project called FileUpload.aspx.**
2. **Drag a FileUpload control from the Toolbox onto the design surface.**
3. **Drag a button onto the surface.**

   The button on the FileUpload control is just for selecting an item on your file system. We still need to postback the form.

   That gives us a good start. The FileUpload has a text box and a button that gives you access to the local file system. The button provides a submit function.

   All the magic happens on the back end for this example. The browser handles the file upload for us. The server is our responsibility.
4. **Double-click the submit button on the design surface to get the Button1_Click event handler.**
5. **Set up a path to save the file.**

```
protected void Button1_Click(object sender, EventArgs e)
{
    String localPath = Server.MapPath("~/UploadedFiles/");
}
```

6. **Add some code to the handler to check if there is a file in the form. The new code is in bold.**

```
protected void Button1_Click(object sender, EventArgs e)
{
    String localPath = Server.MapPath("~/UploadedFiles/");
    if (FileUpload1.HasFile)
    {
    }
}
```

7. **In the body of the** `if` **statement, have the FileUpload control help us save the file.**

   New code is in bold.

   ```
   protected void Button1_Click(object sender, EventArgs e)
   {
       String localPath = Server.MapPath("~/UploadedFiles/");
       if (FileUpload1.HasFile)
       {
           try
           {
               FileUpload1.PostedFile.SaveAs(localPath + FileUpload1.
       FileName);
           }
           catch (Exception ex)
           {
               Response.Write(ex.Message);
           }
       }
   }
   ```

   This is a nice feature. In the old days, we needed to wrangle the bytes themselves. Uphill both ways, in the snow.

To build a comprehensive file upload function, you need a little more stringent programming practices. (Like my error handling, for instance?) The idea here, though, is that there is a `FileUpload` control that gives us significant back-end control.

While we are here, take a look at the `HttpFileCollection`, which is the `System.Web` class that gives the `FileUpload` control its power. All the properties of the `FileUpload` control, like the file's bits, name, and all that, are in the `HttpFileCollection`. Check it out if you need more fine-grained control than the `FileUpload` control gives you.

Baking Cookies

Cookies are the only thing that a Web site can directly save on a client machine without the client's direct permission. It still requires the indirect permission, because a user can disable cookies, but passively a cookie can be saved without actually asking the user, "Is it okay if I save this?"

Cookies are useful for state management. If you know the ID of the client's shopping cart, for instance, you can save that ID in a cookie, and even if the client goes away for a week and comes back, you still will be able to go back to the business layer and look up the information.

Cookies are stored in a collection — actually a dictionary — of keys and values. If you know what you are looking for, you can query the collection for the value you want; if you don't, you can loop through the collection until you find it.

The cookies collection is managed using the Request and Response object — based on the `HttpRequest` and `HttpResponse` classes we cover earlier in this chapter.

Coding for client-side storage

To get a cookie, you have to first leave a cookie. In part of the response to a client — say, after they log in — you want to tell the platform to save information in the Cookies collection.

REMEMBER

Remember that cookies are plain text — anyone can read them. Never store something that can be used by someone wearing a proverbial black hat. I almost always create a `System.Guid` (a globally unique identifier) and use that to track information that I then persist somewhere in my back-end data store.

What is even better is to store information about the session itself and have an understanding that the information will be removed from the database after some time limit. This prevents the impersonation of the user by someone who intercepts the cookie. There are a lot of options, but check out the best practices offered by Microsoft and other organizations before setting up your cookie strategy.

If I want to store information about the session in the cookie, and tell the database that my customer is using that session, I generate a Guid and save it in both places. Then I can retrieve the cookie at the next request, compare it to the available Guids in the user collection, and find the user in question.

Here is an example of setting the cookie based on session information:

```
using System;
using System.Collections.Generic;
using System.Linq;
using System.Web;
using System.Web.UI;
using System.Web.UI.WebControls;

namespace Chapter_4
{
    public partial class Cookies : System.Web.UI.Page
    {
        WebUser currentUser = new WebUser();
        List<WebUser> usersInDatabase = new List<WebUser>();
        protected void Page_Load(object sender, EventArgs e)
        {
```

```
            if (!Page.IsPostBack)
            {
                //This is a first request, so we need to set the cookie
                Guid sessionGuid = new Guid();
                currentUser.SessionId = sessionGuid;
                //Tell the database about the new user
                usersInDatabase.Add(currentUser);
                //Set the cookie
                Response.Cookies.Add(new HttpCookie("SessionId", sessionGuid.
    ToString()));
            }
        }
    }
    //This class would be in the library somewhere,
    //not actually in this file.
    public class WebUser
    {
        public Guid SessionId { get; set; }
    }
}
```

Wrangling cookies on the server

So now the user has the cookie, and the next request comes in. I need to grab the cookie from the collection and search my known user base to get the information that I need. The boldface in the code below indicates the code added:

```
using System;
using System.Collections.Generic;
using System.Linq;
using System.Web;
using System.Web.UI;
using System.Web.UI.WebControls;

namespace Chapter_4
{
    public partial class Cookies : System.Web.UI.Page
    {
        WebUser currentUser = new WebUser();
        List<WebUser> usersInDatabase = new List<WebUser>();
        protected void Page_Load(object sender, EventArgs e)
        {
            if (!Page.IsPostBack)
            {
                //This is a first request, so we need to set the cookie
                Guid sessionGuid = new Guid();
                currentUser.SessionId = sessionGuid;
                //Tell the database about the new user
                usersInDatabase.Add(currentUser);
                //Set the cookie
                Response.Cookies.Add(new HttpCookie("SessionId", sessionGuid.
    ToString()));
            }
            else
            {
```

```
                //The is a postback so we need to get the cookie
                string cookieSession = Request.Cookies.Get("SessionId").Value.
    ToString();
                Guid sessionGuid = new Guid(cookieSession);
                var returningUser = from u in usersInDatabase
                   where u.SessionId.ToString() == sessionGuid.ToString()
                   select u;
                foreach (var user in returningUser)
                {
                    //Better only be one
                    currentUser = user;
                }
        }
    }
    //This class would be in the library somewhere,
    //not actually in this file.
    public class WebUser
    {
        public Guid SessionId { get; set; }
    }
}
```


How ASP.NET manages cookies for you

A lot of the stuff we use to store in a cookie is managed by the ASP.NET engine. Session state, the most common example (discussed earlier), is now handled by the ViewState object. You can store information in the ViewState like you would in a variable, and the information is encoded for you and kept in a special field in the markup.

ViewState has its problems, and a lot of people don't like to use it. In fact, many ASP.NET applications in enterprises have turned it off to save bandwidth and prevent poor coding practices. In these cases, a return to cookies is your best bet to maintain a constant communication with the user.

Tracing with TraceContext

The `TraceContext` class provides all the detailed server processing information about a Web page in ASP.NET. It is exposed in the code-behind as the Trace object and allows you to write messages to the trace log and the screen when certain things happen.

The benefit is that the Trace code runs only when you have tracing turned on. This gives programmers the option to leave tracing code in a working application without it impacting the performance or functionality.

This allows you to think about debugging while you code. When I build a Web application, I just assume that it will break. Fact is, it probably will. Programming is hard, and Web programming is harder. It is likely that either you or the environment will have a fault at some point.

Why not make it easy on yourself later on down the road?

If you decide which parts of the application are most likely to have problems while you code them, you can insert trace messages as you go. It seems like a defeatist attitude, but really I think it is a realist attitude. Even if it is just caused by bad data in two years, you are probably going to spend some time debugging.

To use tracing, you can alter the `@Page` statement at the top of each page in the application, or you can alter the `Web.config` file — which is what we are gonna do. If you want to set up the whole site for tracing, just add the bold code below to the `Web.Config`:

```
<configuration>
  <system.web>
    <trace enabled="true" requestLimit="40" localOnly="false" />
  </system.web>
</configuration>
```

Follow these steps to alter the `Web.config` file for tracing:

1. **Create a new page in the project for tracing.**

   I called it **Tracing.aspx**.

2. **Add the `Trace` statement to the @page directive of the new Tracing. aspx page.**

   ```
   <%@ Page Language="C#" AutoEventWireup="true" CodeBehind="Tracing.aspx.
       cs" Inherits="Chapter_4.Tracing" Trace="true"%>
   ```

3. **In the code-behind, add code to the Page_Load event handler to fake an exception and catch it, and then write to the Trace.**

   This is just to see how Trace works. Book I covers Exception handling in more detail.

   ```
   using System;
   using System.Collections.Generic;
   using System.Linq;
   using System.Web;
   using System.Web.UI;
   using System.Web.UI.WebControls;

   namespace Chapter_4
   {
       public partial class Tracing : System.Web.UI.Page
       {
           protected void Page_Load(object sender, EventArgs e)
           {
               try
               {
                   throw new ApplicationException("This is the fake
    exception.");
               }
   ```

```
                    catch (ApplicationException ex)
                    {
                        Trace.Warn(ex.Message);
                    }
                }
            }
        }
```

4. **Press <F5> to run the application.**

The page will look nothing like you expect. A ton of information is dumped on the page, `Response.Write` style, including our Trace message (check out Figure 4-4).

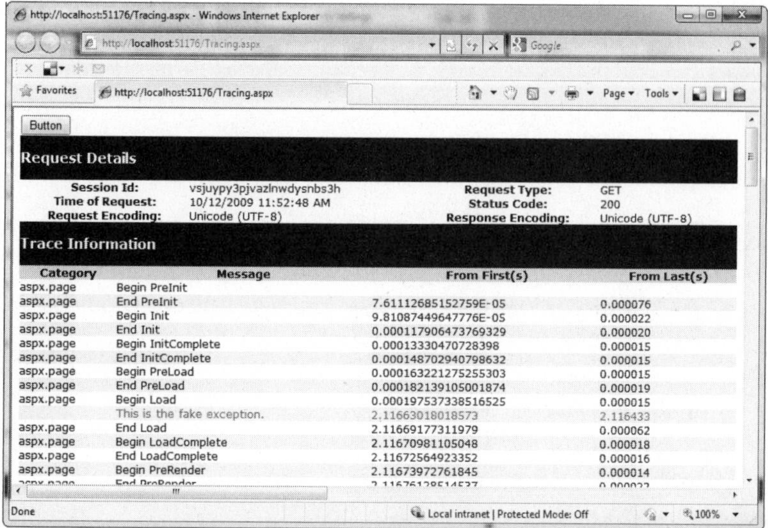

Figure 4-4: An example of ASP.NET tracing.

You don't want to show the user all of this, of course, but if you get word of a problem with the application, wouldn't it be nice to be able to turn on the trace for the page in question? You could give it a little input, and then see how the server processing details respond using the trace.

Chapter 5: Digging into Web Construction

In This Chapter

- Getting started
- Managing files
- Mastering master pages
- Testing the testable
- Deploying your masterpiece

You can know the controls, and you can know the framework, but you don't really know the Web until you understand the little weird bits that make it all work together. No technology has more "glue" components than Web technology.

This chapter is about using some of those "glue" components to build an application. It gives you a chance to do things that you'll have to do every time you make a Web application — set up a master page, test your application, and a few other treats.

ASP.NET shields a lot of that from you, the developer. You don't have to worry about the details of Common Gateway Interface (CGI), for instance. Nonetheless, there are a number of details that you do have to manage in order to get an application on the Internet, such as the following:

- **Setting up a Web project can be ... demanding.** The default options that Microsoft provides are not immediately obvious, and the need to have them right the first time is high.
- **There are templates for ASP.NET sites.** These templates provide all those things that make a site flow as you navigate through it, like the navigation, advertising, headers, and footers.
- **Security for a Web application is ... different.** Because a significant percentage of Web applications are available for public access (quite a shift from Windows applications), you have to consider the reality that people are going to try to use your application as a platform for phishing, XSS, and a hundred other contemporary hacks.
- **Testing Web applications is another consideration, because it is more than unit testing.** If your Web application goes viral, you might have

1,000,000 visitors tomorrow. You don't have to be ready for that today, but you have to know what you need to do to get ready.

✦ **Finally, deploying a Web application is a new pile of joy that you'll get to know and love.** I promise. Remember those UML deployment diagrams you learned in school? They can be useful after all! You actually use them in the Web world.

Managing Files

Setting up an ASP.NET project is not trivial, and there are a lot of wrong ways to do it. I can't tell you the right way — it just depends on your circumstances. What I want to do is give you some of the best practices that will help you form your own path. The idea is to know how the tool works, in order to help you do your work.

Reviewing project types

The first part of the process is making a new project. As with everything else in ASP.NET, this isn't a trivial prospect. You even have to use a different menu item to start the project — New Web Site rather than New Project, as shown in Figure 5-1.

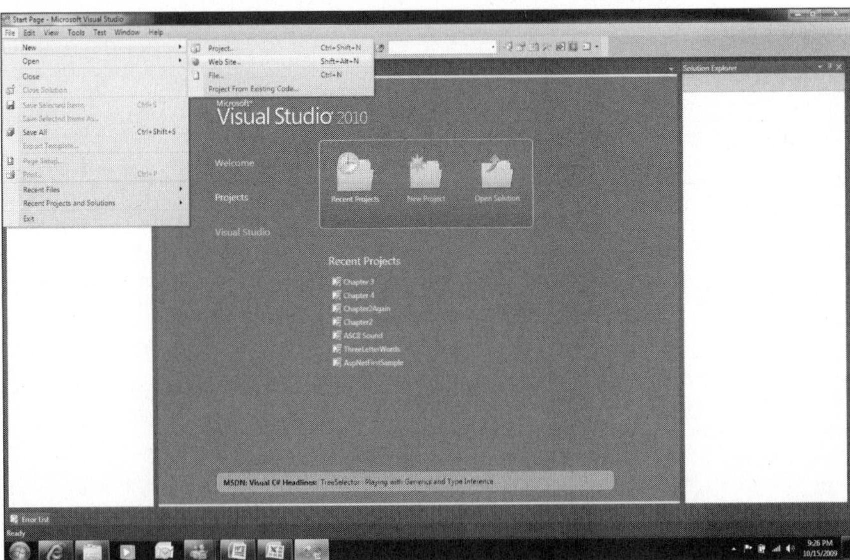

Figure 5-1: There is even a different menu item!

The New Web Site dialog box includes several items, but we are concerned with only one, the ASP.NET Web site. Here are all the options:

- **ASP.NET Web site:** This is what we want. It is a file share that represents just what it says: a Web site made up of ASP.NET files. Fantastic. Not as simple as it sounds, but it is the right start.
- **Silverlight Script Web:** This isn't the right place to talk about Silverlight. Like WPF, Silverlight is a XAML (rhymes with "camel") project, but it is designed for the Web. It is Microsoft's answer to Adobe Flash. Don't sweat it right now.
- **ASP.NET Web service:** Don't use this; use WCF for Web Services.
- **Empty Web site:** Just a folder and a share.
- **WCF Service:** A template for a service. Book VII covers these.
- **ASP.NET Reports Web site:** Same as the first bullet selection except it includes a bunch of references to the RDL reporting structure.
- **Dynamic Data Linq to SQL Web site:** This is a simple, auto-generated forms-over-data site. I don't care for them, and they aren't good examples of C#, so I skip them for now. Plus, Linq to SQL is end-of-life (meaning Microsoft isn't supporting it any more).
- **Dynamic Data Entities Web site:** Again, an auto-generated forms-over-data site. Not what we are looking for.

If you cancel out of the New Web Site dialog box, add a New Project, and then click on Web in the Installed Templates tree view (under C#), you find a whole new list of goodies. (See Figure 5-2.)

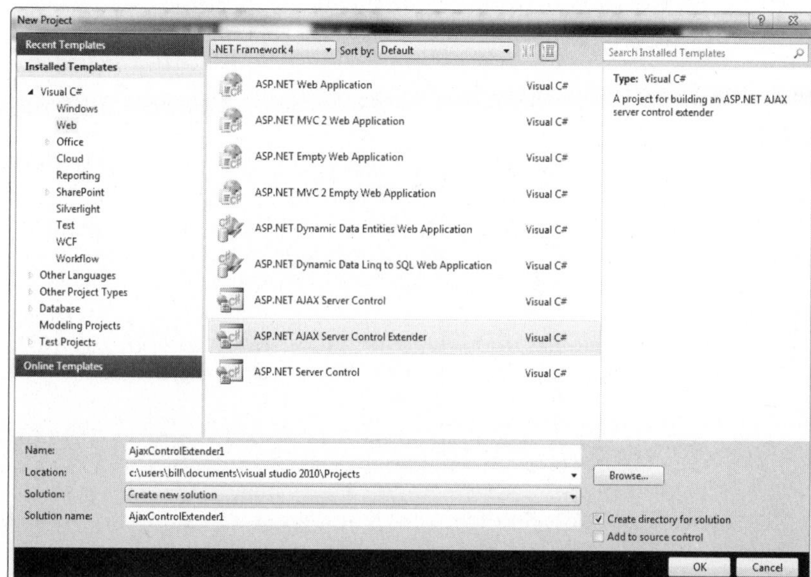

Figure 5-2: What's the difference between a Web site and a Web application?

In Visual Studio 2002 and 2003, Web projects worked like all other projects. They had a project file, needed to be compiled and packaged, and so forth. In Visual Studio 2005, that plan was scrapped for the Web site — just a loose collection of files in any folder, which would be treated like a project. No project file, no compilation of a single resource file — more like classic ASP.

Fact is, there is room for both, and in Visual Studio 2008 and 2010, both are offered. So, if you say you want a new Web Site, you get a federation of files in a folder that can just be copied over to a Web server. If you want a new Web application, you get a real, compiled application. All the same other constraints apply. Here is a breakdown:

✦ **ASP.NET Web Application:** How to make a site more like a regular program. Comes with a project file, and so on.

✦ **ASP.NET Web Service application:** Same advice (use WCF).

✦ **ASP.NET Ajax Server Control:** This allows you to build a new Toolbox item for AJAX. Really a nice feature, but too in-depth for this minibook. Check MSDN.

✦ **WCF Service Application:** How to do service-oriented development in .NET. More in Book VII.

✦ **ASP.NET Server Control:** Like the AJAX control, except it allows you to make a normal control.

✦ **ASP.NET AJAX Server Control Extender:** A template for changing the functionality of an existing AJAX Toolbox item.

✦ **Dynamic Data Linq to SQL Web Application:** As earlier — end of life. Don't use it.

✦ **Dynamic Data Entities Web Application:** Just like the Entities site, except a real application. Preferred implementation for this project type.

So which do you choose? If it is a Web site — literally a public site that will be on a public server and include a handful of pages that an anonymous user views — I use the Web site format. If it is an application — part of a larger initiative for a company with development standards and standard libraries and whatnot — I use the Web application format.

Your mileage may vary. Find out more about the controversy between the project types at `http://Webproject.scottgu.com/`.

Reviewing file types

Make a new ASP.NET Web site called Chapter5, and save it in the default location. Visual Studio makes a new site for you, in the specified folder. Three files are added:

✦ **Default.aspx:** This is the starter markup file. Has the HTML and ASP.NET controls.

✦ **Default.aspx.cs:** The code-behind file for the Default.aspx file.

✦ **Web.config:** The magic configuration file. A lot goes into this one.

There is also an App_Data folder. This is used by Visual Studio and ASP.NET to store, for instance, a SQL Lite database that you might make to store your application data. Just leave it there for a second.

You just know we need a few new files, right? We should add a style sheet, and maybe a script file or two. Right-click on the project and select Add New Item.

You can add an absurd number of files to a site — just look at Figure 5-3. Global Application Class? Silverlight-enabled WCF Service? What *are* these things? Does anyone actually use this stuff?

Yes, but don't sweat it too much. You need to worry about only a few file types to make a good application, like these:

✦ **Master page:** This is the template for the site. We handle these in the next section.

✦ **Style sheet:** This is the CSS 2.0 style for your application. If you aren't familiar, refer to *HTML and CSS For Dummies* — great book.

✦ **Jscript file:** So named because Microsoft can't say JavaScript anymore or the lawyers beat them up.

✦ **Class:** Just your basic C# class, in its own file.

That's what you need. Now to organize them.

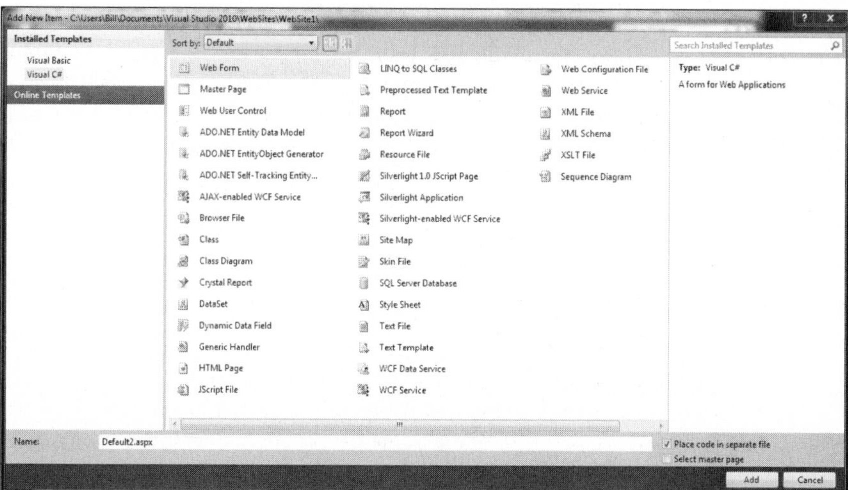

Figure 5-3: Man, that is a lot of files.

Organizing files

You have two choices when organizing your Web site. You can build a few projects to manage your files, or you can build folders into the Web project and put your files there. My usual methodology is to build separate projects for the class files and folders for the Web-related files. This way, if you want to reuse the classes for a Windows Mobile application, you can easily just reference the class file project.

Web files should be in folders in the Web application. Note that this can have some implications for referencing files. If your project isn't the root of a Web server, you might have to carefully consider how to reference files.

If you are deploying your Web site to a domain, like `www.mynewWebsite.com`, you can use a `./` to refer to files, like this:

```
<img src="./images/myImage.png">
```

If you aren't deploying to a domain — for instance, if you are making an application that lives in a folder of a site, such as `www.someoneelsessite.com/myApplication`, you can't use `./` because you don't know how far away the root of the application is, or what the directory really is.

ASP.NET can handle this problem for you. A construct in ASP.NET is implemented with the tilde (~), but it works only in ASP.NET controls. That means that the `img` HTML tag won't work with a tilde; you have to use the `asp:Image` control, like this:

```
<asp:Image ID="Image1" runat="server" ImageUrl="~/images/
   myImage.png"/>
```

For organization, I have a pattern. It may or may not work for you. Please feel free to make your own. Mine breaks down like this:

- I put my class libraries in a separate project. Usually, I have a business logic layer (or controller) in a second project, and a data access layer (or model) in a third project.
- I add a Bits folder, and in that, I put folders for, well, all the bits.
  - Style sheets
  - Images
  - JavaScript files
  - Whatever else
- I then make a root level folder for every section of the site. If I have three top level menu items in my site, I have three folders. If I just have application files, and don't have a regular menu structure, everything will be in the root.

Mastering Master Pages

Now that there is some form and function to the project, the next step is to add some form and function to the site itself. Master pages are exactly what they sound like, structural elements that contain the content of the site as "slave" components.

Master pages are more than page templates. They are fully functional content containers that are supported by Visual Studio in a number of ways. Master pages reduce the complexity of maintaining common content on Web pages by replicating that content automatically and containing the programming to one file from the developer's perspective.

There is no requirement to use master pages. In fact, most of the projects I work on don't use Master Pages, because of dependencies on older security or navigational frameworks. That's okay. If you are building something new, certainly consider using master pages.

Making a master page

We start by making a new master page. Just follow these steps:

1. **Right-click on the Chapter5 Web site and select Add New Item.**
2. **Click on Master Page.**
3. **Keep the default name of MasterPage.Master and click OK.**
4. **Change to Design view.**
5. **Open the Properties panel.**
6. **Click on the designer, outside of the Body marked area, so that the DOCUMENT is selected in the Properties panel.**
7. **Click on the** `BgColor` **property, and pick your favorite color.**
8. **Back in the designer, click on the Body marked area, and type** My Web Site **or something equally fascinating.**
9. **Highlight the text, and select H1 in the HTML Source Editing Toolbar, like I did in Figure 5-4.**
10. **Press Enter to add a blank line under the header.**
11. **From the Toolbox, drag a ContentPlaceholder control under the title.**

Now you have a template for the rest of your pages. You can add navigation here, and I recommend it. To keep things simple for this introduction, however, I move on.

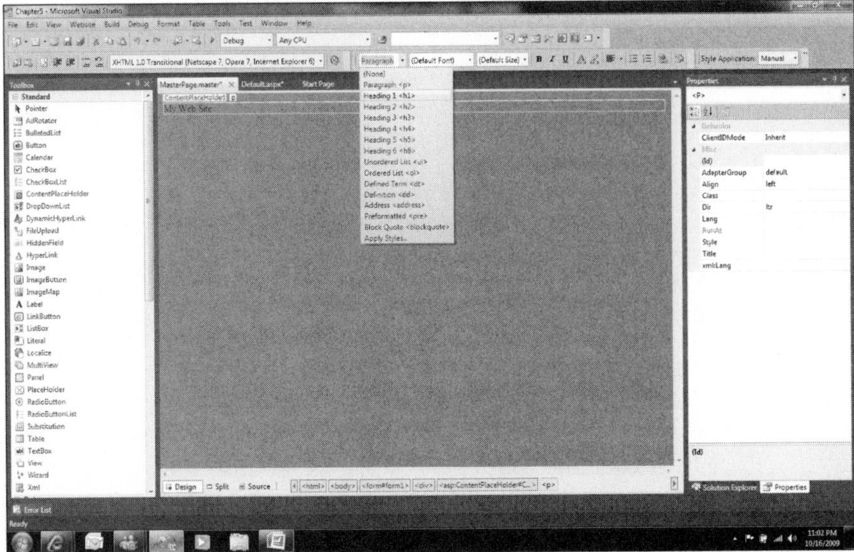

Figure 5-4: Making a header.

Adding content

You won't believe how simple adding content is. You see, the master page is something that the content page adheres to, not something you have to inject content into. You just have to make pages like usual, and they will drop themselves in that content placeholder. Follow these steps to add content:

1. **Right-click on the Web site, and select Add New Item.**
2. **Click on Web Form (the master page is probably still selected) and name it** Home.aspx.

   Wait! Don't click Add yet!
3. **Check the Select Master Page check box in the lower right-hand corner.**
4. ***Now* you can click Add.**

   The Select a Master Page dialog box appears.
5. **You can select which master page you want — as shown in Figure 5-4. We have only one, so click it under Contents of Folder.**
6. **Click OK.**

Notice how different the template content of the page is now that you have a master page. Visual Studio knew how to handle this! There are no HTML headers or footers, because VS knows they are in the master page.

```
<%@ Page Title="" Language="C#" MasterPageFile="~/MasterPage.master"
    AutoEventWireup="true" CodeFile="Home.aspx.cs" Inherits="Home" %>

<asp:Content ID="Content1" ContentPlaceHolderID="head" Runat="Server">
</asp:Content>
<asp:Content ID="Content2" ContentPlaceHolderID="ContentPlaceHolder1"
    Runat="Server">
</asp:Content>
```

There is obviously more to learn about master pages and how to develop sites with them, but my goal here is just to cover the best practice. Now that you know, move to MSDN and see how best to use master pages for your project.

Testing Web Applications with Visual Studio

It's easy to test Web applications using Visual Studio, though it isn't a well-advertised feature.

This is available only in Team System. If you have Professional, you can't do Web tests. Also important: You don't have to test a Web project in your solution — you can write a Web test against any URL.

Follow these steps to test your Web application:

1. **Choose File➪New➪Project and select Test Project.**
2. **In the new project, right-click on the project file and select New Test.**
3. **In the New Test dialog box, select Web Test.**
4. **Change the test name to** GoogleTest.Webtest **and click OK.**

   The Web Test Recorder opens in your browser. (See Figure 5-5.)

   Though I am going to use Google for this test, please don't use a production Web site of your own for testing.
5. **Go to** `www.google.com`**.**
6. **Search for C# 2010 All In One.**
7. **Click on the Amazon link (I assume there is one).**
8. **Click Stop to stop the recording.**

   Visual Studio takes a minute and tries to detect dynamic parameters. It should find (at least) the search criteria in the Promote Dynamic Parameters to Web Test Parameters dialog box shown in Figure 5-6.
9. **Click the search parameter (C# All In One) check box to promote it to a Web test parameter and click OK.**

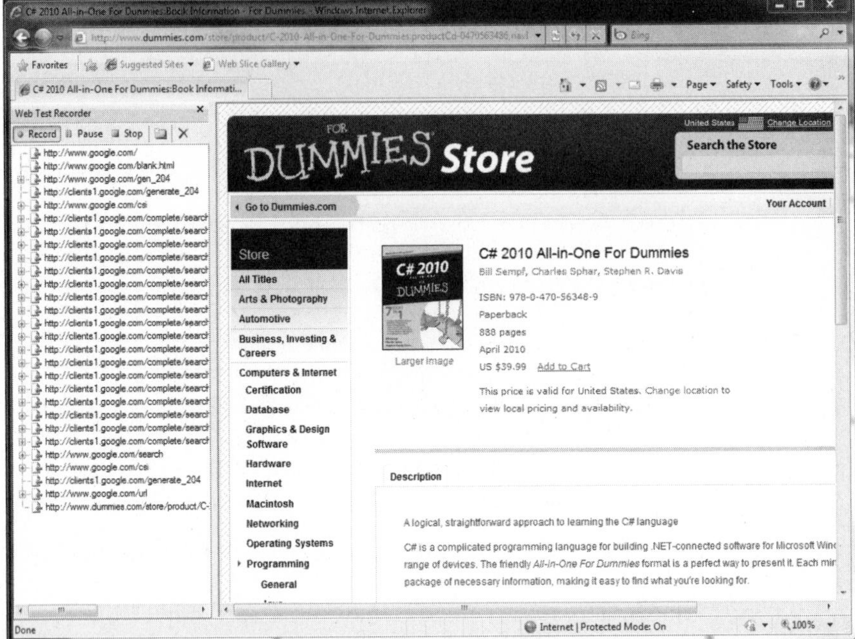

Figure 5-5: Launching the Web test recorder.

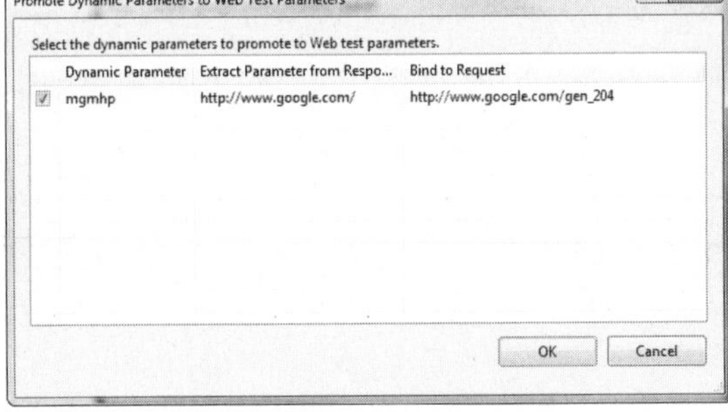

Figure 5-6: The Promote Dynamic Parameters to Web Test Parameters dialog box.

You are returned to the Visual Studio text manager, where you see all the requests you made (all two of them) in the Web Test panel. You can then click on separate items in the request tree and change the parameters — such as the querystring — for any request.

When you run a test, the test manager asks you for any query parameters that you promoted. In our case, the search term was promoted, so you can use the test as a search engine! There are probably more convenient ways to search, however.

Deploying Your Masterpiece

Web deployment has historically been difficult in a number of platforms. Because you need the markup files, and any back-end support (like script files or compiled libraries), and perhaps even any middle support, such as an interpreter for your PHP files, getting a Web application out to a server can be demanding.

Lots of options

When ASP.NET came out, it promised *xcopy deployment* and, in general, it delivered. Because .NET components are versioned, if you strongly name your DLL files you can just use the DOS xcopy command (or drag and drop in Explorer) to drag them right to your server, thus the term *xcopy deployment.* If you have a permissions thing, you can use File Transfer Protocol (FTP) or whatever.

In fact, xcopy deployment has made all sorts of things possible. Dot Net Nuke, an open source content management system for ASP.NET, has taken things to a logical extreme. When you build a new module for the platform, you add the files to a compressed folder and upload them right through a File Upload control on the site. Then the component is installed — you can use it right away. Neat.

For your site, you can use Windows Explorer if you have share permissions for your server, or FTP if you don't. Figure 5-7 shows a Web site that I manage. The left side is my development copy — notice the `.cs` files. The right side has the version on the server.

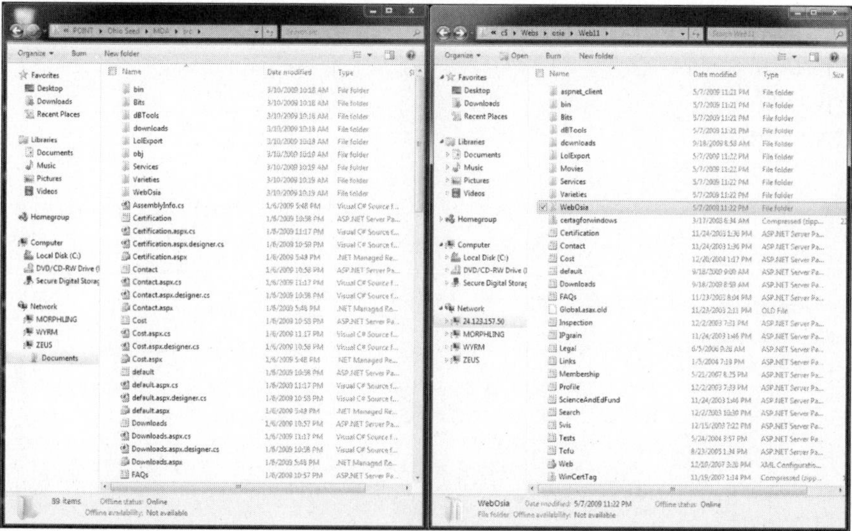

Figure 5-7: An example of xcopy deployment.

If I want, I can just select all the files that I need on the left and drag them to the right. That means I have to get all the ASPX files, but not the .CS files because they are compiled into the DLL. Oh, that's right, I have to get the DLL, too. And the script files.

Oh wait, the directories have be sorted out too, because they have their own ASPX and .CS files. And I can't remember . . . do you have to copy the report files (you don't)? Hmm, this is harder than I thought.

Copying Web sites with "Copy Web"

If you have a Web site project (earlier in this chapter I point out that there are two project types), you have a Visual Studio–driven option for the xcopy option. Because these sites don't compile and you need to move the `.cs` files along with the `.aspx` files, this tool fits the bill.

To run it, look for the Copy Web icon in Solution Explorer. I highlighted it with a red box in Figure 5-8. It launches the Copy Web design surface, which looks a lot like the two Windows Explorer boxes in Figure 5-6, except it comes with neat buttons.

To use the Web Copy tool, find the location for your deployment on the right side of the panel. Use the Connect button to get there. Because it is URI driven, you can easily push to an FTP site or a Windows share, local IIS install, or a remote site using SharePoint extensions.

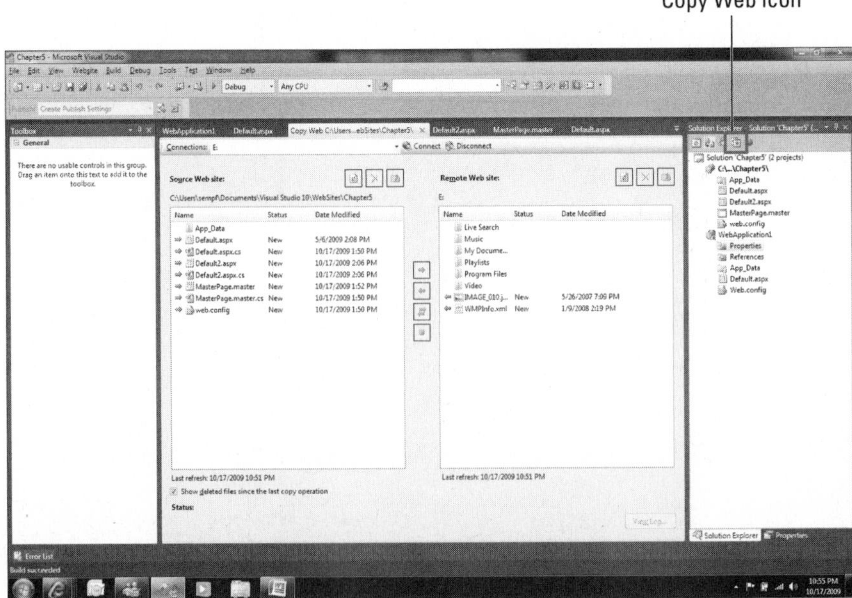

Figure 5-8: Looks a lot like Windows Explorer, doesn't it?

From there, highlight the files you want to copy, and click the direction you want to move them (usually the arrow pointing to the right). Visual Studio gives you a hand by telling you what direction files need to go with the icons to the left of the files.

Package/Publish

For Web applications, there is an answer too — and one that will fix my poor application in the previous section, "Copy Web sites with 'Copy Web.'" Package and Publish is designed to assist with more sophisticated deployments usually found with Web Application projects.

To get to the package and deployment options, double-click on the Properties folder in the project, and then click the Package/Publish tab on the left-hand side of the designer surface. This panel, shown in Figure 5-9, has everything you need to solve most mid-range deployment problems.

Starting at the top — you can isolate 64-bit operating systems with the Platform drop-down list. This is good when you are developing in 32 bit but know your server is 64. Right below that is a link to the Help files, in case you don't have this chapter handy.

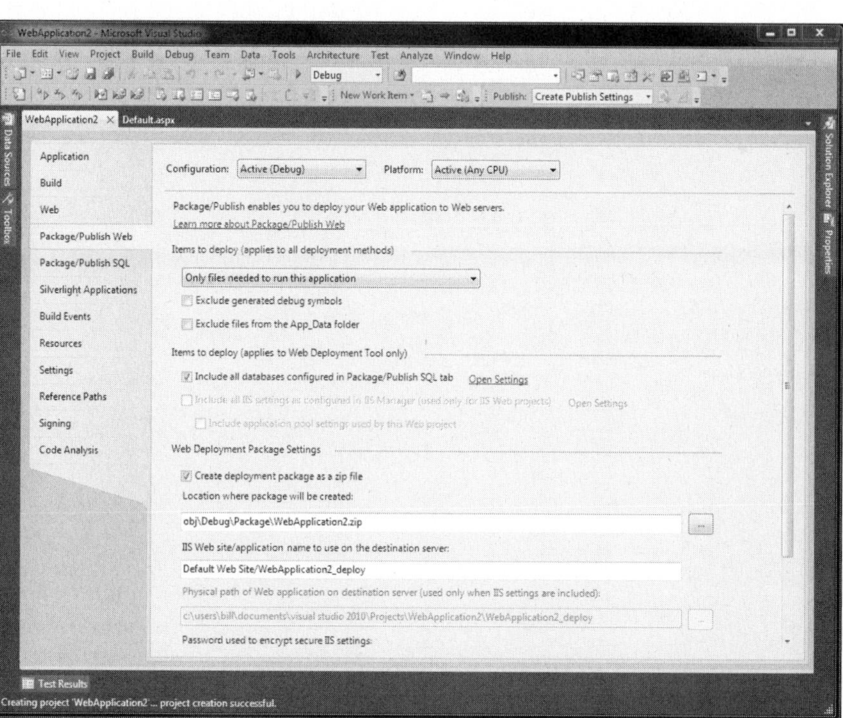

Figure 5-9: Packaging for publishing.

In the Items to Deploy section, you can solve the big problem that I mention earlier. There you can tell the deployment to deploy only markup and compiled files, if that is what you need to do. There are options to exclude debug symbols, too — remember, they don't run if they aren't there, and it all goes a little faster. You can always add them if you need them.

You now can use MsDeploy with Visual Studio. MsDeploy is a new feature of IIS that assists with the deployment of really complex Web applications. Search for it on TechNet for more information. It takes a Zip file, which you can configure in the MsDeploy Package Settings section.

Book VII

Service-Oriented Development

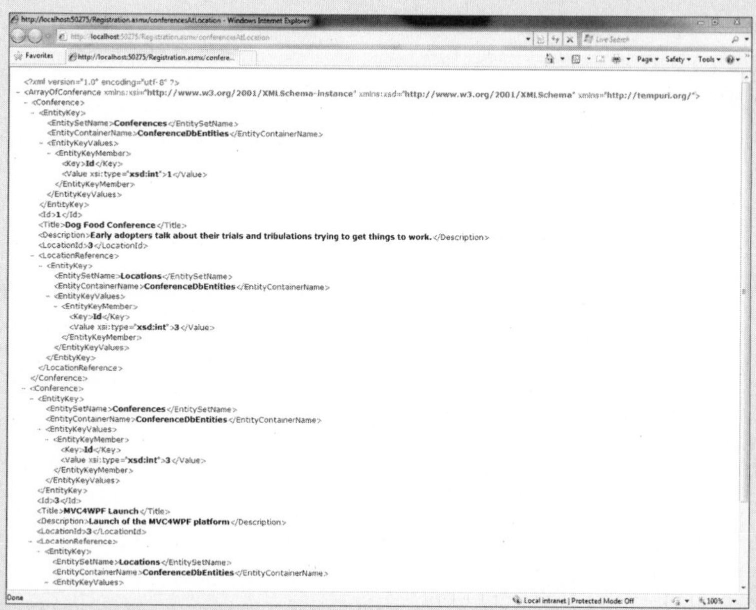

http://localhost:50275/Registration.asmx/conferencesAtLocation - Windows Internet Explorer
Favorites
Page ▾ Safety ▾ Tools ▾
<?xml version="1.0" encoding="utf-8" ?>
- <ArrayOfConference xmlns:xsi="http://www.w3.org/2001/XMLSchema-instance" xmlns:xsd="http://www.w3.org/2001/XMLSchema" xmlns="http://tempuri.org/">
- <Conference>
- <EntityKey>
<EntitySetName>Conferences</EntitySetName>
<EntityContainerName>ConferenceDbEntities</EntityContainerName>
- <EntityKeyValues>
- <EntityKeyMember>
<Key>Id</Key>
<Value xsi:type="xsd:int">1</Value>
</EntityKeyMember>
</EntityKeyValues>
</EntityKey>
<Id>1</Id>
<Title>Dog Food Conference</Title>
<Description>Early adopters talk about their trials and tribulations trying to get things to work.</Description>
<LocationId>3</LocationId>
- <LocationReference>
- <EntityKey>
<EntitySetName>Locations</EntitySetName>
<EntityContainerName>ConferenceDbEntities</EntityContainerName>
- <EntityKeyValues>
- <EntityKeyMember>
<Key>Id</Key>
<Value xsi:type="xsd:int">3</Value>
</EntityKeyMember>
</EntityKeyValues>
</EntityKey>
</LocationReference>
</Conference>
- <Conference>
- <EntityKey>
<EntitySetName>Conferences</EntitySetName>
<EntityContainerName>ConferenceDbEntities</EntityContainerName>
- <EntityKeyValues>
- <EntityKeyMember>
<Key>Id</Key>
<Value xsi:type="xsd:int">3</Value>
</EntityKeyMember>
</EntityKeyValues>
</EntityKey>
<Id>3</Id>
<Title>MVC4WPF Launch</Title>
<Description>Launch of the MVC4WPF platform</Description>
<LocationId>3</LocationId>
- <LocationReference>
- <EntityKey>
<EntitySetName>Locations</EntitySetName>
<EntityContainerName>ConferenceDbEntities</EntityContainerName>
- <EntityKeyValues>
Done
Local intranet | Protected Mode: Off
100%

Making a SOAP service in ASMX

Contents at a Glance

Chapter 1: Getting Acquainted with Web Services

In This Chapter

- Exploring the basic principles of service-oriented apps
- Building service-oriented apps
- Making XML Web services available

A *Web service* is just the provision of functionality over the Internet using an open interface. A Web page provides functionality that you can see; a Web service provides the underlying data, in a format that you can use in another application.

Web services are straightforward — at least until the software manufacturers start messing with them. Web services are standards driven, just as HTML is, and the World Wide Web Consortium (W3C) owns their documentation. Web services have been a hot topic for the past decade, but only in the past five years or so (in step with the ubiquitous nature of the Internet) have they become a viable option for the delivery of hard-to-find software functionality.

A few different Web services formats exist in the .NET world, and they solve two basic problems:

- Making part of your application available past the physical boundary of the application.
- Making a distributed middle to your application so that you can scale paragraphs if your site suddenly has a lot of traffic.

After covering a few Web service principles, I present some code to show you how each format works.

Understanding Web Services

Web services provide a way to extend methods past the normal boundary of a software system. You usually write the something like the following chunk of code in order to start building a problem:

```
public bool AddStuff(String stuff)
{
   //Add it here
   return true;
}
```

and then you call it like this:

```
bool DidItWork = AddStuff("This is the new Stuff");
```

Using Web services, however, you call the method this way:

```
POST /Service1.asmx HTTP/1.1
Host: localhost
Content-Type: application/soap+xml; charset=utf-8
Content-Length: length
<?xml version="1.0" encoding="utf-8"?>
<soap12:Envelope xmlns:xsi="http://www.w3.org/2001/XMLSchema-
    instance" xmlns:xsd="http://www.w3.org/2001/XMLSchema"
    xmlns:soap12="http://www.w3.org/2003/05/soap-envelope">
  <soap12:Body>
    <AddStuff xmlns="http://tempuri.org/">
      <stuff>string</stuff>
    </AddStuff>
  </soap12:Body>
</soap12:Envelope>
```

and then see a response like this one:

```
HTTP/1.1 200 OK
Content-Type: application/soap+xml; charset=utf-8
Content-Length: length
<?xml version="1.0" encoding="utf-8"?>
<soap12:Envelope xmlns:xsi="http://www.w3.org/2001/XMLSchema-
    instance" xmlns:xsd="http://www.w3.org/2001/XMLSchema"
    xmlns:soap12="http://www.w3.org/2003/05/soap-envelope">
  <soap12:Body>
    <AddStuffResponse xmlns="http://tempuri.org/">
      <AddStuffResult>boolean</AddStuffResult>
    </AddStuffResponse>
  </soap12:Body>
</soap12:Envelope>
```

Whoa! Hey, why would anyone want to build a function that way? I'm glad you asked. In the later section "Building Service-Oriented Applications," I answer your questions. For now, I describe some concepts that make building web services easier to handle.

Web services can be defined by three basic principles:

- Loosely coupled: They don't require a constant connection to the server
- Contract driven: They provide an interface that describes all of their functionality
- More likely to be chunky, not chatty: Rather than lots of properties with single values, they provide big methods that return collections.

I discuss these topics more fully in the sections that follow.

Loosely coupled

Because Web services are, like Web applications, *loosely coupled* , Web service conversations aren't guaranteed to make sense. You might get a sentence from three minutes ago, after four other sentences have gone past, or you might not hear from them again after the first line.

When you stop to think about it, louse coupling makes sense: Web service calls are just like navigation in a Web page. Sometimes you click a link and then close your browser, and sometimes you click the link twice. Web applications are up to the whim of the user, and so are Web services.

For this reason, a client of a Web service must be *loosely coupled* to the service. For example, you don't want to make a user wait until a Web service call is complete. You must call x *asynchronously* and have the result show up when it is ready.

Fortunately, .NET handles the asynchronous call. You just tell your application that you're calling a service asynchronously and then provide a delegate for the service to call when it's ready. As long as you handle the code properly, the service will work as expected.

In this example, you can see that we implemented the loose coupling with an asynchronous call:

```
using System;
using System.Collections.Generic;
using System.Linq;
using System.Text;

namespace ConsoleApplication1
{
    class Program
    {
        static void Main(string[] args)
        {
            //Here YOU are calling the service
   asynchronously.
```

```
            AddStuffReference.Service1SoapClient client = new
    AddStuffReference.Service1SoapClient();
            client.AddStuffCompleted += new
    EventHandler(client_AddStuffCompleted);
            client.AddStuffAsynch("This is the stuff");
        }

        //This method is called when the response comes back.
        //No timers or anything.  .NET handles it for you.
        void proxy_AddStuffCompleted(object
    sender, AddStuffReference.Service1SoapClient.
    AddStuffCompletedEventArgs e)
        {
            bool result = e.Result.ToString();
        }
    }
}
```

The example above only protects your user interface from experiencing a tie-up. You still have no real indication that the messages will ever be delivered, so you should never write software that depends on the delivery of the data from the service. It has to fail gracefully.

Contract driven

In client-server development, an interface defines a contract of sorts between the domain model and the user interface. That contract can be used to drive development in the same way as a contract is used to drive a business deal. If you know what I require and I know what you require, we can quickly and easily make a deal.

A Web service is required to have an interface that conforms to the Web Services Description Language (WSDL) standard. WSDL describes expected inputs and allowed outputs just as an interface would, creating a contract between the service provider and the client.

In .NET, your contract is created automatically from the code for the service. If you call a service in the browser (which isn't the way it's designed to be called — I tell you more about that topic later in this minibook) from the development machine, you see the test screen shown in Figure 1-1. Even though the browser gains some basic important information about the service, it isn't the contract. The contract is shown behind the Service Description link.

Clicking the Service Description link appends the text `?WSDL` to the URI, and the Web browser shows the contract. This contract is used by the client system to determine exactly which information the service wants and how it will respond to input. Though the WSDL is displayed in a browser, as shown in Figure 1-2, the interesting part is the XML that's behind the screen.

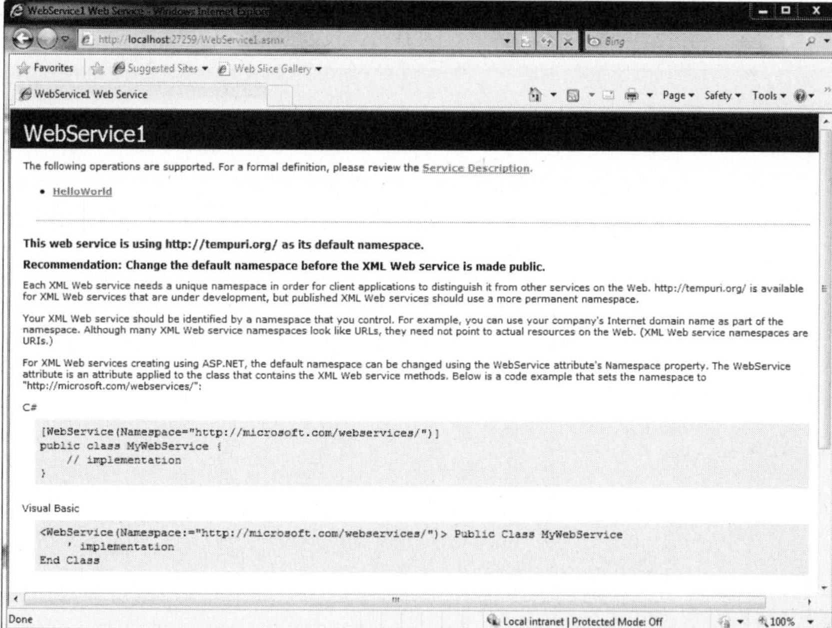

Figure 1-1: The default service overview.

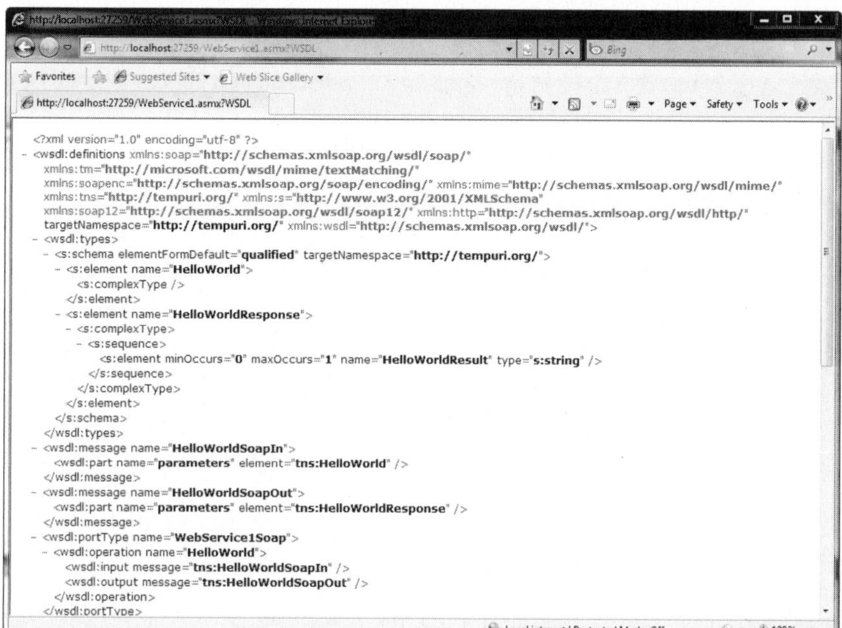

Figure 1-2: The Service Description in WSDL.

For compilable languages, the client machine does essentially the same thing no matter which platform it's on (Java or Basic or PHP or Ruby): At compile time, it reads the WSDL and creates a proxy that the client talks to. This:

- Brokers the communication process between the client and the service
- Provides type safety, if it's supported
- Generally makes your life easier because WSDL (and the contract it provides) is an important part of a service developer's work

The contract isn't legally binding (and contains only a small amount of fine print). The service provider reserves the right to change the service any time it wants, and can even forgo updating the WSDL with no fear of legal reprisal. Because you're a .NET developer, though, your WSDL is generated automatically.

Chunky versus chatty

Although the chunky-versus-chatty services issue might sound like a face-off between candy bars, it isn't.

Rather than perform small, incremental operations via Web services, you use them to make large, sweeping "strokes." The length of individual calls might be larger, but the number of communications is fewer, which reduces network overhead.

Suppose that an application changes the settings of a piece of hardware located miles away from it — perhaps your home heating system (which is a good use of a service). The client application (your computer) is absolutely local, the remote device (your heater) is certainly remote, and a network (probably the Internet) is in the middle. If you have a service with a series of individual controls, such as TurnFanOn and TurnFanOff, it's a common interface for a local application, such as connecting a heater directly to your computer.

The following chunk of code gives an example of that chatty sort of interface:

```
namespace HomeHeater
{
    public class Chatty : IChatty
    {
        public bool TurnFanOn()
        {
            return true;
        }
        public bool TurnFanOff()
        {
            return true;
        }
```

```
        public bool SetTemperature(int newTemperature)
        {
            return true;
        }
        public bool SetFanSpeed(string newFanSpeed)
        {
            return true;
        }
    }
```

The interface in this example is *chatty* (in case you couldn't tell from its class name). Every time you change a knob on the controller, a call is made to a service. Move the temperature to 72 degrees and call the service. Turn the fan to its High setting and call the service. Turn the temperature back down to 71 degrees and call the service. The client "chats" with the service.

Nothing is intrinsically wrong with this implementation. For a service, though, with more network overhead for every call, it isn't the best way to build methods. Instead, you want your client to change settings and then pull a big lever on the side to make all the changes at one time.

A *chunky* interface provides a domain model for the client to use, with properties to set. Then, after all settings are in the model object, you send the whole shootin' match to the service. It looks like this:


```
namespace HomeHeater
{
    public class Chunky : IChunky
    {
        public bool UpdateHeaterSettings(HeaterModule
    heaterModule)
        {
            return true;
        }
    }
    public class HeaterModule
    {
        public int Temperature { get; set; }
        public bool FanOn { get; set; }
        public string FanSpeed { get; set; }
    }
}
```

Now, no matter how often you make changes, the service is called only when you "pull the big lever" (update it). Whether this action prevents users from updating after every change depends on your interface. In general, this design principle is the best one for service development.

You may wonder why anyone would bother with a concept as convoluted as Web services. I can assure you that good reasons exist and that you will want to use this technology on a project.

Building Service-Oriented Applications

The first and most obvious use of a service is to create a Service-Oriented Application, or SOA. This overloaded, overused term means that your application (like the heating system I mention in the previous section) uses services to assist a remote client with communications with a server.

Unfortunately, the term *SOA* is no longer useful in the marketplace. So many so-called "experts" have chimed in with large, unmanageable ideas for the creation of systemwise services that it is impossible for anyone to separate the wheat from the chaff.

The concept is simple: The user interface calls a service at some point in the process to communicate with the server. You do this for two reasons:

- **Scalability:** It's the main reason to use a service inside an application — especially a Web application.

  Up to a point, most Web applications have built-in scaling. If you need more access points, you just add more servers and then use a device to sort the traffic to another machine, as shown in Figure 1-3.

  Web applications are different, though, because layers have different scalability needs. Sometimes the database is loaded, and sometimes the Web server is. You must be able to separate the layers of the application, as shown in Figure 1-4 — that's where services start to become useful.

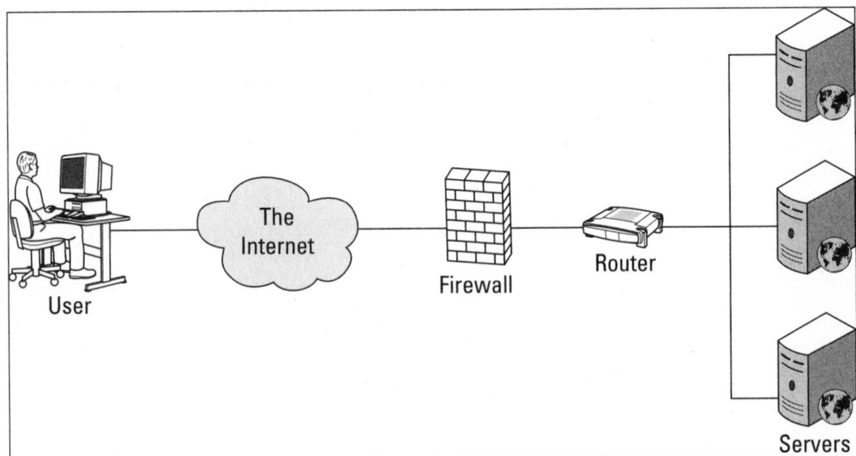

Figure 1-3: Scaling on a simple Web site.

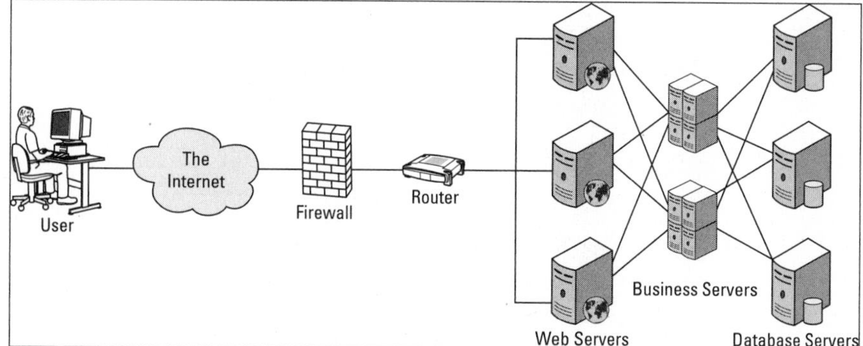

Figure 1-4: Separating the layers.

Because the services use a common format — usually XML over HTTP — you can relatively easily install parts of the application on their own machines to isolate them physically. Because the functionality of the deleted part is called via a service, you can scale the application horizontally.

- **Reusability:** Every organization has a list of its participants — clients, users, voters, cooks, or mailing list subscribers, for example. Regardless of the type of participant, all the people on the list have first and last names and other identifying characteristics.
- It seems like nearly every application written today has a table of People. Savvy programmers use slick tricks to keep these tables in sync or to share information, for example, but only one way exists to share the People table — by using a data silo, as shown in Figure 1-5.

A data silo works this way:

1. A database on some server somewhere contains all participants' demographic information.
2. The database is surrounded by a service layer containing all allowed operations.
3. The service layer is consumed by all other applications in the system, as shown in Figure 1-5.

This set of steps shows you the concept of reuse. It isn't about bits of code (no matter what you might hear) — it's about *data.* Services help to provide access to the data silo.

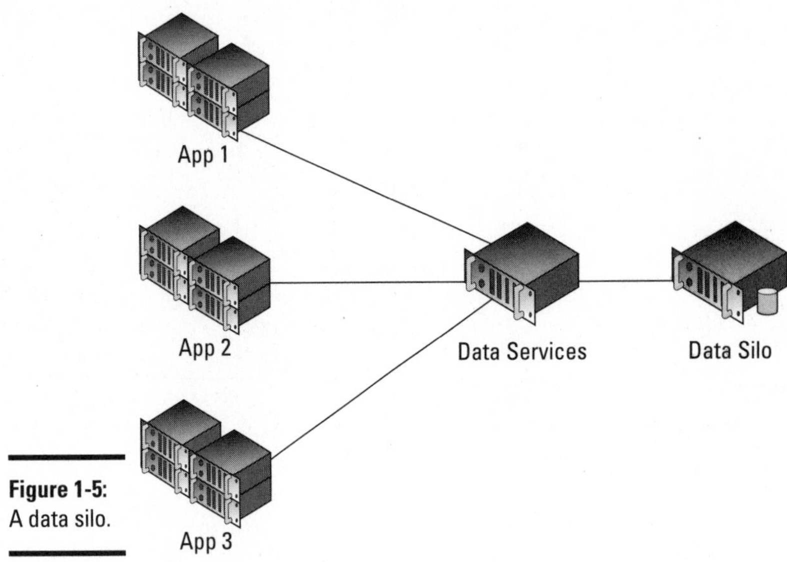

Figure 1-5: A data silo.

Providing XML Web Services

A common use of services is to give other programmers public access to your information by using an open API that can be consumed anywhere. You might recall the WSDL file, described in the earlier section "Contract driven" — it can make your cool function or valuable data available to anyone who needs it.

In the demographic silo example, described in the earlier section "Building Service-Oriented Applications," if you have a valuable mailing list and you want to give your customers access to it, you can send them the list. If you do, however, they can use it forever. Instead, suppose that you could bill your customers every time they use the list. If you provide Web services to implemented functions on the list, you can then track actual usage of the list.

You can see this concept, known as provision past the boundary, everywhere. Take Twitter, for example. Rather than making users to go the Web page to search through billions of messages, Twitter provides a WSDL contract that gives developers the ability to search in their own applications.

Web services can be controlled like any other Web application can. The field-level or operation-level security that used to be handled at the RDBMS level can now be built into a semipublic API.

Building Three Sample Apps

You can build services in C# in a few ways, as described in the next three chapters. This section's heading isn't exactly right, however: I show you how to build *the same app* in three different ways. The app, the SHARP conference management system (or a simple version of it), was built using these formats:

- **ASMX:** This first version is in the venerable ASMX format: ASP.NET Web services. Though this format has been largely superseded by WCF, it's still available. I cover it in this chapter and the next because it's a viable solution for certain situations.
- **WCF:** Windows Communication Foundation (WCF), the most important service platform, is given enough screen time here to get you started. The topic is broad, and you can find lots of references to other resources.
- **REST:** REpresentational State Transfer (REST), the oldest service protocol on the planet, has a new life, thanks to AJAX. REST isn't a first-class citizen in the .NET world, but it's important.

The entire process uses a single entity data model, shown in Figure 1-6, and provides allowed operations to it.

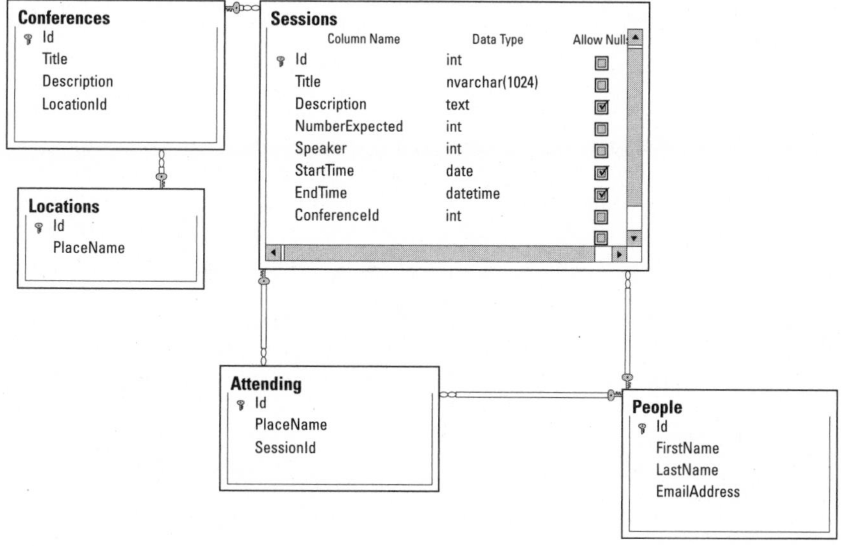

Figure 1-6: The simplified SHARP data model.

The idea is to provide a service model similar to the heating system platform described earlier in this chapter, except using a real, stateful, data-driven application.

Finally, I show you how to solve three different problems. Then you can shoot for three different outcomes. Otherwise, what fun would it be?

Chapter 2: Building Web Services with ASMX

In This Chapter

- Getting acquainted with SOAP
- Creating an ASMX service
- Running an ASMX service
- Building the SHARP code

In Chapter 1 I state that services provide access to functional code over the wire. Though it wasn't covered, it probably became obvious that one just can't call a method on a remote machine without some kind of wrapper. The black magic that makes .NET methods work in a client program don't work over the Internet.

There have been a bunch of remote procedure call (as it is called) protocols over the years. Some you might be familiar with include:

- CORBA
- DCOM
- RCW
- OpenBinder
- LINX
- DLPI
- STREAMS
- DDE
- Even AJAX, in its own way.

The benefit to using services is that they are based on a:

- standard
- human readable
- extendable
- protocol

None of the other messaging protocols are all of those. They all have some small (or occasionally large) problem that prevents the benefits of remote procedure access to really shine. Web services provide what is actually needed. The second Web service protocol to provide these benefits in usable form is SOAP. (ReST is the first, but that is a story for a later chapter.)

Getting to Know SOAP

Simple Object Access Protocol or SOAP is an XML-based protocol for sending messages over the Internet, usually via HTTP. You can think of it as an envelope for remote procedure calls because that is exactly what it is.

The major benefit to SOAP, aside for its rather global acceptance and its longevity, is the rich experience that it provides the client. There are a *lot* of developer features in SOAP, like transactions and security, and they all work pretty well.

SOAP and standards

Standards are discussed in this book elsewhere, but it bears discussing here too. Here is how standards-based development works:

1. Either because of industry need or a company idea, some organization develops a standard. This is usually a recognized organization like the World Wide Web Consortium (W3C) or a company, like Microsoft or IBM.
2. The standard is distributed to the community for review.
3. After community acceptance, the standard is certified, either by the originating organization or an organization like IEEE or ISO.
4. Some company, when developing a product, realizes that it needs a feature that happens to be described by that standard.
5. After reviewing the standard, the company decides to implement the standard.

Realistically, regardless of certification, only when a large number of companies implement a standard does it actually become a genuine standard. Many so-called "Web" browsers over the years supported "standard" protocols like VRML and such that never made it.

It's true, folks. The Internet superhighway is littered with the broken documents of dead standards.

The WS-* standards

The WS-* (usually pronounced WS-*star,* referring to the wildcard * character that references all standards that begin with WS) standards fit right in here. These are Web service standards that apply to protocols like SOAP. They are written by a standards organization, reviewed, certified, and have been used.

What is better is that the additional standards include a lot of really neat functionality that makes SOAP a very rich development experience. Usually, distributed communication standards leave transactions, security, and other such functionality up to the developer.

SOAP isn't like that. It is supposed to have all that stuff baked in.

The WS-* standards include all this useful functionality:

- **Web Services Transactions (WS-TX):** Coordinates the outcome of broadly distributed communications.
- **Web Services Reliable Exchange (WS-RX):** Provides a confirmation of communication for service calls.
- **Web Service Federation (WS-FED):** Allows for a federation of trust between service providers.
- **Web Service Remote Portlets (WS-RP):** A standard for Web parts using services (like you see in SharePoint).
- **Web Service Security (WS-SX):** A supported trusted exchange.
- **Web Services Discovery (WS-DD):** A way to find services in a large enterprise.
- **Building Information Exchange (oBIX):** Allows buildings to talk to each other about their wiring. No, I'm *not* kidding!
- **OASIS ebXML:** A business XML standard that is designed to provide a standardized data model for communications.

In general, these are fantastic additions. They define a set of functionality that all Web service development software providers — Microsoft, IBM, Sun, open source initiatives, whomever — can implement. If you need transactions, they are there. Security? Baked in.

The impact to you

The problem is that these standards were used differently by every company that implemented them.

No, I am not kidding. The problem with standards this detailed in scope is that in order to be useful they must either leave a lot to the imagination or define everything. OASIS erred on the side of being too loose, and the implementations are a mess.

If you are working inside the Microsoft stack — meaning, you are communicating with other .NET projects — you are golden. Within the Microsoft platform, everything is defined the same.

However, if you are communicating outside the .NET Framework — say with IBM or Sun — you should expect problems if you are using WS-* defined functionality.

The take-home is that SOAP includes a lot of standard functionality that isn't found anywhere else. Sure, some distributed message contracts have a lot of features found in SOAP, and SOAP might not be completely implemented the same everywhere, but there isn't anything else that even tries to provide this functionality in a standardized way.

From this perspective, SOAP is a fantastic platform. Need transactions, especially **secure** transactions? SOAP has them. Need large binary attachments? SOAP has that. Have BPEL requirements? There's a SOAP for that.

Big, fat, and slow

All this eating at the trough of standardized features has made SOAP, well, a little large-boned. Let me give you an example. The XML required just to set the context for transactions (the service equivalent of a cookie) is:

```
<wscoor:CoordinationContext
    xmlns:wsa="http://www.w3.org/2005/08/addressing"
    xmlns:wscoor="http://docs.oasis-open.org/
                        ws-tx/wscoor/2006/06"
    xmlns:myApp="http://www.example.com/myApp"
    S11:mustUnderstand="true">
    <wscoor:Identifier>
         http://Fabrikam123.com/SS/1234
    </wscoor:Identifier>
    <wscoor:Expires>3000</wscoor:Expires>
    <wscoor:CoordinationType>
       http://docs.oasis-open.org/ws-tx/wsat/2006/06
    </wscoor:CoordinationType>
    <wscoor:RegistrationService>
        <wsa:Address>
         http://Business456.com/
                     mycoordinationservice/
registration
        </wsa:Address>
        <wsa:ReferenceParameters>
          <myApp:BetaMark> ... </myApp:BetaMark>
```

```
            <myApp:EBDCode> ... </myApp:EBDCode>
          </wsa:ReferenceParameters>
      </wscoor:RegistrationService>
      <myApp:IsolationLevel>
            RepeatableRead
      </myApp:IsolationLevel>
  </wscoor:CoordinationContext>
```

In the Java world, 10MB SOAP messages are not uncommon — although that includes the payload — and that works out to what, 200,000 lines? In one HTTP call? That's probably a bit much.

SOAP dramatically increases your overhead in communication. If you don't need the security, federation, and transaction capabilities of SOAP, consider ReST — covered in Chapter 4. If you are communicating in a homogenous Microsoft environment, consider binary encoding.

On the other hand, if you are communicating in moderately heterogeneous environments and do in fact need an encrypted, federated transaction using a common enterprise data model, by all means look at SOAP.

Making an ASMX Service

You can write a SOAP service in ASMX or WCF.

ASMX doesn't stand for anything — it is ASPX with the *P* changed to an *M*, which means Service. (Try not to laugh.) It is the extension of an ASP.NET Web file that provides a service rather than a Web page.

The thing is, ASMX allows only for SOAP. WCF does other things. Here I cover ASMX; I leave ASMX here because WCF's additional functionality makes WCF a clear winner in this race. (For writing in WCF, check out Chapter 3.)

Nonetheless, if you are making a publically consumable service and need it to be straightforward and simple to deploy, then ASMX might be for you. Certainly, there is a lot of ASMX service code out there which you might have to maintain.

Let's just start by building one.

Creating a new service

ASMX Web services are ASP.NET projects. As such, they seem a lot like ASP. NET Web applications — because they *are* ASP.NET Web applications. You can actually put an ASMX file in a regular ASP.NET application, and a Web file in a Web service application like we do in the following step list. The template is just there to help you get started.

1. **Open Visual Studio and click on New Project.**

   The New Project dialog box appears.

2. **In Installed Templates under the Visual C# node, select Web.**
3. **In the box to the right, click ASP.NET Web Service Application.**
4. **Change the Name to `ANewService` and the Solution to `Book7Chapter2`.**

   An example is shown in Figure 2-1.

5. **Click OK.**

This process generates a project that has all the right references for a Web service project in ASMX and gives you a sample file to start with.

Analyzing the file setup

Note that although a `Service1.asmx` file (and the usual code-behind file) is created, the markup file has only one line in it:

```
<%@ WebService Language="C#" CodeBehind="Service1.asmx.cs"
   Class="ANewService.Service1" %>
```

This is by design. Nothing goes in the markup file. All the magic is in the code-behind.

Figure 2-1: Make a new Web service.

Breaking down the sample code

The `Service1.asmx.cs` file does all the work in our new service, starting with the code in the template. Let's run through that code a line at a time:

```
1  using System;
2  using System.Collections.Generic;
3  using System.Linq;
4  using System.Web;
5  using System.Web.Services;
6
7  namespace ANewService
8  {
9      /// <summary>
10     /// Summary description for Service1
11     /// </summary>
12     [WebService(Namespace = "http://tempuri.org/")]
13     [WebServiceBinding(ConformsTo = WsiProfiles.BasicProfile1_1)]
14     [System.ComponentModel.ToolboxItem(false)]
15     // To allow this Web Service to be called from script, using ASP.NET AJAX,
   uncomment the following line.
16     // [System.Web.Script.Services.ScriptService]
17     public class Service1 : System.Web.Services.WebService
18     {
19
20         [WebMethod]
21         public string HelloWorld()
22         {
23             return "Hello World";
24         }
25     }
26 }
```

There are eight things to point out:

- Line 5 brings in the `System.Web.Services` namespace; it's essential to the rest of the template.
- Line 12 sets the Namespace for the service. The namespace, just like the namespace of your .NET classes, can be anything you want. It doesn't refer to a real place on the Web.
- Line 13 sets the Web Service Binding. WS-I is the Web Services Interoperability organization who (you guessed it) sets *even more* standards for Web services. Basic Profile 1.1 is more or less the industry standard. You can find out more at `http://www.ws-i.org`.
- Line 14 declares if the item should be a Toolbox item in design time environments. This declares whether it should show up in design time Toolboxes.
- Line 16 (when uncommented) activates runtime support for AJAX.
- Line 17 is a normal, everyday class definition, but notice that it inherits `System.Web.Service.WebService`.

- On Line 20, you can see the `[WebMethod]` attribute. This allows you to control what methods are available to the service from the class, and there are a few attributes for fine-grained control.
- The code itself is fairly boring — the functional code is exactly the same as it would be in a normal class. All the things that make it a Web service are in the declaration.

Running the service

Press F5 and run the service. If all goes well, you should see something like Figure 2-2. This is the default visualization for a service — remember that you didn't make a user interface; IIS did this for you, to make it easier to test. External users can't see this.

Clicking the Service Description gives you the WDSL for the whole service. This is what a non-.NET application needs to build its proxy. Note that all it does is append a `?WSDL` to the end of the URL.

Clicking the Hello World link gives you a test screen and implementation guidance for the method. You will have one of these links for every one of the methods in the class marked with `WebMethod`.

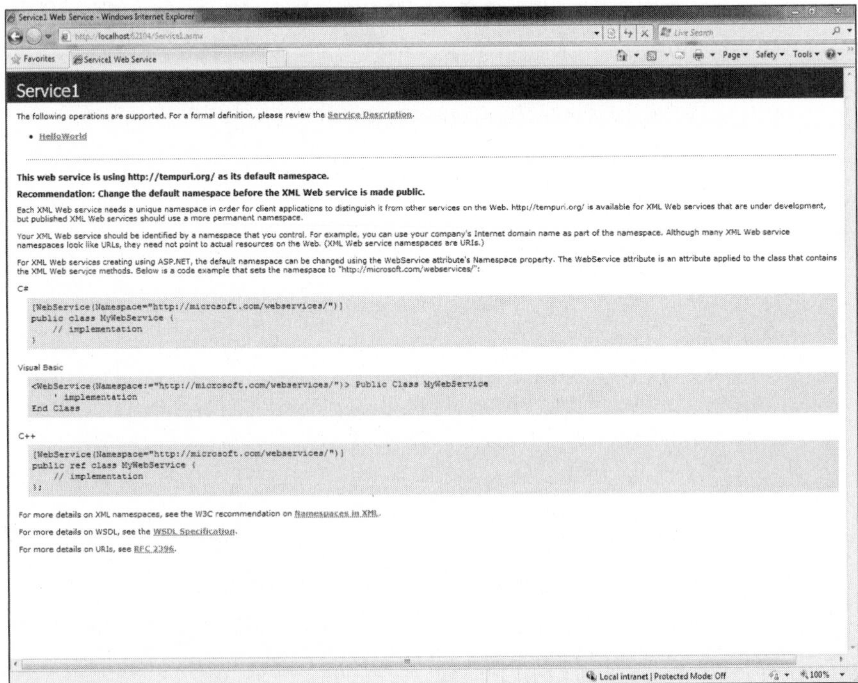

Figure 2-2: Running the default service.

Building the code for SHARP

First you need to get set up. Here's what you need to do to start using the Web template:

1. **Add a new Web Service Application project to the solution by right-clicking the solution and selecting Add New Project. Name the project** `SharpAsmx`.
2. **If you haven't already, add a data connection to the** `ConferenceDB`**. The database is downloadable from** `csharpfordummies.net`.
3. **Right-click on the** `SharpAsmx` **project and add an Entity Data Model by selecting Add ...New Item and picking ADO.NET Entity Data Model from the list. (It's under Data.) I named it** SHARP.edmx.
4. **When the Entity Data Model wizard appears, select Generate from Database and click Next.**
5. **In Choose Your Data Connection, pick the** `ConferenceDb` **you added in Step 1. Keep the rest of the defaults.**
6. **When it asks you to copy the file to your project, choose No.**

   You don't need copies of the database floating around.
7. **In Choose Your Database Objects, pick all the tables except sysdiagrams, and change the Model Namespace to** SharpModel.

   An example appears in Figure 2-3.
8. **Click Finish.**

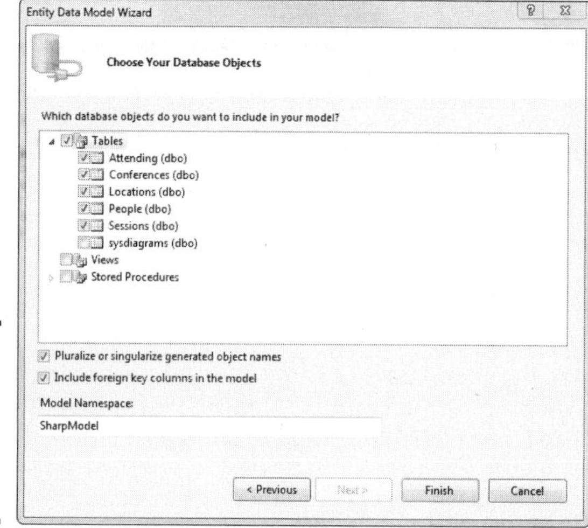

Figure 2-3: Adding the Sharp tables to the model.

That's how you set up an ASMX Web service project. You have a data source, an entity model (you could use your organization's domain model, or hand-rolled procedures and ADO.NET, or whatever), and a starting point for the service.

Next, you set up some services that make sense of your user interface. There are two schools of thought on this. First, you can roll up the entity model in the service signature itself. Second, you could write a separate business layer and just call the Business Layer (BL) methods with the services.

The deciding factor is reuse. If you will later need to roll exactly this logic into a standalone application (anything that won't use the services), then make a separate BL. For simplicity, we will do the former.

1. **Using the default template, delete the default `HelloWorld` method and put in a method signature for a new `conferencesAtLocation` method. It will accept a `conferenceId` (maybe from Web site navigation) and return a list of conferences at that location.**

```
public List<Conference> conferencesAtLocation(int locationId)
{

}
```

2. **The first step is just to get the entities from the Entity Data Model. Add the bold lines. They set up a context for the Entity Framework, then get the list of conferences.**

```
public List<Conference> conferencesAtLocation(int locationId)
{
    ConferenceDbEntities conferenceContext = new ConferenceDbEntities();
    ObjectSet<Conference> allConferences = conferenceContext.Conferences;
}
```

3. **Next, write a Linq query to just get the conferences with the `locationId`. This is in the bold lines below.**

```
public List<Conference> conferencesAtLocation(int locationId)
{
    ConferenceDbEntities conferenceContext = new ConferenceDbEntities();
    ObjectSet<Conference> allConferences = conferenceContext.Conferences;
    var conferenceQuery = from c in allConferences
                          where c.LocationId == locationId
                          select c;
}
```

4. **In order to use the results of the Linq query, you must use an iterator. You need to dispose of the context. Finally, you return the results. These steps are in the bold lines added below:**

```
public List<Conference> conferencesAtLocation(int locationId)
{
    ConferenceDbEntities conferenceContext = new ConferenceDbEntities();
    ObjectSet<Conference> allConferences = conferenceContext.Conferences;
```

```
        var conferenceQuery = from c in allConferences
                              where c.LocationId == locationId
                              select c;
        List<Conference> locationConferences = conferenceQuery.ToList();
        conferenceContext.Dispose();

        return locationConferences;
    }
```

5. To make it a Web service, you need to add the `WebMethod` **decorator on the method signature, and you are done.**

```
[WebMethod]
public List<Conference> conferencesAtLocation(int locationId)
{
  ConferenceDbEntities conferenceContext = new ConferenceDbEntities();
  ObjectSet<Conference> allConferences = conferenceContext.Conferences;
  var conferenceQuery = from c in allConferences
            where c.LocationId == locationId
            select c;
  List<Conference> locationConferences = conferenceQuery.ToList();
  conferenceContext.Dispose();

  return locationConferences;
}
```

6. Press F5 to run the test page, and click on the `conferencesAtLocation` **method link. Enter** 3 **into the Test field, and the result should come back like Figure 2-4 if everything is good.**

So what about all that other stuff that goes into SOAP? Security, transactions, and like that? It's all baked in, but it's well beyond the scope of this book.

For instance, check out the `SoapHeader` attribute. It allows you to specify even the most complex security attributes on your Web methods. There's more, too. Check out MSDN.

Deploying

Deploying an XML Web Service is just like deploying a Web application. They are effectively the same thing.

One benefit of ASMX over WCF is the simple configuration. In fact, if you check out the configuration file for the application you built here, you'll see that the only configuration information revolves around the Entity Model. Adding an ASMX service to a Web project is easy.

Something important that you need to know: After you deploy, the sample test page doesn't run anymore. You'll still get the information service page, but if you try to run the test script, you'll get the message shown in Figure 2-5. This is just for security and can be overridden, though I don't advise overriding it in a production setting.

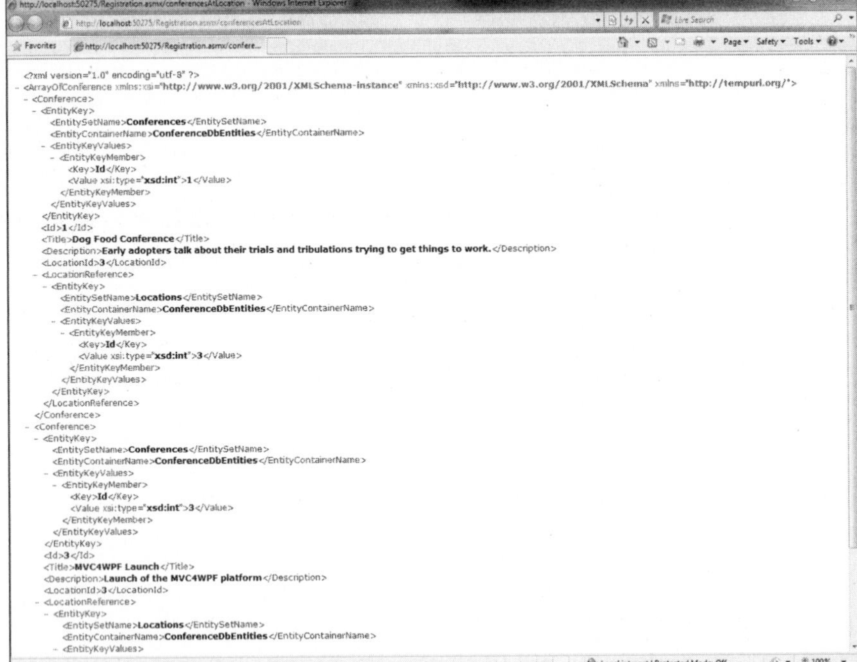

Figure 2-4: Results of our service.

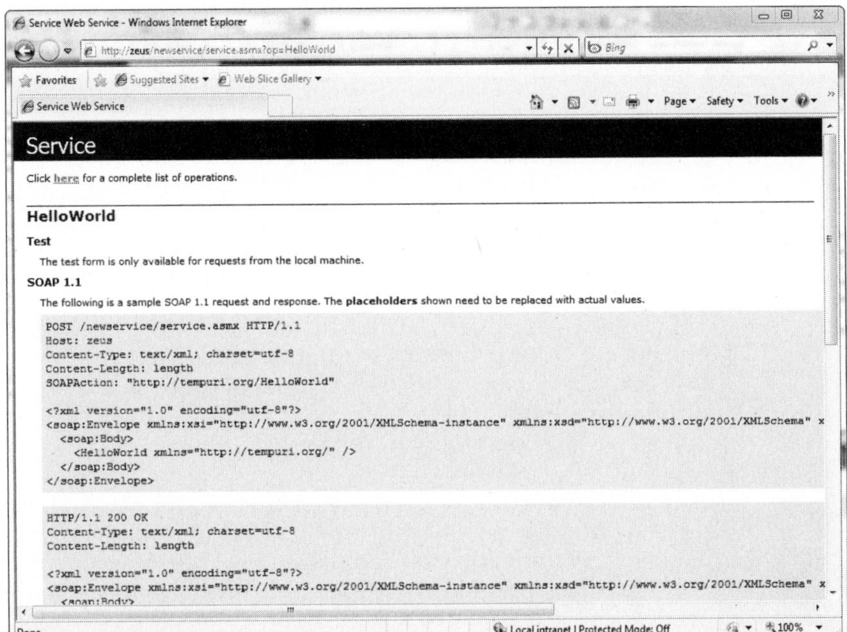

Figure 2-5: Can't run test scripts in production!

Consuming services in your applications

Consuming an ASMX service works just like consuming any other service, from any provider. To see what I mean, follow these steps.

1. **Create a new C# Console application in the project. I called mine** ConsumeSharp.
2. **Right-click on the project and select Add Service Reference.**
3. **Click the Discover button.**

   Visual Studio finds all the services in your solution. In a real project, you probably would put a URL in the Address text box.
4. **Select the** `Registration.asmx` **service and set the Namespace to** `SharpReference`.

   An example is shown in Figure 2-6.
5. **Click OK.**

Visual Studio does a ton of work for you here. There is no magic — Visual Studio reads the WSDL of the service referenced and builds a proxy just as though it were a service written in C++ or Java.

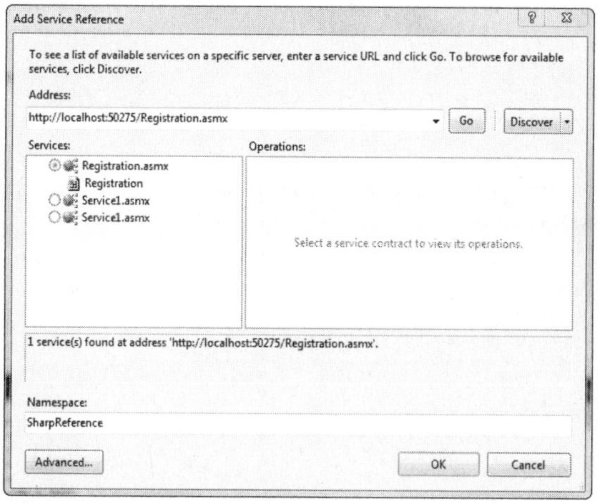

Figure 2-6: Adding a service reference.

As such, the objects returned to you will be more along the lines of a service than what you would expect in C#, especially as delivered by ASMX. The code in the console application to consume your now-proxied service looks like this:

```
using System;
using System.Collections.Generic;
using System.Linq;
using System.Text;
```

```
namespace ConsoleApplication1
{
    class Program
    {
        static void Main(string[] args)
        {
            SharpReference.RegistrationSoapClient serviceReference = new
    SharpReference.RegistrationSoapClient();
            SharpReference.Conference[] conferences = serviceReference.
    conferencesAtLocation(3);
            Console.WriteLine("There will be {0} conferences at location number
    3.", conferences.Length)
            Console.ReadKey();
        }
    }
}
```

Notice that the `conferencesAtLocation` method now returns an array rather than a `List<Conference>`. The consuming language doesn't have to have generics, but it does have to have arrays (if it conforms to WS-I). That's the only assumption we can make. (See Figure 2-7.)

Right-click on the console application and press F5. The console application should start, and it should find the two rows in the array just as it would in the list.

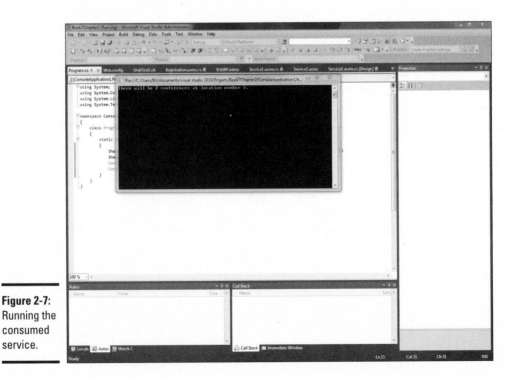

Figure 2-7: Running the consumed service.

Chapter 3: Building Web Services with WCF

In This Chapter

- Getting acquainted with WCF
- Creating WCF services
- Configuring a new service
- Deploying a new service

Windows Communication Foundation is just that — the foundation for communication between Windows computers. It just so happens that thanks to open standards like SOAP and ReST, WCF can communicate with other software systems.

Although ASMX was really designed to make public services — such as, for instance, adding an API to a simple Web application — WCF is a complete distributed computing platform for Windows.

In the early days of .NET, there was a technology called .NET Remoting that replaced DCOM. DCOM was Distributed COM, or the common accepted way to communicate between distributed components. It was replaced by REmoting when .NET came out. Remoting basically took the principles of DCOM and migrated them to .NET.

WCF isn't like that. WCF is a complete rethinking of distributed computing, based on the understanding that computing is becoming more and more distributed. New protocols for communication come out every day.

The goal here then is to define the differences between ASMX and WCF, and see that WCF is a true communications protocol and that ASMX is solely for adding services to Web sites. You can use either technology for both tasks, but one is certainly more suited than the other for each.

In this chapter I look at why WCF works well and then build the SHARP service for a variety of service types. Won't have to change a lick of code to do it, either. It's all in the configuration.

Getting to Know WCF

First there was DCOM. Then there was .NET Remoting.

The path to a distributed computing platform for Microsoft has been a long one. Distributed computing is a hard problem to solve; nothing bad on the Microsoft developers for continuing to hone their platform.

Anyway, there is SOAP, there are Microsoft binary formats, people are creating custom HTTP contexts — the distributed computing platform is a mess. Something needed to happen to enable us to all take our existing code and make it available across the enterprise.

The designers of WCF (largely Doug Purdy, Don Box, and crew) had two diverse issues. On one hand was ASMX, providing SOAP Web service access to business logic. On the other hand was .NET Remoting, providing Microsoft a custom, black box format for the transmission of information between components via known network protocols.

In Chapter 2, I discuss ASMX and its limitations. Taking a deeper look at Remoting makes the case for a comprehensive platform even more clear. (See Figure 3-1.)

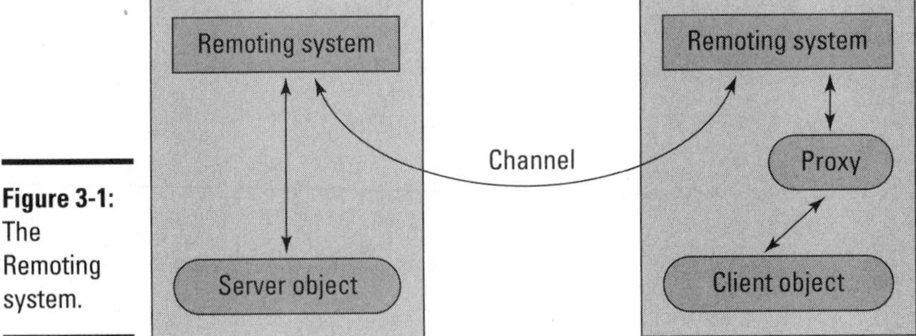

Figure 3-1: The Remoting system.

If each of two systems, say a Client System and a Server System, had a similarly configured Remoting system, then they could communicate. The problem, of course, is that it was never, ever configured correctly (or so it seemed). One side of the equation or the other will make some change, and the whole system will come to a crashing halt.

Clearly, there has to be some product that brings the various formats of remote access together under one umbrella. Something that would accept one block of logic and provide multiple service types.

Eventually, WCF was that solution. Starting as an add-on to .NET 2.0, WCF effectively enabled developers to make specific endpoints for a generic connector.

Let's be clear about the problem we were trying to solve. In Figure 3-2, we see the original problem illustrated by David Chappel for Microsoft back in 2007.

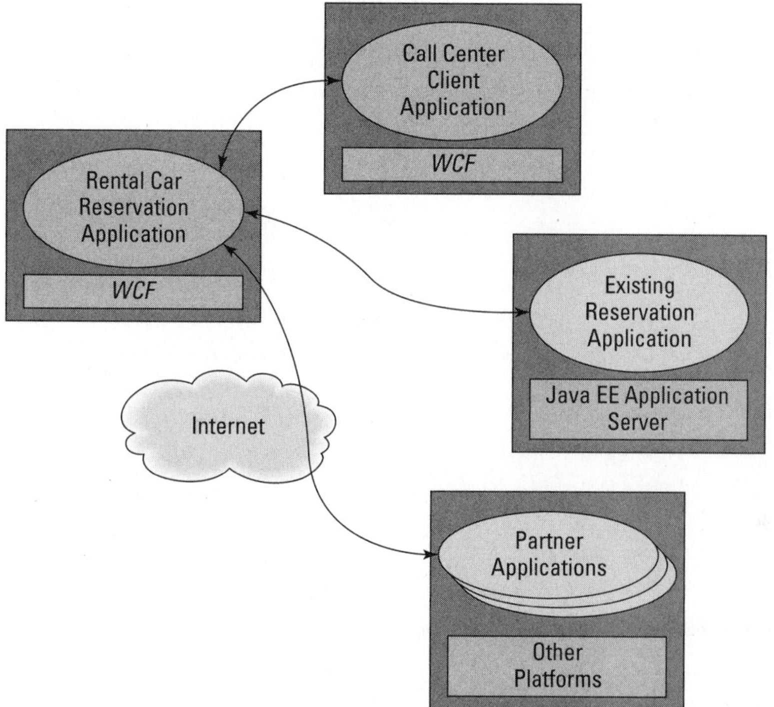

Figure 3-2: The original problem to be solved.

A car dealership is trying to build a new reservation application (similar to the conference management application of SHARP). The business logic needs to be both accessible to outside applications and provide a quality binary transport format for the internal communication.

WCF is the answer. It uses configuration to provide various *endpoints* to consuming applications, from SOAP to ReST to binary associations that resemble DCOM. It doesn't require configuration on both ends of the pipe, only on the server side. If the server serves it, the client can consume it.

Creating a WCF Service

As with so much in working with the .NET Framework, creating a WCF service isn't so much about the code as it is about the configuration. The SHARP project starts out a lot like the ASMX service.

To get started building out the SHARP service in WCF, follow these steps:

1. **Open Visual Studio and click on New Project.**
2. **Select the WCF Service Application in the Web folder of the tree view.**
3. **Configure the project, as shown in Figure 3-3.**
4. **Click OK.**

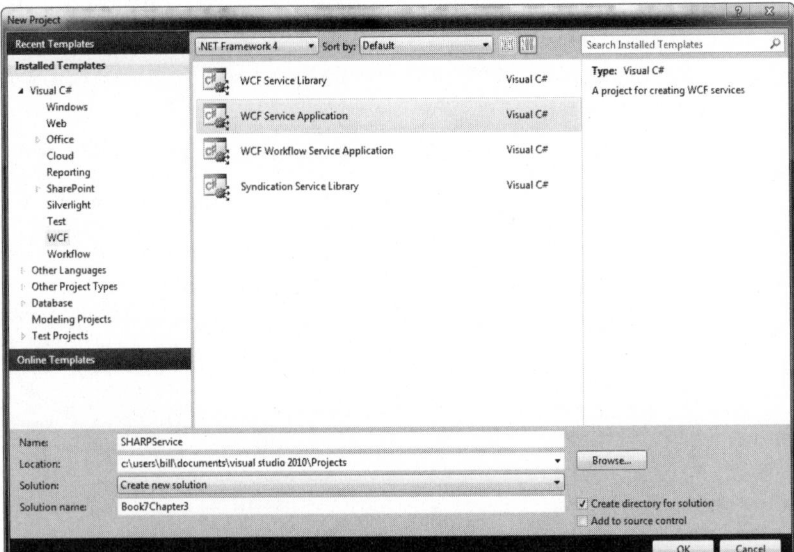

Figure 3-3: Starting the new WCF Service.

Breaking it down

Let's look at the template code for a bit. It's nothing like the ASMX code, because remember — WCF is different. You can get it to do more or less the same thing as ASMX, but it isn't the same technology. Here's what the WCF code looks like:

```
namespace SHARPService
{
    // NOTE: You can use the "Rename" command on the "Refactor" menu to change
  the class name "Service1" in code, svc and config file together.
  public class Service1 : IService1
    {
```

```
        public string GetData(int value)
        {
            return string.Format("You entered: {0}", value);
        }

        public CompositeType GetDataUsingDataContract(CompositeType composite)
        {
            if (composite == null)
            {
                throw new ArgumentNullException("composite");
            }
            if (composite.BoolValue)
            {
                composite.StringValue += "Suffix";
            }
            return composite;
        }
    }
}
```

There are a few of things of interest here:

- **There is no `[WebMethod]` decoration.** You don't need it in WCF. The whole project is a service project.
- **The class implements a custom interface, `IService`.** We'll look at that in a second.
- **There are two sample methods.** The usual old "hello world" style method `GetData`, and a more complex example called `GetDataUsingContract`.

The `GetDataUsingContract` method makes a lot more sense when you take a look at `IService.cs` below.

```
namespace SHARPService
{
    // NOTE: You can use the "Rename" command on the "Refactor" menu to change the interface name "IService1" in both code and config file together.
    [ServiceContract]
    public interface IService1
    {

        [OperationContract]
        string GetData(int value);

        [OperationContract]
        CompositeType GetDataUsingDataContract(CompositeType composite);

        // TODO: Add your service operations here
    }
    // Use a data contract as illustrated in the sample below to add composite types to service operations.
    [DataContract]
    public class CompositeType
    {
        bool boolValue = true;
        string stringValue = "Hello ";

```

```
23         [DataMember]
24         public bool BoolValue
25         {
26             get { return boolValue; }
27             set { boolValue = value; }
28         }
29
30         [DataMember]
31         public string StringValue
32         {
33             get { return stringValue; }
34             set { stringValue = value; }
35         }
36     }
37 }
```

Hey, lookie here! Decorations for the classes! And the mythical `CompositeType`! Don't let the name fool you — this code is just a class, like any other class. It is just like the List<T> of Conference types that we returned from the ASMX service. The Framework doesn't have a Conference class — we defined it in the entity Data Model.

Line 4 has a `[ServiceContract]` attribute that is similar to the `[WebClass]` of ASMX, and the `[OperationContract]` too, is similar to `[WebMethod]`, at least in usage.

Then we have the `DataContract`. This allows us to decorate classes — even in our domain model — with attributes that define which classes and methods get to go out to the service if and when the class is ever called into service (so to speak).

Making a registration service

Like we do in Chapter 2, let's just start with a service that returns the list of our conferences. Follow these steps:

1. **Create a new WCF Service project, just like the earlier example.**

   I called mine `SHARPService`.

2. **Add a Class called `Conference`.**

   This will be a hand-rolled class that won't be connected to a database for now, but will provide a good example of how to set up a `DataContract`. This listing is the code-behind of the service file.

   ```
   using System;
   using System.Collections.Generic;
   using System.Linq;
   using System.Web;
   using System.Runtime.Serialization;

   namespace SHARPService
   {
   ```

```
        public class Conference : SHARPService.IConference
        {
            public int Id { get; set; }
            public String Title { get; set; }
            public String Description { get; set; }
            public int LocationId { get; set; }
        }
    }
```

We want this to be our `DataContract` for the service. Based on what we see in the template, we should add a `[DataContract]` above the class and `[DataMember]` above the properties.

3. **Add the `DataContract` for the service.**

```
using System;
using System.Collections.Generic;
using System.Linq;
using System.Web;
using System.Runtime.Serialization;

namespace SHARPService
{
    [DataContract]
    public class Conference : SHARPService.IConference
    {
        [DataMember]
        public int Id { get; set; }
        [DataMember]
        public String Title { get; set; }
        [DataMember]
        public String Description { get; set; }
        [DataMember]
        public int LocationId { get; set; }
    }
}
```

Now that there is a class to use, it is time to make the service.

4. **Right-click on the SHARPService project and add a new WCF Service.**

   I called mine `Registration.svc`.

5. **Delete the template method and add the code below.**

   Unlike the ASMX sample, this isn't a working version; we are just setting up a mock reply.

```
namespace SHARPService
{
    public class Registration : IRegistration
    {
        public List<Conference> conferencesAtLocation(int locationId)
        {
            List<Conference> locationConferences = new
    List<Conference>();
            return locationConferences;
        }
    }
}
```

6. **Right-click on the `Registration.svc` file and select Set as Start Page.**
7. **Press F5 to run the Project.**

Notice that though the ASP.NET development server runs, your Web browser does not. The WCF Test Client, shown in Figure 3-4, takes the place of the development test page for ASMX. It enables you to add in the request values and see what the response values are without having to depend on HTTP.

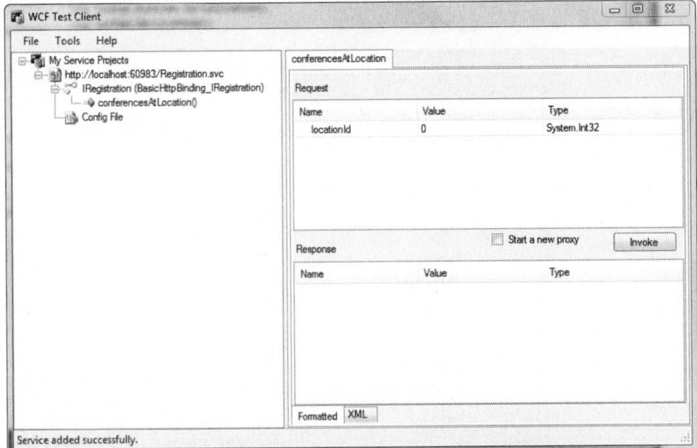

Figure 3-4: The WCF test client.

Why is this? WCF enables you to use things other than HTTP (the protocol that is the backbone of the Web) for transport of message details. (You can find a few examples in the sidebar, "Using different endpoints.")

Configuring

The only downside to WCF is the configuration. Because WCF is the be-all and end-all of the remote procedure call in Windows, there are enough configuration options to handle it all. Gets a little chippy at times.

Fortunately, there is the Service Configuration Editor. Shown in Figure 3-5, the Service Configuration Editor allows you to manage the complex options that are WCF's primary power.

Using different endpoints

The whole point of WCF is that you can write one service and then have IIS accept a lot of different protocols calling on the same code. Sure, we can do SOAP, like we did in ASMX. We also can do a lot of other protocols. Here is the breakdown of all the different endpoints, according to MSDN:

- **BasicHttpBinding:** A binding that is suitable for communicating with WS-Basic Profile conformant Web services (for example, ASP.NET Web services [ASMX]-based services). This binding uses HTTP as the transport and text/XML as the default message encoding.
- **WSHttpBinding:** A secure and interoperable binding that is suitable for non-duplex service contracts.
- **WSDualHttpBinding:** A secure and interoperable binding that is suitable for duplex service contracts or communication through SOAP intermediaries.
- **WSFederationHttpBinding:** A secure and interoperable binding that supports the WS-Federation protocol that enables organizations that are in a federation to efficiently authenticate and authorize users.
- **NetTcpBinding:** A secure and optimized binding suitable for cross-machine communication between WCF applications.
- **NetNamedPipeBinding:** A secure, reliable, optimized binding that is suitable for on-machine communication between WCF applications.
- **NetMsmqBinding:** A queued binding that is suitable for cross-machine communication between WCF applications.
- **NetPeerTcpBinding:** A binding that enables secure, multiple machine communication.
- **MsmqIntegrationBinding:** A binding that is suitable for cross-machine communication between a WCF application and existing Message Queuing applications.
- **BasicHttpContextBinding:** A binding that is suitable for communicating with WS-Basic Profile conformant Web services that enables HTTP cookies to be used to exchange context.
- **NetTcpContextBinding:** A secure and optimized binding suitable for cross-machine communication between WCF applications that enables SOAP headers to be used to exchange context.
- **WebHttpBinding:** A binding used to configure endpoints for WCF Web services that are exposed through HTTP requests instead of SOAP messages.
- **WSHttpContextBinding:** A secure and interoperable binding that is suitable for non-duplex service contracts that enables SOAP headers to be used to exchange context.

So when do you use what? Well, if you want to have two .NET applications communicate, or the layers of a single application communicate, then use NetTcpBinding. If you are cross-platform communicating, then use WSHttpBinding.

Only if for some reason those don't work do you start to look into the others. Oh, and remember that you can have many endpoints for the same service. Don't use SOAP for a data layer. Just make a separate SOAP header if you need cross-platform support.

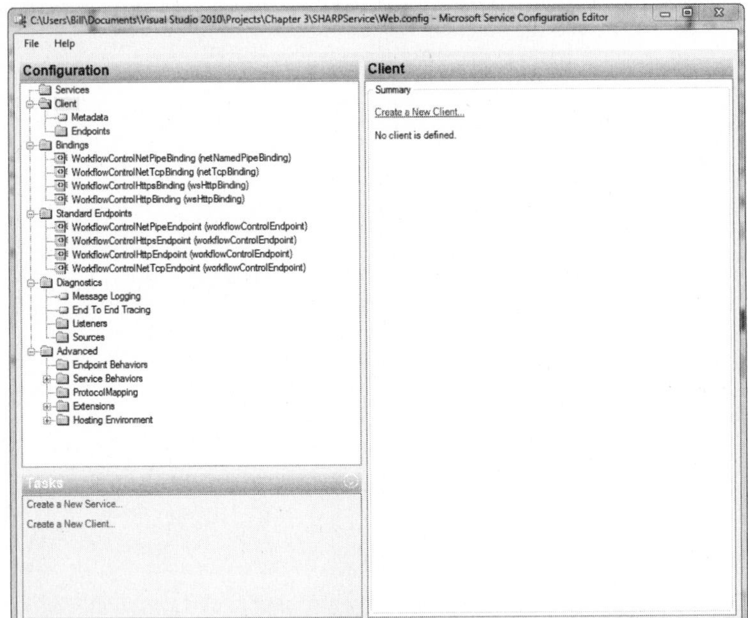

Figure 3-5: The Service Configuration Editor.

Using the Service Configuration Editor for adding a service endpoint seems more complex than it ought to be. Just follow these steps:

1. **Open the Web.config of your project by clicking File... Open and navigate to your Web.config.**
2. **Select File➪Add New then click Create a New Service.**
3. **Click Browse and find the compiled DLL of your project.**

   It should be in the Bin folder, and named `SHARPService.dll` if you used my naming.
4. **Double-click on the DLL, and the services that are represented show up. As shown in Figure 3-6, click the Registration service. Click Open, and then Next.**
5. **Confirm the service contract.**

   (See, I told you it would be useful later!)
6. **Click Next.**

   In the Binding Configuration window, you'll see what I mean about the number of options. Select the Existing Binding Configuration radio button and check out the drop-down list. The items in that list are covered in the sidebar, "Using different endpoints." For now, accept the default.
7. **Click Next.**

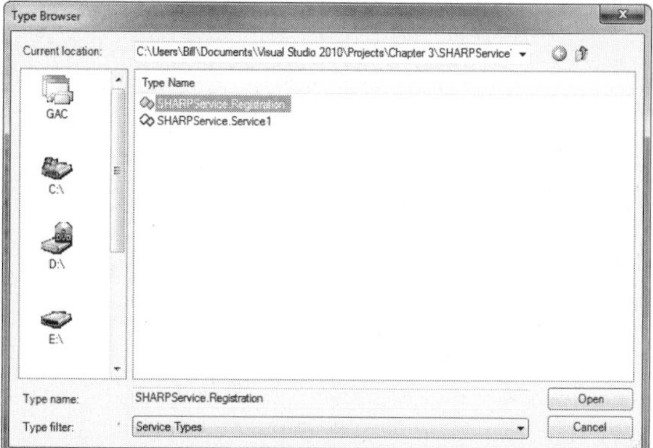

Figure 3-6: Selecting the service in question.

8. **In the endpoint address, enter** http://localhost/ **for the purpose of this walk-through.**
9. **Click Finish on your confirmation window.**
10. **When you are done, an endpoint with no name appears under the `SHARPService.Registration` service. You can click on this endpoint and add a name, like** SharpHttp**. The endpoint panel is shown in Figure 3-7.**
11. **Choose File⇨Save and then close the configuration editor.**

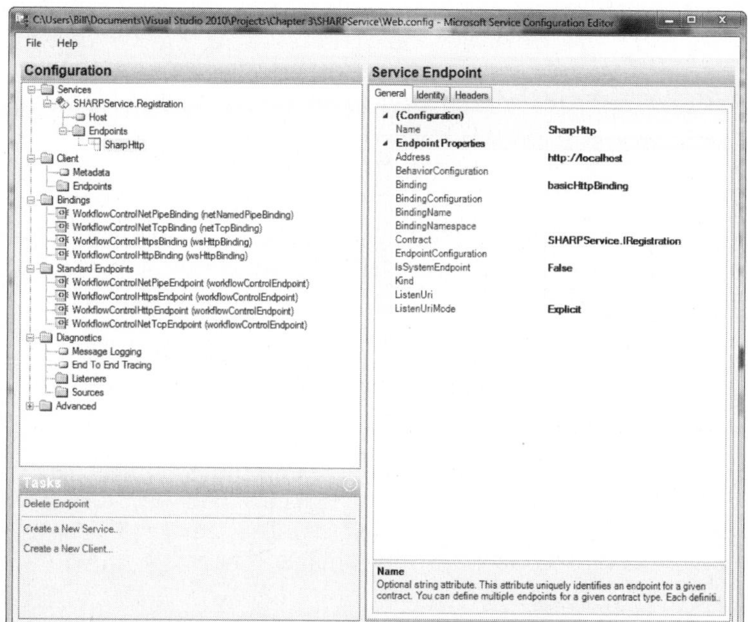

Figure 3-7: A finished endpoint.

Back in Visual Studio–land, open the `Web.Config` file in the code editor by double-clicking it in the Solution Explorer. You'll see that the `ServiceModel` section has been edited with your new endpoint. The code looks like this:

```
<system.serviceModel>
  <services>
    <service name="SHARPService.Registration">
      <clear />
      <endpoint address="http://localhost" binding="basicHttpBinding"
        bindingConfiguration="" name="SharpHttp" contract="SHARPService.
  IRegistration" />
    </service>
  </services>
  <behaviors>
    <serviceBehaviors>
      <behavior>
        <!-- To avoid disclosing metadata information, set the value below to
  false and remove the metadata endpoint above before deployment -->
        <serviceMetadata httpGetEnabled="true" />
        <!-- To receive exception details in faults for debugging purposes, set
  the value below to true.  Set to false before deployment to avoid disclosing
  exception information -->
        <serviceDebug includeExceptionDetailInFaults="false" />
      </behavior>
    </serviceBehaviors>
  </behaviors>
</system.serviceModel>
```

Now, would that have been easier to do in code? Maybe. Why is the service editor around then? Because when you get a lot of bindings, it can get pretty messy in there. Check out the sidebar on using other bindings to get an idea.

Deploying

If you use IIS to host the service, deployment of WCF is the same as ASMX. You can effectively copy the `.svc` and `.config` files with the compiled binaries and have a working Web application.

The better way to deploy in Visual Studio 2010 is to use the Publish Web tool. If you right-click on the project and select Publish, you'll have the option to set up a repeatable profile so that you don't forget anything. (See Figure 3-8.)

This panel does all the things that you would have to do yourself:

- Set the URL of the service
- Name the Application (in the site properties in IIS)
- Set up credentials
- Copy the right files

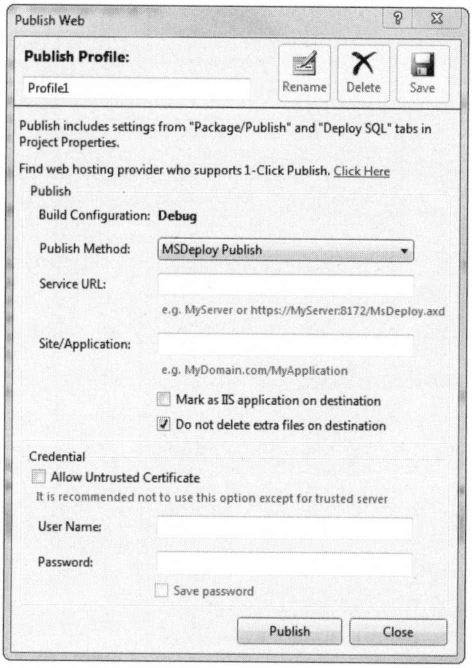

Figure 3-8: The Publish Web dialog box.

You can set up the profile once, and then reuse it every time you have to re-publish the application. Pretty slick.

Consuming

All there is left to do is use it.

As one would expect, setting up a service reference for a WCF service is a lot like setting up a reference for an ASMX service. You still right-click and select Add Service Reference, you still get the dialog box shown in Figure 3-9, and you still can reference the service easily in your code.

Two things to remember:

- ✦ The file extension you are looking for is `.svc`.
- ✦ The binding you set up is abstracted away from you.

The filename thing is workable, but the binding is important. Keep in mind that the selecting of a binding is invisible to the developer, but it has a significant impact on functionality and especially performance. The decision of which to use is not to be made lightly; it should be done only after much research and needs analysis.

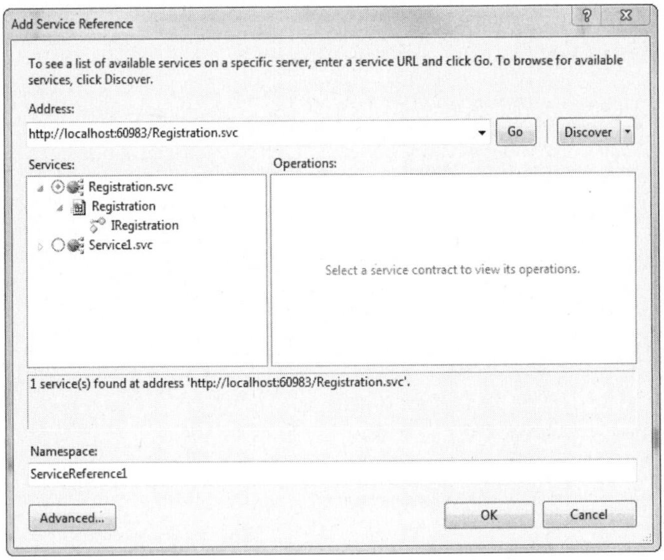

Add Service Reference

To see a list of available services on a specific server, enter a service URL and click Go. To browse for available services, click Discover.

Address:

http://localhost:60983/Registration.svc

Go | Discover

Services:

Registration.svc
Registration
IRegistration
Service1.svc

Operations:

Select a service contract to view its operations.

1 service(s) found at address 'http://localhost:60983/Registration.svc'.

Namespace:

ServiceReference1

Advanced... | OK | Cancel

Figure 3-9: Adding the WCF service reference.

Chapter 4: Building Web Services with ReST

In This Chapter

- Understanding the principles of ReST
- Implementing ReST services using WCF
- Consuming ReST services

Chapter 3 includes a sidebar, "Using Different Endpoints," that has a big list of binding formats you can use with WCF. I point out that for most applications, you use SOAP, or binary. That's not necessarily accurate.

Another binding is pretty popular — it is the binding that your Web browser uses to get pages from Web servers. It is called ReST, and it stands for Representational State Transfer.

In this chapter, I introduce you to ReST and guide you through its advantages and drawbacks.

Getting to Know ReST

ReST is basically the use of the traditional GET and POST patterns the old folks will remember from CGI. For you young pups, it is the basic format of Web requests. For instance, when you click on a link that looks like this:

```
http://mydomain.com/start.aspx?id=3
```

. . . you are using ReST. Remember, we aren't talking about an implementation here. We are talking about a remote procedure call mechanism. It is just a way to get parameters for a query to a remote machine and to get data back.

We also aren't talking about a protocol, like SOAP is. ReST is an architecture. It has guidelines, not rules.

A ReST interface has four goals. They are

- Scalability of component interactions
- Generality of interfaces
- Independent deployment of components
- Intermediary components to reduce latency, enforce security, and encapsulate legacy systems

Use of ReST with WCF meets most but not all of those goals. Let's take a quick ride over the details of the implementation of ReST in WCF, and you can make your own call.

Understanding the Guiding Principles of ReST

There are four guiding principles to ReST. According to the standard, all ReSTful interfaces must provide interfaces that adhere to these principles. In the real world, compliance is up for discussion. Here are the principles:

- **Identification of resources:** Individual resources (like a data item, for instance) are identified in requests (for example, using URIs in Web-based ReST systems). The resources themselves are conceptually separate from the representations that are returned to the client. For example, the server does not send its database, but rather, perhaps, some HTML, XML, or JSON that represents some database records expressed, for instance, in French and encoded in UTF-8, depending on the details of the request and the server implementation.
- **Manipulation of resources through these representations:** When a client holds a representation of a resource, including any metadata attached, it has enough information to modify or delete the resource on the server, provided it has permission to do so.
- **Self-descriptive messages:** Each message includes enough information to describe how to process the message (for example, which parser to invoke). An example of this is the use of Internet media types, previously known as MIME types. From the media type alone, the client must know how to process its contents. If it needs to look inside the message's contents in order to understand it, the message is not self-descriptive. For example, merely using the "application/xml" media type is not sufficient for knowing what to do with its contents, unless code-download is used.
- **Hypermedia as the engine of application state:** If it is likely that the client will want to access related resources, these should be identified in the representation returned (for example, by providing their URIs in sufficient context, such as hypertext links). This creates an environment where the software system consuming the service has more than normal knowledge of the way the data is stored.

Diving into the details of ReST

ReST as a concept is as old as the Web, but as a Web service implementation it is fairly new — about as new as SOAP. The largest implementation of ReST as a standard is the Web itself. CGI is based on the ReST interface.

The call to a ReST interface is clearly smaller than a SOAP call. Seriously. Look at these two examples:

ReST:

```
POST /Start.asmx HTTP/1.1
Host: localhost
Content-Type: http; charset=utf-8
http://mydomain.com/start.aspx?id=3
```

SOAP:

```
POST /Service1.asmx HTTP/1.1
Host: localhost
Content-Type: application/soap+xml; charset=utf-8
Content-Length: length

<?xml version="1.0" encoding="utf-8"?>
<soap12:Envelope xmlns:xsi="http://www.w3.org/2001/XMLSchema-
    instance" xmlns:xsd="http://www.w3.org/2001/XMLSchema"
    xmlns:soap12="http://www.w3.org/2003/05/soap-envelope">
  <soap12:Body>
    <HelloWorld xmlns="http://tempuri.org/" />
  </soap12:Body>
</soap12:Envelope>
```

The XML of SOAP kinda gets in the way.

On the other hand. SOAP has a list of security features. There is a list of transaction features. There is a list of attachment features. SOAP has a lot of features.

ReST, not so much. ReST has only four features:

- GET – Request a resource
- PUT – Upload a resource
- POST – Submit data
- DELETE – Delete resource

Changing a WCF Service to Use ReST

Looking at the WCF service that is built in Chapter 3, it seems that changing the endpoints will solve the problem. This example starts with some of the code created in Chapter 3.Then we will alter the endpoint behavior manually to create a ReST service.

Getting the WCF service

Let's start by getting the code from the WCF service in Chapter 3 and tweaking it. Just follow these steps:

1. **Create a new WCF service application.**

   I called mind `SharpRest`.

2. **Make a new Registration service by right-clicking the folder and choosing Add a New Service File.**

3. **Copy the code into `registration.svc` and `iRegistration.cs` from the similarly named files in the Chapter 3 project.**

4. **Add the Conference class and the iConference interface from Chapter 3.**

Exposing the ReST service

Now for the editing. The class attributes you add here are important because they affect how the compiler sets up the service responses.

To implement ReST on the service side, there have to be three (*Three*!!! That's a bunch!) additional attributes on that service contract:

- **ServiceContractAttribute:** Defines the interface as a service interface.
- **WebInvokeAttribute:** Tells the compiler that this class can be called by a Web-based ReST model.
- **WebGetAttributeClass:** Remember GET, PUT, POST, and DELETE? This tells the runtime that the class will respond to a GET.

All right, ServiceContract we got — it came with the template. We need to add the method contract. The interface now looks like this:

```
namespace SharpRest
{
    [ServiceContract]
    public interface IRegistration
    {
        [OperationContract]
        [WebInvokeAttribute]
        [WebGetAttribute]
```

```
        List<Conference> conferencesAtLocation(int
    locationId);
    }
}
```

What does that do for us? It tells the runtime compiler that a URI can call this directly. You can check out the binding itself by looking at the test client, as shown in Figure 4-1.

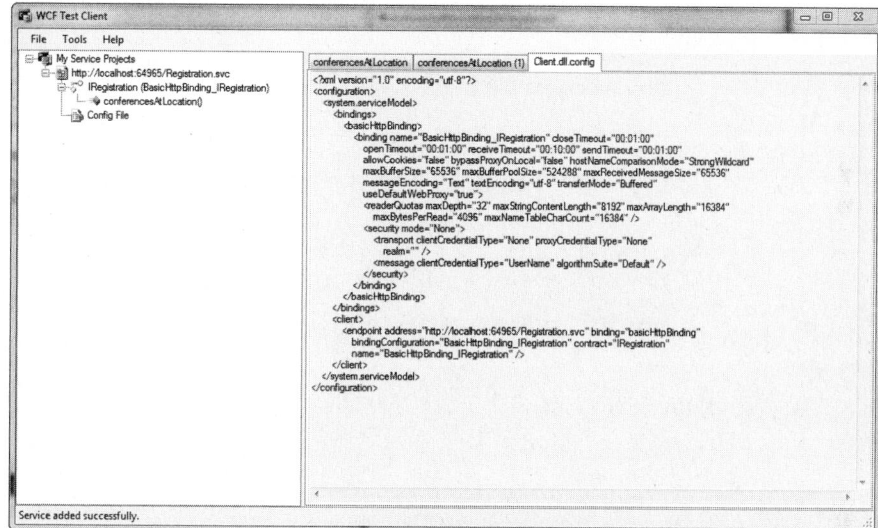

Figure 4-1: A ReST binding.

That isn't all there is to it, though. We need to create a WebServiceHost.

Returning data in different ways

The WebServiceHost is a `ServiceHost` class that happens to handle ReST very well, so we use it for that purpose. There are a few ways to do this, just like there are in WCF. These include the following:

- **Any .NET application running on a box can be a host.** A Windows service, console application, even a running WPF application can host a service. As long as it has access to the network device, it should work.
- **IIS can host the application, and you can configure it in code.** This involves using a WebServiceHost object in the service `codebehind`, and decorating the class with attributes for configuration.
- **The `Web.config` file can be set up to define an endpoint**: This is the easiest way, and the way we do it in Chapter 3. If configured this way, adding other endpoints to the code is a straightforward change.

There isn't a binding in the WCF Configuration tool for the ReST binding, however, so we have to do it another way. Just follow these steps:

1. **Open the `Web.Config` for the service.**

   There should be binding information in there from the SOAP service we built in Chapter 3. Leave that there.

2. **Add the bold listing for the custom POX binding under the ServiceModel section.**

   It is the first bold code in Listing 4-1.

3. **Add the Service information into the Service section. It is the second bold code in Listing 4-1.**

Listing 4-1: The ReST Service Implementation

```
<?xml version="1.0" encoding="utf-8"?>
<configuration>
  <system.web>
    <compilation debug="true" targetFramework="4.0">
      <assemblies>
        <add assembly="System.Data.Entity, Version=4.0.0.0, Culture=neutral, Publ
    icKeyToken=b77a5c561934e089" />
      </assemblies>
    </compilation>
  </system.web>
  <system.serviceModel>
    <bindings>
      <customBinding>
        <binding name="poxBinding">
          <textMessageEncoding messageVersion="None" />
          <httpTransport />
        </binding>
      </customBinding>
    </bindings>
    <services>
      <service name="SHARPService.Registration">
        <clear />
        <endpoint address="http://localhost" binding="basicHttpBinding"
          name="SharpHttp" contract="SHARPService.IRegistration"
    listenUriMode="Explicit">
          <identity>
            <certificateReference storeName="My" storeLocation="LocalMachine"
              x509FindType="FindBySubjectDistinguishedName" />
          </identity>
        </endpoint>
        <endpoint address="http://localhost" binding="wsDualHttpBinding"
          bindingConfiguration="" name="SharpDual" contract="SHARPService.
    IRegistration" />
      </service>
      <service name="SHARPService.Registration">
        <host>
          <baseAddresses>
            <add baseAddress="http://localhost" />
          </baseAddresses>
        </host>
```

```
        <endpoint address="registration"
                  binding="customBinding"
                  bindingConfiguration="poxBinding"
                contract="SHARPService.IRegistration" />
      </service>
    </services>
    <behaviors>
      <serviceBehaviors>
        <behavior>
          <!-- To avoid disclosing metadata information, set the value below to
    false and remove the metadata endpoint above before deployment -->
          <serviceMetadata httpGetEnabled="true" />
          <!-- To receive exception details in faults for debugging purposes, set
    the value below to true.  Set to false before deployment to avoid disclosing
    exception information -->
          <serviceDebug includeExceptionDetailInFaults="false" />
        </behavior>
      </serviceBehaviors>
    </behaviors>
  </system.serviceModel>
  <system.webServer>
    <modules runAllManagedModulesForAllRequests="true" />
  </system.webServer>
  <connectionStrings>
    <add name="ConferenceDbEntities" connectionString="metadata=res://*/
    Sharp.csdl|res://*/Sharp.ssdl|res://*/Sharp.msl;provider=System.Data.
    SqlClient;provider connection string='Data Source=.\SQLEXPRESS;AttachDbFil
    ename=&quot;C:\Program Files\Microsoft SQL Server\MSSQL10.SQLEXPRESS\MSSQL\
    DATA\ConferenceDb.mdf&quot;;Integrated Security=True;Connect Timeout=30;User
    Instance=True;MultipleActiveResultSets=True'" providerName="System.Data.
    EntityClient" />
  </connectionStrings>
</configuration>
```

Book VIII

New Features in C# 4.0

The 5th Wave
By Rich Tennant
With Object Oriented Programming, I understand the "encapsulation" and "inheritance" part. It's that darn "cluttermorphism" that stumps me.

Contents at a Glance

Chapter 1: Programming Dynamically!

In This Chapter

- ✔ **Understanding dynamic typing**
- ✔ **Defining variables**
- ✔ **Putting dynamic to use**
- ✔ **Making static operations dynamic**

For many years, I thought that dynamic programming referred to being really flashy and flamboyant while writing code. So, I started wearing Hawaiian shirts and singing loudly.

Later, I found out this isn't the case.

Dynamic programming is another one of those buzzwords that really doesn't have a clear definition. At its loosest, it means developing something in such a way that the program makes more decisions about the way it runs while running, rather than when you compile it.

Scripting languages are a great example of this. When you write something in VBScript, you don't compile it at all — all of the decisions are made at runtime. Ruby is another good example: Most of the time, an entire program can just be typed into a command prompt and run right from there.

There are examples that are not so good — like VB Classic. Remember the Variant type? You could declare a variable to be Variant and VB wouldn't decide what it was supposed to be for real until the program ran. In the best of cases, this added immense flexibility to the language. In the worst of cases, you got Type Mismatch errors at runtime.

To give a concrete example, when you declare a variable in a dynamically typed language, you don't have to say what type you are making that variable. The compiler will just figure it out for you. In a static language, like C# 3.0, you do have to say what type you are making that variable.

Microsoft originally promised that dynamic types would never be in C#, but later decided that the feature had to be added. Why? Mostly, it's because of the development for Microsoft Office (like the reasoning for much of the rest of Book VIII). Office uses COM, the pre-.NET structure for Microsoft applications.

COM expects that the languages that use it (like VB Classic and C++) will have dynamic types. This made developing for Microsoft Office difficult for C# programmers, which was exactly opposite of what Microsoft wanted to happen. The end result? The dynamic type.

Shifting C# Toward Dynamic Typing

So-called "dynamic languages" are a trend that keeps coming back, like ruffled tux shirts. *Dynamic languages* are languages that allow for loose typing, rather than static. The concept got started in the 1960s with LISP. Dynamic languages came back in the late 1980s for two reasons: network management scripting and the artificial intelligence craze. Thanks to the Web, the buzzword is back yet again.

The World Wide Web, for those of you who aren't old enough to remember, was built on View Source and dynamic languages. Microsoft's original Web development language, Active Server Pages, was built on VBScript — a dynamic language.

The Web is better with a dynamic programming environment, so the trend is probably here to stay this time (until the next big thing, anyway). C# isn't the only language that is adding dynamic language features, and dynamic type isn't the only language feature that has been added to make it more appealing for Web programmers.

Several dynamic languages have been around for a while, like these:

- Perl
- Visual Basic
- Smalltalk
- LISP
- Scheme

While some of these aren't as popular as they once were, they are still out there and have pushed the trend in the newer languages. You can see this trend in all the new or refurbished dynamic languages that have popped up over the last ten years. Many of them have roots in the Web, while others are being newly used for the Web:

- PHP
- Ruby
- JavaScript
- Cold Fusion

- Python
- Cobra (my new favorite)
- Groovy
- Boo
- Newspeak

Programmers who work in dynamic languages — how can I put this gently — feel strongly about their choice of tools. The communities are very strong. Developers who work in dynamic languages use them for practically everything except highly structured team-build kinds of environments, like:

- Scripting infrastructure for system maintenance
- Building tests
- One-use utilities
- Server farm maintenance
- Scripting other applications
- Building Web sites
- File maintenance

Dynamic languages are popular for these kinds of tasks for two reasons. First, they provide instant feedback, because you can try a piece of code outside the constraints of the rest of the program you are writing. Second, you can start building your higher-level pieces of code without building the plumbing that makes it work.

For instance, Ruby has a command line interface that you can simply paste a function into, even out of context, and see how it works. There is even a Web version at `http://tryruby.hobix.com/`. You can type code right in there, even if there are classes referenced that aren't defined, because Ruby will just take a guess at it.

This moves nicely into the next point, that a dynamic language enables you to build a class that refers to a type that you haven't defined elsewhere. For example, you can make a class to schedule an event, without actually having to build the underlying Event type first.

All of this lends itself to a language that is a lot more responsive to change. You can make a logic change in one place and not have to dig through reams of code to fix all the type declarations everywhere. Add this to optional and named parameters (see Chapter 2) and you have a lot less typing to do when you have to change your program.

Other benefits to dynamic languages in general show up as you use them more. For instance, macro languages are usually dynamically typed. If you have tried to build macros in previous versions of Visual Studio, you know what a pain it is to use a static language.

Making C# (and VB.NET, for that matter) more dynamic not only makes it a better language for extending Visual Studio, but it also gives programmers the capability to include the language in the programs they write so that other developers can further extend those applications.

Programming Dynamically

By now, you must be asking, "What exactly are we talking about here?" Fair question. When you define a new variable, you can use the `dynamic` keyword, and C# will let you make assumptions about the members of the variable.

More or less, what I'm talking about it this. If you want to declare a new Course object, you do it like this:

```
Course newCourse = new Course();
newCourse.Schedule();
```

This is, of course, assuming that you have a Course class defined somewhere else in your program, like this:

```
class Course {
   public void Schedule()
   {
       //Something fancy here
   }
}
```

But what if you don't know what class the new object will be? How do you handle that? You could declare it as an Object, because everything derives from Object, right? Here's the code:

```
Object newCourse = new Object();
```

Not so fast, my friend, if you make your next line this:

```
newCourse.Schedule();
```

Note the squiggly line appears almost immediately, and you get the famous "object does not contain a definition for Schedule..." error in the design time Error List.

However, we can do this:

```
dynamic newCourse = SomeFunction();
newCourse.Schedule();
```

All this code needs to have is the stub of a function that returns some value, and we are good to go. What if `SomeFunction()` returns a string? Well, we will get a runtime error. But it will still compile!

About now, if you are anything like me, you have to be thinking: "This is a *good* thing? How!?!" I hear you, trust me. For the time being, you can blame COM.

You see, COM was mostly constructed using C++, which has a variant type. In C++, you could declare a variable to be dynamic, like this:

```
VARIANT newCourse;
```

It worked just like the dynamic type, except C# wasn't invented yet. Anyway, because a lot of the objects in COM used Variant out parameters, it was really tough to handle Interop using .NET.

Because Microsoft Office is mostly made of COM objects, and because it isn't going to change any time soon, and because Microsoft wants us all to be Office developers one day, bam, we have the dynamic type.

Say, for instance, that our `newCourse` is a variant out parameter from a method in a COM class. In order to get the value, we have to declare it an Object, like this:

```
CourseMarshaller cm = new CourseMarshaller(); //a COM object
int courseId = 4;
Object newCourse;
cm.MakeCourse(courseId, newCourse);
//and now we are back to square one
newCourse.Schedule(); //This causes a 'member not found
   exception'
```


Line six will not compile, even if the Schedule method exists, because we can't assume that `newCourse` will always come back as a Course object, because it is declared a variant. We are stuck.

With a dynamic type, though, we are golden once again, with this code:

```
CourseMarshaller cm = new CourseMarshaller(); //a COM object
int courseId = 4;
dynamic newCourse;
cm.MakeCourse(courseId, newCourse);
newCourse.Schedule(); //This now compiles
```

What happens if `newCourse` comes back as something that doesn't have a Schedule method? You get a runtime error. But there are `try/catch` blocks for runtime errors. Nothing will help it compile without the dynamic keyword.

Readers who are long-time Visual Basic programmers, or even newer VB.NET programmers, realize that you can handle this dynamically — and have always been able to — in Visual Basic. For a long time, I have recommended that programmers working with legacy systems use Visual Basic for their new code, and this is exactly why.

In the interest of language parity, now C# can do it, too. In general, this is good, because many organizations are writing legacy code in VB and new code in C# — and it can get pretty messy in the trenches. This change makes the code base slimmer.

Putting Dynamic to Use

When C# encounters a dynamic typed variable, like the variables we created earlier, it changes everything that variable touches into a *dynamic operation*. This dynamic conversion means that when you use a dynamically typed object in an expression, the entire operation is dynamic.

Classic examples

There are six examples of how this works. Say we have the `dynamic` variable `dynaVariable`. Because the dynamic variable will pass through all six examples, they will all be dispatched dynamically by the C# compiler. Here are those examples, with nods to Daniel Ng.

- **`dynamicVariable.someMethod("a", "b", "c");`**: The compiler binds the method `someMethod` at runtime, since `dynaVariable` is `dynamic`. No surprise.
- **`dynamicVariable.someProperty = 42;`**: The compiler binds the property `someProperty` just like it did in the first method.
- **`var newVar = dynamicVariable + 42;`**: The compiler looks for any overloaded operators of "+" with a type of `dynamic`. Lacking that, it outputs a `dynamic` type.
- **`int newNumber = dynamicVariable;`**: This is an implicit conversion to `int`. The runtime determines if a conversion to `int` is possible. If not, it throws a type mismatch error.

✦ **`int newString = (int) dynamicVariable;`**: This is an explicit cast to `int`. The compiler encodes this as a cast — you actually change the type here.

✦ **`Console.WriteLine(dynamicVariable);`**: Because there is no overload of `WriteLine` that accepts a `dynamic` type explicitly, the entire method call is dispatched dynamically.

Making static operations dynamic

If the compiler chooses to make a static operation dynamic — as it did in item 6 in the preceding section — the compiler rebuilds the code on the fly to have it handle the dynamic variable. What does that mean for you? Glad you asked.

Let's take item 6, `Console.WriteLine(dynamicVariable);`. This piece of code forces the compiler to build intermediary code, which checks for the type of variable at runtime in order to come up with something that is writable to the console. The compiled code first checks if the input is a static type that it knows. Next, it checks for a type present in the program. Then it will just try a few things that might work. It will fail with an error if it finds nothing.

If this must happen, that's fine. But remember that it is slower than all git out. This is why `Variant` got such a bad rap in Visual Basic classic. Dynamic is something you don't use until you need it. It puts a tremendous strain on the machine running the program, especially if all variables are dynamic.

Understanding what's happening under the covers

Let's take an example right out of MSDN. Microsoft points out this simple method:

```
class C
{
    public dynamic MyMethod(dynamic d)
    {
        return d.Foo();
    }
}
```

This is pretty straightforward stuff — a method that accepts a dynamic class and returns the results of the type's `Foo` method. Not a big deal.

Here is the compiled C# code:

```
class C
{
    [return: Dynamic]
    public object MyMethod([Dynamic] object d)
    {
        if (MyMethodo__SiteContainer0.p__Site1 == null)
        {
            MyMethodo__SiteContainer0.p__Site1 =
              CallSite<Func<CallSite, object, object>>
              .Create(new CSharpCallPayload(
                CSharpCallFlags.None, "Foo",
typeof(object), null,
                new CSharpArgumentInfo[] {
              new CSharpArgumentInfo(CSharpArgumentInfoFl
ags.None,
            null) }));
        }
        return MyMethodo__SiteContainer0.p__Site1
          .Target(MyMethodo__SiteContainer0.p__Site1, d);
    }

    [CompilerGenerated]
    private static class MyMethodo__SiteContainer0
    {
        public static CallSite<Func<CallSite, object,
object>> p__Site1;
    }
}
```

Yeah, that's what I said, too. I am not going to even begin to try breaking down this code — and fortunately, we don't have to. That's what we have compilers for, right?

Running with the Dynamic Language Runtime

There is more to dynamic languages than just the dynamic typing. You can do some powerful things. Like all power, you have to be careful not to misuse it.

The Dynamic Language Runtime — shown in Figure 1-1 — is a library added to the .NET Framework specifically to provide for adding dynamic languages (like Ruby) to the Visual Studio fold (like IRONRuby), or to add dynamic language features to existing static languages (like C# 4.0).

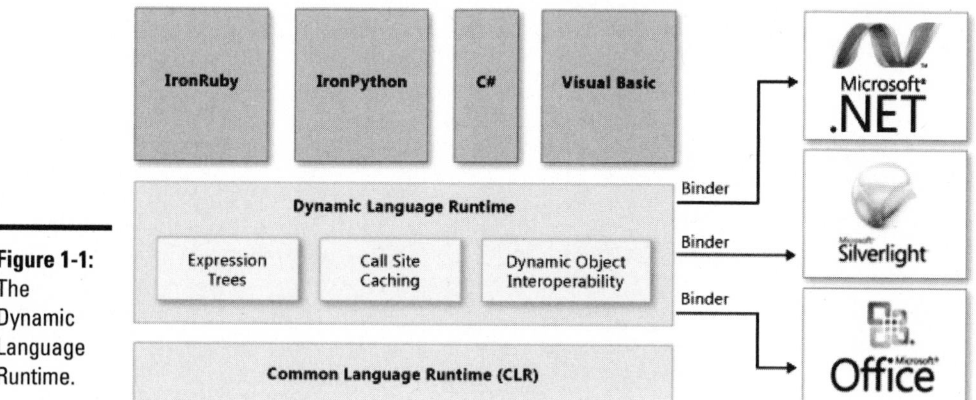

Figure 1-1: The Dynamic Language Runtime.

The runtime helps the compiler to construct code in the compiled assembly that will make a lot of choices dynamically. The code block at the end of the preceding section is an example of the simplest kind.

The DLR assisted in the creation of IRONRuby, which makes it possible to code in Ruby — the current hot dynamic language — right in Visual Studio. Of course, because the DLR enables C# to take on dynamic language features, much that you can do in Ruby you can now do in C#.

Dynamic Ruby

Ruby takes advantage of its dynamic roots in its implementation of the Trabb Pardo-Knuth algorithm. Don't be put off by the name — this is just a straightforward problem that can be solved by computer code.

The program needs to read 11 numbers from an input device — in our case, the console's `ReadLine` method. It stores them in an array. Then, it processes the array backward — starting from the last entered value — with some function. If the value doesn't exceed some arbitrary threshold, it prints the result.

The program looks like this in Ruby:

```
class TPK
  def f( x )
    return Math.sqrt(x.abs) + 5*x **3
  end
```

```
  def main
    Array.new(11) { gets.to_i }.reverse.each do |x|
      y = f(x)
      puts "#{x} #{(y>400) ? 'TOO LARGE' : y}"
    end
  end
end
```

This isn't a Ruby book, and that fact isn't lost on me. Nonetheless, this is the best dynamic language that I can use for an example — bar none.

Two functions are defined: `f` and `main`. `Main` accepts 11 numbers from the console and then moves them to an integer array (that's what `gets.to_i` does). For each value in the array, it sets `y` equal to `f(x)` and then sees if it is higher than our arbitrary value. If so, it prints "TOO LARGE"; otherwise, it prints the number.

Why is being dynamic important for this algorithm? It isn't. You could do it all statically typed. The dynamic bit does have an impact, though.

First, `f(x)` doesn't care what `x` is. The program assumes that whatever comes in gets changed to an integer at `gets.to_i`, but the function itself is case agnostic. This is good and bad, because if we do happen to give it a string or some other type, it will fail.

The array itself isn't typed, either. This can have benefits, because it is possible to drop a differently typed value in there if you know you are just going to write it to the screen.

Dynamic C#

Of course, C# now has similar features, right? We should be able to do the same thing! Yes, in fact, we can. Here's the code:

```
static dynamic f(dynamic x)
{
    return (Math.Sqrt(x) + 5.0 * Math.Pow(x, 3.0));
}
static void Main(string[] args)
{
    dynamic[] array = new Array[11];
    for (int i = 0; i < 11; i++)
    {
        array[i] = Console.ReadLine();
    }
    for (int i = 10; i>=0; i--)
    {
```

```
                    dynamic y = f(array[i]);
                    if (y > 400.0)
                    {
                        Console.WriteLine(string.Format("{0} TOO
LARGE", i));
                    }else{
                        Console.WriteLine("{0} : {1}", i,
array[1]);
                    }
                }
                Console.ReadKey();
            }
```

Line for line, the application does the same thing as the Ruby code, albeit longer. I kept the names the same so it was easier to follow. Because I had to use `for` loops to handle the integrators, it made the body of the program quite a bit beefier. Figure 1-2 shows what the program looks like when it runs.

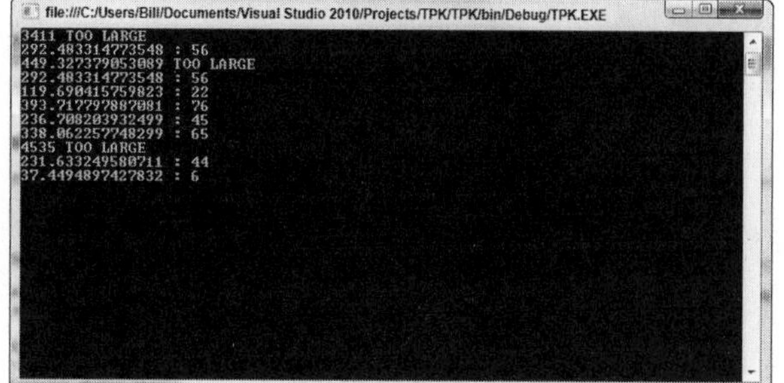

Figure 1-2: The TPK program running.

But why use the dynamic type here? Clearly we could have just used `double` for this. Use of dynamic just made the program easier to create. Try changing the array to an array of `double`, like this:

```
Double[] array = new Double[11];
```

Hey, look at that: Now the `ReadLine` doesn't work. We'll just cast it to a `double`. Nope, can't do that; we have to use `TryParse`. You get the picture. Static types are hard to code with. Dynamic types are easier to code with.

What's the other side of this? Well, obviously, if the user enters a string, she gets a runtime error, and that is bad. If we statically type everything, then we can trap that error much easier, and handle it right on user input.

Add to that the reality that C# is making runtime decisions about every single variable throughout the entire run of the program. That's a whole lot of extra processing that we could have avoided if we had just done that static typing.

The take-home here is that using dynamic types makes your programming job much easier and your troubleshooting job much harder. If you are writing a utility script for your own use, and don't care if it occasionally crashes with a type mismatch, then use dynamic. If you are writing a backup script for a hospital and the lives of thousands are at stake, I advise static types.

Chapter 2: Improving Productivity with Named and Optional Parameters

In This Chapter

- Distinguishing between named and optional parameters
- Using optional parameters
- Implementing reference types
- Declaring Output parameters

Parameters, as you probably remember, are the inputs to methods. They are the values that you put in so that you get a return value. Sometimes, the return values are parameters, too, which confuses things.

In the world of C# and most C-derived languages, parameters can't be optional. Instead of making parameters optional, you are just expected to make a separate overload for every version of the method that you expect your users to need.

This pattern works fairly well, but there are still a lot of problems. Many VB programmers point to the flexible parameterization as a strong reason to use VB over C#.

C# 4.0 has optional parameters. *Optional parameters* are parameters that have a default value right in the method signature — just like the VB.NET implementation. This is one more step toward language parity, and again in the name of COM programming.

It's the same control versus productivity issue that Chapter 1 shows us about the dynamic type. Optional parameters give you just enough rope to hang yourself. A programmer can make mistakes just as easily as he can help himself.

Optional Parameters

Optional parameters depend on having a default value set in order to be optional. For instance, if you are searching for a phone number by name and city, you can default the city name to your city, making the parameter optional.

```
public static string searchForPhoneNumber(string name, string
   city = "Columbus") {...}
```

In C# 3.0, you implement this with two overloaded implementations of the search method. One of them includes the name and the city as parameters. The second only has the name as a parameter. It sets the city in the body of the method and calls the first method. The code looks like this:

```
public static string searchForPhoneNumber(string name, string
   city) {...}
public static string searchForPhoneNumber(string name) {
   string city = "Columbus";
   return searchForPhoneNumber(name, city);
}
```

The canonical example of this is the `addit` method. It's silly, but it illustrates the realities of multiple overloads. So, before we had this:

```
public static int addit(int z, int y)
{
    return z + y;
}
public static int addit(int z, int y, int x)
{
    return z+y+x;
}
public static int addit(int z, int y, int x, int w)
{
    return z + y + x + w;
}
public static int addit(int z, int y, int x, int w, int v)
{
    return z + y + x + w + v;
}
```

With optional parameters, we now have this:

```
public static int addit(int z, int y, int x = 0, int w = 0,
   int v = 0)
{
    return z + y + x + w + v;
}
```

If we need to add two numbers, we can do it easily.

```
int answer = addit(10, 4),
```

If we need to add four numbers, we have no problems either.

```
int answer = addit(10, 4, 5, 12);
```

So why are optional parameters dangerous? Because sometimes default values can have unintended consequences. For instance, you don't want to make a `divideit` method and default the parameters to 0. Someone could call it and get an undebuggable division by zero error. Setting the optional values in `additall` to 1 inside the method body would be bad.

```
public static int addit(int z, int y, int x = 0, int w = 0,
   int v = 1)
{
    //You CLEARLY don't want this
    return z + y + x + w + v;
}
```

And sometimes problems can be very subtle, so use optional parameters carefully. For instance, say you have a base class, and then a derived class that implements the base, like this:

```
public abstract class Base
{
    public virtual void SomeFunction(int x = 0)
    {...}
}

public sealed class Derived
{
    public override void SomeFunction(int x = 1)
    {...}
}
```

What happens if you declare a new instance?

```
Base ex1 = new Base();
ex1. SomeFunction ();                    // SomeFunction (0)

Base ex2 = new Derived();
ex2. SomeFunction ();                    // SomeFunction (0)

Derived ex3 = new Derived();
ex3. SomeFunction ();                    // SomeFunction (1)
```

What happened here? Depending on how you implement the classes, the default value for the optional parameter is set differently. The first example, `ex1`, is an implementation of `Base`, and the default optional parameter is 0. In the second example, `ex2` is cast to a type of `Derived` (which is legal, since `Derived` is a subclass of `Base`) and the default value is also 0. However, in the third example, `Derived` is instantiated directly and the default value is 1. This is not particularly expected behavior, though I have to admit that I am not sure WHAT expected behavior is in a case like this. No matter how you slice it, it's a gotcha and something to watch out for.

Reference types

A reference type, as Book 1 discusses, types a variable that stores reference to actual data, instead of the data itself. Reference types are usually referred to as objects, though this is a little inaccurate since everything in the .NET Framework is an object.

New reference types are implemented with

- Class
- Interface
- Delegate

These need to be built before you use them; class itself isn't a reference type, but the `Calendar` class is.

There are three built-in reference types in the .NET Framework:

- String (who knows why this isn't a static type)
- Object
- Dynamic

You can pass a reference type into a method just like you can pass a static type. It is still considered a parameter. You still use it inside the method like any other variable.

But can reference types be passed, like static types can? Let's try. For instance, if we have a `Schedule` method for our `Calendar` class, we could pass in the `CourseId` or we could pass in the whole `Course`. It all depends on how we structure the application.

```
public class Course
{
    public int CourseId;
    public string Name;
    public void Course(int id, string name)
```

```
        {
            CourseId = id;
            Name = name;
        }
    }
    public class Calendar
    {
        public static void Schedule(int courseId)
        {
        }
        public static void Schedule(Course course)
        {
           //Something interesting happens here
        }
    }
```

In this example, we have an overloaded method for `Schedule` — one that accepts a `CourseId` and one that accepts a `Course` reference type. The second is a reference type, because `Course` is a class, rather than a static type, like the `Integer` of the `CourseId`.

What if we want the second `Schedule` method to support an optional `Course` parameter? Say, if I just want it to create a `New Course` by default if I omit the parameter. This would be similar to setting a static integer to "0" or whatever, wouldn't it?

```
        public static void Schedule(Course course = New
    Course())
        {
            //Implementation here
        }
```

This isn't allowed, however. Visual Studio allows optional parameters only on static types, and the compiler tells you so. If I want to do this, I have to accept the `CourseId` in the `Schedule` method and construct a new `Course` in the body of the event.

Output parameters

As Book 1 discusses, Output parameters are parameters in the method signature that actually change the value of the variable that is passed into them by the user. The parameter references the location of the original variable, rather than creating a "working copy."

Output parameters are declared in a method signature with the `out` keyword. You can have as many as you like (well, within reason), although if you use more than a few, you probably should use something else (a generic list, maybe?).

An Output parameter might look like this in a method declaration:

```
    public static void Schedule(int courseId, out string
name, out DateTime scheduledTime)
    {
        name = "something";
        scheduledTime = DateTime.Now;
    }
```

Following the rules, we should be able to make one of these parameters optional by presetting a value. But, sigh, it doesn't work, as shown in Figure 2-1.

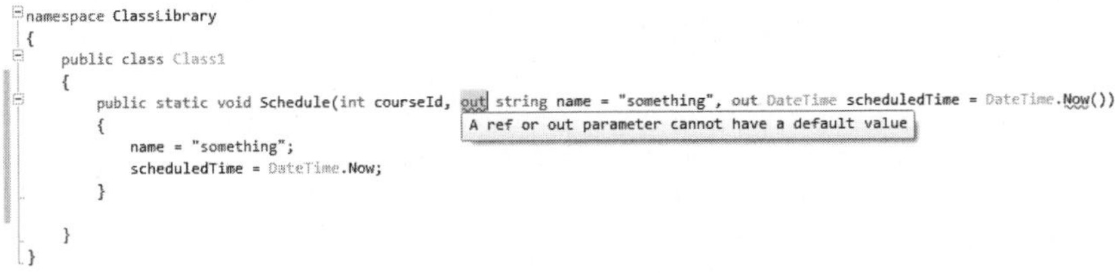

```
namespace ClassLibrary
{
    public class Class1
    {
        public static void Schedule(int courseId, out string name = "something", out DateTime scheduledTime = DateTime.Now())
        {                                         A ref or out parameter cannot have a default value
            name = "something";
            scheduledTime = DateTime.Now;
        }

    }
}
```

Figure 2-1: Visual Studio error on default optional parameter value.

Unlike reference parameters, it makes sense that Output parameters don't support default values. The Output parameter is exactly that — output, and setting the value should happen inside the method body.

Keep in mind the purpose of optional parameters — resolving the need for heavily overloaded methods. Because Output parameters aren't expecting a value coming in any way, it doesn't benefit the programmer to have default values.

Named Parameters

Hand in hand with the concept of optional parameters are named parameters. If you have more than one default parameter, you need a way to tell the compiler which parameter you are supplying!

For example, look at the `additall` method earlier in this chapter, after optional parameters are implemented:

```
public static int addit(int z, int y, int x = 0, int w = 0,
    int v = 0)
{
    return z + y + x + w + v;
}
```

Clearly the order of the parameters doesn't matter in this implementation, but if this were in a class library you might not know that the order of the parameters is a non-issue! How would you tell the compiler to skip `x` and `w` if you want to supply `v`? In the old days, you would do this:

```
int answer = additall(3,7, , ,4);
```

Fortunately, we don't have to do that anymore. Now, with named parameters, we can say:

```
int answer = additall(z:3, y:7, v:4);
```

The nonoptional parameters don't have to be named, because the position is assumed since they are required anyway. Nonetheless, it is good practice to name them. If you skip naming them, you have this instead:

```
int answer = additall(3, 7, v:4);
```

You have to admit that this is a little harder to read. One would have to go back to the method signature to figure out what is happening.

Overload Resolution

Problems begin when you have optional arguments and overloaded methods in the same method signature. Because C# allows for differently named parameters in overloads, things can get sort of hairy. Take for example:

```
class Course
{
        public void New(object course)
        {
        }
        public void New(int courseId)
        {
        }
}
```

Try calling the `New` method with something like this:

```
Course course = new Course();
course.New(10);
```

Here, the runtime picks the second overload because 10 better matches an `int` than an `object`. The same is true when dealing with overloaded method signatures with optional parameters. The tiebreaker goes to the overload with the fewest casts required to make it work.

Chapter 3: Helping Out with Interop

In This Chapter

- Using Dynamic Import
- Deploying without primary Interop assemblies
- Skipping the ref statement

The Component Object Model, usually called COM, is a standard for the interface of software bits at the binary level. Because it is binary, it is language-neutral, which was Microsoft's goal when the company introduced COM in 1993. COM is a language-neutral way to implement objects in a lot of different environments.

COM is as an umbrella term for a lot of different technologies in the Microsoft world. OLE, OLE2, ActiveX, COM+, and DCOM are all versions of the same idea — just implemented in different ways.

The problem with COM is networking. Although a thorough explanation is outside the scope of this book, it is important to understand that Microsoft's answer to broadly distributed applications in the 1990s was less than good. DCOM, or Distributed COM, was fraught with problems.

When XML Web services entered the scene in the late 1990s with SOAP, Microsoft just put a wrapper around COM that translated to and from SOAP. In the background, however, they were planning a much more sophisticated messaging system for Windows. That system eventually became ASP.NET Web services, and then WCF in its latest iteration.

Applications that are sewn to the desktop don't really use DCOM, though, so they have been slow to move to services, and therefore slow to move to .NET. These applications still live in COM, so we still need to interact with COM — even in this service-oriented, .NET world we live in.

What applications could be so Neanderthal? How about Microsoft Office. Yup — Microsoft Office is the biggie, and it is why C# 4.0 includes a bunch of COM interoperability features, collectively called Interop Improvements.

Principally, the optional parameters discussed in Chapter 2 of this book were implemented for COM Interop. We cover three other major improvements here: using Dynamic Import, deploying without primary Interop assemblies (PIAs), and skipping the ref statement.

If you plan on coding against Microsoft Office, trust me — this is information you need.

Using Dynamic Import

Many COM methods accept and return variant types, which are represented in the primary Interop assemblies as objects. In most cases, a programmer calling these methods already knows the static type of a returned object from context, but explicitly has to perform a cast on the returned value to make use of that knowledge. These casts are so common in day-to-day development that they constitute a major nuisance.

To create a smoother experience, you can import these COM APIs in such a way that variants are represented using the type dynamic. In other words, from your point of view, COM signatures have occurrences of dynamic instead of object in them.

This means that you can easily access members directly off a returned object, or you can assign an object to a strongly typed local variable without having to cast. To illustrate, you can now say

```
excel.Cells[1, 1].Value = "Hello";
```

instead of

```
((Excel.Range)excel.Cells[1, 1]).Value2 = "Hello";
```

and

```
Excel.Range range = excel.Cells[1, 1];
```

instead of

```
Excel.Range range = (Excel.Range)excel.Cells[1, 1];
```

Why is this a big deal? One reason is that it simplifies the programmer's work. Code from Microsoft Office is tremendously difficult to read. Take a look at this code block from an Office application I wrote for the *VSTO For Dummies* book:

```
Office.CommandBars commandBars = default(Office.CommandBars);
Office.CommandBar commandBar = default(Office.CommandBar);
Office.CommandBarButton runStoreReport = default(Office.
    CommandBarButton);
commandBars = (Microsoft.Office.Core.CommandBars)Application.
    CommandBars;
commandBar = commandBars.Add("VSTOAddinToolbar", Office.
    MsoBarPosition.msoBarTop, , true);
commandBar.Context = Visio.VisUIObjSets.visUIObjSetDrawing +
    "*";
runStoreReport = (Microsoft.Office.Core.CommandBarButton)
    commandBar.Controls.Add(Office.MsoControlType.
    msoControlButton);
runStoreReport.Tag = "Store Report";
runStoreReport.Click += VisualizeSales;
```

Here's what the code block looks like in C# 4.0:

```
Office.CommandBars commandBars = Office.CommandBars;
Office.CommandBar commandBar = Office.CommandBar;
Office.CommandBarButton runStoreReport = Office.
    CommandBarButton;
commandBars = Application.CommandBars;
commandBar = commandBars.Add("VSTOAddinToolbar", msoBarTop, ,
    true);
commandBar.Context = Visio.VisUIObjSets.visUIObjSetDrawing +
    "*";
runStoreReport =commandBar.Controls.Add(msoControlButton);
runStoreReport.Tag = "Store Report";
runStoreReport.Click += VisualizeSales;
```

It's a lot simpler to read. Keep in mind, though, that all those casts still exist — they are just handled by the compiler. Microsoft didn't redo the Office components into .NET; the company just made the compiler communicate better. The compiler still builds code that speaks to the primary Interop assemblies as they are.

Working without Primary Interop Assemblies

Speaking of PIAs (excuse the similarity to another well-known, three-letter acronym), they are handled a lot better in .NET 4.0 in general.

PIAs are large .NET assemblies generated from COM interfaces to facilitate strongly typed interoperability. They provide great support at design time, where your experience of the Interop is as good as if the types were really defined in .NET. However, at runtime these large assemblies can easily bloat your program and also cause versioning issues because they are distributed independently of your application.

The no-PIA feature allows you to continue to use PIAs at design time without having them around at runtime. Instead, the C# 4.0 compiler bakes the small part of the PIA that a program actually uses directly into its assembly. The PIA doesn't have to be loaded at runtime.

To see how this works, try these steps in both Visual Studio 2010 and Visual Studio 2008 (if you have it):

1. **Create a new console application by choosing File⇨New⇨Project and picking C#⇨Console application. Name your project** PIAs.
2. **After the project loads, right-click on References.**
3. **Click Add Reference.**
4. **Select Microsoft.Office.Interop.Excel, version 12, if you have it. Otherwise, use the latest version you have loaded.**
5. **Click OK.**
6. **Add** using Microsoft.Office.Interop.Excel; **to the header.**
7. **Change the Main procedure to the following (just enough to get Excel rolling):**

```
static void Main(string[] args)
{
    Microsoft.Office.Interop.Excel.Application
xl = new Application();
    xl.Quit();
}
```

8. **Right-click on the Solution and select Add Project.**
9. **Add a new Setup project.**
10. **Right-click on the Setup project and choose Add⇨Project Output.**
11. **Select Primary Output.**
12. **Click OK.**

The setup project will automatically determine what to deploy with the application. In Visual Studio 2008, with C# 3.0, it will deploy the primary Interop assemblies, as shown in Figure 3-1.

In Visual Studio 2010, the setup doesn't deploy the PIAs. The specific parts being used are compiled right into the EXE for the application. This is demonstrated in Figure 3-2.

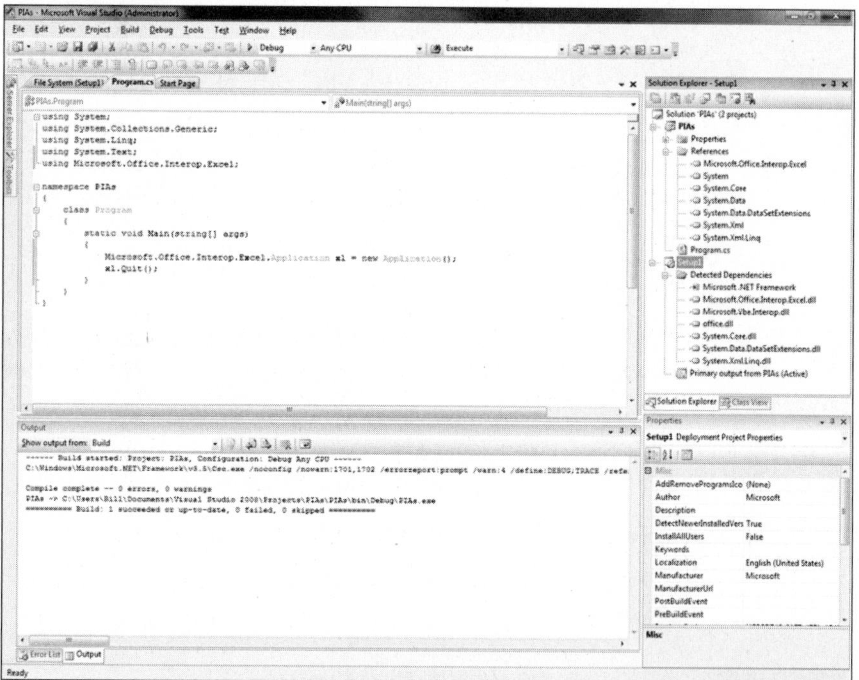

Figure 3-1: Deploying the PIAs in C# 3.0.

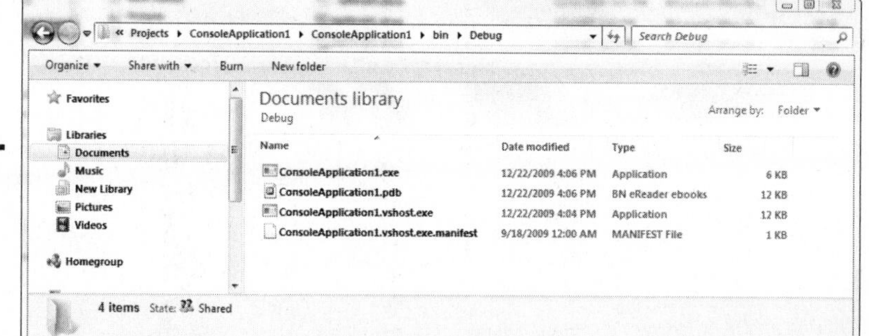

Figure 3-2: Deploying without PIAs in C# 4.0.

Skipping the Ref Statement

Because of a different programming model, many COM APIs contain a lot of reference parameters. Contrary to refs in C#, these are typically not meant to mutate a passed-in argument for the subsequent benefit of the caller but are simply another way of passing value parameters.

It therefore seems unreasonable that a C# programmer should have to create temporary variables for all such ref parameters and pass these by reference. So let's delete them.

Instead, specifically for COM methods, the C# compiler allows you to pass arguments by values to such a method and automatically generates temporary variables to hold the passed-in values, subsequently discarding these when the call returns. In this way, the caller sees value semantics and doesn't experience any side effects, but the called method still gets a reference.

You can see this in action in the canonical optional parameter example from Chapter 2. In the usual `SaveAs` from Microsoft Word, everything is a reference parameter.

```
object filename = "test.docx";
object missing = System.Reflection.Missing.Value;

doc.SaveAs(ref filename,
           ref missing, ref missing, ref missing,
           ref missing, ref missing, ref missing,
           ref missing, ref missing, ref missing,
           ref missing, ref missing, ref missing,
           ref missing, ref missing, ref missing);
```

In C# 4.0, you can skip both the "missing" optional parameters and the ref statement.

```
object filename = "test.docx";
doc.SaveAs(filename);
```

Chapter 4: Revising Generics

In This Chapter

- Understanding variance
- Working with contravariance
- Using covariance

Generics are covered in length in Books I and II, as they relate to creating collections of objects or business concepts, and how they impact object-oriented programming. They also play a large role in dynamic design and programming, which Chapter 1 of this book covers.

The generics model implemented in C# 2.0 was incomplete. Although parameters in C# all allow for variance in several directions, generics do not.

Variance has to do with types of parameters and return values. *Covariance* means that an instance of a subclass can be used when an instance of a parent class is expected, while *Contravariance* means that an instance of a superclass can be used when an instance of a subclass is expected. When neither is possible, it is called *Invariance.*

All fourth-generation languages support some kind of variance. In C# 3.0 and earlier versions, parameters are covariant and return types are contravarient. So, this works because string and integer parameters are covariant to object parameters:

```
public static void MessageToYou(object theMessage)
{
   if (theMessage != null)
      Console.Writeline(theMessage)
}
//then:
MessageToYou("It's a message, yay!");
MessageToYou(4+6.6);
```

And this works because object return types are contravarient to string and integer return types (for example):

```
object theMessage =  MethodThatGetsTheMessage();
```

Generics are nonvariant in C# 2.0 and 3.0. This means that if `Basket<apple>` is of type `Basket<fruit>`, those `Baskets` are not interchangeable like strings and objects are in the preceding example.

Variance

If we look at a method like the preceding one:

```
public static void WriteMessages()
{
    List<string> someMessages = new List<string>();
    someMessages.Add("The first message");
    someMessages.Add("The second message");
    MessagesToYou(someMessages);
}
```

and then we try to call that method like we did earlier with a string type:

```
//This doesn't work in C#3!!
public static void MessagesToYou(IEnumerable<object>
   theMessages)
{
    foreach (var item in theMessages)
        Console.WriteLine(item);
}
```

this fails in Visual Studio 2008. Generics are invariant in C# 3.0. But, in Visual Studio 2010 this complies because `IEnumerable<T>` is covariant — you can use a more derived type as a substitute for a higher-order type. Let's look at a real example.

Contravariance

In my scheduling application, I have `Events`, which have a date, and then a set of subclasses, one of which is `Course`. A `Course` is an `Event`. Courses know their own number of students.

Anyway, back at the ranch, I have a method called `MakeCalendar`.

```
public void MakeCalendar(IEnumerable<Event> theEvents)
{
    foreach (Event item in theEvents)
    {
        Console.WriteLine(item.WhenItIs.ToString());
    }
}
```

Pretend it makes a calendar; for now, all it does is print the date to the console. MakeCalendar is systemwide, so it expects some enumerable list of events.

I also have a Sort algorithm at the main system, called EventSorter. This is used to pass into the Sort method of collections. It expects to be called from a list of Events. Here is the EventSorter class:

```
class EventSorter : IComparer<Event>
{
    public int Compare(Event x, Event y)
    {
        return x.WhenItIs.CompareTo(y.WhenItIs);
    }
}
```

I am writing the Instructor Led Training section of the event manager, and I need to make a list of courses, sort them, and then make a calendar. So I make my list of courses in ScheduleCourses, then I call sort and pass in the EventSorter:

```
public void ScheduleCourses()
{
    List<Course> courses = new List<Course>()
    {
        new Course(){NumberOfStudents=20, WhenItIs = new
   DateTime(2009,2,1)},
        new Course(){NumberOfStudents=14, WhenItIs = new
   DateTime(2009,3,1)},
        new Course(){NumberOfStudents=24, WhenItIs = new
   DateTime(2009,4,1)},
    };
    //Now I am passing an ICompare<Event> class to my
   List<Course> collection.
    //It should be an ICompare<Course> but I can use
   ICompare<Event> because of contravariance
    courses.Sort(new EventSorter());


    //I am passing a List of courses, where a List of Events
   was expected.
    //We can do this because generic parameters are covariant
    MakeCalendar(courses);
}
```

But wait, this is a list of courses I am calling Sort from, right, not a list of events. Doesn't matter — IComparer<Event> is a contravariant generic for T (its return type) as compared to IComparer<Course> so I can still use the algorithm.

Now I have to pass my list into the `MakeSchedule` method, but that method expects an enumerable collection of `Events`. Because parameters are covariant for generics now, I can pass in a List of Courses, as `Course` is covariant to `Event`. Make sense?

There is another example of contravariance, using parameters rather than return values. If I have a method that returns a generic list of `Courses`, I can call that method expecting a list of `Events`, because `Event` is a superclass of `Course`.

You know how you can have a method that returns a `String` and assign the return value to a variable that you have declared an object? Now you can do that with a generic collection, too.

In general, the C# compiler makes assumptions about the generic type conversion. As long as you are working up the chain for parameters, or down the chain for return types, C# will just magically figure the type out.

Covariance

I now have to pass my list into the `MakeSchedule` method, but that method expects an enumerable collection of `Events`. Because parameters are covariant for generics now, I can pass in a List of Courses, as `Course` is covariant to `Event`. This is covariance for parameters.

Index

Special Characters

A

B

C

D

E

F

J

K

L

M

N

O

P

Q

R

T

U

V

W

X

Y

Z

Business/Accounting & Bookkeeping

Bookkeeping For Dummies
978-0-7645-9848-7

eBay Business All-in-One For Dummies, 2nd Edition
978-0-470-38536-4

Job Interviews For Dummies, 3rd Edition
978-0-470-17748-8

Resumes For Dummies, 5th Edition
978-0-470-08037-5

Stock Investing For Dummies, 3rd Edition
978-0-470-40114-9

Successful Time Management For Dummies
978-0-470-29034-7

Computer Hardware

BlackBerry For Dummies, 3rd Edition
978-0-470-45762-7

Computers For Seniors For Dummies
78-0-470-24055-7

Phone For Dummies, nd Edition
78-0-470-42342-4

Laptops For Dummies, 3rd Edition
978-0-470-27759-1

Macs For Dummies, 10th Edition
978-0-470-27817-8

Cooking & Entertaining

Cooking Basics For Dummies, 3rd Edition
978-0-7645-7206-7

Wine For Dummies, 4th Edition
978-0-470-04579-4

Diet & Nutrition

Dieting For Dummies, 2nd Edition
978-0-7645-4149-0

Nutrition For Dummies, 4th Edition
978-0-471-79868-2

Weight Training For Dummies, 3rd Edition
978-0-471-76845-6

Digital Photography

Digital Photography For Dummies, 6th Edition
978-0-470-25074-7

Photoshop Elements 7 For Dummies
978-0-470-39700-8

Gardening

Gardening Basics For Dummies
978-0-470-03749-2

Organic Gardening For Dummies, 2nd Edition
978-0-470-43067-5

Green/Sustainable

Green Building & Remodeling For Dummies
978-0-470-17559-0

Green Cleaning For Dummies
978-0-470-39106-8

Green IT For Dummies
978-0-470-38688-0

Health

Diabetes For Dummies, 3rd Edition
978-0-470-27086-8

Food Allergies For Dummies
978-0-470-09584-3

Living Gluten-Free For Dummies
978-0-471-77383-2

Hobbies/General

Chess For Dummies, 2nd Edition
978-0-7645-8404-6

Drawing For Dummies
978-0-7645-5476-6

Knitting For Dummies, 2nd Edition
978-0-470-28747-7

Organizing For Dummies
978-0-7645-5300-4

SuDoku For Dummies
978-0-470-01892-7

Home Improvement

Energy Efficient Homes For Dummies
978-0-470-37602-7

Home Theater For Dummies, 3rd Edition
978-0-470-41189-6

Living the Country Lifestyle All-in-One For Dummies
978-0-470-43061-3

Solar Power Your Home For Dummies
978-0-470-17569-9

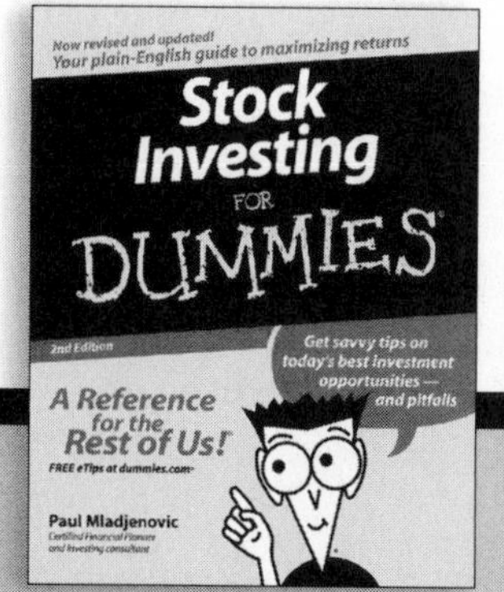

Available wherever books are sold. For more information or to order direct: U.S. customers visit www.dummies.com or call 1-877-762-2974. U.K. customers visit www.wileyeurope.com or call (0) 1243 843291. Canadian customers visit www.wiley.ca or call 1-800-567-4797.

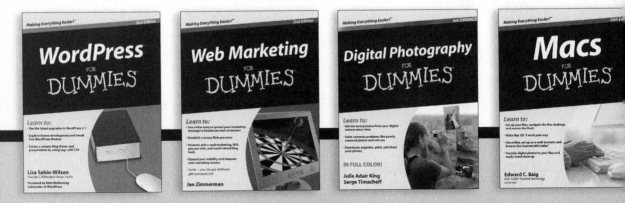